Street by Street

DERBY, LEICESTER NOTTINGHAM

BELPER, ILKESTON, LOUGHBOROUGH, RIPLEY

Beeston, Castle Donington, Coalville, Eastwood, Heanor, Hucknall, Long Eaton, Shepshed, Stapleford, West Bridgford

1st edition May 2001

© Automobile Association Developments Limited 2001

This product includes map data licensed from Ordnance Survey® with the permission of the Controller of Her Majesty's Stationery Office. © Crown copyright 2000. All rights reserved. Licence No: 399221.

Published by AA Publishing (a trading name of Automobile Association Developments Limited, whose registered office is Norfolk House, Priestley Road, Basingstoke, Hampshire, RG24 9NY. Registered number 1878835).

Mapping produced by the Cartographic Department of The Automobile Association.

A CIP Catalogue record for this book is available from the British Library.

Printed by G. Canale & C. s.p.a., Torino, Italy

The contents of this atlas are believed to be correct at the time of the latest revision. However, the publishers cannot be held responsible for loss occasioned to any person acting or refraining from action as a result of any material in this atlas, nor for any errors, omissions or changes in such material. The publishers would welcome information to correct any errors or omissions and to keep this atlas up to date. Please write to Publishing, The Automobile Association, Fanum House, Basing View, Basingstoke, Hampshire, RG21 4EA.

Ref: MX087

Key to map pages ii-iii

Key to map symbols iv-1

Enlarged scale pages 2-9

Street by Street 10-147

Index – towns & villages 148

Index – streets 149-183

Index – featured places 183-188

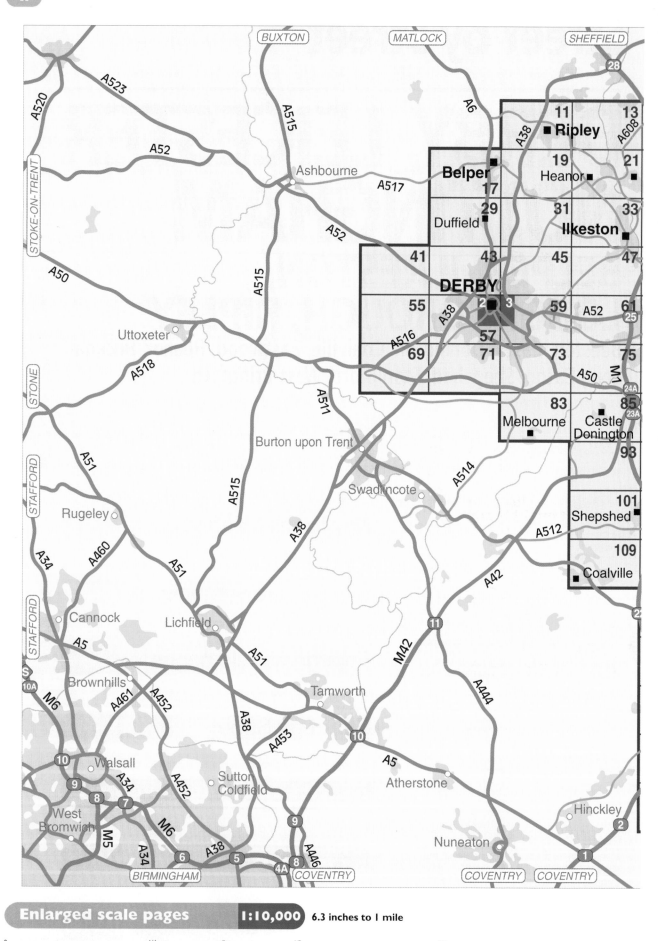

1:10,000 6.3 inches to 1 mile

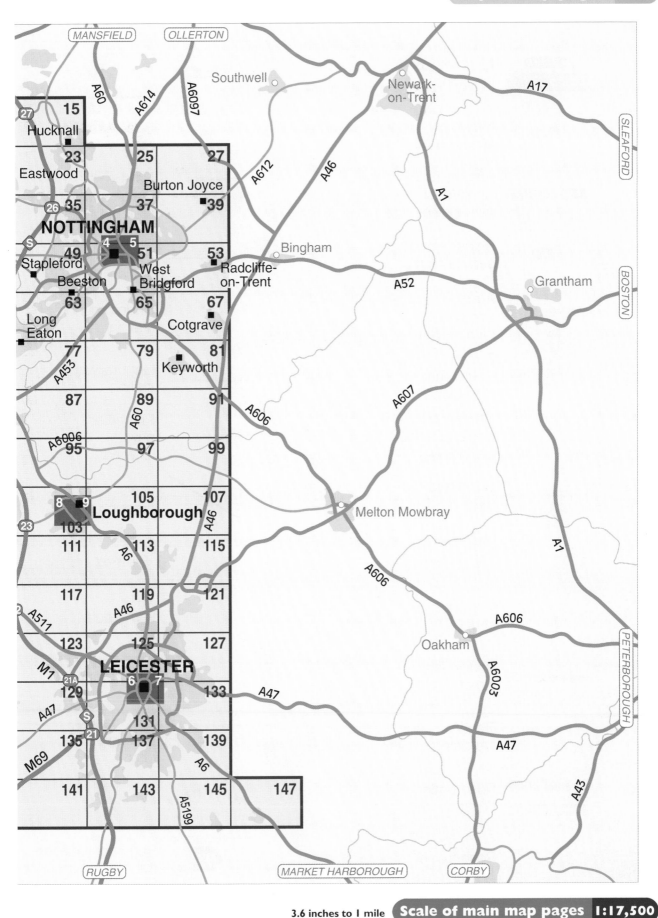

MANSFIELD OLLERTON

Southwell

Newark-on-Trent

A17

SLEAFORD

A60 A614 A6097

A612

A46

A1

27 15
Hucknall

23 25 27
Eastwood Burton Joyce

26 35 37 39

NOTTINGHAM

Bingham

A52

Grantham

BOSTON

4 5
S
49 51 53
Stapleford West Radcliffe-
Beeston Bridgford on-Trent

63 65 67
Long Cotgrave
Eaton

77 79 81
A453 Keyworth

A60

A607

87 89 91

A606

A6006
95 97 99

8 9
105 107
Loughborough
23 103 A46

Melton Mowbray

111 113 115
A6

A1

117 119 121
A511 A46

A606

123 125 127

M1

Oakham A606

A6003

21A
129 6 7 133 A47
LEICESTER
S
131

21
135 137 139
M69 A6

A47

141 143 145 147
A5199

RUGBY MARKET HARBOROUGH CORBY

A43

PETERBOROUGH

3.6 inches to 1 mile **Scale of main map pages 1:17,500**

0 1/2 miles 1

0 1/2 kilometres 1 1/2 2

Junction 9	Motorway & junction
Services	Motorway service area
	Primary road single/dual carriageway
Services	Primary road service area
	A road single/dual carriageway
	B road single/dual carriageway
	Other road single/dual carriageway
	Restricted road
	Private road
← ←	One way street
	Pedestrian street
	Track/ footpath
	Road under construction
	Road tunnel
P	Parking

P+🚌	Park & Ride
	Bus/coach station
	Railway & main railway station
	Railway & minor railway station
⊖	Underground station
⊖	Light railway & station
+++++++++++++	Preserved private railway
LC	Level crossing
•—•—•—•—•	Tramway
- - - - - - - -	Ferry route
·················	Airport runway
—·—·—·—·	Boundaries- borough/ district
▼▼▼▼▼▼▼▼	Mounds
93	Page continuation 1:17,500
7	Page continuation to enlarged scale 1:10,000

River/canal lake, pier		Toilet with disabled facilities	
Aqueduct lock, weir		Petrol station	
Peak (with height in metres) 465 ▲ Winter Hill		Public house	
Beach		Post Office	
Coniferous woodland		Public library	
Broadleaved woodland		Tourist Information Centre	
Mixed woodland		Castle	
Park		Historic house/ building	
Cemetery		Wakehurst Place NT National Trust property	
Built-up area		Museum/ art gallery	
Featured building		Church/chapel	
City wall		Country park	
A&E Accident & Emergency hospital		Theatre/ performing arts	
Toilet		Cinema	

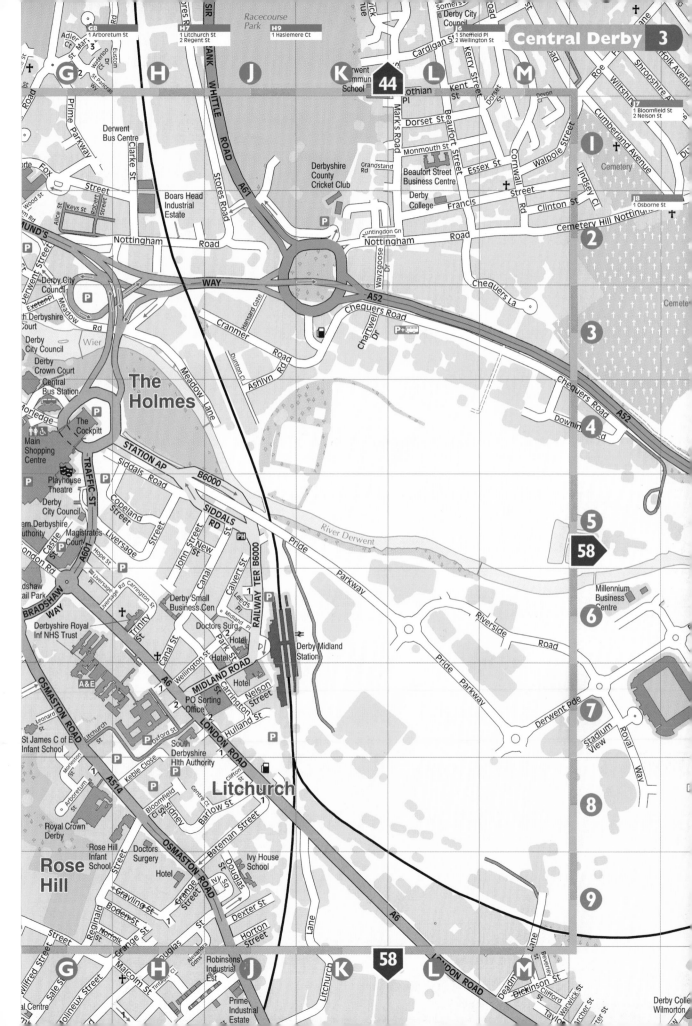

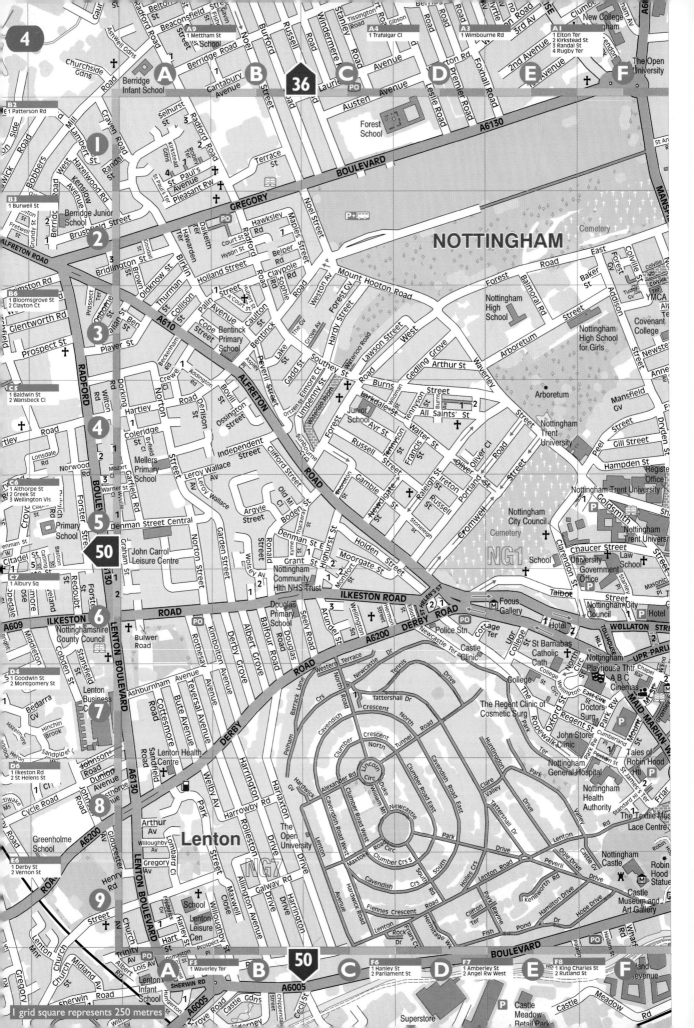

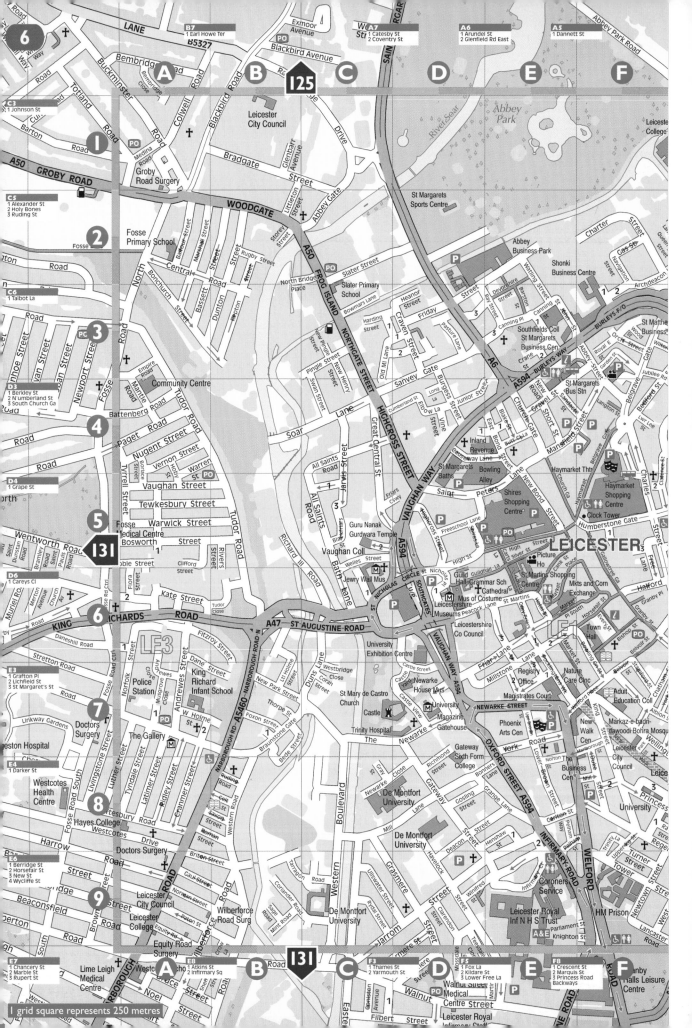

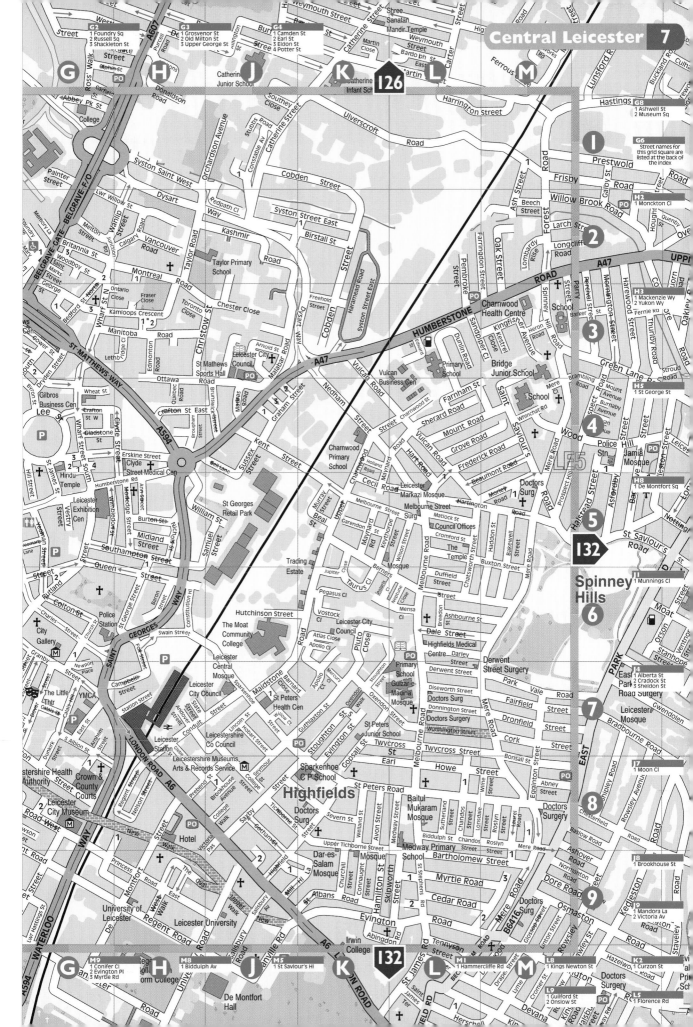

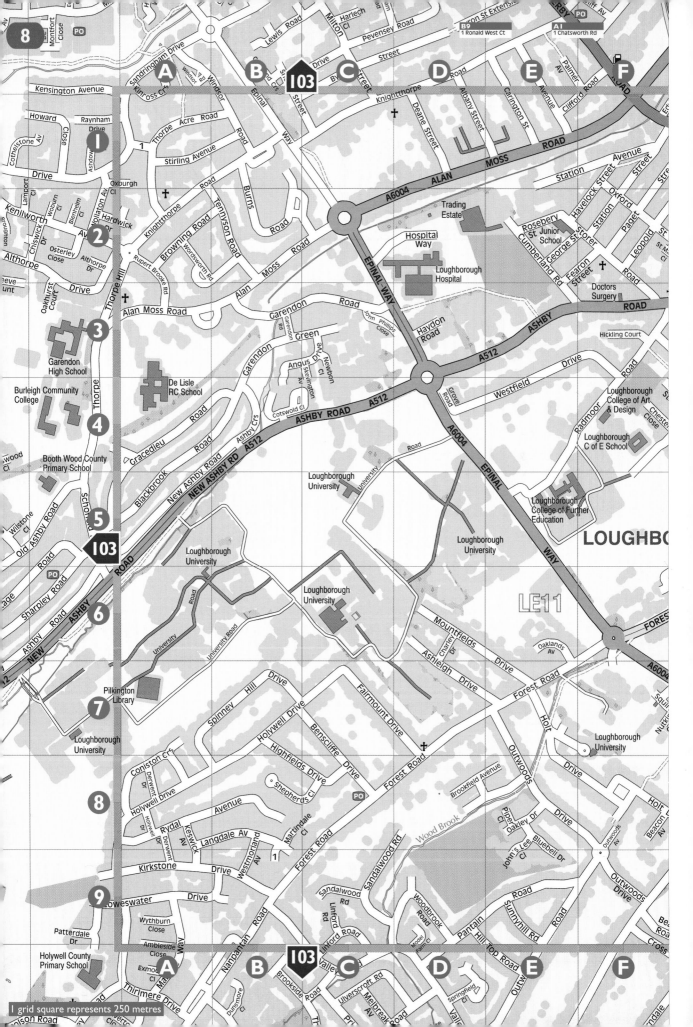

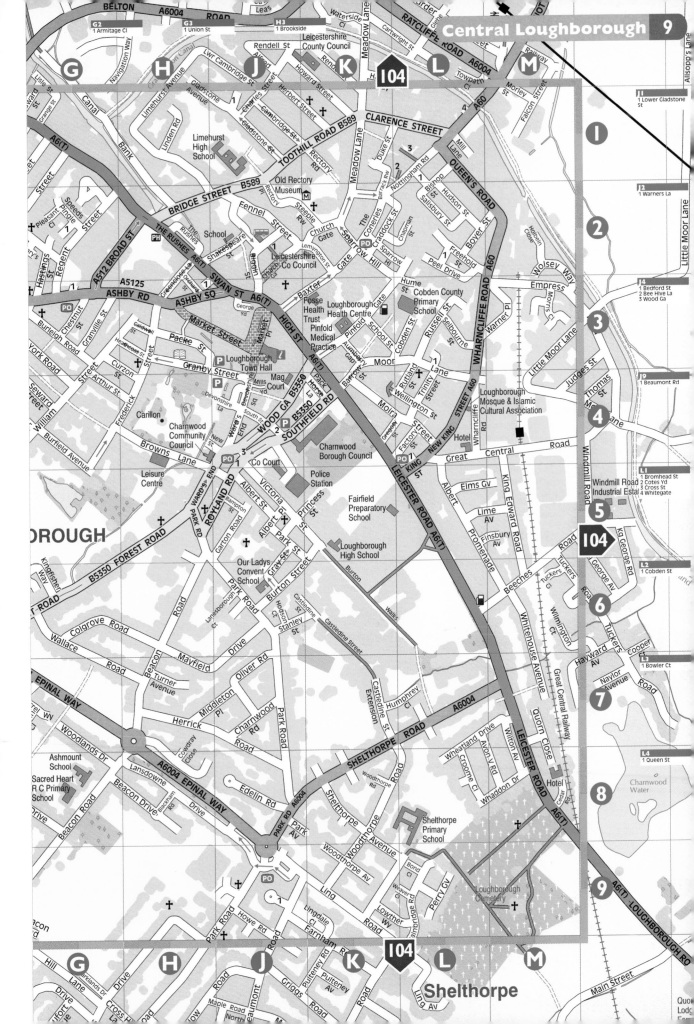

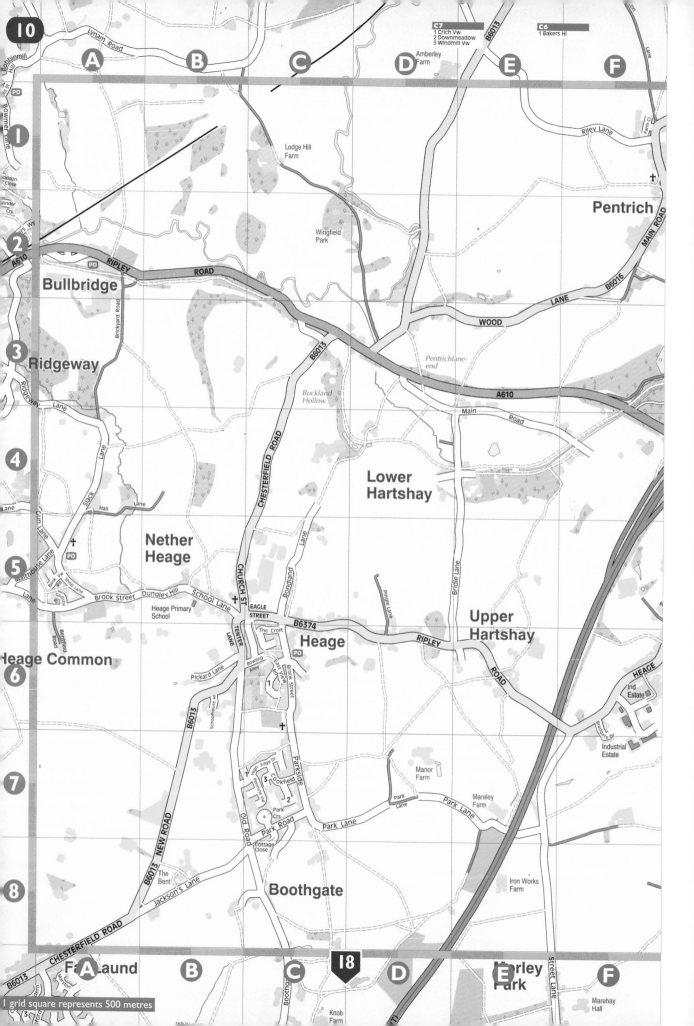

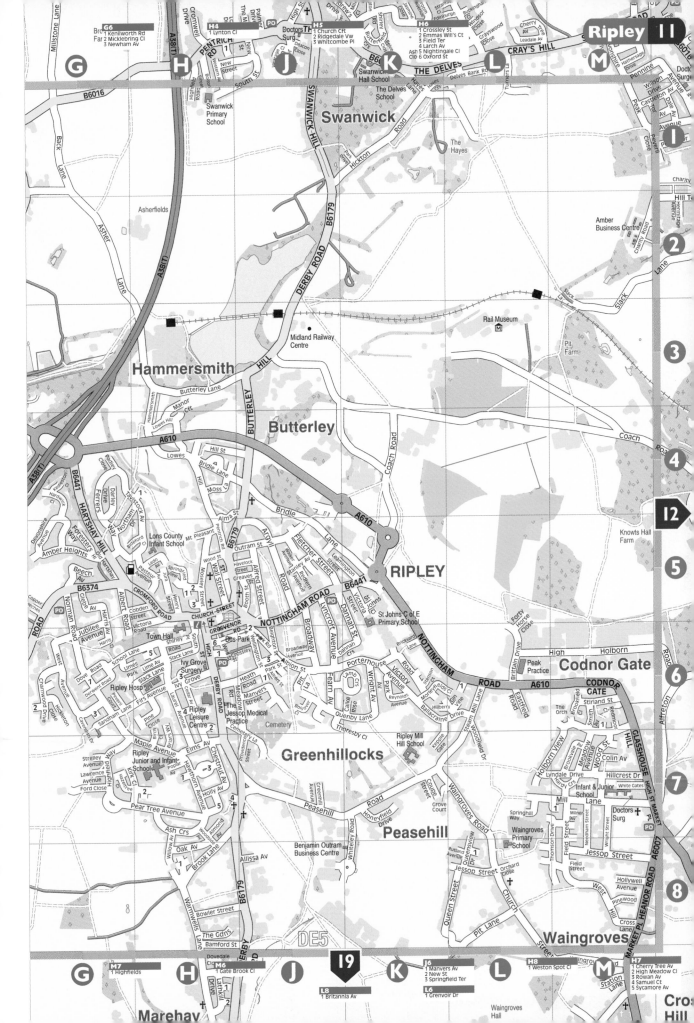

Swanwick

Hammersmith

Butterley

RIPLEY

Greenhillocks

Peasehill

Codnor Gate

Waingroves

Marehay

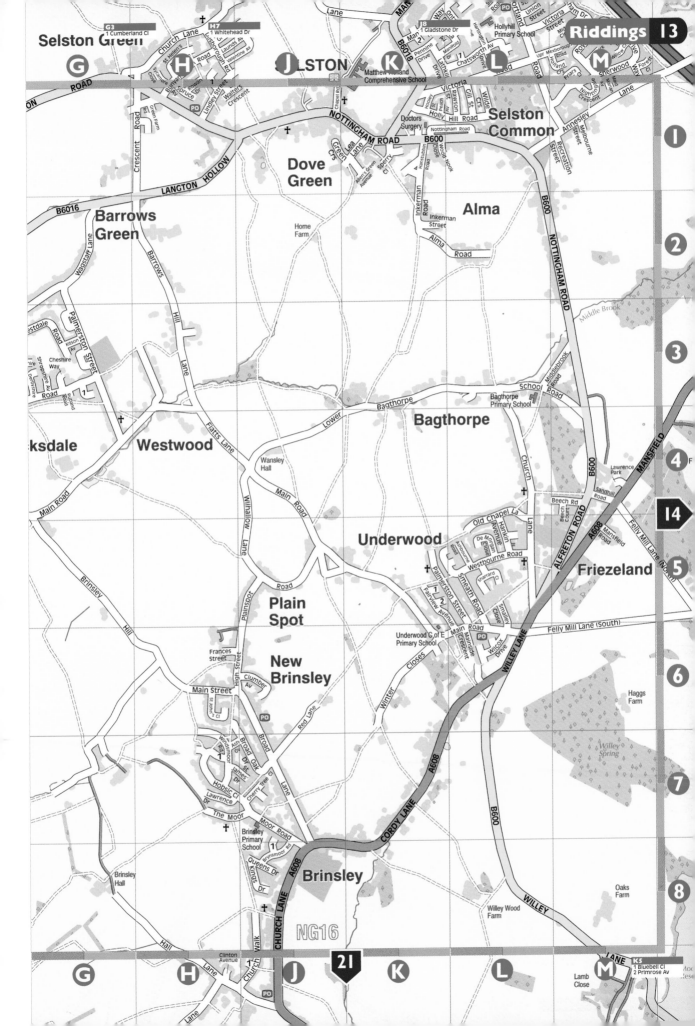

Selston Green

G3 1 Cumberland Cl

H7 1 Whitehead Dr

G

H

Church Lane

St Helen's Cl

Bunyard Cl

Spruce Cl

Rowan Cl

Lindley Street

Walters Crescent

Lounds Av

Valentine Av

ROAD

Green Farm

Green Rd

PO

J LSTON

Chapel Rd

Matthew Holland Comprehensive School

NOTTINGHAM ROAD

Dove Green

Merry Green Avenue

Lea Lane

Green Crs

Sperry Cl

Inkerman Road

Inkerman Street

Alma Road

Doctors Surgery

Nottingham Road

Wood Nook

Hanstubbin Road

B600

Way Off

Gladstone Dr

Man

B6018

Pennine Drive

Manifold

Hollyhill Primary School

J8

Hosley

Holly

Hill

Chatsworth Av

Victoria Street

Portland Road

Union Road

Dr

Way

Rawson

Gill St

Wilde Cl

PO

Holland

Crs

Friars Cl

Roy

L

Sherwood

Dr

Willow

Forest

Way

M

Melbourne Street

Annesley Street

Nightingale Crescent

B600

NOTTINGHAM ROAD

Selston Common

Alma

Recreation Street

Upr Mexborough Road

Mid

Wm Dr

1

2

3

14

4

5

6

7

8

B6016

Barrows Green

Crescent Road

Home Farm

Langton Hollow

Wagstaff Lane

Palmerston Street

Kitson Av

Cheshire Way

Shropshire Av

Derbyshire

Rutland Road

westdale Road

Hill Lane

ksdale

Westwood

Barrows Lane

Flatts Lane

Wansley Hall

Lower

Bagthorpe

Bagthorpe Primary School

School Road

Middlebrook Road

Middle Brook

Beech Rd

Beech Court

Sandhill Road

Lawrence Park

B600

ALFRETON ROAD

A608

Felly Mill Lane (North)

MANSFIELD

Main Road

Brinsley

Hill

Main Road

Wilhallow Lane

Road

Plainspot

Plain Spot

New Brinsley

Frances Street

High Street

Clumber Av

Main Street

St John's Cl

Wadsmoor Rd

Ash Dr

James Dr

PO

Broad Oak Cl

Broad

Red Lane

Lane

Winter Closes

Smeath Road

Underwood

Old Chapel La

Hankin Avenue

De Morgan Cl

Annecourse

Westbourne Road

Palmerston Street

Fairview Avenue

Sharrard

Smalley Close

Main Road

Mainside Crescent

PO

Wilcox Drive

Underwood C of E Primary School

Felly Mill Lane (South)

WILLEY LANE

Friezeland

Mansfield Road

Haggs Farm

Willey Spring

Lawrence Dr

Hobsic Cl

Cherry Tree Cl

The Moor

Moor Road

Brinsley Primary School

Brynsmoor Rd

Queens Dr

Kings Dr

Brinsley Hall

Hall

Clinton Avenue

Church Walk

CHURCH LANE

A608

Brinsley

NG16

Cordy Lane

B600

WILLEY

Willey Wood Farm

Oaks Farm

Lamb Close

LANE

K6 1 Bluebell Cl

2 Primrose Av

14

A B C D E F

Salmon Lane

Little Oa

A
Two Dale
Farm

Osler Drive

Willow

Lake View Drive

M1

1

MANSFIELD ROAD

A608

†

Annesley
Hall

2

Millington
Springs

Junction 27

A608

ANNESLEY

Weavers La

Home Farm

Dog

Bear

ROAD

3

MANSFIELD

William
Wood

Weaver's Lane

Kennel Lane

4

Feller Priory

13

Mill Lane (North)

America
Farm

M1

5

Kennel Lane

6

Haggs
Farm

7

Morning Springs

Robin
Hood's
Well

High
Park
Wood

M1

8

Beauvale
House

Moor
Reserve

A B C D E F

22

New Road

1 grid square represents 500 metres

G H J K L M

I
2
3
4
5
6
7
8

Annesley
Plantation

Stafford Way

Tilford Rd
PO
Newstead
Primary
School
Fraser St
Markham St
Webb St
Station Road
Musters Rd
1
Byron Street
Abbey Rd
Livingstone St

Newstead Station

Station Avenue

Newstead

Cemetery
Cemetery

Aldercar Wood

A611

Hucknall Road

ROAD

A611

Hays Farm

Quarry Banks

NG15

Quarry Lane

Linby

Linby
Papplewick C of E
School

LINBY

Top Wighay
Farm

ANNESLEY ROAD

A611

Main St
MAIN ST

LC

Church

WIGHAY ROAD   B6011

Waterloo

Union St

Sherwood Wk

Robey Cl

Road

Church Lane

Hayden Lane

Bernard Av

Frances Cv
Susan Cv
Dorothy Av
Down Cl
Alison Av
Della Av
Ethel Av

Vaughan Avenue

Rosslyn Drive

Eric Av
Coates Av
Beardsmore Cv
Barbara Sq
Ward Avenue
Broadway Dr

Hucknall National
Secondary School

Wighay

Annesley Road

Quarry Cl

Linby Walk

Holbeck Rd

The Drift

Leen Mills

Holy Cross RC
School

Infant
School

Balmoral Gv

Buckingham Avenue

Copeland Road
Leadale
Av

Whyburn
House Farm

Washdyke
Lane

Dobpark
Washdyke La

Misk Hollows

Bentinck St
Victoria Street
St Mary's Way
Newstead
Terrace

National Junior
& Infant School

Hucknall
Leisure
Centre

Carlingford Road

Palmer Av

Co-Operative Av

Linby Rd

Linby Av

Perlethorpe Av

A611

Addison Drive
Greenwood Vale
Greenwood Av
Rydal Dr
Coniston Road
Ullswater
Windermere
Belvoir St
Grassmere Cl
Pevril Cl
George Street
Allen St
Montague Road

Spring Street
PO
Ogle Street
North Hill Lane
North Hill
Primary
School

Silo Farm

HUCKNALL

Primary
School
Robert's Lane

Cranbourne
Grove

Charnwood
Grove

Forest Vw Dr

Portland Gra

Priory Rd

Abbey Close
Private Road

Wood Lane

Park Rd
Park Av

St Patrick's Rd
Garden Rd
Hawthorn Av
Munks Avenue
Aitchison Av
Plumb Rd
Moss Rd
Spring Rd

West Street
West Ter
South Street
Charles Av
Derbyshire Lane
Beech Av
Ladycroft Av
Hanson Crescent

Titchfield St
Baker St
Church Drive

Ashfield
District
Council

William St
Central Av
Belle Isle Rd
Byron St
Chatsworth
Windmill
Storth Av

Vine Terrace
High St
Duke St
Albert St
Pale St
Thoresby Dr

Station Road

Station Ter
Bolsover St

Vaughan
Gardens

Hucknall
Hucknall
Baths
Lane
College of Continuing
Education

School Av

District
Council

Beauvale

Whyburn Lane
Long Acre
Common Lane

Beauvale Road

23

A611

Long Hill

Annie Holgate
Junior &

G H J K L M

M8
1 Kersall Gdns
2 Kneesall Gv

M7
1 Windsor Cl

M6
1 Alexander Cl
2 Parkgate
3 Piper Cl

L8
1 Turner St

Rockwood Crescent
Dawlish Close
Hillcrest
Laxton Drive
Spr Road
Abbots Drive

Yorke St
Portland Rd
Woodford Rd
Oakfield Rd
Bearfield

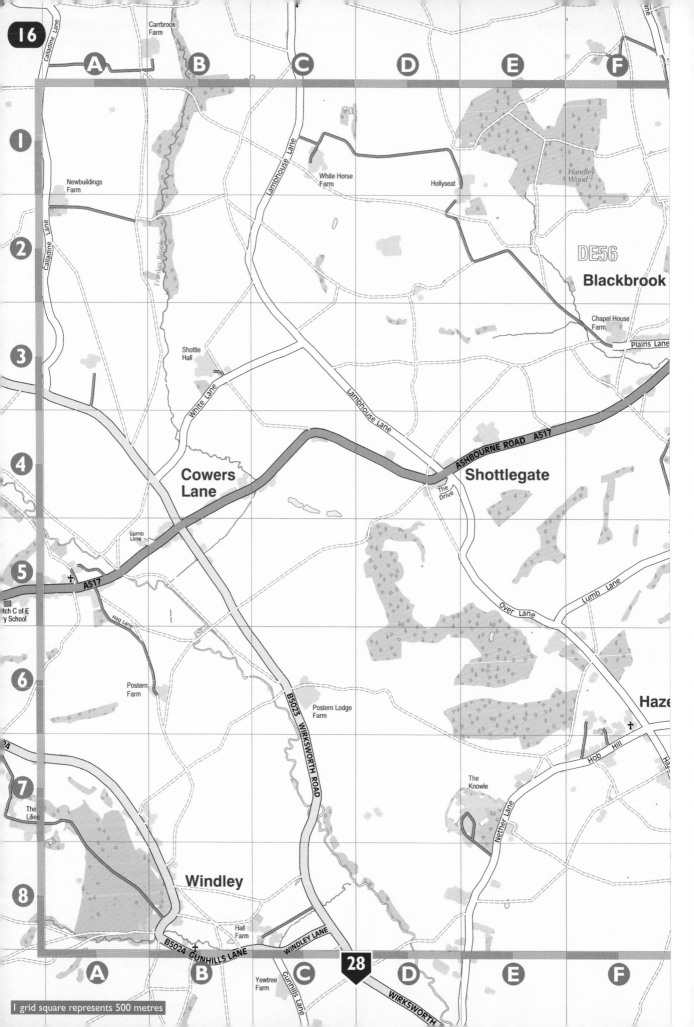

A B C D E F

Calladine Lane

Carrbrook Farm

1

Newbuildings Farm

Calladine Lane

Franker Brook

White Horse Farm

Hollyseat

Handley Wood

2

DE56

Blackbrook

Chapel House Farm

Plains Lane

3

Shottle Hall

White Lane

Lambhouse Lane

Lambhouse Lane

ASHBOURNE ROAD A517

4

Cowers Lane

Shottlegate

The Drive

Lumb Lane

5

A517

Over Lane

Lumb Lane

itch C of E y School

Hag Lane

6

Postern Farm

Postern Lodge Farm

B5023 WIRKSWORTH ROAD

Haze

Hob Hill

Nether Lane

7

The Lilies

24

The Knowle

8

Windley

Hall Farm

Windley Lane

Gunhills Lane

A B B5024 GUNHILLS LANE C 28 D E F

Yewtree Farm

WIRKSWORTH

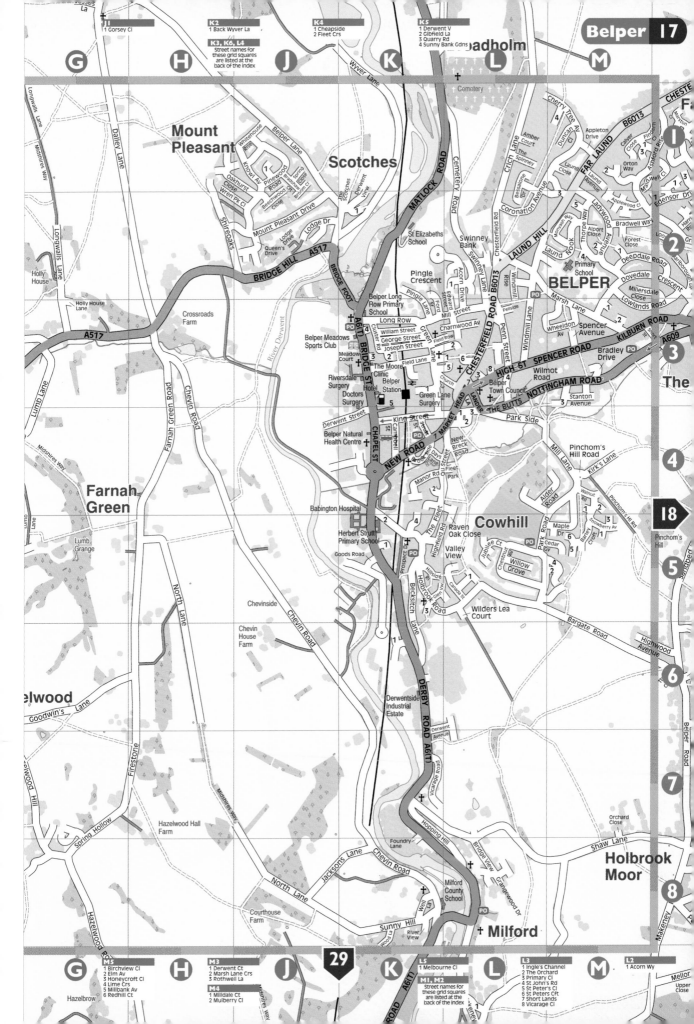

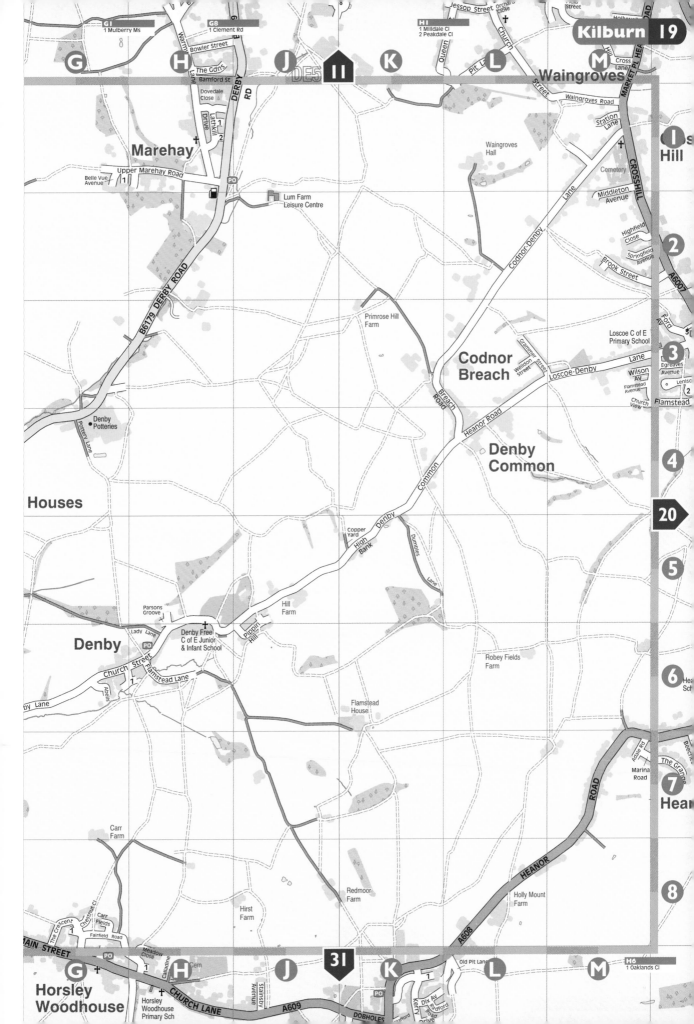

G G1 1 Mulberry Ms
G8 1 Clement Rd
H H1 1 Milldale Ci 2 Peakdale Cl

G H Bowler Street
J DE5 11 K
L Waingroves
M Cross Lane

The Gdns
Bamford St
Dovedale Close

Marehay

Lathkill Drive

Belle Vue Avenue
Upper Marehay Road
PO

Lum Farm Leisure Centre

B6179 DERBY ROAD

Denby Potteries
Pottery Lane

Houses

Primrose Hill Farm

Waingroves Hall

Waingroves Road

Station Lane

CROSSHILL
Cemetery

Middleton Avenue

Highfield Close
Springfield Avenue

Brook Street

I Hill

2

A6007

Ford AV

Codnor-Denby Lane

Codnor Breach

Grammer Street
Weldon Street

Loscoe C of E Primary School

3

Egreaves Avenue

Lenisc

Flamstead

Wilson AV
Flamstead Avenue

Church View

Loscoe-Denby

Breach Road

Heanor Road

Denby Common

4

20

Common

Copper Yard

Denby

High Bank

Dumbles Lane

5

Hill Farm

Parsons Groove

Denby Free C of E Junior & Infant School

Pippin Hill

Robey Fields Farm

6

Hea Sch

Denby

Lady Lane
PO

Church Street

Flamstead Lane

Abells
Denby Lane

Flamstead House

Adale Rd

Marina Road

The Grange

Beech

7

Hea

Carr Farm

Redmoor Farm

HEANOR ROAD

Holly Mount Farm

8

Carr Fields
Chestnut Cl

The Crescent
Fairfield Road
MAIN STREET
PO

Meadow Close
Calladine

Hirst Farm

A608

Horsley Woodhouse

G
H

Horsley Woodhouse Primary Sch

CHURCH LANE

Cem

Avenue
Stainsby

J 31 K

A609

DOBHOLES

Old Pit Lane

L

1

Kerry Drive
Dix AV
Stafford

M H6 1 Oaklands Cl

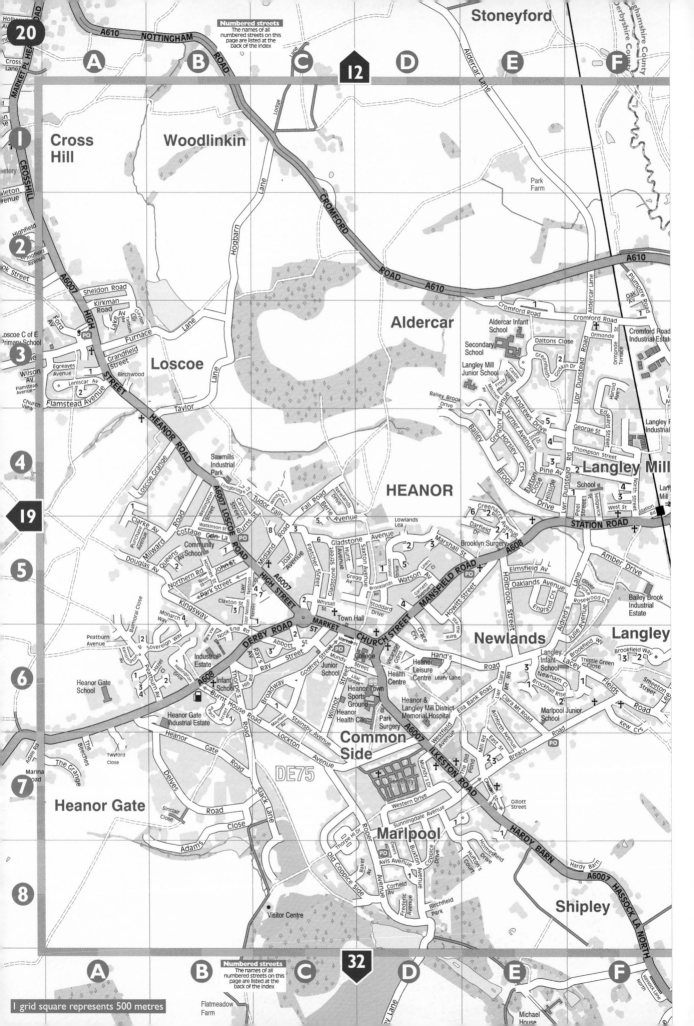

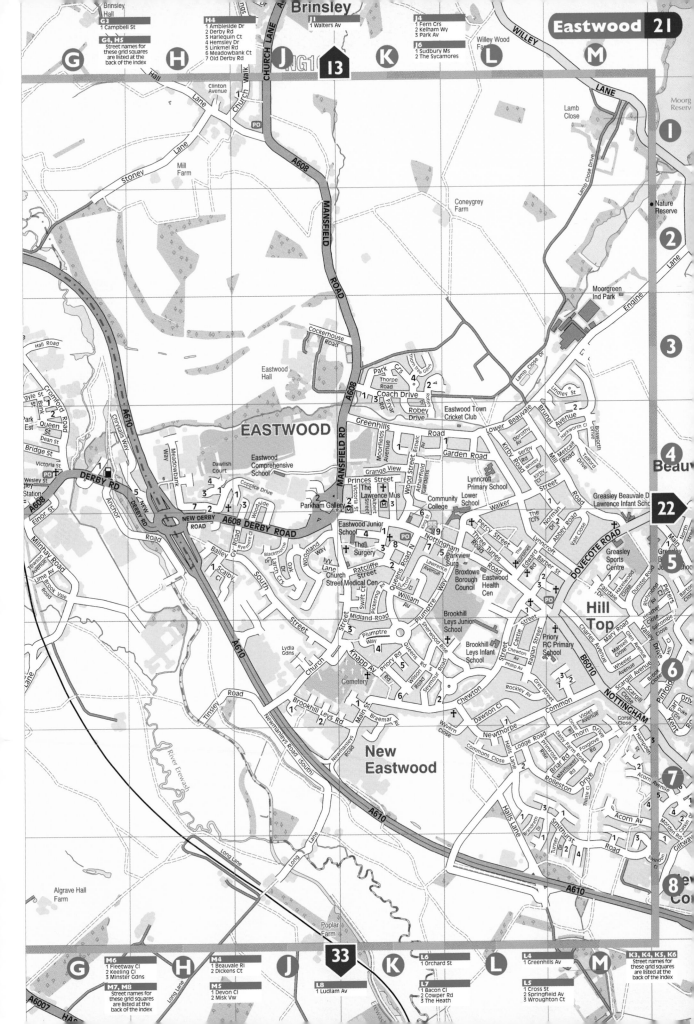

A B C 14 D E F

Beauvale

G2
1 Bethel Gdns
2 Pinehurst Av
3 Suffolk Av
4 Tudor Ct

H2
1 Meadow Cl
2 Norfolk Cl

H3
1 Oaktree Cl
2 Woodlands Farm Cl

J2
1 Elizabeth Cl
2 Seymour Rd
3 Strathmore Cl

K2
1 Eastwood Cl
2 Kingsway Gdns
3 Marchesi Cl
4 Norman Dr

G H J 15 K L M

Ruffs

The Holgate School

Hazelgrove

Broomhill

Cemetery

Hucknall Town Football Club

Annie Holgate Junior & Infant School

Torkard Hill Medical Centre

Westville

Edgewood Drive Primary School

Daniels Way

24

Hucknall Airfield

Eel Hole Farm

Woodhall Farm

Nottinghamshire County
City of Nottingham

Golf Course

Riseborough Walk

NG6

SANDHURST ROAD

New Farm

Blenheim Farm

Blenheim Lane

CAMBERLEY ROAD

Alderman Derbyshire School

Dabell

Snape Wood Medical Centre

Snapewood Primary School

Nature Reserve

Bulwell

Broad Eadow Road

Cemetery

Bulwell Business Centre

Springfield Surgery

Bulwell Medical Centre

Health Centre

I
2
3
4
5
6
7
8

G H 35 J K L M

M7
1 Bacton Gdns
2 Cawston Gdns
3 Hazel St
4 Saxelby Gdns

M3
1 Chestnut Gv
2 Mulberry Gv

M6
1 Acle Gdns

L2, M1, M2, M8
Street names for these grid squares are listed at the back of the index

L8
1 Alder Gdns
2 Downes Cl
3 Gunn Cl
4 Uttle Gdns

L3
1 Belmont Cl
2 Derwent Dr

L7
1 Camberley Ct
2 Harwich Cl
3 Welton Gdns

35
Street names for these grid squares are listed at the back of the index

WATNALL ROAD

M1

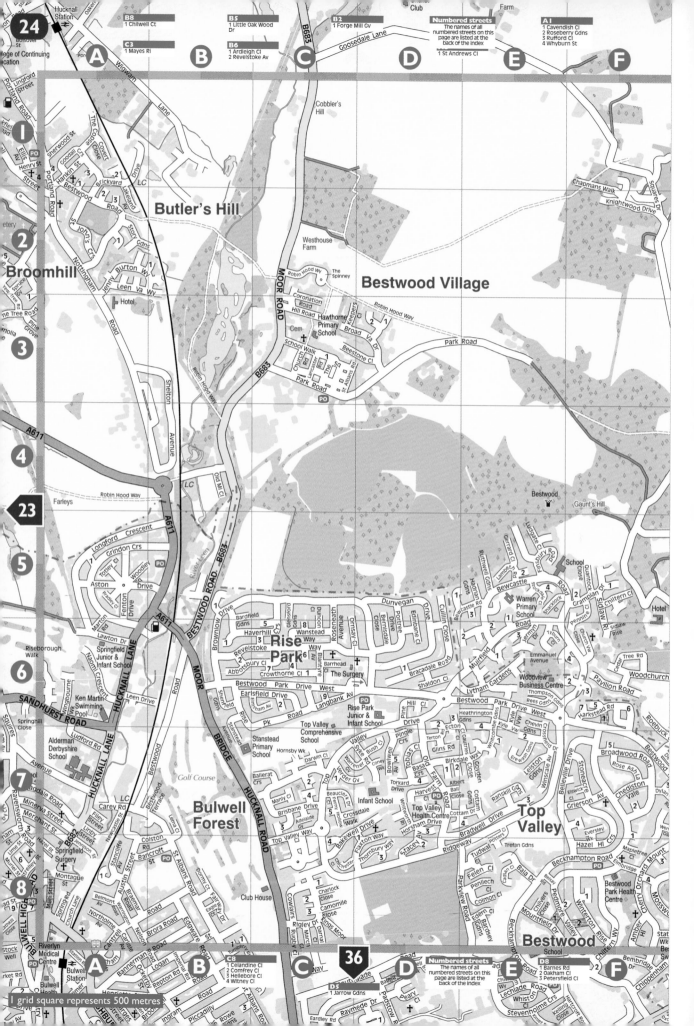

Hucknall
Station

A   B   C   D   E   F

1

Butler's Hill

Cobbler's Hill

2   Broomhill

Westhouse Farm

Bestwood Village

The Spinney

Coronation Road

Hill Road   Hawthorne Primary School   Robin Hood Way

3   Cem   Broad Va Dr   Beestone Cl

Park Road

School Walk   St Albans Rd   The Sq

Park Road

PO

A611

4

LC

23   Robin Hood Way   Farleys   Old Ml Cl

Bestwood   Gaunt's Hill

5   Longford Crescent   Grindon Crs   Woodley Drive   Aston   Fenton Drive

Brownlow Drive   Bardfield Gdns   Haverhill   Revelstoke   Abbotsbury Cl   Crowthorne Cl   Wanstead Way   Blantyre   Barrhead Cl   The Surgery   Bracadale Road   Sheldon Cl

Rise Park

Warren Primary School

Bewcastle   Quantock   Grampian   Sidlaw   Chiltern Rd   Hotel

School Close

6   Riseborough Walk   Springhill Close   Ken Martin Swimming Pool   Lawton Dr   Springfield Junior & Infant School   Naomi Crescent   Leen Drive

Bestwood Park Drive West   Earlsfield Drive   Langbank Av   Rise Park Junior & Infant School   PO

Lytham Gardens   Woodview Business Centre   Emmanuel Avenue   Cedar Tree Rd   Woodchurch   Pavilion Road

SANDHURST ROAD

7   Alderman Derbyshire School   Ludford Rd   Carey Rd   LC   Bestwood Terrace   Bulwell Forest   Golf Course   Stanstead Primary School   Top Valley Comprehensive School   Top Valley Way   Harkstead Rd   Roebuck   Belleville Drive   Broadwood Road   Rose Ash La   Chediston Vale

Minerva Street   Merchant St   Filey Street   Linby St

Top Valley Health Centre   Top Valley   Beckhampton Road   Bestwood Park Health Centre

8   Riverlyn Medical Centre   Bulwell Station   Springfield Surgery   Colston Rd   Bancroft   St Albans Road   Club House   Bestwood School   Bestwood

1 grid square represents 500 metres

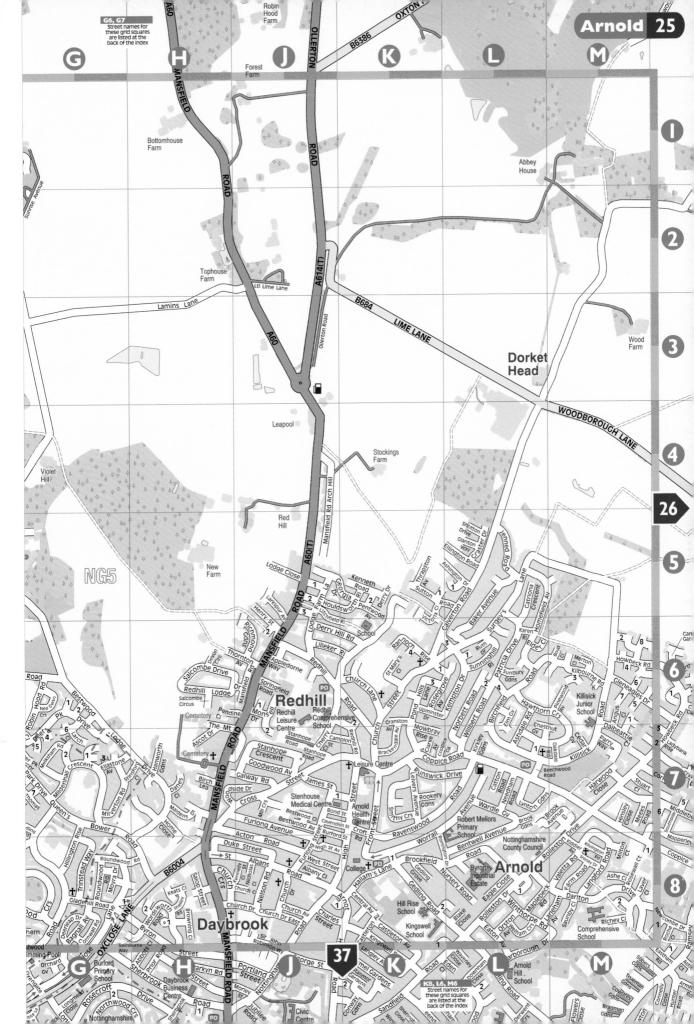

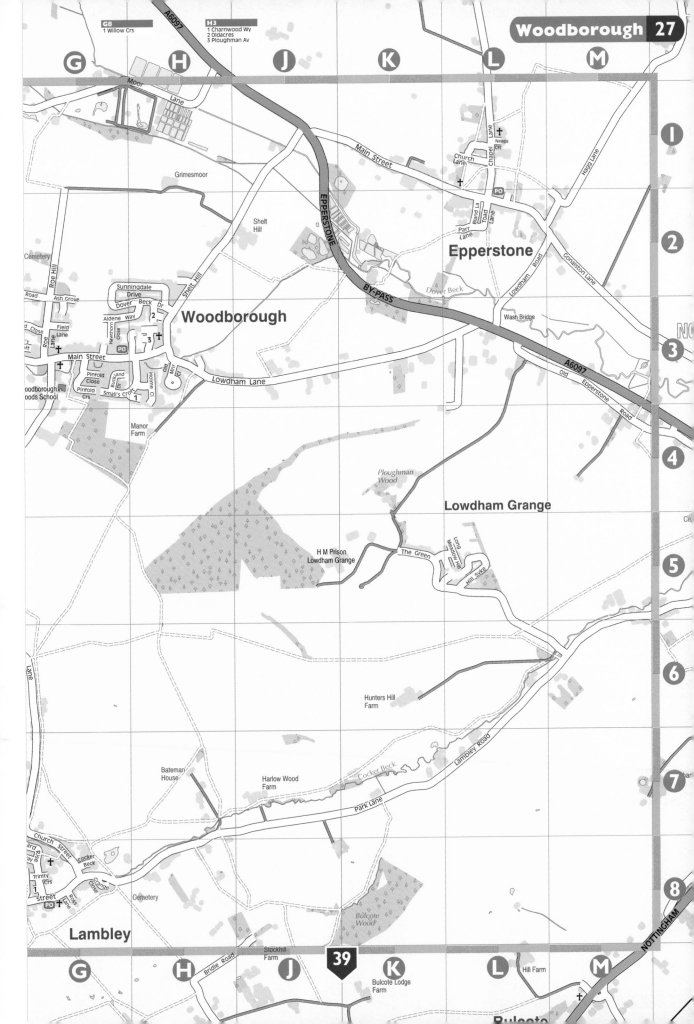

G H J K L M

I
2
3
4
5
6
7
8

Moor Lane

Grimesmoor

Main Street

Church Lane

Chapel Lane

Neeps Cft

Epperstone

PO

Bland La Toad Lane

Parr Lane

Hagg Lane

Shelt Hill

EPPERSTONE

BY-PASS

Dover Beck

Lowdham Road

Gonalston Lane

Wash Bridge

A6097

Old Epperstone Road

Cemetery

Roe Hill

Ash Grove

Road

Close

Field Lane

Roe Lane

Sunningdale Drive

Dover Beck Dr

Aldene Way

Hawthorn Close

Woodborough

Shelt Hill

2

3

PO

Main Street

Pinfold Close

Pinfold Crs

Small's Croft

Bucks and

Holme Cl

Old Mnr

1

Lowdham Lane

Woodborough Woods School

Manor Farm

Ploughman Wood

Lowdham Grange

H M Prison Lowdham Grange

The Green

Long Meadow Hill

Hill Syke

Hunters Hill Farm

Lambley Road

Bateman House

Harlow Wood Farm

Cocker Beck

Park Lane

Church Street

Rise

Cocker Beck

Trinity Crs

Grange Close

1

Street

Ross Lane

PO

Cemetery

Bulcote Wood

Lambley

Bridle Road

Stockhill Farm

39

Bulcote Lodge Farm

Hill Farm

NOTTINGHAM

G H J K L M

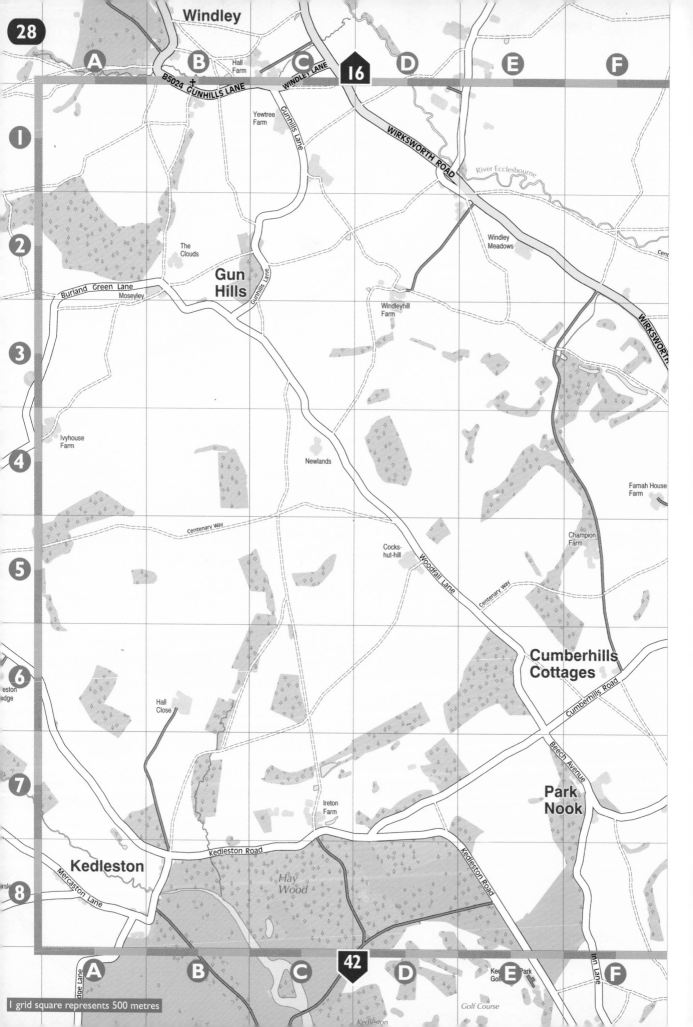

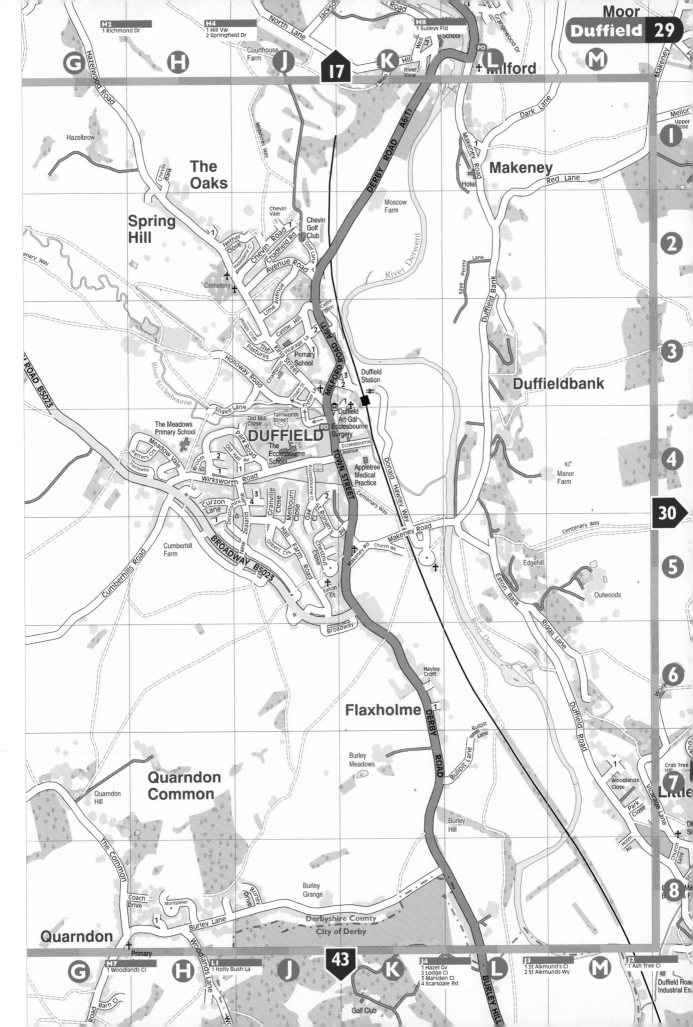

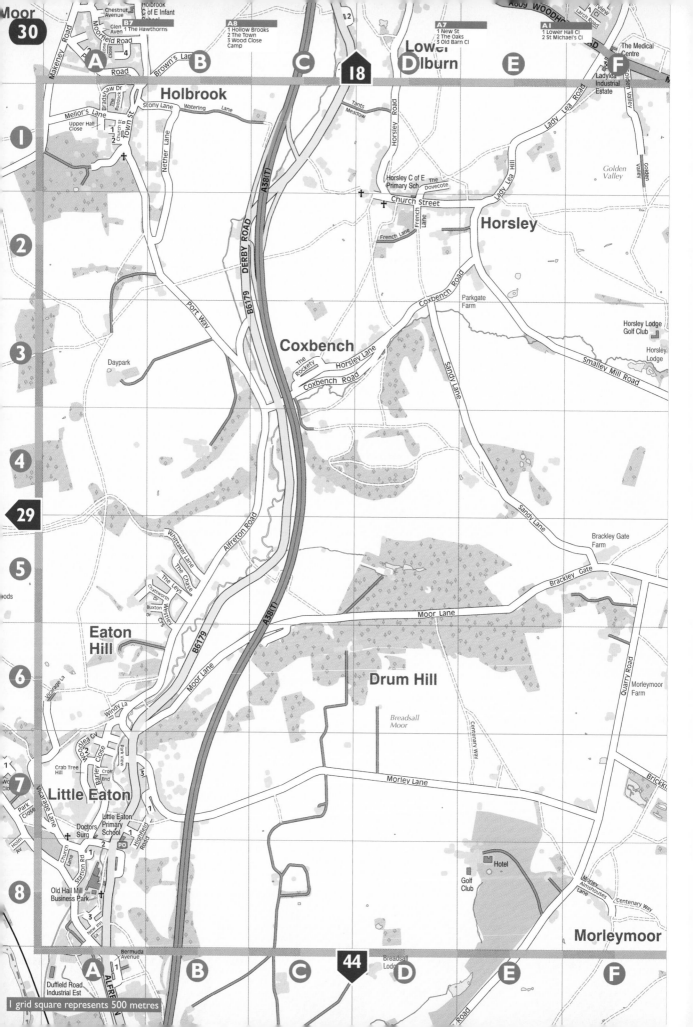

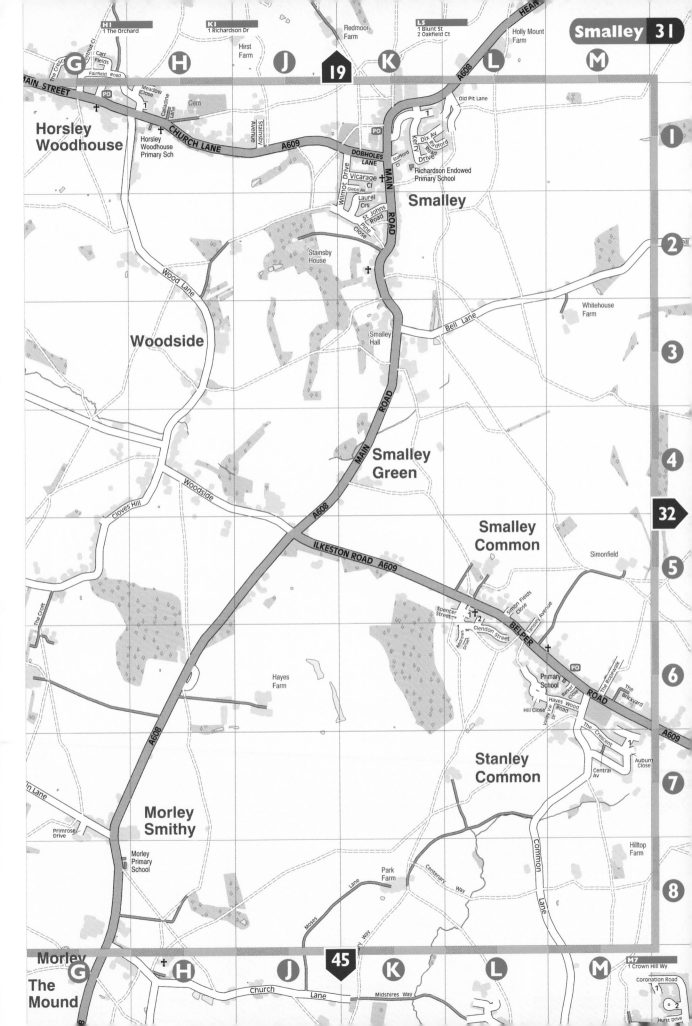

32

20

46

31

A B C D E F

I
2
3
4
5
6
7
8

C8
1 Burncroft
2 School Sq

C7
Street names for
this grid square are
listed at the back of
the index

B7
1 Burnham Cl
2 Chertsey Ct
3 Richmond Cl
4 Sunninghill Cl
5 Twyford Cl
6 Weybridge Cl
7 Windsor Ct

A6007 HASSOCK LA NORTH

Hassock
Lane
North

Pit Lane

ey

Oppice Side

Corfield
AV

Frederic
Avenue

Avenue

Bl

Visitor Centre

Michael
House
School

Flatmeadow
Farm

Prospect
Farm

Bell Lane

Bell Lane

Shipley Lane

Home
Farm

Shipley
Country Park

The American
Adventure
Theme Park

Mapperley
Reservoir

Shipley Lane

Mapperley Park

Mapperley

Lodge
Farm

The Limes

Main Street   PO   Coachways
Primary
School

Lodge

Slack Road

Slack Road

Head House
Farm

Park Hall Lane

Mapperley

Lane

field

The
Brickyard

A609 HIGH LANE CENTRAL

HIGH LANE WEST

A609

Lewcote
Lane

HIGH

LANE

Auburn
Close

Kiln
Cl

Lechlade Close

Surgton

Whilton
Crs

Derbyshire   Avenue

2

8

Bracington Rd

4

Chilel

7

Derwent AV

**West
Hallam**

Nutbro
Cricket
Club

Newdigate Street

Station

Hallam
Way

Newbrdge
Crs

Wilton
Cl

7

Elizabeth
Cl

Henley
Way

3

6

1

Crescent

5

Hardwick

6

Ferntree
Close

Whitefurrows

Centenary Way

Bagot
St

Caversham
Way

Hampton
Ct

Harpur
Ct

Ashford
Cl

Kingston

Cl

Hurley
Court

Peveril
Cl

Scargill Road

Lathkill Close

Road

Slack Road

DE7

Hilltop
Farm

West Hallam
Cricket Club

Scargill C of E
Primary School

Holme
Cft

Nursery
West

Avenue

St

Hallam Medical Cen

PO

Centenary Way

Hilltop
Farm

Centenary Way

Beech
Lane

The Dales
Medical Cen

Orchard Close   2   The
Village
Hall
Ct

Coronation Road
1

Cat   And   Fiddle   Lane

Thacker
Barn

Hurst Drive

Stanley

Station Rd

I grid square represents 500 metres

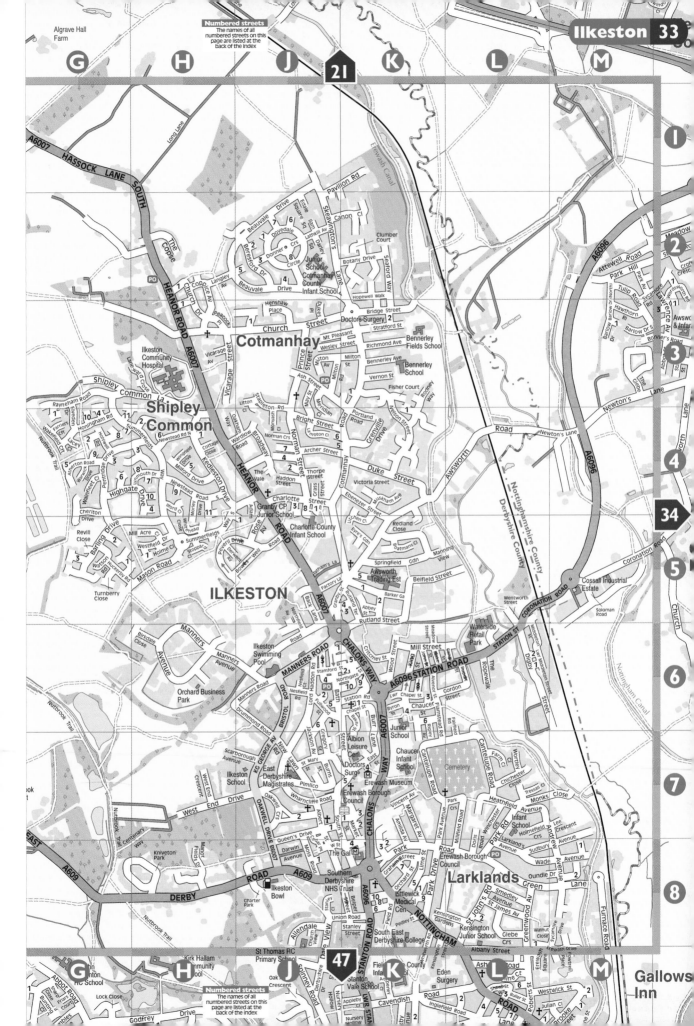

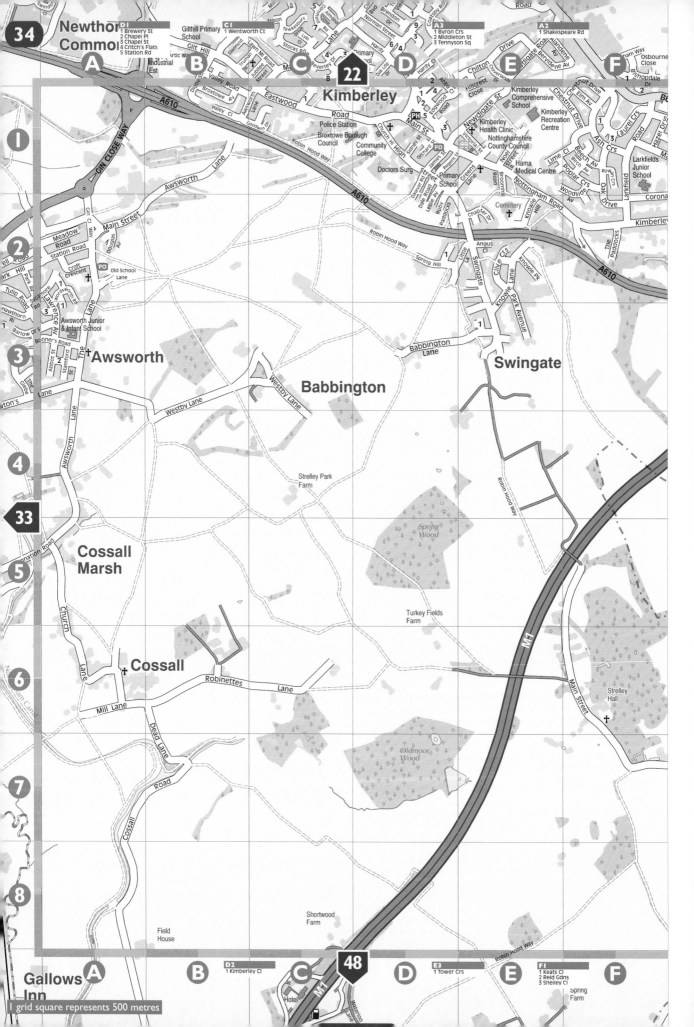

34

Newthor
Common

A   **B**   **22**   Kimberley   **D**   **E**   **F**

A   1 Brewery St
2 Chapel Pl
3 Chapel St
4 Critch's Flats
5 Station Rd

C   1 Wentworth Ct

A3   1 Byron Crs
2 Middleton St
3 Tennyson Sq

A2   1 Shakespeare Rd

Gilthill Primary
School

Kimberley
Comprehensive
School

Kimberley
Recreation
Centre

Kimberley
Health Clinic

Nottinghamshire
County Council

Hama
Medical Centre

Police Station
Broxtowe Borough
Council
Community College

Doctors Surg

Larkfields
Junior
School

Corona

I

2   Meadow Road   Station Road   Main Street

3   Awsworth

Awsworth Junior
& Infant School

Swingate

Babbington Lane

4

Westby Lane   **Babbington**

Strelley Park
Farm

Spring
Wood

Robin Hood Way

33

5   Cossall
Marsh

Turkey Fields
Farm

6   Cossall

Robinettes   Lane

Mill Lane

Strelley
Hall

7

Oldmoor
Wood

8

Field
House

Shortwood
Farm

Gallows
Inn

A   **B**   **48**   **D**   **E**   **F**

D2   1 Kimberley Cl

E3   1 Tower Crs

F   1 Keats Cl
2 Reid Gdns
3 Shelley Cl

Spring
Farm

Hotel

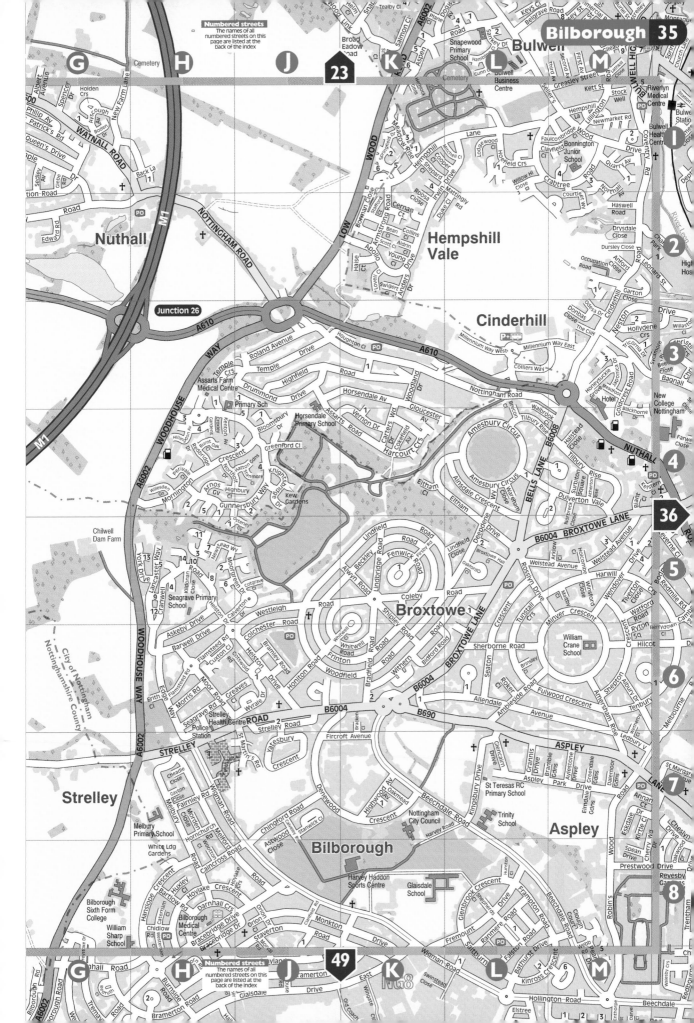

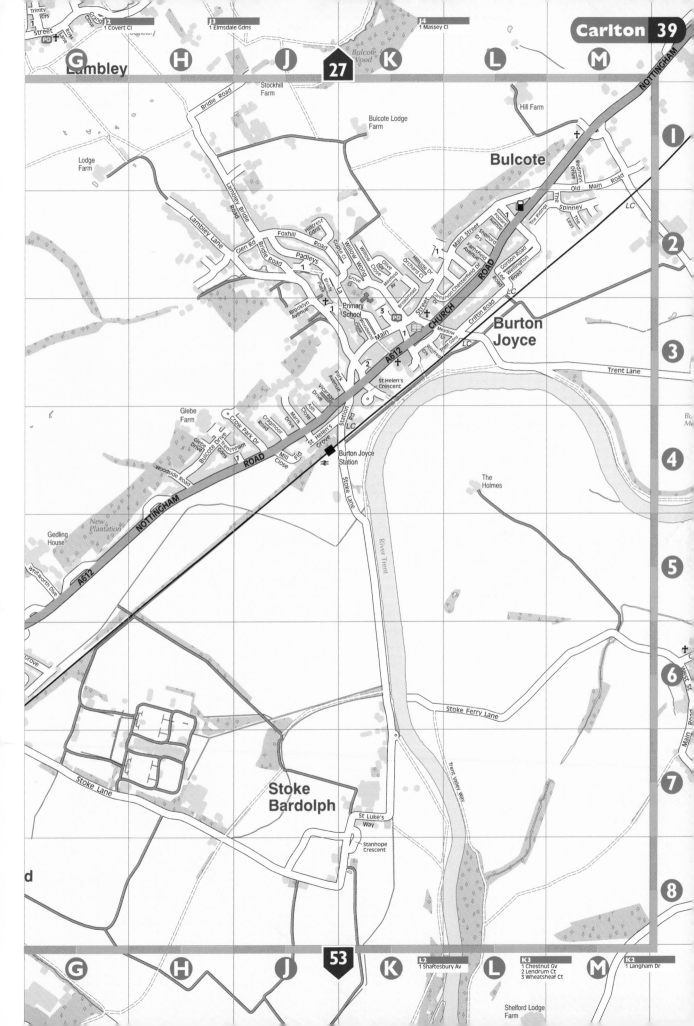

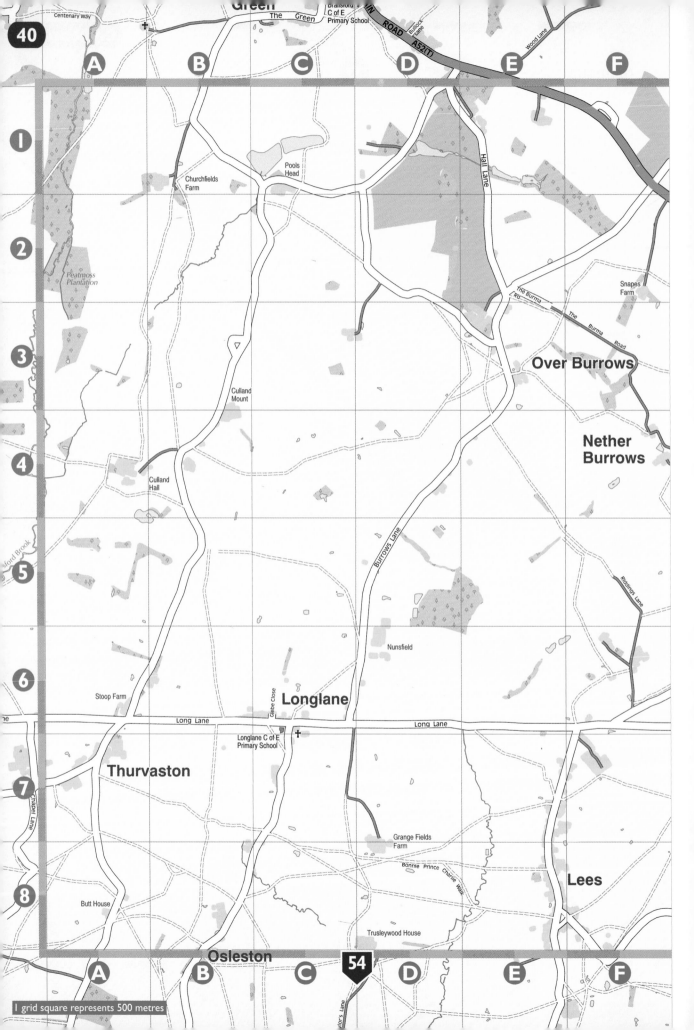

G H J K L M

K5
1 Fieldon Cl

I

Wildpark Lane

Buck
Hazels

2

Windy
Arbour

Meynell Langley

Priestwood
Farm

Me
La

ASHBOURNE ROAD A52(T)

Hilltop
Farm

Flagshaw Lane

Lodge Lane

3

Lodge Farm

4

42

Langley
Hall

Flagshaw Lane

5

Church   Lane

Kirk Langley
C of E
Primary School

PO

The Cannery

Kirk Langley

ASHBOURNE ROAD A52(T)

Petty

Close

Lane

Langley Green

The Green

MOOR LANE

6

Petty Close Lane

B5020

Poyser Lane

The
Pastures

Pimm's
Road

Long Lane

Long Lane

Adams Road

Pole's Road

Wheathill
Farm

Brun   Lane

7

**Langley
Common**

B5020

8

*Radbourne
Common*

Foxfields Farm

G H J K L M

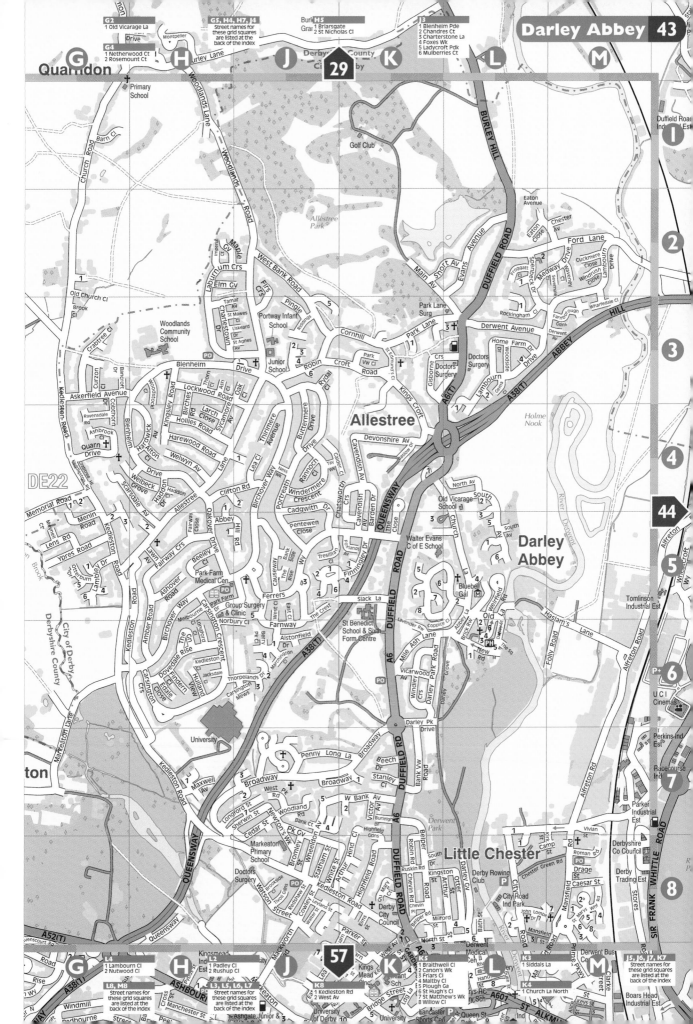

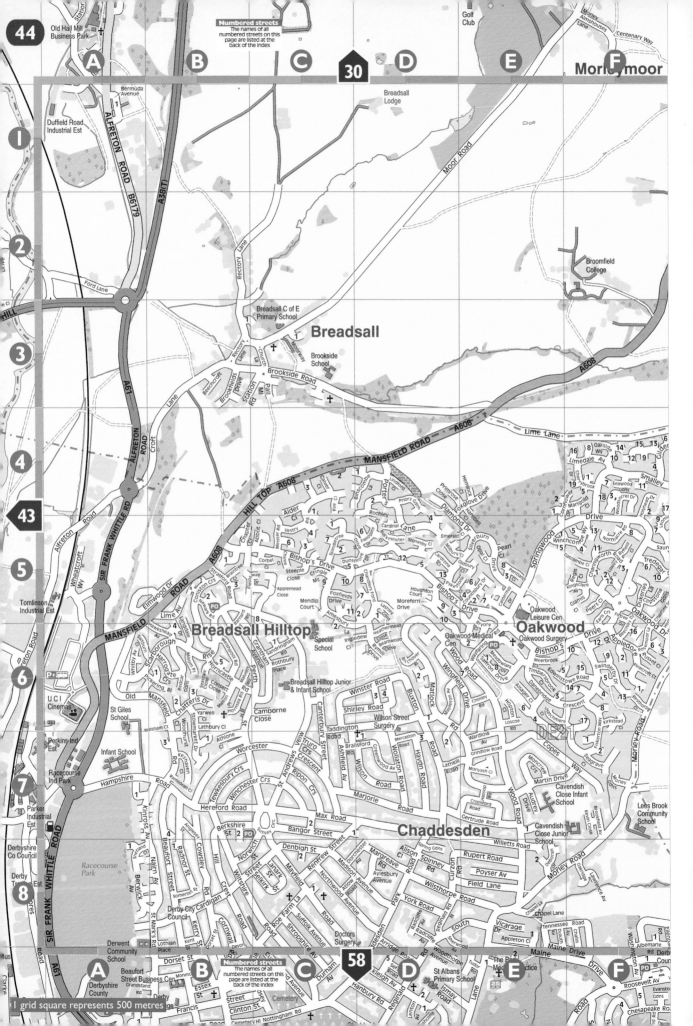

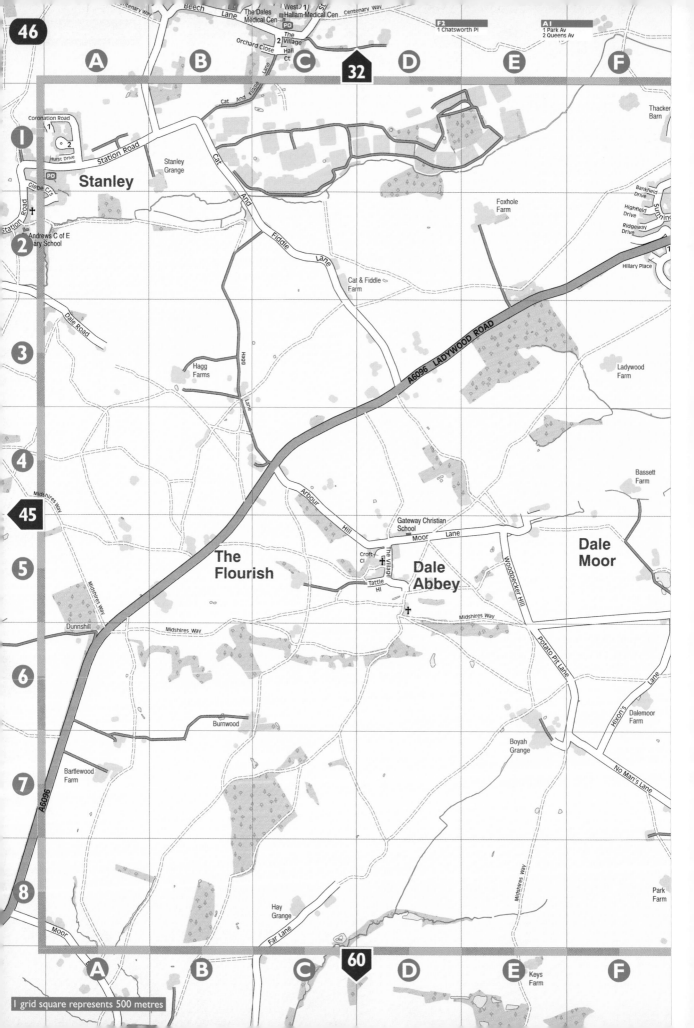

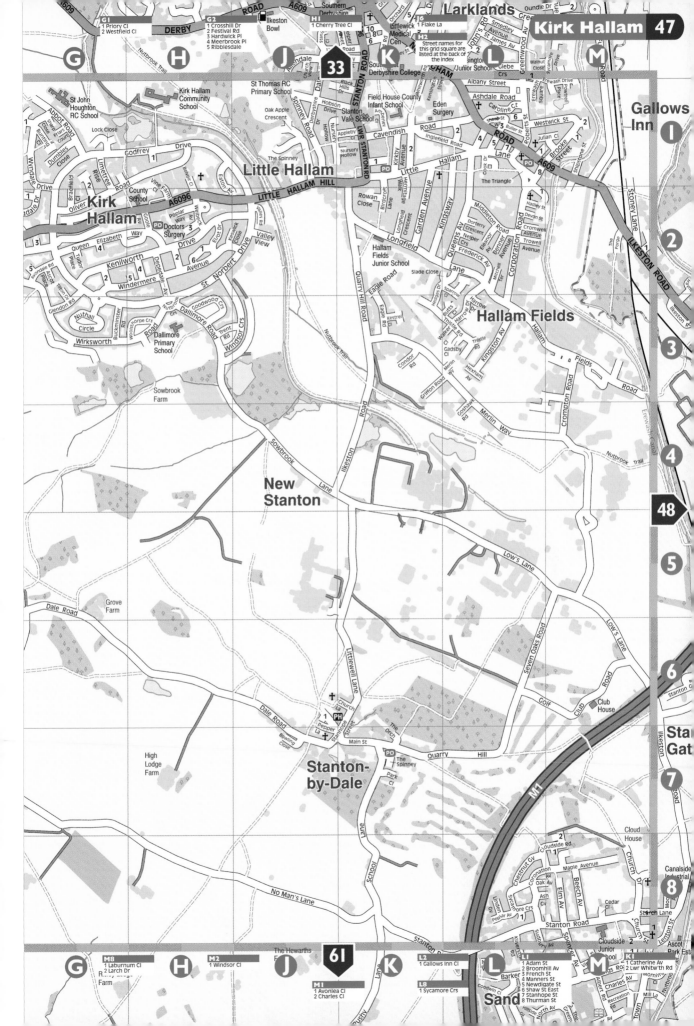

Larklands

Gallows Inn

Kirk Hallam

Little Hallam

Hallam Fields

New Stanton

Stanton-by-Dale

Sand

G1
1 Priory Cl
2 Westfield Cl

G2
1 Crosshill Dr
2 Festival Rd
3 Hardwick Pl
4 Meerbrook Pl
5 Ribblesdale

H1
1 Cherry Tree Cl

H2
Street names for
this grid square are
listed at the back of
the index

33

61

48

M8
1 Laburnum Cl
2 Larch Dr

M2
1 Windsor Cl

M1
1 Avonlea Cl
2 Charles Cl

L2
1 Gallows Inn Cl

L8
1 Sycamore Crs

1 Adam St
2 Broomhill Av
3 French St
4 Manners St
5 Newdigate St
6 Shaw St East
7 Stanhope St
8 Thurman St

K1
1 Catherine Av
2 Lwr Whitw'th Rd

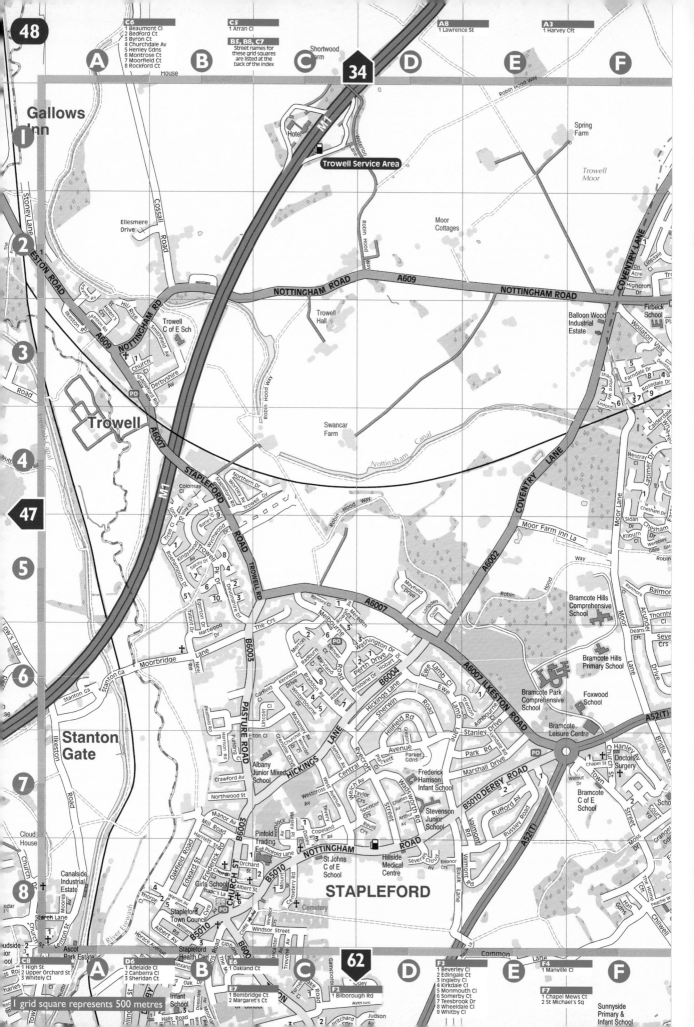

48

A   B   C   34   D   E   F

C6
1 Beaumont Cl
2 Bedford Ct
3 Byron Ct
4 Churchdale Av
5 Henley Gdns
6 Montrose Ct
7 Moorfield Ct
8 Rockford Ct

C5
1 Arran Cl

B5, B8, C7
Street names for
these grid squares
are listed at the
back of the index

A8
1 Lawrence St

A3
1 Harvey Cft

Gallows Inn

1

Shortwood Farm

Spring Farm

Trowell Moor

Hotel

Trowell Service Area

2

ESTON ROAD

Ellesmere Drive

NOTTINGHAM ROAD   A609   NOTTINGHAM ROAD

Robin Hood Way

Moor Cottages

Firbeck School

Wollaton Vale

Trowell Hall

Balloon Wood Industrial Estate

Coventry Lane

3

Trowell C of E Sch

Church

PO

Trowell

Swancar Farm

Nottingham Canal

Moor Farm Inn La

4

STAPLEFORD ROAD

A6007

Coventry Lane

A6002

47

5

Robin Hood Way

Bramcote Hills Comprehensive School

TROWELL RD

Bramcote Hills Primary School

6

Moorbridge

B6003

A6007 ILKESTON ROAD

Bramcote Park Comprehensive School

Foxwood School

Bramcote Leisure Centre

A52(T)

Stanton Gate

HICKINGS LANE

PASTURE ROAD

Albany Junior Mixed School

Frederick Harrison Infant School

Stevenson Junior School

Bramcote C of E School

B5010 DERBY ROAD

Doctors Surgery

7

Cloud House

Canalside Industrial Estate

Pinfold Trading Est

St Johns C of E School

NOTTINGHAM ROAD

Hillside Medical Centre

8

Ascot Park Estate

Stapleford Health Cen

Girls School

Stapleford Town Council

STAPLEFORD

B5010

B6003

Cemetery

A   D   B   E   62   C   D   E   F

D4
1 Adelaide Cl
2 Canberra Cl
3 Montrose Ct

E6
1 Oakland Ct

F3
1 Beverley Cl
2 Edingale Ct
3 Ingleby Cl
4 Kirkdale Cl
5 Monmouth Cl
6 Somerby Ct
7 Teesbrook Dr
8 Wheeldale Cl
9 Whitby Cl

F4
1 Manville Cl

C8
1 High St
2 Upper Orchard St
3 Whitely Cl

E2
1 Bembridge Ct
2 Margaret's Ct

F2
1 Bilborough Rd

F7
1 Chapel Mews Ct
2 St Michael's Sq

1 grid square represents 500 metres

Sunnyside Primary & Infant School

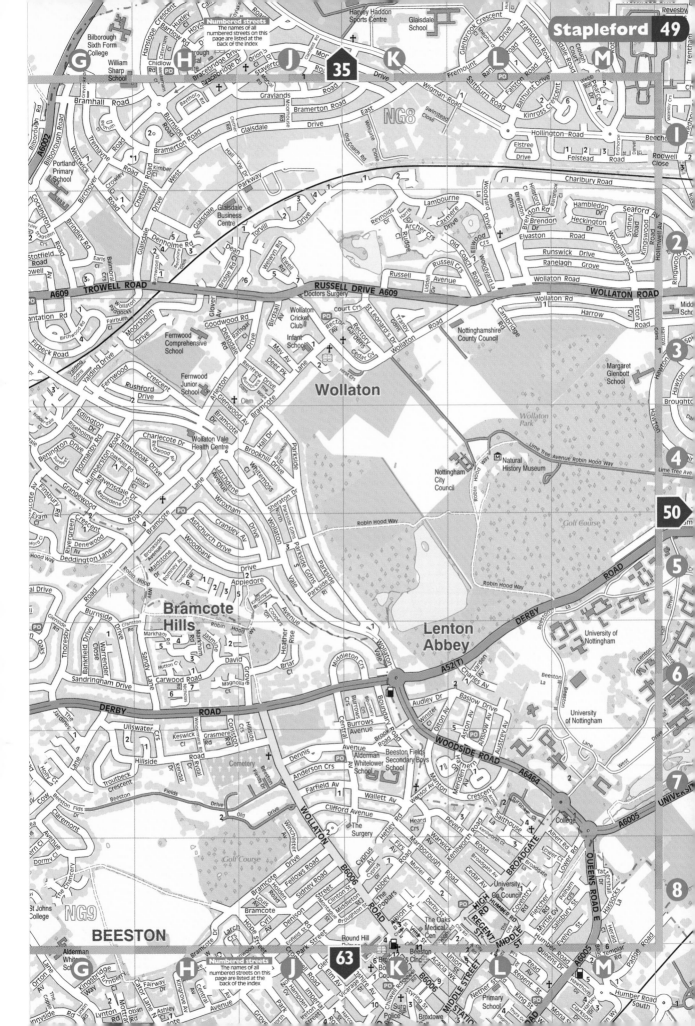

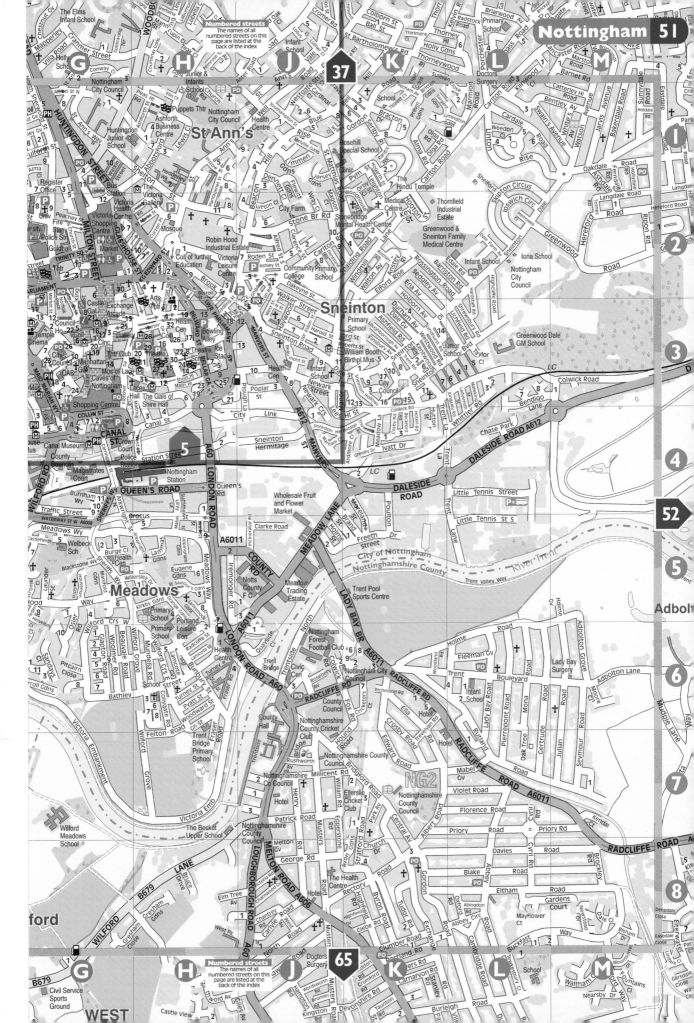

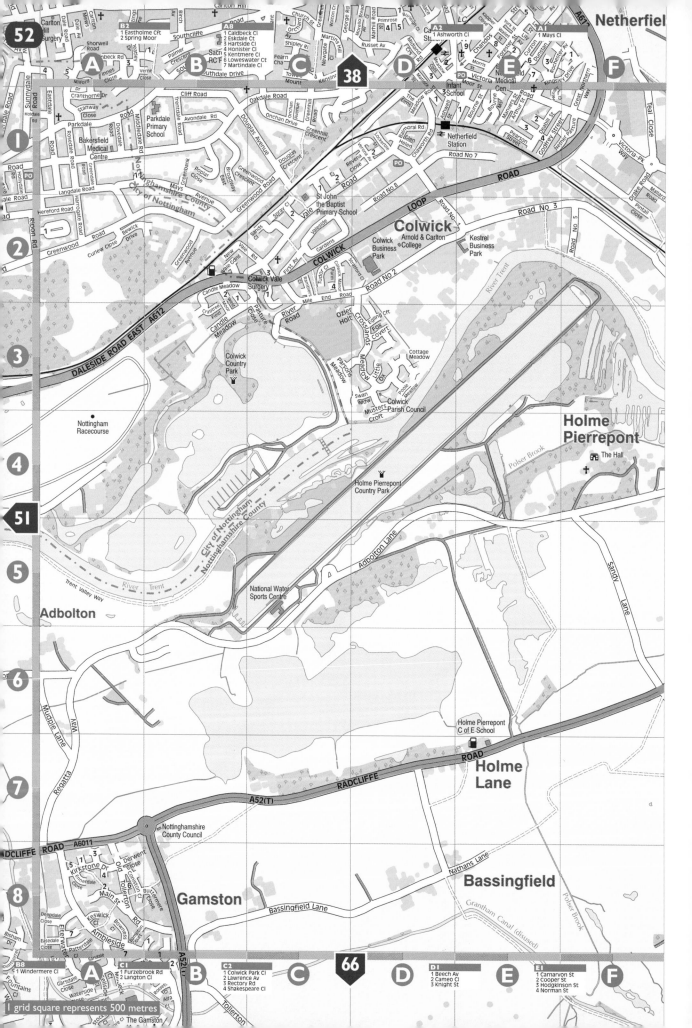

J4
1 Lamcote Ms
2 Mount Pleasant
3 Orchard Cl
4 The Woodlands

J5
1 Barrington Cl
2 Jasper Cl
3 Portage Cl
4 Regina Cl
5 St Catherines St
6 Saskatoon Cl
7 Yonge Cl

K3
1 Richmond Dr

K5
1 Douglas Cl

G   H   J   39   K   L   M

RADCLIFFE
ON TRENT

River Trent

Ouse Dyke

Road No 4

Polser Brook

Holme Lane

Trent Vale Way

Shelford Lodge
Farm

Valley Road

Ridge Lane

Shelford Road

Park Road

Cliff Drive

Hopewell Close

Clumber Drive
Chatsworth Av
Webeck Rd
Westcliffe Avenue

Grandfield Crs
Cliff Way
Rockley Av
Cliff Crs
Cliff St

Grandfield Av

Hamilton Drive

Oak Tree Av

Birkin Av
Butler Av
Penrith Av
Wakefield Av

Newstead

Queen's Road
Malkin Av
Newton Av
Thoresby Av

Summer Way
Centre Wy
Oak Avenue
Cliff Lane
Fernwood Drive

Shelford Grove
Chestnut Grove

The Crescent

Radcliffe Stn

Brookfield Cl

Gatcombe Close

Golf Road

Harewood Close

Nursery Cl
Woodside Av
Dormy Cl

Nursery Rd

GRANTHAM
Thomas Av
Northfield Avenue

PO

Harle

Carter Av
Marl Rd
Blakeney Road
Woodland Cl

John's Road

Covert Crs

Rushcliffe Avenue
New Lome Cv
Bingham Road
Eastwood Road
Cropwell Road

Hillside Rd

The Green
Greenway
Sydney Gv
Pinfold Cl
Lamcote Gdns

Main Road
Hogg Ln
Hall Cl
Vicarage La
Shadwell Grove

Walnut Grove

Health Centre

PO

Dayncourt School

Cemetery

Albert St
Lincoln St
Victoria Gv

Glebe Lane
Cropwell Gardens

Radcliffe on Trent Golf Club

Dewberry Lane

Yew Tree Close

Water Road

Prince Edward Crs

Paddock Cl
Bailey Lane

Oxford Avenue

Whitworth Drive

Ume Cl
Maple Cl
Beech Cl
Sycamore Cl
Willow Cl

Radcliffe Junior School

Cherry Tree Close

St Lawrence Bvd
Kingsway
Granville Cl

Nottingham

GRANTHAM ROAD A52(T)

A52(T)

Lees Barn Road

Lees Barn

Lamcote Field

Holme House

Hall Farm

Shepherd's Path

North Farm

Cotgrave Place

I
2
3
4
5
6
7
8

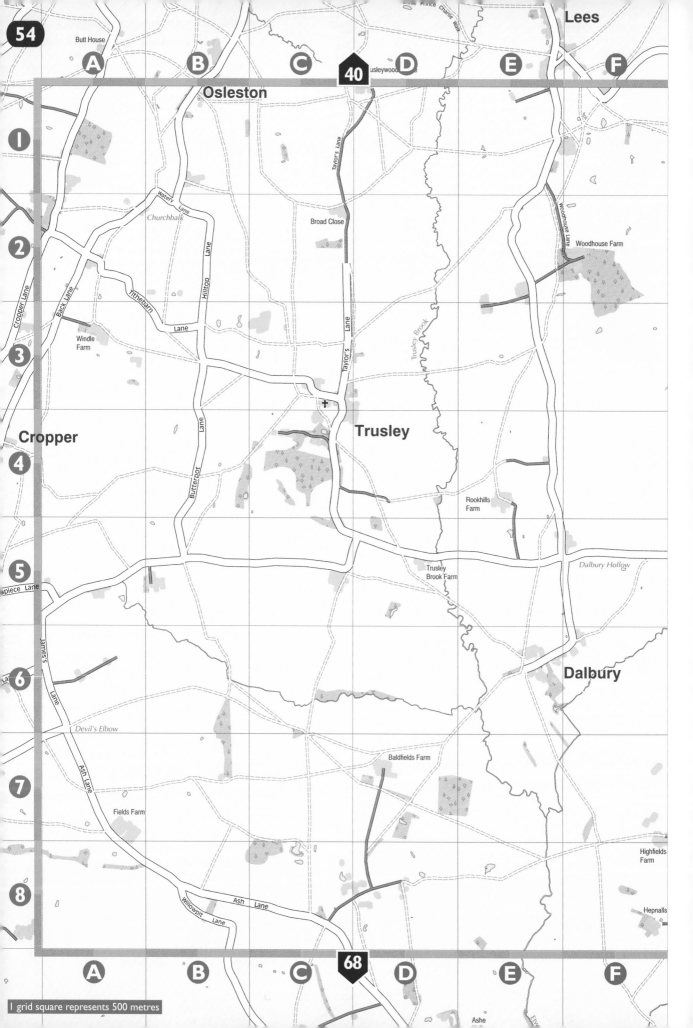

54

Lees

A   B   C   **40** usleywood   D   E   F

Butt House

Osleston

I

Watery Lane

Churchbalk

Broad Close

2

Cropper Lane

Back Lane

Tithebarn

Hilltop Lane

Windle Farm

Lane

3

Woodhouse Lane

Woodhouse Farm

Trusley Brook

Cropper

Butterpot Lane

Taylor's Lane

Taylor's Lane

†

Trusley

4

Rookhills Farm

5

piece Lane

Trusley Brook Farm

Dalbury Hollow

James's Lane

Dalbury

6

Devil's Elbow

Ash Lane

Baldfields Farm

7

Fields Farm

Highfields Farm

8

Willowpit Lane

Ash Lane

Hepnalls

Ashe

A   B   C   **68**   D   E   F

M8
1 Kingfisher Cl

G

H

J

41

K

L

M

I

Foxfields Farm

Bonnie Prince Charlie Walk

Radbourne

Silverhill Farm

2

Bonnie Prnce Charlie Walk

3

Birch Wood

Potlocks Farm

Sandown Av

4

Doc Surg

Naseby Close

Swayfield

56

Terrel Hays

4

2

Cherts Cl

5

Smerrills Farm

Treeside Cl

Ladybank

6

Bonehill Farm

Bearwardcote Hall

Heage Lane

7

Bannells Lane

A516(T)

ETWALL ROAD

The Grange

Hospital Lane

8

Bearwardcote Farm

Merlin Way

1

G

H

Heage Lane

A516(T)

J

69

K

Dee Lane

Grassy Lane

L

M

Oakdene Farm

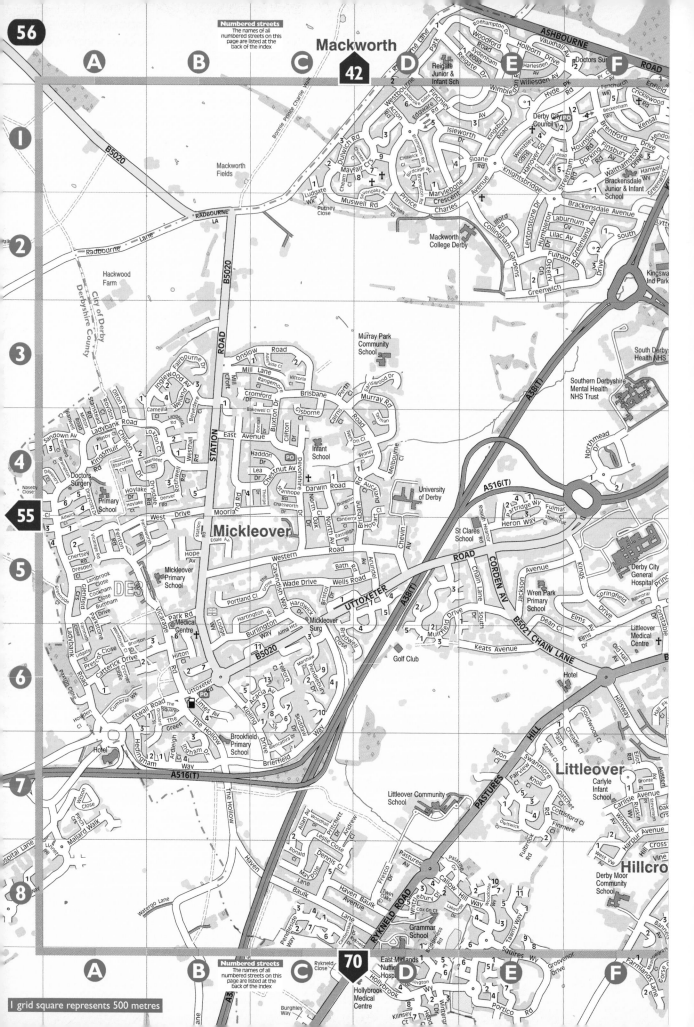

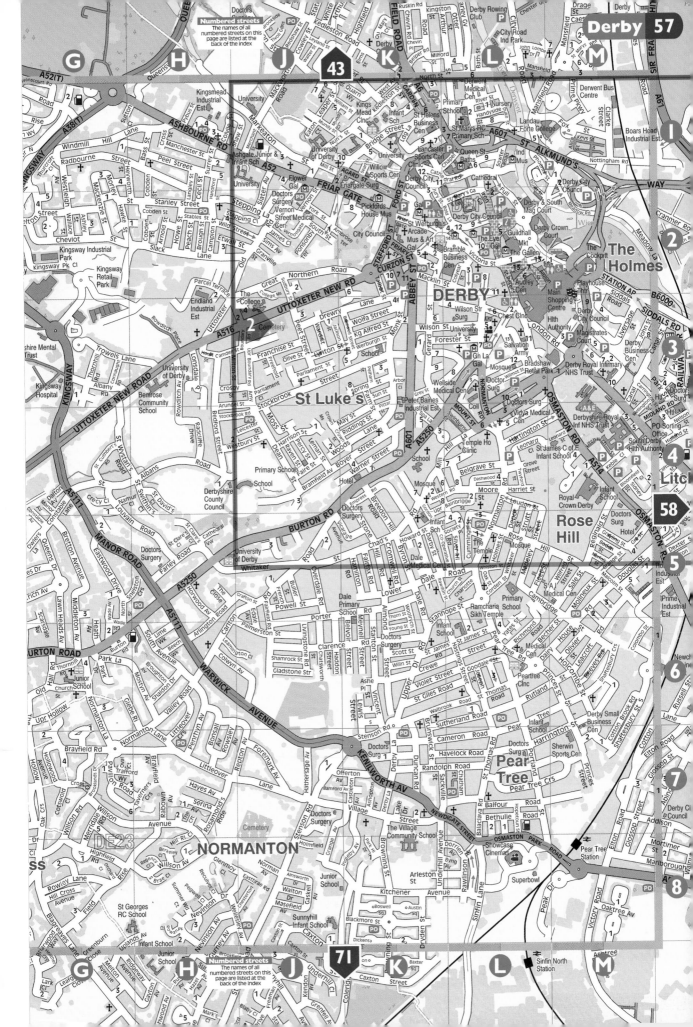

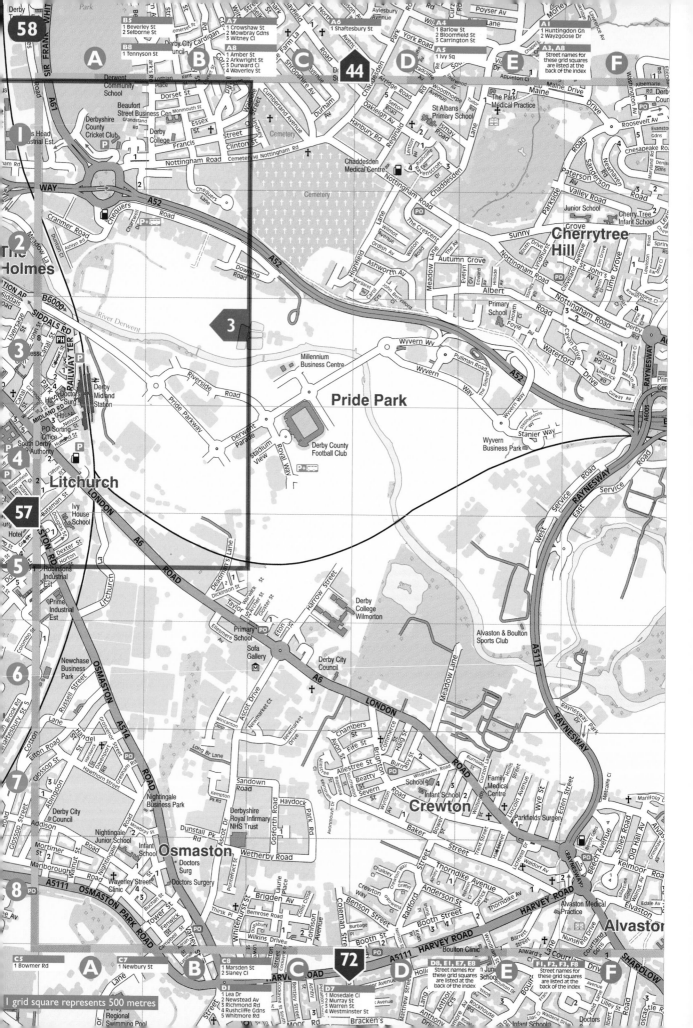

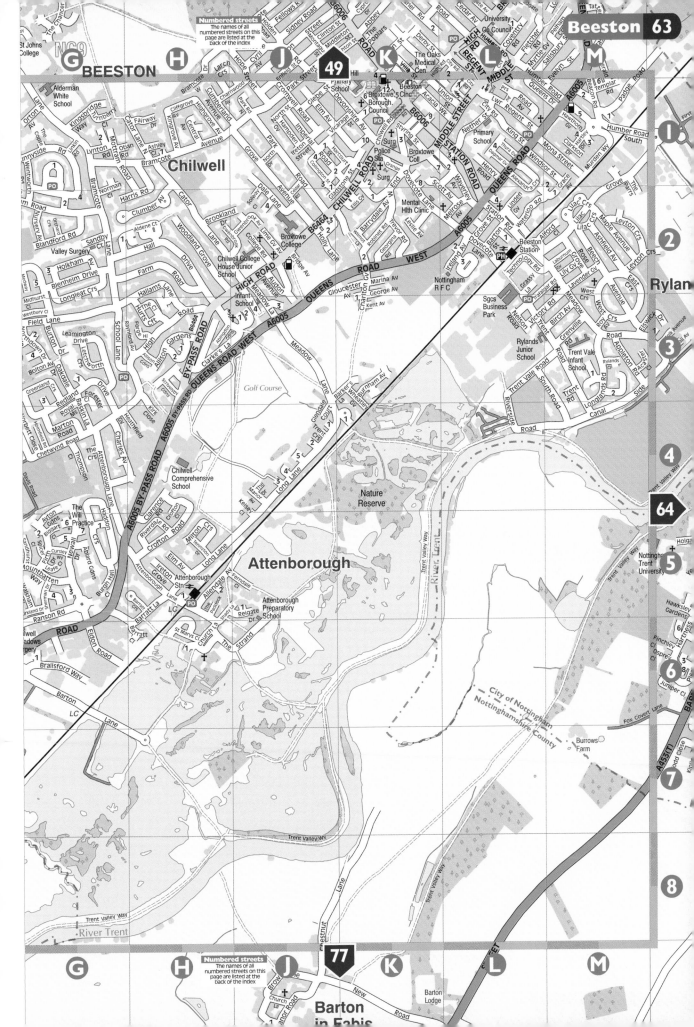

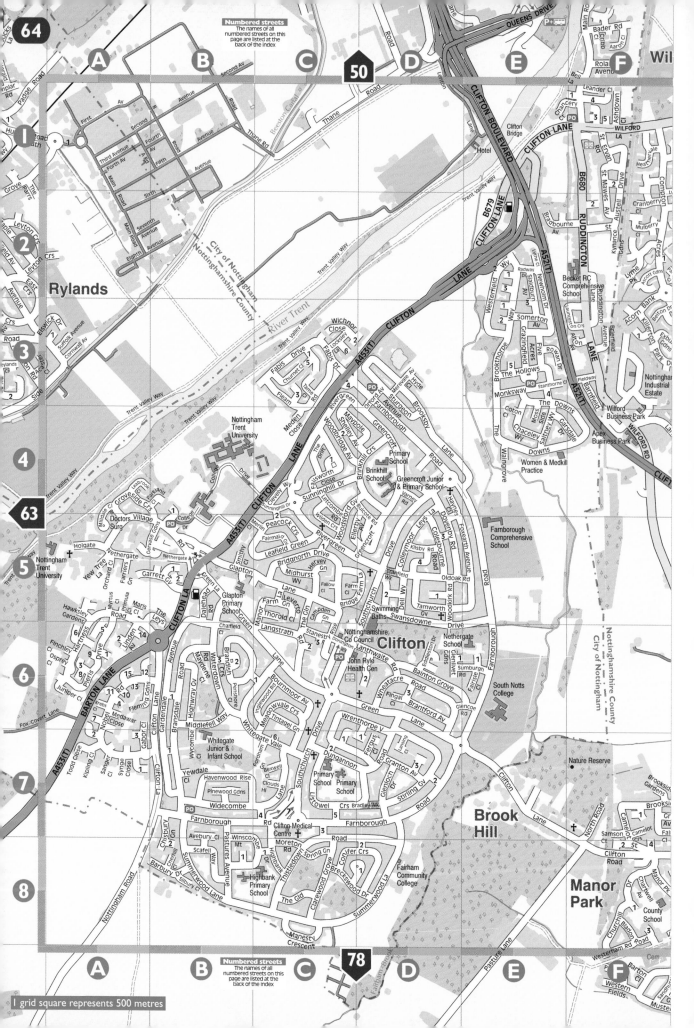

G H J K L M

53

1 Chichester Dr — J3
1 Lamplands — J4
1 Ingleby Cl — J5

I
2
3
4
5
6
7
8

Hollygate Lane

Grantham Canal (disused)

Peashill Farm

Windmill Hill

High Hazles Road

The Old Park

Main Road

Mill La

Morkinshire La

Primary School

Wyne Farm

Thurman

Church Lane

PO

Bingham

Lawrence Cl

Chapel La

East Acres

The Park

Pinfold Cl

Colston Gate

Rivermead

Glenbrook

Health Centre

Deanscourt

Avondale

Ring

Grassmere

Fir Dale

Crosshill

Willowdene

Lingford

Meadow Spring

Cotgrave

Hales Close

Rectory Road

Woodgate Lane

Baker's Hollow

Woodlands

Mensing Av

Plumtree Road

Cherry Orch

Broad Meering

Scrimshire La

Risedale

Risegate

Candleby Lane

Candleby Gardens

Candleby Close

County Infant School

Ash Lea School

Manvers Junior School

Green Platt

Forest

White

Furrows

Daisy Cl

Fern La

Fern Lea

Corn Cl

Owthorpe Road

Ash Lea Close

Sandive

Flagholme

Woodview

Cartindale

Ritchie Cl

Meadow

Whitelands

Phoenix

Thornhons

Marshwood

Burhill

Cloverdale

Flaxendale

Eastwold

Briar Ga

Barn

Manns Leys

Toft Cl

Miller's Br

Daleside

Westway

The Dial

Fox Cl

Bonny Md

Cripps Com

Runcie

Woulds Pl

Ring

Moor Leas

Brambleway

Thirlbeck

East Cl

Warwick Gardens

Saxon Way

Hickling Way

NG12

Woodgate Lane

Plumtree Road

Cotgrave Road

Clipston

Gilliver La

Church Gate

Glebe Farm

Wolds Lane

Cotgrave Wolds

Owthorpe Road

A46(T)

Borders Wood

Owthorpe Wolds

e-Wold G H J K L M

81

1 West Furlong — L6

1 Chennel Nook — L5
2 Edgington Cl

1 Hazelwood — L4
2 Troutbeck

1 GreenfIelds Dr — K5
2 Hawthorn Av
3 Manorwood Rd
4 Spinney Cl
5 The Warren
6 Woodland Cl

C6
1 Bentley Rd
2 Blithe Cl
3 Dale Brook
4 Huntspill Rd
5 Marston Brook
6 Mill Fleam
7 Sandford Brook

C5
1 Churchill Dr
2 Falaise Wy
3 Lancaster Dr
4 Montgomery Cl
5 Shaef Cl
6 Utah Cl

B5
1 Cherry Tree Cl

A5
1 Dove Ri
2 Percy Wood Cl
3 Shady Gv
4 Willowbrook Cl

A B C 54 D E F

1

2

3 Burntheath

4

5 Hilton

6 DE65

7

8

Hepnalls

Park Farm

Ashe Hall

Hilton Fields

A516(T)

Sutton Lane

Willowpit Lane

Ashe Lane

Etwall Brook

Church Hill

John Port School

Etwall Leisure Centre

PO

Etwall Primary School

Etw

Derby Road

Hilton Road

Sutton Lane

Mill Meadow Way

The Bancroft

Etta's Way

Chestnut Grove

Windmill Rd

Springfield

Eggington Road

Grove P

Hilton Lodge

Derby Road

A516(T)

A50(T)

Hilton Industrial Estate

Dale End Lane

Sutton Lane

Mill Grove

West Avenue

Main Street

Bembrose Community School

Mill Lane

Back Lane

Peacroft Lane

Field Cl

Bancroft Close

Ivy Ct

Hawthorn Cl

Alders Brook

Bloomfield Close

Calder Close

Wyston Brook

Welland Road

Tinsell Brook

Avon Way

Nene Way

Washford Road

The Mease

The Mease

Derby Airfield

Blacksmith's

Primary School

Derby Road

A5132

Eggington Road

New Road

Willowfield

Peacroft Ct

Pegasus Way

Normandy Road

Mulberry Way

Bader Wy

Nithan Cl

Lucas Lane

Rodney Cl

Halifax

Enfield

A50(T)

A5132

Eggington Road

Hargate Manor

Oldfield Lane

Blakeley Lane

Blakeley Lodge

Eggington Road

LC

LC

HILTON ROAD

Etwall Road

C7
1 Stour Cl

F3
1 Ash View Cl
2 Mansfields Cft

F4
1 Blakelow Dr
2 Melville Ct

A B C D E F

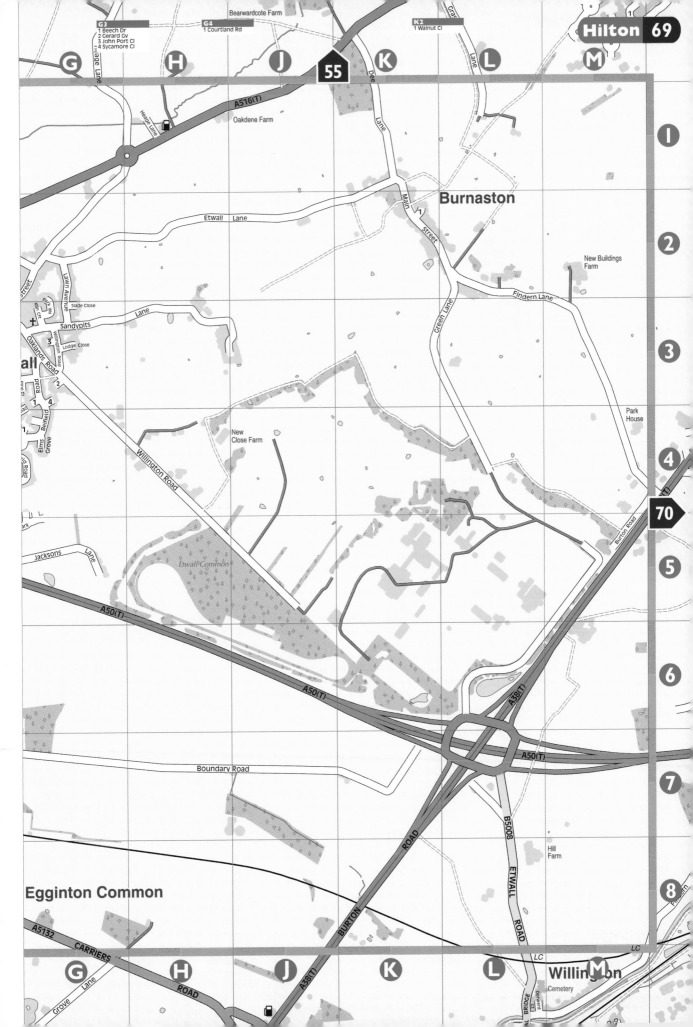

G3
1 Beech Dr
2 Gerard Gv
3 John Port Cl
4 Sycamore Cl

G4
1 Courtland Rd

K2
1 Walnut Cl

Bearwardcote Farm

G H J 55 K L M

A516(T)

Oakdene Farm

Etwall Lane

Main Street

Burnaston

New Buildings Farm

Findern Lane

Lawn Avenue

Sandypits Lane

Slade Close

Lodge Close

Willington Road

Green Lane

Park House

Oaklands Road

Belfield Grove

Elms

New Close Farm

70

Burton Road

Jacksons Lane

Etwall Common

Willington Road

A50(T)

A50(T)

A38(T)

A50(T)

Boundary Road

B5008

ETWALL ROAD

Hill Farm

Egginton Common

A5132 CARRIERS

BURTON ROAD

Willington

Cemetery

LC

LC

Grove Lane

ROAD

BRIDGE

G H J K L M

I 1
2
3
4
5
6
7
8

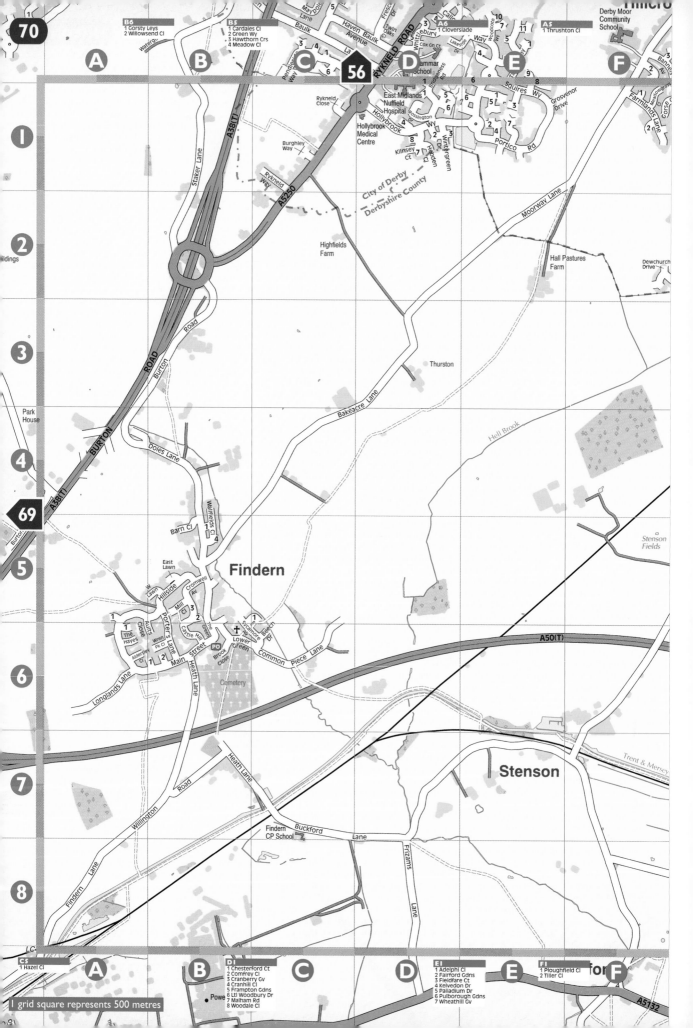

B6
1 Gorsty Leys
2 Willowsend Cl

B5
1 Cardales Cl
2 Green Wy
3 Hawthorn Crs
4 Meadow Cl

A6
1 Cloverslade

A5
1 Thrushton Cl

Derby Moor
Community
School

A B C 56 D E F

RYKNELD ROAD

Rykneld
Close

East Midlands
Nuffield
Hospital

Hollybrook
Medical
Centre

Kilnsey
Ct

Winegreen

CDr.
Hebden

Portico Rd

Squires Wy

Grosvenor
Drive

Burghley
Way

Rykneld
Way

A5250

City of Derby
Derbyshire County

Highfields
Farm

Moorway Lane

Hall Pastures
Farm

Dewchurch
Drive

1

2

3

4

69

5

6

7

8

Staker Lane

A38(T)

BURTON ROAD

Burton Road

Park
House

Doles Lane

Bakeacre Lane

Hell Brook

Thurston

Stenson
Fields

Barn Cl

Wallfields Cl

East
Lawn

Findern

Hillside

Mill Cl

Cromwell Av

W Lawn

Aults Close

Porter's Lane

The Hayes

Aldersley Cl

Wren Cl

Pk Cl

Main Street

Castle Hill

Heath Lane

Green Lane

Brook
Close

Lower
Green

Sycamore Av

Beech Dr

Common Piece Lane

Cemetery

Longlands Lane

A50(T)

Stenson

Trent & Mersey

Willington Road

Heath Lane

Findern Lane

Findern
CP School

Buckford Lane

Frizams Lane

A5132

LC

C5
1 Hazel Cl

D1
1 Chesterford Ct
2 Comfrey Cl
3 Cranberry Gv
4 Cranhill Cl
5 Frampton Gdns
6 Ltl Woodbury Dr
7 Malham Rd
8 Woodale Cl

E1
1 Adelphi Cl
2 Fairford Gdns
3 Fieldfare Ct
4 Kelvedon Dr
5 Palladium Dr
6 Pulborough Gdns
7 Wheathill Gv

F1
1 Ploughfield Cl
2 Tiller Cl

A B C D E F

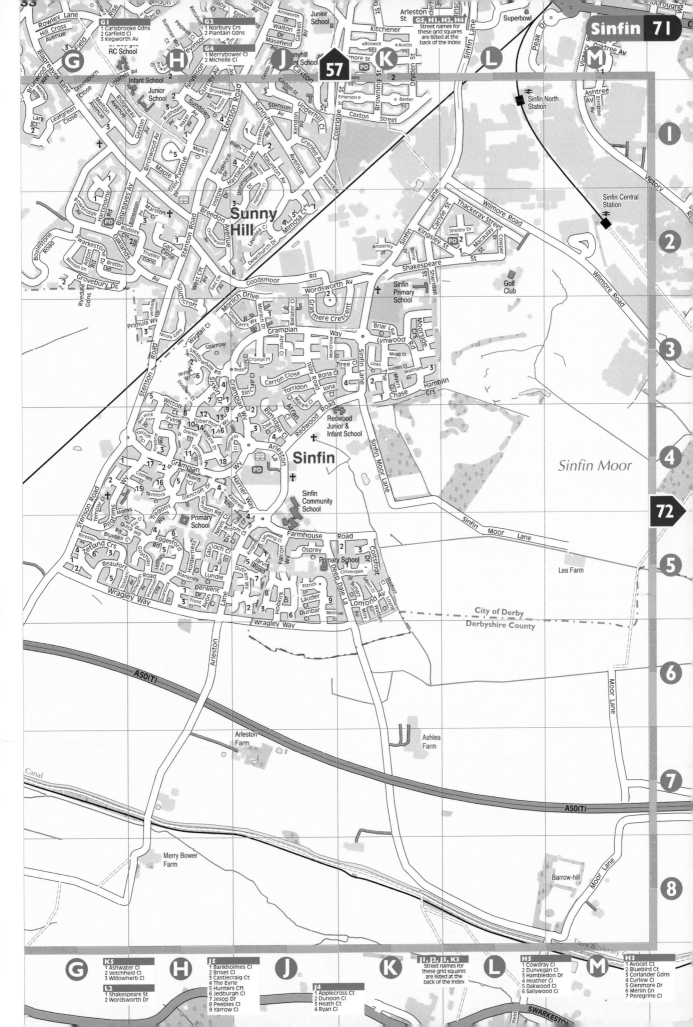

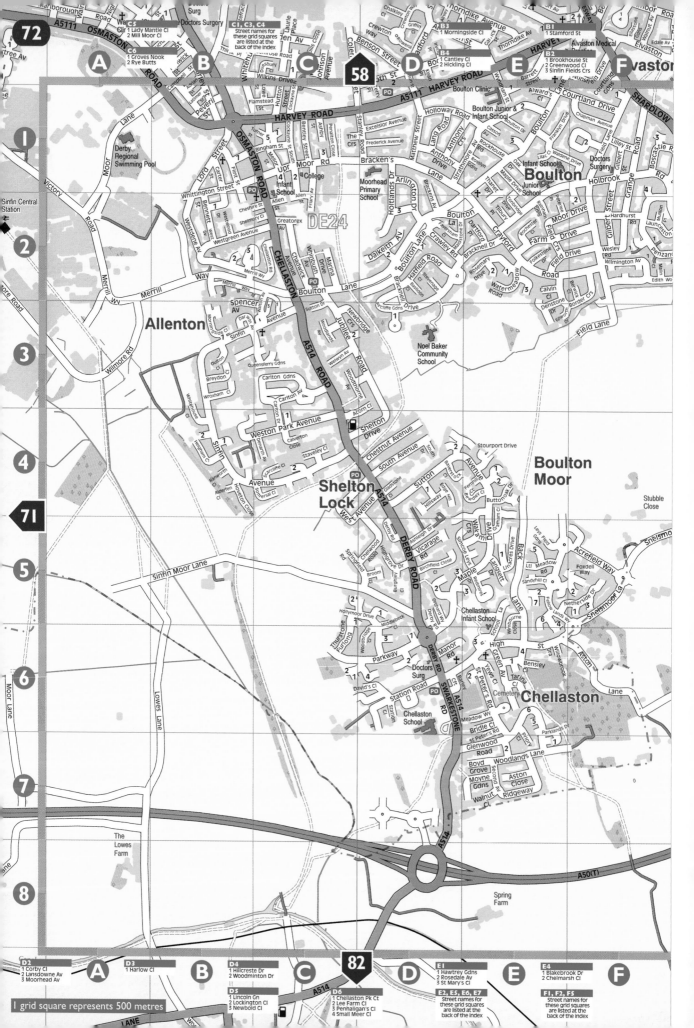

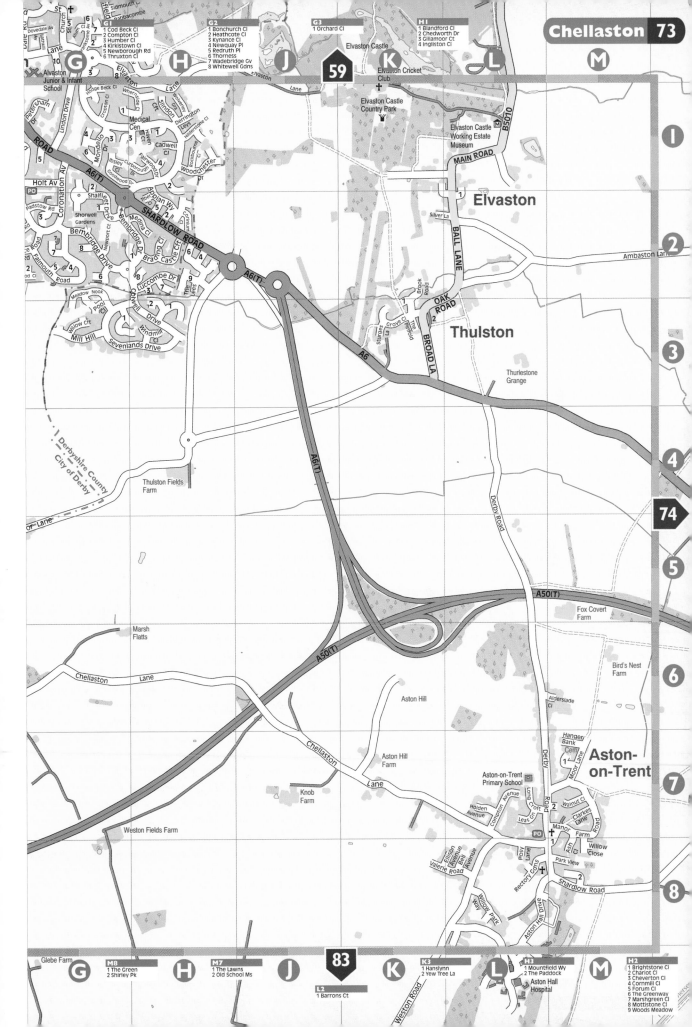

G1
1 Cod Beck Cl
2 Compton Cl
3 Humber Cl
4 Kirkistown Cl
5 Newborough Rd
6 Thruxton Cl

G2
1 Bonchurch Cl
2 Heathcote Cl
3 Kynance Cl
4 Newquay Pl
5 Redruth Pl
6 Thorness
7 Wadebridge Gv
8 Whitewell Gdns

G3
1 Orchard Cl

H1
1 Blandford Cl
2 Chedworth Dr
3 Gillamoor Ct
4 Ingliston Cl

59

G H J K L M

I

Elvaston Castle

Elvaston Cricket Club

Elvaston Castle Country Park

Elvaston Castle Working Estate Museum

MAIN ROAD

Elvaston

Alvaston Junior & Infant School

Medical Cen

Silver La

BALL LANE

B5010

2

Ambaston Lane

ROAD

A6(T)

SHARDLOW ROAD

Brook Road

OAK ROAD

Thulston

Sturges Grove Cl
La
The Pinfold

3

BROAD LA

Thurlestone Grange

A6

4

A6(T)

Derby Road

74

Thulston Fields Farm

Derbyshire County
City of Derby

5

Marsh Flatts

A50(T)

Fox Covert Farm

6

Bird's Nest Farm

Aston Hill

Alderslade Cl

Chellaston Lane

A50(T)

Aston Hill Farm

Hanger Bank Cem
1

Aston-on-Trent

7

Chellaston Lane

Knob Farm

Aston-on-Trent Primary School

Long Croft
Leas Cn

Walnut Cl

Clarkes Lane

Moor Lane

Derby Road

Weston Fields Farm

Holden Avenue

Compton Avenue

Manor Farm

Ash Lane

Willow Close

PO

Park View

Ellison Avenue
Bell Avenue
Valerie Road

Posy Lane

Rectory Cdns

Shardlow Road

8

Willow Park Way

Aston Hall Drive

Aston Hall Hospital

Glebe Farm

G
M8
1 The Green
2 Shirley Pk

H
M7
1 The Lawns
2 Old School Ms

J
83

K
K3
1 Hanslynn
2 Yew Tree La

L
H3
1 Mountfield Wy
2 The Paddock

M
H2
1 Brightstone Cl
2 Chariot Cl
3 Cheverton Cl
4 Cornmill Cl
5 Forum Cl
6 The Greenway
7 Marshgreen Cl
8 Mottistone Cl
9 Woods Meadow

L2
1 Barrons Ct

Weston Road

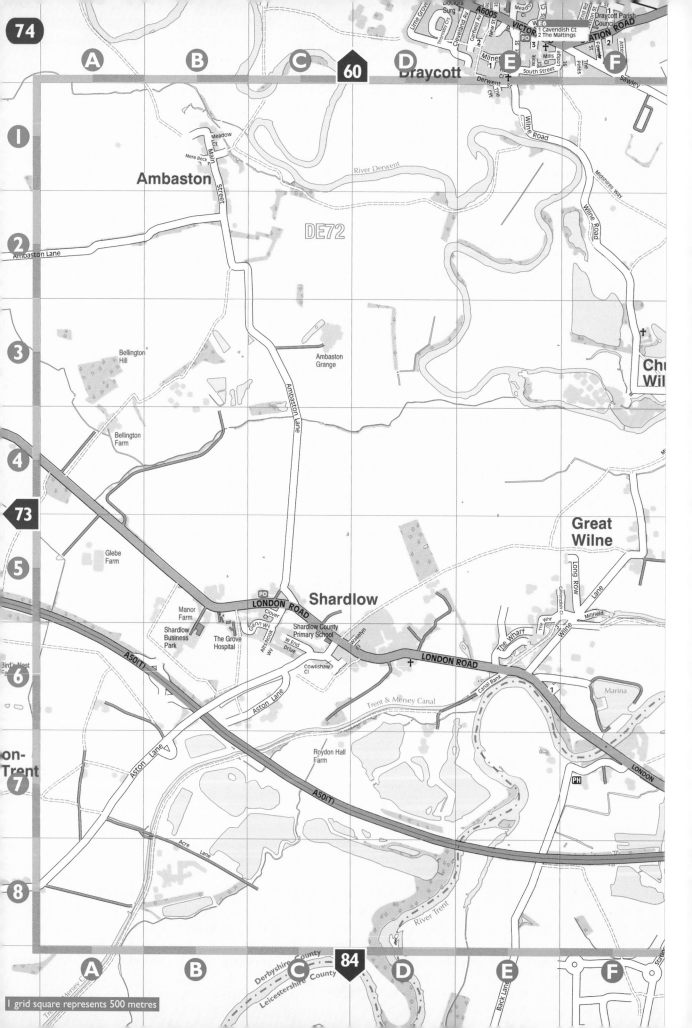

A   B   C   **60**   D Draycott

I

Meadow Ct
Mere Beck
Ambaston
Main Street

River Derwent

DE72

Wilne Road

2
Ambaston Lane

Midshires Way

Wilne Road

3
Bellington Hill

Ambaston Grange

Ch
Wil

4
Bellington Farm
Ambaston Lane

A50(T)

73

Great Wilne

5
Glebe Farm

Long Row

Cavendish Cl
Wilne Lane

Millfield

Manor Farm
PO
LONDON ROAD
Clover Ct
Shardlow

The Wharf
Wharf
The

Shardlow Business Park
Alte Nook Wy
Glenn Wy
The Grove Hospital

Shardlow County Primary School
W End Drive
Wavelyn

LONDON ROAD
LONDON

Bird's Nest
6

Cowlishaw Cl

Aston Lane

Canal Bank

Marina

on-Trent
7

A50(T)

Roydon Hall Farm

Trent & Mersey Canal

PH

Acre Lane

8

River Trent

A   B   Derbyshire County   C   **84**   D   E   F
Leicestershire County

Back Lane

Station

Top right area labels:
Lime Grove
A6005
VICTOR
1 Cavendish Ct
2 The Maltings
TION ROAD
Draycott Parish Council
Milne
Derwent Ct
South Street
PO
3
Mills
The Pines
Sawley

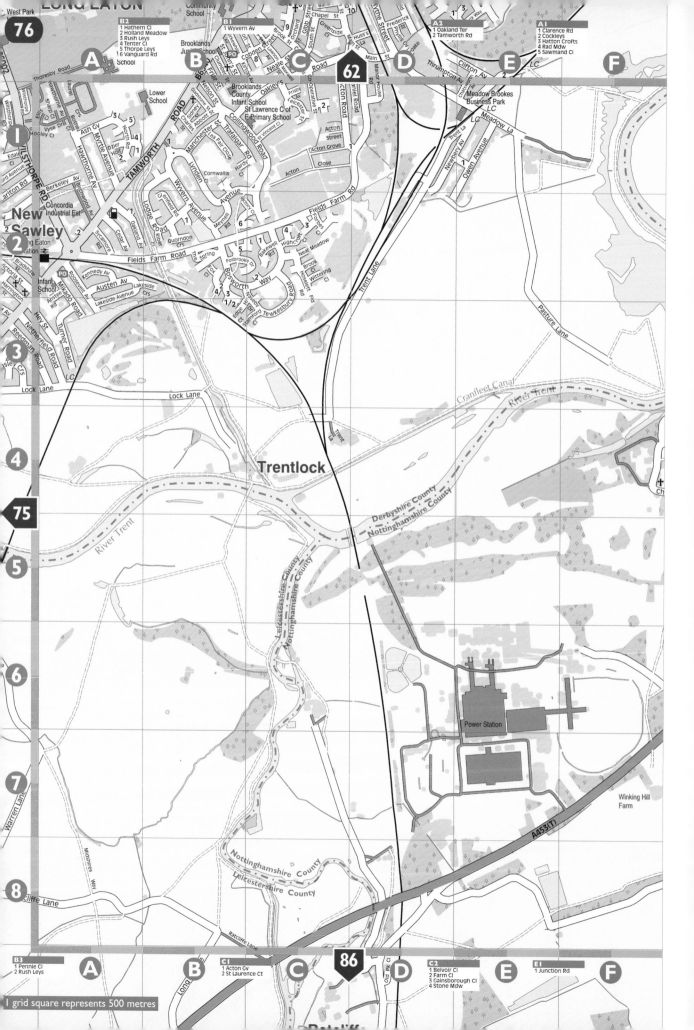

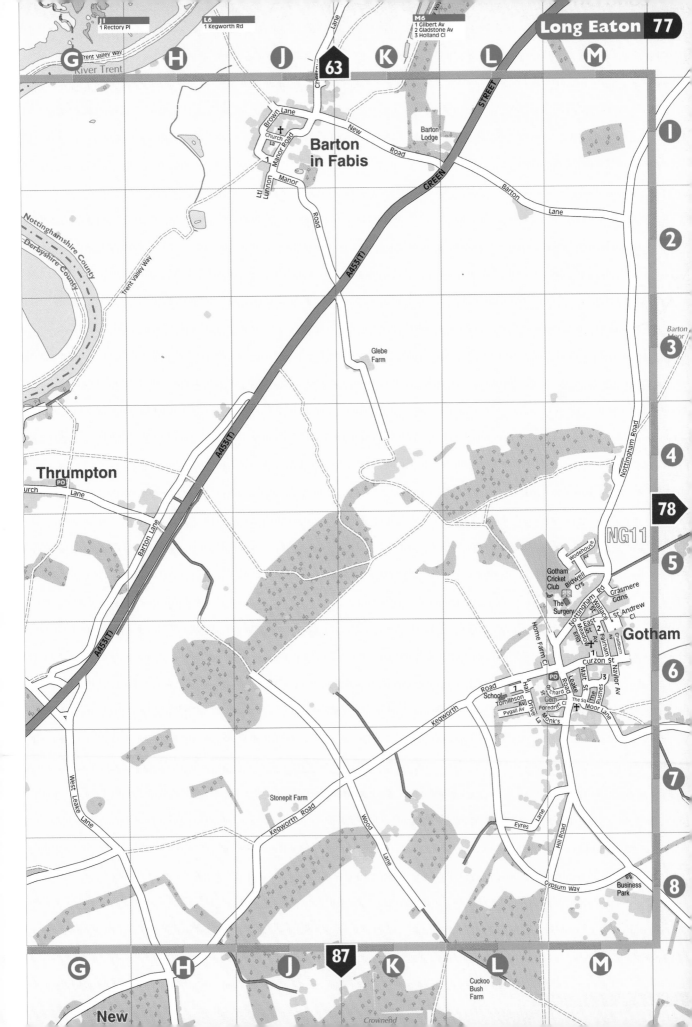

1 Rectory Pl

L6
1 Kegworth Rd

M6
1 Gilbert Av
2 Gladstone Av
3 Holland Cl

G H J K L M

63

I

Barton in Fabis

Brown Lane

Church La

New Road

Barton Lodge

GREEN STREET

Manor Road

Ltl Lunnon

Manor Road

2

Barton Lane

3

Nottinghamshire County

Derbyshire County

Trent Valley Way

River Trent

Glebe Farm

A453(T)

Nottingham Road

4

Thrumpton

PO

Church Lane

Barton Lane

A453(T)

78

NG11

5

Wodehouse Av

Gotham Cricket Club

Bidwell Crs

Grasmere Gdns

The Surgery

Nottingham Rd

St Andrew Cl

East End

Wallace Av

Fairham Av

Meadow

Chadburn

St Andrew Cl

Gotham

Curzon St

6

Road School

Tomlinson Av

Pygall Av

PO

Hall Drive

Home Farm Cl

Chard St

Gem

Forednt Cl

Monk's

Leake Road

Malt St

St

The Sq

Naylor Av

Moor Lane

Kegworth Road

7

A453(T)

West Leake Lane

Stonepit Farm

Kegworth Road

Wood Lane

Eyres Lane

Hill Road

Gypsum Way

Business Park

8

G H J K L M

87

New

Cuckoo Bush Farm

Crownend

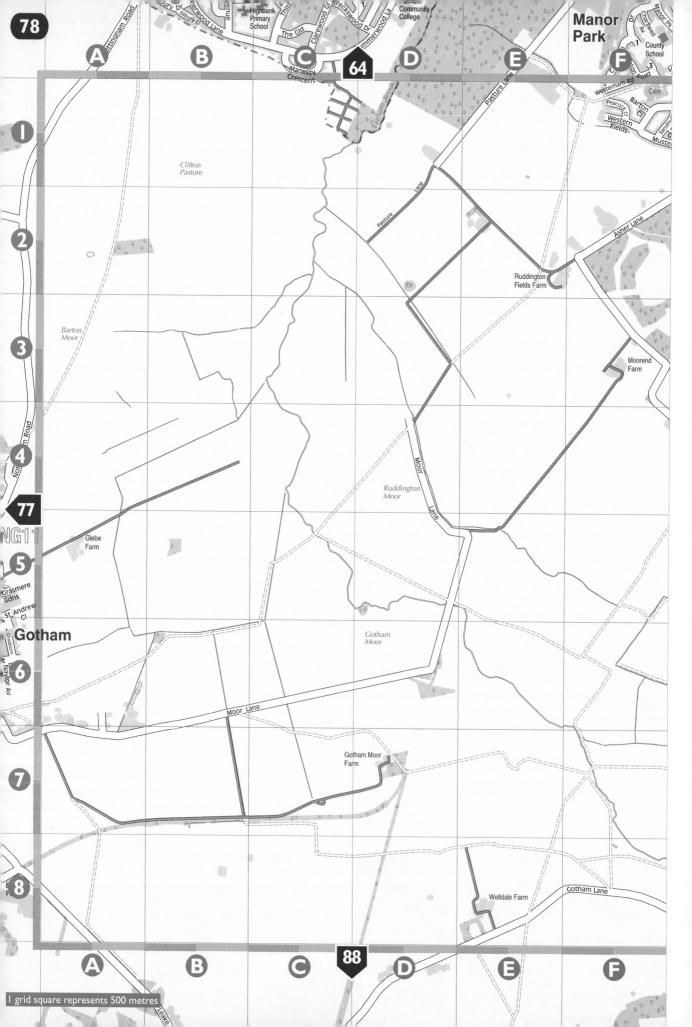

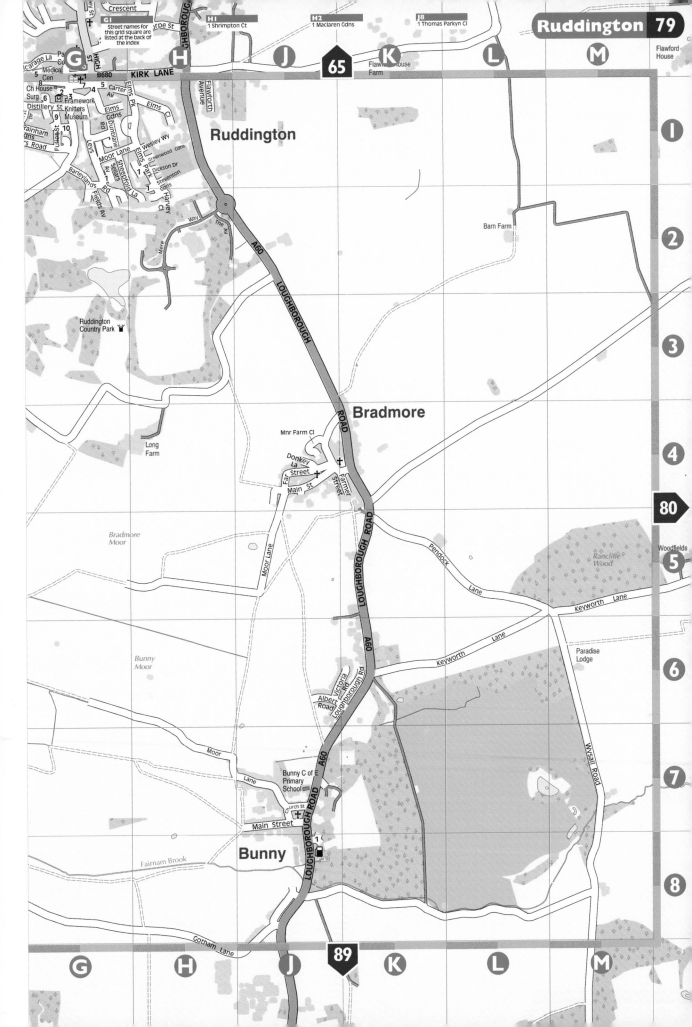

Crescent

G1 Street names for this grid square are listed at the back of the index

H1 1 Shrimpton Ct

H2 1 Maclaren Gdns

J8 1 Thomas Parkyn Cl

Flawford House

G

H

J

65

K

L

M

Flawford House

KIRK LANE

B680

Medical Cen

Ch House

Distillery St

Surg

Framework Knitters Museum

Fulwell St

Carter Av

Elms Pk

Elms Cl

Elms Gdns

Moor Lane

Wesley Wy

Greenwood Gdns

Dickson Dr

Stevenson Gdns

Harvey Cl

Dumblane

Sellars Av

Elms Park

Barleylands

Fields Av

Sheepfold La

Leys

Ruddington

Flawforth Avenue

A60

The Av

Mere

Way

1

Ruddington Country Park

2

Barn Farm

3

LOUGHBOROUGH

Long Farm

Bradmore

Mnr Farm Cl

Donkey La

Far Street

Main St

Farmer Street

ROAD

4

80

Bradmore Moor

Moor Lane

Pendock Lane

Rancliffe Wood

Woodfields

5

Bunny Moor

LOUGHBOROUGH ROAD

A60

Victoria Rd

Albert Road

Loughborough Rd

Keyworth Lane

Keyworth Lane

Paradise Lodge

6

Moor

Lane

Bunny C of E Primary School

A60

Wysall Road

7

Church St

Main Street

LOUGHBOROUGH ROAD

1

Bunny

Fairnam Brook

8

Gotham Lane

89

G

H

J

K

L

M

A   B   C   66   D   E   F

Plumtree

Normanton-on-the

E5
1 Laburnum Av

Clipston
C4
1 Charnwood Av
2 Far Pastures Cl

The
C3
1 Beaumont Cl
2 Franklyn Gdns
3 Sidmouth Cl

Flawford
House

Chestnut
Farm

Church La
Saddlers Yard
Old
Plumtree
School

1

**Plumtree
Park**

Park Road
Park Avenue

Crossdale Drive
Primary School

Green
Cl
Poplars Cl

Platt

Parkside

Normanton
Wolds

Hillcrest
Rd
Highfield
Rd
Abbot
Close
Bishops
Close

Crossdale Drive

Brockwood
Gdns'

Rose Gv
Blair
Close

Villa Road

Lowlands
Drive

Wolds

Drive
Covert

Rancliffe Av
Delville Avenue
Highbury Road

Brockwood
Crs

Adams Hill
Clifford
Close
Normanton Lane

Lyncombe
Gdns

Keyworth

Debdale
Lane

Wynbreck
Drive

Wolds
Rd

Spinney Road
Hayes Road
Plantation Road

Gorse Rd
Fairham Close

Thelda Avenue
Dale Road

Ashley Road

Ashley
Cl
Crs
Watton

Drive
Crantock
Gdns

Cherry
Hl

High View
Avenue

Meadow Drive

Nicker Hill

Intake
Road
Croft Road

Rose

Nottingham Road

Church
Drive

Rannock
Gardens

Wolds

PO

Mount Pleasant

The
Ridings

Park Avenue
West

Infant
School

Park
Avenue
East

Manor
Road
Woodleigh
West Cl
East

Keyworth
Parish
Council

South Wolds
Comprehensive
School

Fairway

Larch
Wy

Rowan Dr
Maple Cl

Willow Brook

County Primary
School

Golf Course Road

79

Woodfields

1

Health
Centre

Elm Av
Elm

Beech
Avenue

Lilac Cl

Stanton

Club
House

Bunny Lane

Roseland
Close

Hawthorn Cl
Wrights Orchard
The Square

PO

Windmill
Court

Laurel
Av
Limetree Cl
Ash Grove

Selby Lane

Lane

Widmerpool Lane

Lane

Barrow Blade
2
Holme

Main Street

Cedar
Drive

The Pastures

Brook
View
Lings Lane

Wolds Lane

Wembley
Lodge

*Keyworth
Wolds*

Wembley
Farm

Wysall Lane

Lings Lane

North Lodge
F

A   B   C   90   D   E   F

Longcliffe

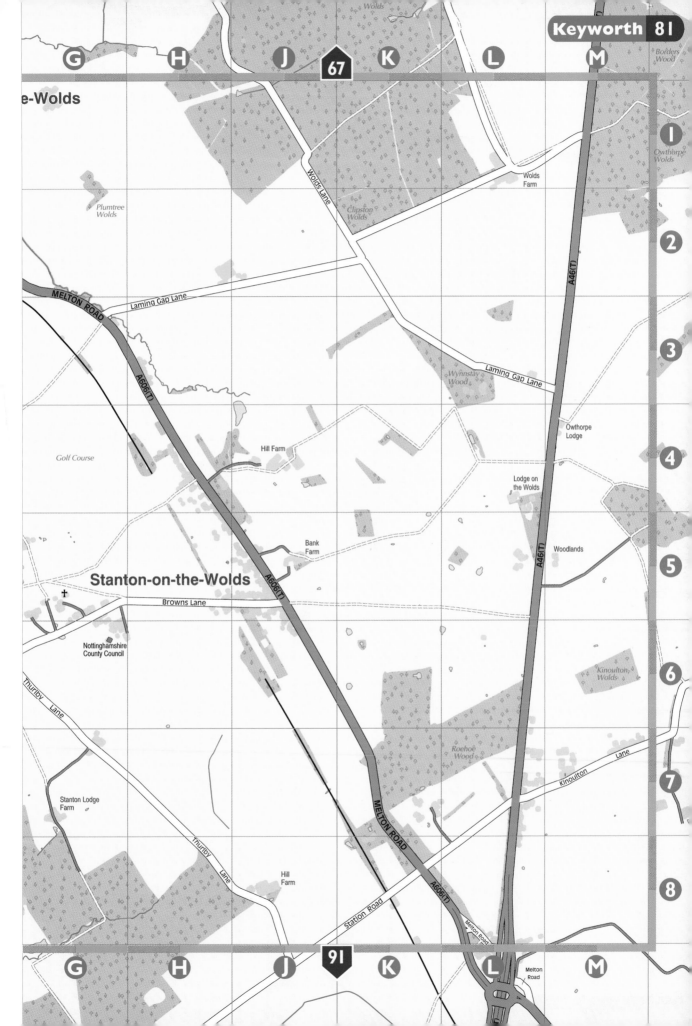

e-Wolds

G H J **67** K L M

1

Borders Wood

Owthorpe Wolds

2

Plumtree Wolds

Wolds Farm

Clipston Wolds

Wolds Lane

A46(T)

MELTON ROAD

Laming Gap Lane

Laming Gap Lane

3

A606(T)

Wynnstay Wood

Owthorpe Lodge

4

Golf Course

Hill Farm

Lodge on the Wolds

Woodlands

5

Bank Farm

Stanton-on-the-Wolds

✝

Browns Lane

A606(T)

Kinoulton Wolds

6

Nottinghamshire County Council

Thurlby Lane

Roehoe Wood

Kinoulton Lane

Kinoulton Lane

7

Stanton Lodge Farm

MELTON ROAD

8

Thurlby Lane

Hill Farm

Station Road

A606(T)

Melton Road

Melton Road

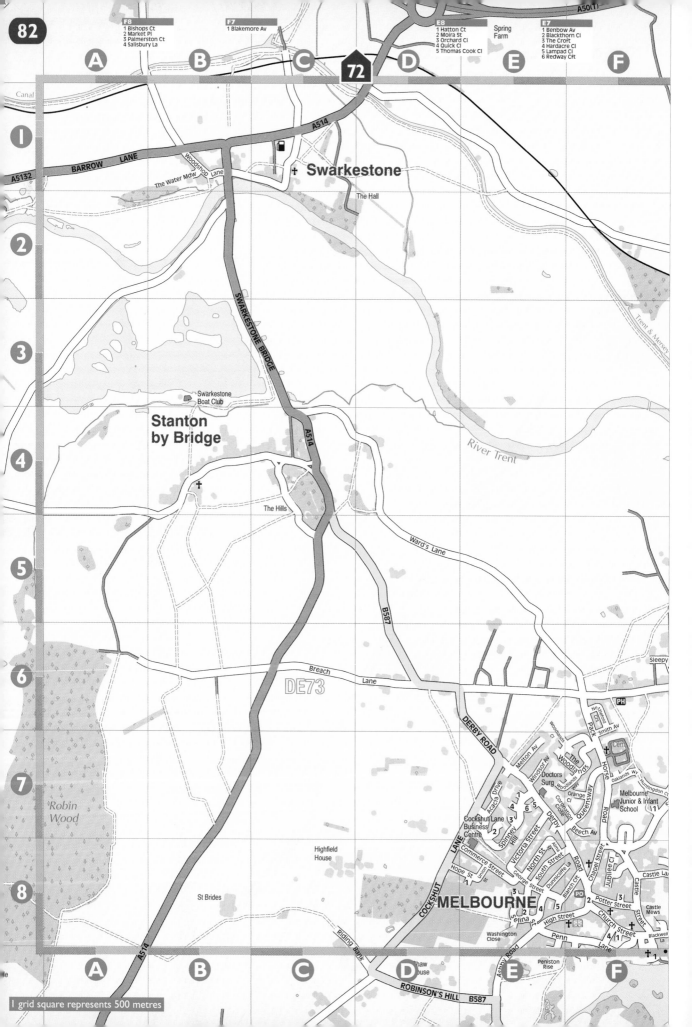

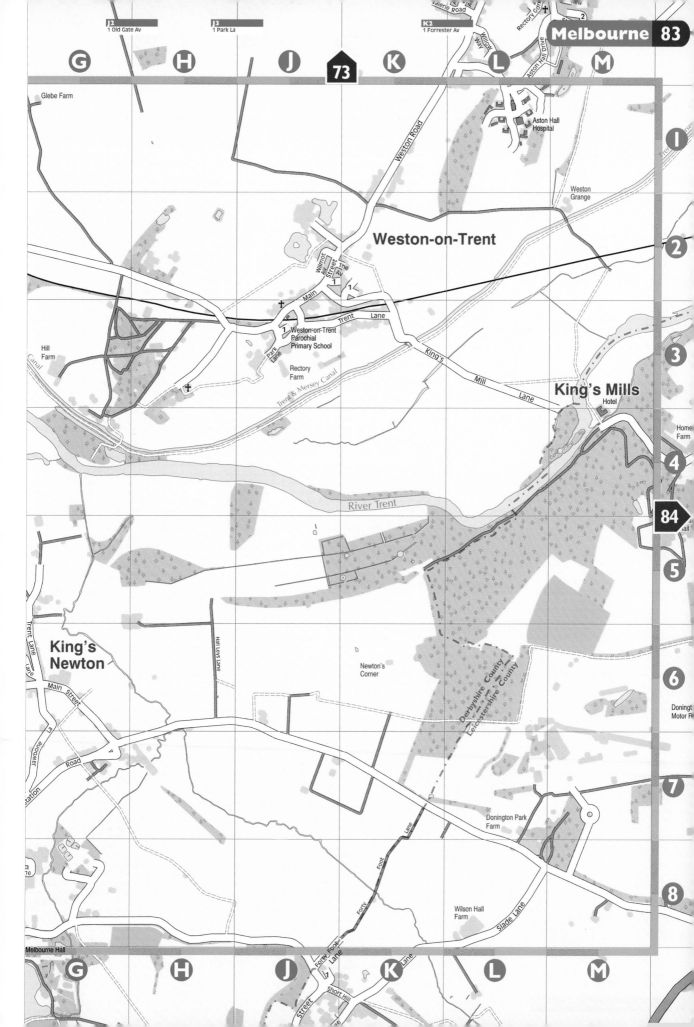

J2 1 Old Gate Av
J3 1 Park La
K2 1 Forrester Av

G   H   J   73   K   L   M

I

Glebe Farm

Weston Road

Weston-on-Trent

Weston Grange

Aston Hall Hospital

2

Wilmot Av
Street
The Av

Main

Trent   Lane

Park Lane

Weston-on-Trent Parochial Primary School

Rectory Farm

King's

Mill

Lane

King's Mills

Hotel

Home Farm

3

Hill Farm

Canal

Trent & Mersey Canal

4

84

River Trent

5

King's Newton

Hall Leys Lane

Newton's Corner

Derbyshire County

Leicestershire County

Donington Motor R

6

Trent Lane

Lane

Main Street

Jawbone La

Station Road

Donington Park Farm

7

Foot

Lane

Fox

Foot

Lane

Wilson Hall Farm

Slade Lane

8

Melbourne Hall

Street

Short Hill

G   H   J   K   L   M

F3
1 The Moat
2 Monteith Pl
3 Montford Ms

E5
1 Cavendish Cl

E4
1 Carrs Cl
2 Delven La
3 Lothian Pl
4 Peartree Cl

E3
1 Loudoun Pl
2 Rawdon Cl
3 Selina Cl
4 The Spinney

A   B   C   74   D   E   F

I

Trent & Mersey Canal

Derbyshire County
Leicestershire County

2

River Trent

Short Lane

LC

Trent Lane
Industrial Estate

Sycamore Road
Willow Road
Gasny Av
Station Road
Newbold Drive

Hawthorn Road
Trent Lane
Victoria Street

3

Bentley Road

Hazelrigg
Walton Hi
Campion Hill
Spittal

Tanyard Close

Fox Road
Foxbrook Dr
Shirley Cl
Darsway
Salter Cl
Queens Way
Staunton
School La
Huntingdon Dr
Orchard CP School
Haulton Drive
Harcourt Place
Bondgate
The Hollow
Castle Hill
The

Roby Lea
Minton Rd

Studbrook Close

Ferrers Close
Kirkland Close
The Green
Grange Rd
Tipnal
Drive

Doctors Surg
PO
St Borough St
Clapgun Street
Garden Crs

4

Home Farm

Park Lane

Cordwell Close
Bosworth
Orchard Avenue

Park Lane
Towles Pastures

Apiary Gate
Hotel
Eastway

Barn
St Edwards Junior School
Castle D Community College

83

Donington Hall

Paddock Cl

Starkie Avenue
Park Av
Shields Cresct

Cooks Av

Cherbrough Road
High Street

Hall Farm Close
Delven Lane Close

Orly Av
Crabtree Close
Bakewell Drive
Hallam Fields Rd
St Edward's Rd
Harvey Rd
Hastings St
Eaton Road
Meadow Crs
Stonehill
Cedar Road
Eastway

5

6

Donington Park Motor Racing Circuit

Hill Top Farm
PH
Hill Top
Diseworth Road

7

The Donington Collection Racing Car Museum
M

Anson Road

Dakota Road
Swan Rivers
Ambassador Road
Viscount

8

WALTON HILL

Isley Walton

A453 ASHBY
Green Lane

A   B   **F4**
1 The Biggin
2 Mount Pleasant
3 St Anne's La   C   92   D   **F5**
1 Routh Av
2 Windmill Cl   E   F

I grid square represents 500 metres

85

76

B5
1 The Croft

B4
1 Borrowell
2 Queens Rd

A5
1 Bulstode Pl
2 Langley Dr
3 Ropewalk
4 Stonehills

A4
1 Jeffares Cl
2 Wyvelle Crs

A B C D E F

1
2
3
4
5
6
7
8

Ratcliffe
on Soar

Long Lane
Farm

Long Lane

Ratcliffe Lane

Kegworth Road

Kingston
on Soar

Kegworth Rd

Kingston Lane

Station Road

Station Road

Old Bull
Farm Cl

Melton Lane

College Road

University of
Nottingham

Sutton
Fields
House

Derby Road

Kegworth
Squash Club

Hotel

Packington Hill

Kegworth
Museum

High Street

Nottingham Road

Station Road

New Street

Bridge Fields

Moore
Av

Kirk Av

The
Osiers

River Soar

Mill La

Orchard Surgery

PO

PH

Primary
School

Pleasant Pl

Heathfield

KEGWORTH

Whatton Road

Cem

Sutton
Rd

Thomas
Road

Hillside

Roberts
Close

The Lodge

Bedford
Cl

Gerrard
Crescent

Burley
Rise

Brickyard Lane

New

London Road

A6(T)

Soar Lane

Cemetery

Marle Pit Hill

Main Street

St Ann's
Manor

Bollard's La

Buck's La

A453(T)

A6(T)

tion 24

Windmill
Way

Sibson
Drive

Pep
Drive

Suthers
Road

Nine
Acres

Langley Drive

Springfield

Oldershaw
Av

W Bank

Broadhill Road

Foxhills

Shepherd
Wk

Kirby
Drive

St Andrew's Rd

Staffords
Acre

Whatton
Road

Whatton
Road

Slade
Farm

Spring House
Farm

River Soar

Devil's
Elbow

Sutton Bonington
Primary School

Side
Av

Ley

Frederick
Av

Hotel

River Soar

A B C D E F

1 grid square represents 500 metres

G   H   J   77   K   L   M

I

2

3

Cuckoo
Bush
Farm

Crownend
Wood

New
Kingston

Road

Kingston Fields
Farm

Wossock Lane

Ash
Spinney

4

88

5

West Leake Lane

Kingston Brook

Scotland Farm

Dark Lane

Village Farm
Cl

Main   Street   West
Leake

6

Kingston Brook

West Leake Road

Melton Lane

Pithouse Lane

PH

Manor Farm

Landcroft Lane

Trowell Lane

Brickyard Lane

Midshires Way

7

California Farm

Hungary Lane

Hills Farm

Travell's Hill

8

Hungary La

Sutton
Bonington

G   H   J   95   K   Cold Harbour
Farm   L   REMPSTONE   M

A6006   ROAD

D5
1 Brickcliffe Rd

C6
1 De Ferrers Cl
2 Manor Fm Mdw
3 Southwell Cl
4 Winchester Cl

C5
1 Wootton Cl

C4
1 Sweet Leys Dr
2 Towson Fld

A   B   C   D   E   F

I
2
3
4
87
5
6
7
8

Leake Road

Highthorn Farm

Midshires Way

Golf Course

Bunny Lane

Gotham Rd

Rushcliffe
Golf Club

Stocking Lane

Rushcliffe Gv

Hill
Top Farm

Midshires Way

Rouli Cope Crs

Angrave Rd

Hollis
Meadow

Sharpley Dr

St. Mary's Crescent

Weavers

Elm Av

Manor Rd

Ryeham

Taft Leys
Farm

Midshires Way

Thistle

Blink

Northfields Wy

Harefield

Towson Fld

Home Av

The Crs

Lantern   Lane

Brookfields Wy

Halls Brook

Lantern Lane
Primary School

Brook Furlong
Farm

The Burrows

East
Leake

Harry Carlton
Comprehensive School

Carlton
Crs

Taft Leys Rd

Fisher

7

Kingston Brook

Gotham   Rd

Stonebridge

Moore Rd

Monks Mdw

Drive

Bateman   Rd

York

Turo

Exeter Cl

3

2

Doctors
Surgery

Health Centre

Leake   Road

Birch Lea

Rope Wk

Cl

4

PO

1

Costock   Road

West Leake Road

Field End Cl

Station

Road

Twentylands Dr

Church
Cl

School Cl

The
green

Main   Street

Sainsbury Av

Cromwell Dr

Oldershaw Rd

Brickley Crs

The Kerp

Meadow Rise Cl

Leivers Cl

Old
Rectory
Cl

The
Nook

Primary
School

Hawley

Castle Hill

Brookside   Av

Burton

Burton
Wk

Burton
Wk

Potters Lane

Hall
Gdns

Maple
Twll

Ash
Twll

Willow

Poplar

Beech

Oak Crs

Pine

Yew
Cl

Brookside

Orchard
Cl

Bay Av

Kirk Ley Rd

Mill
La

Manor Farm

Woodgate Rd

Rempstone Road

Loughborough   Road

Woodgate Farm

Sheepwash Brook

The Lings
Farm

A   B   C   D   E   F

Whitehills
Farm

Rempstone Road

ROAD

I grid square represents 500 metres

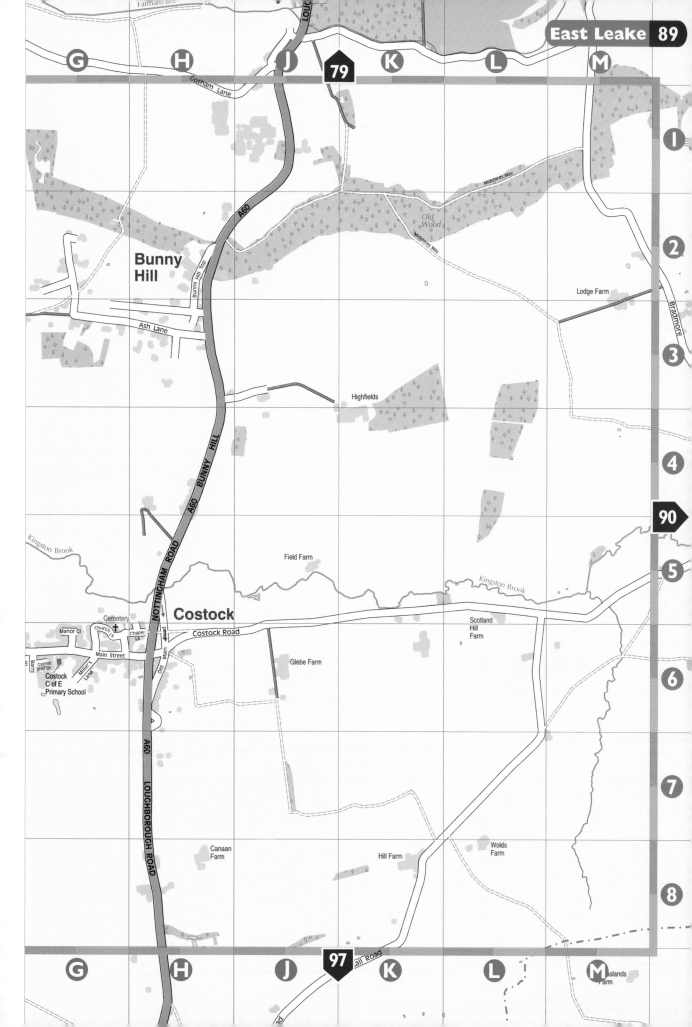

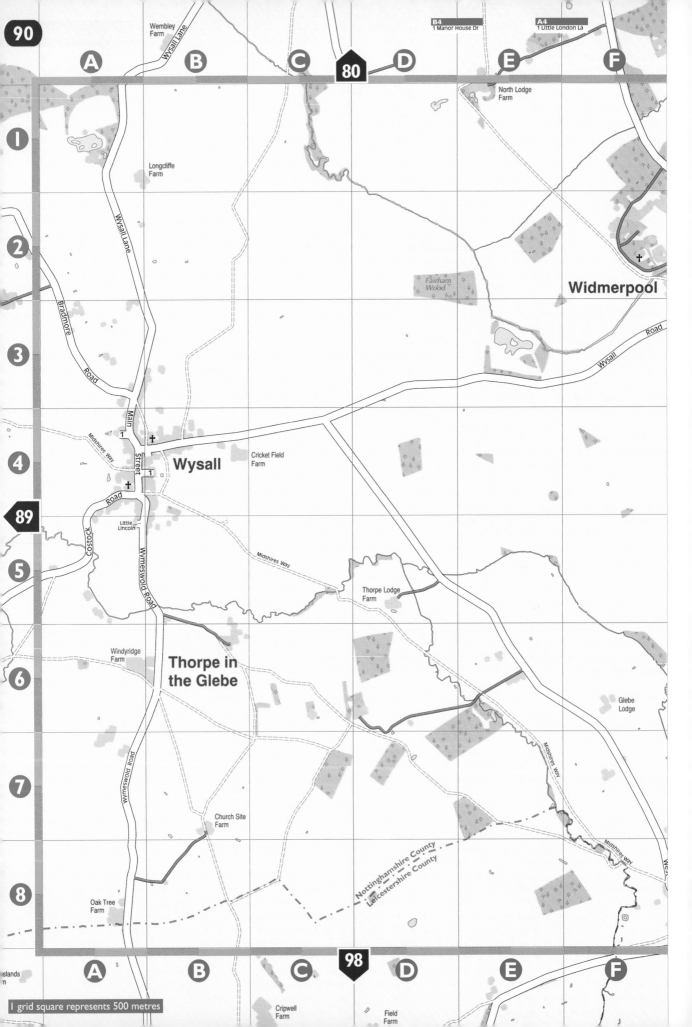

(A) (B) (C) **80** (D) (E) (F)

B4
1 Manor House Dr

A4
1 Little London La

Wembley
Farm

Wysall Lane

1

Longcliffe
Farm

North Lodge
Farm

2

Bradmore Road

Fairham
Wood

Widmerpool

3

Wysall Road

Main

Street

Midshires Way

4

Costock Road

† Wysall

Cricket Field
Farm

† Little
Lincoln

89

Midshires Way

5

Wymeswold Road

Thorpe Lodge
Farm

Glebe
Lodge

Windyridge
Farm

6

**Thorpe in
the Glebe**

Midshires Way

7

Wymeswold Road

Church Site
Farm

Nottinghamshire County
Leicestershire County

Midshires Way

8

Oak Tree
Farm

Wes

slands
n

(A) (B) (C) **98** (D) (E) (F)

Cripwell
Farm

Field
Farm

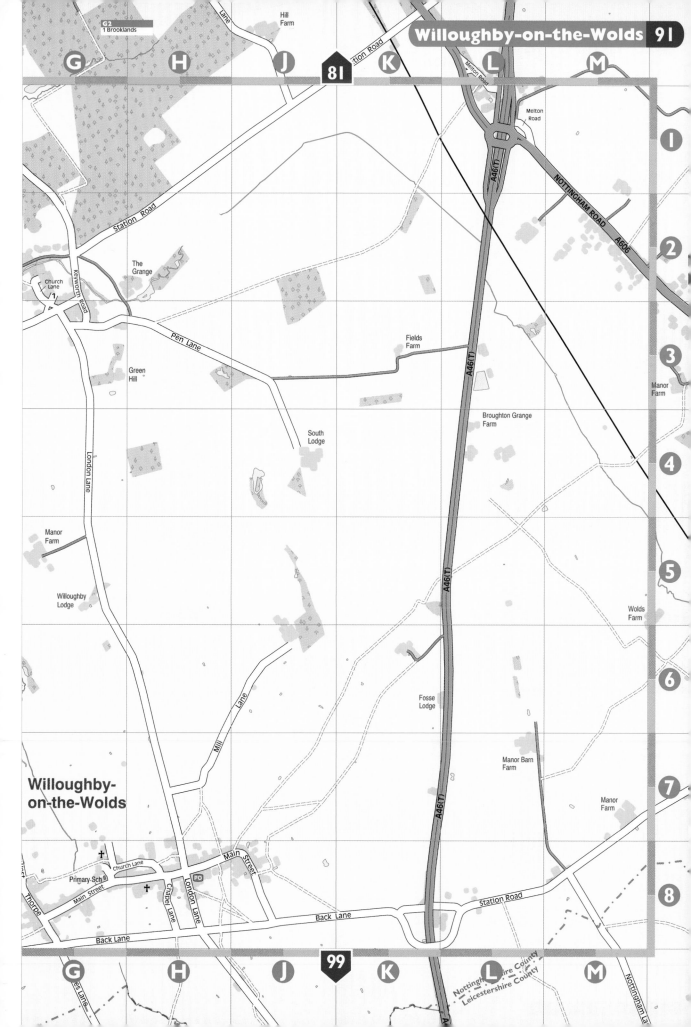

G2
1 Brooklands

G **H** **J** **81** **K** **L** **M**

I

2

3

4

5

6

7

8

Hill Farm

Station Road

Melton Road

NOTTINGHAM ROAD A606

Melton Road

The Grange

Church Lane

Keyworth Road

Pen Lane

Fields Farm

A46(T)

Manor Farm

Green Hill

South Lodge

Broughton Grange Farm

London Lane

A46(T)

Manor Farm

Wolds Farm

Willoughby Lodge

Mill Lane

Fosse Lodge

Manor Barn Farm

Willoughby-
on-the-Wolds

Manor Farm

Primary Sch

Church Lane

Main Street

Thorpe

Main Street

Chapel Lane

London Lane

PO

Back Lane

Back Lane

Station Road

A46(T)

Nottingham La

G **H** **J** **99** **K** **L** **M**

Nottinghamshire County
Leicestershire County

WALTON HILL

Is By Walton

84

A453 ASHBY

Green Lane

The Bowley

High Barn Farm

A453

MOOR LANE

Moor Lane

Woodhouse Farm

Langley Priory

Tonge

Field Lane

Close

A453

Scaffacre Farm

A42(T)

Long Mere Lane

A42(T)

A42(T)

Gelscoe Lane

Gelscoe Lodge Farm

Long Mere Farm

Breedon Lodge Farm

Merril Grange

Westmeadow Brook

Bromley Lane

Pasture Wood

Top Merril Grange

Mill Lane

100

Woodside Farm

Hillparks Farm

Bromley Lane

Belton Primary

PO

School Lane

Presents La

Church

G2
1 Brookside

M3
1 Barnfield Cl

Donington Park Service Area

G   H   J   **85**   K   L   M

Bleak House

ROAD

Hyam's Lane

Diseworth Junior School

Diseworth

Junction 23a

Clements Gate

Hall Gate

Gate

Orchard Cl

Page Lane

Lady Gate

The Woodcroft

Shakespeare Close

Green

Wind Farm

Long Mere Lane

Wood Nook Farm

West End

Main Street

PO

Long Whatton

Long Whatton C of E School

A42(T)

Westmeadow Lane

Kegworth Lane

Whatton Road

94

M1

Riste Farm

Dry Pot Lane

Glebe Farm

Smithy Lane

Piper Farm

Piper Wood

ASHBY ROAD

B5324

Highfields Farm

B5324 ASHBY ROAD

Hallamford Road

Woodlands Farm

Oakley Road

G   H   J   **101**   K   L   M

Street

Grace Dieu

Black Brook

Avenue

ROAD

I   2   3   4   5   6   7   8

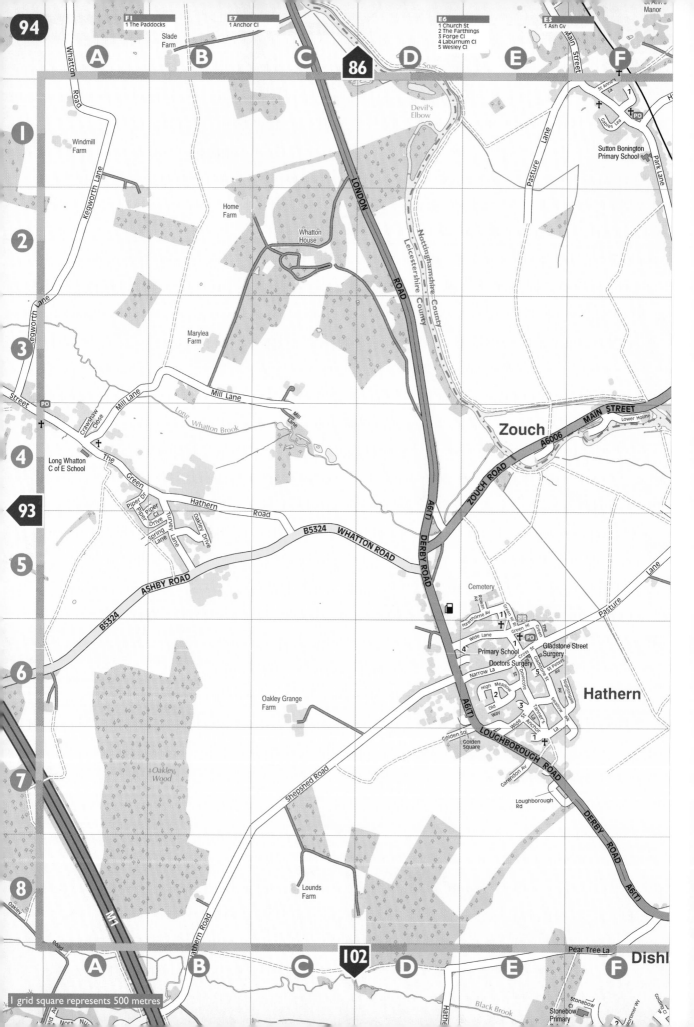

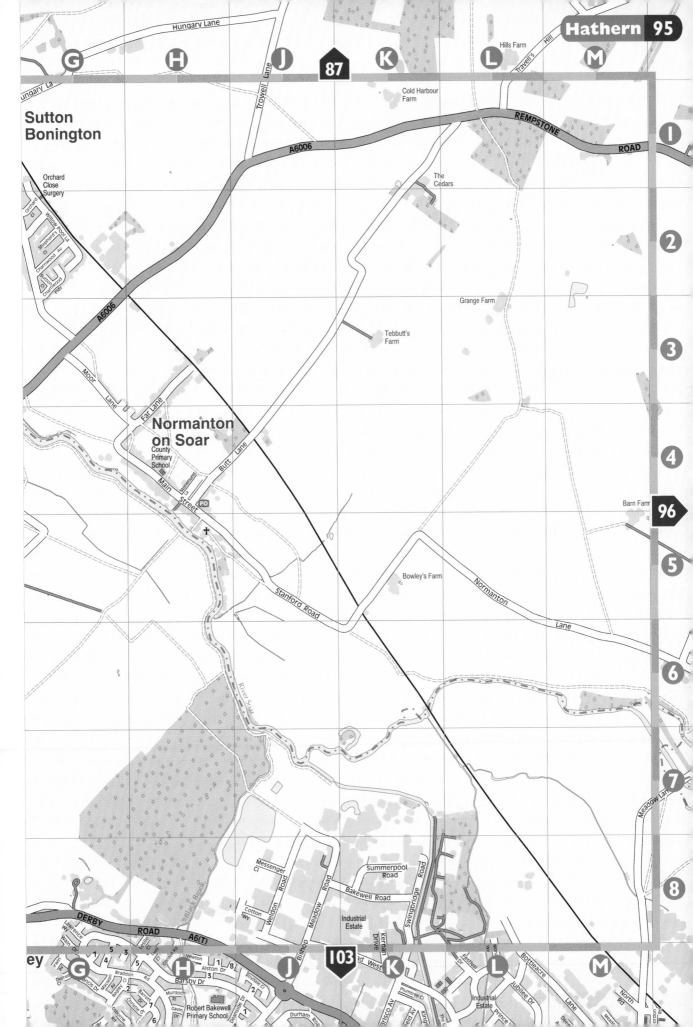

G   H   J   87   K   L   M

Hungary Lane

Travellers' Hill

Hills Farm

Cold Harbour
Farm

REMPSTONE

ROAD

I

**Sutton
Bonington**

Orchard
Close
Surgery

Orchard

Willow Pool La

Shepherd's Cl

Charnwood Av

Charnwood Rd

Burt

The Cedars

A6006

A6006

2

Grange Farm

3

Tebbutt's
Farm

Moor Lane

Far Lane

**Normanton
on Soar**

County
Primary
School

Butt Lane

Main Street

PO

✝

Stanford Road

4

Barn Farm   96

Bowley's Farm

Normanton

Lane

5

River Soar

6

Meadow Lane

7

Black Brook

Messenger
Cl

Weldon
Road

Cotton
Wy

Bishop Meadow Road

Summerpool
Road

Bakewell Road

Swinbridge
Road

Industrial
Estate

Kernan
Drive

Festival Dr

Jubilee Dr

Bottleacre

Lane

North
Rd

8

DERBY   ROAD   A6(T)

Lawrence
Wy

Irwin

Main Dr

Durrell Dr

Francis Dr

Leslie
Cl

Macaulay

Bagley

Cordell Rd

Barrett Dr

Christie Dr

Osborne

Gavin
Dr

Braddon
Rd

Murdoch
Dr

Alston Dr

Barsby Dr

Deanside Dr

**Robert Bakewell
Primary School**

Durham Rd

Royalale Ct

Plumtree Cl

Brisco Av

King Edward

The

Field Av West

Prince

Rd West

Industrial
Estate

Mc

Festival Dr

Jubilee Dr

North

Deep

Gordon Rd

Meadow

ey

G   H   J   103   K   L   M

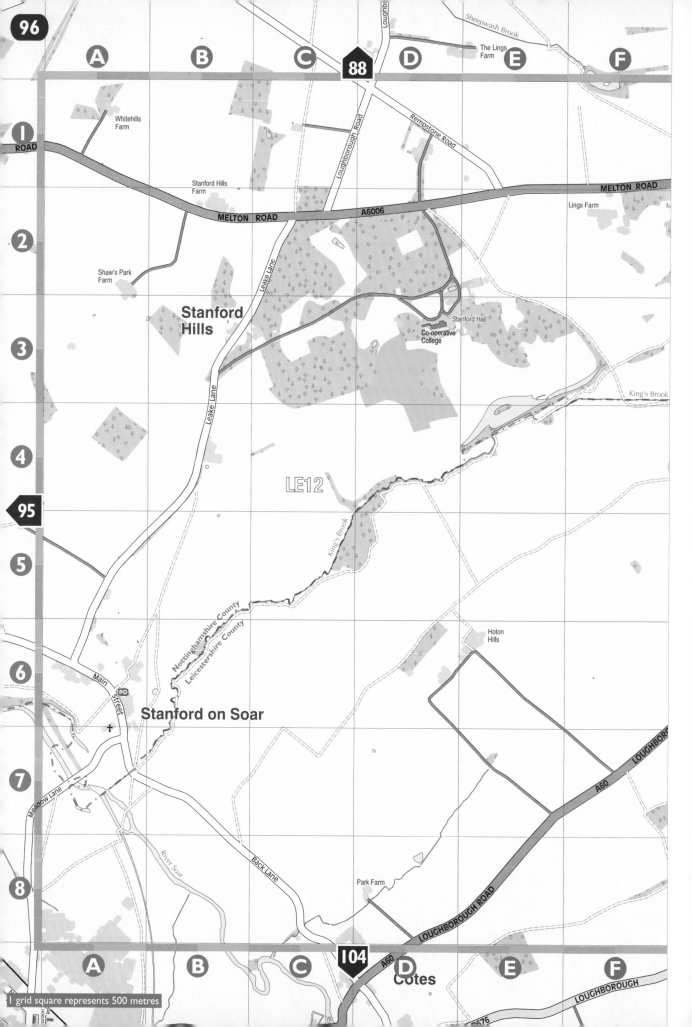

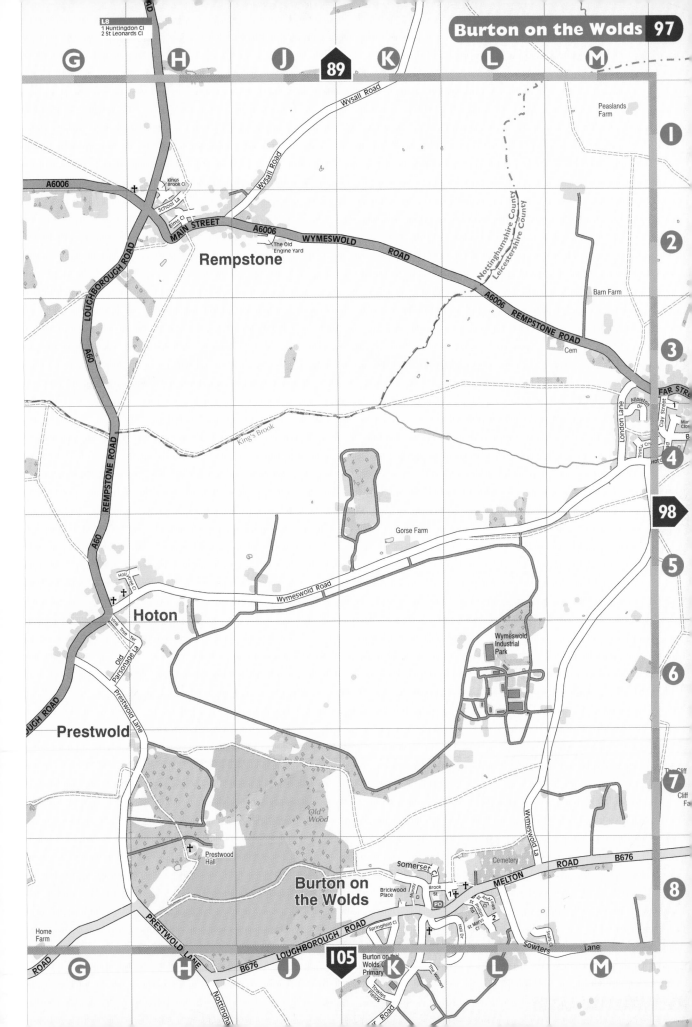

G H J 89 K L M

L8
1 Huntingdon Cl
2 St Leonards Cl

Peaslands
Farm

I

2

A6006

Wysall Road

Kings
Brook Cl

School La

Wysall Road

Elms Cl

MAIN STREET

A6006

WYMESWOLD

ROAD

The Old
Engine Yard

Rempstone

LOUGHBOROUGH ROAD

A60

A6006

REMPSTONE ROAD

Nottinghamshire County
Leicestershire County

Barn Farm

Cem

3

FAR STREET

London Lane

Appleton
Dr

Clay Street

1

Mar
Clos

Trinity Crs

B

King's Brook

Hot Cl

4

98

Gorse Farm

5

REMPSTONE ROAD

A60

Holly Tree Cl

Wymeswold Road

Hoton

Lime Tree Ter

Old Parsonage La

Wymeswold
Industrial
Park

6

Prestwold

Prestwold Lane

UGH ROAD

Wymeswold La

The Cliff

7

Cliff Fa

Old
Wood

Prestwood
Hall

Cemetery

MELTON

ROAD

B676

8

Somerset Cl

Brickwood
Place

Mercury

Brook
St

St Andrews

PO

St Phillips

St Marys

2

Hall Dr

**Burton on
the Wolds**

Home
Farm

PRESTWOLD LANE

Springfield Cl

ROAD

G

B676

LOUGHBOROUGH ROAD

H

Nottingha

J

105

Burton on the
Wolds C
Primary

K

The Willows

Trowles
Fields

Seals

Sowters

Lane

L

M

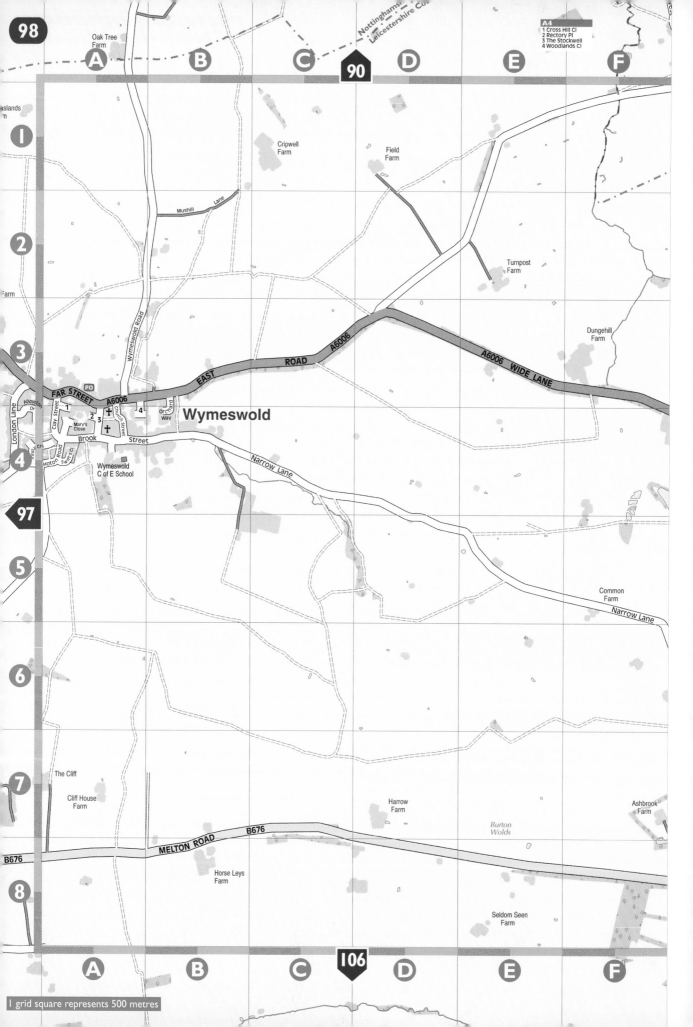

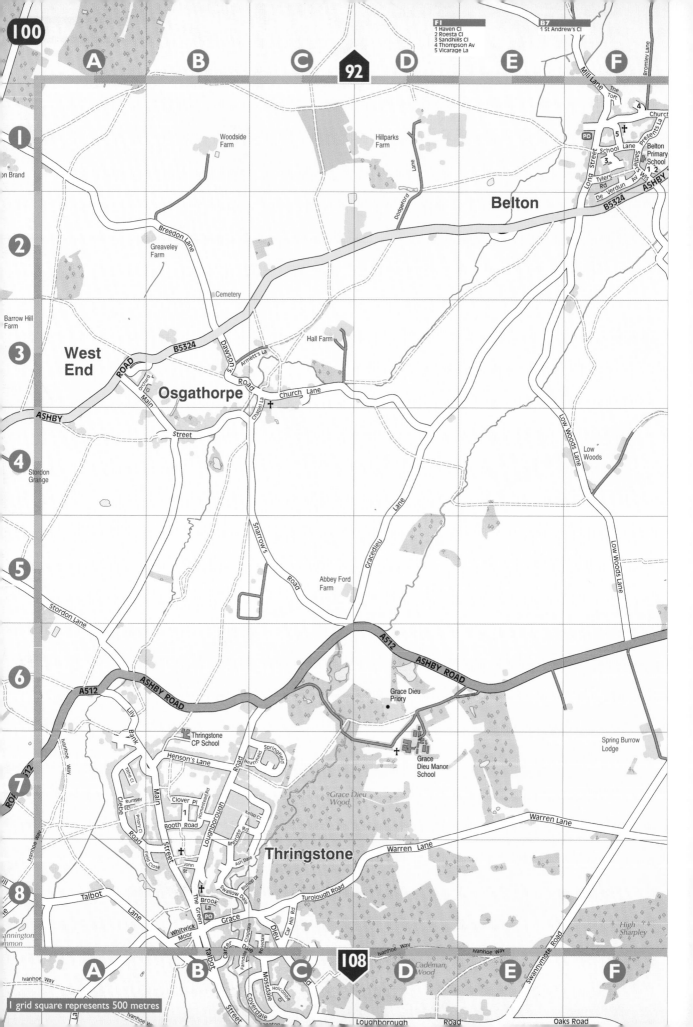

A B C 92 D E F

1

on Brand

Woodside Farm

Hillparks Farm

Dodgeford Lane

Mill Lane

The Toft

4

Church

PO

5

School Lane

Belton Primary School

Long Street

3

Snells

presents La

2

1

Tylers Rd

De Verdun Av

Belton

ASHBY

B5324

2

Breedon Lane

Greaveley Farm

3

Barrow Hill Farm

West End

B5324

Dawson's

Road

Armett's La

Hall Farm

ROAD

ASHBY

Osgathorpe

Main

Chapel La

Church Lane

Street

Low Woods Lane

Low Woods

4

Stordon Grange

Snarrow's Road

Gracedieu Lane

5

Stordon Lane

Abbey Ford Farm

6

A512

ASHBY ROAD

A512

ASHBY ROAD

Grace Dieu Priory

Spring Burrow Lodge

Lily Bank

Ivanhoe Way

Thringstone CP School

Henson's Lane

Loughborough Road

Springfield

Heather side

Grace Dieu Manor School

7

ROI 512

Glebe Road

Rumsey Cl

Priory Cl

Main Street

Clover Pl

1

Booth Road

Homestead Rd

Kelso Ct

Melrose Rd

Ash Dale

Grace Dieu Wood

Warren Lane

Warren Lane

Thringstone

Flagg Close

John St

Swallow Dale

Bishop Dr

Turolough Road

8

Talbot Lane

The Green

Brook La

PO

Grace

Dieu

Whitwick Moor

Carter Dale

Ferndale

Crageale

Kessdale

Carr Hill Rd

Ivanhoe Way

Ivanhoe Way

Swannymore Road

High Sharpley

Ivanhoe Way

A B 108 C D E F

Mossdale

Coverdale

Holcombe

Cademan Wood

Loughborough Road

Oaks Road

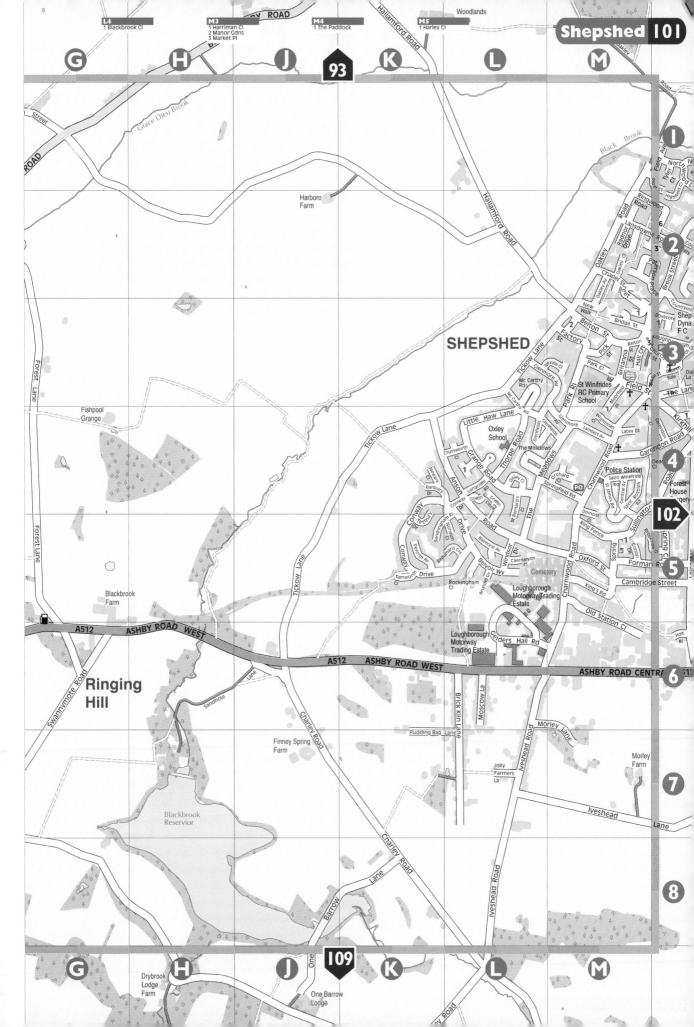

SHEPSHED

Ringing Hill

Blackbrook Reservoir

Blackbrook Farm

Fishpool Grange

Harboro Farm

Woodlands

Grace Dieu Brook

Black Brook

A512 ASHBY ROAD WEST

A512 ASHBY ROAD WEST

ASHBY ROAD CENTRAL

Loughborough Motorway Trading Estate

Loughborough Motorway Trading Estate

St Winifrides RC Primary School

Oxley School

Police Station

Cemetery

Finney Spring Farm

Morley Farm

Drybrook Lodge Farm

One Barrow Lodge

Hallamford Road

Forest Lane

Forest Lane

Swannymore Road

Charley Road

Iveshead Road

Iveshead Lane

Tickow Lane

Tickow Lane

Charnwood Road

Oxford St

Cambridge Street

Old Station Cl

Gelders Hall Rd

Brick Kiln Lane

Moscow La

Morley Lane

Pudding Bag Lane

Barrow Lane

Sandhole Lane

93
109
102

L4
1 Blackbrook Cl

M3
1 Harriman Cl
2 Manor Gdns
3 Market Pl

M4
1 The Paddock

M5
1 Harley Cl

A5
1 Nook Cl
2 Snowdon Cl

A4
1 Freehold St

Lounds
Farm

A3
1 Cheapside

A2
1 Blacksmiths Av
2 Coachmans Ct
3 Lansdowne Av
4 Ploughmans Dr
5 Shepherds Cl
6 Woodlands Dr
7 Woodmans Wy

A1
1 Wortley Cl

(A) (B) (C) **94** (D) (E) (F)

Pear Tree La

Dishl

(1)

Black Brook

Stonebow
Primary
School

Stonebow
Cl

(2)

Butthole Lane

Hind Leys
Community
College

Shepshed
Dynamo
FC

St Botolphs
C of E (C)
Primary School

Garendon
Park

Dunholme
Avenue

Prestbury
Road

(3)

PO

Danve's
La

The Lane

Smithy Wy

Westoby
Nelson

(4)

Garendon Road

Police Station
Saint Winefride

Forest
House
Surgery

Temple
of Venus

Cropston
Avenue

Cropston
Av

Leighton
Barden Cl
Rowbank

Windleden
Road

Butterley
Dr

Old Ashby Rd
Surgery

101

Newcroft
County
Primary
School

Malvern
Av

Grassholme
Dr

Bowden
Close

Lanesm...

Naseby Drive

Pitsford Drive

Old
Ashby Rd

Herr

(5)

Cambridge Street

Fairway

Brendon Cl

Abberton Way

Fox...
Belmont...
Wy Dr

Hotel

New Ashby Rd

Sharpl

Snell's
Nook

(6) **ENTRAL** A512

Junction 23

ASHBY ROAD EAST

A512 NEW ASHBY ROAD

Oakwood Drive

Holywell
Hall

Gas...
Cen...

Hurst
Farm

(7)

Morley
Farm

Lane

Ingleberry
Lodge

Nanpantan

(8)

INGLEBERRY ROAD

Bodkin
Farm

Longcliffe
Golf Course

Longcliffe
Gdns

Nanpantan
Reservoir

B4
1 Peartree Av

(A)

F1
1 Archer Cl
2 Forsyth Cl
3 Melville Cl
4 Sheldon Cl
5 Wyndham Rd

(B)

F2
1 Byland Wy
2 St Olaves Cl
3 Trelissick Cl
4 Waverley Cl
5 Whitby Cl

(C) **110** (D)

F4
1 Ladybower Rd
2 Winterburn Wy

(E)

F5
1 Butterley Dr
2 De Lisle Ct
3 Ravensthorpe Dr
4 Rudyard Cl

(F)

1 grid square represents 500 metres

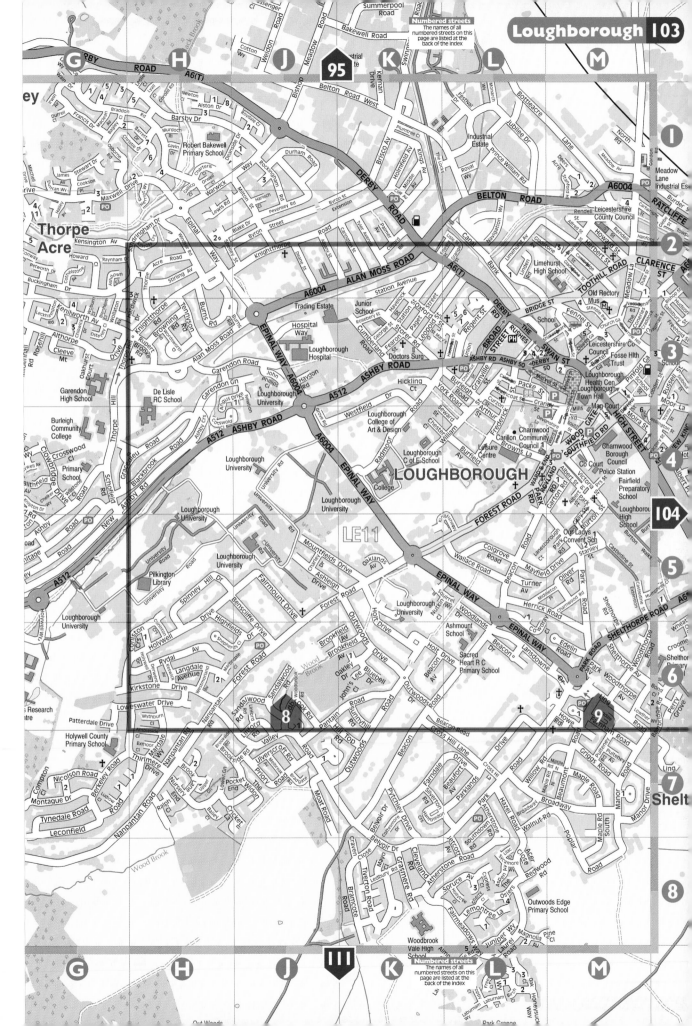

A   B   C   96   D   E   F

A5
1 Shelthorpe Rd
2 Tuckers Cl
A4
1 Finsbury Av
2 Queen St
A3
1 Bowler Ct
2 Cobden St
3 Hume St
A2
1 Bromhead St
2 Cotes Yd

Park Farm

LOUGHBOROUGH ROAD

Cotes

I

A6004

LOUGHBOROUGH

Gordon Rd

Meadow Lane Industrial Est
Loughborough Station
PO
Border Street
Railway Ter
Towpath La

A60 NOTTINGHAM ROAD
BARROW ROAD
B676

Burton Bandalls

Cotes Road

2

CLARENCE ST
RATCLIFFE RD
Meadow La
Hanford
Nettleham Rd
Falcon
A60
Mill La

LC

River Soar

3
PO
Pinfold Ga
Primary School
QUEEN'S ROAD
Hudson St
Salisbury Rd
Freehold St
Peel Dr
Rover Rd
Wolsey Way
Russell St
Empress
WHARNCLIFFE RD
Warner
Morris
Little
Judges St
Thomas St

Moor Lane

HIGH STREET

4
KG ST NEW KING ST
Moira St
Cobden St
Wellington St
Trinity St
Loughborough Mosque & Islamic Cultural Association
Great Central
Moor Lane
Moor Lane
Windmill Rd
Windmill Road Industrial Est
KG George Rd

Loughborough Moors

Ryecroft Farm

9

103
Hotel
Albert Promenade
Elms Gv
Lime Av
Beeches
Edward Road
KG George Avenue
Tuckers

Grand Union Canal

5
LEICESTER
Whitehouse
Winnington
Whitehouse Ct
Hayward
Naylor Av
Cooper Ct
Cooper Ct

A6004
SHELTHORPE ROAD
Wheatland Dr
Avon Rd
Witton Av
Quorn Cl
A6(T)

6
Shelthorpe Primary School
Croome Cl
Cooper Cl
Whaddon Dr
Hotel
Charnwood Water

Pilling's Lock

Flesh Hovel Lane

Bull-in-the-Hollow Farm

Loughborough Cem

7
Shelthorpe
Ling Av
Manor Drive
Main Street
Great Central Railway
Quorn Lodge
A6(T) LOUGHBOROUGH ROAD

Lodge Farm

River Soar

8
Woodthorpe

Loughborough Road

A6(T)
Beacon View Farm
Way
Farley
Pepper Dr
Allen Av
Kercey Rd
Freeman
Turner
Alexander
Meynell
Quorn (Quorndon)
Barrow
A6(T)

A   B   C   112   D   E   F

A6
1 Cedar Rd
2 Weaver Cl
D8
1 Bayliss Cl
2 Gamble Wy
3 Long Cl
4 Rupert Law Cl
5 Russ Cl
6 Stirling Cl
E8
1 Dexters Cl
2 Parkers Flds

Warwick Road
Rumsey
Rawlins School
Soar Road

1 grid square represents 500 metres

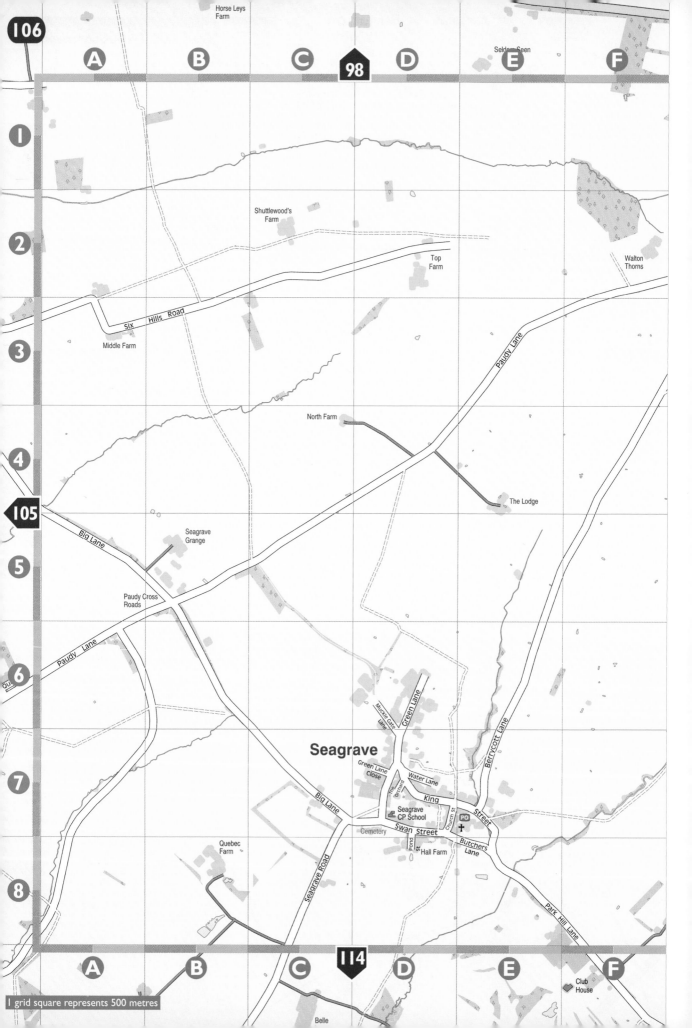

Ⓐ   Ⓑ   Ⓒ   **98**   Ⓓ   Ⓔ   Ⓕ

Horse Leys
Farm

Seldom Seen

Ⓘ

Shuttlewood's
Farm

❷

Walton
Thorns

Top
Farm

Six Hills Road

Paudy Lane

❸

Middle Farm

North Farm

❹

The Lodge

105

Big Lane

Seagrave
Grange

❺

Paudy Cross
Roads

Paudy Lane

❻

qu

Green Lane

Muckle Gate Lane

Berrycott Lane

Seagrave

Green Lane
Close

The Orchard

Water Lane

❼

Big Lane

King Street

Seagrave
CP School

Church St

PO

Quebec
Farm

Cemetery

Swan Street

Butchers
Lane

Seagrave Road

Pond St

Hall Farm

❽

Park Hill Lane

Ⓐ   Ⓑ   Ⓒ   **114**   Ⓓ   Ⓔ   Ⓕ

Club
House

Belle

MELTON ROAD

B676

G **H** B676 **J** 99 **K** SIX HILLS **L** **M**

B676

†

Six Hills

Old Park Farm

Paudy Lane

The Oaks Farm

1

2

Ragdale Wolds Farm

Six Hills Road

Wolds Farm

Ragdale Hall

Main Street

3

Seagrave Wolds

A46(T)

A46(T)

4

Bunker Hill Farm

Charlton Gorse Farm

5

Thrussington Grange

6

North Hill Farm

Ox Brook

7

The Lodge Farm

8

Motel

G **H** **J** 115 **K** **L** **M**

Hilltop

The Elms

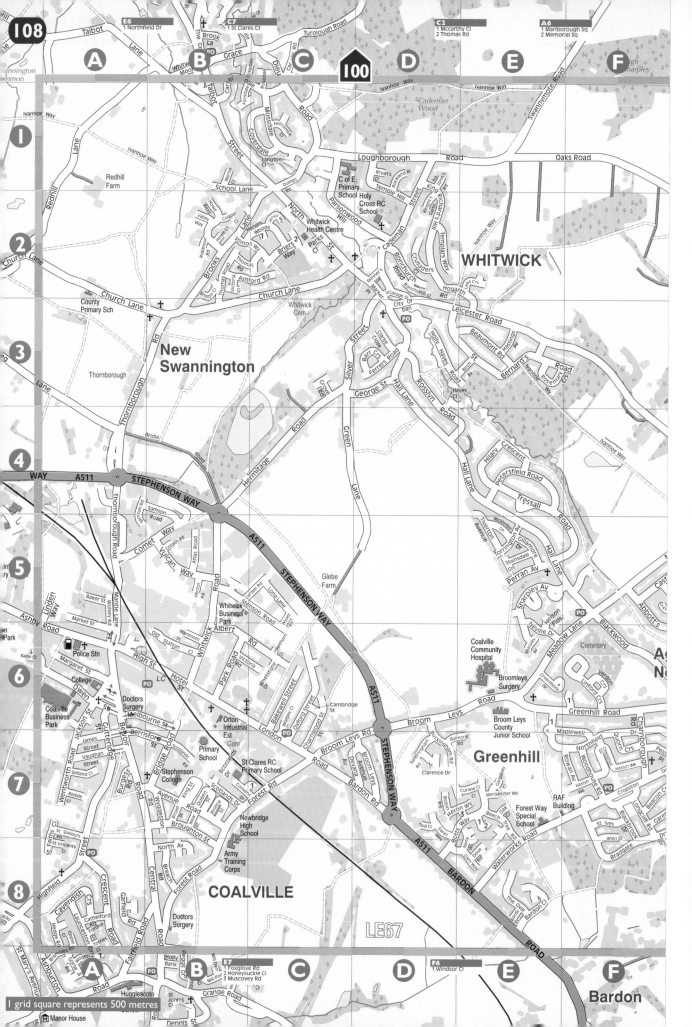

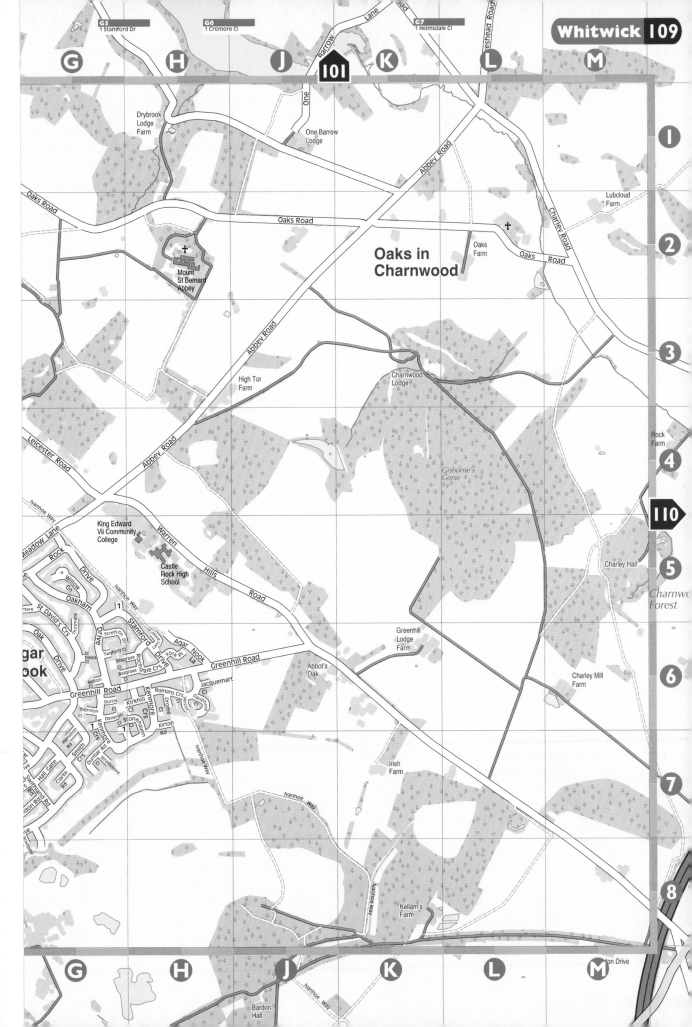

110

A B C **102** D E ✝ F

1

Longcliffe Lodge Farm

Bodkin Farm

Nanpantan Road

Woodhouse Lane

Newtown Reservoir

ubcloud arm

2

B591

Wood Brook

3

B591

Rock Farm

Dean's Lane

4

Bawdon Lodge

M1

109

5

Louella Stud

Charnwood Forest

Hill Farm

B591

6

Hall Farm

Charley Road

Bawdon Castle Farm

M1

7

Bess Bagley

B591

8

Ulverscroft Lodge Farm

n Drive

A B C **116** D E F

Whitcrofts Lane

M1

B591

Poultney Wood

1 grid square represents 500 metres

Oak

L1
1 Copse Gv
2 Fishpond Wy
3 Honeysuckle Wy
4 Lavender Cl
5 Mimosa Cl
6 Silverbirch Wy

G H J **103** K L M

Woodbrook Vale High School

Primary School

Out Woods Farm

Out Woods

Charnwood Hall

Pocket Gate Farm

Blackbird's Nest

Brook Road

Brook Road

Woodhouse Lane

Golf Course

Breakback Road

Beacon Hill County Park

Club House

Beacon Road

Beacon Road

Park Grange

Beaumanor Hall

Leicestershire County Council

Beaumanor Drive

Briscoe Lane

Woo

Home Farm Cl

Forest Rd

School La

112

Woodhouse Eaves

Perry Cl
Herrick Rd
Tuckett Rd
Bird
Main
Windmill
Paterson Dr
Paterson Dr

Brand Lane

Woodhouse Parish Council

St Pauls C of E Primary School

Leicestershire Round

Raxhills Cl
Meadow

Mill Road

Hill Road

PH
PO

The Dr
Hill Rise

Church Hill

Hastings Rd
Victoria Road
Charnwood Rd
Nanhill Dr

Brand Hill

Upper Broombriggs

Maplewell Road

Maplewell Hall School

Joe Moore's Lane

Priory Lane

Benscliffe Road

The Brand

Main Street

House

Golf Course

Benscliffe

G H J **117** K L M

I
2
3
4
5
6
7
8

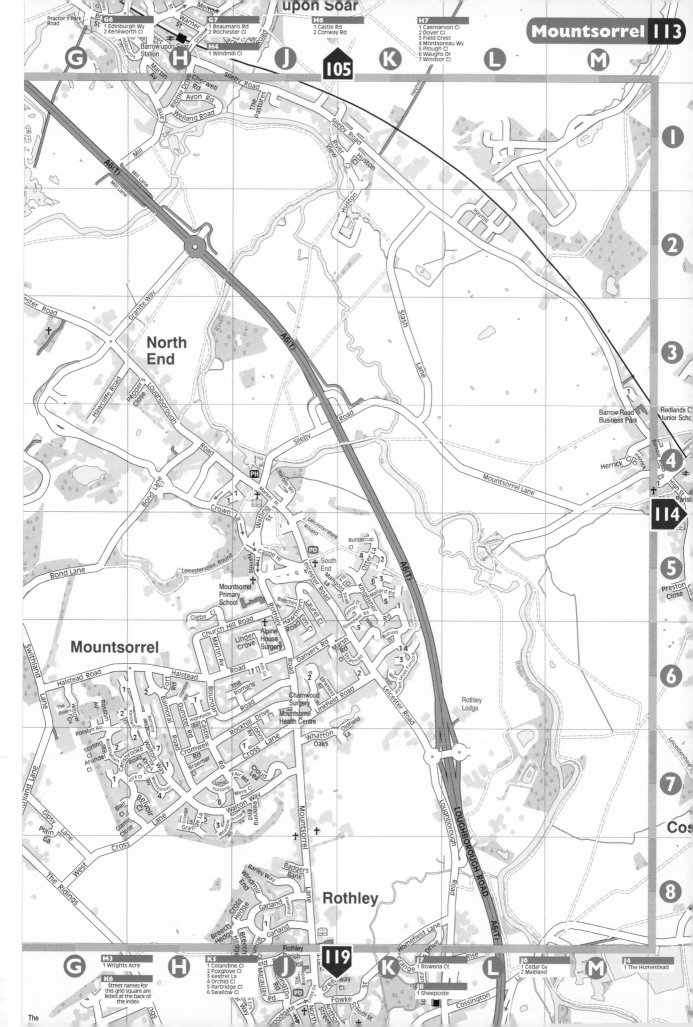

B3
1 Dickens Cl

A6
1 Middle Orch

A4
1 Church La Ltl

A3
1 Hudson Rd

A B C 106 D E F

1

Club House

Belle Isle

Hanover Lodge

Golf Course

2

Jubilee Avenue

Greedon Rise

Highgate Primary School

3

Forest Dr

Greedon Rd

Barradale AV

Homefield Road

St Mary's Road

Park Road

Pryor Road

Weldon AV

Collingwood Drive

Heathcote Drive

Albert Springfield Rd

Brunsfield

Gibson Road

Lakes Close

Parsons Drive

Banards Drive

Highgate Farm

Stanage Road

Ainsworth Dr

Redlands County Junior School

Marshall AV

Pochin Way

Moreton Dl

Haybrooke

Hickling

Nesfield

Nether Cl

Hanover Drive

St Gregory's Road

Caroe Cl

Caney

Highgate Wellbrook Drive Avenue

Highgate Surgery

Stanford Cl

Finsbury AV

Leicestershire Way

SILEBY

Barrow Road Business Park

Kestrick

Barrow Road

Highbridge

King Street

Swan Street

PO

PH

Sileby Station

The Banks Surgery

The Banks

Ratcliffe Road

Brook St

Ward Cl Cl's

Cemetery Rd

Cemetery

Peashill Close

Ratcliffe College (Sch)

4

113

Sileby Parish Council

High St

Back La

Albion Road

Avenue Road

Staveley Close

Kendal Road

Phoenix Drive

A46(T)

5

Preston Close

Cossington Road

Charles Street

Milner Close

Sherrard Dr

Quaker Rd

West Wilbourne Crescent End

Moyneux Drive

Charles Street

Chalfont Drive

LC

Ratcliffe Road

Humble Lane

PO

6

Leicestershire Way

C of E Primary School

Fisher Close

Homestead Close

Hall Cl

Main Street

Back Lane

Bennett's Lane

Humble Lane

Glebe Lodge Farm

Blackberry Lane

Home Farm

Wreake House Farm

River Wreake

7

Cossington

Middlefield Road

8

Platts Lane

Syston Road

A607 SYSTON ROAD

A607

COSSINGTON LANE

Lewin Bridge

A Grange B
B7
1 Hall Cl
C 120 D E F

Chestnut Farm

C3
1 Heathcote Dr

C4
1 Highgate Rd

1 grid square represents 500 metres

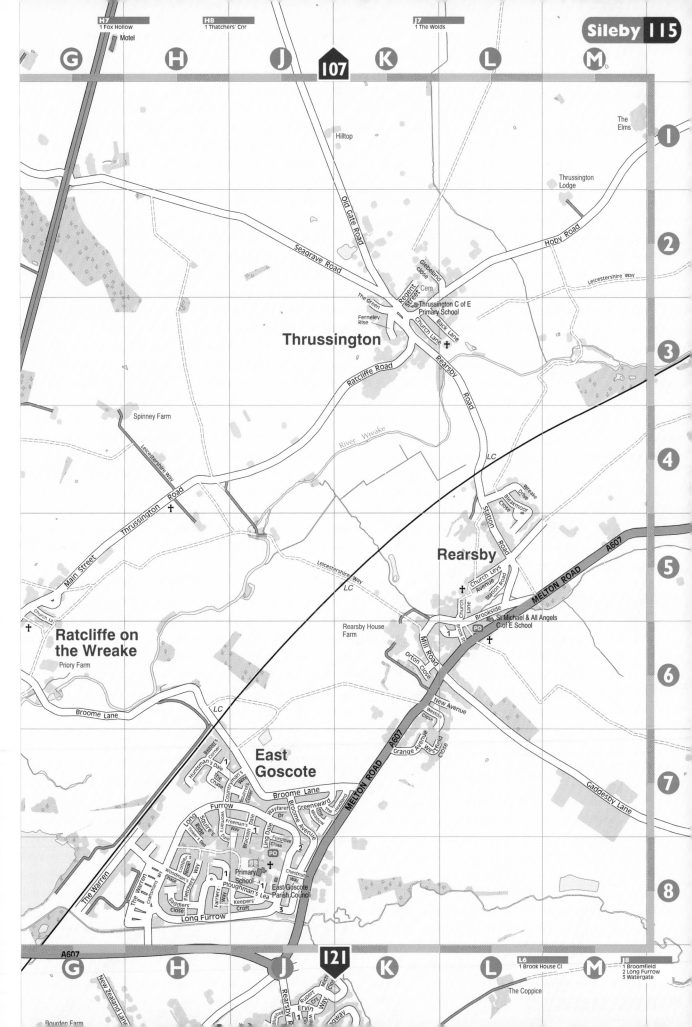

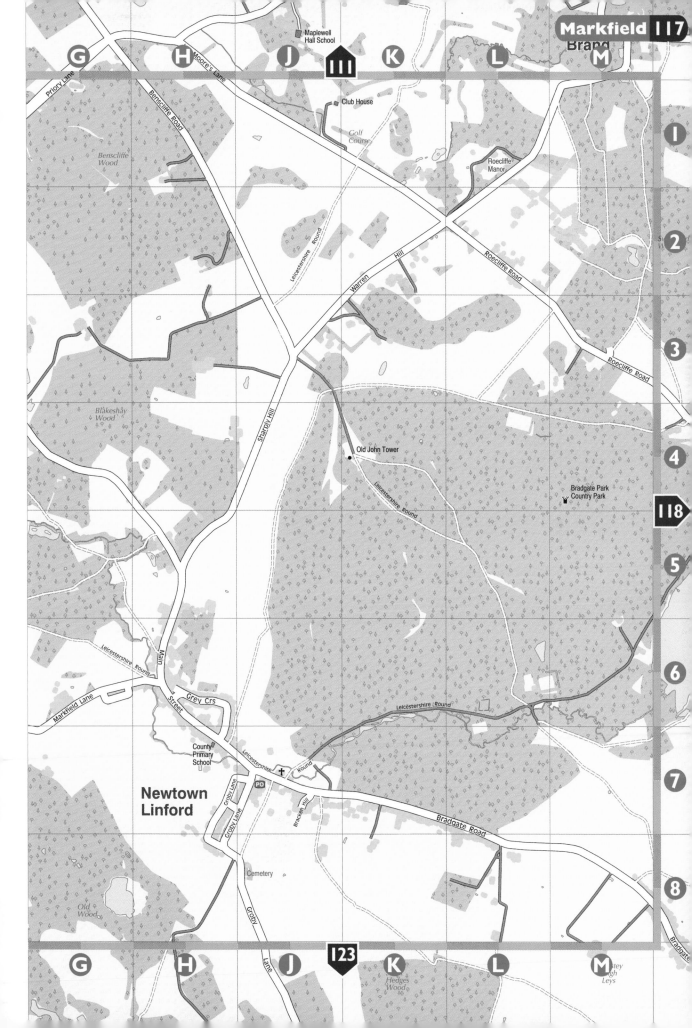

G H J K L M

Priory Lane

Benscliffe Road

Benscliffe Wood

Moore's Lane

Maplewell Hall School

Club House

Golf Course

Warren Hill

Leicestershire Round

Roecliffe Manor

Roecliffe Road

Roecliffe Road

I

2

3

4

118

Sharply Hill

Blakeshay Wood

Old John Tower

Leicestershire Round

Bradgate Park Country Park

5

6

Leicestershire Round

Main Street

Markfield Lane

Grey Crs

County Primary School

Leicestershire Round

Leicestershire Round

Newtown Linford

Groby Lane

PO

Groby Lane

Cemetery

Bracken Hill

Bradgate Road

Old Wood

Groby Lane

Hedges Wood

stey gh Leys

Bradgate

7

8

G H J K L M

A   B   C   D   E   F

Syston Road

Grange

Chestnut Farm

Lewin Bridge

A607 SYSTON ROAD

COSSINGTON LANE

114

1

2

3

4

119

5

6

7

8

Wanlip

A46(T)

Grand Union Canal

Meadow Lane

Meadow Lane

A46(T)

Wanlip Road

Glebe Way

Glebe Way

Moorland Rd

Martin Drive

Swift Close

Swallow Drive

Glebe Way

Teal Way

Wren Close

Cygnet

Blackthorn

Scorefield Dr

Heath Av

Gorse Walk

Willow

Mallard Drive

4

5

1

3

2

St Columba Wy

Iona Rd

Priory Close

Lindisfarne

Abbots

Cromer Dr

Harwick Dr

Chatsworth Dr

Haddon Close

Wolsey Way

Worsey Way

Syston Station

High Street

Church

Lower Church

Bath St

Harcourt Close

Turn St

West St

North St

Chapel St

School St

Walkers

Brookside

The Stiles

Necton St

St Peter's Street

Broad St

Brookfield St

Brookfield St

Barkby Rd

St Peter & St Paul C of E Primary School

Upper Church St

Syston Health Centre

PO

Clumber Close

Badminton Road

Avery Drive

Beatty Road

Northfields

Northfields

Shir

Parkst

Melton Road

Victoria St

Albert Street

Sandford Road

Wellington St

Halford

Necton St

Trinity Close

University Close

College Road

Montague Rd

Plumtree Way

Southfield

Orien

Per

Maiden Street

Archdale Street

Bruxby St

Upxham

Hadrian Close

Marcus Close

Augustus Close

Trojan Close

Roman Wy

Simpson Close

The Pastures

Roundhill Close

Wanlip Road

Station Rd

Goode's Lane

Millers Close

Holmdale Dr

Paul's Drive

Crescent

Copford

Goode's Av

Ash Dr

Beech Dr

Oak

Cedar Dr

Lime Dr

Pine Dr

Cherry Dr

Merton C Primary

The Meadway

PO

Melton Road

Britannia Way

Roundhill College

Barkby Lane

Barkby Lodge

Russet Way

Melba Wy

Worcester Av

Ashmead Crescent

Allington Dr

Allington Drive

Worcester Av

Watermead Country Park

Feature Road

A607

St Crispin's Way

Post Rd

Solar Rd

Wreave St

Soar Road

Norman Road

Winster Dr

Barkby Thorpe Lane

Bishop Ellis RC Primary School

Bridge

Brampton Rd

Thorpe Field Drive

Barkby Thorpe Lane

Eastfield County Primary School

Charnwood Av

Checkland Rd

Millcroft

Sanders Rd

Charnwood Av

Highway

Eastfield Rd

Athlone Rd

Canal St

Unicorn St

Alexandra

Elizabeth

Victoria St

Wharf St

Forest Av

Mill La

Red Hill Lane

Earls Close Industrial Est

Earls Cl

Knight Cl

Dukes Cl

Bradgate Av

Earls Close Industrial Estate

Earls Way

Field Vw

The Coppice

Meadow La

Bourne Rd

Bramley Road

chard Road

Whiles Lane

Blenheim

PO

Doctors Surgery

Lea Close

Brook St

Bridge Pk Rd

Assured Dr

Garden St

MELTON ROAD

NEWARK DRIVE

B667

Chappell Dr

Church

Beverley

Cem

Church Hill County Infant School

Church Hill

Dovedale Road

Rutland Dr

Spencer

Thorndale

Beacon Avenue

Dickinson

Dyke

Gregory Cl

Shenton

Gladstone

West

Church Road

Lakeside Business Park

Dorothy

A607

Humberstone Lane

126

Thurmaston

A   B   C   D   E   F

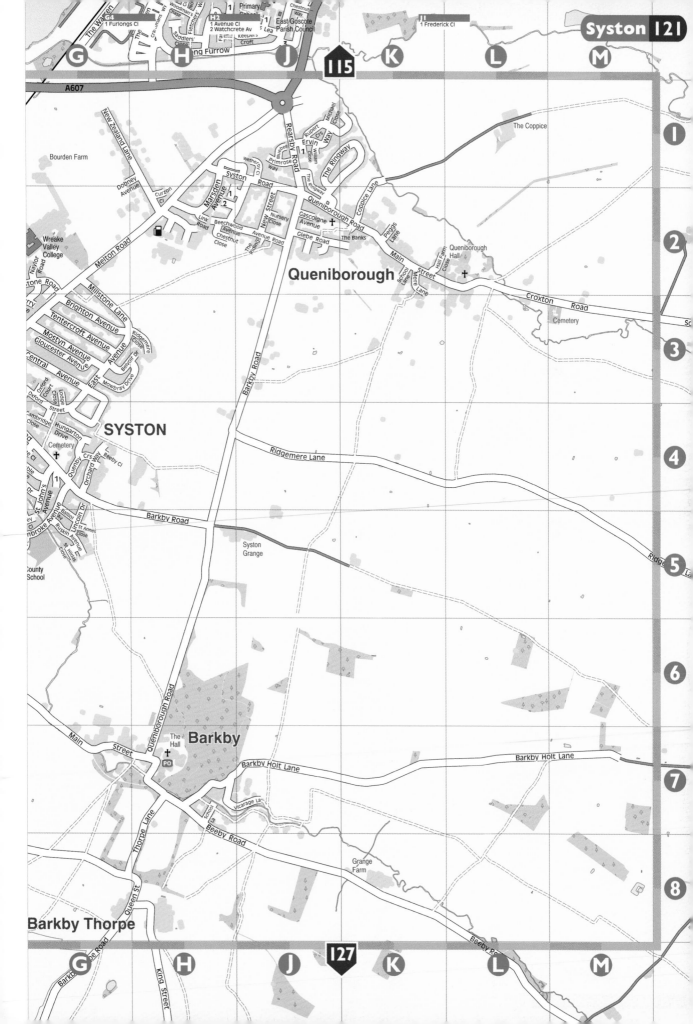

The Waren

G4
1 Furlongs Cl

H2
1 Avenue Cl
2 Watchcrete Av

Primary

Woodman's Close

Fletchers W

Sadlers' Close

ng Furrow

Chestnut Way

East Goscote Parish Council

Keepers Croft

J1
1 Frederick Cl

G **H** **J** ◆**115** **K** **L** **M**

A607

The Coppice

Bourden Farm

New Zealand Lane

Dobney Avenue

Curzon Cl

Rearsby Road

Rupert Crs

Michael Close

Ervin

Bluebell
Primrose
Way

1

William Close

The Ringway

Wetherby Cl

Melton Road

Marsden Avenue

Syston Road

New Street

Queniborough Road

Coppice Lane

Link Road

Beechwood Avenue

Chestnut Close

Avenue Road

The Pound

Nursery Close

Gascoigne Avenue

Glebe Road

The Banks

Peggs Lane

Main Street

Queniborough Hall

Queniborough

School Lane

Mere Lane

Hall Farm Close

Queniborough

Croxton Road

Cemetery

Wreake Valley College

Naylor Road

Millstone Lane

Ridgemere Close

Ridgemere Lane

Barkby Road

Ridge La

Brighton Avenue

Tentercroft Avenue

Mostyn Avenue

Gloucester Avenue

Central Avenue

Avenue East

Mowbray Drive

Belvoir Dr

Hungarton Drive

SYSTON

Cemetery

Queniby Crs

Orchard Way

Beeby Cl

St John's Avenue

Cambridge Close

Oxford Court
Close

Lodge Street

1

Pembroke Avenue

Balliol Ave

Lincoln Dr

St Annes Close

Ruskin Avenue

St Hildas Close

Barkby Road

Syston Grange

County School

Queniborough Road

Main Street

Barkby

The Hall

PO

Barkby Holt Lane

Barkby Holt Lane

Thorpe Lane

School La

Vicarage La

Beeby Road

Grange Farm

Queen St

Barkby Thorpe

Barkt e Road

King Street

Beeby Rd

G **H** **J** ◆**127** **K** **L** **M**

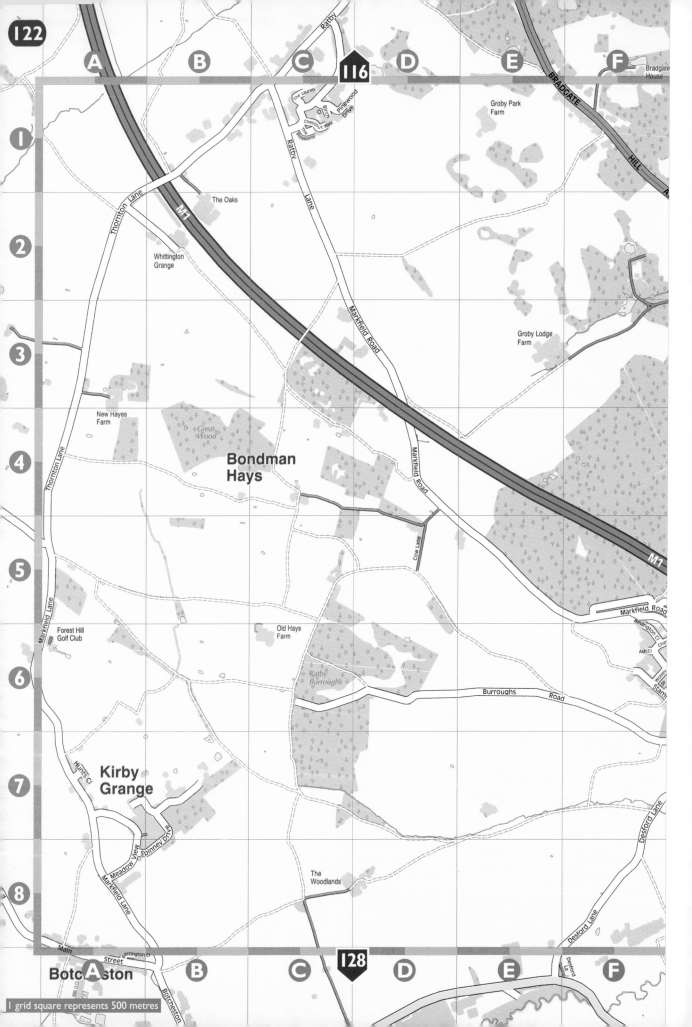

A   B   C   116   D   E   F   BRADGATE

Bradgate House

I

2

3

4

5

6

7

8

Thornton Lane

M1

The Oaks

Whittington Grange

Ratby

Ratby Lane

The Laurels
Birch Cl
Chestnut Walk
The Blossoms

Pinewood Drive

Groby Park Farm

Groby Lodge Farm

Markfield Road

HILL

New Hayes Farm

Great Wood

Bondman Hays

Markfield Road

Cow Lane

M1

Markfield Road

Bevington Cl

Ash Cl

Thornton Lane

Markfield Lane

Forest Hill Golf Club

Old Hays Farm

Ratby Burroughs

Burroughs   Road

Stam

Hunts Cl

Kirby Grange

Meadow View
Spinney Drive

Markfield Lane

The Woodlands

Desford Lane

Desford La

Botc A ston

Main Street

Berrington Cl

Botcheston

B   C   128   D   E   F

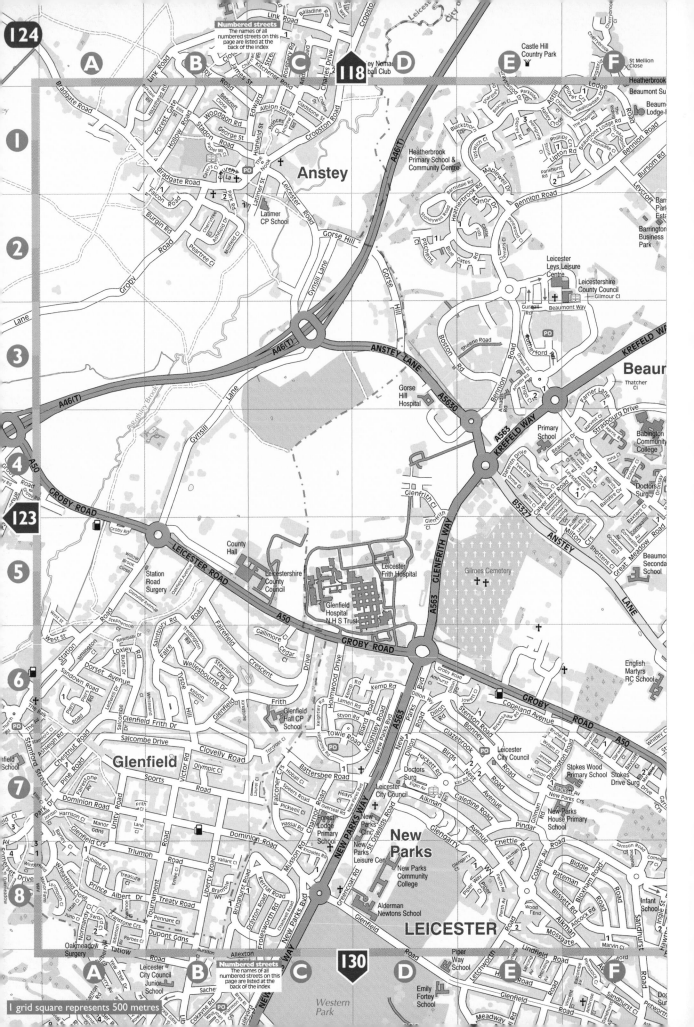

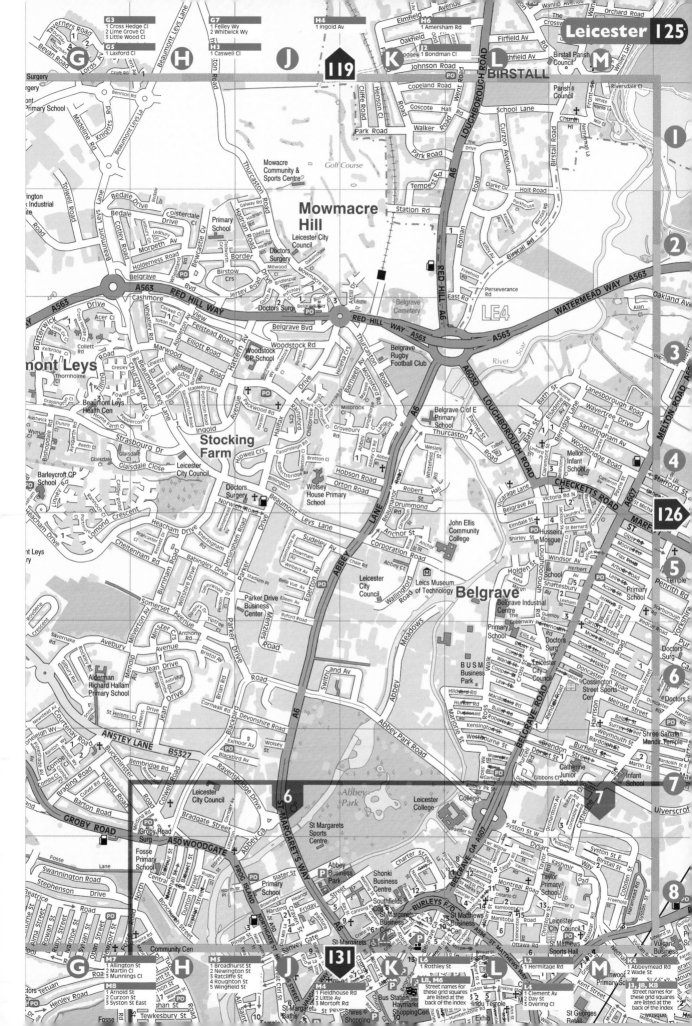

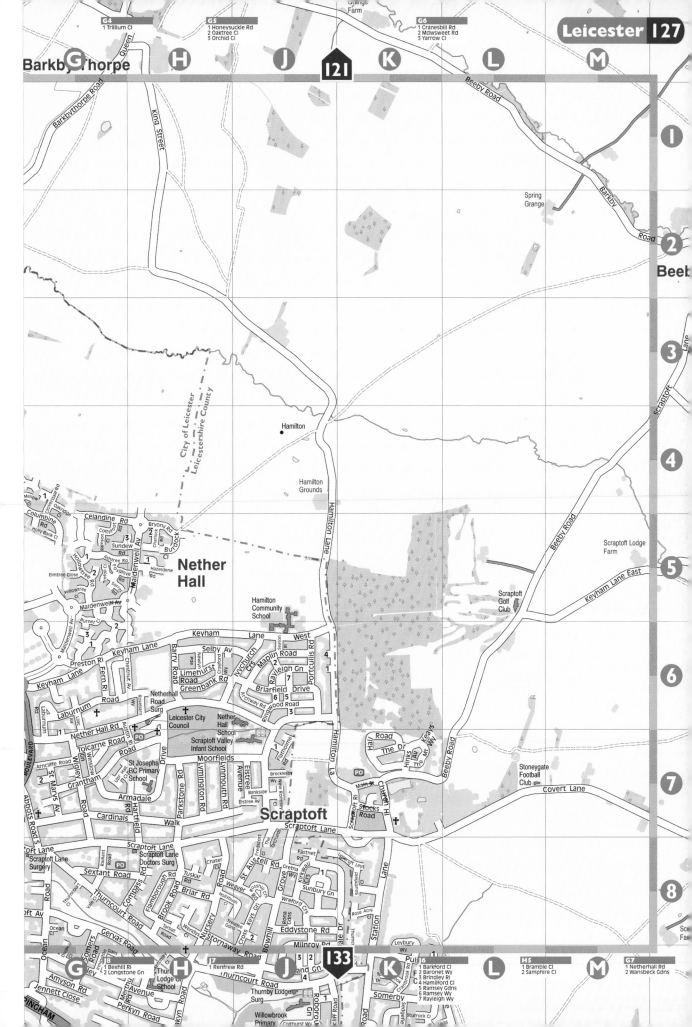

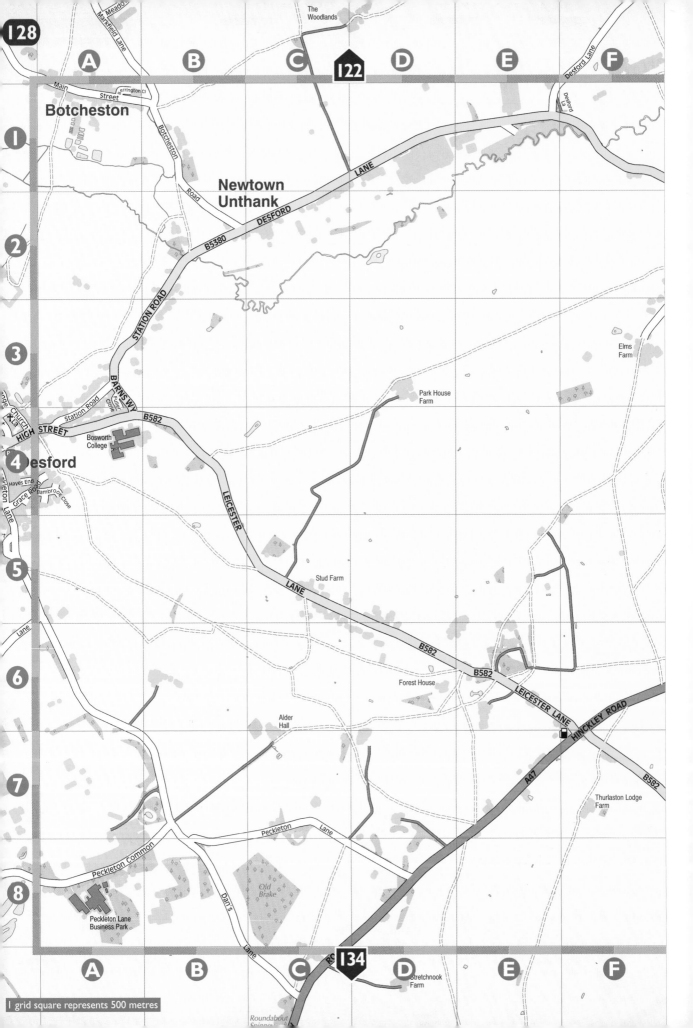

A   B   C   **122**   D   E   F

1

Botcheston

Meadow
Markfield Lane
Main Street
errington Cl
Botcheston Road

Newtown
Unthank

The Woodlands

Desford Lane
Desford La

LANE

2

DESFORD

B5380

STATION ROAD

3

BARNS W'Y

Fuller Close

Station Road

Park House Farm

Elms Farm

Desford

Church
K'la
HIGH STREET

B582

Bosworth College

LEICESTER

4

Hayes End
Grace Road
Bambrook Close
eton
Lane

5

LANE

Stud Farm

B582

Lane

6

Forest House

B582

LEICESTER LANE

HINCKLEY ROAD

7

Alder Hall

A47

Thurlaston Lodge Farm

B582

Peckleton Lane

8

Peckleton Common

Dan's Lane

Old Brake

Peckleton Lane Business Park

A   B   C   **134**   D   Stretchnook Farm   E   F

Roundabout Spinney

Kirby Muxloe

Kirby Fields

Leicester Forest East

Junction 21a

Leicester Forest East Service Area

County Primary School

Golf Club

Oaks Farm

Leicester Ivanhoe C C

Kingstand Farm

Lawn Farm

Old Warren Farm

Enderby Lodge

New House Farm

Huncote Grange

Hoefields

Parsons Gallery
KM Sports Club
Cemetery
Hunters Lodge
Medical Centre
Holmfield CP School
Doctor Surge

Roads and places

DESFORD ROAD
RATBY LANE
B5380
B5380
RATBY LANE
HINCKLEY ROAD
HINCKLEY ROAD
A47
A47
M1
Station Road
Princess Drv
Main Street
Hedgerow Lane
Ladysmith Rd
Pretoria Rd
Fox Lane
Castle Rd
Barwell Rd
Armson Av
Garfit Rd
Oakcroft Av
Court Cl
The Keep
Lime Gv
Wilshere Cl
Links Road
Gullet Lane
The Huntings
Barons Cl
Barns Cl
Wentworth Gn
Stamford Road
Forest Drive
Hastings Road
Portland Rd
Roundhill
Holmewood
The Fairway
Holt Dr
Rosedene
Walton Cl
Linden Lane
Hewitt Dr
Beechwood Av
Kirby Lane
Beechwood Av
Priory Walk
Charnwood
Charnwood Drive
Packer Avenue
Churchill
Bignal Dr
Elliott Drive
Stratt
Birchwood
Walsingham Crs
Wardens
South Av
Holmfield Av
Park Drive
Scudamore Road
Wanstead Road
Wembley Road
Carrow Road
Elland Rd
Sunningdale
St Davids Rd
Cherry Hills Rd
Oakme
Surge
Murr
Towers Drive
Station Cl
Station Dr
Towers
Kirby Drive
Forest Rise
Barry Av
Cherry Tree Av
Barry
Martin Av
Avenue
Ellis Dr
Maytree Av
Maytree Drive
Harene Crs
Highland Av
Pine Tree Gv
Hawthorn
Barbara
Shepherd Cl
Stafford Leys
Boyers Wk
Regents
Rushmere Wk
Acres Rd
Queens Dr
Lowland Av
Kings Wk
Kings Wk
Chapel Gn
Chapel Green
Kennedy Way
Webb
Hobill Close
Baines Lane
Baines La
Chapel Gn
Brickman Lane
Blue Pots Cl
Kingcup
Pleasant Close
Teal Cl
Warren
Mallard
Woodpecker
Swallo
Copse
Forest View Close
Harvester
Harrow
Carnation Cl
House Lane
Acacia Cl
Acacia Way
Pendragon Wy
Lancelot Lane
Excalibur Wy
Guinevere Wy
Tristram Cl
Birchwood Cl
Galahad Cl
Beggar's Lane
Beggar's Lane
Lark Wy
Seymour
Grange Av
Kings Drive
Kinloe Av
Glenfield La
Farley Way
Primrose Way

123

130

135

Leicestershire County
City of Leicester

G H J K L M I
2 3 4 5 6 7 8

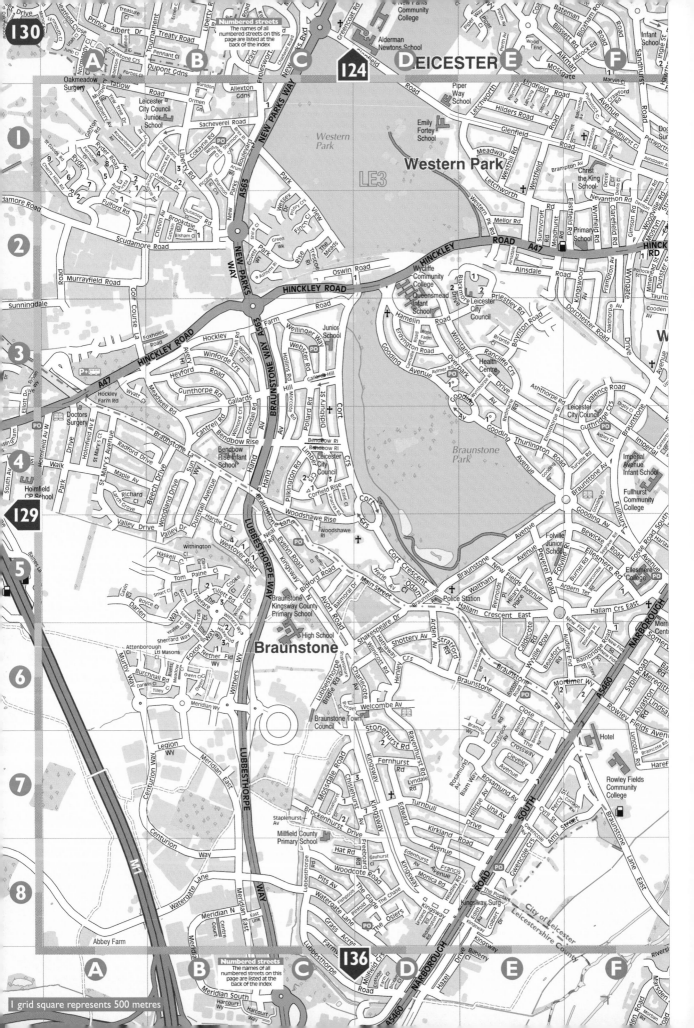

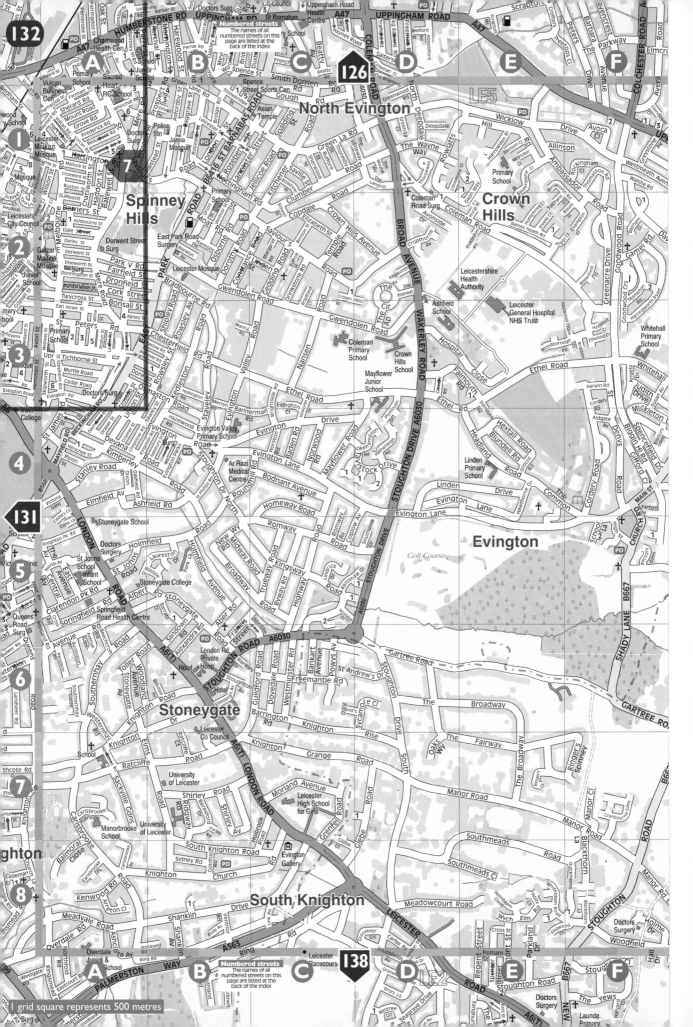

A B C **128** D E F

I

2

3

4

5

6

7

8

A B **140** D E F

Peckleton

Old Brake

Dan's Lane

Stretchnook Farm

Roundabout Spinney

HINCKLEY ROAD

A47

Desford Road

Knoll Farm

Newhall Park Farm

Clump Farm

Bassett Farm

Long Spinneys

HINCKLEY ROAD

Bungalow Farm

Hill Farm

Holt Crs

Enderby Road

Primary Rd School PO

Desford Rd

Main Street

Tyers Cl

Thurlaston

Holmes

Church St

Nursery Cl

Normanton Cl

Croft Road

Earl Shilton Road

LE9
Normanton
Turville

Dairy Farm

Yennards Farm

M69

ane

ard's

Mirfield Farm

Watery Gate Lane

Pingle Lane

Croft Lane

Sandpit Cotts

Thurlaston Lane

Mill Lane

Huit Farm

M69

ton Lane

G H J K L M

J8
1 Robotham Cl

K6
1 Camellia Cl

L3
1 Gayton Heights

129

L4
1 Barbara Cl
2 Cherry Tree Gv
3 Columbia Cl
4 Jacques Cl
5 The Nook
6 Rossetti Rd
7 Sloane Cl

K5
1 Needwood Wy

I

New House Farm

Huncote Grange

B582 DESFORD ROAD

B582

Hoefields Farm

Enderby Road

MILL HILL   M69

Warren Park Way

Harolds Lane

2

The Park

Mill Hill Industrial Est

Quarry La

Granite Cl

Froanes Cl

Leicester Lane

3

Cook's Lodge

Forest Road

Seine Lane

Capers Lane

Coney Lane

Moores La

Chapel

High St

Cross

Enderby

B582

BLABY

4

Pope Crs

Drummond Rd

Crays

Blake Cl

Carter Cl

Jarrett

Mitchell Rd

Sloane Cl

Alexander Av

Brook

Danemill CP School

Leisure Cen

Barnam La

Kirk

M69

Herrick

Keats

Sheridan

Coleridge Drive

George St

Jacob

Equinn Road

King St

Rawson

John St

Salt Close

136

Hardwicke Lodge Farm

Forest Road

Kiplin Drive

Shelley Rd

Holyoake St

Danemill CP School

Highcroft High Com

5

Pastures CP School

Radnor Cl

Stalmore Av

Souttrey

West Street

Stewart Avenue Surgery

The Rise

Kleider

Meller Cl

Stewart Av

Grizedale Gv

Camelot Wy

6

Green's Lodge

Hemlock Close

Broom Wy

The Pastures

Buttercup

Milton

Pimpernel

Meadow

Boswell St

Browning St

Tennyson St

Burns

Forest Rd

Woodland

Speedwell

Orchid Cl

Chaucer St

Foxglove

Clover

Leicestershire County Council

Alyssum Wy

Teasel Cl

The Pastures

Copt Oak Road

Narborough

Marigold Wy

Hardwicke Rd

The Burrows

Copt Oak Road

Woodlands Day Hospital

Holland Wy

KING EDWARD

7

Huncote Cem

Huncote Leisure Centre

Sports Fld

Denman

Langley Cl

Red Hill

School

Red Hill Av

Canons

B4114

Blaby District Council

Cem

Health Centre

Lodge Cl

Critchlow Rd

Hobill Cl

Masons Cl

Woodside Cl

Woodhouse Cl

Greenhill Rd

Squirrel Cl

Coltbeck Avenue

Langham Drive

Desford Rd

Narborough Parish Council

School La

Huncote CP School

Cooper Rd

Thornborough

Acan Wy

Narborough Hall Gallery

Coventry Rd

Bell

Jubilee

8

Forest Rd

Main St

Brook Street

St James Cl

Carey Rd

Narborough Rd

Fitchley

Duncan

School La

The Gn

Ratcliffe Drive

Huncote

Huncote Road

Elms Farm

Finch Cl

Linnett Wy

Oaks Industrial Est

Cutters Close

Burrows Close

Sharpe Wy

McDowell Wy

Chestnut

Croft

Hill Road

Mortimer Road

Oak Rd

G H J K L M

M7
1 Bushey Cl
2 Greenwich Cl
3 Hampstead Cl

M2
1 Feldspar Cl

141

L7
1 Campion Cl
2 Kingsbridge Cl
3 Milford Cl
4 Thistle Cl
5 Whitebeam Cl

L6
1 Kingsley Cl
2 Wordsworth Crs

L5
1 Meadow Edge
2 Thornhills
3 Thornhills Gv

M8
1 Cedar Crs
2 Desford Rd
3 Fletchers Cl
4 Masons Cl
5 Spiers Cl
6 William St

M4
1 Co-operation St
2 The Cross
3 Gumley Sq

L8
1 Badger Cl
2 Elmhurst Cl
3 Lapwing Ct
4 Overfield Cl
5 Wakeley Cl

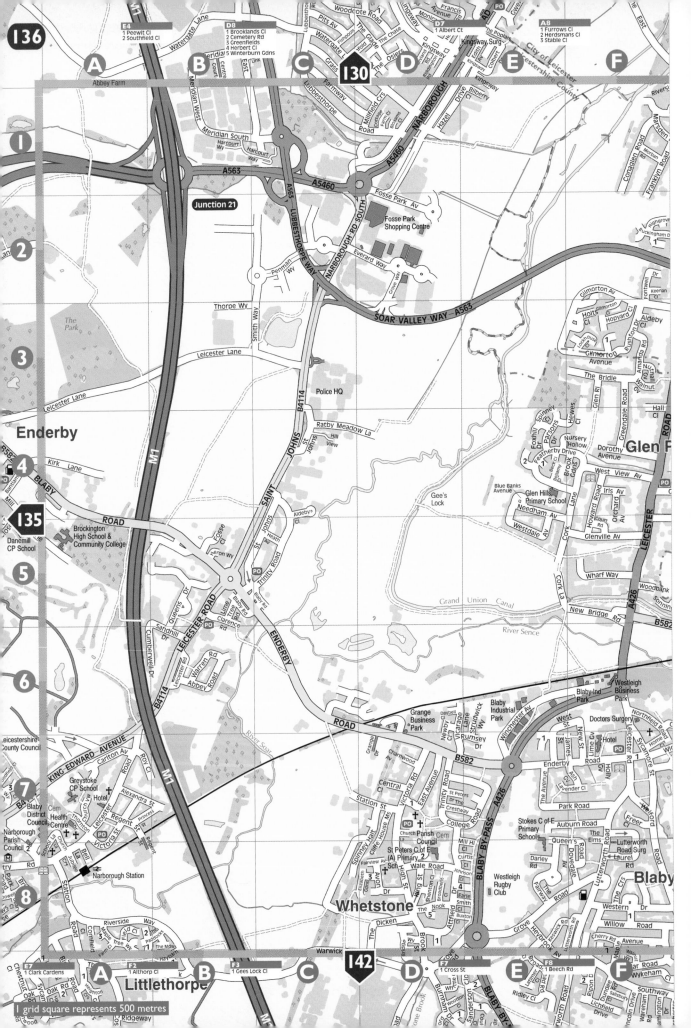

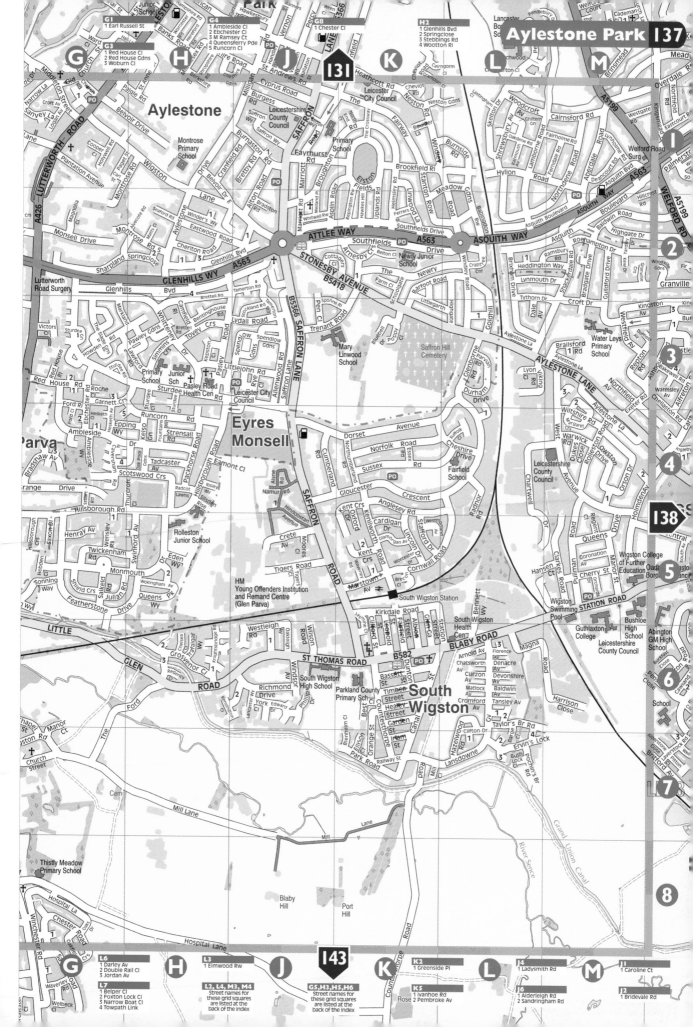

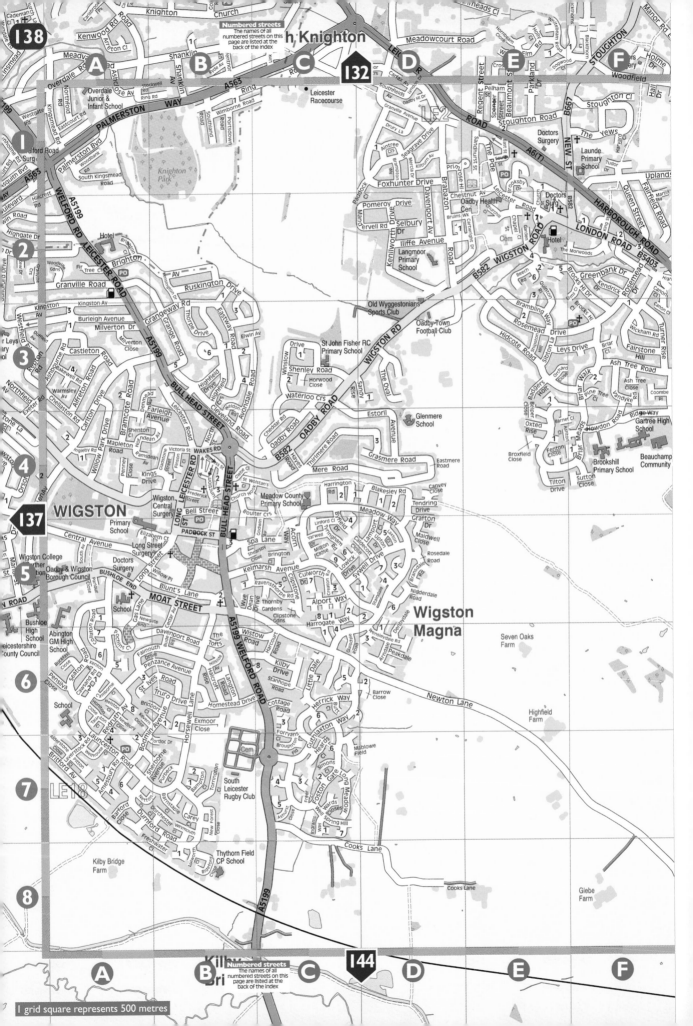

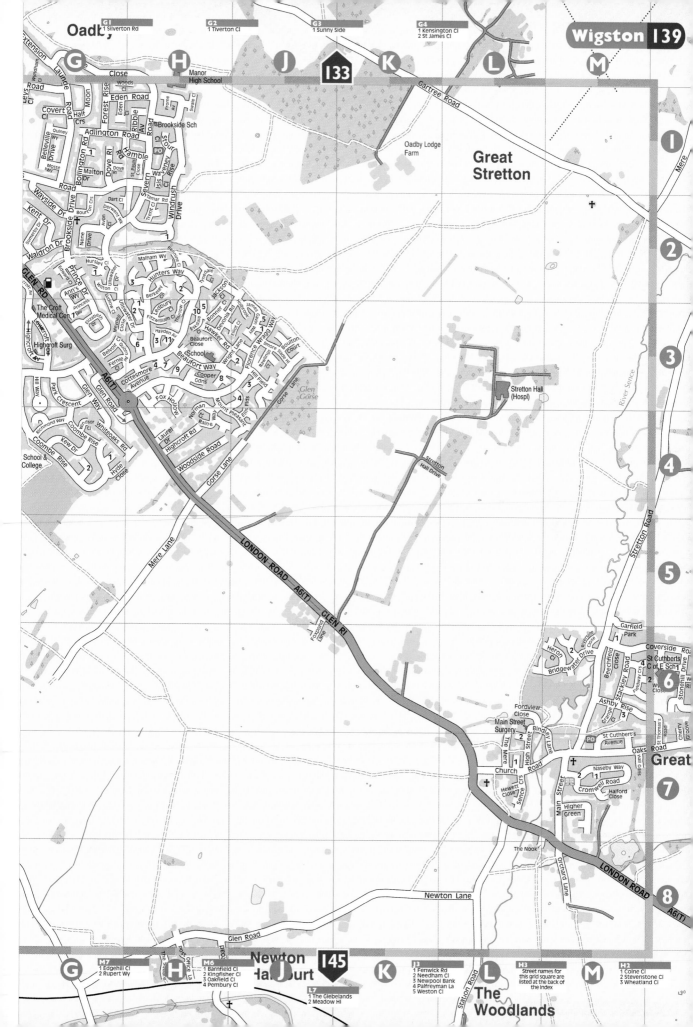

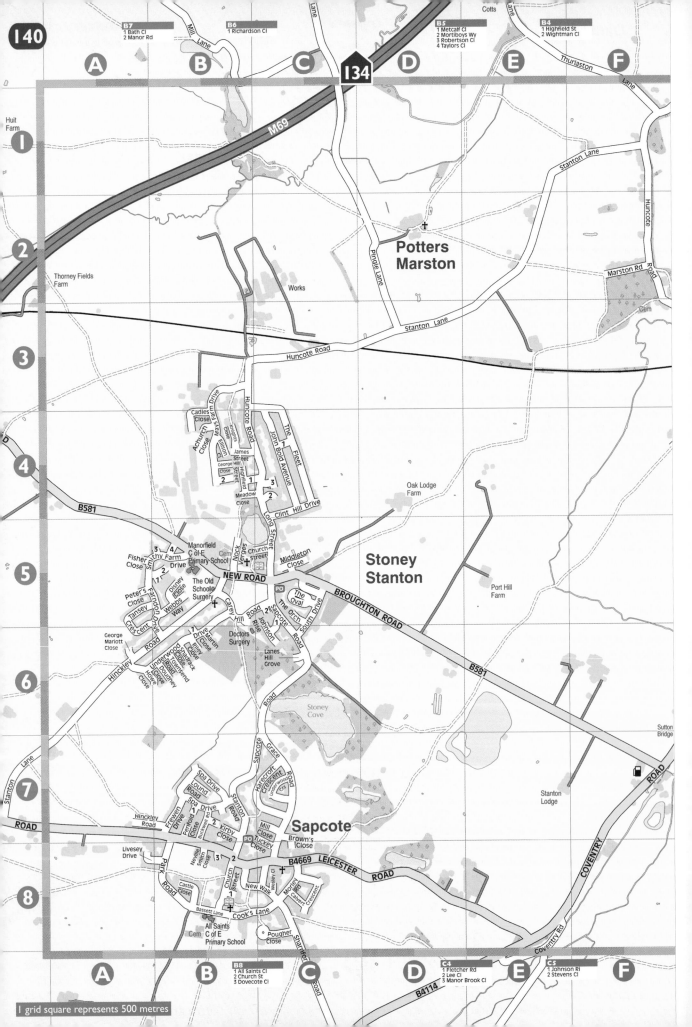

134

B7
1 Bath Cl
2 Manor Rd

B6
1 Richardson Cl

B5
1 Metcalf Cl
2 Mortiboys Wy
3 Robertson Cl
4 Taylors Cl

B4
1 Highfield St
2 Wightman Cl

A   B   C   D   E   F

I

2

3

4

5

6

7

8

Huit Farm

Thorney Fields Farm

M69

M69

Potters Marston

Works

Cotts

Thurlaston Lane

Stanton Lane

Marston Rd

Huncote Road

Stanton Lane

Huncote Road

Cem

Cadles Close
Achurch Close
May's Farm Drive
Knights Close
Elliston Close
James Street
George Hill
Highfield Street
Huncote Road
The Fleet
John Bold Avenue
1
2
1
3
2
Meadow Close
Clint Hill Drive
Long Street

Oak Lodge Farm

Stoney Stanton

Port Hill Farm

B581

Manorfield C of E Primary School
Fisher Close
Smithy Farm
Drive
3   4
2
1
Dicney Close
Peter's Close
Farndon Drive
Tansey Crescent
Webbs Way
The Old School Surgery
Cem
Nock Verges
Church Street
Middleton Close
NEW ROAD
PO
The Oval
The Orch
Carey Hill Road
Sapcote Rise
Johnson
1
Doctors Surgery
South Drive
BROUGHTON ROAD

B581

George Mariott Close
Hinckley Road
Underwood Close
Shadrack Close
Douchey Close
Hovle Close
townsend
Drive
Martin
Riley
Close
1
Lanes Hill Grove

Road

Stoney Cove

Sutton Bridge

Stanton Lane
ROAD

Sapcote
Spa Drive
Lound Road
Frewen Drive
Spa Drive
Penfold Close
Buckwell Rd
Kirby Close
Hinckley Road
Livesey Drive
Newlifel Smith Close
3
2
Park Road
Castle Close
Bassett Lane
Cook's Lane
Church Street
New Walk
1
All Saints C of E Primary School
Cem
Harecroft Crescent
Sapcote Road
Grace Road
Underwood Cfs
Stanton Road
Mill Close
Tuckey Close
PO
Brown's Close
B4669 LEICESTER ROAD
Morley Rd
Calver Crescent
Wason Cl
Pougher Close

Stanton Lodge

Shamford Road
COVENTRY ROAD
Coventry Rd

B4114

A   B   C   D   E   F

B8
1 All Saints Cl
2 Church St
3 Dovecote Cl

C4
1 Fletcher Rd
2 Lee Cl
3 Manor Brook Cl

C5
1 Johnson Rl
2 Stevens Cl

I grid square represents 500 metres

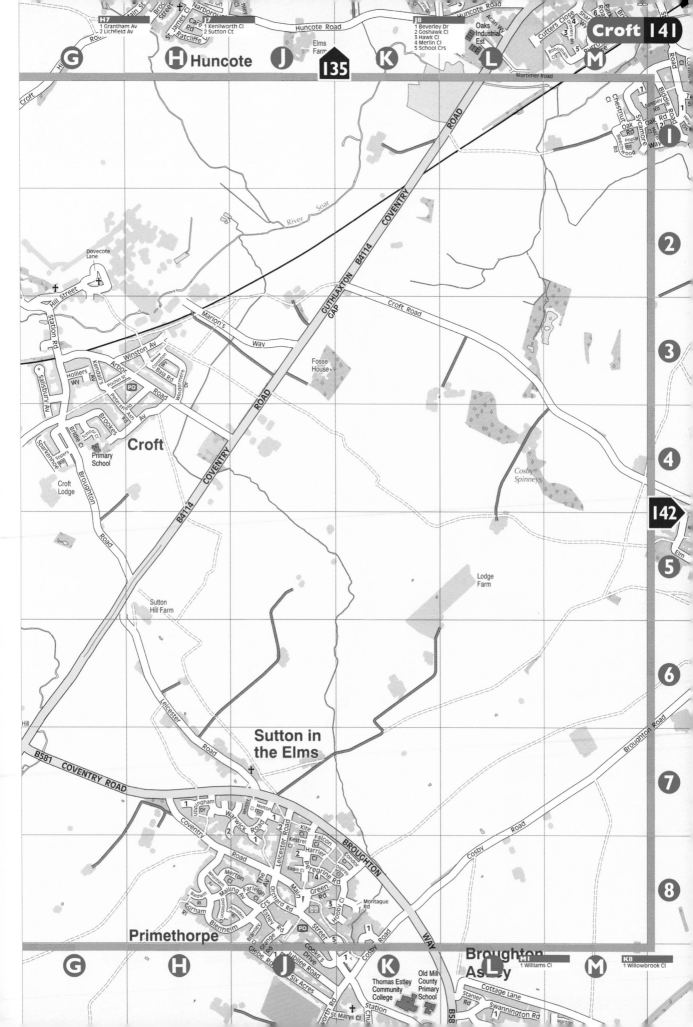

H7
1 Grantham Av
2 Lichfield Av

J7
1 Kenilworth Cl
2 Sutton Ct

J8
1 Beverley Dr
2 Goshawk Cl
3 Hawk Cl
4 Merlin Cl
5 School Crs

G

H Huncote

J

135

K

L

M

Huncote Road

Oaks Industrial Est

Cutters Close

Mortimer Road

I

2

River Soar

COVENTRY

ROAD

3

Dovecote Lane

Hill Street

GUTHLAXTON GAP

B4114

Croft Road

Fosse House

4

Cosby Spinneys

Station Rd

Salisbury Av

Marion's

Way

Winston Av

Arbor

Bala Rd

Windermere Dr

Coventry Rd

Holliers Wy

Kendall's Av

PO

Petersfield

Ash

Brookes

Bridle Cl

Sopers

School

Sparkenhoe

Croft

Primary School

Croft Lodge

Broughton Road

COVENTRY ROAD

B4114

142

5

Elm

Lodge Farm

Sutton Hill Farm

6

Leicester Road

Hill

Broughton Road

B581 COVENTRY ROAD

Sutton in the Elms

7

Cosby Road

Uppingham Dr

Warwick Rd

Melton Cl

Kite Cl

Falcon Cl

Kestrel Cl

Harrier

Condor

Osprey

8

BROUGHTON

Coventry Road

Merton

Malling Av

Farleigh

The Orchard Rd

Peregrine Rd

Eagle Cl

Green Rd

Montague Rd

Whinham

Baldwin Rl

Gorham

Blenheim

Penistone Av

Amsden

Bramley

Grange

Estley Rd

Main Street

Hobby Cl

PO

WAY

Primethorpe

Cooke's Drive

Clebe Road

Jubilee Road

Six Acres

Thomas Estley Community College

St Marys Cl

Old Mill County Primary School

Cosby Road

Station Church

Broughton Astley

K8
1 Williams Cl

1 Willowbrook Cl

Cottage Lane

Stanier Rd

Swannington Rd

B58

G

H

J

K

L

M

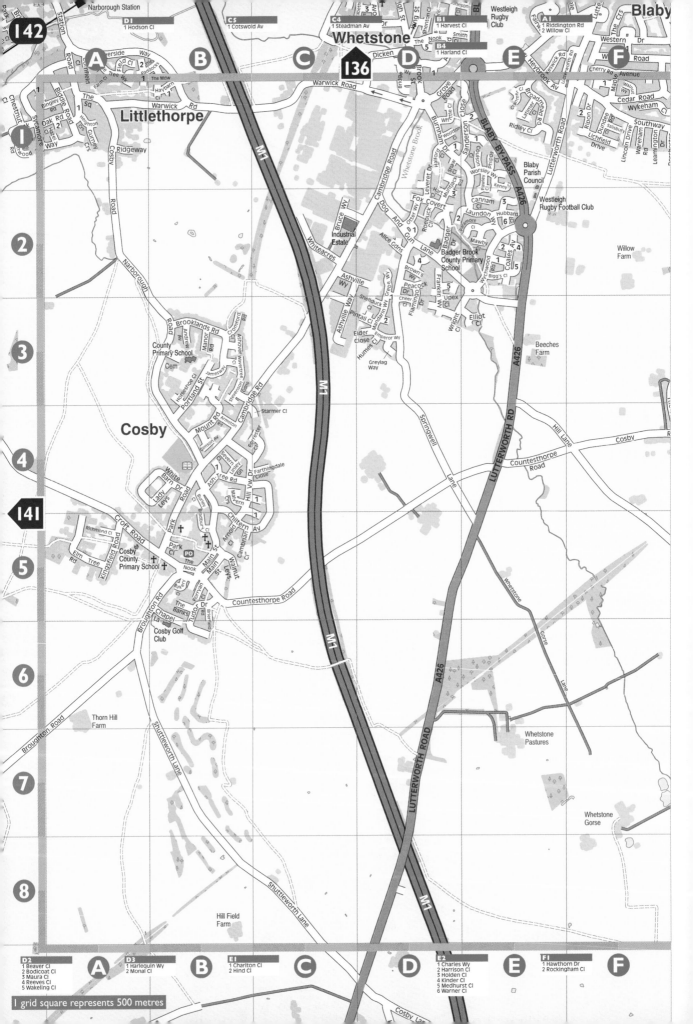

Primary School

137
144

G1
1 Wynton Cl

G3
1 Ludlam Cl
2 Old Field Cl

H3
1 Broomleys
2 Leopold Cl
3 The Woodlands

H4
1 The Vineries

G   H   J   K   L   M

Hospital Lane

Keepers
Farm

Rose Farm

Winchester Rd

Oaks Dr

Oakfield Crs

Saville Road

Waverley Road

Welbeck Cl

Leysland
High
School

Clinic

Borrowcup
Cl

Scalborough Close

Broadfield Wy

Wheatland Dr

Leysland
Av

The Dales

Sunburn Rd

Benson Cl

The Rowans

Linden Farm Drive

Fir Tree Av

Pinewood Dr

Walnut

Almond

Cherrytree Cl

Chestnuts

The Plantation

Laurel

Gwendoline Dr

Spring Well Dr

Barnley

Poplar

Aspen Av

Holyrood Dr

Westfield

Penfold Dr

Linden Avenue

The Elms

Willow Drive

Beechwood Infant School

Junior School

Edgeley Av

Maple Av

Spinney Av

Paddock

Buckingham Rd

Ladbroke Gv

Judith Dr

Foston Lane

Hazelbank Rd

Regent Rd

New St

Roseloand Cl

Rosebank Rd

Cem

Countesthorpe

Foston Lane

Countesthorpe
Community
College

The Drive

Cosby Road

Station

Bassett Av

Maurice Dr

Beechings

Stonecroft

Mennecy Cl

Waterloo Crs

Glebe Dr

Road

Gillam Butts

Tophall Dr

Marston Crs

Hallcroft Av

Health Centre

Green La

Central St

The Sq

Main St

Mull Wy

Arran Wy

Orchard La

Scotland Way

Shetland

Brook

Dale Acre

Skye Wy

Lewis Wy

Fairisle

Orkney Wy

Jona

Church

Willoughby Road

Glebe
Farm

Soars Lodge
Farm

Peatling Road

Hill Lane

Bambury Lane

Red Pool Spinney

Westdale
Farm

Bambury Lane

Folly Br

Barley Lane

Peatling
Lodge Farm

Bambury

Watt St

School La

I
2
3
4
5
6
7
8

K4
1 Bute Wy
2 Stroma Wy

K3
1 Archery Cl
2 Kirkfield Rd

J4
1 Christopher Cl

J3
1 The Hawthorns
2 Larchwood
3 Springwell Cl
4 Stanyon Cl

Willoughby

Peatling

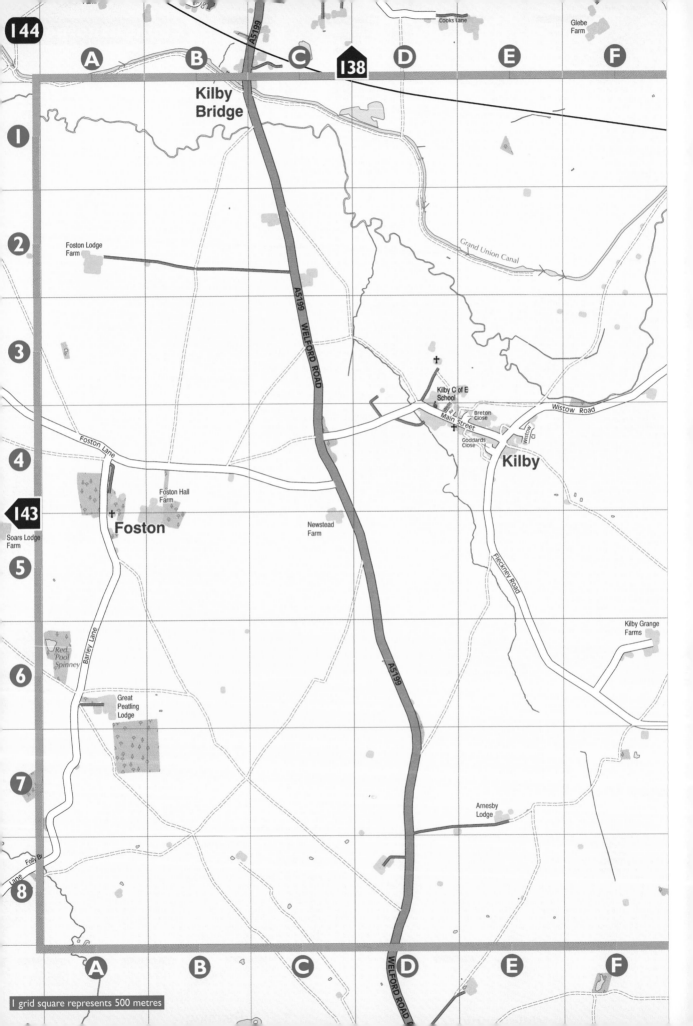

144

A   B   C   138   D   E   F

Kilby
Bridge

Cooks Lane

Glebe
Farm

1

Grand Union Canal

2

Foston Lodge
Farm

A5199

WELFORD ROAD

3

Kilby C of E
School

Kilby

Wistow Road

Breton
Close

Main Street

Goddards
Close

Wistow Cl

Foston Lane

4

143

Foston Hall
Farm

Foston

Newstead
Farm

Fleckney Road

Soars Lodge
Farm

5

Kilby Grange
Farms

Red
Pool
Spinney

Barley Lane

6

Great
Peatling
Lodge

A5199

7

Arnesby
Lodge

Folly Br

Lane

8

A   B   C   D   WELFORD ROAD   E   F

1 grid square represents 500 metres

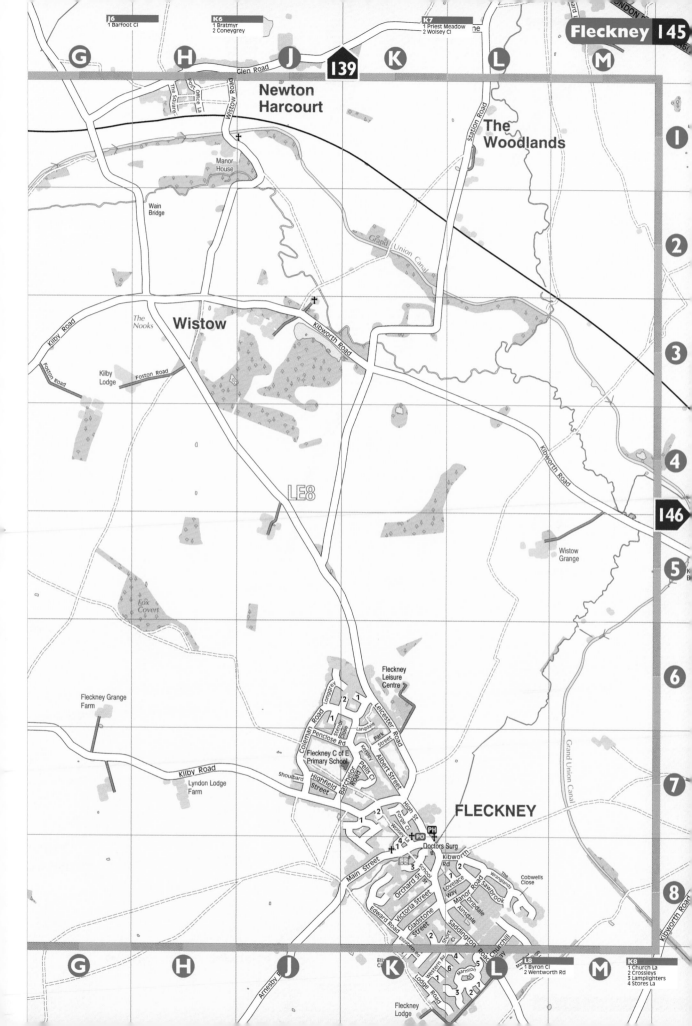

G   H   J   K   L   M

J6
1 Barfoot Cl

K6
1 Bratmyr
2 Coneygrey

K7
1 Priest Meadow
2 Wolsey Cl

Glen Road

139

**Newton
Harcourt**

The Square

Post Office La

Wistow Road

Manor
House

Wain
Bridge

Station Road

**The
Woodlands**

I

1

2

Grand Union Canal

Kilby Road

The
Nooks

Wistow

Kibworth Road

3

Foston Road

Kilby
Lodge

Foston Road

Kibworth Road

4

146

LE8

Wistow
Grange

5

Fox
Covert

6

Fleckney
Leisure
Centre

Fleckney Grange
Farm

Longrav

Exeter Close

Coleman Road

Penclose Rd

2

1

1

Langdale

Leicester Road

Park
Street

Kersey

Albert Street

Grand Union Canal

Kilby Road

Fleckney C of E
Primary School

Shoulbard

Pells Cl

Batchelor Road

Highfield
Street

Lyndon Lodge
Farm

7

2

1

High St

Parade Cl

FLECKNEY

Wolsey

4 1

PH

PO

Doctors Surg

Kibworth
Rd

2

8

Main Street

Orchard St

School St

Lovelace
Way

Manor Road

Oriedale

The
Wranglands

Cobwells
Close

Sawbrook

Ainsdale

Edward Road

Victoria Street

Gladstone
Street

Elizabeth Rd

Saddington Road

Churchill

Kibworth Road

L8
1 Byron Cl
2 Wentworth Rd

K8
1 Church La
2 Crossleys
3 Lamplighters
4 Stores La

Eliz
Cl

Western Av

Marmion

Lodge Road

Fleckney
Lodge

G   H   J   K   L   M

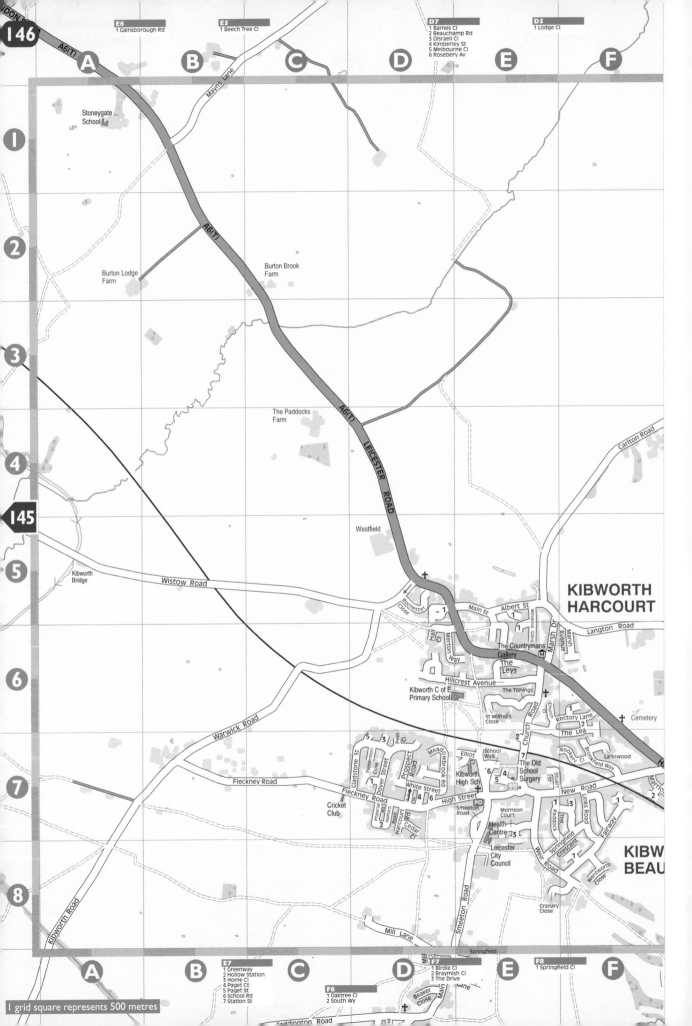

A6(T)

Mavis Lane

Stoneygate School

Burton Lodge Farm

Burton Brook Farm

A6(T)

The Paddocks Farm

LEICESTER ROAD

Carlton Road

Westfield

Kibworth Bridge

Wistow Road

KIBWORTH HARCOURT

Rochester Close

Main St

Albert St

Langton Road

Hall Croft

Merton Way

Windmill Gdns

Marsh Dr

Marsh Avenue

The Countrymans Gallery

The Leys

Hillcrest Avenue

The Tithings

Warwick Road

Kibworth C of E Primary School

St Wilfrid's Close

Church

Church Road

Rectory Lane

The Lea

Cemetery

Fleckney Road

Gladstone St

Palmerston Close

Peel St

Prospect Road

Meadowbrook Rd

White Street

Elliot Cl

Kibworth High Sch

School Walk

The Old School Surgery

Rookery Cl

Brookfield Way

Larkswood

Fleckney Road

Dover Street

Cricket Club

Imperial Close

Halford

Harcourt

Cedar St

High Street

Smeeton Road

PO

Stuart St

New Road

Links Road

The Paddock

KIBW BEAU

Leicester City Council

Morrison Court

Health Centre

Springfield Crescent

Fairway

Weir Road

Wentworth Close

Kibworth Road

Smeeton Road

Granary Close

Mill Lane

Springfield

Beaker Close

Main Lane

Geddington Road

1 grid square represents 500 metres

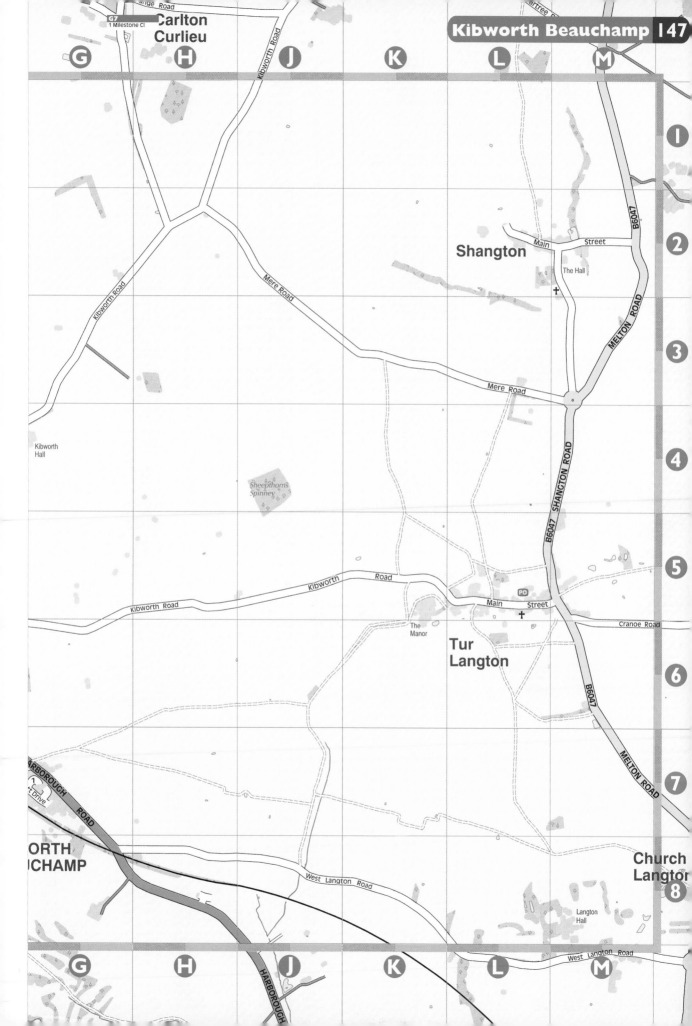

Adbolton 51 M5	Cosby 142 A4	The Holmes 3 H4	New Sawley 75 M2	Smalley Common 31 L5
Agar Nook 108 F6	Cossall 34 A6	Horsley Woodhouse 31 C1	New Stanton 47 J4	Smalley Green 31 K4
Aldercar 20 D3	Cossall Marsh 34 A5	Hoton 97 H5	Newstead 15 J1	Smithy Houses 18 F4
Allenton 72 A3	Cossington 114 A7	Hucknall 15 H7	New Swannington 108 B3	South Knighton 132 B8
Allestree 43 K4	Costock 89 H5	Humberstone 126 D8	Newthorpe 22 A6	South Wigston 137 K6
Alma 13 L2	Cotes 104 D1	Huncote 135 H8	Newthorpe Common 22 A8	Spondon 59 L2
Alvaston 58 F8	Cotgrave 67 M5	Ilkeston 33 H5	Newton Harcourt 145 J1	Spring Hill 29 H2
Ambaston 74 A1	Cotmanhay 33 J3	Ironville 12 C3	Newtown Linford 117 H7	Stanford Hills 96 B3
Anstey 124 C1	Countesthorpe 143 K3	Isley Walton 84 B8	Newtown Unthank 128 B1	Stanford on Soar 96 A6
Arnold 25 L8	Cowers Lane 16 B4	Jacksdale 12 F4	Normanton 57 H8	Stanley 46 A1
Aspley 35 M7	Cowhill 17 L5	Kedleston 28 A8	Normanton on Soar 95 H4	Stanley Common 31 L7
Aston-on-Trent 73 M7	Crewton 58 D7	Kegworth 85 M6	Normanton-on-the-Wolds 80 E1	Stanton-by-Bridge 82 B4
Attenborough 63 J5	Croft 141 H4	Keyworth 80 E4	Normanton Turville 134 B6	Stanton-by-Dale 47 J7
Awsworth 34 A3	Cropston 118 D5	Kibworth Beauchamp 146 F8	North End 113 H3	Stanton Gate 48 A7
Aylestone 137 H1	Cross Hill 20 A1	Kibworth Harcourt 146 F5	North Evington 132 C1	Stanton-on-the-Wolds 81 G5
Aylestone Park 131 J8	Crown Hills 132 E2	Kilburn 18 E7	Nottingham 4 D2	Stapleford 48 C8
Babbington 34 C3	Cumberhills Cottages 28 E6	Kilby 144 E4	Nuthall 35 G2	Stenson 70 E7
Bagthorpe 13 K4	Dalbury 54 F6	Kilby Bridge 144 B1	Oadby 133 G8	Stocking Farm 125 H4
Bargate 18 A6	Dale Abbey 46 D5	Kimberley 34 C1	Oaks in Charnwood 109 K2	Stoke Bardolph 39 J7
Barkby 121 H7	Dale Moor 46 F5	King's Mills 83 M3	The Oaks 29 H1	Stoneyford 12 E8
Barkby Thorpe 120 F8	Darley Abbey 43 L5	King's Newton 83 G6	Oakwood 44 E6	Stoneygate 132 B6
Barrows Green 13 G2	Daybrook 25 H8	Kingston on Soar 86 E3	Ockbrook 60 B2	Stoney Stanton 140 D5
Barrow upon Soar 105 J8	Denby 19 G6	Kirby Fields 129 K2	Old Basford 36 C3	Stoughton 133 H6
Barton in Fabis 77 J1	Denby Bottles 18 E6	Kirby Grange 122 A7	Openwoodgate 18 B4	Street Lane 18 F2
Bassingfield 52 E8	Denby Common 19 L4	Kirby Muxloe 129 H1	Osgathorpe 100 B3	Strelley 35 G2
Beaumont Leys 124 F3	Derby 2 E5	Kirk Hallam 47 G2	Osleston 54 B1	Sunny Hill 71 H2
Beauvale 15 H8	Diseworth 93 H1	Kirk Langley 41 J5	Osmaston 58 B8	Sutton Bonington 95 G1
Beauvale 22 A4	Dishley 102 F1	Knighton 131 M8	Over Burrows 40 E3	Sutton in the Elms 141 J7
Beeston 49 G8	Dorket Head 25 L3	Knighton Fields 131 K6	Park Nook 28 E7	Swanwick 11 J1
Belgrave 125 L5	Dove Green 13 J1	Lambley 27 C8	Pear Tree 57 L7	Swarkestone 82 C1
Belper 17 M2	Draycott 60 D8	Langley 20 F6	Peasehill 11 K7	Swingate 34 E3
Belton 100 E2	Drum Hill 30 D6	Langley Common 41 M7	Pentrich 10 F2	Swithland 112 B8
Bestwood 24 E8	Duffield 29 J4	Langley Green 41 H6	Plain Spot 13 J5	Syston 121 G4
Bestwood Village 24 D2	Duffieldbank 29 L3	Langley Mill 20 F4	Plumtree 80 D1	Thorneywood 37 L7
Bilborough 35 J8	Dunkirk 50 B5	Larklands 33 L8	Plumtree Park 80 C2	Thorpe Acre 103 G2
Birstall 119 L8	East Goscote 115 J7	Lees 40 F8	Porchester 37 M5	Thorpe in the Glebe 90 B6
Blaby 136 F8	East Leake 88 C5	Leicester 6 E5	Potters Marston 140 D2	Thringstone 100 C8
Blackbrook 16 F2	Eastwood 21 J4	Leicester Forest East 129 K5	Prestwold 97 C7	Thrumpton 77 G4
Bogend 22 D5	Eaton Hill 30 A6	Lenton 4 A8	Pride Park 58 C3	Thrussington 115 J3
Bondman Hays 122 B4	Edwalton 65 L4	Lenton Abbey 49 K6	Primethorpe 141 H8	Thulston 73 L3
Boothgate 10 D3	Egginton Common 69 G8	Linby 15 L4	Pye Hill 12 E2	Thurcaston 118 E5
Borrowash 59 M5	Elvaston 73 L2	Litchurch 3 J8	Quarndon 29 G8	Thurlaston 134 F4
Botcheston 128 A1	Enderby 135 M4	Little Chester 43 L8	Quarndon Common 29 H7	Thurmaston 120 E8
Boulton 72 E1	Epperstone 27 L2	Little Eaton 30 A7	Queniborough 121 J2	Thurnby 133 J3
Boulton Moor 72 E4	Etwall 68 F3	Little Hallam 47 J1	Quorndon 104 E8	Thurvaston 40 A7
Bradmore 79 K4	Evington 132 E5	Littleover 56 E7	Radbourne 55 H2	Tollerton 66 B6
Bramcote Hills 49 H5	Eyres Monsell 137 H4	Littlethorpe 142 A1	Radcliffe on Trent 53 J3	Top Valley 24 E7
The Brand 111 M8	Far Laund 18 A1	Lockington 85 K3	Radford 50 B2	Toton 62 E5
Braunstone 130 C6	Farnah Green 17 G4	Long Eaton 62 A8	Ratby 123 G7	Trentlock 76 C4
Breadsall 44 C3	Field Head 116 D7	Longlane 40 C6	Ratcliffe on Soar 86 C1	Trowell 48 A4
Breadsall Hilltop 44 B6	Findern 70 B5	Long Whatton 93 M4	Ratcliffe on the Wreake 115 G6	Trusley 54 D4
Breaston 61 G7	Flaxholme 29 K6	Loscoe 20 B3	Rawson Green 18 D5	Tur Langton 147 L6
Brinsley 13 J8	Fleckney 145 L1	Loughborough 8 F5	Rearsby 115 K5	Underwood 13 K5
Brook Hill 64 E7	The Flourish 46 B5	Lowdham Grange 27 K4	Redhill 25 J6	Upper Hartshay 10 E5
Broomhill 23 M2	Foston 144 A5	Lower Hartshay 10 D4	Red Hill 135 L7	Waingroves 11 L8
Broxtowe 35 K5	Friezeland 13 M5	Lower Kilburn 18 D8	Rempstone 97 H2	Walton on the Wolds 105 M3
Bulcote 39 L1	Gallows Inn 47 M1	Mackworth 42 C8	Riddings 12 B1	Wanlip 120 A5
Bullbridge 10 A2	Gamston 52 B8	Makeney 29 L1	Ringing Hill 101 G6	Watnall 22 E7
Bulwell 23 L8	Gedling 38 D5	Manor Park 64 F8	Ripley 11 K5	West Bridgford 65 G1
Bulwell Forest 24 B7	Giltbrook 22 A7	Mapperley 32 D4	Rise Park 24 C6	Westcotes 130 F3
Bunny 79 J8	Glenfield 124 A7	Mapperley 37 J4	Risley 61 J3	West End 100 A3
Bunny Hill 89 H2	Glen Parva 136 F4	Mapperley Park 37 G6	Rose Hill 3 G9	Western Park 130 D1
Burnaston 69 K2	Golden Valley 12 A4	Marehay 19 H1	Rothley 113 J8	West Hallam 32 D7
Burton Joyce 39 L3	Gotham 77 M6	Markeaton 42 F7	Rothley Plain 112 F7	West Leake 87 K6
Burton on the Wolds 97 J8	Greasley 22 C4	Markfield 116 A6	Ruddington 79 H1	Weston-on-Trent 83 K2
Bushby 133 M2	Great Stretton 139 L1	Marlpool 20 D7	Ruffs 23 J2	Westville 23 J3
Butler's Hill 24 B2	Great Wilne 74 F5	Meadows 51 G5	Rushey Mead 126 C3	Westwood 13 H4
Butterley 11 J4	Greenhill 108 E7	Melbourne 82 D8	Rylands 64 A2	Whetstone 136 C8
Carlton 38 A6	Greenhillocks 11 J7	Mickleover 56 B5	St Ann's 5 K3	White Moor 18 A2
Carrington 36 E6	Greenhill 123 K3	Milford 17 L8	St Luke's 2 B6	Whitemoor 36 B6
Castle Donington 85 G5	Gun Hills 28 B2	Moorgreen 22 B3	Sandiacre 61 L1	Whitwick 108 E2
Cavendish Bridge 75 G7	The Gutter 18 A3	Moravian Settlement 59 M3	Sapcote 140 C7	Widmerpool 90 F2
Chaddesden 44 D7	Hallam Fields 47 L3	Morley 45 G1	Sawley 75 K3	Wigston 138 A4
Chellaston 72 E6	Hammersmith 11 H3	Morleymoor 30 F8	Scotches 17 J1	Wigston Magna 138 D5
Cherrytree Hill 58 E2	Hathern 94 F6	Morley Park 18 E1	Scraptoft 127 J7	Wilford 50 F8
Chilwell 63 H1	Hazelgrove 23 L2	Morley Smithy 31 H7	Seagrave 106 C7	Willoughby-on-the-Wolds 91 G7
Church Langton 147 M8	Hazelwood 16 F6	Mount Pleasant 17 H1	Selston Common 13 L1	Wilsthorpe 61 L7
Church Wilne 74 F3	Heage 10 C6	Mountsorrel 113 G6	Shacklecross 60 B6	Windley 16 B8
Cinderhill 18 B5	Heanor 20 D4	Mowmacre Hill 125 J2	Shangton 147 L2	Wistow 145 H3
Cinderhill 35 L3	Heanor Gate 20 A7	Nanpantan 102 F8	Shardlow 74 C5	Wollaton 49 J3
Clarendon Park 131 L6	Hemington 85 H2	Narborough 135 J7	Shelthorpe 104 A7	Woodborough 27 H3
Clifton 64 D6	Hempshill Vale 35 K2	Nether Burrows 40 F4	Shelton Lock 72 C4	Woodhouse 112 A4
Clipston 67 H6	Highbury Vale 36 A1	Netherfield 38 F8	Shepshed 101 L3	Woodhouse Eaves 111 L5
Coalville 108 B8	Highfields 7 J8	Nether Hall 127 H5	Sherwood 36 F4	The Woodlands 145 L1
Codnor 12 A8	Hillcross 56 F8	Nether Heage 10 B5	Shipley 20 E8	Woodlinkin 20 B1
Codnor Breach 19 L3	Hill Top 21 M5	New Basford 36 D6	Shipley Common 33 H4	Woodside 31 H3
Codnor Gate 11 M6	Hilton 68 B5	New Brinsley 13 J6	Shottlegate 16 E4	Woodthorpe 37 K3
Codnor Park 12 D4	Holbrook 30 B1	New Eastwood 21 K7	Sileby 114 B4	Woodthorpe 104 A8
Colwick 52 D2	Holbrook Moor 17 M8	New Kingston 87 G1	Sinfin 71 J4	Wymeswold 98 B4
Common Side 20 C7	Holme Lane 52 E7	Newlands 20 E6	Six Hills 107 K1	Wysall 90 B4
Copt Oak 116 A1	Holme Pierrepont 52 E4	New Parks 124 D8	Smalley 31 K2	Zouch 94 E4

USING THE STREET INDEX

Street names are listed alphabetically. Each street name is followed by its postal town or area locality, the Postcode District, the page number, and the reference to the square in which the name is found.

Example: **Abbey Dr** *BSTN/STPLFD* NG9 .... **49** K8 🔟

Some entries are followed by a number in a blue box. This number indicates the location of the street within the referenced grid square. The full street name is listed at the side of the map page.

GENERAL ABBREVIATIONS

ACC .... ACCESS	CLFS .... CLIFFS	DR .... DRIVE	GDNS .... GARDENS	INT .... INTERCHANGE
ALY .... ALLEY	CMP .... CAMP	DRO .... DROVE	GLD .... GLADE	IS .... ISLAND
AP .... APPROACH	CNR .... CORNER	DRY .... DRIVEWAY	GLN .... GLEN	JCT .... JUNCTION
AR .... ARCADE	CO .... COUNTY	DWGS .... DWELLINGS	GN .... GREEN	JTY .... JETTY
ASS .... ASSOCIATION	COLL .... COLLEGE	E .... EAST	GND .... GROUND	KG .... KING
AV .... AVENUE	COM .... COMMON	EMB .... EMBANKMENT	GRA .... GRANGE	KNL .... KNOLL
BCH .... BEACH	COMM .... COMMISSION	EMBY .... EMBASSY	GRG .... GARAGE	L .... LAKE
BLDS .... BUILDINGS	CON .... CONVENT	ESP .... ESPLANADE	GT .... GREAT	LA .... LANE
BND .... BEND	COT .... COTTAGE	EST .... ESTATE	GTWY .... GATEWAY	LDG .... LODGE
BNK .... BANK	COTS .... COTTAGES	EX .... EXCHANGE	GV .... GROVE	LGT .... LIGHT
BR .... BRIDGE	CP .... CAPE	EXPY .... EXPRESSWAY	HGR .... HIGHER	LK .... LOCK
BRK .... BROOK	CPS .... COPSE	EXT .... EXTENSION	HL .... HILL	LKS .... LAKES
BTM .... BOTTOM	CR .... CREEK	F/O .... FLYOVER	HLS .... HILLS	LNDG .... LANDING
BUS .... BUSINESS	CREM .... CREMATORIUM	FC .... FOOTBALL CLUB	HO .... HOUSE	LTL .... LITTLE
BVD .... BOULEVARD	CRS .... CRESCENT	FK .... FORK	HOL .... HOLLOW	LWR .... LOWER
BY .... BYPASS	CSWY .... CAUSEWAY	FLD .... FIELD	HOSP .... HOSPITAL	MAG .... MAGISTRATE
CATH .... CATHEDRAL	CT .... COURT	FLDS .... FIELDS	HRB .... HARBOUR	MAN .... MANSIONS
CEM .... CEMETERY	CTRL .... CENTRAL	FLS .... FALLS	HTH .... HEATH	MD .... MEAD
CEN .... CENTRE	CTS .... COURTS	FLS .... FLATS	HTS .... HEIGHTS	MDW .... MEADOWS
CFT .... CROFT	CTYD .... COURTYARD	FM .... FARM	HVN .... HAVEN	MEM .... MEMORIAL
CH .... CHURCH	CUTT .... CUTTINGS	FT .... FORT	HWY .... HIGHWAY	MKT .... MARKET
CHA .... CHASE	CV .... COVE	FWY .... FREEWAY	IMP .... IMPERIAL	MKTS .... MARKETS
CHYD .... CHURCHYARD	CYN .... CANYON	FY .... FERRY	IN .... INLET	ML .... MALL
CIR .... CIRCLE	DEPT .... DEPARTMENT	GA .... GATE	IND EST .... INDUSTRIAL ESTATE	ML .... MILL
CIRC .... CIRCUS	DL .... DALE	GAL .... GALLERY	INF .... INFIRMARY	MNR .... MANOR
CL .... CLOSE	DM .... DAM	GDN .... GARDEN	INFO .... INFORMATION	MS .... MEWS

MSN	MISSION
MT	MOUNT
MTN	MOUNTAIN
MTS	MOUNTAINS
MUS	MUSEUM
MWY	MOTORWAY
N	NORTH
NE	NORTH EAST
NW	NORTH WEST
O/P	OVERPASS
OFF	OFFICE
ORCH	ORCHARD
OV	OVAL
PAL	PALACE
PAS	PASSAGE
PAV	PAVILION
PDE	PARADE
PH	PUBLIC HOUSE
PK	PARK
PKWY	PARKWAY
PL	PLACE
PLN	PLAIN
PLNS	PLAINS
PLZ	PLAZA
POL	POLICE STATION
PR	PRINCE
PREC	PRECINCT
PREP	PREPARATORY
PRIM	PRIMARY
PROM	PROMENADE
PRS	PRINCESS
PRT	PORT
PT	POINT
PTH	PATH
PZ	PIAZZA
QD	QUADRANT
QU	QUEEN
QY	QUAY
R	RIVER
RBT	ROUNDABOUT
RD	ROAD
RDG	RIDGE
REP	REPUBLIC
RES	RESERVOIR
RFC	RUGBY FOOTBALL CLUB
RI	RISE
RP	RAMP
RW	ROW
S	SOUTH
SCH	SCHOOL
SE	SOUTH EAST
SER	SERVICE AREA
SH	SHORE
SHOP	SHOPPING
SKWY	SKYWAY
SMT	SUMMIT
SOC	SOCIETY
SP	SPUR
SPR	SPRING
SQ	SQUARE
ST	STREET
STN	STATION
STR	STREAM
STRD	STRAND
SW	SOUTH WEST
TDG	TRADING
TER	TERRACE
THWY	THROUGHWAY
TNL	TUNNEL
TOLL	TOLLWAY
TPK	TURNPIKE
TR	TRACK
TRL	TRAIL
TWR	TOWER
U/P	UNDERPASS
UNI	UNIVERSITY
UPR	UPPER
V	VALE
VA	VALLEY
VIAD	VIADUCT
VIL	VILLA
VIS	VISTA
VLG	VILLAGE
VLS	VILLAS
VW	VIEW
W	WEST
WD	WOOD
WHF	WHARF
WK	WALK
WKS	WALKS
WLS	WELLS
WY	WAY
YD	YARD
YHA	YOUTH HOSTEL

POSTCODE TOWNS AND AREA ABBREVIATIONS

ALFN	Alfreton
ARN	Arnold
ASH	Sutton in Ashfield/Kirkby in Ashfield
ASHB	Ashbourne
BLWL	Bulwell
BPR/DUF	Belper/Duffield
BSTN/STPLFD	Beeston/Stapleford
BWSH/BRSTN	Borrowash/Breaston
CALV/BJ	Calverton/Burton Joyce
CARL	Carlton
CDON/KEG	Castle Donington/Kegworth
CFTN/RUD	Clifton/Ruddington
COAL	Coalville
COT/KEY/RAD	Cotgrave/Keyworth/Radcliffe on Trent
DERBY	Derby
DERBYSE	Derby southeast
DERBYW	Derby west
EWD/SEL/PNX	Eastwood/Selston/Pinxton
GBY/RBY	Groby/Ratby
HEANOR	Heanor
HUCK/RAV	Hucknall/Ravenshead
ILK	Ilkeston
LBORO	Loughborough
LEI	Leicester
LEIE	Leicester east
LEIN	Leicester north
LEIS	Leicester south
LEIW	Leicester west
LGEAT	Long Eaton
MAPPK/POR/STA	Mapperley Park/Porchester/St Ann's
MCKLVR	Mickleover
MELB/CHEL	Melbourne/Chellaston
MKTHBORO	Market Harborough
NORM/LIT	Normanton/Littleover
NOTT	Nottingham
NOTTE	Nottingham east
RDERBYSW	Rural Derby southwest
RIPLEY	Ripley
RLBORO	Rural Loughborough
RLEINE/SYS	Rural Leicester north & east/Syston
RLEIW/BAR	Rural Leicester south/Barwell
RLEIW/BBY	Rural Leicester south/Blaby
RMMWB	Rural Melton Mowbray
WBRGFD	West Bridgford
WGSTN	Wigston
WOL/BIL/BRX	Wollaton/Bilborough/Broxtowe

Index - streets

1st - Ame

1st Av NOTTE NG7 ....36 F7
2nd Av NOTTE NG7 ....36 F7
3rd Av NOTTE NG7 ....36 F7

A

Aaron Cl CFTN/RUD NG11 ....50 F8
Abba Cl EWD/SEL/PNX NG16 ....22 D8
Abberton Wy LBORO LE11 ....102 E5
Abbey Br NOTTE NG7 ....50 C5
Abbey Circ WBRGFD NG2 ....51 L8
Abbey Cl HUCK/RAV NG15 ....15 J8
Abbey Cl LEIN LE4 ....125 K5
Abbey Court Rd LEIN LE4 ....125 K4
  LEIN LE4 ....125 K4
Abbey Dr BSTN/STPLFD NG9 ....49 K8
  LEIN LE4 ....125 K4
Abbeyfield Rd NOTTE NG7 ....50 D7
Abbeyfields Cl DERBYSE DE22 ....43 L5
Abbey Ga LEIW LE3 ....6 C2
Abbey Gv MAPPK/POR/STA NG3 ....37 K8
Abbey HI DERBYW DE22 ....43 M3
Abbey Hill Rd DERBYW DE22 ....43 H5
Abbey La DERBYW DE22 ....43 L6
  LEIN LE4 ....125 J3
Abbey Mdw LEIN LE4 ....125 K4
Abbeymead Rd LEIN LE4 ....125 K4
Abbey Park Rd LEI LE1 ....125 K6
Abbey Park St LEIN LE4 ....7 G1
Abbey Ri LEIN LE4 ....125 K4
Abbey Rd BSTN/STPLFD NG9 ....49 K8
  COAL LE67 ....109 H4
  EWD/SEL/PNX NG16 ....21 M5
  HUCK/RAV NG15 ....15 J1
  RLEIW/BAR LE9 ....136 B6
  WBRGFD NG2 ....51 L8
Abbey St DERBYW DE22 ....2 D6
  ILK DE7 ....33 K5
  LEI LE1 ....6 F3
  NOTTE NG7 ....50 C5
Abbey Yd DERBYW DE22 ....43 L6
Abbot Cl COT/KEY/RAD NG12 ....80 C3
  DERBYE DE21 ....44 C5
Abbot Rd ILK DE7 ....47 G1
Abbotsbury Cl ARN NG5 ....24 B6
Abbots Cl ARN NG5 ....37 H1
  LEIE LE5 ....126 F7
Abbots Dr HUCK/RAV NG15 ....23 J1
Abbotsford Dr
  MAPPK/POR/STA NG3 ....5 K3
Abbotsford Ms ILK DE7 ....33 H4
Abbotsford Rd LEIE LE5 ....126 D8
Abbots Rd HUCK/RAV NG15 ....23 J1
Abbot's Rd North LEIE LE5 ....126 F7
Abbots Rd South LEIE LE5 ....126 F7
Abbot St EWD/SEL/PNX NG16 ....34 A3
Abbots Wy WOL/BIL/BRX NG8 ....50 A5
Abbotts Cl RLEINE/SYS LE7 ....120 D4
Abbotts Barn Cl DERBYW DE22 ....2 D5
Abbott's Oak Dr COAL LE67 ....108 F5
Abbott St HEANOR DE75 ....20 C6
  LGEAT NG10 ....76 B1
Abells RIPLEY DE5 ....19 G6
Abercarn Cl BLWL NG6 ....23 M8
Aberdale Rd LEIS LE2 ....137 M1
Aberdare Cl DERBYE DE21 ....45 G5
Aberdeen St
  MAPPK/POR/STA NG3 ....5 L6
Aberford Av WOL/BIL/BRX NG8 ....36 B7
Aber Rd LEIS LE2 ....132 B6
Abingdon Dr CFTN/RUD NG11 ....65 H7
Abingdon Gdns ARN NG5 ....37 L2
  BSTN/STPLFD NG9 ....63 H3
Abingdon Rd LEIS LE2 ....7 K9
  WBRGFD NG2 ....51 L8
Abingdon Sq
  WOL/BIL/BRX NG8 ....36 A6
Abingdon St DERBYSE DE24 ....58 A7
Ablard Gdns BSTN/STPLFD NG9 ....63 G5
Abney Cl MCKLVR DE3 ....56 D5
Abney St LEIE LE5 ....7 M8
Acacia Av LEIN LE4 ....119 M7
  MCKLVR DE3 ....56 C6
Acacia Cl HUCK/RAV NG15 ....23 M2
  LEIW LE3 ....129 K5
Acacia Crs CARL NG4 ....38 D7
Acacia Dr MELB/CHEL DE73 ....82 E7

Acacia Gdns
  EWD/SEL/PNX NG16 ....22 D7
Acacia Wk BSTN/STPLFD NG9 ....63 K1
Acan Wy RLEIW/BAR LE9 ....135 L8
Acaster Cl BSTN/STPLFD NG9 ....63 M3
Acer Cl LBORO LE11 ....103 L8
  LEIN LE4 ....125 C3
  RLEIW/BAR LE9 ....135 L7
Acer Cft DERBYE DE21 ....44 C4
Achurch Cl RLEIW/BAR LE9 ....140 B4
Acle Gdns BLWL NG6 ....23 M6
Acorn Av EWD/SEL/PNX NG16 ....21 M7
Acorn Bank CFTN/RUD NG11 ....64 F3
Acorn Cl DERBYSE DE24 ....72 C4
Acorn Dr BPR/DUF DE56 ....17 L2
  CARL NG4 ....38 E5
Acorn Pk NOTTE NG7 ....50 C7
Acorn St LEIN LE4 ....125 M5
Acorn Wy BPR/DUF DE56 ....17 L2
  DERBYE DE21 ....45 G6
  DERBYE DE21 ....59 G2
  WGSTN LE18 ....138 C5
A'court St NOTTE NG7 ....4 B3
Acrefield Wy MELB/CHEL DE73 ....72 F5
Acre La BWSH/BRSTN DE72 ....74 B8
Acres Rd LEIW LE3 ....124 E6
Acton Av BLWL NG6 ....36 B3
Acton Gv LGEAT NG10 ....76 C1
Acton Rd ARN NG5 ....25 H7
  DERBYW DE22 ....56 B1
  LGEAT NG10 ....62 C8
Adale Rd HEANOR DE75 ....19 M7
Adams Cl HEANOR DE75 ....20 B8
Adams Ct ILK DE7 ....33 J4
Adams HI COT/KEY/RAD NG12 ....80 D4
  NOTTE NG7 ....50 A5
Adam's Rd ASHB DE6 ....41 L7
Adam St ILK DE7 ....47 L1
Adbolton Av CARL NG4 ....38 C6
Adbolton Gv WBRGFD NG2 ....51 M5
Adbolton La COT/KEY/RAD NG12 ....52 D5
  WBRGFD NG2 ....51 M6
Adcock Rd LEIE LE3 ....124 F8
Adderley Rd LEIS LE2 ....131 M6
Addington Rd NOTTE NG7 ....4 A3
Addison Dr HUCK/RAV NG15 ....15 J7
Addison Rd CARL NG4 ....37 M7
  DERBYSE DE24 ....57 M7
Addison St NOTT NG1 ....4 F5
Adelaide Cl BSTN/STPLFD NG9 ....48 D6
  LEIN LE4 ....119 C8
  MCKLVR DE3 ....56 C3
Adelaide Gv ARN NG5 ....24 C7
Adelaide Wk
  EWD/SEL/PNX NG16 ....12 D3
Adel Dr CARL NG4 ....38 C6
Adelphi Cl NORM/LIT DE23 ....70 E1
Adenburgh Dr
  BSTN/STPLFD NG9 ....63 H6
Adler Ct DERBY DE1 ....43 M8
Adlington Rd LEIS LE2 ....139 C1
Admiral Cl HEANOR DE75 ....20 C5
Adrian Cl BSTN/STPLFD NG9 ....62 D6
Adrian St DERBYSE DE24 ....72 B1
Adwick Cl MCKLVR DE3 ....56 A5
Afton Cl LBORO LE11 ....102 F4
Agar Ct DERBY DE1 ....2 C2
Agar Nook La COAL LE67 ....109 H6
Agar St LEIN LE4 ....125 M6
Agnes Vls
  MAPPK/POR/STA NG3 ....37 J5
Aikman Av LEIW LE3 ....124 E3
Aikman Cl LEIW LE3 ....124 D5
Aimploy Ct NORM/LIT DE23 ....57 L6
Ainley Cl DERBYSE DE24 ....58 D8
Ainsdale RLEIW/BBY LE8 ....145 L8
Ainsdale Crs WOL/BIL/BRX NG8 ....35 L4
Ainsdale Rd LEIW LE3 ....130 C2
Ainsley Rd WOL/BIL/BRX NG8 ....50 B1
Ainsworth Dr NORM/LIT DE23 ....57 M8
  RLBORO LE12 ....114 C4
Aintree Cl LEIW LE3 ....133 H5
Aintree Crs LEIS LE2 ....138 D1
Aira Cl WBRGFD NG2 ....66 B1
Airedale Cl LGEAT NG10 ....75 L1
  RDERBYSW DE65 ....62 E3
Aisne Rd WGSTN LE18 ....137 L4
Alan Cl LEIN LE4 ....125 M3

Alandene Av
  EWD/SEL/PNX NG16 ....22 E8
Alan Moss Rd LBORO LE11 ....8 B3
Albany Cl ARN NG5 ....25 J8
  HUCK/RAV NG15 ....23 G2
Albany Ct BSTN/STPLFD NG9 ....48 C6
Albany Rd DERBYW DE22 ....57 G3
  NOTTE NG7 ....36 E7
Albany St ILK DE7 ....47 L1
  LBORO LE11 ....103 J2
Albemarle Rd ARN NG5 ....37 H3
  DERBYE DE21 ....58 F1
Alberta St LEIE LE5 ....7 J4
Alberta Ter NOTTE NG7 ....36 E7
Albert Av BSTN/STPLFD NG9 ....48 B8
  CARL NG4 ....37 M8
  EWD/SEL/PNX NG16 ....12 F3
  EWD/SEL/PNX NG16 ....35 G1
  RLBORO LE12 ....114 B3
  WOL/BIL/BRX NG8 ....36 B7
Albert Ball Cl ARN NG5 ....24 D7
Albert Ct RLEIW/BBY LE8 ....136 D7
Albert Crs DERBYE DE21 ....58 F3
Albert Gv NOTTE NG7 ....4 B6
Albert Pl LBORO LE11 ....9 J5
Albert Prom LBORO LE11 ....9 L5
Albert Rd BSTN/STPLFD NG9 ....49 L7
  BWSH/BRSTN DE72 ....60 F8
  CFTN/RUD NG11 ....79 J6
  COAL LE67 ....108 B6
  DERBYE DE21 ....58 E2
  LEIS LE2 ....132 A5
  LGEAT NG10 ....61 M1
  LGEAT NG10 ....62 B8
  MAPPK/POR/STA NG3 ....37 H6
  NOTTE NG7 ....50 C4
  RIPLEY DE5 ....11 G5
  WBRGFD NG2 ....51 K7
Albert Street Central
  MAPPK/POR/STA NG3 ....5 H3
Albert St North
  MAPPK/POR/STA NG3 ....5 G3
Albert St South
  MAPPK/POR/STA NG3 ....5 L5
Albion Ri ARN NG5 ....25 K6
Albion Rd LGEAT NG10 ....62 C7
  RLBORO LE12 ....114 A4
Albion St BSTN/STPLFD NG9 ....49 K8
  DERBY DE1 ....2 F4
  ILK DE7 ....33 K6
  LEI LE1 ....6 F7
  LEIS LE2 ....138 E2
  NOTT NG1 ....5 G9
  RIPLEY DE5 ....11 J6
  RLEINE/SYS LE7 ....120 F4
  RLEIW/BBY LE8 ....145 K7
  RLEIW/BBY LE8 ....146 E5
  WGSTN LE18 ....138 A3
Albury Dr WOL/BIL/BRX NG8 ....35 M6
Albury Sq NOTTE NG7 ....4 C7
Alcester Dr LEIE LE5 ....133 H5
Alcester St NOTTE NG7 ....50 C7
Aldeby Cl LEIE LE3 ....136 F5
  RLEIW/BAR LE9 ....136 C4
Aldene Ct BSTN/STPLFD NG9 ....63 H2
Aldene Wy CALV/BJ NG14 ....27 G3
Aldercar La EWD/SEL/PNX NG16 ....12 E8
  EWD/SEL/PNX NG16 ....20 F3
Alder Cl DERBYE DE21 ....44 C5
  LEIW LE3 ....129 K5
Alderfen Cl DERBYSE DE24 ....72 B4
Alder Gdns BLWL NG6 ....23 L8
Alderleigh Rd WGSTN LE18 ....137 J6
Alderley Ct DERBYSE DE24 ....58 C7
Aldermens Cl WBRGFD NG2 ....51 G5
Alderney St NOTTE NG7 ....50 D4
Alder Rd BPR/DUF DE56 ....17 L4
Alders Brook RDERBYSW DE65 ....68 B6
Aldersgate DERBYW DE22 ....42 D8
Alderslade
  BWSH/BRSTN DE72 ....73 M6
Aldersley Rd RDERBYSW DE65 ....70 A6
Alderstone Cl WGSTN LE18 ....138 A7

Alderton Cl LEIN LE4 ....126 A2
Alderton Rd ARN NG5 ....37 G2
Alder Wy COT/KEY/RAD NG12 ....80 E5
Aldgate Av LEIE LE5 ....132 F4
Aldgate Cl BLWL NG6 ....23 L8
Aldred's La HEANOR DE75 ....20 E6
Aldridge Cl BSTN/STPLFD NG9 ....62 C5
Aldrin Cl BLWL NG6 ....35 K2
Aldworth Cl ARN NG5 ....37 G1
Aldwych Cl ARN NG5 ....24 E5
Aldwych Cl ARN NG5 ....35 H5
  WOL/BIL/BRX NG8 ....35 H5
Alexander Cl BSTN/STPLFD NG9 ....63 L2
Alexander Rd NOTTE NG7 ....4 C8
  RLBORO LE12 ....104 D8
Alexander St LEIW LE3 ....6 C5
Alexandra Crs
  BSTN/STPLFD NG9 ....63 L1
Alexandra Gdns
  NORM/LIT DE23 ....57 M5
Alexandra Rd LEIS LE2 ....132 B6
  LGEAT NG10 ....62 B7
Alexandra St ARN NG5 ....37 F7
  BSTN/STPLFD NG9 ....62 B1
  EWD/SEL/PNX NG16 ....21 K5
  LEIN LE4 ....120 C7
Alexandre Cl NORM/LIT DE23 ....71 H1
Alford Cl BSTN/STPLFD NG9 ....63 L2
Alford Rd COT/KEY/RAD NG12 ....65 M3
  WBRGFD NG2 ....65 M1
Alfred Av MAPPK/POR/STA NG3 ....37 L5
Alfred Cl MAPPK/POR/STA NG3 ....5 H3
Alfred Dr BPR/DUF DE56 ....18 E7
Alfred St ALFN DE55 ....12 B1
  LBORO LE11 ....103 M2
  LBORO LE11 ....9 J5
  RIPLEY DE5 ....11 J5
Alfred Street Central
  MAPPK/POR/STA NG3 ....5 H3
Alfred St North
  MAPPK/POR/STA NG3 ....5 G3
Alfred St South
  MAPPK/POR/STA NG3 ....5 L5
Alfreton Rd ALFN DE55 ....12 F1
  DERBYE DE21 ....30 B5
  DERBYE DE21 ....43 M7
  DERBYE DE21 ....44 A1
  EWD/SEL/PNX NG16 ....13 M5
  NOTTE NG7 ....4 B3
  RIPLEY DE5 ....12 A6
  WGSTN LE18 ....138 A3
Alice Gdns RLEIW/BBY LE8 ....142 D2
Alice St DERBY DE1 ....3 G2
Alison Cl DERBYE DE21 ....44 D8
Allan Av NORM/LIT DE23 ....56 C7
Allandale Rd HEANOR DE75 ....20 B5
  LEIS LE2 ....132 C5
Allen Av RLBORO LE12 ....104 D8
Allendale ILK DE7 ....33 J8
Allendale Av BSTN/STPLFD NG9 ....63 H3
  WOL/BIL/BRX NG8 ....35 L6
Allen's Green Av
  EWD/SEL/PNX NG16 ....13 K1
Allen St DERBYSE DE24 ....72 C2
  HUCK/RAV NG15 ....15 J7
Allen's Wk ARN NG5 ....25 K6
Allenwood Rd WGSTN LE18 ....137 J3
Allestree Cl DERBYSE DE24 ....58 C7
Allestree La DERBYW DE22 ....43 H5
Allestree St DERBYSE DE24 ....58 C7
Allexton Gdns LEIW LE3 ....130 B1
All Hallows Dr CARL NG4 ....38 D5
Alliance Rd LEIW LE3 ....124 A8
Allington Av NOTTE NG7 ....4 B9
Allington Dr RLEINE/SYS LE7 ....119 M7
Allington St LEIN LE4 ....125 M7
Allinson Cl LEIS LE2 ....132 E1
Allison Gdns BSTN/STPLFD NG9 ....63 H3
Allissa Av RIPLEY DE5 ....11 J8
Alloway Cl LEIN LE4 ....126 B3
All Saints Cl RLEIW/BAR LE9 ....140 B8
All Saints Ct MCKLVR DE3 ....56 B6
  RLEINE/SYS LE7 ....118 F5
All Saints' St NOTTE NG7 ....4 D4
Allwood Dr CARL NG4 ....38 C7
Allwood Gdns
  HUCK/RAV NG15 ....23 M1

Alma Cl CARL NG4 ....38 E5
  NOTT NG1 ....5 G4
Alma Hts MCKLVR DE3 ....56 C6
Alma HI EWD/SEL/PNX NG16 ....22 C7
Alma Rd EWD/SEL/PNX NG16 ....13 L2
  MAPPK/POR/STA NG3 ....51 K1
Alma St DERBYW DE22 ....131 G1
  LEIW LE3 ....131 G1
  MELB/CHEL DE73 ....82 E8
  NOTTE NG7 ....36 E6
  RIPLEY DE5 ....11 H7
Almond Av RIPLEY DE5 ....11 H7
Almond Cl EWD/SEL/PNX NG16 ....22 C8
  HUCK/RAV NG15 ....23 M2
  RLBORO LE12 ....111 K1
  RLEIW/BBY LE8 ....143 J3
Almond Rd LEIS LE2 ....131 K4
Almond St NORM/LIT DE23 ....57 K5
Almond Wk CARL NG4 ....38 E5
Alnwick Cl BLWL NG6 ....36 B1
Alpha Ter NOTT NG1 ....4 F3
Alpine St BLWL NG6 ....36 B3
Alport Cl BPR/DUF DE56 ....17 M2
Alport Wy WGSTN LE18 ....138 C5
Alsager Cl DERBYE DE21 ....44 E6
Alston Dr LBORO LE11 ....103 H1
Alstonfield Dr DERBYW DE22 ....43 H3
Altar Stones La COAL LE67 ....116 A3
Althorp Cl LEIS LE2 ....136 F2
Althorpe Dr LBORO LE11 ....103 G3
Althorpe St NOTTE NG7 ....4 C6
Alton Av CFTN/RUD NG11 ....64 F3
Alton Cl CFTN/RUD NG11 ....65 G4
  DERBYW DE22 ....43 H4
Alton Rd BPR/DUF DE56 ....18 A3
  LEIS LE2 ....137 J2
Alts Nook Wy
  BWSH/BRSTN DE72 ....74 C6
Alum Cl DERBYSE DE24 ....59 G8
Alvaston Rd LEIW LE3 ....130 F6
Alvaston St DERBYSE DE24 ....58 F7
Alvecote Rd LEIS LE2 ....137 H2
Alvenor St ILK DE7 ....33 K6
Alverstone Rd
  MAPPK/POR/STA NG3 ....37 G6
Alverton Cl MCKLVR DE3 ....56 A6
Alward's Cl DERBYSE DE24 ....72 E1
Alwood Gv CFTN/RUD NG11 ....64 B4
Alwyn Rd WOL/BIL/BRX NG8 ....35 K5
Alyssum Wy RLEIW/BAR LE9 ....135 K6
Amadis Rd LEIN LE4 ....124 C5
Amanda Rd LEIS LE2 ....136 F3
Ambassador Rd
  CDON/KEG DE74 ....84 F8
  LEIE LE5 ....132 E1
Ambaston La
  BWSH/BRSTN DE72 ....73 M2
Amber Ct BPR/DUF DE56 ....17 L1
Amber Dr EWD/SEL/PNX NG16 ....20 F5
Ambergate Dr LEIN LE4 ....119 K7
Ambergate Rd
  WOL/BIL/BRX NG8 ....35 L8
Amber Hts RIPLEY DE5 ....11 H5
Amber HI ARN NG5 ....24 F8
Amberley Cl ILK DE7 ....47 K1
  LEIN LE4 ....126 C1
Amberley Dr DERBYSE DE24 ....71 K2
Amberley St NOTT NG1 ....4 F7
Amber Rd DERBYW DE22 ....43 H6
Amber St DERBYSE DE24 ....58 A8
Ambler Cl WGSTN LE18 ....138 B6
Ambleside WBRGFD NG2 ....52 A8
Ambleside Cl LBORO LE11 ....103 H1
  LEIS LE2 ....137 G4
Ambleside Dr
  EWD/SEL/PNX NG16 ....21 H4
  LEIS LE2 ....137 G4
Ambleside Rd WOL/BIL/BRX NG8 ....35 L4
Ambleside Wy CARL NG4 ....38 F7
  LEIS LE2 ....137 G4
Ambrose Cl LEIW LE3 ....130 F1
Ambrose Ter DERBY DE1 ....2 B3
Amen Aly DERBY DE1 ....2 E3
Amersham Rd LEIN LE4 ....125 H6
Amesbury Circ
  WOL/BIL/BRX NG8 ....35 L4
Amesbury La DERBYSE DE21 ....44 C5
Amesbury Rd WGSTN LE18 ....138 A7

Amhurst Cl *LEIW* LE3 .... 124 D6
Amilda Av *ILK* DE7 .... 33 K7
Amis Cl *LBORO* LE11 .... 103 G2
Amos Rd *LEIW* LE3 .... 130 B1
Ampthill Ri *ARN* NG5 .... 36 F3
Amsden Ri *RLEINE/BAR* LE9 .... 141 H8
Amyson Rd *LEIE* LE5 .... 133 C1
Amy St *DERBYW* DE22 .... 2 A6
   LEIW LE3 .... 130 E8
Ancaster Gdns
   WOL/BIL/BRX NG8 .... 49 L3
Anchor Cl *RLBORO* LE12 .... 94 E7
   WOL/BIL/BRX NG8 .... 35 M5
Anchor La *RLBORO* LE12 .... 94 E6
Anchor Rd *EWD/SEL/PNX* NG16 .. 21 L4
Anchor St *LEIS* LE2 .... 125 K5
Anders Dr *BLWL* NG6 .... 35 K2
Anderson Crs *BSTN/STPLFD* NG9 . 49 J7
Anderson St *DERBYSE* DE24 ... 58 D8
Andover Cl
   WOL/BIL/BRX NG8 .... 49 M1
Andover St *LEIS* LE2 .... 7 H7
   RLEIW/BAR LE9 .... 142 B3
Andrew Av *ILK* DE7 .... 33 L7
Andrew Cl *NORM/LIT* DE23 ... 56 C7
Andrewes Cl *LEIW* LE3 .... 6 A6
Andrewes St *LEIW* LE3 .... 6 A7
Andrew Rd *RLEINE/SYS* LE7 .... 124 F7
   ILK DE7 .... 31 L6
Andrews Dr *EWD/SEL/PNX* NG16.. 20 E3
Aneford Rd *LEIN* LE4 .... 126 C6
Anfield Cl *ARN* NG5 .... 25 J5
Anford Cl *BLWL* NG6 .... 35 M2
Angela Cl *ARN* NG5 .... 25 J5
Angela Dr *LEIE* LE5 .... 132 F5
Angel Rw West *NOTT* NG1 .... 4 F2
Anglers' La *DERBYE* DE21 ..... 59 J5
Anglesey Rd *WGSTN* LE18 .... 137 K4
Anglesey St *DERBYSE* DE21 ... 44 B7
Angletarn *WBRGFD* NG2 ..... 66 A1
Angrave Cl *MAPPK/POR/STA* NG3 .. 5 M2
Angrave Rd *RLBORO* LE12 ..... 88 C4
Angus Cl *ARN* NG5 .... 25 M6
   EWD/SEL/PNX NG16 .... 34 E2
   RLEINE/SYS LE7 .... 133 K1
Angus Dr *LBORO* LE11 .... 8 B3
Anmer Cl *WBRGFD* NG2 ..... 50 F6
Annan St *WOL/BIL/BRX* NG8.. 35 M7
Anne Potter Cl
   BWSH/BRSTN DE72 .... 60 A2
Anne's Cl *MAPPK/POR/STA* NG3.. 37 L5
Annesley Gv *NOTT* NG1 ..... 4 F3
Annesley La
   EWD/SEL/PNX NG16 .... 13 M1
Annesley Rd *HUCK/RAV* NG15.. 14 F2
   WBRGFD NG2 .... 65 K1
Ann St *LEIE* LE5 .... 7 H5
Ann's Wy *LEIS* LE2 .... 139 G2
Anslow Av *BSTN/STPLFD* NG9 .. 49 L7
Anson Rd *CDON/KEG* DE74 .. 84 F7
   RLBORO LE12 .... 101 L4
Anstee Rd *LGEAT* NG10 ..... 76 A3
Anstey Ct *DERBYE* DE21 ..... 44 E6
Anstey La *GBY/RBY* LE6 .... 123 M5
   LEIN LE4 .... 124 D3
   LEIW LE3 .... 124 E5
   RLEINE/SYS LE7 .... 118 D7
   RLEINE/SYS LE7 .... 124 D3
Anstey Ri *MAPPK/POR/STA* NG3 .. LE12
Answorth Dr *WBRGFD* NG2 ... 50 F6
Anthony Crs *DERBYSE* DE24 ... 72 C1
Anthony Dr *DERBYSE* DE24 ... 72 D1
   RLEINE/SYS LE7 .... 133 K2
Anthony Rd *LEIN* LE4 .... 125 H6
Anthony St *RLEINE/SYS* LE7 .. 119 J1
Antill St *BSTN/STPLFD* NG9 ... 62 B1
Apiary Ga *CDON/KEG* DE74 ... 84 F4
Apollo Cl *LEIS* LE2 .... 7 K6
Apollo Ct *LEIS* LE2 .... 7 K7
Apollo Dr *BLWL* NG6 .... 35 K2
Appian Cl *BWSH/BRSTN* DE72 .. 60 A6
Appian Wy *DERBYSE* DE24 .. 73 H1
Appleby Cl *ILK* DE7 .... 47 K1
   LEIW LE3 .... 130 A1
Appleby Rd *LEIN* LE4 .... 128 E8
Applecross Cl *DERBYSE* DE24 .. 71 J4
Appledore Av *WOL/BIL/BRX* NG8.. 49 H5
Appledore Dr *DERBYE* DE21 .. 44 F6
Appledorne Wy *ARN* NG5 .... 25 J6
Applegate Cl *DERBYE* DE21 ... 44 F4
Applemead Cl *DERBYE* DE21 .. 44 C5
Appleton Av *LEIN* LE4 .... 125 H3
Appleton Cl *DERBYE* DE21 ... 44 E8
Appleton Dr *BPR/DUF* DE56 .. 17 M1
   RLBORO LE12 .... 97 M3
Appleton Rd *BSTN/STPLFD* NG9.. 63 M3
Appletree Cl *BWSH/BRSTN* DE72 .. 60 A6
Apple Tree Cl
   COT/KEY/RAD NG12 .... 65 L3
Applewood Cl *BPR/DUF* DE56 .. 17 M2
Applewood Gv *ARN* NG5 .... 37 H4
The Approach *LEIE* LE5 ..... 132 D3
Aquitaine Cl *RLEIW/BAR* LE9 .. 135 L4
Arbor Cl *DERBYW* DE22 ..... 2 D1
Arboretum St *NORM/LIT* DE23 .. 3 G8
   NOTT NG1 .... 4 E3
Arbor Rd *RLEIW/BAR* LE9 .... 141 G3
Arbour Hl *ILK* DE7 .... 46 C4
Arbour Rd *LEIN* LE4 .... 125 M5
Arbrook Dr *WOL/BIL/BRX* NG8 .. 50 B8
Arbury Dl *RLBORO* LE12 ..... 102 A5
Arbutus Cl *CFTN/RUD* NG11.. 64 A6
Archdale Rd *ARN* NG5 ..... 37 C1
Archdale St *RLEINE/SYS* LE7 .. 120 D5
Archdeacon La *LEIE* LE1 ..... 6 F5
   LEIN LE4 .... 126 C3
Archer Cl *LBORO* LE11 ..... 102 F1
Archer Crs *WOL/BIL/BRX* NG8.. 49 J2
Ardath Rd *LEIN* LE4 .... 126 A6
Arden Av *LEIN* LE4 .... 130 D5
Arden Cl *BSTN/STPLFD* NG9 ... 49 L7
   HUCK/RAV NG15 .... 24 A2

NORM/LIT DE23 .... 57 J5
Ardern Ter *LEIW* LE3 .... 130 E5
Ardleigh Cl *ARN* NG5 .... 24 B6
   MCKLVR DE3 .... 56 B7
Ardmore Cl *WBRGFD* NG2 .... 5 M9
Ardsley Cl *HEANOR* DE75 ..... 20 E5
Argosy Rd *CDON/KEG* DE74 ... 85 J7
Argyle St *DERBYW* DE22 ..... 2 C8
   EWD/SEL/PNX NG16 .... 20 F3
   NOTT NG7 .... 4 B5
Argyll Cl *DERBYE* DE21 .... 59 K2
Argyll Rd *RIPLEY* DE5 .... 11 J5
Ariel Cl *ARN* NG5 .... 36 D2
Arkers Cl *BLWL* NG6 .... 36 B4
Arklow Cl *WOL/BIL/BRX* NG8 ... 35 M5
Arkwright Av *BPR/DUF* DE56 ... 141 H6
Arkwright St *DERBYSE* DE21 ... 58 A8
Arkwright St North
   WBRGFD NG2 .... 51 G4
Arkwright St South
   WBRGFD NG2 .... 51 H6
Arkwright Wk *WBRGFD* NG2 .. 51 H6
Arleston Dr *WOL/BIL/BRX* NG8... 49 H3
Arleston La *DERBYSE* DE24 ... 71 H6
Arleston St *NORM/LIT* DE23 ... 57 K8
Arlington Dr *DERBYSE* DE24 ... 72 D1
   MAPPK/POR/STA NG3 .... 37 G6
Arlington Rd *NORM/LIT* DE23... 57 G6
Armadale Cl *ARN* NG5 .... 26 A7
Armadale Dr *LEIE* LE5 .... 127 G2
Arnett's La *RLBORO* LE12 ..... 100 B3
Armfield Rd *ARN* NG5 .... 38 A1
Armitage Cl *LEIN* LE4 .... 9 G2
Armitage Dr *LGEAT* NG10 ..... 62 E8
Armscote Cl *DERBYE* DE21 ... 44 F5
Armson Av *RLEIW/BAR* LE9 ... 129 J2
Armstrong Av *RLEIW/BAR* LE9 . 142 B4
Armstrong Rd *BLWL* NG6 ..... 35 K2
Arncliff Cl *WOL/BIL/BRX* NG8 ... 49 G5
Arncliffe Rd *LEIE* LE5 .... 127 G7
Arndale Av *WGSTN* LE18 ..... 138 D6
Arndale Rd *ARN* NG5 .... 37 G2
Arnesby Crs *WGSTN* LE18 ..... 137 K2
Arnesby Rd *NOTTE* NG7 ..... 50 B4
Arnhem St *LEIE* LE1 .... 7 G7
Arnheim Ter *DERBYE* DE21 ..... 59 J4
Arno Av *NOTTE* NG7 .... 36 F7
   WGSTN LE18 .... 137 L6
Arnold Av *LGEAT* NG10 ..... 75 L3
   WGSTN LE18 .... 137 L6
Arnold Cl *RLEIW/BAR* LE9 .... 142 B5
Arnold Crs *LGEAT* NG10 ..... 75 L3
Arnold La *MAPPK/POR/STA* NG3 .. 38 A3
Arnold Rd *ARN* NG5 .... 36 E2
Arnold St *DERBYW* DE22 ..... 57 H2
   LEI LE1 .... 7 J3
Arnos Gv *WOL/BIL/BRX* NG8 .. 35 H4
Arnot Hill Rd *ARN* NG5 ..... 25 J8
Arno Vale Gdns *ARN* NG5 .... 37 K2
Arno Vale Rd *ARN* NG5 ..... 37 K2
Arnside *BSTN/STPLFD* NG9 ... 62 C2
Arnside Cl *ARN* NG5 .... 36 F2
Arnside Rd *ARN* NG5 .... 36 F2
   R BSTN/STPLFD NG9 .... 64 A1
Arran Cl *BSTN/STPLFD* NG9 ... 48 C5
   DERBYSE DE24 .... 71 J4
Arran Rd *LEIN* LE4 .... 126 B3
Arran Wy *RLEIW/BBY* LE8 ... 143 K4
Arreton Cl *LEIS* LE2 .... 132 A8
Arridge Rd *DERBYE* DE21 ..... 44 D8
Arthur Av *BSTN/STPLFD* NG9 .. 48 D7
   NOTT NG7 .... 4 A8
Arthur Crs *CARL* NG4 .... 52 E1
Arthur Hind Cl *DERBYW* DE22.. 43 K8
Arthur Mee Rd
   BSTN/STPLFD NG9 .... 62 C2
Arthur St *BWSH/BRSTN* DE72 .. 60 A2
   CARL NG4 .... 52 E1
   DERBY DE1 .... 43 K8
   LBORO LE11 .... 9 G4
   NOTTE NG7 .... 4 D3
Artic Wy *EWD/SEL/PNX* NG16.... 22 B8
Arum Wy *LEIW* LE3 .... 130 B1
Arundel Av *MCKLVR* DE3 ..... 56 D5
Arundel Cl *LGEAT* NG10 ..... 61 M3
   RLEINE/SYS LE7 .... 113 C7
Arundel Dr *BSTN/STPLFD* NG9 .. 48 F5
   DERBYE DE21 .... 59 K2
Arundel Gv *RLBORO* LE12 ..... 101 L5
Arundel St *DERBYW* DE22 ..... 57 H4
   LEIW LE3 .... 6 A6
Ascot Av *EWD/SEL/PNX* NG16 .. 22 B8
Ascot Dr *ARN* NG5 .... 25 H7
   DERBYSE DE24 .... 58 B8
   HUCK/RAV NG15 .... 23 H2
Ascot Pl *ILK* DE7 .... 47 G2
Ascot Rd *LEIN* LE4 .... 125 M5
   WOL/BIL/BRX NG8 .... 36 B8
Ascott Gdns *WBRGFD* NG2 ... 64 F2
Asfordby St *LEIE* LE5 .... 132 B1
Ash Acre *BPR/DUF* DE56 ..... 18 B3
Asha Margh *LEIN* LE4 ..... 125 L5
Ashbourne Cl *BSTN/STPLFD* NG9.. 48 E6
Ashbourne Rd *ASHB* DE6 ... 41 L5
   ASHB DE6 .... 41 L5
   BPR/DUF DE56. .... 16 D4
   DERBYW DE22 .... 42 B6
   DERBYW DE22 .... 57 H1
   EWD/SEL/PNX NG16 .... 13 L5
   WGSTN LE18 .... 138 A3
Ashbourne St *LEIS* LE2 ..... 7 L6
Ashbrook Av *BWSH/BRSTN* DE72.. 60 A5
Ashbrook Cl *DERBYW* DE22 ... 43 G4
Ashburnham Av *NOTTE* NG7..... 4 A7
Ashby Crs *LBORO* LE11 ..... 8 B4
Ashby Gld *LEIE* LE5 .... 133 G2
Ashby Ri *RLEIW/BBY* LE8 ... 139 M6
Ashby Rd *CDON/KEG* DE74 ... 85 L7
   COAL LE67 .... 100 A6
   COAL LE67 .... 116 B5
   LBORO LE11 .... 8 B5
   LBORO LE11 .... 100 F1
Ashby Road Central
   RLBORO LE12 .... 101 M6
Ashby Rd East *RLBORO* LE12 .. 102 B6
Ashby Rd West *RLBORO* LE12.. 101 G6
Ashby Sq *LBORO* LE11 ..... 9 H3

Ashby St *DERBYSE* DE24 ..... 72 C1
Ashchurch Dr *WOL/BIL/BRX* NG8.. 49 H5
Ash Cl *BWSH/BRSTN* DE72 ... 73 M8
   CALV/BJ NG14 .... 39 J3
   DERBYW DE22 .... 43 H3
   GBY/RBY LE6 .... 122 F6
   RLBORO LE12 .... 105 H6
Ashclose Av *LEIS* LE2 .... 132 A8
Ashcombe Gdns
   DERBYE DE21 .... 44 F6
Ash Ct *GBY/RBY* LE6 .... 123 J5
Ash Crs *EWD/SEL/PNX* NG16..... 34 F1
   RIPLEY DE5 .... 11 H7
Ashcroft Cl *DERBYSE* DE24 ... 58 D8
Ash Dl *COAL* LE67 .... 100 B8
Ashdale Av *LEIW* LE3 .... 135 K6
Ashdale Rd *ARN* NG5 .... 25 L7
   ILK DE7 .... 47 L1
   MAPPK/POR/STA NG3 .... 51 M1
Ashdown Av *LEIW* LE3 ..... 130 F1
Ashdown Cl *CFTN/RUD* NG11.... 64 F1
   LBORO LE11 .... 103 G2
Ashdown Rd *WGSTN* LE18 ... 138 B3
Ash Dr *RLEINE/SYS* LE7 ..... 120 F5
Ashe Cl *ARN* NG5 .... 25 M8
Ashe La *RDERBYSW* DE65 ... 68 E2
Ashe Pl *NORM/LIT* DE23 ..... 57 K6
Asher La *CFTN/RUD* NG11 ... 78 F2
   RIPLEY DE5 .... 11 G2
Ashfield Av *BSTN/STPLFD* NG9 .. 63 M2
   DERBYE DE21 .... 44 C7
Ashfield Dr *RLEINE/SYS* LE7 .. 124 B2
Ashfield Rd *LEIN* LE4 .... 120 D7
   LEIS LE2 .... 132 A4
   WBRGFD NG2 .... 51 K3
Ashford Cl *ILK* DE7 .... 32 B7
Ashford Pl *ILK* DE7 .... 33 J2
Ashford Ri *WOL/BIL/BRX* NG8 ... 35 M4
   WOL/BIL/BRX NG8 .... 49 H5
Ashford Rd *COAL* LE67 ..... 108 B2
   LEIS LE2 .... 131 L6
Ashforth Av *HEANOR* DE75 ... 20 E8
Ashforth St *MAPPK/POR/STA* NG3.. 5 J3
Ash Gv *EWD/SEL/PNX* NG16 .. 13 H7
   CALV/BJ NG14 .... 27 G2
   COT/KEY/RAD NG12 .... 80 D5
   EWD/SEL/PNX NG16 .... 13 H7
   LGEAT NG10 .... 47 L8
   LGEAT NG10 .... 76 A1
   RLBORO LE12 .... 94 E5
   RLBORO LE12 .... 113 J6
   RLEIW/BBY LE8 .... 136 F7
Ashgrove Ct *DERBYE* DE21 .... 44 F6
Ashington Cl *LEIW* LE3 ..... 124 F7
Ashington Dr *ARN* NG5 ..... 25 K5
Ashlands Wy *RLEIW/BAR* LE9 .. 135 K6
Ash La *ASHB* DE6 .... 54 A7
   RLBORO LE12 .... 89 H3
Ash Lea Cl *COT/KEY/RAD* NG12... 67 K5
Ashleigh Dr *LBORO* LE11 ..... 8 D6
   MELB/CHEL DE73 .... 72 D5
Ashleigh Rd *LEIW* LE3 ..... 123 M7
   LEIW LE3 .... 131 G3
Ashley Cl *BSTN/STPLFD* NG9 .. 63 H1
Ashley Crs *COT/KEY/RAD* NG12.. 80 C4
Ashley Rd *COT/KEY/RAD* NG12.. 80 D4
Ashley St *DERBYW* DE22 ..... 57 G2
   MAPPK/POR/STA NG3 .... 5 L3
Ashling St *WBRGFD* NG2 ..... 51 J5
Ashlyn Rd *DERBYE* DE21 ..... 3 J4
Ashlyns Ri *LEIW* LE3 ..... 130 C2
Ashmead Crs *RLEINE/SYS* LE7 .. 120 A6
Ashmeadow *BWSH/BRSTN* DE72 .. 59 M6
Ash Mount Rd
   EWD/SEL/PNX NG16 .... 20 F4
Ashness Cl *WBRGFD* NG2 ... 66 A1
Ashop Rd *BPR/DUF* DE56 ..... 18 B2
Ashopton Av *NORM/LIT* DE23.... 57 K7
Ashover Cl *DERBYE* DE21 ..... 44 D7
   MAPPK/POR/STA NG3 .... 37 J7
   RLEIW/BAR LE9 .... 142 B3
Ashover Rd *DERBYW* DE22 .. 43 H5
   LEIE LE5 .... 7 M8
Ashridge Wy
   COT/KEY/RAD NG12 .... 66 A3
Ash Rd *RLEIW/BAR* LE9 .... 141 H4
Ash St *ILK* DE7 .... 33 J3
   LEIE LE5 .... 7 M2
Ashthorpe Rd *LEIW* LE3 ..... 130 E3
Ashton Av *ARN* NG5 .... 25 K5
Ashton Cl *LEIS* LE2 .... 138 E4
   MCKLVR DE3 .... 56 A4
   WGSTN LE18 .... 138 A6
Ashton Wy *BPR/DUF* DE56 ... 18 B3
Ashtree Av *DERBYSE* DE24 ... 71 M1
Ash Tree Cl *BPR/DUF* DE56 ... 29 J2
   ILK DE7 .... 44 C3
   LEIS LE2 .... 138 F5
Ashtree Rd *LEIE* LE5 .... 127 G5
Ash Tree Rd *LEIS* LE2 .... 132 B4
Ash-Tree Rd *RLEIW/BAR* LE9 .. 142 B4
Ashurst Cl *WGSTN* LE18 ..... 138 C7
Ashurst Rd *LEIW* LE3 ..... 130 D7
Ashview Cl *LGEAT* NG10 ..... 79 H2
Ash View Cl *RDERBYSW* DE65 .. 68 F3
Ashville Cl *WBRGFD* NG2 ... 50 E6
Ashville Wy *RLEIW/BBY* LE8 .. 142 C2
Ash Wk *RLBORO* LE12 ..... 113 H1
Ashwater Cl *DERBYSE* DE24 ... 71 K5
Ashwater Dr
   MAPPK/POR/STA NG3 .... 38 B1
Ashwell Gdns *NOTTE* NG7 ... 36 C7
Ashwell St *CARL* NG4 .... 52 E1
   LEI LE1 .... 7 G8
Ashwick Cl *CFTN/RUD* NG11... 64 E2
Ashworth Av *CFTN/RUD* NG11... 65 C7
   DERBYE DE21 .... 58 D2
Ashworth Cl
   MAPPK/POR/STA NG3 .... 52 A2
Ashworth Crs
   MAPPK/POR/STA NG3 .... 37 M5
Askeby Dr *WOL/BIL/BRX* NG8.. 35 H6
Askew La *RDERBYSW* DE22 ... 43 G4
Askrigg Wy *WGSTN* LE18 ... 138 C5
Aslockton Dr *WOL/BIL/BRX* NG8.. 35 L8
Aspen Av *LBORO* LE11 ..... 103 L8
Aspen Dr *DERBYE* DE21 ..... 59 C3
   RLEIW/BBY LE8 .... 143 J3

Aspen Rd *BLWL* NG6 .... 23 K8
Asper St *CARL* NG4 .... 38 E8
Aspley La *WOL/BIL/BRX* NG8 ... 35 M7
Aspley Park Dr
   WOL/BIL/BRX NG8 .... 35 L7
Aspley Pl *NOTTE* NG7 .... 4 B3
Asplin Rd *LEIS* LE2 .... 137 J2
Asquith Bvd *LEIS* LE2 ..... 137 M1
   WGSTN LE18 .... 137 M2
Asquith Wy *WGSTN* LE18 ... 137 L2
Assarts Rd *EWD/SEL/PNX* NG16... 35 J4
Assured Dr *LEIN* LE4 .... 120 B8
Astcote Cl *HEANOR* DE75 ... 20 E6
Aster Rd *MAPPK/POR/STA* NG3 .. 5 L2
Astill Dr *LEIN* LE4 .... 125 K3
Astill Lodge Rd *LEIN* LE4 .... 124 E1
Astle Ct *ARN* NG5 .... 38 A1
Astley Cl *LEIS* LE2 .... 130 F4
Astley Dr *MAPPK/POR/STA* NG3.. 37 K6
Astlow Dr *BPR/DUF* DE56 ... 17 M1
Aston Av *BSTN/STPLFD* NG9 .. 49 L7
Aston Cl *BLWL* NG6 .... 24 A5
Aston Gn *BSTN/STPLFD* NG9 .. 62 C4
Aston Hall Dr
   BWSH/BRSTN DE72 .... 73 L8
Aston Hl *LEIS* LE2 .... 131 L7
Aston La *BWSH/BRSTN* DE72 .. 74 A7
   MELB/CHEL DE73 .... 72 F6
Aston Rd *NORM/LIT* DE23 ... 71 G2
   DERBYE DE21 .... 44 C7
Astral Gv *HUCK/RAV* NG15..... 23 H3
Astwood Cl *WOL/BIL/BRX* NG8.. 35 J8
Atchison Gdns *DERBYE* DE21 .. 44 F8
Atherfield Gdns
   EWD/SEL/PNX NG16 .... 21 K4
Atherstone Cl *LEIS* LE2 ..... 139 H3
Atherstone Rd *LBORO* LE11 .. 103 K8
Atherton Ri *WOL/BIL/BRX* NG8 .. 35 M4
Atherton Rd *ILK* DE7 .... 33 G4
Athlone Cl *DERBYE* DE21 ..... 44 B7
Athol Cl *DERBYSE* DE24 ..... 71 J3
Athorpe Gv *BLWL* NG6 ..... 24 A5
Atkins St *LEIS* LE2 .... 6 E8
Atlas Cl *LEIS* LE2 .... 7 K6
Atlas Rd *COAL* LE67 .... 108 B5
Atlow Rd *DERBYE* DE21 ..... 44 C8
Attenborough Cl *LEIW* LE3 .. 130 A6
Attenborough La
   BSTN/STPLFD NG9 .... 63 G4
Attercliffe Ter *WBRGFD* NG2 ... 51 C6
Attewell Cl *BWSH/BRSTN* DE72 .. 60 F8
Attewell Rd *EWD/SEL/PNX* NG16... 33 M2
Attfield Dr *RLEIW/BBY* LE8 ... 136 D8
Attingham Cl *LEIE* LE5 ..... 126 B7
Attlebridge Cl *DERBYE* DE21 .. 44 B7
Attlee Wy *WGSTN* LE18 ..... 137 J3
Atworth Gv *NORM/LIT* DE23 ... 56 D8
Aubrey Rd *ARN* NG5 .... 36 F5
Auburn Cl *RLEIW/BBY* LE8 ... 136 E1
Auburn Rd *RLEIW/BBY* LE8 ... 136 E1
Auckland Cl *MCKLVR* DE3 ... 56 C5
   NOTTE NG7 .... 50 C2
Auckland Rd *HUCK/RAV* NG15 .. 23 H2
Auden Cl *LEIN* LE4 .... 124 F5
Audley Cl *ILK* DE7 .... 33 H4
Audley Dr *BSTN/STPLFD* NG9 .. 49 K6
Audley End *LEIW* LE3 ..... 130 E6
Audon Av *BSTN/STPLFD* NG9 .. 63 J2
Audrey Dr *DERBYE* DE21 ..... 44 E7
Augusta Cl *LEIS* LE2 .... 130 A1
Augusta St *NORM/LIT* DE23 ... 57 M5
Augustine Gdns *ARN* NG5 ... 24 E6
Aults Cl *RDERBYSW* DE65 .... 70 A6
Aumberry Gap *LBORO* LE11 ... 9 K3
Austen Av *LGEAT* NG10 ..... 76 A2
   NORM/LIT DE23 .... 56 F7
   NOTTE NG7 .... 4 C1
Austin Rd *LEIS* LE5 .... 127 G6
Austins Dr *LGEAT* NG10 ..... 61 M3
Austin Sq *NORM/LIT* DE23 ... 57 K8
Austin St *BLWL* NG6 .... 24 A5
Austrey Av *BSTN/STPLFD* NG9 .. 49 L7
Austwick Cl *LEIN* LE4 .... 125 G4
Autumn Gv *DERBYE* DE21 ... 58 D2
Avalon Cl *BLWL* NG6 .... 36 C1
Avebury Av *LEIS* LE2 ..... 125 G6
Avebury Cl *CFTN/RUD* NG11... 64 A4
Aveline Cl *ARN* NG5 .... 24 D7
Avenue A *NOTT* NG1 .... 5 K7
Avenue B *NOTT* NG1 .... 5 K7
Avenue C *NOTT* NG1 .... 5 L7
Avenue D *NOTT* NG1 .... 5 L7
Avenue E *NOTT* NG1 .... 5 L7
Avenue Gdns *LEIS* LE2 ..... 132 A6
Avenue Rd *BPR/DUF* DE56 ... 29 J2
   COAL LE67 .... 108 B7
   LEIS LE2 .... 132 A6
   RLBORO LE12 .... 114 B4
   RLEINE/SYS LE7 .... 121 J2
Avenue Road Extension
   LEIS LE2 .... 131 L6
The Avenue *BWSH/BRSTN* DE72.. 83 J2
   CFTN/RUD NG11 .... 79 H2
   DERBY DE1 .... 2 F6
   DERBYE DE21 .... 58 D2
   LEIS LE2 .... 132 A5
   LEIW LE3 .... 123 M6
   RLEIW/BAR LE9 .... 141 J4
   RLEIW/BBY LE8 .... 143 H3
Averham Cl *DERBYE* DE21 ... 44 F6
Averil Rd *LEIE* LE5 .... 132 F1
Averton Sq *WOL/BIL/BRX* NG8 .. 50 B4
Avery Dr *COAL* LE67 .... 116 B6
Avery Hl *LEIW* LE3 .... 130 B3
   RLEINE/SYS LE7 .... 120 F3
Aviemore Cl *ARN* NG5 .... 24 D8
Aviemore Wy *DERBYSE* DE24 .. 71 J3
Avis Av *HEANOR* DE75 ..... 20 D8
Avoca Cl *LEIE* LE5 .... 132 F1
Avocet Ct *DERBYSE* DE24 ... 71 H3
Avonbridge Cl *ARN* NG5 ..... 26 A6
Avon Cl *DERBYSE* DE24 ..... 71 H5
   LEIS LE2 .... 139 G2
Avondale Cl *LGEAT* NG10 ... 75 L1
Avondale Rd *CARL* NG4 ..... 52 B1
   DERBYE DE21 .... 59 H1

ILK DE7 .... 47 G2
   NORM/LIT DE23 .... 2 E7
   WGSTN LE18 .... 138 B4
Avon Dr *RLEIW/BBY* LE8 ..... 136 D8
Avon Gdns *WBRGFD* NG2 ... 51 K8
Avonlea Cl *ILK* DE7 .... 32 F7
Avonmouyh Dr *DERBYSE* DE24... 58 C7
Avon Pl *BSTN/STPLFD* NG9 ... 49 L8
Avon Rd *CARL* NG4 .... 38 D5
   LEIS LE2 .... 130 C5
   MAPPK/POR/STA NG3 .... 51 M2
   RLBORO LE12 .... 113 H1
Avonside Dr *LEIE* LE5 ..... 132 C2
Avon St *DERBYSE* DE24 ..... 58 C7
   LEIS LE2 .... 7 K8
Avon Vale Rd *LBORO* LE11 ... 9 L7
Avon Wy *RDERBYSW* DE65 .. 68 C6
Awsworth La
   EWD/SEL/PNX NG16 .... 34 A4
Awsworth Rd *ILK* DE7 .... 33 L4
Axbridge Cl *LEIN* LE4 .... 125 H6
Axford Cl *CARL* NG4 .... 38 D5
Aycliffe Gdns *DERBYSE* DE21 .. 44 D8
Aylesbury Av *DERBYE* DE21 .. 44 D8
Aylesham Av *ARN* NG5 ..... 37 K1
Aylestone Dr *LEIS* LE2 ..... 137 H2
   WOL/BIL/BRX NG8 .... 35 M7
Aylestone La *WGSTN* LE18... 137 L3
Aylestone Rd *LEIS* LE2 ..... 131 K4
   LEIS LE2 .... 131 K4
Aylestone Wk *LEIS* LE2 ..... 131 K4
Aylmer Rd *LEIW* LE3 ..... 130 D3
Ayr Cl *DERBYE* DE21 .... 59 H3
Ayr St *NOTTE* NG7 .... 4 C4
Ayscough Av
   MAPPK/POR/STA NG3 .... 38 B1
Aysgarth Rd *LEIN* LE4 ..... 125 G4
Ayston Rd *LEIW* LE3 ..... 130 E6
Ayton Cl *WBRGFD* NG2 ..... 51 J8
Ayton Gdns *BSTN/STPLFD* NG9.. 63 G5
Azalea Ct *EWD/SEL/PNX* NG16... 22 A7

B

Babbacombe Cl *ARN* NG5 ..... 36 F1
   DERBYSE DE24 .... 59 G8
Babbacombe Wy
   HUCK/RAV NG15. .... 23 H1
Babbington Crs *CARL* NG4 ... 38 C5
Babbington La
   EWD/SEL/PNX NG16 .... 34 D3
Babbington Rw *LEIS* LE2 ..... 137 L2
Babingley Dr *LEIN* LE4 ..... 125 H5
Babington Ct
   BSTN/STPLFD NG9 .... 63 G2
   DERBYE DE21 .... 2 E6
Babington Rd *RLBORO* LE12 .. 105 J7
   RLEINE/SYS LE7 .... 119 J1
Back La *CDON/KEG* DE74 .... 84 E1
   COT/KEY/RAD NG12 .... 80 A6
   EWD/SEL/PNX NG16 .... 35 H1
   ILK DE7 .... 33 J5
   MELB/CHEL DE73. .... 72 E5
   RDERBYSW DE65 .... 55 G5
   RIPLEY DE5 .... 11 G1
   RLBORO LE12 .... 91 G8
   RLBORO LE12 .... 96 C8
   RLBORO LE12 .... 114 A4
   RLEINE/SYS LE7 .... 114 B8
   RLEINE/SYS LE7 .... 115 K3
Back Sitwell St *DERBY* DE1. .. 2 F5
Back Wyver La
   BPR/DUF DE56 .... 17 K2
Bacon Cl *EWD/SEL/PNX* NG16 .. 21 L7
Bacton Av *BLWL* NG6 .... 23 M7
Bacton Gdns *BLWL* NG6 ..... 23 M7
Baddeley Dr *WGSTN* LE18 ... 137 M3
Baden Powell Rd
   WBRGFD NG2 .... 51 J3
Baden Rd *LEIE* LE5 .... 132 C4
Bader Rd *CFTN/RUD* NG11 ... 50 F8
Badger Cl *DERBYE* DE21 ..... 59 K1
   HUCK/RAV NG15. .... 23 G1
   RLEIW/BAR LE9 .... 135 L8
Badger Dr *RLEIW/BBY* LE8 ... 142 C2
Badgers Bank *RLEINE/SYS* LE7... 113 J8
Badger's Cnr *RLEINE/SYS* LE7... 115 H7
Badgers Holt *LEIS* LE2 ..... 138 E3
Badgers Wk *RLBORO* LE12 ... 112 C2
Badmington Rd *LEIN* LE4 ... 126 B2
Badminton Cl *RLEINE/SYS* LE7.. 120 F2
Baggrave St *LEIE* LE5 ..... 132 B1
Bagley Cl *LBORO* LE11 ..... 103 G1
Bagnall Av *ARN* NG5 .... 25 G8
Bagnall Rd *BLWL* NG6 ..... 36 A3
Bagot St *ILK* DE7 .... 32 A7
Bagshaw St *DERBYSE* DE24 ... 58 C7
Bagthorpe Cl *ARN* NG5 ..... 36 E4
Bailey Brook Crs
   EWD/SEL/PNX NG16 .... 20 E4
Bailey Brook Dr
   EWD/SEL/PNX NG16 .... 20 E4
Bailey Cl *ARN* NG5 .... 25 H8
   LBORO LE11 .... 103 H7
Bailey Grove Rd
   EWD/SEL/PNX NG16 .... 21 H5
Bailey La *COT/KEY/RAD* NG12... 53 J5
Bailey St *BLWL* NG6 .... 36 C5
   BSTN/STPLFD NG9 .... 62 A1
   CARL NG4 .... 38 E8
   NORM/LIT DE23 .... 2 D8
Bainbridge Rd *LBORO* LE11.... 104 A7
   LEIN LE4 .... 130 F6
   WGSTN LE18 .... 138 C6
Bainbridge St *NORM/LIT* DE23 .. 2 B8
Baines La *LEIW* LE3 ..... 129 M4
Bains Dr *BWSH/BRSTN* DE72 ... 60 B6
Bainton Gv *CFTN/RUD* NG11... 64 D6
Bakeacre La *RDERBYSW* DE65 ... 70 C4
Bakehouse La
   BWSH/BRSTN DE72 .... 59 M2
Baker Av *ARN* NG5 .... 25 H5
   HEANOR DE75 .... 20 D8
Bakerdale Rd
   MAPPK/POR/STA NG3 .... 51 M1
Baker Rd *EWD/SEL/PNX* NG16 .. 22 A7
Bakers Hl *BPR/DUF* DE56 ..... 10 C6

Baker's Hollow COT/KEY/RAD NG12 .... 67 J4
Baker St COAL LE67 .... 108 A5
DERBYSE DE24 .... 58 D7
HUCK/RAV NG15 .... 15 L8
ILK DE7 .... 33 K6
NOTT NG1 .... 4 F2
Bakery Cl RLEIW/BAR LE9 ..... 142 B5
Bakewell Av LEIW LE3 .... 38 C6
Bakewell Cl MCKLVR DE3 .... 56 B4
Bakewell Dr ARN NG5 .... 24 C8
CDON/KEG DE74 .... 84 E5
Bakewell Rd LBORO LE11 ...... 95 K8
LGEAT NG10 .... 76 C2
WGSTN LE18 .... 138 A3
Bakewell St COAL LE67 .... 108 C6
DERBY DE22 .... 2 C5
LEIS LE2 .... 7 M5
Balaclava Rd NORM/LIT DE23... 57 L8
Bala Dr ARN NG5 .... 24 E8
Bala Rd RLEIW/BAR LE9 .... 141 H3
Balcombe Av LEIW LE3 .... 130 F1
Balderstone Cl LEIE LE5 ...... 132 E2
Baldwin Av LEIW LE18 .... 137 L6
Baldwin Ri RLEIW/BAR LE9 .... 141 H8
Baldwin Rd WGSTN LE18 ...... 137 M2
Baldwin St EWD/SEL/PNX NG16 .... 22 A6
NOTTE NG5 .... 4 C5
Bale Rd LEIN LE4 .... 126 C6
Balfour Rd BSTN/STPLFD NG9 ... 62 B1
NORM/LIT DE23 .... 57 L7
NOTTE NG7 .... 4 B6
Balfour St LEIW LE3 .... 6 A2
Balisfire Gv LEIN LE4 .... 124 F4
The Balk LEIW LE3 .... 123 M6
Ballacraine Dr RIPLEY DE5 .... 11 K6
Balladine Rd RLEINE/SYS LE7 .. 118 C3
Ballantrae Cl ARN NG5 .... 26 A7
Ballards Cl LEIN LE4 .... 124 F4
Ballards Wy BWSH/BRSTN DE72... 60 B6
Ballater Cl DERBYSE DE24 ..... 71 J3
LEIE LE5 .... 133 H4
Balleny Cl DERBYE DE21 ...... 44 D5
Ballerat Crs ARN NG5 .... 24 C7
Balliol Av RLEINE/SYS LE7 .... 121 G5
Ball La BWSH/BRSTN DE72 ..... 73 L2
Ball St MAPPK/POR/STA NG3 ... 37 K8
Balmoral Av RLBORO LE12 ..... 101 L5
WBRGFD NG2 .... 51 J7
Balmoral Cl HEANOR DE75 ..... 20 A6
LEIS LE2 .... 132 A8
LGEAT NG10 .... 61 M4
NORM/LIT DE23 .... 56 F5
Balmoral Crs WOL/BIL/BRX NG8 ... 49 G2
Balmoral Dr BSTN/STPLFD NG9 ... 48 F5
LEIW LE3 .... 130 C5
Balmoral Gv HUCK/RAV NG15 ... 15 M7
Balmoral Rd BWSH/BRSTN DE72... 60 A6
CARL NG4 .... 52 D1
COAL LE67 .... 108 D7
ILK DE7 .... 47 H2
NOTT NG1 .... 4 E2
RLBORO LE12 .... 113 H6
Bamburgh Cl DERBYE DE21 ..... 59 H3
Bambury La RLEIW/BBY LE8 .... 143 H6
Bamford Av NORM/LIT DE23 ... 57 J7
Bamford Cl RIPLEY DE5 .... 11 H8
Bamkin Cl HUCK/RAV NG15 .... 23 M1
Bampton Cl WGSTN LE18 ...... 138 B7
Bampton Ct WBRGFD NG2 ...... 52 A8
Bampton St LBORO LE11 .... 9 J5
Banbury Av BSTN/STPLFD NG9 ... 62 D4
Banbury Dr RLBORO LE12 ...... 101 K4
Bancroft Cl RDERBYSW DE65 ... 68 B5
Bancroft Dr DERBYW DE22 ..... 43 G3
Bancroft St BLWL NG6 .... 24 A8
The Bancroft RDERBYSW DE65 ... 68 F4
Bandalls La RLBORO LE12 ...... 105 G3
Bangor St DERBYE DE21 .... 44 C7
Bankart Av LEIE LE2 .... 132 C6
Bank Ct DERBYW DE22 .... 43 G1
Bankfield Dr BSTN/STPLFD NG9... 49 G6
Bank Field Dr DERBYE DE21 .... 59 K3
Bankfield Dr ILK DE7 .... 46 F1
Bank Hl CALV/BJ NG14 .... 26 D4
Bankholmes Cl DERBYSE DE24 .. 71 J5
Bank Pl NOTT NG1 .... 5 H7
Banksburn Cl HEANOR DE75 .... 20 A6
Banks Cl ARN NG5 .... 37 M2
Bank Side DERBYW DE22 .... 43 J5
Bankside LEIE LE2 .... 127 J7
Banks Rd BSTN/STPLFD NG9 .... 62 C5
LEIS LE2 .... 131 H4
The Banks RLBORO LE12 .... 105 H7
RLBORO LE12 .... 114 A4
RLEINE/SYS LE7 .... 121 K2
RLEIW/BAR LE9 .... 142 B5
Bank St EWD/SEL/PNX NG16 ... 21 G3
LGEAT NG10 .... 62 D8
Bank View Rd BPR/DUF DE56 ... 10 A5
DERBYW DE22 .... 43 K7
Bankwood Cl WOL/BIL/BRX NG8 .... 35 L6
Bannell's La MCKLVR DE3 ...... 55 K7
Bannels Av NORM/LIT DE23 .... 56 F8
Bannerman Rd BLWL NG6 ...... 36 A1
LEIE LE5 .... 132 B4
Bantlam La RLEIW/BAR LE9 .... 135 M4
Banwell Cl MCKLVR DE3 .... 56 A4
Barbara Av LEIE LE5 .... 126 F8
LEIW LE3 .... 129 K4
Barbara Cl RLEIW/BAR LE9 .... 135 L4
Barbara Rd LEIW LE3 .... 130 F6
Barbara Sq HUCK/RAV NG15 ... 15 K6
Barber Cl ILK DE7 .... 33 J4
Barber St EWD/SEL/PNX NG16 ... 21 L5
Barbrook Cl WOL/BIL/BRX NG8 ... 49 M2
Barbury Dr CFTN/RUD NG11 ... 64 B8
Barchester Cl DERBYE DE21 ... 44 F5
Barclay Cl ILK DE7 .... 33 H4
Barclay St LEIW LE3 .... 131 G3
Barden Cl LBORO LE11 .... 102 F4
Barden Rd ARN NG5 .... 37 L3
Bardfield Gdns ARN NG5 ...... 24 B6
Bardney Dr BLWL NG6 .... 23 L7
Bardolph Cl LEIN LE4 .... 125 M7

Bardolph St East LEIN LE4 .... 126 A7
Bardon Cl LE67 .... 108 E8
Bardon Rd COAL LE67 .... 108 C7
Bardsey Ct DERBYE DE21 ...... 44 F4
Bardsey Gdns ARN NG5 .... 24 E8
Bare La BWSH/BRSTN DE72 ..... 60 A2
Barent Cl ARN NG5 .... 36 D1
Barent Wk ARN NG5 .... 36 D1
Barf Cl MCKLVR DE3 .... 56 C6
Barfoot Cl RLEIW/BBY LE8 .... 145 J6
Barfoot Rd WGSTN LE18 ...... 137 K2
Barford Cl WGSTN LE18 ...... 138 A7
Barford Rd BPR/DUF DE56 ..... 18 A6
Bargate Cl BPR/DUF DE56 ..... 17 M5
Bargate Rd BPR/DUF DE56 ..... 17 M5
Barge Cl WGSTN LE18 .... 137 L7
Barkby Holt La RLEINE/SYS LE7... 121 J7
Barkby La RLEINE/SYS LE7 .... 120 F6
Barkby Rd LEIN LE4 .... 126 C5
RLEINE/SYS LE7 .... 120 F4
RLEINE/SYS LE7 .... 127 M1
Barkby Thorpe La RLEINE/SYS LE7 .... 120 C6
Barkbythorpe Rd LEIN LE4 .... 126 D3
Barker Av EWD/SEL/PNX NG16... 12 F3
Barker Av East LGEAT NG10 ... 61 M1
Barker Av North LGEAT NG10 ... 61 L1
Barker Ga ILK DE7 .... 31 M6
NOTT NG1 .... 5 J7
Barker's La BSTN/STPLFD NG9 ... 63 J5
Barker St LEIE LE5 .... 126 B8
Barkford Cl LEIE LE5 .... 127 J6
Barkla Cl CFTN/RUD NG11 ..... 64 A7
Bar La WOL/BIL/BRX NG8 ...... 36 A5
Barley Cl DERBYE DE21 .... 30 A7
LEIW LE3 .... 124 A7
Barley Corn Cl DERBYE DE21 ... 45 G5
Barley Cft BPR/DUF DE56 ..... 17 M5
MELB/CHEL DE73 .... 72 D6
WBRGFD NG2 .... 65 G3
Barley Dale Dr BSTN/STPLFD NG9 .... 48 B5
Barleylands CFTN/RUD NG11 ... 79 G1
Barley La RLEIW/BBY LE8 ..... 143 M8
Barley Wy RLEINE/SYS LE7 .... 113 J8
Barling Dr ILK DE7 .... 33 G5
Barling Rd LEIE LE5 .... 126 D7
Barlock Rd BLWL NG6 .... 36 A2
Barlow Dr EWD/SEL/PNX NG16 ... 33 M3
Barlow Dr (North) EWD/SEL/PNX NG16 .... 33 M3
Barlow Dr South EWD/SEL/PNX NG16 .... 33 M3
Barlow St DERBY DE1 .... 3 H8
Barmouth Av LEIS LE2 .... 137 L1
Barnard Cl LEIS LE2 .... 7 J7
Barnard Rd DERBYE DE21 ..... 44 B6
Barnards Dr RLBORO LE12 .... 114 C3
Barnard Wy RLBORO LE12 ..... 113 H6
Barnby Av WGSTN LE18 .... 138 A3
Barnby Wk ARN NG5 .... 37 G3
Barn Cl CDON/KEG DE74 ...... 84 E4
COT/KEY/RAD NG12 .... 67 J5
DERBYW DE22 .... 43 G1
RDERBYSW DE65 .... 70 B5
WGSTN LE18 .... 138 C7
Barn Cft BSTN/STPLFD NG9 .... 62 F1
Barndale Cl WBRGFD NG2 ..... 65 G4
Barnes Cl LEIN LE4 .... 126 C2
RLEIW/BBY LE8 .... 146 D7
Barnes Heath Rd LEIE LE5 .... 132 E2
Barnes Rd ARN NG5 .... 24 D8
Barnet Cl LEIS LE2 .... 138 E4
Barnet Rd MAPPK/POR/STA NG3... 37 M8
Barnfield CFTN/RUD NG11 .... 64 F3
Barnfield Cl RLBORO LE12 ..... 93 M3
RLEIW/BBY LE8 .... 139 M6
Barngate Cl LEIN LE4 .... 119 K7
Barnhill Gv NORM/LIT DE23 ... 56 E8
Barnley Cl RLEIW/BBY LE8 .... 143 J3
Barns Cl RLEIW/BAR LE9 ...... 129 G2
Barnsdale Rd LEIN LE4 .... 124 D2
Barnsley Ter WBRGFD NG2 .... 51 G6
Barnstaple Cl DERBYE DE21 ... 44 E5
WGSTN LE18 .... 138 B7
Barnstaple Rd LEIE LE5 ...... 133 H4
Barnston Rd WBRGFD NG2 .... 51 K2
Barns Wy RLEIW/BAR LE9 ..... 128 A3
Barnwell Av LEIN LE4 .... 125 K3
Barnwood Cl MCKLVR DE3 .... 56 A5
Baron Cl DERBYE DE21 .... 45 H4
Baronet Wy LEIE LE5 .... 127 J6
Barons Crs CARL NG4 .... 38 C6
RLEIW/BAR LE9 .... 129 G2
Baron St LEI LE1 .... 7 H6
Barons Wy RLBORO LE12 ...... 113 J4
Barrack La NOTTE NG7 .... 4 B7
Barrack Rw CFTN/RUD NG11 ... 9 K2
Barradale Av RLBORO LE12 .... 114 A3
Barra Ms WBRGFD NG2 .... 50 F5
Barratt Crs BSTN/STPLFD NG9... 63 H5
Barratt La BSTN/STPLFD NG9 ... 63 H6
Barr Crs COAL LE67 .... 108 D3
Barrett Dr LBORO LE11 .... 103 H1
Barrett St DERBYSE DE24 ..... 58 E8
Barrhead Cl ARN NG5 .... 24 C6
Barrie Dr DERBYSE DE24 ...... 71 K2
Barrington Cl COT/KEY/RAD NG12 .... 53 J5
Barrington Rd LEIS LE2 ...... 132 C6
Barrique Rd BPR/DUF DE56 .... 50 C6
Barrons Ct BWSH/BRSTN DE72 ... 73 L2
Barron's Wy BWSH/BRSTN DE72 .... 60 A6
The Barroon CDON/KEG DE74 ... 84 F4
Barrowcliffe Ct RLBORO LE12 .. 105 G7
Barrow Ct WGSTN LE18 .... 138 D6
Barrow La MELB/CHEL DE73 ... 82 A1
Barrow Rd RLBORO LE12 ...... 104 F3
RLBORO LE12 .... 114 A4
Barrows Hill La EWD/SEL/PNX NG16 .... 13 H2
Barrow Slade COT/KEY/RAD NG12 .... 80 C5
Barrow St LBORO LE11 .... 9 K4

Barrs Hl RLBORO LE12 .... 89 G6
Barry Cl LEIW LE3 .... 129 J4
Barrydale Av BSTN/STPLFD NG9... 63 K2
Barry Dr LEIW LE3 .... 129 J4
RLEINE/SYS LE7 .... 120 F5
Barry Rd LEIW LE3 .... 127 H6
Barry St BLWL NG6 .... 23 M8
Barsby Dr LBORO LE11 .... 103 H1
Barston St LEI LE1 .... 6 E3
Bartholomew St LEIS LE2 ..... 7 L9
Bartlow Rd WOL/BIL/BRX NG8 ... 35 H8
Barton Cl CFTN/RUD NG11 ..... 78 F1
GBY/RBY LE6 .... 123 H8
WGSTN LE18 .... 138 A3
Barton Knowle BPR/DUF DE56 .... 18 B3
Barton La BSTN/STPLFD NG9 ... 63 G6
CFTN/RUD NG11 .... 64 A6
CFTN/RUD NG11 .... 77 L2
Barton Rd LEIN LE3 .... 125 G7
LGEAT NG10 .... 62 E8
Bartons Cl EWD/SEL/PNX NG16 ... 22 A5
Barton St EWD/SEL/PNX NG16 ... 22 A5
Barwell Dr WOL/BIL/BRX NG8 ... 35 H6
Barwell Rd RLEIW/BAR LE9 .... 129 H2
Basa Crs ARN NG5 .... 24 D7
Basford Rd BLWL NG6 .... 36 B6
Basildon Cl DERBYSE DE24 .... 72 D2
Baskin La BSTN/STPLFD NG9 ... 63 G3
Baslow Av CARL NG4 .... 38 B6
Baslow Cl LGEAT NG10 .... 75 L2
Baslow Dr BSTN/STPLFD NG9 ... 49 L6
DERBYW DE22 .... 43 K4
Baslow Rd LEIE LE5 .... 7 M8
Bassett Av RLEIW/BBY LE8 .... 143 J4
Bassett Cl EWD/SEL/PNX NG16 .... 22 C8
ILK DE7 .... 33 G4
Bassett La RLEIW/BAR LE9 .... 140 B8
Bassett Rd EWD/SEL/PNX NG16... 22 C8
Bassett St LEIW LE3 .... 6 A3
WGSTN LE18 .... 137 K6
Bassford Av HEANOR DE75 .... 20 D5
Bassingfield La COT/KEY/RAD NG12 .... 52 C8
Bassingham Cl DERBYE DE21 ... 44 F6
Bass St DERBYW DE22 .... 57 H1
Bastion St NOTTE NG7 .... 50 C2
Batchelor Rd RLEIW/BBY LE8 ... 145 K7
Bateman Rd LEIW LE3 .... 124 E8
RLBORO LE12 .... 88 B5
Bateman St DERBY DE1 .... 3 J9
Bath Cl RLEIW/BAR LE9 .... 140 B7
Bath La LEI LE1 .... 6 C5
Bathley St WBRGFD NG2 ...... 51 G6
Bath Rd MCKLVR DE3 .... 56 C5
Baths La HUCK/RAV NG15 ..... 15 M8
Bath St DERBY DE1 .... 43 L8
ILK DE7 .... 33 J5
LEIN LE4 .... 125 L4
NOTT NG1 .... 5 K6
RLEINE/SYS LE7 .... 120 E3
Bathurst Dr WOL/BIL/BRX NG8 ... 49 L1
Bathurst Rd LEIS LE2 .... 133 H3
Battenberg Rd LEIW LE3 ...... 131 G1
Batten St LEIS LE2 .... 131 J6
Battersbee Rd WOL/BIL/BRX NG8... 35 L7
Battersbee Wy LEIW LE3 ...... 124 C7
Baulk La BSTN/STPLFD NG9 .... 62 D2
Baverstock Cl MELB/CHEL DE73... 72 D4
Baxter Ga LBORO LE11 .... 9 J3
Baxters Cl LEIN LE4 .... 124 F5
Baxter Sq NORM/LIT DE23 ..... 71 K1
Baycliff Cl LEIW LE3 .... 124 F7
Bayham Cl LEIE LE5 .... 132 F2
Bayleaf Crs DERBYE DE21 ..... 44 F8
Bayliss Cl RLBORO LE12 ...... 104 D8
Bayliss Rd CARL NG4 .... 38 B4
Baysdale WGSTN LE18 .... 138 D5
Bay St LEI LE1 .... 6 D3
Bayswater Cl DERBYW DE22 ... 56 D1
Bayswater Dr WGSTN LE18 ... 137 H6
Bayswater Rd EWD/SEL/PNX NG16 .... 22 D8
Baythorn Rd WOL/BIL/BRX NG8... 49 H1
Beackden Cl BPR/DUF DE56 ... 18 C3
Beacon Av LBORO LE11 .... 8 C4
RLBORO LE12 .... 120 D8
RLBORO LE12 .... 112 C2
Beacon Cl COAL LE67 .... 116 C6
GBY/RBY LE6 .... 123 J5
LEIN LE4 .... 124 C1
Beacon Crs COAL LE67 .... 108 F7
Beacon Dr LBORO LE11 .... 9 G8
Beacon Hill Dr HUCK/RAV NG15... 23 G2
Beacon Hill Ri MAPPK/POR/STA NG3 .... 5 L5
Beacon Rd BSTN/STPLFD NG9 ... 63 M1
LBORO LE11 .... 8 C4
RLBORO LE12 .... 111 G6
Beaconsfield Rd LEIW LE3 ..... 131 G3
Beaconsfield St LGEAT NG10 ... 62 C8
NOTTE NG7 .... 36 D7
Beal St LEIS LE2 .... 7 K5
Beamwood Cl DERBYE DE21 ... 44 D6
Bean Cl BLWL NG6 .... 35 K2
Beardall St HUCK/RAV NG15 ... 23 M1
Beardmore Cl DERBYE DE21 ... 44 F8
Beardsley Gdns WBRGFD NG2 ... 50 F5
Beardsley Rd RLBORO LE12 ... 112 C1
Beardsmore Gv HUCK/RAV NG15... 15 K6
Beast Market Hl NOTT NG1 ... 5 G7
Beatrice Rd LEIE LE4 .... 124 F8
Beatty Av LEIE LE5 .... 126 C8
Beatty Rd LEIE LE5 .... 126 C8
RLEINE/SYS LE7 .... 120 F3
Beatty St DERBYSE DE24 ...... 58 D7
Beauchamp Rd RLEIW/BBY LE8 .... 146 D7
Beauclerk Dr ARN NG5 .... 24 C7
Beaufort Av LBORO LE11 ..... 103 L7
Beaufort Cl LEIS LE2 .... 139 H3
RLEIW/RUD NG11 .... 65 G4
Beaufort Dr BSTN/STPLFD NG9 .... 63 G2
Beaufort Rd DERBYSE DE24 ... 71 G5
LEIW LE3 .... 130 E6
Beaufort St DERBYE DE21 ..... 44 B7

Beaufort Wy LEIS LE2 .... 139 H3
Beaulieu Gdns WBRGFD NG2 ... 65 G2
Beaumanor Rd RLBORO LE12 ... 112 A3
Beaumanor Gdns RLBORO LE12... 112 A3
Beaumanor Rd LEIN LE4 ...... 125 K5
Beaumaris Ct DERBYE DE21 ... 59 K2
Beaumaris Crs RLBORO LE12 ... 101 K5
Beaumaris Dr BSTN/STPLFD NG9... 62 F3
CARL NG4 .... 38 F6
Beaumaris Rd RLBORO LE12 ... 113 G7
Beaumont Cl BSTN/STPLFD NG9 .... 48 C6
COT/KEY/RAD NG12 .... 80 C3
Beaumont Gdns WBRGFD NG2 .... 65 H3
Beaumont Gn GBY/RBY LE6 ... 123 K5
Beaumont Leys La LEIN LE4 ... 125 H3
Beaumont Lodge La LEIN LE4 ... 124 F1
Beaumont Rd COAL LE67 ...... 108 A7
LBORO LE11 .... 9 J3
LBORO LE11 .... 103 M7
LEIE LE5 .... 7 L5
RLBORO LE12 .... 105 G7
Beaumont St LEIS LE2 .... 138 E1
WBRGFD NG2 .... 5 L1
Beaumont Wy LEIN LE4 .... 124 E3
Beaurepaire Crs BPR/DUF DE56 .... 17 M2
Beaureper Av DERBYW DE22 ... 43 J4
Beauvale EWD/SEL/PNX NG16 ... 22 A5
Beauvale Crs HUCK/RAV NG15 ... 23 H1
Beauvale Dr ILK DE7 .... 33 J2
Beauvale Ri EWD/SEL/PNX NG16 .... 21 M4
Beauvale Rd HUCK/RAV NG15 ... 23 J1
WBRGFD NG2 .... 51 G6
Beauville Dr LEIN LE4 .... 124 E4
Beaver Cl RLEIW/BBY LE8 ..... 142 D2
Becher St NORM/LIT DE23 ..... 57 L6
Beck Cl LEIS LE2 .... 136 E4
Beckenham Rd NOTTE NG7 .... 4 A3
Beckenham Wy DERBYW DE22 ... 56 F1
Becket St DERBY DE1 .... 2 D4
Beckett St LEIE LE5 .... 126 C7
Beckford Rd WBRGFD NG2 .... 51 K4
Beckhampton Rd ARN NG5 .... 24 E8
Beckingham Rd LEIS LE2 ...... 7 M3
Beckitt Cl DERBYSE DE24 ..... 58 E7
Beckley Rd WOL/BIL/BRX NG8 ... 35 K5
Beckside COT/KEY/RAD NG12 ... 66 A3
Becksitch La BPR/DUF DE56 ... 17 K5
Beck St CARL NG4 .... 38 C7
NOTT NG1 .... 5 J6
Bedale Cl COAL LE67 .... 108 A7
Bedale Cl BSTN/STPLFD NG9 ... 62 E3
Bedale Dr LEIN LE4 .... 125 G2
Bedale Rd ARN NG5 .... 37 G2
Bedarra Gv NOTTE NG7 .... 50 C3
Bede St LEIS LE2 .... 6 B8
Bedford Cl CDON/KEG DE74 ... 86 B6
DERBYW DE22 .... 57 H4
Bedford Ct BSTN/STPLFD NG9 ... 48 C6
Bedford Dr GBY/RBY LE6 ..... 123 K5
Bedford Gv BLWL NG6 .... 36 B2
Bedford Rd WGSTN LE18 ...... 137 L4
Bedford St DERBYW DE22 ..... 57 H4
LBORO LE11 .... 9 J4
LBORO LE11 .... 103 M7
Bedford St North LEI LE1 ..... 7 G3
Bedford St South LEI LE1 ..... 6 F4
Bedlington Gdns MAPPK/POR/STA NG3 .... 37 J6
Beeby Cl RLEINE/SYS LE7 ..... 121 G4
Beeby Rd LEIE LE5 .... 132 B1
RLEINE/SYS LE7 .... 121 H7
RLEINE/SYS LE7 .... 127 L2
Beecham Av MAPPK/POR/STA NG3 .... 37 K8
Beech Av BSTN/STPLFD NG9 ... 63 M2
BWSH/BRSTN DE72 .... 60 A4
BWSH/BRSTN DE72 .... 61 K7
CARL NG4 .... 52 D1
COT/KEY/RAD NG12 .... 80 D5
DERBYSE DE24 .... 58 F8
DERBYW DE22 .... 28 E7
EWD/SEL/PNX NG16 .... 34 F1
GBY/RBY LE6 .... 123 J6
HUCK/RAV NG15 .... 15 L8
LGEAT NG10 .... 47 M8
LGEAT NG10 .... 62 C6
MAPPK/POR/STA NG3 .... 37 L3
MELB/CHEL DE73 .... 82 F7
NOTTE NG7 .... 36 F7
RIPLEY DE5 .... 11 G5
RLBORO LE12 .... 88 B7
Beech Cl BLWL NG6 .... 36 A3
BPR/DUF DE56 .... 18 F7
COAL LE67 .... 116 C7
COT/KEY/RAD NG12 .... 53 K5
COT/KEY/RAD NG12 .... 65 L3
EWD/SEL/PNX NG16 .... 13 M5
Beech Ct DERBYE DE21 .... 59 H3
EWD/SEL/PNX NG16 .... 34 F1
Beechcroft ILK DE7 .... 44 B3
Beechcroft Av DERBYE DE21 ... 130 E7
Beechcroft Rd LEIS LE3 ...... 132 A6
Beechdale Rd WOL/BIL/BRX NG8... 35 L7
WOL/BIL/BRX NG8 .... 49 M1
Beech Dr DERBYW DE22 ...... 43 K7
LEIW LE3 .... 130 B4
RDERBYSW DE65 .... 69 G3
RDERBYSW DE65 .... 70 B7
RLEINE/SYS LE7 .... 120 F5
Beeches Av DERBYE DE21 ..... 59 H4
RLBORO LE12 .... 113 J5
Beeches Rd LBORO LE11 ...... 9 M6
The Beeches HEANOR DE75 ... 20 A7
Beechfield Av LEIE LE4 ...... 119 L8
Beechfield Cl RLEIW/BBY LE8 ... 139 M6
Beech Gdns DERBYSE DE21 ... 58 F8
Beechings Cl RLEIW/BBY LE8 ... 143 J4
Beech La ILK DE7 .... 32 B8
Beechley Dr DERBY DE21 ..... 44 B6
Beech Rd EWD/SEL/PNX NG16 ... 13 L4
LEIS LE2 .... 138 C2
RLEIW/BBY LE8 .... 136 F8
Beech St LEIE LE5 .... 7 M2

Beech Tree Cl RLEIW/BBY LE8 .... 146 E5
Beech Tree Rd COAL LE67 .... 108 E7
Beech Wk NORM/LIT DE23 .... 57 H6
LEIW LE3 .... 126 C1
LEIW LE3 .... 129 K4
RLEINE/SYS LE7 .... 121 H2
RLEINE/SYS LE7 .... 129 K3
Beechwood Av LEIN LE4 ...... 38 F6
LEIW LE3 .... 17 J2
LEIE LE5 .... 133 G2
Beechwood Cl BPR/DUF DE56 ... 17 J2
Beechwood Crs NORM/LIT DE23 .... 57 G6
Beechwood Rd ARN NG5 ...... 25 L7
LEIE LE4 .... 141 M1
Bee Hive La LBORO LE11 ..... 9 J4
Beeley Cl BPR/DUF DE56 ..... 18 A1
DERBYW DE22 .... 43 H5
Beeston Cl BLWL NG6 .... 36 B1
Beestone Cl BLWL NG6 .... 24 C3
Beeston Fields Dr BSTN/STPLFD NG9 .... 49 G7
Beeston La NOTTE NG7 .... 49 L6
Beeston Rd BLWL NG6 .... 50 B6
Beggar's La LEIN LE4 .... 129 G5
Begonia Cl LEIW LE3 .... 129 K5
Beighton St RIPLEY DE5 ...... 11 J6
Belconnen Rd ARN NG5 .... 36 D2
Belfield Rd RDERBYSW DE65 ... 69 G4
Belfield St ILK DE7 .... 33 K5
Belford Cl BLWL NG6 .... 23 K7
Belfry Cl MCKLVR DE3 .... 56 D6
Belfry Dr LEIW LE3 .... 130 A2
Belfry Wy COT/KEY/RAD NG12... 66 A3
Belgrave Av LEIN LE4 .... 125 L4
COAL LE67 .... 109 G6
Belgrave Bvd LEIN LE4 .... 125 J3
Belgrave Cl BPR/DUF DE56 .... 18 A2
Belgrave F/O LEI LE1 .... 7 G2
Belgrave Ga LEI LE1 .... 7 G2
Belgrave Ms CFTN/RUD NG11 ... 65 G4
Belgrave Rd BLWL NG6 .... 23 L8
LEIN LE4 .... 125 L7
Belgrave St NORM/LIT DE23 ... 2 E8
Bellamy Cl LEIS LE2 .... 136 E4
Bellar Ga NOTT NG1 .... 5 K7
Bell Av BWSH/BRSTN DE72 .... 73 L8
Bell Cl GBY/RBY LE6 .... 123 H7
Belle-Isle Rd HUCK/RAV NG15 ... 23 L1
Belleville Dr ARN NG5 .... 24 C7
Belle Vue Av LEIN LE4 .... 125 J5
RIPLEY DE5 .... 11 G5
Bellevue Ct MAPPK/POR/STA NG3... 5 L3
Bellflower Rd LEIE LE5 .... 126 F5
Bellholme Cl LEIN LE4 .... 125 M4
Bellingham Ct DERBYW DE22 ... 43 G5
Bell La CFTN/RUD NG11 .... 50 F8
ILK DE7 .... 31 L3
LEIE LE5 .... 7 J4
RLEIW/BAR LE9 .... 136 A3
Belimore Gdns WOL/BIL/BRX NG8 .... 49 H2
Bells La WOL/BIL/BRX NG8 .... 35 L4
Bell St CARL NG4 .... 38 B7
WGSTN LE18 .... 138 B4
Belmont Av BLWL NG6 .... 24 A8
BWSH/BRSTN DE72 .... 61 J7
Belmont Cl BSTN/STPLFD NG9 ... 62 F3
HUCK/RAV NG15 .... 23 L3
Belmont Dr BWSH/BRSTN DE72... 59 M6
Belmont St LEIS LE2 .... 131 H8
Belmont Wy LBORO LE11 ...... 102 F5
Belper Av CARL NG4 .... 38 B6
Belper Cl ILK DE7 .... 33 K8
WGSTN LE18 .... 137 L7
Belper Crs CARL NG4 .... 38 B6
Belper La BPR/DUF DE56 ..... 17 J1
Belper Rd BPR/DUF DE56 ..... 43 K7
DERBY DE1 .... 31 L6
ILK DE7 .... 4 B2
NOTTE NG7 .... 33 K8
Belper St ILK DE7 .... 125 M4
LEIN LE4 .... 22 E8
Belsay Rd ARN NG5 .... 56 D3
Belsford Cl EWD/SEL/PNX NG16... 22 E7
Belsize Cl DERBYW DE22 ..... 56 D1
Belton Cl COAL LE67 .... 109 G6
LGEAT NG10 .... 61 M3
WGSTN LE18 .... 137 K2
Belton Dr WBRGFD NG2 .... 64 F3
Belton Rd LBORO LE11 .... 103 L2
LEIW LE3 .... 130 E7
Belton Rd West LBORO LE11 ... 103 J1
Belton St NOTTE NG7 .... 36 D7
RLBORO LE12 .... 101 M3
Belvedere Av NOTTE NG7 ..... 36 D7
Belvedere Cl COT/KEY/RAD NG12 .... 80 C3
MCKLVR DE3 .... 56 B4
Belvoir Cl BWSH/BRSTN DE72 ... 61 G8
ILK DE7 .... 47 H1
LEIS LE2 .... 139 G3
LGEAT NG10 .... 76 C2
RLBORO LE12 .... 113 H7
Belvoir Dr LBORO LE11 .... 103 K8
LEIS LE2 .... 137 G1
RLEINE/SYS LE7 .... 121 G3
Belvoir Dr East LEIS LE2 ..... 137 H1
Belvoir Hl WBRGFD NG2 ...... 51 K3
Belvoir Rd CARL NG4 .... 38 E8
COAL LE67 .... 108 A6
WBRGFD NG2 .... 51 L6
Belvoir St HUCK/RAV NG15 ... 15 K7
LEI LE1 .... 6 F4
MAPPK/POR/STA NG3 .... 37 K5
NORM/LIT DE23 .... 57 K5
Belvoir Wy RLBORO LE12 ..... 101 L5
Belward St NOTT NG1 .... 5 K7
Belwood Cl CFTN/RUD NG11 ... 64 D5
Beman Cl LEIN LE4 .... 126 C2
Bembridge Ct BSTN/STPLFD NG9 .... 48 D7
DERBYSE DE24 .... 73 G2
Bembridge Dr ARN NG5 .... 36 F1
Bembridge Rd LEIW LE3 ...... 125 G7
Bemrose Rd DERBYSE DE24 ... 58 C8
Benbow Av MELB/CHEL DE73 ... 82 E7

Bencroft Cl *RLEINE/SYS* LE7 .... 124 B1
Bendall Gn *NORM/LIT* DE23 .... 71 G2
Bendbow Ri *LEIW* LE3 .... 130 C4
Bendigo La *WBRGFD* NC2 .... 51 L4
Benington Dr *WOL/BIL/BRX* NG8... 49 G4
Benmore Ct *DERBYE* DE21 .... 44 F4 🄰
Benner Av *ILK* DE7 .... 47 L2
Bennerley Av *ILK* DE7 .... 33 K3
Bennerley Rd *BLWL* NG6 .... 23 K7
Bennett Ri *RLEIW/BAR* LE9 .... 135 J2
Bennett Rd
  MAPPK/POR/STA NG3 .... 37 L2
Bennett's La *RLBORO* LE12 .... 114 B7
Bennett St *DERBYSE* DE24 .... 72 B2
  LGEAT NG10 .... 61 M1
  LGEAT NG10 .... 62 A5
Bennett Wy *WGSTN* LE18 .... 137 L5
Benneworth Cl *HUCK/RAV* NG15 ... 23 K2
Bennion Rd *LEIN* LE4 .... 124 E3
  RLEINE/SYS LE7 .... 133 L3
Benscliffe Dr *LBORO* LE11 .... 8 C7
Benscliffe Rd *GBY/RBY* LE6......... 117 H1
Benskins Ov *LEIN* LE4 .... 119 C8
Benskyn Cl *RLEIW/BBY* LE8 .... 143 H3
Bensley Cl *MELB/CHEL* DE73... 72 E6
Benson St *DERBYSE* DE24 .... 58 C8
  LEIE LE5 .... 132 C2
Ben St *NOTTE* NG7 .... 4 A3
Bentfield Rd *BPR/DUF* DE56....... 10 A6
Bentinck Av *COT/KEY/RAD* NG12... 66 B6
Bentinck Rd *CARL* NG4 .... 38 A5
  NOTTE NG7 .... 4 A3
Bentinck St *HUCK/RAV* NG15 ..... 15 K7
Bentingham Rd *LEIS* LE2 .... 137 H3
Bentley Av
  MAPPK/POR/STA NG3 .... 51 L1
Bentley Rd *CDON/KEG* DE74 ..... 84 D3
  LEIN LE4 .... 119 L7
  RDERBYSW DE65 .... 68 C6 🄰
Bentley St *DERBYSE* DE24 .... 72 C1
Bentwell Av *ARN* NG5 .... 25 L8
Beresford Dr *DERBYE* DE21 .... 59 J3 🄰
  ILK DE7 .... 33 J2
  LEIS LE2 .... 132 B7
Beresford Rd *LGEAT* NG10 .... 75 L2
Beresford St *NOTTE* NG7 .... 50 C2 🄰
Berkeley Av *LGEAT* NG10 .... 76 A2
  MAPPK/POR/STA NG3 .... 37 G7
Berkeley Cl *LEIS* LE2 .... 139 H2
  NORM/LIT DE23 .... 57 H8
Berkeley Rd *LBORO* LE11 .... 103 C7
Berkley St *LEI* LE1 .... 6 D3
Berkshire Rd *LEIS* LE2 .... 131 H8
Berkshire St *DERBYE* DE21 .... 44 B7
Berle Av *HEANOR* DE75 .... 20 C4
Bermuda Dr *DERBYE* DE21 .... 44 A1 🄰
Bernard Av *HUCK/RAV* NG15..... 15 M6
Bernard St *ARN* NG5 .... 36 F6
Berners St *LEI* LE1 .... 7 K6
Bernisdale Cl *ARN* NG5 .... 24 D5
Berridge Dr *LEIS* LE2 .... 138 F1 🄰
Berridge La *LEIN* LE4 .... 125 M4
Berridge Rd *NOTTE* NG7 .... 36 C8
Berridge Rd West *NOTTE* NG7 ... 36 C8
Berridge St *LEI* LE1 .... 6 E6 🄰
Berriedale Cl *LEIE* LE5 .... 26 A7 🄰
Berrington Cl *LEIE* LE5 .... 126 C7 🄰
  RLEIW/BAR LE9 .... 128 A1
Berrisford St *COAL* LE67 .... 108 A7
Berrycott La *RLBORO* LE12 .... 106 E7
Berrydown Cl *WOL/BIL/BRX* NG8.. 35 M6
Berry Hill Gv *CARL* NG4 .... 38 C5
Berry's La *GBY/RBY* LE6 .... 123 C7
Berwick Av *DERBYE* DE21 .... 44 A8
Berwick Cl *ARN* NG5 .... 37 G1
  DERBYSE DE24 .... 72 F2
Berwick Dr *DERBYSE* DE24 .... 71 H4
Berwin Cl *LGEAT* NG10 .... 61 L6 🄰
Beryldene Av
  EWD/SEL/PNX NG16 .... 22 E8
Besecar Av *CARL* NG4 .... 38 C5 🄰
Besecar Cl *CARL* NG4 .... 38 C5
Bessabone Dr *BPR/DUF* DE56 ... 17 L2
Bessell La *BSTN/STPLFD* NG9 ... 62 A2
Best Cl *WGSTN* LE18 .... 137 K6
Besthorpe Ct *DERBYE* DE21 ..... 44 F6
Bestwick Av *HEANOR* DE75 ...... 20 F6 🄰
Bestwood Av *ARN* NG5 .... 25 J7
Bestwood Cl *ARN* NG5 .... 25 J7
Bestwood Lodge Dr *ARN* NG5 ... 25 G6
Bestwood Park Dr *ARN* NG5 ..... 24 F7
Bestwood Park Dr West
  ARN NG5 .... 24 D6
Bestwood Rd *BLWL* NG6 .... 24 B7
  HUCK/RAV NG15.................... 24 A1
Bestwood Ter *BLWL* NG6 .... 24 B7
Bethel Gdns *HUCK/RAV* NG15 ... 23 G2 🄰
Bethulie Rd *NORM/LIT* DE23 ..... 57 L7
Betula Cl *CFTN/RUD* NG11 .... 64 A6 🄰
Bevan Rd *LEIN* LE4 .... 119 C8
Beveridge Sr *RLBORO* LE12...... 105 H8
Beverley Av *LEIN* LE4 .... 125 M6 🄰
Beverley Cl *LEIN* LE4 .... 120 C8
  WOL/BIL/BRX NG8 .... 48 F5 🄰
Beverley Dr *EWD/SEL/PNX* NG16... 22 C2 🄰
  RLEIW/BAR LE9 .... 141 J8 🄰
Beverley Gdns *CARL* NG4 .... 38 D6
Beverley Rd *CDON/KEG* DE74... 85 H7
Beverley St *DERBYSE* DE24 ...... 58 B5 🄰
Bevington Cl *GBY/RBY* LE6 .... 122 C7
Bewcastle Gv *LEIN* LE4 .... 125 H2
Bewcastle Rd *ARN* NG5 .... 24 E6 🄰
Bewdley Cl *MELB/CHEL* DE73 ... 72 E4
Bewick Dr *MAPPK/POR/STA* NG3.. 52 A2
Bewicke Rd *LEIW* LE3 .... 130 F5
Bexhill Ri *LEIE* LE5 .... 127 J8 🄰
Bexwell Cl *CFTN/RUD* NG11 ..... 64 C7
Biam Wy *LEIW* LE3 .... 130 E7
Biant Cl *WOL/BIL/BRX* NG8 .... 35 M4
Bicester Av *DERBYSE* DE24 ...... 71 G5
Bickley Moss *DERBYE* DE21 ..... 44 F6
Biddle Rd *LEIW* LE3 .... 124 F8
  RLEIW/BAR LE9 .... 142 A1
Biddulph Av *LEIE* LE5 .... 7 M8 🄰
Biddulph St *LEIS* LE2 .... 7 L8
Bideford Cl *RIPLEY* DE5 .... 11 G5
  WGSTN LE18 .... 138 B8

Bideford Dr *NORM/LIT* DE23........ 71 H1
Bideford Rd *LEIE* LE5 .... 133 H4
Bidford Cl *LEIW* LE3 .... 130 C5
Bidford Rd *LEIW* LE3 .... 130 C5
  WOL/BIL/BRX NG8 .... 49 G4
Bidwell Crs *CFTN/RUD* NG11 .... 77 M5
Biggart Cl *BSTN/STPLFD* NG9 ... 63 G5
Biggin Hill Rd *LEIE* LE5 .... 132 F4
Biggin St *LBORO* LE11 .... 9 J2
The Biggin *CDON/KEG* DE74 ..... 84 F4 🄰
Bigg's Cl *RLEIW/BBY* LE8 .... 142 E2
Big La *RLBORO* LE12 .... 106 A5
Bignal Dr *LEIW* LE3 .... 129 M3
Bilberry Cl *LEIW* LE3 .... 136 E1
Bilborough Rd
  WOL/BIL/BRX NG8 .... 48 F2 🄰
Billesdon Dr *ARN* NG5 .... 36 D3
Billington Cl *LEIN* LE4 .... 125 J4
Bilsdale Rd *WGSTN* LE18 .... 138 D6 🄰
Bindley La *RLEIW/BBY* LE8 .... 139 L6
Bingham Rd *ARN* NG5 .... 37 G5
  COT/KEY/RAD NG12 .... 53 K4
  COT/KEY/RAD NG12 .... 67 K4
Bingham St *DERBYSE* DE24 ...... 72 C1
Bingley Rd *RLEIW/BAR* LE9 ...... 141 M1
Binscombe La *DERBYE* DE21 .... 44 D4
Birch Av *BSTN/STPLFD* NG9 ..... 63 M3
  CARL NG4 .... 38 B8
  COAL LE67 .... 108 E3
  EWD/SEL/PNX NG16 .... 34 F1
  ILK DE7 .... 33 L8 🄰
  RLBORO LE12 .... 105 H6
Birch Cl *COAL* LE67 .... 122 C1
  DERBYE DE21 .... 59 L1
  LEIN LE4 .... 126 B6
  RIPLEY DE5 .... 11 H7
  RLBORO LE12 .... 111 L1
Birchdale Av *HUCK/RAV* NG15 ... 23 L2
Birches Rd *DERBYW* DE22 .... 43 H4
Birchfield Av *COAL* LE67 .... 116 B7
Birchfield Cl *MELB/CHEL* DE73 .. 72 D5
Birchfield Pk *HEANOR* DE75 ..... 20 D8
Birchfield Rd *ARN* NG5 .... 25 L6
Birch Lea *ARN* NG5 .... 25 H7
  RLBORO LE12 .... 88 B6
Birchover Pl *ILK* DE7 .... 33 J2 🄰
Birchover Ri *DERBYE* DE21 .... 59 J3
Birchover Rd *WOL/BIL/BRX* NG8 .. 49 G2
Birchover Wy *DERBYW* DE22 ..... 43 H6
Birch Tree Av *RLEINE/SYS* LE7 ... 119 L6
Birchtree Rd *WGSTN* LE18 .... 138 B3 🄰
Birchview Cl *BPR/DUF* DE56 ..... 17 M5 🄰
Birchwood *HEANOR* DE75 .... 20 A3
Birchwood Av
  BWSH/BRSTN DE72 .... 61 K8
  LGEAT NG10 .... 76 A1
  NORM/LIT DE23 .... 71 H1
Birchwood Cl *LEIW* LE3 .... 129 K5
Birchwood Rd
  WOL/BIL/BRX NG8 .... 35 H8
Bircumshaw's Rd
  HEANOR DE75 .... 20 C5 🄰
Birdcage Wk *DERBYW* DE22 ..... 56 D1
Birdcroft La *ILK* DE7 .... 47 K2
Bird Hill Rd *RLBORO* LE12 .... 111 K5
Birdie Cl *RLEIW/BBY* LE8 .... 146 F7 🄰
Birdsall Av *WOL/BIL/BRX* NG8.. 49 J3
Birds Nest Av *LEIW* LE5 .... 124 D7
Birdwood St *NORM/LIT* DE23 .... 57 K6 🄰
Birkdale Av *LEIE* LE5 .... 132 B6
Birkdale Cl *COT/KEY/RAD* NG12 ... 65 L5
  ILK DE7 .... 33 H6
  MCKLVR DE3 .... 56 E5 🄰
Birkdale Rd *RLEINE/SYS* LE7 ..... 124 A1
Birkdale Wy *ARN* NG5 .... 24 D7 🄰
Birkenshaw Rd *LEIW* LE3 .... 124 E6
Birkin Av *BSTN/STPLFD* NG9 .... 62 E5 🄰
  CFTN/RUD NG11 .... 65 G7
  COT/KEY/RAD NG12 .... 53 L3
  NOTTE NG7 .... 4 A2
Birkland Av
  MAPPK/POR/STA NG3 .... 37 L3
  NOTT NG1 .... 5 G3
Birley St *BSTN/STPLFD* NG9 ..... 62 B2
Birling Cl *BLWL* NG6 .... 23 J8
Birrell Rd *NOTTE* NG7 .... 36 E7
Birsmore Av *LEIN* LE4 .... 126 B3
Birstall Rd *LEIN* LE4 .... 125 L2
Birstall St *LEI* LE1 .... 7 K2
Biscay Ct *DERBYE* DE21 .... 45 G5 🄰
Bisham Dr *WBRGFD* NG2 .... 51 M8
Bishop Dl *COAL* LE67 .... 100 B8
Bishopdale Cl *LGEAT* NG10 ...... 75 L1
Bishopdale Dr
  EWD/SEL/PNX NG16 .... 22 E5 🄰
Bishopdale La *LEIN* LE4 .... 125 G4
Bishop Meadow Rd
  LBORO LE11 .... 103 J1
Bishops Cl *COT/KEY/RAD* NG12 ... 80 C3
Bishops Ct *MELB/CHEL* DE73 ... 82 F8 🄰
Bishop's Dr *DERBYE* DE21 .... 44 E6
Bishop St *EWD/SEL/PNX* NG16 .. 21 K5 🄰
  LBORO LE11 .... 9 L2
  LEI LE1 .... 7 K2
Bishops Wy *HUCK/RAV* NG15 ... 15 M6
Bisley St *LEIS* LE2 .... 131 H4
Bispham Dr *BSTN/STPLFD* NG9 ... 62 D4
Blaby By-pass *RLEIW/BBY* LE8.. 136 E8
Blaby Cl *NORM/LIT* DE23 .... 71 H1
Blaby Rd *RLEIW/BAR* LE9 .... 135 M4
  WGSTN LE18 .... 137 L6
Blackberry La *RLEINE/SYS* LE7 ... 114 C7
Blackberry Wy *BPR/DUF* DE56... 18 D5
Blackbird Av *LEIE* LE5 .... 124 D7
Blackbird La *LEIN* LE4 .... 6 B1
Blackbird Rw *BPR/DUF* DE56 .... 18 A6
Blackbrook Cl *RLBORO* LE12 ..... 101 L4 🄰
Blackbrook Dr *COAL* LE67 .... 108 F7
Blackbrook Rd *LBORO* LE11 .... 8 A5
Blackburn Pl *ILK* DE7 .... 33 J4 🄰
Blackett Av *LEIW* LE3 .... 124 E7 🄰
Blackfriars Cl
  WOL/BIL/BRX NG8 .... 35 H4 🄰
Blackfriars St *LEI* LE1 .... 6 C5
Blackham Rd *LBORO* LE11 .... 9 H8
Blackhill Dr *CARL* NG4 .... 38 D7

Black Hills Dr *ILK* DE7 .... 47 L5 🄰
Black La *RLBORO* LE12 .... 105 L3
Blackmore Br *LEIS* LE2 .... 130 E2
Blackmore St *NORM/LIT* DE23 ... 57 K8
Blackmount Ct
  DERBYE DE21 .... 71 H4 🄰
Blackrod Cl *BSTN/STPLFD* NG9 ... 62 E5 🄰
Blacksmiths Av
  RLBORO LE12 .... 102 A2 🄰
Blackstone Wk *WBRGFD* NG2... 51 G5
Blackthorn Cl *DERBYE* DE21 ..... 44 C5 🄰
  MELB/CHEL DE73 .... 82 E7 🄰
Blackthorn La *LEIN* LE4 .... 124 D1
  RLEINE/SYS LE7 .... 120 C4
Blackthorne Cl
  BPR/DUF DE56 .... 18 D5 🄰
Blackthorne Dr *BLWL* NG6 .... 35 M4
  EWD/SEL/PNX NG16 .... 21 J5
Blackthorn La *LEIS* LE2 .... 132 F7
Blackthorn Wk *LEIE* LE5 .... 123 M8
Blackwell Rd *WGSTN* LE18 .... 138 C6 🄰
Blackwell Rd *MELB/CHEL* DE73.. 82 F8
Blackwood *COAL* LE67 .... 108 F5
Bladen Cl *RLEIW/BBY* LE8 .... 143 H3
Bladon Cl *MAPPK/POR/STA* NG3 .. 37 J5
Bladon Rd *CFTN/RUD* NG11 ..... 64 F8
Blagreaves Av *NORM/LIT* DE23 .. 71 G2
Blagreaves La *NORM/LIT* DE23... 57 C8
Blair Cl *RLBORO* LE12 .... 113 C7
Blair Gv *LGEAT* NG10 .... 61 L3
Blairmore Rd *LEIW* LE3 .... 130 A1 🄰
Blaise Cl *CFTN/RUD* NG11 .... 64 C7 🄰
Blaise Gv *LEIN* LE4 .... 126 B2
Blakebrook Dr
  MELB/CHEL DE73 .... 72 E4 🄰
Blake Cl *ARN* NG5 .... 25 L8
Blake Cl *LGEAT* NG10 .... 75 M2 🄰
  RLEIW/BAR LE9 .... 135 L4
Blake Dr *LBORO* LE11 .... 103 J2
Blakeley La *RDERBYSW* DE65 ... 68 F5
Blakelow Dr *RDERBYSW* DE65 ... 68 F4 🄰
Blakemore Av
  MELB/CHEL DE73 .... 82 F7 🄰
Blakeney Ct *DERBYE* DE21 .... 45 C6
Blakeney Rd
  COT/KEY/RAD NG12 .... 53 M4
  WBRGFD NG2 .... 51 L7
Blakenhall Cl *RLEIW/BAR* LE9 ... 135 K7 🄰
Blakenhall Rd *LEIE* LE5 .... 132 E2
Blake St *BSTN/STPLFD* NG9 ..... 62 C1
  WBRGFD NG2 .... 51 L8
Blakesley Rd *WGSTN* LE18 .... 138 D4
Blake St *ILK* DE7 .... 33 K6
  LEI LE1 .... 6 E4
Blanch Cft *MELB/CHEL* DE73 .... 82 F8
Blandford Av *LGEAT* NG10 .... 75 M2
Blandford Cl *DERBYSE* DE24 .... 73 H1
Blandford Rd *BSTN/STPLFD* NG9 .. 63 C2
Bland La *CALV/BJ* NG14 .... 27 L2
Bland Rd *LEIW* LE3 .... 124 D7
Blandford Gdns *WBRGFD* NG2 ... 65 G2
Blankley Dr *LEIS* LE2 .... 132 B6
Blanklyn Av *LEIE* LE5 .... 132 B2
Blankney Cl *DERBYSE* DE24 ..... 71 H5
Blankney St *BLWL* NG6 .... 36 C3
Blantyre Av *BLWL* NG6 .... 24 C6 🄰
Blaydon Cl *LEIW* LE3 .... 124 F7
Bleaberry Cl *WBRGFD* NG2 ...... 66 A2 🄰
Bleachers Yd *NOTTE* NG7 .... 36 C6
Bleakmoor Cl *RLEINE/SYS* LE7 ... 115 L4
Bleasby Cl *LEIN* LE4 .... 126 E3 🄰
Bleasby St *WBRGFD* NG2 .... 51 K3 🄰
Bleasdale Cl *CARL* NG4 .... 38 E5 🄰
Blencathra Cl *WBRGFD* NG2 ..... 66 A2
Blencathra Dr *MCKLVR* DE3 ..... 56 C7
Blenheim Av
  MAPPK/POR/STA NG3 .... 38 A5
Blenheim Cl *CFTN/RUD* NG11 ... 64 F8 🄰
  LBORO LE11 .... 103 C3
  WGSTN LE18 .... 137 K7
Blenheim Ct *BPR/DUF* DE56 ..... 18 B2 🄰
Blenheim Crs *RLEIW/BAR* LE9 ... 141 H8
Blenheim Dr *BSTN/STPLFD* NG9 .. 63 C2
  DERBYW DE22 .... 43 G4
Blenheim La *BLWL* NG6 .... 23 J3
Blenheim Pde *DERBYW* DE22 ... 43 J5 🄰
Blenheim Rd *LEIN* LE4 .... 119 M7
Blenheim Wy *LEIN* LE4 .... 125 J3
Blenheim St *LGEAT* NG10 .... 61 M3 🄰
Bley Av *RLBORO* LE12 .... 88 B7
Blidworth Rd
  WOL/BIL/BRX NG8 .... 35 H5 🄰
Blind La *BWSH/BRSTN* DE72 .... 61 H7
Blissett Rd *LEIW* LE3 .... 130 A1
Blithe Rd *RDERBYSW* DE65 ...... 68 C6 🄰
Blithfield Av *LBORO* LE11 .... 102 F4
Blithfield Gdns
  MELB/CHEL DE73 .... 72 E5 🄰
Bloomfield Cl *DERBY* DE1 .... 3 H8
  RDERBYSW DE65 .... 68 B8
Bloomfield Rd *LEIS* LE2 .... 131 K8
Bloomfield St *DERBY* DE1 .... 3 J7 🄰
Bloomsbury Dr
  EWD/SEL/PNX NG16 .... 33 K5
Bloomsgrove Rd *ILK* DE7 .... 33 K5 🄰
Bloomsgrove St *NOTTE* NG7 ...... 4 B6 🄰
The Blossoms *COAL* LE67 .... 122 C1
Blount St *LEI* LE1 .... 126 D1
Bloxams Ct *LEIW* LE5 .... 136 D1
Bloxham St *LEIE* LE5 .... 124 F8
Blue Banks Av *LEIE* LE5 .... 136 E4
Bluebell Cl *DERBYSE* DE24 ...... 71 G5
  EWD/SEL/PNX NG16 .... 13 K5 🄰
  HUCK/RAV NG15.................... 23 G1
  RLEINE/SYS LE7 .... 121 J1
  RLEIW/BAR LE9 .... 129 J1 🄰
Bluebell Dr *LBORO* LE11 .... 8 E8
  WGSTN LE18 .... 137 K3
Blue Bell Hill Rd
  MAPPK/POR/STA NG3 .... 5 M3
Bluebird Dr *DERBYSE* DE24 ...... 71 H3 🄰
Bluecoat Ct *NOTT* NG1 .... 5 G4
Bluecoat St *NOTT* NG1 .... 5 G4
Blue Gates Rd *LEIE* LE5 .... 124 D2
Blue Pots Cl *LEIW* LE3 .... 129 J5
Blundell Cl
  MAPPK/POR/STA NG3 .... 37 K7
Blundell Rd *LEIE* LE5 .... 132 E4
Blunt's La *WGSTN* LE18 .... 138 B5

Blunt St *ILK* DE7 .... 31 L5 🄰
Blyth Gdns
  MAPPK/POR/STA NG3 .... 37 J5 🄰
Blyth Pl *DERBYE* DE21 .... 44 B6 🄰
Blyth St *MAPPK/POR/STA* NG3 ... 37 J6
Blyton Wk *ARN* NG5 .... 24 F3 🄰
Boat La *EWD/SEL/PNX* NG16 .... 12 E8
Boatmans Cl *ILK* DE7 .... 33 K5
Bobbers Mill Br *NOTTE* NG7 ..... 36 B8
Bobbers Mill Rd *NOTTE* NG7 .... 36 C8
Boden Dr *EWD/SEL/PNX* NG16... 35 G1
Bodenham Cl *WGSTN* LE18 ...... 138 A7 🄰
Boden St *NORM/LIT* DE23 .... 2 C8 🄰
  NOTTE NG7 .... 4 B5
Bodicote Cl *RLEINE/SYS* LE8 .... 142 D2 🄰
Bodmin Av *HUCK/RAV* NG15 ..... 23 G2
  WGSTN LE18 .... 138 A7
Bodmin Cl *DERBYSE* DE24 .... 71 H4 🄰
Bodmin Dr *WOL/BIL/BRX* NG8 ... 36 A5
Bodnant Av *LEIE* LE5 .... 132 C4
Body Rd *BSTN/STPLFD* NG9 ..... 62 F4
Bohem Rd *LGEAT* NG10 .... 62 A4
Bold Cl *BLWL* NG6 .... 23 M7
Bold La *DERBY* DE1 .... 2 E5
Bolero Cl *WOL/BIL/BRX* NG8 ..... 49 J2 🄰
Bolingey Wy *HUCK/RAV* NG15... 23 G2
Bollard's La *RLBORO* LE12 .... 86 E8
Bollington Rd *LEIS* LE2 .... 139 G1
Bolsover Cl *RIPLEY* DE5 .... 11 J6
Bolsover St *HUCK/RAV* NG15 ... 15 M8
  LEIE LE5 .... 132 C1
Bolton Av *BSTN/STPLFD* NG9 ... 63 G3
Bolton Cl *WBRGFD* NG2 .... 51 L8 🄰
Bolton Rd *LEIW* LE3 .... 131 G2
Bolton Ter *COT/KEY/RAD* NG12 ... 53 K4
Bonchurch Cl *COAL* LE67 .... 108 C2
  DERBYSE DE24 .... 73 G2 🄰
Bonchurch St *LEIE* LE5 .... 6 A2
Bond Cl *LBORO* LE11 .... 9 L3
Bondgate *CDON/KEG* DE74 ...... 84 F4
Bondland La *BPR/DUF* DE56 ..... 10 C5
Bond La *RLEINE/SYS* LE7 .... 113 C5
Bondman Cl *LEIN* LE4 .... 125 J2 🄰
Bond St *ARN* NG5 .... 25 J7
  WBRGFD NG2 .... 5 L7
Bonetti Cl *ARN* NG5 .... 38 A2 🄰
Bonington Cl *BLWL* NG6 .... 35 L1
Bonington Dr *ARN* NG5 .... 25 K8
Bonington Rd
  MAPPK/POR/STA NG3 .... 37 L4 🄰
Bonner Cl *LEIS* LE2 .... 139 H3
Bonner Hl *CALV/BJ* NG14 .... 26 D1
Bonners La *LEIS* LE2 .... 6 D8
Bonner's Rd
  EWD/SEL/PNX NG16 .... 33 M3
Bonney Rd *LEIW* LE3 .... 124 E6
Bonnie Prince Charlie Wk
  DERBYW 56 C1
Bonnington Crs *ARN* NG5 .... 37 G3
Bonnington Rd *LEIS* LE2 .... 131 M6
Bonny Md *COT/KEY/RAD* NG12 ... 67 J6
Bonnyrigg Dr *DERBYE* DE21 .... 44 E5 🄰
Bonsall Av *NORM/LIT* DE23 ...... 57 H7
Bonsall Dr *MCKLVR* DE3 .... 56 C4
Bonsall St *LEIS* LE2 .... 7 M8
  LGEAT NG10 .... 62 C7
Bonser Cl *CARL* NG4 .... 38 C8
Bonville Pl *LEIW* LE3 .... 130 F6
Booth Cl *LEIE* LE5 .... 132 F2
  MAPPK/POR/STA NG3 .... 5 J3
Boothgate *BPR/DUF* DE56 .... 18 C1
Booth Rd *COAL* LE67 .... 100 B7
Booth St *DERBYSE* DE24 .... 58 D8
  RIPLEY DE5 .... 11 J5
Border Crs *DERBYSE* DE24 ...... 72 F3
Border Dr *LEIN* LE4 .... 125 H2
Borlace Crs *BSTN/STPLFD* NG9 ... 62 C1 🄰
Borlace St *LEIW* LE3 .... 6 A4
Borman Cl *BLWL* NG6 .... 35 K2
Borough St *CDON/KEG* DE74 ... 84 F4
  CDON/KEG DE74 .... 86 B5
Borrowash By-pass
  DERBYE DE21 .... 58 F4
Borrowash Rd *DERBYE* DE21 ... 59 K4
Borrowcup Cl *RLEIW/BBY* LE8 ... 143 C3
Borrowdale Cl *WBRGFD* NG2 ... 66 B3 🄰
Borrowdale Dr *LGEAT* NG10 .... 75 L1
Borrowell *CDON/KEG* DE74 ...... 86 B3 🄰
Borrowfield Rd *DERBYE* DE21 ... 59 J4
Borrowfields
  BWSH/BRSTN DE72 .... 59 M6 🄰
Boscastle Rd *DERBYSE* DE24 ... 72 F1
Bosden Cl *WOL/BIL/BRX* NG8 ... 49 H1 🄰
Bosley Sq *BSTN/STPLFD* NG9 ... 49 L7 🄰
Bostock's La *BWSH/BRSTN* DE72.. 61 K3
  LGEAT NG10 .... 62 A1
Boston Ct *DERBYE* DE21 .... 59 G1
Boston Rd *LEIN* LE4 .... 124 D3
Boston St *NOTT* NG1 .... 5 K7
Boswell Sq *NORM/LIT* DE23 ..... 57 K8
Boswell St *NOTTE* NG7 .... 50 C2 🄰
  RLEIW/BAR LE9 .... 135 L6
Bosworth Av *NORM/LIT* DE23 ... 71 J1 🄰
Bosworth Dr
  EWD/SEL/PNX NG16 .... 21 M4
Bosworth Rd *CDON/KEG* DE74 ... 84 D4
Bosworth St *LEIW* LE3 .... 6 A5
Bosworth Wy *LGEAT* NG10 ...... 76 B2
Botany Av *MAPPK/POR/STA* NG3 .. 37 J7
Botany Cl *CFTN/RUD* NG11 ...... 65 G4 🄰
Botany Dr *ILK* DE7 .... 33 K2
Botcheston Rd *GBY/RBY* LE6 ... 128 B1
Bothe Cl *LGEAT* NG10 .... 76 A1
Bottleacre La *LBORO* LE11 .... 103 K5
Botts Wy *COAL* LE67 .... 108 D8
Boulder La *LEIS* LE2 .... 137 K1
Boulter Crs *WGSTN* LE18 .... 138 B4
Boulton Cl *LEIS* LE2 .... 139 J3
Boulton Dr *DERBYSE* DE24 ...... 72 E1
Boulton La *DERBYSE* DE24 ...... 72 E1
  DERBYSE DE24 .... 72 E1
Boundary Crs *BSTN/STPLFD* NG9.. 49 K6
Boundary La
  EWD/SEL/PNX NG16 .... 21 G4 🄰
Boundary Rd *BSTN/STPLFD* NG9 .. 49 K6 🄰
  DERBYW DE22 .... 2 A5
  LEIS LE2 .... 131 H6
  RDERBYSW DE65 .... 69 H7

  RLBORO LE12 .... 113 H6
  WBRGFD NG2 .... 65 J3
Boundary Wy *RLBORO* LE12 ..... 102 A2
Bourne Br *BSTN/STPLFD* NG9 ... 49 H6 🄰
Bourne Ms *CARL* NG4 .... 52 E1
Bourne Sq *BWSH/BRSTN* DE72 ... 61 J7 🄰
Bourne St *CARL* NG4 .... 52 E1
  DERBY DE1 .... 2 F6
Bournmoor Ct *RLEIW/BBY* LE8... 143 C3
Bourton Crs *LEIS* LE2 .... 139 G2
Bovill St *NOTTE* NG7 .... 4 B4
Bowbridge Av *NORM/LIT* DE23 ... 71 G2
Bowden Dr
  BSTN/STPLFD NG9 .... 63 M1 🄰
Bowers Av *MAPPK/POR/STA* NG3... 5 J1
Bower St *DERBYSE* DE24 .... 58 D7
Bowes Well Rd *ILK* DE7 .... 33 J5
Bowhill Gv *LEIE* LE5 .... 133 J1
Bowland Cl
  MAPPK/POR/STA NG3 .... 37 L8 🄰
  MCKLVR DE3 .... 56 C6 🄰
Bowlees Ct *NORM/LIT* DE23 ..... 56 C8 🄰
Bowler Dr *BPR/DUF* DE56 .... 18 E8 🄰
Bowler St *RIPLEY* DE5 .... 11 H8
The Bowley *CDON/KEG* DE74 ... 92 F2
Bowling Aly *BPR/DUF* DE56 ...... 10 C6
Bowling Cl *ILK* DE7 .... 47 J7
Bowling Green St *LEI* LE1 .... 6 F6
Bowlwell Av *ARN* NG5 .... 24 D7
Bowmans Wy *LEIW* LE3 .... 123 M7
Bowmar La *LEIW* LE3 .... 6 C3
Bowmer Rd *DERBYSE* DE24 ..... 58 C5 🄰
Bown Cl *BPR/DUF* DE56 .... 18 E7
Bowness Av *WBRGFD* NG2 .... 66 A5
Bowness Cl *WBRGFD* NG2 .... 52 A8
Bowscale Cl *WBRGFD* NG2 ...... 66 A2 🄰
Boxley Dr *WBRGFD* NG2 .... 65 H3
Boxmoor Cl *NORM/LIT* DE23 .... 56 D8 🄰
Boyce Gdns
  MAPPK/POR/STA NG3 .... 37 K6
Boycroft Av
  MAPPK/POR/STA NG3 .... 37 K6
Boyd Cl *ARN* NG5 .... 25 M6
Boyd Gv *MELB/CHEL* DE73 ...... 72 E7
Boyer St *DERBYW* DE22 .... 2 C8
  LBORO LE11 .... 9 L2
Boyers Wk *LEIW* LE3 .... 129 K4
Boylestone Rd *NORM/LIT* DE23 ... 71 G2
Boynton Dr
  MAPPK/POR/STA NG3 .... 37 K6
Boynton Rd *LEIW* LE3 .... 130 E3
Brabazon Cl *LEIS* LE2 .... 138 D2 🄰
Brabazon Rd *LEIS* LE2 .... 138 D1
Bracadale Rd *ARN* NG5 .... 24 D6 🄰
Bracebridge Dr
  WOL/BIL/BRX NG8 .... 35 H8
  WOL/BIL/BRX NG8 .... 49 H1
Bracey Ri *WBRGFD* NG2 .... 65 J4
Bracken Cl *CARL* NG4 .... 38 B5 🄰
  LEIE LE5 .... 132 F3
  LEIW LE3 .... 129 K5 🄰
  LGEAT NG10 .... 61 M6
  WOL/BIL/BRX NG8 .... 35 K6
Bracken Dl *RLEINE/SYS* LE7 ..... 115 J8
Brackendale Av *ARN* NG5 .... 25 K7
Brackenfield Dr
  EWD/SEL/PNX NG16 .... 21 M8 🄰
Brackenfield Wk *LEIE* LE5 .... 120 D7
Bracken Hl *GBY/RBY* LE6 .... 117 J7
Bracken Rd *LGEAT* NG10 .... 61 M6
Brackens Av *DERBYSE* DE24 .... 72 D1
Brackensdale Av *DERBYW* DE22... 56 F2
Bracken's La *DERBYSE* DE24 ... 72 D1
Brackenthwaite *LEIN* LE4 .... 126 B4
Bracken Wy *COAL* LE67 .... 116 C6
Brackley Dr *DERBYE* DE21 .... 59 J2
Brackley Ga *ILK* DE7 .... 30 E5
Bracknell Crs *WOL/BIL/BRX* NG8 .. 36 B6
Bracknell Dr *DERBYSE* DE24 .... 72 D2
Bracton Dr
  MAPPK/POR/STA NG3 .... 51 L1
Bradbourne Av *CFTN/RUD* NG11 .. 64 E2
Bradbourne Rd *LEIE* LE5 .... 132 B2
Bradbury Cl
  BWSH/BRSTN DE72 .... 60 A6 🄰
  RLEIW/BAR LE9 .... 142 B4
Bradbury St *WBRGFD* NG2 .... 51 L3 🄰
Braddock Cl *NOTTE* NG7 .... 50 C3 🄰
Braddon Av *BSTN/STPLFD* NG9 ... 48 C6
Braddon Rd *LBORO* LE11 .... 103 C1
Bradfield Cl *LEIE* LE5 .... 132 C3
Bradfield Rd *WOL/BIL/BRX* NG8... 35 K6
Bradgate Av *LEIN* LE4 .... 120 D8
Bradgate Cl *LGEAT* NG10 .... 61 M3 🄰
  RLEINE/SYS LE7 .... 133 J1
Bradgate Ct *NORM/LIT* DE23 .... 71 J1 🄰
Bradgate Dr *COAL* LE67 .... 108 F7
  GBY/RBY LE6 .... 123 C6
  RIPLEY DE5 .... 10 F6
  WGSTN LE18 .... 137 M2
Bradgate Hl *GBY/RBY* LE6 .... 116 E8
Bradgate Rd *COAL* LE67 .... 116 C6 🄰
  GBY/RBY LE6 .... 117 K7
  LBORO LE11 .... 103 J7
  NOTTE NG7 .... 36 F6
  RLEINE/SYS LE7 .... 118 C4
Bradgate St *LEIN* LE4 .... 6 A4
Brading Cl *DERBYSE* DE24 .... 73 H2
Brading Rd *LEIW* LE3 .... 125 G7
Bradley Dr *BPR/DUF* DE56 .... 17 M3
Bradley St *DERBYW* DE22 .... 43 J7 🄰
  LGEAT NG10 .... 62 A2
Bradley's Yd
  COT/KEY/RAD NG12 .... 66 C8
Bradley Wk *CFTN/RUD* NG11 ... 64 C7
Bradman Gdns *ARN* NG5 .... 37 M1
Bradmoor Gv
  MELB/CHEL DE73 .... 72 F5 🄰
Bradmore Av
  CFTN/RUD NG11 .... 65 G7 🄰
Bradmore La
  COT/KEY/RAD NG12 .... 80 B2
Bradmore Rd
  COT/KEY/RAD NG12 .... 37 J3 🄰
Bradmore Rd
  COT/KEY/RAD NG12 .... 90 A3
Bradshaw Av *ALFN* DE55 .... 12 B1
  LEIS LE2 .... 137 G4
Bradshaw Cft *BPR/DUF* DE56 ... 17 J1

Bradshaw Dr *BPR/DUF* DE56 ...... 30 A1
Bradshaw St *LGEAT* NG10 ...... 75 M2
Bradshaw Wy *DERBY* DE1 ...... 3 C6
Bradston Rd *LEIS* LE2 ...... 137 J2
Bradwell Cl
  EWD/SEL/PNX NG16 ...... 22 A7 2
  MCKLVR DE3 ...... 56 C6
Bradwell Dr *ARN* NG5 ...... 24 E7
Bradwell Wy *BPR/DUF* DE56 ...... 17 M2
Braefield Cl *ILK* DE7 ...... 47 C2
Braefell Cl *COT/KEY/RAD* NG12 ...... 66 B2
Braemar Av *EWD/SEL/PNX* NG16.. 21 K6
Braemar Cl *DERBYSE* DE24 ...... 71 H4 2
  RLBORO LE12 ...... 113 H7
Braemar Dr *CARL* NG4 ...... 38 F6
  LEIN LE4 ...... 126 A3
Braemar Rd *BLWL* NG6 ...... 24 A8
Brafield Cl *BPR/DUF* DE56 ...... 18 B3
Brailsford Rd *DERBY* DE21 ...... 44 C7
  NOTTE NG7 ...... 50 C6 1
  WGSTN LE18 ...... 137 M3
Brailsford Wy *BSTN/STPLFD* NG9.. 63 C6
Braintree Cl *DERBYE* DE21 ...... 44 B5
Braithwell Dr *DERBYW* DE22 ...... 43 K5 1
Bramall Ct *LEIE* LE5 ...... 126 C8 1
Bramall Rd *LEIE* LE5 ...... 126 B8
Bramber Cl *LEIN* LE4 ...... 126 C1 1
Bramber Gv *CFTN/RUD* NG11 ...... 64 C8 1
Brambleberry Ct
  DERBYE DE21 ...... 44 F4 2
Bramble Cl *BLWL* NG6 ...... 36 B4
  BSTN/STPLFD NG9 ...... 63 H5 1
  LEIE LE5 ...... 127 H5 1
  LGEAT NG10 ...... 61 M6
Bramble Dr
  MAPPK/POR/STA NG3 ...... 37 L8
Bramble Gdns
  WOL/BIL/BRX NG8 ...... 35 M7
Bramble Ms *MCKLVR* DE3 ...... 56 B6 2
Bramble St *DERBY* DE1 ...... 2 D4
Bramble Wy *BPR/DUF* DE56 ...... 18 D5
  LEIW LE3 ...... 124 B8
  LEIW LE3 ...... 130 E6
Brambleway
  COT/KEY/RAD NG12 ...... 67 L5
  LEIE LE5 ...... 132 B1 2
Brambling Rd *LEIE* LE5 ...... 7 M4
Brambling Wy *LEIS* LE2 ...... 138 E3
Bramcote Av *BSTN/STPLFD* NG9 .. 63 H1
Bramcote Dr *BSTN/STPLFD* NG9 ... 49 J8
  WOL/BIL/BRX NG8 ...... 49 H4
Bramcote Dr West
  BSTN/STPLFD NG9 ...... 63 H1
Bramcote La *RLBORO* LE12 ...... 63 G1
  WOL/BIL/BRX NG8 ...... 49 J4
Bramcote Rd *BSTN/STPLFD* NG9 .. 49 J8
  LBORO LE11 ...... 103 K8
  LEIW LE3 ...... 130 F7
  WGSTN LE18 ...... 138 A4
Bramcote St *NOTTE* NG7 ...... 50 C2
Bramerton Rd
  WOL/BIL/BRX NG8 ...... 49 H1
Bramfield Av *DERBYW* DE22 ...... 2 A8
Bramhall Rd *WOL/BIL/BRX* NG8 ... 49 G1
Bramley Cl *DERBYE* DE21 ...... 45 G4 1
  RLEINE/BAR LE9 ...... 141 J8
Bramley Ct *LEIW* LE3 ...... 123 M7
Bramley Orch *RLEINE/SYS* LE7 .. 133 L2
Bramley Rd *LEIN* LE4 ...... 119 M8
  LEIW LE3 ...... 131 G1 1
  LEIW LE3 ...... 130 E1
Brampton Av *HEANOR* DE75 ... 20 E5 2
Brampton Cl *MCKLVR* DE3 ...... 56 A4
Brampton Ct *BPR/DUF* DE56 .. 18 B3 2
Brampton Ct *BSTN/STPLFD* NG9 .. 62 C2
Brampton Wy *LEIS* LE2 ...... 138 D1
Brancaster Cl *BLWL* NG6 ...... 35 M3 1
  LEIN LE4 ...... 125 H5
Brandelhow Ct *DERBYE* DE21 ... 44 F4 2
Brand Hl *RLBORO* LE12 ...... 111 J7
Brandish Crs *CFTN/RUD* NG11 ... 64 B6
Brandon St *LEIN* LE4 ...... 125 L7
Brandreth Av
  MAPPK/POR/STA NG3 ...... 37 J7
Brandreth Dr
  EWD/SEL/PNX NG16 ...... 21 L8
Brand St *WBRGFD* NG2 ...... 51 J5
Branklene Cl
  EWD/SEL/PNX NG16 ...... 22 C8 2
Branksome Av *DERBYSE* DE24 ... 59 G8
Bransdale Cl *LGEAT* NG10 ...... 75 M1
Bransdale Rd *CFTN/RUD* NG11.... 64 B7
  WGSTN LE18 ...... 138 D5
Branston Av *RLBORO* LE12 ...... 105 J7
Branston Gdns *WBRGFD* NG2 ... 65 H3 1
Branston Wk *ARN* NG5 ...... 37 G3 1
Brantford Av *CFTN/RUD* NG11 .... 64 D6
Branting Hi *GBY/RBY* LE6 ...... 123 M4
Branting Hill Av *LEIW* LE3 ...... 123 M5
Branting Hill Gv *LEIW* LE3 ...... 123 M5
Brassington Cl
  EWD/SEL/PNX NG16 ...... 21 M8 2
  ILK DE7 ...... 32 C7
Brassington Rd *DERBY* DE21 .. 44 D6 1
Bratmyr *RLEIW/BBY* LE8 ...... 145 K6 1
Braunstone Av *LEIW* LE3 ...... 130 E5
Braunstone Cl *LEIW* LE3 ...... 130 D6
Braunstone Ga *LEIS* LE2 ...... 6 B7
Braunstone La *LEIW* LE3 ...... 130 E6
Braunstone La East *LEIW* LE3 ... 130 F7
Braunstone Wy *LEIW* LE3 ...... 130 C4
Braunton Av *HUCK/RAV* NG15 .... 23 J4
Braybrooke Rd *LEIN* LE4 ...... 126 C6
Brayfield Av *NORM/LIT* DE23 .... 57 H7
Brayfield Rd *NORM/LIT* DE23 .... 57 G7
Braymish Cl *LEIW* LE3 ...... 124 F7 2
Brayton Crs *BLWL* NG6 ...... 36 B2
Brazil St *LEIS* LE2 ...... 131 J4
Breachfield Rd *RLBORO* LE12 .... 105 H8
Breach La *MELB/CHEL* DE73 .... 82 C6
Breach Rd *COAL* LE67 ...... 108 B8
  HEANOR DE75 ...... 20 E7
  RIPLEY DE5 ...... 19 K3
Breadcroft La *RLBORO* LE12 ...... 105 H4
Breakback Rd *RLBORO* LE12 .... 111 H4
Breaston La *BWSH/BRSTN* DE72.. 61 H3

Brechin Cl *ARN* NG5 ...... 25 M6 2
Breck Hill Rd *ARN* NG5 ...... 37 J3
Breckswood Dr *CFTN/RUD* NG11.. 64 C8
Brecon Cl *DERBYE* DE21 ...... 59 J2
  LGEAT NG10 ...... 61 L7
  WGSTN LE18 ...... 137 K5
  WOL/BIL/BRX NG8 ...... 35 L3
Bredon Cl *LGEAT* NG10 ...... 61 L7
Breech Hedge *RLEINE/SYS* LE7 .. 113 H8
Breedon Av *NORM/LIT* DE23 .... 71 H2
  WGSTN LE18 ...... 138 A4 1
Breedon Hill Rd *NORM/LIT* DE23 .. 2 C8
Breedon La *RLBORO* LE12 ...... 100 B2
Breedon St *LEIS* LE2 ...... 7 L6
  LGEAT NG10 ...... 75 M3
Brendon Cl *RLBORO* LE12 ...... 102 A6
Brendon Dr *EWD/SEL/PNX* NG16 .. 22 D8
  WOL/BIL/BRX NG8 ...... 49 L2
Brendon Gdns
  WOL/BIL/BRX NG8 ...... 49 L2
Brendon Rd *WOL/BIL/BRX* NG8 .. 49 L2
Brendon Wy *LGEAT* NG10 ...... 61 L6
Brentcliffe Av
  MAPPK/POR/STA NG3 ...... 37 L8 2
Brentford Dr *DERBYW* DE22 .... 56 F1
Brent Knowle Gdns *LEIE* LE5 .... 133 H2
Brentwood Dr *LEIS* LE2 ...... 131 L6
Bren Wy *RDERBYSW* DE65 ...... 68 C5
Bressingham Dr
  CFTN/RUD NG11 ...... 65 G4
Bretby Rd *LEIS* LE2 ...... 137 J1
Bretby Sq *NORM/LIT* DE23 ...... 71 H2
Breton Cl *WGSTN* LE18 ...... 144 C4
Brett Cl *HUCK/RAV* NG15 ...... 23 J3
Brettell Rd *LEIS* LE2 ...... 137 H3
Bretton Av *NORM/LIT* DE23 ...... 57 G5
Bretton Cl *LEIN* LE4 ...... 125 J4
Bretton Rd *BPR/DUF* DE56 ...... 18 C2 1
Brewer Cl *LEIN* LE4 ...... 126 C2
Brewery St
  EWD/SEL/PNX NG16 ...... 34 D1 1
Brewsters Rd
  MAPPK/POR/STA NG3 ...... 37 K7
Brex Ri *LEIW* LE3 ...... 130 B1
Breydon Cl *DERBYSE* DE24 ...... 72 B3
Brian Rd *LEIN* LE4 ...... 125 H6
The Brianway *LEIE* LE5 ...... 126 D8
Briar Av *LGEAT* NG10 ...... 61 L4
Briarbank Av
  MAPPK/POR/STA NG3 ...... 37 L7
Briar Cl *BSTN/STPLFD* NG9 ...... 49 J6
  BWSH/BRSTN DE72 ...... 60 A6
  COT/KEY/RAD NG12 ...... 80 D3
  DERBYE DE21 ...... 58 F2
  HUCK/RAV NG15 ...... 23 H2
  LEIS LE2 ...... 138 F3
Briarfield Dr *LEIE* LE5 ...... 127 J6
Briar Ga *COT/KEY/RAD* NG12 .... 67 L5
  LGEAT NG10 ...... 61 L5
Briargate Dr *LEIN* LE4 ...... 119 J7
Briar Lea Cl *DERBYSE* DE24 ...... 71 K3
Briar Meads *LEIS* LE2 ...... 138 F4
Briar Rd *EWD/SEL/PNX* NG16 .... 21 M7
  LEIE LE5 ...... 127 H8
Briarsgate *DERBYW* DE22 ...... 43 H5 1
Briars Wk *RIPLEY* DE5 ...... 11 H7
Briar Wk *LEIS* LE2 ...... 138 F3
Briarwood Av
  MAPPK/POR/STA NG3 ...... 37 L8
Briarwood Wy *NORM/LIT* DE23 .. 71 G1
Brickcliffe Rd *RLBORO* LE12 .... 88 D5 1
Brickenell Rd *CALV/BJ* NG14 .... 26 D1
Bricklin La *ILK* DE7 ...... 30 F7
Brick Kiln La *RLBORO* LE12 ...... 101 L6
Brickley Crs *RLBORO* LE12 ...... 88 D6
Brickman St *LEIW* LE3 ...... 129 J5
Brick Rw *DERBY* DE22 ...... 43 L6
Brickwood Pl *RLBORO* LE12 ...... 97 K8
Brickyard Dr *HUCK/RAV* NG15 .... 24 A2
Brickyard La *BPR/DUF* DE56 ...... 18 D6
  COT/KEY/RAD NG12 ...... 53 M4 1
  RIPLEY DE5 ...... 11 K6
  RLBORO LE12 ...... 87 K7
Brickyard Rd *BPR/DUF* DE56 ...... 10 A3
The Brickyard *ILK* DE7 ...... 31 M6
Bridevale Rd *LEIS* LE2 ...... 137 J2 1
Bridge Av *BSTN/STPLFD* NG9 .... 63 J2
Bridge Cl *LEIN* LE4 ...... 120 D7
Bridge Ct *HUCK/RAV* NG15 ...... 23 L2
Bridge Farm La *CFTN/RUD* NG11.. 64 C5
Bridge Fld *BWSH/BRSTN* DE72 .. 61 G8
Bridge Flds *CDON/KEG* DE74 ...... 86 C4
Bridge Foot *BPR/DUF* DE56 ...... 17 J2
Bridge Gv *WBRGFD* NG2 ...... 51 J7
Bridge Hl *BPR/DUF* DE56 ...... 17 J2
Bridgend Cl *BSTN/STPLFD* NG9 .. 62 B2
Bridgeness Rd *NORM/LIT* DE23 .. 70 D1
Bridge Park Rd *LEIN* LE4 ...... 120 B8
Bridgeport Rd *DERBYE* DE21 .... 59 G1
Bridge Rd *COAL* LE67 ...... 108 B7
  LEIE LE5 ...... 126 B8
  LEIE LE5 ...... 132 B1
  WOL/BIL/BRX NG8 ...... 49 H2
Bridge St *BPR/DUF* DE56 ...... 17 K3
  DERBY DE1 ...... 2 C2
  EWD/SEL/PNX NG16 ...... 21 G4
  ILK DE7 ...... 33 K3
  LBORO LE11 ...... 9 H2
  LGEAT NG10 ...... 62 B6
  RLBORO LE12 ...... 101 M3
  RLBORO LE12 ...... 105 G8
Bridge Vw *BPR/DUF* DE56 ...... 17 L8
Bridgewater Dr
  RLEIW/BBY LE8 ...... 139 M6
Bridge Wy *RLEIW/BBY* LE8 ...... 142 D1
Bridgford Rd *WBRGFD* NG2 ...... 51 K7
Bridgnorth Dr *CFTN/RUD* NG11 .. 64 C5
Bridgnorth Wy
  BSTN/STPLFD NG9 ...... 62 C4
Bridgwater Cl *DERBYSE* DE24 .. 59 C8 1
Bridle Cl *MELB/CHEL* DE73 ...... 72 E6
  RLEIW/BBY LE8 ...... 141 G4
Bridle La *BPR/DUF* DE56 ...... 10 E5
  RIPLEY DE5 ...... 11 H4
Bridle Rd *BSTN/STPLFD* NG9 .... 48 F7
  CALV/BJ NG14 ...... 39 H1
  COAL LE67 ...... 108 A4

Bridlesmith Ga *NOTT* NG1 ...... 5 H7 3
Bridlespur Wy *BLWL* NG6 ...... 125 J2
The Bridle *LEIS* LE2 ...... 136 F3
Bridlington St *NOTTE* NG7 ...... 36 M3
Bridport Av
  WOL/BIL/BRX NG8 ...... 50 B2 1
Bridport Rd *WGSTN* LE18 ...... 138 A6
Brielen Rd *COT/KEY/RAD* NG12 .. 53 L4
Brierfield Av *CFTN/RUD* NG11 .... 64 F3
Brierfield Rd *RLEIW/BAR* LE9 .... 142 B5
Brierfield Wy *MCKLVR* DE3 ...... 56 B7
Brierley Gn *CARL* NG4 ...... 38 E8 3
Briers Cl *RLEIW/BAR* LE9 ...... 135 M8
Briers Wy *COAL* LE67 ...... 108 C2
Brigden Av *DERBYSE* DE24 ...... 58 C8
Brightmoor St *NOTT* NG1 ...... 5 J7
Brighton Av *RLEINE/SYS* LE7 .... 121 G3
  WGSTN LE18 ...... 138 A2
Brighton Cl *WGSTN* LE18 ...... 138 A2
Brighton Rd *DERBYE* DE24 ...... 58 D7
  LEIE LE5 ...... 126 B7
Brightside Rd *LEIE* LE5 ...... 132 A1
Brightstone Cl *DERBYSE* DE24 .. 73 H2 1
Bright St *DERBYW* DE22 ...... 57 H2 1
  ILK DE7 ...... 33 J4
Brightwell Dr *LEIW* LE3 ...... 129 M3
Brindley Ri *LEIE* LE5 ...... 127 J6 3
Brindley Rd *WOL/BIL/BRX* NG8 .. 143 K3
Bringhurst Rd *LEIW* LE3 ...... 124 B8 1
Brington Cl *WGSTN* LE18 ...... 138 C5
Brinkhill Crs *CFTN/RUD* NG11 .... 64 D4
The Brinks *RLBORO* LE12 ...... 112 F2
Brinsley Cl *WOL/BIL/BRX* NG8.... 35 L6
Brinsley Hl *EWD/SEL/PNX* NG16... 13 G5
Brinsmead Rd *LEIS* LE2 ...... 131 M8
Brisbane Dr *ARN* NG5 ...... 24 C7
  BSTN/STPLFD NG9 ...... 71 H1
Brisbane Rd *MCKLVR* DE3 ...... 56 C3
Brisco Av *RLBORO* LE12 ...... 103 K1
Briscoe La *RLBORO* LE12 ...... 111 M3
Briset Cl *DERBYSE* DE24 ...... 71 J5 2
Bristol Av *LEIN* LE4 ...... 125 H6
Bristol Dr *MCKLVR* DE3 ...... 56 C5
Bristol Rd *ILK* DE7 ...... 33 J6
  RIPLEY DE5 ...... 11 L8 1
Britannia Rd *LGEAT* NG10 ...... 62 B6
Britannia St *LEI* LE1 ...... 7 G2
  RLBORO LE12 ...... 101 M3
Britannia Wy *RLEINE/SYS* LE7 .. 120 C6
Britford Av *WGSTN* LE18 ...... 137 M7
Briton St *LEIS* LE2 ...... 6 A9
Brittain Dr *RIPLEY* DE5 ...... 11 L6
Britten Gdns
  MAPPK/POR/STA NG3 ...... 51 K1
Brixham Dr *WGSTN* LE18 ...... 137 L2
Brixham Rd *HUCK/RAV* NG15 .... 23 H2
Brixton Rd *NOTTE* NG7 ...... 50 C2 3
Brixworth Rd *LEIE* LE5 ...... 133 J1 1
Broad Av *LEIE* LE5 ...... 132 D2
Broad Bank *DERBYW* DE22 ...... 43 J7 3
Broadbent Cl *RLEIW/BBY* LE8 .. 136 D8
Broad Cl *CALV/BJ* NG14 ...... 26 F3
Broad Eadow Rd
  EWD/SEL/PNX NG16 ...... 23 K8
Broadfields Cl *DERBYW* DE22 ... 43 K7 1
Broadfield Wy *RLEIW/BBY* LE8.. 143 G3
Broadford Cl *LEIN* LE4 ...... 126 B3 2
Broadgate *BSTN/STPLFD* NG9 .. 63 H1
Broadgate Av *BSTN/STPLFD* NG9.. 49 L8
Broadgate La *BSTN/STPLFD* NG9.. 49 L8
Broadhill Rd *CDON/KEG* DE74 .... 86 A5
Broadholme St *NOTTE* NG7 ...... 50 D4 1
Broadhurst Av *BLWL* NG6 ...... 36 B5
Broadhurst St *LEIN* LE4 ...... 125 M5 1
Broadlands *LGEAT* NG10 ...... 61 M3
Broad La *BWSH/BRSTN* DE72 ... 73 K3
  EWD/SEL/PNX NG16 ...... 13 J7
Broadleaf Cl *DERBYE* DE21 .... 44 C5 2
Broadleigh Cl
  CFTN/RUD NG11 ...... 65 G4 3
Broadmead *CALV/BJ* NG14 ...... 39 K3
Broad Meadow *WGSTN* LE18 .. 138 C6 1
Broadmead Rd *RLEINE/BBY* LE8.. 142 E1
Broad Meer *COT/KEY/RAD* NG12.. 67 J4
Broad Oak Cl
  MAPPK/POR/STA NG3 ...... 5 J2
Broad Oak Dr *BSTN/STPLFD* NG9.. 62 B1
  EWD/SEL/PNX NG16 ...... 13 H7
Broadstairs Rd
  BSTN/STPLFD NG9 ...... 62 D5 1
Broadstone Cl *WBRGFD* NG2 ...... 65 H3
Broad St *COAL* LE67 ...... 108 B7
  LBORO LE11 ...... 9 G2
  LGEAT NG10 ...... 62 B8
  NOTT NG1 ...... 5 J6
  RLEINE/SYS LE7 ...... 120 C4
  RLEIW/BAR LE9 ...... 135 M4
Broad Valley Dr *BLWL* NG6 ...... 24 C3
Broad Wk *BLWL* NG6 ...... 36 A4 1
Broadway *BPR/DUF* DE56 ...... 29 J6
  DERBYW DE22 ...... 43 J7
  HEANOR DE75 ...... 20 C6
  ILK DE7 ...... 33 J4
  LBORO LE11 ...... 103 L7
  NOTT NG1 ...... 5 J8 1
  RIPLEY DE5 ...... 11 J5
  RLEINE/SYS LE7 ...... 120 E4 1
Broadway Av *RIPLEY* DE5 ...... 11 J6
Broadway East *CARL* NG4 ...... 52 B7
Broadway Furlong
  RLEINE/SYS LE7 ...... 118 C8
Broadway Park Cl
  DERBYW DE22 ...... 43 J7 3
Broadway Rd *LEIS* LE2 ...... 132 B5
The Broadway *LEIS* LE2 ...... 132 E7
Broadwood Ct
  BSTN/STPLFD NG9 ...... 49 L7 2
Broadwood Rd *ARN* NG5 ...... 24 F7
Brockdale Gdns
  COT/KEY/RAD NG12 ...... 80 C3
Brockenhurst Ri *HEANOR* DE75 .. 20 E6
Brockhole Cl *WBRGFD* NG2 ...... 66 B2 1
Brockhurst Gdns
  MAPPK/POR/STA NG3 ...... 51 K1 1
  COAL LE67 ...... 108 A4
Brocklesby Wy *LEIE* LE5 ...... 127 J7

Brockley *DERBYE* DE21 ...... 59 J2
Brockley Rd *WBRGFD* NG2 ...... 51 M8
Brocks Hill Cl *LEIS* LE2 ...... 138 F3
Brocks Hill Dr *LEIS* LE2 ...... 138 E2
Brockwood Crs
  COT/KEY/RAD NG12 ...... 80 C3
Bromfield Cl
  MAPPK/POR/STA NG3 ...... 38 A8 1
Bromhead St *LBORO* LE11 ...... 9 M1 1
Bromley Cl *BLWL* NG6 ...... 35 M1 1
Bromley La *RLBORO* LE12 ...... 92 F8
Bromley Pl *NOTT* NG1 ...... 4 F7
Bromley Rd *WBRGFD* NG2 ...... 65 J1
Brompton Cl *ARN* NG5 ...... 24 E5 2
Brompton Rd *DERBYW* DE22 .... 56 D1
Bronte Cl *LEIW* LE3 ...... 130 E3
Bronte Pl *NORM/LIT* DE23 ...... 56 F7
Bronze *WGSTN* LE18 ...... 138 D6 2
Brook Av *ARN* NG5 ...... 25 L7
Brook Cl *BLWL* NG6 ...... 35 M1 1
  DERBYW DE22 ...... 43 C3
  EWD/SEL/PNX NG16 ...... 21 M6
  LGEAT NG10 ...... 76 C2
  RDERBYSW DE65 ...... 70 B6
Brook Ct *RLEIW/BBY* LE8 ...... 143 K3
Brookdale Ct *ARN* NG5 ...... 37 H2
Brookdale Rd *LEIE* LE5 ...... 130 B2
Brookes Av *RLEIW/BAR* LE9 .... 141 G4
Brooke St *ILK* DE7 ...... 47 M1
  LGEAT NG10 ...... 61 M2
Brook Gdns *ARN* NG5 ...... 25 L7
  LEIS LE2 ...... 136 F4
Brookhill Cl *WOL/BIL/BRX* NG8 .. 49 J4
Brookhill Dr *WOL/BIL/BRX* NG8 .. 49 J4
Brookhill Leys Rd
  EWD/SEL/PNX NG16 ...... 21 M3
Brookhouse Av *LEIS* LE2 ...... 7 J8
Brook House Cl
  RLEINE/SYS LE7 ...... 115 L6 1
Brookhouse St
  DERBYSE DE24 ...... 72 B2 1
  LEIS LE2 ...... 7 J8 1
Brookland Dr *BSTN/STPLFD* NG9.. 63 H2
Brooklands
  COT/KEY/RAD NG12 ...... 91 G2 1
Brooklands Av *HEANOR* DE75.... 20 D5
Brooklands Cl
  RLEIW/BBY LE8 ...... 136 D8 1
Brooklands Crs *CARL* NG4 ...... 38 E6 1
Brooklands Dr *CARL* NG4 ...... 38 E6
  NORM/LIT DE23 ...... 57 G7
Brooklands Rd
  MAPPK/POR/STA NG3 ...... 37 M8
  RLEIW/BAR LE9 ...... 142 B3
Brook La *COAL* LE67 ...... 100 B8
  LBORO LE11 ...... 103 H7
  RIPLEY DE5 ...... 11 H8
  RLBORO LE12 ...... 105 J7
Brooklyn Av *CALV/BJ* NG14 ...... 39 J3
Brooklyn Cl *BLWL* NG6 ...... 36 B2
Brooklyn Rd *BLWL* NG6 ...... 36 B2
Brook Rd *BSTN/STPLFD* NG9 .... 49 K7
  BWSH/BRSTN DE72 ...... 59 M6
  DERBYSE DE24 ...... 73 K2
  LEIE LE5 ...... 127 H8
  RLBORO LE12 ...... 111 H3
Brooksby Dr *LEIS* LE2 ...... 138 E2
Brooksby La *CFTN/RUD* NG11 .... 64 F7
Brooksby St *LEIS* LE2 ...... 131 J6 1
Brook Side *BPR/DUF* DE56 ...... 17 K4
Brookside *CDON/KEG* DE74 ...... 93 G2 2
  EWD/SEL/PNX NG16 ...... 21 K3 1
  LBORO LE11 ...... 9 H5 1
  RLBORO LE12 ...... 88 C7
  RLEINE/SYS LE7 ...... 115 L5
  RLEINE/SYS LE7 ...... 120 E3
Brookside Av *BSTN/STPLFD* NG9.. 49 H5
  LGEAT NG10 ...... 61 M7
  RLBORO LE12 ...... 88 B6
  RLBORO LE12 ...... 105 M6 1
Brookside Cl *DERBYW* DE22 ...... 43 J8
  LGEAT NG10 ...... 61 M7
  RLBORO LE12 ...... 97 K8
  RLBORO LE12 ...... 98 A4
  RLBORO LE12 ...... 102 A2
  RLBORO LE12 ...... 114 A4
  RLEINE/SYS LE7 ...... 115 L6
  RLEINE/SYS LE7 ...... 120 E3
  RLEIW/BAR LE9 ...... 135 H8 1
  RLEIW/BAR LE9 ...... 136 D8
Brookside Gdns
  CFTN/RUD NG11 ...... 64 F7
Brookside Rd *CFTN/RUD* NG11.... 64 F7
  ILK DE7 ...... 44 C3
  LBORO LE11 ...... 103 H7
Brooks La *COAL* LE67 ...... 108 B2
Brook St *BPR/DUF* DE56 ...... 10 A5
  DERBY DE1 ...... 2 C1
  HEANOR DE75 ...... 19 M2
  LEIN LE4 ...... 120 B8
  NOTT NG1 ...... 5 J6
  RLBORO LE12 ...... 97 K8
  RLBORO LE12 ...... 98 A4
  RLBORO LE12 ...... 102 A2
  RLBORO LE12 ...... 114 A4
  RLEINE/SYS LE7 ...... 115 L6
  RLEINE/SYS LE7 ...... 120 E3
  RLEIW/BAR LE9 ...... 135 H8 1
  RLEIW/BAR LE9 ...... 136 D8
Brookthorpe Wy
  RLEINE/SYS LE7 ...... 64 E3
Brookvale Av *RIPLEY* DE5 ...... 11 M7
  RIPLEY DE5 ...... 18 E5
Brookvale Ri *RIPLEY* DE5 ...... 18 E5

Brook Vale Rd
  EWD/SEL/PNX NG16 ...... 21 G5
Brookvale Rd *RIPLEY* DE5 ...... 18 E5
Brook View Dr
  COT/KEY/RAD NG12 ...... 80 C5
Brookwood Crs *CARL* NG4 ...... 38 A8
Broom Av *RLBORO* LE12 ...... 103 L8 1
Broom Cl *BPR/DUF* DE56 ...... 17 J2
  BPR/DUF DE56 ...... 29 H4
  DERBYSE DE24 ...... 71 H5
  MELB/CHEL DE73 ...... 72 D5
Broome Av *RLEINE/SYS* LE7 .... 115 J7
Broome La *RLEINE/SYS* LE7 .... 115 G6
Broomfield *RLEINE/SYS* LE7 .... 115 J8 1
Broomfield Cl *LGEAT* NG10 ...... 61 L2 1
Broomhill Av *ILK* DE7 ...... 47 L1 2
Broomhill Cl *MCKLVR* DE3 ...... 56 B4 1
  EWD/SEL/PNX NG16 ...... 34 L1
  HUCK/RAV NG15 ...... 23 L2
Broomhill Rd *BLWL* NG6 ...... 36 A1
Broomhills *RLEIW/BAR* LE9 ...... 135 K7
Broomleys *RLEIW/BBY* LE8 ...... 143 H3 1
Broom Leys Av *COAL* LE67 ...... 108 D7
Broom Leys Rd *COAL* LE67 ...... 108 C7
Broom Wy *RLEINE/BAR* LE9 .... 135 K6
Brora Rd *BLWL* NG6 ...... 24 B8
Brougham St *LEI* LE1 ...... 7 H4
Brough St *DERBYW* DE22 ...... 57 H2
Broughton Av *NORM/LIT* DE23 .. 57 H6
Broughton Cl *ILK* DE7 ...... 33 J5 1
  LBORO LE11 ...... 103 G3 1
  RLEINE/SYS LE7 ...... 118 C8
Broughton Dr
  WOL/BIL/BRX NG8 ...... 50 A4 1
Broughton Fld *WGSTN* LE18 ...... 138 C7
Broughton Rd *LEIS* LE2 ...... 137 J1
  RLEINE/BAR LE9 ...... 140 C5
  RLEINE/BAR LE9 ...... 141 G4
  RLEINE/BAR LE9 ...... 141 G4
Broughton St *BSTN/STPLFD* NG9.. 49 J8
  COAL LE67 ...... 108 B7
Broughton Wy *RLEINE/BAR* LE9 .. 141 K8
Brown Av *RLBORO* LE12 ...... 112 E1
Brownhill Crs *RLEINE/SYS* LE7 .. 118 F2
Browning Cl *ARN* NG5 ...... 37 H2
Browning Rd *LBORO* LE11........ 8 A2
Browning St *LEIW* LE3 ...... 131 G3
  NORM/LIT DE23 ...... 57 K8
  NORM/LIT DE23 ...... 71 K1
  RLEIW/BAR LE9 ...... 135 L6
Brown La *CFTN/RUD* NG11 ...... 77 J1
Brownlow Dr *BLWL* NG6 ...... 24 B6
Brown's Cl *RLEIW/BAR* LE9 ...... 140 C7
Browns Cft *BLWL* NG6 ...... 36 C4 1
Brown's Flats
  EWD/SEL/PNX NG16 ...... 22 D8 2
Brown's La *BPR/DUF* DE56 ...... 18 B8
  COT/KEY/RAD NG12 ...... 81 H5
  LBORO LE11 ...... 9 H4
Browns Rd *LGEAT* NG10 ...... 62 C7
Brown St *NOTTE* NG7 ...... 4 A2
Brown's Wy *RLEIW/BBY* LE8 .... 142 D2
Broxburn Cl *LEIN* LE4 ...... 126 B3 1
Broxfield Cl *LEIS* LE2 ...... 138 E4
Broxtowe Av
  EWD/SEL/PNX NG16 ...... 34 B1
  WOL/BIL/BRX NG8 ...... 35 M6
Broxtowe Dr *HUCK/RAV* NG15 .. 15 K6
Broxtowe Hall Cl
  WOL/BIL/BRX NG8 ...... 35 L5
Broxtowe La
  WOL/BIL/BRX NG8 ...... 35 L5 1
Bruce Cl *WBRGFD* NG2 ...... 51 H5 1
Bruce Dr *WBRGFD* NG2 ...... 51 H8
Bruce St *LEIS* LE2 ...... 131 H4
Bruin St *LEIN* LE4 ...... 125 L6
Bruins Wk *LEIS* LE2 ...... 138 D2
Brunel Av *EWD/SEL/PNX* NG16.... 21 L4
  LEIW LE3 ...... 124 E6
Brun La *ASHB* DE6 ...... 41 M7
Brunswick Dr
  BSTN/STPLFD NG9 ...... 62 D2 1
Brunswick St *LEI* LE1 ...... 7 J4
  NORM/LIT DE23 ...... 57 K6
Brunswood Cl *DERBYE* DE21 .... 59 J2
Brunton Cl *MCKLVR* DE3 ...... 56 A6
Brushfield Av *RLBORO* LE12 .... 114 B3
Brushfield St *NOTTE* NG7 ...... 36 C8
Brussels Ter *ILK* DE7 ...... 33 J6 1
Brusty Pl *CALV/BJ* NG14 ...... 39 J2
Bruxby St *RLEINE/SYS* LE7 .... 120 D4
Bryan Cl *RLBORO* LE12 ...... 105 H7
Bryan's Cl *COAL* LE67 ...... 108 D1
Bryngarth Crs *LEIE* LE5 ...... 126 F8 1
Brynsmoor Rd
  EWD/SEL/PNX NG16 ...... 13 J8
Bryony Cl *DERBYE* DE21 ...... 44 E5
Bryony Rd *LEIE* LE5 ...... 127 H5
Buchanan St *DERBY* DE1 ...... 2 E1 1
Buchan St *DERBYSE* DE24 ...... 58 B8
Buckfast Cl *LEIE* LE5 ...... 132 D4 1
  WGSTN LE18 ...... 138 A6
Buckfast Wy *WBRGFD* NG2 ...... 65 L1
Buckford La *RDERBYSW* DE65 .... 70 C7
Buckhaven Cl *LEIN* LE4 ...... 126 B3
Buckhazels La *ASHB* DE6 ...... 41 L1
Buckingham Av *DERBYE* DE21 .. 44 B7 2
  HUCK/RAV NG15 ...... 15 M7
Buckingham Cl *GBY/RBY* LE6 .... 123 J3
Buckingham Ct *LGEAT* NG10 .. 61 L4 2
  LEIS LE2 ...... 136 F2
Buckingham Dr *LBORO* LE11 .... 103 G2
Buckingham Rd *ARN* NG5 ...... 37 J2
  COAL LE67 ...... 108 D7
  LGEAT NG10 ...... 61 L4
  RLEIW/BBY LE8 ...... 143 K3
Buckingham Wy
  EWD/SEL/PNX NG16 ...... 22 F8
Buckland Cl *DERBYW* DE22 ...... 2 A2
Buckland Dr *CALV/BJ* NG14 ...... 27 G7
Buckland Rd *LEIE* LE5 ...... 126 B7
Bucklow Cl *WOL/BIL/BRX* NG8 .. 49 J4 2
Buckminster Cl *DERBYE* DE21 ... 44 D5
Buckminster Rd *ILK* DE7 ...... 33 H5
  LEIW LE3 ...... 125 G7
Buck's La *RLBORO* LE12 ...... 86 E8

Buckwell Rd RLEIW/BAR LE9 ...... 140 B7
Budby Ri HUCK/RAV NG15....... 15 M8
Buddon La RLBORO LE12....... 112 C3
Bude Dr LEIW LE3........ 124 A6
Bude Rd WGSTN LE18........ 138 B6
Bulcote Dr CALV/BJ NG14....... 39 H4
Bulcote Rd CFTN/RUD NC11....... 64 C4
Bullace Rd MAPPK/POR/STA NG3 .. 5 M2
  MAPPK/POR/STA NG3........ 37 K8
Bull Close Rd NOTTE....... 50 C7
Buller Rd LEIN LE4....... 125 L6
Buller St ILK DE7....... 47 L1
  NORM/LIT DE23........ 57 J5
  RLEIW/BBY LE8....... 146 D7
Buller Ter ARN NG5....... 37 H4 ▯
Bullfinch Rd BLWL NG6........ 36 B3
Bull Head St WGSTN LE18....... 138 B5
Bullins Cl ARN NG5....... 25 J7
Bullivant St MAPPK/POR/STA NG3.. 5 J3
Bullock La ALFN DE55....... 12 C2
Bullpit La BPR/DUF DE56....... 29 L7
Bulrush Cl RLBORO LE12....... 113 K6
Bulstode Pl CDON/KEG DE74....... 86 A5 ▯
Bulwell High Rd BLWL NG6....... 35 M1
Bulwell La BLWL NG6....... 36 B3
Bulwer Rd LEIS LE2....... 131 M6 ▯
  NOTTE NG7....... 4 A6
Bunbury Rd WBRGFD NG2....... 51 H6
Bunny Hl RLBORO LE12....... 89 H4
Bunny Hill Top RLBORO LE12....... 89 H2
Bunny La COT/KEY/RAD NG12.... 80 B5
  RLBORO........ 88 C2
Bunting Cl ILK DE7....... 47 G1
Buntings La CARL NG4....... 38 A3
Bunting St NOTTE NG7....... 50 B5
Bunyan Green Rd
  EWD/SEL/PNX NG16....... 13 H1
Burbage Cl BPR/DUF DE56....... 18 B3
  LBORO LE11....... 103 J1 ▯
Burbage Pl DERBYSE DE24....... 58 D8
Burchnall Rd LEIW LE3....... 130 A6
Burcot Cl ILK DE7....... 32 C7
Burder St LBORO LE11....... 104 A3
Burdet Cl LEIW LE3....... 130 C6
Burdett Wy LEIN LE4....... 125 H3
Burdock Cl DERBYE DE21....... 44 C5 ▯
  LEIE LE5....... 127 H5
Burfield Av LBORO LE11....... 9 G4
Burfield St LEIN LE4....... 125 M7
Burford Rd NOTTE NG7....... 36 D7
Burford St ARN NG5....... 25 J7
Burgass Rd
  MAPPK/POR/STA NG3....... 37 L8
Burge Cl WBRGFD NG2....... 51 K5
Burgess Rd COAL LE67....... 108 A7
  LEIS LE2....... 137 J1
Burgess St LEI LE1....... 6 D3
  WGSTN LE18....... 138 B4
Burgh Hall Cl BSTN/STPLFD NG9 ... 63 G5
Burghley Cl MELB/CHEL DE73 ... 74 F7
Burghley Wy NORM/LIT DE23....... 70 C1
Burgin Rd RLEINE/SYS LE7....... 124 B2
Burhill COT/KEY/RAD NG12....... 67 L5
Burland Green La ASHB DE6....... 28 A2
Burleigh Av WGSTN LE18....... 138 A3
Burleigh Cl CARL NG4....... 38 D8
Burleigh Dr DERBYW DE22....... 43 K7
Burleigh Rd LBORO LE11....... 9 G3
  WBRGFD NG2....... 65 K1
Burleigh St ILK DE7....... 33 K6 ▯
Burley Cl RLEIW/BAR LE9....... 142 B4
Burley Dr DERBYW DE22....... 29 J8
Burley Hl DERBYW DE22....... 43 L1
Burley La DERBYW DE22....... 29 H8
Burley Ri CDON/KEG DE74....... 86 B6
Burleys F/O LEI LE1....... 6 F3
Burleys Wy LEI LE1....... 6 E3
Burlington Cl
  BWSH/BRSTN DE72....... 61 H7
Burlington Rd ARN NG5....... 37 G4
  CARL NG4....... 38 D7
  DERBYW DE22....... 56 D1 ▯
  LEIS LE2....... 132 A6
Burlington Wy MCKLVR DE3....... 56 B6
The Burma Rd ASHB DE6....... 40 F3
Burnaby Av LEIE LE5....... 132 B1 ▯
Burnaby St BLWL NG6....... 36 B3 ▯
  DERBYSE DE24....... 58 D7
Burnaston Rd LEIS LE2....... 137 J1
Burnbank Cl WBRGFD NG2....... 66 B2 ▯
Burnbreck Gdns
  WOL/BIL/BRX NG8....... 49 J3
Burncroft ILK DE7....... 32 C8 ▯
Burndale Wk ARN NG5....... 24 C7
Burnel Rd LEIW LE3....... 130 F5
Burneston Wy WGSTN LE18....... 138 C5 ▯
Burnet Cl LEIE LE5....... 127 G5
Burnham Av BSTN/STPLFD NG9 ... 63 K3
Burnham Cl ILK DE7....... 32 B7 ▯
  WGSTN LE18....... 138 B8 ▯
Burnham Dr LEIN LE4....... 125 H5
  MCKLVR DE3....... 56 A5
  RLEIW/BBY LE8....... 142 D1
Burnham St ARN NG5....... 37 G5
Burnham Wy WBRGFD NG2....... 51 G4
Burnmoor St LEIS LE2....... 131 J5
Burns Av NOTTE NG7....... 4 A4
Burnside Cl DERBYSE DE24 .... 71 H4 ▯
Burnside Dr BSTN/STPLFD NG9 ... 49 G5
  DERBYE DE21....... 59 K3
Burnside Gv COT/KEY/RAD NG12.... 66 A6
Burnside Rd LEIS LE2....... 137 L1
  WBRGFD NG2....... 65 J2
  WOL/BIL/BRX NG8....... 49 H1
Burnside DERBYSE DE24....... 58 E7
Burns Rd DERBYW DE22....... 8 B1
  ILK DE7....... 33 J2
  NOTTE NG7....... 4 C4
  RLEIW/BAR LE9....... 135 L6
Burnt House Rd HEANOR DE75 ... 20 B6
Burnt Oak Cl
  EWD/SEL/PNX NG16....... 35 H4
Burnwood Dr
  WOL/BIL/BRX NG8....... 49 H2 ▯

Burr La ILK DE7....... 33 K6
Burroughs Rd GBY/RBY LE6....... 122 E6
Burrows Av BSTN/STPLFD NG9 .... 49 K6
Burrows Cl RLEIW/BAR LE9....... 135 M8
Burrows Crs BSTN/STPLFD NG9 ... 49 K6
Burrows La ASHB DE6....... 40 D5
The Burrows RLBORO LE12....... 88 C5
  RLEIW/BAR LE9....... 135 K7
Bursdon Cl LEIW LE3....... 130 B1
Bursom Rd LEIN LE4....... 124 F1
Burtness Rd CFTN/RUD NG11 .... 64 A8
Burton Av CARL NG4....... 37 M7
Burton Cl CARL NG4....... 38 E7
  LEIS LE2....... 139 H3 ▯
Burton Dr BSTN/STPLFD NG9 .... 63 G3
Burton Rd DERBY DE1....... 2 E6
  NORM/LIT DE23....... 56 F6
  RDERBYSW DE65....... 70 A4
Burton St HEANOR DE75....... 20 C5 ▯
  LBORO LE11....... 9 J6
  LEI LE1....... 7 H5
  NOTT NG1....... 5 G6
Burton Wk RLBORO LE12....... 88 C7
Burton Wks LBORO LE11....... 9 K6
Burwell St NOTTE NG7....... 4 B3 ▯
Buscot Cl LEIN LE4....... 126 B7
Bushby Rd LEIE LE5....... 126 B8
Bush Cl ARN NG5....... 24 D7
Bushey Cl RLEIW/BAR LE9....... 135 M7 ▯
Bush Lock Cl WGSTN LE18....... 137 L7
Bushloe End WGSTN LE18....... 138 A5
Bushy Cl LGEAT NG10....... 75 L1
Butchers La RLBORO LE12....... 106 E8
Butcombe Rd LEIN LE4....... 125 H6
Bute Av NOTTE NG7....... 4 A7
Bute Wy RLEIW/BAR LE9....... 143 K4 ▯
Butler Av COT/KEY/RAD NG12 .... 53 L3
Butler Cl LEIN LE4....... 126 C3
Butlers Cl HUCK/RAV NG15....... 24 A2 ▯
Butt Cl WGSTN LE18....... 138 C6
Butt Close La LEI LE1....... 6 E4
Buttercup Cl RLBORO LE12....... 113 K5
  RLEIW/BAR LE9....... 135 L6
Butterley Dr LBORO LE11....... 102 F5 ▯
Butterley Hl RIPLEY DE5....... 11 J4
Butterley La RIPLEY DE5....... 11 H3
Buttermead Cl
  BSTN/STPLFD NG9....... 48 B5 ▯
Buttermere Cl LGEAT NG10....... 61 L5 ▯
  WBRGFD NG2....... 52 A8
Buttermere Ct ARN NG5....... 37 G5 ▯
Buttermere Dr
  BSTN/STPLFD NG9....... 49 H7 ▯
  DERBYW DE22....... 43 J4
Buttermere St LEIS LE2....... 131 L6 ▯
Buttermere Wy RLBORO LE12....... 105 G6
Butterpot La ASHB DE6....... 54 B4
Butterton Cl ILK DE7....... 33 L8 ▯
Butterwick Cl NORM/LIT DE23... 71 J2 ▯
Butterwick Dr LEIN LE4....... 125 G3
Butthole La RLBORO LE12....... 102 B2
Butt La RLBORO LE12....... 95 H4
Buttonoak Dr MELB/CHEL DE73 .. 72 E4
Butts Cl ILK DE7....... 47 L3
The Butts BPR/DUF DE56....... 17 L4
Butt St LGEAT NG10....... 61 M2 ▯
  HEANOR DE75....... 20 D8 ▯
Buxton Av CARL NG4....... 38 B6
Buxton Cl LEIN LE4....... 125 G3
  MCKLVR DE3....... 56 C4
Buxton Rd DERBYE DE21....... 44 D6
Buxton St LEIS LE2....... 7 L5
Byfield Cl DERBYE DE21....... 44 F5
  NOTTE NG7....... 4 A4
Byfield Dr WGSTN LE18....... 138 C4
Byford Cl
  MAPPK/POR/STA NG3....... 37 J5 ▯
Byford Rd LEIN LE4....... 125 J5
Byland Wy LBORO LE11....... 102 F2 ▯
Byley Rd WOL/BIL/BRX NG8 .... 48 F2 ▯
Byng Av NORM/LIT DE23....... 57 K8
By-pass Rd BSTN/STPLFD NG9 ... 49 K4
Byrne Ct ARN NG5....... 37 M2 ▯
Byron Av LGEAT NG10....... 61 M4
Byron Cl RLEIW/BAR LE9....... 135 L5
  RLEIW/BBY LE8....... 145 L8 ▯
Byron Ct BSTN/STPLFD NG9 .... 48 C6 ▯
Byron Crs
  EWD/SEL/PNX NG16....... 34 A3 ▯
Byron Gv ARN NG5....... 37 G4
Byron Rd WBRGFD NG2....... 51 K8
Byron St ARN NG5....... 25 H8
  HUCK/RAV NG15....... 15 H1
  HUCK/RAV NG15....... 23 L1
  ILK DE7....... 33 K6
  LBORO LE11....... 103 J2
  LEI LE1....... 7 G7
  NORM/LIT DE23....... 2 D9
Byron Street Extension
  LBORO LE11....... 103 J2
Byway Rd LEIE LE5....... 132 C5
Bywell La BPR/DUF DE56....... 18 D7

C

Cabin Leas LBORO LE11....... 103 M2 ▯
Caddaw Av HUCK/RAV NG15....... 23 L1
Cadeby Cl ALFN DE55....... 12 M1 ▯
Cademan Cl LEIS LE2....... 131 M8 ▯
Cademan St COAL LE67....... 108 D2
Cadgwith Dr DERBYW DE22....... 43 J5
Cadlan Cl ARN NG5....... 24 E8
Cades Cl RLEIW/BAR LE9....... 140 B4
Cadwell Cl DERBYSE DE24....... 73 H1
Caerhays Ct DERBYSE DE24....... 71 H4 ▯
Caernarvon Cl DERBYE DE21....... 59 K2
  RLBORO LE12....... 101 L5
  RLBORO LE12....... 113 H7 ▯
Caernarvon Pl
  BSTN/STPLFD NG9....... 62 F3 ▯
Caesar St DERBY DE1....... 43 L8
Caincross Rd WOL/BIL/BRX NG8 .. 35 H8
Cairngorm Cl LEIS LE2....... 131 K8
Cairngorm Dr ARN NG5....... 24 F5 ▯

DERBYSE DE24....... 71 H4
Cairns Cl ARN NG5....... 36 E2
  MCKLVR DE3....... 56 C4
Cairnsford Rd LEIS LE2....... 137 M1
Cairnsmore Cl LGEAT NG10 .... 61 L6 ▯
Cairns St NOTT NG1....... 5 H5
Cairo St NOTTE NG7....... 36 D6
Caister Rd CFTN/RUD NG11....... 64 C7 ▯
Calais Hl LEI LE1....... 7 G7
Calais St LEI LE1....... 7 G7
Caldbeck Cl WBRGFD NG2....... 52 A8 ▯
Caldbeck Ct BSTN/STPLFD NG9 ... 62 F3
Caldbeck Wk ARN NG5....... 24 F8 ▯
Caldecote Rd LEIW LE3....... 130 E6
Caldecott Cl WGSTN LE18....... 138 C5
Calder Cl DERBYW DE22....... 43 J4
  RDERBYSW DE65....... 68 B6
Calderdale WOL/BIL/BRX NG8 .... 48 F4
Calderdale Dr LGEAT NG10....... 75 L1
Calderhall Gdns ARN NG5....... 25 G7 ▯
Caldermill Dr DERBYE DE21....... 44 C5
Calder Rd LEIE LE4....... 125 G4
Caldwell Rd LBORO LE11....... 9 H3
Caledine Rd LEIW LE3....... 124 D7
Caledon Rd ARN NG5....... 36 F5
Calgary Rd LEI LE1....... 7 H2
California Gdns
  DERBYW DE22....... 57 G3 ▯
Calke Ri RIPLEY DE5....... 11 K6
Calladine La BPR/DUF DE56....... 16 A2
  ILK DE7....... 31 H1
Calladine Rd HEANOR DE75....... 20 B5 ▯
Callan Cl RLEIW/BAR LE9....... 135 L4
Callaway Cl WOL/BIL/BRX NG8 .. 49 J2 ▯
Callow Hill Wy NORM/LIT DE23 ... 56 D8
Caloe Cl RLBORO LE12....... 114 C4
Calstock Rd ARN NG5....... 37 J2
Calveley Rd WOL/BIL/BRX NG8 .. 35 J7
Calver Cl BPR/DUF DE56....... 17 M1
  DERBYE DE21....... 44 C4
  WOL/BIL/BRX NG8....... 50 A3
Calver Hey Rd LEIN LE4....... 124 E4
Calvert Crs RLEIW/BAR LE9....... 140 C8
Calverton Av CARL NG4....... 37 M6 ▯
  WGSTN LE18....... 138 A3 ▯
Calverton Cl BSTN/STPLFD NG9 .. 62 E5
  DERBYSE DE24....... 72 C4
  GBY/RBY LE6....... 123 H7
Calverton Dr WOL/BIL/BRX NG8 .. 35 H5
Calverton Rd ARN NG5....... 25 L6
Calvert St DERBY DE1....... 3 J6
Calvin Cl DERBYSE DE24....... 72 E2
Camberley Ct BLWL NG6....... 23 L7 ▯
Camberley Rd BLWL NG6....... 23 L7
Camberwell Av DERBYW DE22.... 56 E1
Camborne Cl DERBYE DE21....... 44 C6
  WGSTN LE18....... 138 A6
Camborne Dr WOL/BIL/BRX NG8 .. 36 A5
Cambria Ms
  MAPPK/POR/STA NG3....... 5 H2
Cambrian Cl RLEIW/BAR LE9....... 142 B5
Cambridge Cl RLEINE/SYS LE7 ... 120 F4
Cambridge Crs
  BSTN/STPLFD NG9....... 48 B5 ▯
Cambridge Gdns ARN NG5....... 37 M2
Cambridge Rd RLEIW/BAR LE9 ... 142 B4
  WBRGFD NG2....... 51 L8
  WOL/BIL/BRX NG8....... 49 L3
Cambridge St CARL NG4....... 38 C7
  COAL LE67....... 108 C6
  DERBYE DE21....... 59 J4
  LBORO LE11....... 9 J1
  LEIW LE3....... 131 G3
  NORM/LIT DE23....... 57 L5
  RLBORO LE12....... 101 M5
Camdale Cl BSTN/STPLFD NG9 ... 62 F2
Camden Cl WBRGFD NG2....... 5 M7
Camden Rd LEIW LE3....... 130 E6
Camden St DERBYW DE22....... 57 H3
  LEI LE1....... 7 G4 ▯
Camelford Rd COAL LE67....... 108 A8
Camelia Av CFTN/RUD NG11....... 64 A6 ▯
Camellia Cl MCKLVR DE3....... 56 B4
  RLEIW/BAR LE9....... 135 K6 ▯
Camelot Av ARN NG5....... 36 E5
Camelot Crs CFTN/RUD NG11 .... 64 F7
Camelot St CFTN/RUD NG11....... 64 F7
Camelot Wy RLEIW/BAR LE9....... 135 L6
Cameo Cl CARL NG4....... 52 D1 ▯
Cameron Av LEIE LE5....... 125 M4
Cameron Rd NORM/LIT DE23....... 57 K7
Cameron St ARN NG5....... 37 G5 ▯
Camfield Ri LEIE LE5....... 137 H3
Camomile Cl ARN NG5....... 24 C8
Campbell Av LEIN LE4....... 126 C1
Campbell Dr CARL NG4....... 38 A7
Campbell Gdns ARN NG5....... 26 A6
Campbell St BPR/DUF DE56....... 17 K4
  DERBYSE DE24....... 72 B1
  EWD/SEL/PNX NG16....... 21 G3 ▯
  LEI LE1....... 7 G7
  MAPPK/POR/STA NG3....... 5 L5 ▯
Campden Gn CFTN/RUD NG11 .... 64 C6
Campion Cl RLEIW/BAR LE9....... 135 L7 ▯
Campion Hl CDON/KEG DE74....... 84 E3
Campion St ARN NG5....... 25 J7
  DERBYW DE22....... 57 H2
Campsie Ct DERBYSE DE24....... 71 H4 ▯
Camp St DERBY DE1....... 43 L8
Camrose Cl WOL/BIL/BRX NG8 .. 35 K7
Camville Rd LEIW LE3....... 130 D3
Canada St BPR/DUF DE56....... 17 L5
Canal Bank BWSH/BRSTN DE72 .. 74 E6
  LBORO LE11....... 9 G1
  LBORO LE11....... 103 L2
Canal Side BSTN/STPLFD NG9 .... 63 M4
Canal St DERBY DE1....... 3 H6
  ILK DE7....... 33 L6
  LEIN LE4....... 120 B7
  LEIS LE2....... 131 G8
  LGEAT NG10....... 61 M2
  NOTT NG1....... 5 H9
  NOTTE....... 137 K7

Candleby Cl COT/KEY/RAD NG12 .. 67 K4
Candleby La COT/KEY/RAD NG12.. 67 K4
Candle Meadow WBRGFD NG2.... 52 B3
Cank St LEI LE1....... 6 E6
Canning Pl LEI LE1....... 6 E3
Canning St LEI LE1....... 6 E3
Canning Wy LBORO LE11....... 103 G1 ▯
Cannock St LEIE LE4....... 126 E4
Cannock Wy LGEAT NG10....... 62 E8
Cannon St ARN NG5....... 37 G4
Canon Cl ILK DE7....... 33 J2
Canons Cl RLEIW/BAR LE9....... 135 M7
Canonsleigh Rd LEIN LE4....... 125 J4
Canon's Wk DERBYW DE22....... 43 K5 ▯
Canon St ILK DE7....... 33 K7
Canterbury Cl
  EWD/SEL/PNX NG16....... 35 H3 ▯
Canterbury Rd
  WOL/BIL/BRX NG8....... 50 B2
Canterbury St DERBYE DE21....... 44 C6
Canterbury Ter LEIE LE3....... 130 F4
Cantley Av CARL NG4....... 38 C5
Cantley Cl DERBYSE DE24....... 72 B4 ▯
Cantrell Rd BLWL NG6....... 36 A1
  LEIW LE3....... 130 B4
Canver Cl WOL/BIL/BRX NG8 .... 49 G1 ▯
Canvey Cl WGSTN LE18....... 138 D4
Canwick Cl WOL/BIL/BRX NG8 .. 49 G2 ▯
Capers Cl RLEIW/BAR LE9....... 135 L4
Capesthorne Cl LEIE LE5....... 126 B7 ▯
Caporn Cl BLWL NG6....... 36 A1
Carbery Cl LEIS LE2....... 139 H3 ▯
Cardale Rd
  MAPPK/POR/STA NG3....... 51 L1
Cardales Cl RDERBYSW DE65 .... 70 B5 ▯
Cardean Dr DERBY DE1....... 43 M8 ▯
Cardigan Dr WGSTN LE18....... 137 K5
Cardigan St DERBYE DE21....... 44 B8
Cardinal Cl DERBYE DE21....... 44 D5
  GBY/RBY LE6....... 123 H7
  MAPPK/POR/STA NG3....... 5 M3
Cardinals Wk LEIE LE5....... 127 C7
Cardington Cl ARN NG5....... 24 C6 ▯
Cardrona Dr DERBYE DE21....... 59 K2
Cardwell St NOTTE NG7....... 36 D7 ▯
Carew Rd CFTN/RUD NG11....... 64 C5 ▯
Carey Cl WGSTN LE18....... 138 B7
Carey Hill Rd RLEIW/BAR LE9 .... 140 B5
Carey Rd BLWL NG6....... 24 A7
  RLEIW/BAR LE9....... 135 H8
Careys Cl LEI LE1....... 6 D6 ▯
Carfax Av LEIS LE2....... 132 D8
Car Hill Rd COAL LE67....... 100 C8
Carington St LBORO LE11....... 103 K2
Carisbrooke Av
  BSTN/STPLFD NG9....... 49 L7 ▯
  CARL NG4....... 38 F6
  LEIS LE2....... 132 A8
  MAPPK/POR/STA NG3....... 37 G6
Carisbrooke Dr
  MAPPK/POR/STA NG3....... 37 G6
Carisbrooke Gdns LEIS LE2....... 132 A7
  NORM/LIT DE23....... 71 G1 ▯
Carisbrooke Pk LEIS LE2....... 132 A8
Carisbrooke Rd LEIS LE2....... 132 A7
  RLBORO LE12....... 113 C7
Carlile Rd CARL NG4....... 38 C7
Carlin Cl BWSH/BRSTN DE72 .... 61 J7
Carlingford Rd HUCK/RAV NG15 .. 15 L7
Carlin St BLWL NG6....... 23 M8 ▯
Carlisle Av BLWL NG6....... 24 A8
  NORM/LIT DE23....... 56 F7
Carlisle Cl LEIW LE3....... 130 F2
Carl St LEIS LE2....... 137 G1
Carlton Av DERBYSE DE24....... 72 C3
  RLEIW/BAR LE9....... 136 A7
Carlton Cl HEANOR DE75....... 20 E4 ▯
Carlton Crs RLBORO LE12....... 88 D5
Carlton Dr DERBYSE DE24....... 72 C3
  WGSTN LE18....... 138 A4
Carlton Gdns DERBYSE DE24....... 72 C3
Carlton Hl CARL NG4....... 38 B8
Carlton Ms CARL NG4....... 38 A8
Carlton Rd LGEAT NG10....... 75 M2
  NORM/LIT DE23....... 57 H6
  RLEIW/BBY LE8....... 146 F4
Carlton St LEI LE1....... 6 E8
  NOTT NG1....... 5 J7
Carlton Vale Cl CARL NG4....... 38 C6
Carlyle Ct WBRGFD NG2....... 65 J1 ▯
Carlyle Rd WBRGFD NG2....... 51 J8
Carlyle St DERBYSE DE24....... 71 K2
  HEANOR DE75....... 20 D8
Carman Cl EWD/SEL/PNX NG16 ... 22 E7
Carmel Gdns ARN NG5....... 37 K1
Carmen Gv GBY/RBY LE6....... 123 H4
Carnarvon Gv CARL NG4....... 38 B7
Carnarvon Rd WBRGFD NG2....... 65 K1
Carnarvon St CARL NG4....... 52 E1 ▯
Carnation Cl LEIW LE3....... 129 K5
Carnation St LEIN LE4....... 125 K5
Carnegie St NORM/LIT DE23....... 57 J7
Carnforth Cl BSTN/STPLFD NG9 .. 62 B2
  MCKLVR DE3....... 56 C6 ▯
Carnoustie Cl LEIW LE3....... 130 B1
Carnoustie Dr LEIS LE2....... 137 K5
Carnwood Rd ARN NG5....... 36 E1
Carol Crs DERBYE DE21....... 58 D3
Caroline Cl DERBYE DE21....... 59 G4
Caroline Ct ILK DE7....... 47 L1
  LEIS LE2....... 137 J1 ▯
Carpenter's La LEIW LE3....... 123 M8 ▯
Carpe Rd LEIN LE4....... 126 B6
Carradale Cl ARN NG5....... 26 A7 ▯
Carrfield Av BSTN/STPLFD NG9 .. 62 D6
  LGEAT NG10....... 62 D7
Carr Fids ILK DE7....... 19 G8
Carriers Rd RDERBYSW DE65 .... 69 G8
Carrington Ct ARN NG5....... 37 G6 ▯
Carrington St DERBY DE1....... 3 H6
  NOTT NG1....... 5 H9
Carroll Gdns WBRGFD NG2....... 50 F6

Carron Cl DERBYSE DE24....... 71 J3
Carrow Rd LEIW LE3....... 129 M2
Carrs Cl CDON/KEG DE74....... 84 E4 ▯
Carsington Crs DERBYW DE22 .... 43 H6
Carsington Ms DERBYW DE22 .... 43 H6
Carson Rd DERBYE DE21....... 58 F1 ▯
Cartbridge COT/KEY/RAD NG12 .. 67 K5
Carter Av CFTN/RUD NG11....... 79 G1
  COT/KEY/RAD NG12....... 53 M4
Carter Cl LGEAT NG10....... 61 M8
  RLEIW/BAR LE9....... 135 L4
Carter Dl COAL LE67....... 108 B1
Carter Ga NOTT NG1....... 5 K8
Carter Rd BSTN/STPLFD NG9 .... 62 E4 ▯
  LEIN LE4....... 126 A7
Carters Wood Dr
  EWD/SEL/PNX NG16....... 35 K4
Cartland Dr LBORO LE11....... 103 G1 ▯
Carts La LEI LE1....... 6 E5
Cartwright Dr LEIS LE2....... 138 C2
Cartwright St LBORO LE11....... 103 M2
Carver St NOTTE NG7....... 36 D7
Carwood Rd BSTN/STPLFD NG9 .. 49 H6
Cascade Gv NORM/LIT DE23....... 56 E8 ▯
Cashmore Vw LEIN LE4....... 125 H3
Casson Av DERBYSE DE24....... 72 C1
Casson St EWD/SEL/PNX NG16.... 12 C3
Castellan Ri ARN NG5....... 25 G7 ▯
Castell Dr GBY/RBY LE6....... 123 K4
Casterton Rd ARN NG5....... 24 F7 ▯
Castings Rd NORM/LIT DE23 .... 57 M7 ▯
Castle Bvd NOTT NG1....... 5 G8
  NOTTE....... 50 E4
Castle Bridge Rd WBRGFD NG2 ... 50 E5
Castle Cl BWSH/BRSTN DE72....... 60 B5
  LEIE LE9....... 140 B8
Castlecraig Ct DERBYSE DE24 ... 71 J5 ▯
Castle Cft DERBYSE DE24....... 73 H2
Castledine Av RLBORO LE12....... 104 E8
Castledine St LBORO LE11....... 9 K8
  RLBORO LE12....... 112 D1
Castledine Street Extension
  LBORO LE11....... 9 K7
Castle Dr RIPLEY DE5....... 12 A7
  EWD/SEL/PNX NG16 .. 12 D4
Castle Flds LEIN LE4....... 124 E2 ▯
Castlefields WBRGFD NG2....... 50 F5
Castleford Rd LEIE LE5....... 130 C7 ▯
Castle Gdns NOTTE NG7....... 50 D4
Castle Ga NOTT NG1....... 5 G8
Castlegate Av LEIN LE4....... 119 K7
Castle Gv NOTTE NG7....... 4 F8
Castle Hl BPR/DUF DE56....... 29 J3
  CDON/KEG DE74....... 84 F3
  RDERBYSW DE65....... 70 B8
  RLBORO LE12....... 88 D7
  RLBORO LE12....... 113 J5
Castle La EWD/SEL/PNX NG16 ... 12 C5
  MELB/CHEL DE73....... 82 F8
Castle Marina Rd WBRGFD NG2.. 50 E5
Castle Meadow WBRGFD NG2 .... 5 G9
Castle Ms MELB/CHEL DE73....... 82 F8
Castle Orch BPR/DUF DE56....... 29 J3
Castle Ri GBY/RBY LE6....... 123 K5
  RLBORO LE12....... 113 H6 ▯
  RLEIW/BAR LE9....... 129 H2
Castle Rock Dr COAL LE67....... 108 F5
Castleshaw Dr NORM/LIT DE23 .. 56 C8
Castle St DERBY DE1....... 3 G5
  EWD/SEL/PNX NG16....... 21 L6
  LEI LE1....... 6 D7
  MELB/CHEL DE73....... 82 F8
  WBRGFD NG2....... 51 K5 ▯
Castle Yd LEI LE1....... 6 D7
Castleton Av ALFN DE55....... 11 M1
  ARN NG5....... 25 K8
  ARN NG5....... 37 K1
  CARL NG4....... 38 F6
  ILK DE7....... 33 J2 ▯
Castleton Cl HUCK/RAV NG15 .... 23 H1 ▯
  WBRGFD NG2....... 50 F6 ▯
Castleton Ct
  EWD/SEL/PNX NG16....... 35 K1 ▯
Castleton Rd WGSTN LE18....... 138 A3
Castle Vw EWD/SEL/PNX NG16 ... 20 E5
  LEI LE1....... 6 D7
  WBRGFD NG2....... 65 H1
Caswell Cl LEIN LE4....... 125 H3 ▯
Cat & Fiddle La ILK DE7....... 46 B1
Caterham Cl WOL/BIL/BRX NG8 ... 35 H8
Caters Cl RLEINE/SYS LE7....... 124 B1
Catesby St LEIW LE3....... 6 A7 ▯
Catfoot La CARL NG4....... 26 B7
Cathedral Rd DERBY DE1....... 2 D2
Cathedral Vw NORM/LIT DE23 .... 57 H5
Catherine Av ILK DE7....... 47 K1 ▯
Catherine Cl RLBORO LE12....... 112 F1
Catherine St LEIN LE4....... 7 J1
  NORM/LIT DE23....... 57 M5 ▯
Cathkin Cl LEIW LE3....... 130 B2
Catkin Dr EWD/SEL/PNX NG16 ... 22 A8
Catlow Wk ARN NG5....... 25 G7 ▯
Cator Cl CARL NG4....... 38 B4
Cator La BSTN/STPLFD NG9....... 63 H2
Cator La North
  BSTN/STPLFD NG9....... 63 G1
Catriona Crs ARN NG5....... 25 L5
Catterick Dr MCKLVR DE3....... 56 A6
Catterley Hill Rd
  MAPPK/POR/STA NG3....... 51 M1
Cattle Market Rd
  WBRGFD NG2....... 51 H5 ▯
Catton Rd ARN NG5....... 25 L7
Cauby St RLBORO LE12....... 114 C4
Caudle Cl RLEINE/SYS LE7....... 118 D4
Caulton St NOTTE NG7....... 4 B3
Caunton Av
  MAPPK/POR/STA NG3....... 37 J6
Causeway DERBYW DE22....... 43 J5
Causeway La GBY/RBY LE6....... 118 B5
  LEI LE1....... 6 D4
Causeway Ms WBRGFD NG2....... 50 F5 ▯
Cavan Dr DERBYE DE21....... 58 F3

Cavell Cl CFTN/RUD NG11 64 B5 1
Cavendish Av CARL NG4 38 B5
DERBYW DE22 43 K4
Cavendish Cl BPR/DUF DE56 29 H5 1
BWSH/BRSTN DE72 74 E5
CDON/KEG DE74 84 E5 1
HUCK/RAV NG15 24 A1 1
Cavendish Ct
BWSH/BRSTN DE72 74 E6 1
DERBY DE1 2 D3 1
Cavendish Crs
BSTN/STPLFD NG9 48 B5 3
CARL NG4 38 A5
COAL LE67 108 A8
Cavendish Crs North NOTTE NG7 4 C7
Cavendish Crs South NOTTE NG7 4 C9
Cavendish Dr CARL NG4 38 C7
RIPLEY DE5 11 G6
Cavendish Pl
BSTN/STPLFD NG9 63 K1 1
Cavendish Rd CARL NG4 38 A5
ILK DE7 47 K1
LEIS LE2 131 J7
LGEAT NG10 62 A5
Cavendish Rd East NOTTE NG7 4 D7
Cavendish Rd West NOTTE NG7 4 C8
Cavendish St ARN NG5 25 J7
DERBY DE1 2 D3 2
NOTTE NG7 50 C7
Cavendish V ARN NG5 37 H4
Cavendish Wy MCKLVR DE3 56 C5
Cave Rd RLBORO LE12 105 H7
Caversfield Cl NORM/LIT DE23 56 E7 1
Caversham Rd LEIS LE2 137 G4
Caversham Wy ILK DE7 32 B7
Cawsand Rd WGSTN LE18 138 A6
Cawston Gdns BLWL NG6 23 M7 2
Caxmere Dr WOL/BIL/BRX NG8 49 K2
Caxton Cl CARL NG4 38 E8 1
Caxton Ct NORM/LIT DE23 57 J8 1
Caxton St NORM/LIT DE23 57 J8
Caythorpe Crs ARN NG5 37 G3 1
Caythorpe Ri ARN NG5 37 G3
Cecilia Rd LEIS LE2 131 M5
Cecil Rd LEIS LE2 7 K5
Cecil St DERBYW DE22 57 H2
WBRGFD NG2 50 D4
Cedar Av BSTN/STPLFD NG9 49 L8
LEIN LE4 119 L8
LGEAT NG10 76 A2
RIPLEY DE5 11 H6
RLBORO LE12 88 B7
WGSTN LE18 138 B6
Cedar Cl LEIW LE3 124 C6
LGEAT NG10 47 M8
RLEIW/BBY LE8 146 D7
Cedar Ct GBY/RBY LE6 123 K5
Cedar Crs RLEIW/BAR LE9 135 M8 1
Cedar Cft BPR/DUF DE56 18 F8 1
Cedar Dr BWSH/BRSTN DE72 60 A3
COT/KEY/RAD NG12 80 C5
RLEINE/SYS LE7 120 F5
Cedar Gv ARN NG5 25 M7
BPR/DUF DE56 17 L5
HUCK/RAV NG15 23 M2 3
RLBORO LE12 113 J6 1
WOL/BIL/BRX NG8 49 K3
Cedar Pk ILK DE7 33 J7
Cedar Rd BSTN/STPLFD NG9 63 J2
CDON/KEG DE74 84 F5
LBORO LE11 9 M8
LEIS LE2 7 L9
NOTTE NG7 36 E7
RLEIW/BBY LE8 142 F1
Cedars Ct LEIS LE2 132 A5
The Cedars LEIS LE2 131 M8
Cedar St DERBYW DE22 43 J8
Cedar Tree Rd ARN NG5 24 F6
Cedarwood Cl LEIN LE4 126 B6 1
Cedarwood Ct DERBYE DE21 44 C5 1
Celandine Cl ARN NG5 24 C8 1
DERBYE DE21 44 D5 1
RLBORO LE12 113 K5 1
Celandine Rd LEIE LE5 127 G5
Celanese Rd DERBYE DE21 59 G4
Celia Dr CARL NG4 38 B8
Celt St LEIS LE2 6 B8
Cemetery Hill Nottingham Rd
DERBYE DE21 3 M2
Cemetery La RIPLEY DE5 11 H6
Cemetery Rd BPR/DUF DE56 17 L1
BSTN/STPLFD NG9 48 C8
RLBORO LE12 114 B4
RLEIW/BBY LE8 136 D8 2
Centenary Wy ASHB DE6 28 B5
BPR/DUF DE56 29 M5
ILK DE7 33 G8
Central Av ARN NG5 25 K8
BSTN/STPLFD NG9 48 C7
BWSH/BRSTN DE72 59 M6
HUCK/RAV NG15 23 L1
ILK DE7 31 M7
LEIS LE2 132 A5
LGEAT NG10 61 M1
MAPPK/POR/STA NG3 37 L3
NOTTE NG7 36 E6
RLBORO LE12 101 M4
RLEINE/SYS LE7 120 F3
WBRGFD NG2 51 K7
WGSTN LE18 138 A5
Central Cl RLEIW/BBY LE8 136 D7
Central Ct NOTTE NG7 50 D6
Central Rd COAL LE67 108 B8
LEIW LE3 6 A2
Central St MAPPK/POR/STA NG3 5 M3
RLEIW/BBY LE8 143 K4
Centre Ct DERBY DE1 3 H8
LEIW LE3 130 B8
Centre Wy COT/KEY/RAD NG12 53 J3
Centurion Wy NOTTE NG7 50 E7
RLEIW/BAR LE9 130 B7
Cernan Ct BLWL NG6 35 K2
Cerne Cl CFTN/RUD NG11 64 D7 1
Chaceley Wy CFTN/RUD NG11 64 E4
Chadborn Av CFTN/RUD NG11 77 M6
Chadderton Cl LEIS LE2 131 L8
Chaddesden La DERBYE DE21 58 D2
Chaddesden Park Rd
DERBYE DE21 58 D1
Chadfield Rd BPR/DUF DE56 29 J2
Chad Gdns ARN NG5 24 E5 3
Chadwell Rd LEIW LE3 124 C8
Chadwick Av DERBYSE DE24 72 C2
Chadwick Rd NOTTE NG7 36 C8
Chaffinch Cl DERBYE DE21 59 K1
LEIN LE4 124 E1
Chainama Cl LEIW LE3 130 A1 3
Chain La MCKLVR DE3 56 E5
NORM/LIT DE23 56 E6
NOTTE NG7 50 C6 3
Chale Rd LEIN LE4 125 K5
Chalfield Cl CFTN/RUD NG11 64 B6
Chalfont Dr RLBORO LE12 114 A6
WOL/BIL/BRX NG8 50 A1
Chalfont Sq DERBYE DE21 44 F5
Chalkley Cl DERBYSE DE24 58 D8
Challis Av DERBYE DE21 44 F8
Chalons Cl ILK DE7 33 K6 3
Chalons Wy ILK DE7 33 K7
Chalvington Cl LEIE LE5 133 G4
Chamberlain Cl
CFTN/RUD NG11 64 A6 4
Chambers Av ILK DE7 33 M8 1
Chambers Cl COAL LE67 116 D7
Chambers St DERBYSE DE24 58 C7
Champion Av ILK DE7 33 G4 2
Champion Cl LEIE LE5 132 F2
Champion Hl BPR/DUF DE56 29 J3
Chancel Rd LEIN LE4 119 H7
Chancery Ct CFTN/RUD NG11 64 E1
Chancery St LEI LE1 6 E7 1
The Chancery BSTN/STPLFD NG9 49 G8
Chandlers Ford DERBYE DE21 44 D5
Chandos Av CARL NG4 38 E7 1
Chandos Pole St
DERBYW DE22 57 H1 1
Chandos St CARL NG4 38 E8
LEIS LE2 7 L8
MAPPK/POR/STA NG3 5 M1
Chandres Ct DERBYW DE22 43 J3 2
Chandwick Ct DERBYSE DE24 71 H4 7
Chantrey Cl
BSTN/STPLFD NG9 63 H3 1
Chantrey Rd WBRGFD NG2 51 J8
Chantry Cl LGEAT NG10 75 L3 1
MCKLVR DE3 56 A6 2
RLEIW/BAR LE9 135 G7
Chapel Bar NOTT NG1 4 F7
Chapel Cl RLEINE/SYS LE7 120 E3
Chapel Gn LEIW LE3 129 M4
Chapel Hl GBY/RBY LE6 123 J4
Chapel La ARN NG5 25 J7 1
CALV/BJ NG14 27 L1
CARL NG4 26 F8
COT/KEY/RAD NG12 67 K4
DERBYE DE21 44 E8
DERBYE DE21 59 J2
GBY/RBY LE6 123 G7
LEIS LE2 131 M8
MELB/CHEL DE73 72 E6 1
RLBORO LE12 89 H6
RLBORO LE12 91 H8
RLBORO LE12 100 C4
RLEIW/BAR LE9 142 B5
Chapel Mews Ct
BSTN/STPLFD NG9 48 F7 1
Chapel Pl EWD/SEL/PNX NG16 34 D1 2
Chapel Rd EWD/SEL/PNX NG16 13 J1
RLEINE/SYS LE7 118 F4
Chapel Rw
BWSH/BRSTN DE72 59 M5 1
Chapel St BPR/DUF DE56 17 K4
BPR/DUF DE56 18 A8
BPR/DUF DE56 18 E7
BPR/DUF DE56 29 K3 1
BSTN/STPLFD NG9 48 F7
CFTN/RUD NG11 79 G1 2
DERBY DE1 2 D2
DERBYE DE21 59 J2
EWD/SEL/PNX NG16 21 K6 1
EWD/SEL/PNX NG16 34 D1 3
HEANOR DE75 20 E7
ILK DE7 33 K6
LEIS LE2 138 E2
LGEAT NG10 62 C8
MELB/CHEL DE73 82 F8
RIPLEY DE5 11 H5
RLBORO LE12 101 M2
RLEINE/SYS LE7 120 E3
RLEIW/BAR LE9 135 L4
RLEIW/BBY LE8 136 F6
Chapman Av DERBYSE DE24 72 F1
Chapman St LBORO LE11 9 L2
Chapmans Wk ARN NG5 24 F1
Chappell Cl LEIN LE4 120 C8
Chapter Cl DERBYE DE21 44 B5
Chapter Dr EWD/SEL/PNX NG16 34 E2 2
Chard St NOTTE NG7 36 D5
Charing Ct DERBY DE1 43 M8 3
Charingworth Rd
DERBYE DE21 44 F5 3
Chariot Cl DERBYSE DE24 73 H2 2
Charity Rd ALFN DE55 11 M2
Charlbury Cl NORM/LIT DE23 56 E7 2
Charlbury Rd WOL/BIL/BRX NG8 49 M1
Charlecote Av LEIW LE3 130 C6
Charlecote Dr
WOL/BIL/BRX NG8 49 H4
Charlecote Park Dr
WBRGFD NG2 65 G3 1
Charles Av BSTN/STPLFD NG9 48 D7
BSTN/STPLFD NG9 49 L6
BSTN/STPLFD NG9 63 G4
DERBYE DE21 59 H1
EWD/SEL/PNX NG16 21 M6
LGEAT NG10 61 M1
Charles Cl CARL NG4 38 D5
ILK DE7 47 M1 1
Charles Dr RLEINE/SYS LE7 124 C1
Charles Pk BLWL NG6 36 A2
Charles St ARN NG5 25 J8
CFTN/RUD NG11 65 G8 1
HUCK/RAV NG15 15 L8
LBORO LE11 9 J1
LEI LE1 7 G6
LGEAT NG10 76 B1
RLBORO LE12 114 A6
Charleston Rd DERBYE DE21 59 G1
Charlestown Dr DERBYW DE22 43 H3
Charles Wy RLEIW/BBY LE8 142 E2 1
Charlesworth Av NOTTE NG7 36 C7
Charley Dr LBORO LE11 8 D6
Charley Rd RLBORO LE12 101 J6
RLBORO LE12 110 E6
Charlock Cl ARN NG5 24 C8
Charlock Rd LEIE LE5 127 H5
Charlotte Cl ARN NG5 25 J5 2
Charlotte Gv
BSTN/STPLFD NG9 49 H6 2
Charlotte St ILK DE7 33 J4
NORM/LIT DE23 57 L5
Charlton Av LGEAT NG10 62 D7
Charlton Cl RLEIW/BBY LE8 142 E1 1
Charlton Gv BSTN/STPLFD NG9 63 K3
Charnborough Rd COAL LE67 108 F6
Charnock Av WOL/BIL/BRX NG8 50 B4
Charnor Rd LEIW LE3 124 C7
Charnwood GBY/RBY LE6 122 F6
Charnwood Av BPR/DUF DE56 17 K3
BSTN/STPLFD NG9 63 H1
BWSH/BRSTN DE72 60 A5
CDON/KEG DE74 85 G4
COT/KEY/RAD NG12 80 C5 1
LEIN LE4 120 D7
LGEAT NG10 61 L3
LGEAT NG10 75 M3
NORM/LIT DE23 71 H2
RLBORO LE12 95 G2
RLEIW/BBY LE8 136 D7
Charnwood Cl LEIN LE4 120 D7
LEIW LE3 129 L3
Charnwood Dr COAL LE67 116 D7 1
LEIW LE3 129 L4
RIPLEY DE5 11 G6
RLEINE/SYS LE7 133 K2
Charnwood Flds RLBORO LE12 95 G2
Charnwood Gv HUCK/RAV NG15 15 J8
WBRGFD NG2 51 J8
Charnwood La ARN NG5 37 L1
Charnwood Ri RLBORO LE12 111 K7
Charnwood Rd LBORO LE11 9 J7
RLBORO LE12 101 M5
RLEINE/SYS LE7 118 B8
Charnwood St COAL LE67 108 C7
DERBY DE1 2 E7
LEIE LE5 7 L4
Charnwood Wy
CALV/BJ NG14 27 H3 1
Charterhouse Cl
DERBYE DE21 44 D4 1
Charteris Cl LBORO LE11 103 H1
Charter Pk ILK DE7 33 J8
Charterstone La
DERBYW DE22 43 J3 3
Charter St LEI LE1 6 F2
Chartley Rd LEIW LE3 131 G4
Chartwell Av CFTN/RUD NG11 64 F8
Chartwell Dr DERBYE DE21 3 K3
WGSTN LE18 137 L4
Chartwell Gv
MAPPK/POR/STA NG3 38 A2
Chase Pk WBRGFD NG2 51 L4
The Chase BPR/DUF DE56 18 F7
COAL LE67 116 C7
DERBYE DE21 30 B5
DERBYSE DE24 71 K3
LEIW LE3 130 D8
RLEINE/SYS LE7 115 H7
Chater Cl LEIE LE5 126 F8
Chatham Ct BPR/DUF DE56 18 B3 3
Chatham St LEI LE1 6 F7
NORM/LIT DE23 57 L7
NOTT NG1 5 G3 1
Chatsworth Av
BSTN/STPLFD NG9 63 G5 1
CARL NG4 38 C7
COT/KEY/RAD NG12 53 L3
LGEAT NG10 76 E1
NOTTE NG7 36 D5
WGSTN LE18 137 L6
Chatsworth Cl LGEAT NG10 61 M3 5
RLBORO LE12 101 L4
Chatsworth Ct ILK DE7 32 C7 2
Chatsworth Crs DERBYW DE22 43 K5
Chatsworth Dr DERBYE DE21 30 B5
HUCK/RAV NG15 23 L1
MCKLVR DE3 56 C4
RLEINE/SYS LE7 120 D4
Chatsworth Pl ILK DE7 46 F2 1
Chatsworth Rd LBORO LE11 8 A1 1
WBRGFD NG2 51 M7 1
Chatsworth St LEIS LE2 7 L6
NORM/LIT DE23 57 J6
Chatteris Av LEIE LE5 133 H4
Chatteris Dr DERBYE DE21 44 B6
Chaucer St ILK DE7 33 K6
LEIS LE2 132 A4
NOTT NG1 4 E5
RLEIW/BAR LE9 135 L6
Chaveney Ct RLBORO LE12 112 C2
Chaveney Rd RLBORO LE12 112 C2
Chaveney Wk RLBORO LE12 112 C2
Chaworth Av
EWD/SEL/PNX NG16 22 D6 1
Chaworth Rd CARL NG4 52 D1
WBRGFD NG2 65 J1
Cheadle Cl
MAPPK/POR/STA NG3 37 M5 1
NORM/LIT DE23 56 F6
WOL/BIL/BRX NG8 35 H7
Cheam Cl DERBYW DE22 56 C1
Cheapside BPR/DUF DE56 17 K4 1
DERBY DE1 2 D3
RLBORO LE12 102 A3 1
Checketts Cl LEIN LE4 125 M5
Checketts Rd LEIN LE4 125 M4
Checkland Rd LEIN LE4 120 C7
Cheddar Rd CFTN/RUD NG11 64 C7 3
WGSTN LE18 138 C4
Chedington Av
MAPPK/POR/STA NG3 38 B1
Chediston V ARN NG5 24 F7
Chedworth Cl
MAPPK/POR/STA NG3 51 K2 1
Chedworth Dr DERBYSE DE24 73 H1 2
Cheer Cl RLEIW/BBY LE8 142 D3
Chelker Wy LBORO LE11 103 G4
Chellaston La
BWSH/BRSTN DE72 73 J7
MELB/CHEL DE73 73 G6
Chellaston Park Ct
MELB/CHEL DE73 72 D6 1
Chellaston Rd DERBYSE DE24 72 C3 1
WGSTN LE18 138 A3
Chelmarsh Cl
MELB/CHEL DE73 72 E4 2
Chelmorton Pl DERBYE DE21 44 D7 2
Chelmsford Cl MCKLVR DE3 56 A4 2
Chelmsford Rd NOTTE NG7 36 D5 1
Chelsbury Ct ARN NG5 25 J8 1
Chelsea Cl DERBYW DE22 56 C1
EWD/SEL/PNX NG16 35 J4 1
WGSTN LE18 137 H6
Chelsea St NOTTE NG7 36 D6
Cheltenham Cl
BSTN/STPLFD NG9 62 D5 2
Cheltenham Rd LEIN LE4 125 G5
Cheltenham St BLWL NG6 36 C3 2
Chelwood Rd MELB/CHEL DE73 72 D5
Cheney End RLEIW/BAR LE9 135 H7
Cheney Rd LEIN LE4 126 E2
Chennel Nook
COT/KEY/RAD NG12 67 L5 1
Chepstow Rd
CFTN/RUD NG11 64 C7 4
LEIS LE2 132 A4
Chequers La DERBYE DE21 3 L3
Chequers Rd DERBYE DE21 3 K3
Cherhill Cl CFTN/RUD NG11 64 B8
Cheribough Rd CDON/KEG DE74 84 E5
Cheriton Dr ILK DE7 33 G4
Cheriton Gdns
NORM/LIT DE23 56 C8 2
Cheriton Rd LEIS LE2 137 H2
Cherry Av HUCK/RAV NG15 23 M2
Cherrybrook Cl LEIN LE4 118 F8
Cherrybrook Dr DERBYE DE21 44 F4
Cherry Cl ARN NG5 25 J7
BWSH/BRSTN DE72 61 J7
LBORO LE11 103 L8
Cherry Dr RLEINE/SYS LE7 120 F5
Cherry Hl COT/KEY/RAD NG12 80 D4
Cherry Hills Rd LEIW LE3 130 A1
Cherryleas Dr LEIW LE3 131 G3
Cherry Orch COT/KEY/RAD NG12 67 J4
Cherry Orchard Mt ARN NG5 24 F8
Cherry Rd RLEIW/BBY LE8 136 F8
Cherry St WGSTN LE18 137 M5
Cherry Tree Av BPR/DUF DE56 17 L1
LEIW LE3 129 J4
RIPLEY DE5 11 H7 1
Cherry Tree Cl
BWSH/BRSTN DE72 61 K3
COT/KEY/RAD NG12 53 K5
EWD/SEL/PNX NG16 13 J7
ILK DE7 47 H1 1
RDERBYSW DE65 68 B5 1
Cherrytree Cl RLEINE/SYS LE7 124 B2
RLEIW/BBY LE8 143 H3
Cherry Tree Gv
RLEIW/BAR LE9 135 L4 2
Cherry Tree La
COT/KEY/RAD NG12 65 M4
Cherry Tree Ms DERBYE DE21 58 F3 2
Cherry Wood Dr
WOL/BIL/BRX NG8 35 M8
Cherrywood Gdns
MAPPK/POR/STA NG3 37 L7
Chertsey Cl
MAPPK/POR/STA NG3 37 K6 1
Chertsey Ct ILK DE7 32 B7 2
Chertsey Rd MCKLVR DE3 56 A5
Cherwell Ct BLWL NG6 35 K1 1
Cherwell Rd RLBORO LE12 105 H8
Chesapeake Rd DERBYE DE21 58 F1
Chesham Dr ARN NG5 36 F5 1
BSTN/STPLFD NG9 48 F5
Cheshire Dr WGSTN LE18 137 L4
Cheshire Gdns LEIS LE2 131 H8
Cheshire Rd LEIS LE2 131 H8
Cheshire St DERBYSE DE24 72 B2
Cheshire Wy
EWD/SEL/PNX NG16 13 G3
Chesil Av WOL/BIL/BRX NG8 50 B2 2
Cheslyn Dr WOL/BIL/BRX NG8 36 A7
Chester Av DERBYW DE22 43 M2
Chester Cl LBORO LE11 8 F4
LEI LE1 7 J3
RLEIW/BBY LE8 137 G8 1
Chesterfield Av CARL NG4 38 B5
LGEAT NG10 62 D8
Chesterfield Dr CALV/BJ NG14 39 L2
Chesterfield Rd BPR/DUF DE56 10 C4
BPR/DUF DE56 17 L2
LEIE LE5 132 B3
Chesterfield St CARL NG4 38 B8
Chesterford Ct
NORM/LIT DE23 70 D1 1
Chester Gn BSTN/STPLFD NG9 62 C5
Chester Green Rd DERBY DE1 43 L8
Chesterman Cl
EWD/SEL/PNX NG16 33 M3 1
Chester Rd RLEIW/BBY LE8 137 G8
Chesterton Av NORM/LIT DE23 57 J8
Chesterton Rd DERBYE DE21 59 J1
Chestnut Av ALFN DE55 12 B2
BPR/DUF DE56 17 L5
BSTN/STPLFD NG9 63 K1 1
LEIE LE5 127 G6
LEIS LE2 138 D2
MAPPK/POR/STA NG3 37 M5
MCKLVR DE3 56 C4
MELB/CHEL DE73 72 D4
NORM/LIT DE23 2 E9
RIPLEY DE5 11 H7
Chestnut Cl BPR/DUF DE56 29 J5
ILK DE7 19 G8
RLBORO LE12 102 A4
RLBORO LE12 112 C3
RLEINE/SYS LE7 120 F5 1
RLEINE/SYS LE7 121 H2
RLEIW/BAR LE9 141 M1
Chestnut Dr
EWD/SEL/PNX NG16 34 E1
RLEINE/SYS LE7 133 L3
Chestnut Gv ARN NG5 25 L7
BWSH/BRSTN DE72 60 A4
CALV/BJ NG14 39 K3 1
CARL NG4 38 D6
COAL LE67 108 F7
COT/KEY/RAD NG12 53 K3
HUCK/RAV NG15 23 M3 1
LGEAT NG10 47 L8
MAPPK/POR/STA NG3 5 G1
RDERBYSW DE65 68 F3
WBRGFD NG2 51 J8 1
Chestnut La CFTN/RUD NG11 77 J1
Chestnut Rd
EWD/SEL/PNX NG16 20 E4 3
LEIW LE3 124 A7
The Chestnuts LGEAT NG10 61 L7
MAPPK/POR/STA NG3 37 K6 2
RLEIW/BBY LE8 143 J3
Chestnut St LBORO LE11 9 G3
Chestnut Wk COAL LE67 122 C1
GBY/RBY LE6 123 K5
Chestnut Wy RLEINE/SYS LE7 115 J8
Chettle Rd LEIW LE3 124 E8
Chetwin Rd WOL/BIL/BRX NG8 49 H2
Chetwynd Rd
BSTN/STPLFD NG9 62 E5 3
Chevely Ct DERBYE DE21 44 B7 3
Cheverton Cl DERBYSE DE24 73 H2 3
Chevin Av BWSH/BRSTN DE72 60 A5
LEIW LE3 130 B2
MCKLVR DE3 56 D5
Chevin Bank BPR/DUF DE56 29 H1
Chevin Gdns ARN NG5 24 E6
Chevin Pl DERBYW DE22 43 K8
Chevin Rd BPR/DUF DE56 17 H3
BPR/DUF DE56 29 J2
DERBYW DE22 43 K8
Chevin V BPR/DUF DE56 29 J2
Cheviot Av EWD/SEL/PNX NG16 12 D4
Cheviot Cl ARN NG5 24 F5 2
Cheviot Dr BLWL NG6 23 K7 2
RLBORO LE12 102 A4
Cheviot Rd LEIS LE2 131 K8
LEIS LE2 137 K1
LGEAT NG10 61 L6
Cheviot St DERBYW DE22 57 G2
Chewton Av
EWD/SEL/PNX NG16 21 L6
Chewton St EWD/SEL/PNX NG16 21 L6
Cheyenne Gdns DERBYE DE21 58 F2
Cheyny Cl WBRGFD NG2 51 G6 3
Chichester Cl ARN NG5 24 C8
ILK DE7 33 L7
LBORO LE11 103 G7 1
Chichester Dr
COT/KEY/RAD NG12 67 J3 1
Chidlow Rd WOL/BIL/BRX NG8 35 H8
Chigwell Cl WOL/BIL/BRX NG8 35 J4 2
Chilcombe Cl LEIN LE4 125 J4
Chillon Wy HUCK/RAV NG15 23 H1
Chilson Dr MCKLVR DE3 56 A4
Chiltern Av RLBORO LE12 102 B4
RLEIW/BAR LE9 142 B5
Chiltern Cl ARN NG5 24 F5
Chiltern Dr ILK DE7 32 C7
Chiltern Gdns LGEAT NG10 61 L6
Chiltern Gn LEIS LE2 137 L1
Chiltern Wy ARN NG5 36 F1
Chilton Dr EWD/SEL/PNX NG16 22 E8
Chilvers Cl ARN NG5 24 E8
Chilwell Ct BLWL NG6 24 B8 1
Chilwell La BSTN/STPLFD NG9 48 F8
Chilwell Rd BSTN/STPLFD NG9 63 K1
Chilwell St NOTTE NG7 50 D4 2
Chime Cl DERBYE DE21 44 C5
Chingford Ct DERBYW DE22 56 F1 1
Chingford Rd WOL/BIL/BRX NG8 35 J7
Chinley Rd DERBYE DE21 44 E6
Chippendale St NOTTE NG7 50 D4 3
Chippenham Rd ARN NG5 36 F1
Chisbury Gn CFTN/RUD NG11 64 B8
Chisholm Wy ARN NG5 36 E1
Chislehurst Av LEIW LE3 130 C7
Chiswick Cl DERBYW DE22 56 D1
Chiswick Dr LBORO LE11 103 G3 3
Chiswick Rd LEIS LE2 131 K6
Chitterman Wy COAL LE67 116 C7
Chorley Wood Rd LEIE LE5 133 H3
Chrisett Cl LEIE LE5 132 F1 1
Christchurch Rd
HUCK/RAV NG15 23 H3
Christie Dr LBORO LE11 103 G1
Christina Av BLWL NG6 36 A3
Christina Crs BLWL NG6 36 A3
Christopher Cl
RLEIW/BBY LE8 143 J4 1
WOL/BIL/BRX NG8 49 K1 1
Christopher Dr LEIN LE4 126 D3
Christow St LEI LE1 7 H3
Chrysalis Wy
EWD/SEL/PNX NG16 21 G4
Church Av ARN NG5 25 J8
LEIW LE3 131 G2 1
Church Cl ARN NG5 25 H8
BSTN/STPLFD NG9 48 A3
COT/KEY/RAD NG12 53 J4
MAPPK/POR/STA NG3 5 H3 2
MELB/CHEL DE73 72 E6 2
RLBORO LE12 88 C6
RLEINE/SYS LE7 120 F3
RLEIW/BBY LE8 146 E6
Church Crs ARN NG5 25 H8
BSTN/STPLFD NG9 62 E3
Church Cft RIPLEY DE5 11 H5 1
WBRGFD NG2 51 K7 1
Churchdale Av
BSTN/STPLFD NG9 48 C6 4
Churchdown Cl DERBYE DE21 44 F5 4
Church Dr East ARN NG5 25 J8
Church Dr ARN NG5 25 J8
ARN NG5 36 F6
COAL LE67 116 B7
COT/KEY/RAD NG12 80 C4

HUCK/RAV NG15 ... 15 L8
ILK DE7 ... 33 H2
LGEAT NG10 ... 47 M8
WBRGFD NG2 ... 51 K8
Churchfield La NOTTE NG7 ... 50 C1
Church Ga COT/KEY/RAD NG12 ... 67 G2
LEI LE11 ... 9 K2
LEI LE1 ... 6 E5
RLBORO LE12 ... 102 A3
Church HI EWD/SEL/PNX NG16 ... 34 D1
LEIN LE4 ... 125 M1
RDERBYSW DE65 ... 68 F2
RLBORO LE12 ... 111 L7
RLEINE/SYS LE7 ... 127 K7
Church Hill RLEIN LE4 ... 120 C8
RLBORO LE12 ... 113 H6
Churchill CI ARN NG5 ... 37 K1
BWSH/BRSTN DE72 ... 61 H7
LEIS ... 138 E2
Churchill Dr BSTN/STPLFD NG9 ... 48 C7
CFTN/RUD NG11 ... 64 F8
LEIW LE3 ... 129 M3
RDERBYSW DE65 ... 68 C5
Churchill St LEIS LE2 ... 7 K9
Churchlands LBORO LE11 ... 103 H1
Church La ARN NG5 ... 25 K6
ASHB DE6 ... 41 J5
BLWL NG6 ... 24 A8
BPR/DUF DE56 ... 17 K3
BSTN/STPLFD NG9 ... 48 B8
BSTN/STPLFD NG9 ... 63 H6
CALV/BJ NG14 ... 27 L1
CDON/KEG DE74 ... 85 H3
CFTN/RUD NG11 ... 76 F4
CFTN/RUD NG11 ... 77 J1
COT/KEY/RAD NG12 ... 66 C8
COT/KEY/RAD NG12 ... 67 J4
COT/KEY/RAD NG12 ... 91 K2
DERBYE DE21 ... 30 A8
DERBYE DE21 ... 58 E1
DERBYW DE22 ... 42 D7
EWD/SEL/PNX NG16 ... 13 L4
EWD/SEL/PNX NG16 ... 21 J1
EWD/SEL/PNX NG16 ... 34 A5
GBY/RBY LE6 ... 123 G7
HUCK/RAV NG15 ... 15 M5
ILK DE7 ... 31 H1
ILK DE7 ... 44 C3
ILK DE7 ... 45 J1
ILK DE7 ... 47 J6
LEIN LE4 ... 120 B8
LEIS ... 131 M8
LEIS ... 133 J6
RLBORO LE12 ... 89 G6
RLBORO LE12 ... 91 G8
RLBORO LE12 ... 100 C3
RLBORO LE12 ... 105 H7
RLEINE/SYS LE7 ... 115 L5
RLEINE/SYS LE7 ... 124 B1
RLEINE/SYS LE7 ... 133 K3
RLEIW/BAR LE9 ... 136 A7
RLEIW/BBY LE8 ... 136 D7
RLEIW/BBY LE8 ... 145 K8
Church Lane Little
RLBORO LE12 ... 114 A4
Church La North
DERBYW DE22 ... 43 K4
Church Leys Av RLEINE/SYS LE7 ... 115 L5
Church Ms DERBYE DE21 ... 59 H3
WBRGFD NG2 ... 51 H6
Church Nook WGSTN LE18 ... 138 B4
Church Rd BLWL NG6 ... 24 C3
CALV/BJ NG14 ... 39 K3
DERBYW DE22 ... 43 G1
EWD/SEL/PNX NG16 ... 22 C5
LEIE LE5 ... 132 F5
LEIS ... 137 G1
LEIW LE3 ... 123 M6
MAPPK/POR/STA NG3 ... 5 K2
RLEINE/SYS LE7 ... 120 A5
RLEIW/BAR LE9 ... 129 H2
RLEIW/BBY LE8 ... 139 L7
RLEIW/BBY LE8 ... 146 E7
Church Side RLBORO LE12 ... 102 A3
Churchside Gdns NOTTE NG7 ... 36 C7
Church St ALFN DE55 ... 12 B1
ARN NG5 ... 25 K7
BLWL NG6 ... 36 C5
BPR/DUF DE56 ... 10 B5
BPR/DUF DE56 ... 18 D2
BPR/DUF DE56 ... 30 A1
BSTN/STPLFD NG9 ... 48 B8
BSTN/STPLFD NG9 ... 48 F7
BSTN/STPLFD NG9 ... 63 K1
BWSH/BRSTN DE72 ... 60 A3
CARL NG4 ... 27 G7
CARL NG4 ... 38 C8
CDON/KEG DE74 ... 85 K3
CFTN/RUD NG11 ... 79 J7
CFTN/RUD NG11 ... 79 G1
DERBYE DE21 ... 30 D2
DERBYE DE21 ... 59 H3
DERBYE DE24 ... 59 G8
EWD/SEL/PNX NG16 ... 21 J6
HEANOR DE75 ... 20 D6
ILK DE7 ... 33 J3
LEI LE1 ... 7 G6
LEIN LE4 ... 126 B1
LEIS ... 138 E2
LGEAT NG10 ... 47 M8
MELB/CHEL DE73 ... 82 F8
NORM/LIT DE23 ... 57 L5
NORM/LIT DE23 ... 57 G6
NOTTE NG7 ... 50 C4
RIPLEY DE5 ... 11 H5
RIPLEY DE5 ... 19 C6
RLBORO LE12 ... 94 E6
RLBORO LE12 ... 98 A4
RLBORO LE12 ... 100 F1
RLBORO LE12 ... 101 M3
RLBORO LE12 ... 105 H7
RLBORO LE12 ... 106 D7
RLEINE/SYS LE7 ... 119 K1
RLEIW/BAR LE9 ... 134 E4
RLEIW/BAR LE9 ... 140 B8
RLEIW/BAR LE9 ... 140 B5
RLEIW/BBY LE8 ... 137 G7

RLEIW/BBY LE8 ... 143 K4
Church Vw BWSH/BRSTN DE72 ... 61 J8
HEANOR DE75 ... 19 M3
ILK DE7 ... 33 J8
RLEIW/BAR LE9 ... 136 A7
Church View CI ARN NG5 ... 24 F6
Church Wk ALFN DE55 ... 12 C1
BPR/DUF DE56 ... 29 K5
EWD/SEL/PNX NG16 ... 21 K5
Churchward Av LEIN LE4 ... 125 C3
Churnet CI CFTN/RUD NG11 ... 64 C3
Cinder Bank
EWD/SEL/PNX NG16 ... 12 D3
Cinderhill Gv CARL NG4 ... 38 C5
Cinderhill Rd BLWL NG6 ... 35 M3
The Circle DERBYSE DE24 ... 71 J2
LEIE LE5 ... 132 D3
Citadel St NOTTE NG7 ... 50 C2
City of Dan COAL LE67 ... 108 D3
City Rd BSTN/STPLFD NG9 ... 49 L8
DERBY DE1 ... 43 L8
NOTTE NG7 ... 50 B6
The City BSTN/STPLFD NG9 ... 63 L1
BSTN/STPLFD NG9 ... 63 L1
Clandon Dr ARN NG5 ... 36 F5
Clanfield Rd WOL/BIL/BRX NG8 ... 35 J5
Clapgun St CDON/KEG DE74 ... 84 F4
Clapham St NOTTE NG7 ... 50 C2
Clara Mount Rd HEANOR DE75 ... 20 E6
Clarborough Dr ARN NG5 ... 37 L1
Clarefield Rd LEIW LE3 ... 130 F2
Clare Gv LEIE LE5 ... 130 B5
Clarehaven BSTN/STPLFD NG9 ... 62 C2
Claremont Av BSTN/STPLFD NG9 ... 49 C7
HUCK/RAV NG15 ... 23 L2
Claremont Dr CFTN/RUD NG11 ... 65 C4
Claremont Rd ARN NG5 ... 36 F6
Claremont St LEIN LE4 ... 125 L4
Clarence Dr COAL LE67 ... 108 D7
Clarence Rd BSTN/STPLFD NG9 ... 63 H5
LGEAT NG10 ... 76 A1
NORM/LIT DE23 ... 57 J6
RLEIW/BAR LE9 ... 136 D5
Clarence St LBORO LE11 ... 9 K1
LEI LE1 ... 6 F5
MAPPK/POR/STA NG3 ... 5 M5
Clarendon Pk ARN NG5 ... 36 F7
Clarendon Park Rd LEIS LE2 ... 132 A5
Clarendon St LEIS LE2 ... 6 D9
NOTT NG1 ... 4 E5
Clare St NOTT NG1 ... 5 H6
Clare Va NOTTE NG7 ... 4 D8
Clarewood Gv CFTN/RUD NG11 ... 64 C8
Clarges St BLWL NG6 ... 36 A1
Clark Cardens
RLEIW/BBY LE8 ... 136 E7
Clarke Av ARN NG5 ... 25 K7
HEANOR DE75 ... 20 A4
Clarke CI COAL LE67 ... 108 D3
Clarke Dr LGEAT NG10 ... 75 L3
Clarke Gv LEIN LE4 ... 125 L1
Clarke Rd COAL LE67 ... 109 C7
WBRGFD NG2 ... 51 J5
Clarke's La BSTN/STPLFD NG9 ... 63 K5
BWSH/BRSTN DE72 ... 73 M7
Clarkes Rd WGSTN LE18 ... 137 M5
Clarke St DERBY DE1 ... 3 H1
LEIN LE4 ... 125 M4
Clarkson Dr BSTN/STPLFD NG9 ... 63 M1
Claude St NOTTE NG7 ... 50 C6
Clawson Ct LBORO LE11 ... 103 H1
Claxton St HEANOR DE75 ... 20 B5
Claxton Ter HEANOR DE75 ... 20 B5
Claybrook Av LEIW LE3 ... 130 E7
Claydon Rd LEIE LE5 ... 126 C7
Claye St LGEAT NG10 ... 62 C8
Clayfield CI BLWL NG6 ... 35 L1
Claygate MAPPK/POR/STA NG3 ... 37 L8
Clay La HEANOR DE75 ... 20 D5
Claymill Rd LEIN LE4 ... 126 D3
Claypole Rd NOTTE NG7 ... 4 B2
Clay St BWSH/BRSTN DE72 ... 60 E8
RLBORO LE12 ... 98 A4
Clayton Ct NOTTE NG7 ... 4 B6
Clayton Dr LEIN LE4 ... 126 D1
Clayton Gv HEANOR DE75 ... 20 A3
Claytons Dr NOTTE NG7 ... 50 C5
Cleeve Mt LBORO LE11 ... 103 G3
Clematis CI LEIN LE4 ... 124 E2
Clement Av LEIN LE4 ... 125 L4
Clement Rd ILK DE7 ... 47 J7
Clements Ga CDON/KEG DE74 ... 93 G1
Clether Rd WOL/BIL/BRX NG8 ... 49 H1
Cleve Av BSTN/STPLFD NG9 ... 62 C4
Clevedon Crs LEIN LE4 ... 126 C7
Cleveland Av BWSH/BRSTN DE72 ... 60 D8
DERBYE DE21 ... 58 F2
LGEAT NG10 ... 62 D7
Cleveland Ct NOTTE NG7 ... 50 C2
Cleveland Rd LBORO LE11 ... 103 K8
WGSTN LE18 ... 138 B3
Cleveleys Av LEIW LE3 ... 130 E7
Cleveleys Rd
BSTN/STPLFD NG9 ... 62 C4
Clevely Wy CFTN/RUD NG11 ... 64 C4
Cliff Av LBORO LE11 ... 103 K2
Cliff Bvd EWD/SEL/PNX NG16 ... 22 D8
Cliff Crs COT/KEY/RAD NG12 ... 53 K3
Cliff Dr COT/KEY/RAD NG12 ... 53 L2
Cliffe Hill Av BSTN/STPLFD NG9 ... 48 B8
Cliffe House Ms RLEIW/BBY LE8 ... 136 D8
Cliffe Rd LEIN LE4 ... 125 K1
Cliffgrove Av BSTN/STPLFD NG9 ... 63 H1
Cliffmere Wk CFTN/RUD NG11 ... 64 B6
Clifford Av BSTN/STPLFD NG9 ... 49 J7
Clifford CI COT/KEY/RAD NG12 ... 80 D3
LGEAT NG10 ... 75 L3
Clifford Rd LBORO LE11 ... 8 E1
Clifford St LEIW LE3 ... 6 C8
LGEAT NG10 ... 62 C8
NOTTE NG7 ... 4 B4
WGSTN LE18 ... 137 K5
Cliff Rd CARL NG4 ... 38 B8
COT/KEY/RAD NG12 ... 53 J3
NOTT NG1 ... 5 J8
The Cliff BLWL NG6 ... 35 M3

Cliff Wy COT/KEY/RAD NG12 ... 53 K3
Cliffwood Av LEIN LE4 ... 119 K8
Clifton Av COT/KEY/RUD NG11 ... 65 C7
LGEAT NG10 ... 62 E8
Clifton Br NOTTE NG7 ... 50 B5
Clifton Crs BSTN/STPLFD NG9 ... 63 J4
Clifton Dr MCKLVR DE3 ... 56 C4
WGSTN LE18 ... 137 L7
Clifton Gv CARL NG4 ... 38 C5
Clifton La CFTN/RUD NG11 ... 64 E7
CFTN/RUD NG11 ... 64 E1
CFTN/RUD NG11 ... 64 B6
CFTN/RUD NG11 ... 64 E2
Clifton Rd CFTN/RUD NG11 ... 64 F8
DERBYW DE22 ... 43 H4
LEIS ... 131 J7
Clifton St BSTN/STPLFD NG9 ... 63 L1
DERBY DE1 ... 3 J8
Clifton Ter NOTTE NG7 ... 4 D9
Clint Hill Dr RLEIW/BAR LE9 ... 140 C4
Clinton Av ARN NG5 ... 36 F7
EWD/SEL/PNX NG16 ... 21 H1
Clinton Ct NOTT NG1 ... 5 G4
Clinton St BSTN/STPLFD NG9 ... 49 J8
DERBYE DE21 ... 3 M2
Clipper Rd LEIN LE4 ... 126 D4
Clipstone Av
MAPPK/POR/STA NG3 ... 37 L3
NOTT NG1 ... 4 F3
Clipstone CI WGSTN LE18 ... 138 C5
WOL/BIL/BRX NG8 ... 35 H5
Clipstone Gdns DERBYE DE21 ... 44 F5
WGSTN LE18 ... 138 C5
Clipston La COT/KEY/RAD NG12 ... 66 D8
Clive Crs EWD/SEL/PNX NG16 ... 34 E2
Cliveden Gn CFTN/RUD NG11 ... 64 B6
Cloisters Ct DERBYE DE21 ... 44 D5
The Cloisters
BSTN/STPLFD NG9 ... 49 L7
Cloister St NOTTE NG7 ... 50 C5
Close Quarters
BSTN/STPLFD NG9 ... 49 G7
The Close ARN NG5 ... 37 G4
BSTN/STPLFD NG9 ... 63 H3
DERBYW DE22 ... 43 K5
NORM/LIT DE23 ... 57 H5
RLEINE/SYS LE7 ... 118 B8
Cloud Av BSTN/STPLFD NG9 ... 48 D8
Cloud Lea RLBORO LE12 ... 113 J7
Clouds HI CFTN/RUD NG11 ... 64 C7
Cloudside Rd LGEAT NG10 ... 47 L8
Cloudwood CI NORM/LIT DE23 ... 56 F5
Clough St WOL/BIL/BRX NG8 ... 35 M8
Clovelly Rd LEIE LE5 ... 132 D5
LEIW LE3 ... 124 B7
Clover CI DERBYE DE21 ... 59 K2
RLEIW/BAR LE9 ... 135 L7
Clover Ct BWSH/BRSTN DE72 ... 74 C5
Cloverdale COT/KEY/RAD NG12 ... 67 L5
Cloverdale Dr DERBYSE DE24 ... 71 K5
Cloverdale Rd LEIE LE5 ... 127 G5
Clover Gn BLWL NG6 ... 36 A5
Clover Lands CFTN/RUD NG11 ... 65 G4
Cloverlands Dr
EWD/SEL/PNX NG16 ... 22 E8
Clover La RLBORO LE12 ... 113 K6
Clover PI COAL LE67 ... 100 B7
Clover Ri EWD/SEL/PNX NG16 ... 21 M6
Cloverslade RDERBYSW DE65 ... 70 A3
Cloves HI ILK DE7 ... 31 C5
Clowbridge Dr LBORO LE11 ... 103 C4
Clumber Av ARN NG5 ... 36 F7
BSTN/STPLFD NG9 ... 48 D8
CARL NG4 ... 38 E8
EWD/SEL/PNX NG16 ... 13 J6
MAPPK/POR/STA NG3 ... 37 L3
Clumber CI RLEINE/SYS LE7 ... 120 F2
Clumber CI ILK DE7 ... 33 K2
Clumber Crs North NOTTE NG7 ... 4 C8
Clumber Crs South NOTTE NG7 ... 4 C9
Clumber Dr COT/KEY/RAD NG12 ... 53 L3
Clumber Rd LEIE LE5 ... 132 C2
WBRGFD NG2 ... 65 K1
Clumber Rd East NOTTE NG7 ... 4 C8
Clumber Rd West NOTTE NG7 ... 4 C8
Clumber St LGEAT NG10 ... 62 B8
Cluster Rd BPR/DUF DE56 ... 17 K3
Clusters Ct BPR/DUF DE56 ... 17 K3
Clyde St LEI LE1 ... 7 H4
Coach Dr DERBYW DE22 ... 29 C8
EWD/SEL/PNX NG16 ... 21 K3
Coachmans Ct RLBORO LE12 ... 102 A2
Coachmans Cft
WOL/BIL/BRX NG8 ... 49 L2
Coach Rd RIPLEY DE5 ... 11 K4
Coachways ILK DE7 ... 32 C4
Coalbourn CI LEIN LE4 ... 125 J3
Coales Av RLEIW/BBY LE8 ... 142 E2
Coatbridge Av LEIN LE4 ... 126 C7
Coates Av HUCK/RAV NG15 ... 15 K6
LEIW LE3 ... 124 B1
Coatsby Rd EWD/SEL/PNX NG16 ... 22 D8
Cobden St DERBYE DE22 ... 9 L2
LBORO LE11 ... 9 L2
LEI LE1 ... 7 K3
LGEAT NG10 ... 62 B8
NOTTE NG7 ... 50 C2
RIPLEY DE5 ... 11 C5
Cobham CI DERBYSE DE24 ... 71 H4
Cobthorn Dr DERBYW DE22 ... 43 G3
Cobwells CI RLEIW/BBY LE8 ... 145 L8
Cockayne CI LGEAT NG10 ... 61 M4
Cockayne St North
DERBYSE DE24 ... 72 C1
Cockayne St South
DERBYSE DE24 ... 72 C1
Cocker Beck CARL NG4 ... 27 C8
Cockerhouse Rd
EWD/SEL/PNX NG16 ... 21 J3
Cockington Rd
WOL/BIL/BRX NG8 ... 49 C2
Cockleys LGEAT NG10 ... 76 A1
Cockshut La MELB/CHEL DE73 ... 82 D8
Cod Beck CI DERBYSE DE24 ... 73 G1
Codnor-denby La RIPLEY DE5 ... 19 L2
Codnor Ga RIPLEY DE5 ... 11 M6
Codnor La ALFN DE55 ... 2 A5

Common Piece La
RDERBYSW DE65 ... 70 C6
Commons CI
EWD/SEL/PNX NG16 ... 21 L7
The Common DERBYW DE22 ... 29 G7
LEIE LE5 ... 132 E4
Compton Acres WBRGFD NG2 ... 64 F5
Compton Av BWSH/BRSTN DE72 ... 73 L7
Compton CI DERBYSE DE24 ... 73 G1
LBORO LE11 ... 103 G7
Compton Rd ARN NG5 ... 36 F5
LEIS ... 131 C5
Comyn Gdns
MAPPK/POR/STA NG3 ... 5 J4
Conaglen Rd LEIS LE2 ... 136 F1
Condon CI RLBORO LE12 ... 105 J8
Condor CI RLEIW/BAR LE9 ... 141 K8
Condor Rd ILK DE7 ... 47 K3
Conduit CI WBRGFD NG2 ... 51 G5
Conduit St LEIS LE2 ... 7 H7
Cone La LEIS LE5 ... 132 A5
The Coneries LBORO LE11 ... 9 K2
Conery La RLEIW/BAR LE9 ... 135 L4
Coneygrey RLEIW/BBY LE8 ... 145 K8
Coney Wk NOTTE NG7 ... 24 D7
Conifer CI LEIE LE5 ... 7 M9
Conifer Wk CFTN/RUD NG11 ... 64 C8
Coningsby Gdns East
ARN NG5 ... 37 K3
Coningsby Rd ARN NG5 ... 37 K2
Coningswath Rd CARL NG4 ... 38 A5
Coninsby CI LEIW LE3 ... 130 F6
Conisborough Ter
WBRGFD NG2 ... 51 G6
Conisbrough Av CARL NG4 ... 38 F6
Coniston Av BLWL NG6 ... 36 A5
DERBYE DE21 ... 59 J1
LEIS ... 131 J4
Coniston CI WBRGFD NG2 ... 52 A8
Coniston Crs DERBYE DE21 ... 44 B5
LBORO LE11 ... 8 A8
Coniston Dr ILK DE7 ... 47 H2
Coniston Rd BSTN/STPLFD NG9 ... 49 H6
HUCK/RAV NG15 ... 15 K7
LGEAT NG10 ... 61 L5
RLBORO LE12 ... 105 H7
Coniston Wy RLEIW/BAR LE9 ... 141 H3
Connaught Rd DERBYW DE22 ... 57 G3
Connaught St LEIS LE2 ... 7 K9
Connelly CI ARN NG5 ... 38 A1
Connery Ms
BSTN/STPLFD NG9 ... 62 F6
The Connery HUCK/RAV NG15 ... 15 H8
Consett CI DERBYE DE21 ... 44 B6
Consort Gdns DERBYE DE21 ... 45 G4
Constable Av DERBYW DE22 ... 57 G4
Constable Dr NORM/LIT DE23 ... 56 F5
Constable La NORM/LIT DE23 ... 56 E6
Constance Rd LEIE LE5 ... 132 B2
Constance St LEIE LE5 ... 36 E6
Constitution HI LEI LE1 ... 7 H6
Convent Dr COAL LE67 ... 108 B7
Convent St NOTT NG1 ... 5 J6
Conway Av BWSH/BRSTN DE72 ... 60 E8
CARL NG4 ... 38 E8
Conway CI LBORO LE11 ... 102 F2
MAPPK/POR/STA NG3 ... 5 H2
Conway Crs CARL NG4 ... 38 E7
Conway Dr RLBORO LE12 ... 101 K4
Conway Gdns ARN NG5 ... 37 K1
Conway Rd CARL NG4 ... 38 E8
HUCK/RAV NG15 ... 23 H4
LEIS ... 132 B4
LGEAT NG10 ... 62 C7
RLBORO LE12 ... 113 H6
Conway St LGEAT NG10 ... 62 D7
Cooden Av LEIW LE3 ... 130 F3
Cook CI BPR/DUF DE56 ... 18 C2
Cook Dr ILK DE7 ... 47 L1
Cooke CI LBORO LE11 ... 61 M8
Cookfield BPR/DUF DE56 ... 10 C7
Cookham CI MCKLVR DE3 ... 56 A5
Cooks Av CDON/KEG DE74 ... 84 E4
Cook's La RLEIW/BAR LE9 ... 140 B8
WGSTN LE18 ... 138 C8
Cookson Av CARL NG4 ... 38 B5
Cookson PI LBORO LE11 ... 103 C1
Coombe CI RLBORO LE12 ... 102 A5
WOL/BIL/BRX NG8 ... 50 A4
Coombe PI LEIS LE2 ... 138 F3
Coombe Ri LEIS LE2 ... 139 G4
Co-operation St
RLEIW/BAR LE9 ... 135 M4
Co-operative Av
HUCK/RAV NG15 ... 15 M7
Co-operative St LGEAT NG10 ... 62 C8
NORM/LIT DE23 ... 2 D9
Cooper CI ARN NG5 ... 38 A1
BLWL NG6 ... 35 K1
COAL LE67 ... 108 B2
LEIS ... 137 G1
RLEIW/BAR LE9 ... 135 H7
Cooper Ct LBORO LE11 ... 104 B5
Cooper Gdns LEIS LE2 ... 139 H3
Coopers CI
BWSH/BRSTN DE72 ... 60 B6
Coopers Gn WOL/BIL/BRX NG8 ... 49 J5
Cooper's Nook RLEINE/SYS LE7 ... 115 H8
Coopers St CARL NG4 ... 52 E1
DERBYW DE22 ... 57 G1
LEIN LE4 ... 125 L6
Copdale Rd LEIE LE5 ... 132 C2
Copeland Av BSTN/STPLFD NG9 ... 48 C7
LEIW LE3 ... 124 E6
Copeland Crs LBORO LE11 ... 103 H2
Copeland Rd LEIN LE4 ... 125 K1
Copeland St DERBY DE1 ... 3 G5
Cope St NOTTE NG7 ... 4 A3
Copes Wy DERBYE DE21 ... 44 F7
Copinger Rd LEIS LE2 ... 131 K8
Coplow Av LEIE LE5 ... 132 C5
Coplow Crs RLEINE/SYS LE7 ... 120 E5
Copper Beeches RIPLEY DE5 ... 10 F5
Copperleaf CI DERBYW DE22 ... 2 C6

Copper Yd *RIPLEY* DE5 .... 19 K5
Coppice Av *ILK* DE7 .... 33 H2
Coppice Cl *BPR/DUF* DE56 ..... 18 E7 ▣
  DERBYSE DE21 .... 43 K6
Coppice Dr *EWD/SEL/PNX* NG16 ... 20 J4
Coppice Ga *ARN* NG5 .... 25 K7
Coppice Gv
  MAPPK/POR/STA NG3 .... 37 K5 ▣
Coppice La *RLEINE/SYS* LE7 .... 121 K2
Coppice Rd *ARN* NG5 .... 25 K7
The Coppice *COAL* LE67 .... 116 C7 ▣
  LEIN LE4 .... 120 E8
  RLBORO LE12 .... 112 F3
  RLEIW/BAR LE9 .... 135 L7
Copplestone Dr
  MAPPK/POR/STA NG3 .... 38 A1 ▣
Copse Cl *CALV/BJ* NG14 .... 39 J2
  COAL LE67 .... 108 A8
  LEIS LE2 .... 133 C8
  LEIW LE3 .... 129 J6
Copse Gv *NORM/LIT* DE23 ..... 56 E8 ▣
  RLBORO LE12 .... 111 L1 ▣
Copseside Cl *LGEAT* NG10 ...... 61 L7
The Copse *BSTN/STPLFD* NG9 ... 63 G1
  HUCK/RAV NG15 .... 24 A1
  ILK DE7 .... 33 H2
Copthorne Cl *LEIW* LE3 .... 130 B1 ▣
Copt Oak Rd *RLEINE/BAR* LE9 .. 135 K6
Corah St *LEI* LE1 .... 6 C7
Coral St *LEIN* LE4 .... 125 L6
Corbel Cl *DERBYE* DE21 .... 44 C5
Corben Gdns *RLBORO* NG6 ...... 23 K8
Corbet Cl *LEIN* LE4 .... 124 F4
Corbridge Gv *NORM/LIT* DE23 ... 56 E8 ▣
Corby Cl *DERBYSE* DE24 .... 72 D2 ▣
Corby Rd *MAPPK/POR/STA* NG3 ... 37 J6
Cordelia Cl *LEIE* LE5 .... 126 C7
Cordell Rd *LBORO* LE11 .... 103 H1
Corden Av *MCKLVR* DE3 .... 56 E5
Corden St *NORM/LIT* DE23 ..... 57 L5
Cordery Rd *LEIE* LE5 .... 132 F4
Cordville Cl *DERBYE* DE21 ...... 58 F2 ▣
Cordy La *EWD/SEL/PNX* NG16 .. 13 K8
Corfe Cl *NORM/LIT* DE23 .... 71 H1 ▣
Corfield Av *HEANOR* DE75 .... 20 D8
Corfield Ri *LEIW* LE3 .... 130 C4 ▣
Coriander Dr *BLWL* NG6 .... 36 B4
Coriander Gdns
  NORM/LIT DE23 .... 71 H3 ▣
Coriander Rd *LEIS* LE2 .... 6 B9
Corinium Dr *DERBYSE* DE24 ..... 73 H2
Corinth St *CFTN/RUD* NG11 .... 64 C5 ▣
Cork La *LEIS* LE2 .... 136 E5
Cork St *LEIS* LE2 .... 7 M7
Corn Cl *COT/KEY/RAD* NG12 .... 67 J5
Corncrake Av *BLWL* NG6 .... 36 B4 ▣
Cornell Dr *ARN* NG5 .... 26 A7
Cornfield Cl *RLEIW/BAR* LE9 .. 136 A8
Cornfield Rd
  EWD/SEL/PNX NG16 .... 22 C8
Cornflower Dr *DERBYE* DE21 ... 44 E5
Cornhill *DERBYW* DE22 .... 43 K3
Cornhill Rd *CARL* NG4 .... 37 M7
Corn Market *DERBY* DE1 .... 2 F5
Cornmill Cl *DERBYSE* DE24 ..... 73 H2 ▣
Cornwall Av *BSTN/STPLFD* NG9 ... 64 A3
Cornwallis Av *LEIN* LE4 .... 124 F5
Cornwallis Cl *LGEAT* NG10 ..... 76 B1
Cornwall Rd *ARN* NG5 .... 25 G8
  DERBYE DE21 .... 3 M1
  DERBYE DE21 .... 44 B8
  LEIN LE4 .... 125 H6
  WGSTN LE18 .... 137 K5
Cornwall St *RLEIW/BAR* LE9 .. 135 M4
Coronation Av *BPR/DUF* DE56 ... 17 L2
  CFTN/RUD NG11 .... 50 F7
  DERBYSE DE24 .... 73 C2
  LGEAT NG10 .... 47 L8
  WGSTN LE18 .... 137 M5
Coronation Cl *MELB/CHEL* DE73 ... 82 E7
Coronation Rd *BLWL* NG6 .... 24 C3
  EWD/SEL/PNX NG16 .... 33 M5
  EWD/SEL/PNX NG16 .... 34 F7
  HUCK/RAV NG15 .... 15 K6 ▣
  ILK DE7 .... 33 L5
  ILK DE7 .... 45 M1
  MAPPK/POR/STA NG3 .... 37 K3
Coronation St *ILK* DE7 .... 33 K7 ▣
  NORM/LIT DE23 .... 57 M7 ▣
Coronation Wk *CARL* NG4 ...... 38 C6
Coronet Ct *DERBYE* DE21 .... 45 H4 ▣
Corporation Rd *ILK* DE7 .... 47 L2
  LEIN LE4 .... 125 K5
Corporation St *DERBY* DE1 .... 2 F3
Corsham Gdns
  MAPPK/POR/STA NG3 .... 37 L8 ▣
Cort Crs *LEIS* LE2 .... 130 C5
Cosby Rd *RLEIW/BAR* LE9 ..... 141 L8
  RLEIW/BAR LE9 .... 142 A1
  RLEIW/BBY LE8 .... 142 F4
  WBRGFD NG2 .... 51 K4
Cossall Rd *BSTN/STPLFD* NG9 .. 34 A7
  BSTN/STPLFD NG9 .... 48 B2
Cossington La *RLEINE/SYS* LE7 .. 119 L1
Cossington Rd *RLBORO* LE12 .. 114 A5
Cossington St *LEIN* LE4 .... 125 M6
Costock Av *ARN* NG5 .... 36 F3
Costock Rd *COT/KEY/RAD* NG12 ... 90 A5
  RLBORO LE12 .... 88 D6
  RLBORO LE12 .... 89 H6
Cotes Rd *RLBORO* LE12 .... 104 F4
Cotes Rd *LBORO* LE11 .... 9 L1 ▣
  LBORO LE11 .... 104 F3
Cotgrave Av *CARL* NG4 .... 38 D5 ▣
Cotgrave Cl *WOL/BIL/BRX* NG8 .. 35 J5
Cotgrave La *COT/KEY/RAD* NG12 ... 66 C5
Cotgrave Rd
  COT/KEY/RAD NG12 .... 66 D8
Cothelstone Av *LBORO* LE11 .. 103 L4
Cotley Rd *LEIN* LE4 .... 125 C2
Cotmanhay Rd *ILK* DE7 .... 33 K4
Coton Cl *CFTN/RUD* NG11 ...... 64 E4
Cotswold Av *RLEIW/BAR* LE9 .. 142 C5 ▣
Cotswold Cl *LBORO* LE11 .... 8 B4
  LGEAT NG10 .... 61 M7 ▣
  NORM/LIT DE23 .... 57 G7

Cotswold Rd *WOL/BIL/BRX* NG8 .. 35 H6
Cottage Cl *BPR/DUF* DE56 ..... 10 C8
  GBY/RBY LE6 .... 123 C6
  ILK DE7 .... 33 H4
Cottage Farm Cl *LEIW* LE3 .... 136 D1
Cottage Garden La
  HEANOR DE75 .... 20 B5
Cottage La *COAL* LE67 .... 116 A4
Cottage Meadow *CARL* NG4 .... 52 D3
Cottage Rd *WGSTN* LE18 .... 138 C6
Cottage Rw *LEIW* LE3 .... 130 F7
Cottagers Cl *WGSTN* LE18 ..... 137 J2
Cottage Ter *NOTT* NG1 .... 4 D6
Cottam Dr *ARN* NG5 .... 24 D7
Cottam Gdns *ARN* NG5 .... 24 E7
Cottesbrooke Cl
  WGSTN LE18 .... 138 B5 ▣
Cottesmore Av *LEIS* LE2 .... 139 C3
Cottesmore Dr *LBORO* LE11 .. 103 K7
Cottesmore Rd *LEIS* LE2 .... 126 B8
  NOTTE NG7 .... 4 A7
Cottisford Cl *NORM/LIT* DE23 .. 56 E7
Cotton Brook Rd
  NORM/LIT DE23 .... 57 M7
Cotton Cl *LEIN* LE4 .... 126 B2
Cotton Cft *RLBORO* LE12 ...... 101 M5
Cotton La *DERBYSE* DE24 ...... 57 M7
Cotton Wy *LBORO* LE11 .... 95 J8
Coulson Cl *RLEIW/BBY* LE8 ... 142 E1
Countesthorpe Rd
  RLEIW/BBY LE8 .... 142 B5
  RLEIW/BBY LE8 .... 142 E4
  RLEIW/BBY LE8 .... 143 K1
Counting House Rd *LEIS* LE2 .. 131 K5
Countisbury Dr *DERBYE* DE21 .. 44 E5
Countrymans Wy *RLBORO* LE12.. 102 A3
  RLEINE/SYS LE7 .... 115 H7
Countryman Wy *COAL* LE67 .. 116 C7
County Cl *BSTN/STPLFD* NG9 .. 63 L2 ▣
County Rd *CARL* NG4 .... 38 A4
  WBRGFD NG2 .... 51 J5
Coupe St *RIPLEY* DE5 .... 11 K7
Court Cl *RLEIW/BAR* LE9 ...... 129 J2
Court Crs *WOL/BIL/BRX* NG8 .. 49 J3
Courtenay Gdns
  MAPPK/POR/STA NG3 .... 5 J2
Courtenay Rd *LEIW* LE3 .... 125 C6
Court Gdns *CFTN/RUD* NG11 .. 64 F3 ▣
Courtland Dr *DERBYSE* DE24 .. 72 E1
Courtland Gdns *DERBYSE* DE24 .. 72 F1
Courtland Rd
  RDERBYSW DE65 .... 69 C4 ▣
Courtleet Wy *BLWL* NG6 .... 35 M2
Courtney Cl
  WOL/BIL/BRX NG8 .... 49 J2 ▣
Courtney Wy *BPR/DUF* DE56 .. 18 B2 ▣
Court Rd *LEIS* LE2 .... 136 F5
  RLEINE/SYS LE7 .... 133 K3
Court St *NOTTE* NG7 .... 4 B2
The Court *DERBYSE* DE24 ...... 72 F1 ▣
Court Vw *BSTN/STPLFD* NG9 .. 48 F7
Covedale Rd *ARN* NG5 .... 37 G2
Coventry La *BSTN/STPLFD* NG9 .. 48 E5
  WOL/BIL/BRX NG8 .... 48 F7
Coventry Rd *BLWL* NG6 .... 23 M8 ▣
  BLWL NG6 .... 35 M1
  BSTN/STPLFD NG9 .... 49 L8
  RLEIW/BAR LE9 .... 135 M8
  RLEIW/BAR LE9 .... 140 F8
  RLEIW/BAR LE9 .... 141 H4
  RLEIW/BAR LE9 .... 141 K2
  RLEIW/BAR LE9 .... 141 G7
Coventry St *LEIW* LE3 .... 6 A7 ▣
Coverdale *WGSTN* LE18 .... 138 D6 ▣
Coverside Rd *RLEIW/BBY* LE8 .. 139 M6
Covert Cl *CALV/BJ* NG14 .... 39 J2 ▣
  COT/KEY/RAD NG12 .... 80 D3
  HUCK/RAV NG15 .... 24 A1
  LEIS LE2 .... 139 J1
  RLEINE/SYS LE7 .... 120 C4 ▣
Covert Crs *COT/KEY/RAD* NG12 .. 53 M4
Covert La *RLEINE/SYS* LE7 .... 127 L7
Covert Rd *WBRGFD* NG2 .... 65 M1
The Covert *DERBYE* DE21 ...... 59 J3
Covett Wy *LEIW* LE3 .... 130 C2
Cowan St *NOTT* NG1 .... 5 J6
Cowdall Rd *LEIW* LE3 .... 130 B4
Cowdray Cl *DERBYSE* DE24 ... 71 H5 ▣
  LBORO LE11 .... 9 H8
Cowdrey Gdns *ARN* NG5 .... 37 M1
Cowlairs *ARN* NG5 .... 24 C8
Cow La *BSTN/STPLFD* NG9 .... 49 G7
  GBY/RBY LE6 .... 122 D5
Cowley St *BLWL* NG6 .... 36 B4
  DERBYW DE22 .... 43 J8
Cowley Wy *LEIW* LE3 .... 133 J1 ▣
Cowlishaw Cl
  BWSH/BRSTN DE72 .... 74 C6
Cowper Rd *ARN* NG5 .... 37 J3
  EWD/SEL/PNX NG16 .... 21 L7 ▣
Cowper St *DERBYSE* DE24 ...... 71 L2
Cowsley Rd *DERBYE* DE21 ...... 44 B8
Cowslip Cl *RLEIW/BAR* LE9 .. 135 K7 ▣
Coxbench Rd *DERBYE* DE21 ... 30 C3
Cox Green Cl *NORM/LIT* DE23 .. 56 D8
Coxon St *DERBYE* DE21 .... 59 J2
Crabtree Cl *CDON/KEG* DE74... 84 E5
  DERBYW DE22 .... 43 C3
Crabtree Fld *WBRGFD* NG2 ..... 52 B3
Crab Tree Hl *DERBYE* DE21 ... 30 A7
Crabtree Hill Keddleston Rd
  DERBYW DE22 .... 43 C4
Crabtree Rd *BLWL* NG6 .... 35 L1
Craddock Av *DERBYE* DE21 .... 59 J4
Craddock St *LBORO* LE11 .... 9 K2
Cradock Dr *DERBYE* DE21 .... 112 D2
Cradock Rd *LEIS* LE2 .... 131 M5
Cradock St *LEIS* LE2 .... 7 J4 ▣
Crafton St East *LEI* LE1 .... 7 H4
Crafton St West *LEI* LE1 .... 7 G4
Craftsmans Wy
  RLEINE/SYS LE7 .... 115 H8
Cragdale *COAL* LE67 .... 100 B8
Cragdale Rd *ARN* NG5 .... 37 G2
Cragmoor Rd *CALV/BJ* NG14... 39 J4
Craig Gdns *LEIW* LE3 .... 130 B1

Craighill Rd *LEIS* LE2 .... 131 M7
Craiglee Ct *DERBYSE* DE24 .... 71 H4 ▣
Craig St *LGEAT* NG10 .... 62 C8
Crammond Cl *WBRGFD* NG2 ... 50 F5 ▣
Cramps Cl *RLBORO* LE12 .... 105 H8
Crampton Ct *ARN* NG5 .... 24 E7 ▣
Cramworth Dr *ARN* NG5 .... 37 H4 ▣
Cranberry Cl *CFTN/RUD* NG11 .. 64 F2
Cranberry Gv *NORM/LIT* DE23 .. 70 D1 ▣
Cranbourne Cl
  BSTN/STPLFD NG9 .... 48 B5 ▣
Cranbourne Gdns *LEIS* LE2 .. 132 F7
Cranbourne Gv *HUCK/RAV* NG15 .. 15 J8
Cranbrook Rd *RLEINE/SYS* LE7 .. 133 K1
Cranbrook St *NOTT* NG1 .... 5 J6
Cranbury Rd *RLEINE/SYS* LE7 .. 127 C6 ▣
Crane-ley Rd *GBY/RBY* LE6 ... 123 J4
Crane St *LEI* LE1 .... 6 E5
Cranfield Rd *LEIS* LE2 .... 137 H1
Cranfield Wk *CFTN/RUD* NG11 .. 64 D5
Cranfleet Wy *LGEAT* NG10 ..... 61 M8
Cranford Gdns *WBRGFD* NG2 .. 65 G3 ▣
Cranhill Cl *NORM/LIT* DE23 ... 70 D1 ▣
Cranmer Cl *RLEIW/BBY* LE8 .. 142 E1
Cranmer Dr *RLEINE/SYS* LE7 .. 120 D4
Cranmer Rd *DERBYE* DE21 ...... 3 J3
Cranmer St *ILK* DE7 .... 33 K6 ▣
  LEIW LE3 .... 6 A8
  LGEAT NG10 .... 62 B6
  MAPPK/POR/STA NG3 .... 5 C2
Cranmore Cl *ARN* NG5 .... 25 L5 ▣
Cranoe Rd *RLEIW/BBY* LE8 .. 147 M6
Cransley Av *WOL/BIL/BRX* NG8 .. 49 H5
Cranston Av *ARN* NG5 .... 25 K6
Cranstone Crs *LEIW* LE3 ...... 124 A8
Cranston Rd *BSTN/STPLFD* NG9 .. 49 G6
Cranthorne Dr
  MAPPK/POR/STA NG3 .... 52 A1
Crantock Cl *LEIE* LE5 .... 133 C4
Crantock Gdns
  COT/KEY/RAD NG12 .... 80 D4
Cranwell Cl *LEIE* LE5 .... 132 F5 ▣
Cranwell Rd
  WOL/BIL/BRX NG8 .... 35 H5 ▣
  EWD/SEL/PNX NG16 .... 22 A7 ▣
  NOTTE NG7 .... 4 D5
Craster Dr *ARN* NG5 .... 25 L5
  BLWL NG6 .... 23 K7 ▣
Craven Cl *LBORO* LE11 .... 103 K7
Craven Rd *NOTTE* NG7 .... 36 C8
Craven's Rough *COAL* LE67 .. 116 F3
Crawford Av *BSTN/STPLFD* NG9 .. 48 B7
Crawford Cl
  WOL/BIL/BRX NG8 .... 49 J2 ▣
Crawford Ri *ARN* NG5 .... 26 A7
Crawley Rd *DERBYSE* DE24 ... 72 D2
Crawshaw Cl *RLBORO* LE12 .. 94 A4
Crayford Dr *ARN* NG5 .... 26 E2
Crayford Wy *LEIE* LE5 .... 127 H6
Craythorne Wy *WGSTN* LE18 .. 138 D5 ▣
Creaton Ct *WGSTN* LE18 ...... 138 C5 ▣
Creaton Rd *WGSTN* LE18 ...... 138 C5
Crecy Cl *NORM/LIT* DE23 ...... 57 G4
Crediton Cl *WGSTN* LE18 ...... 138 B7 ▣
Crescent Av *CARL* NG4 .... 38 C6 ▣
Crescent Rd *COAL* LE67 .... 108 A8
  EWD/SEL/PNX NG16 .... 13 H1
Crescent St *LEI* LE1 .... 6 F8 ▣
The Crescent *ARN* NG5 .... 37 J3
  BSTN/STPLFD NG9 .... 48 C6
  BSTN/STPLFD NG9 .... 62 E5
  BSTN/STPLFD NG9 .... 63 G4
  BWSH/BRSTN DE72 .... 61 G8
  COT/KEY/RAD NG12 .... 53 L3
  DERBYE DE21 .... 58 D2
  DERBYSE DE24 .... 72 C1
  EWD/SEL/PNX NG16 .... 21 L5
  ILK DE7 .... 19 G8
  ILK DE7 .... 31 M6
  MAPPK/POR/STA NG3 .... 37 H7
  RLBORO LE12 .... 88 D5
  RLEIW/BBY LE8 .... 136 F8
  WGSTN LE18 .... 138 A3 ▣
Cressbrook Wy *DERBYE* DE21 .. 44 F4 ▣
Cresswell Cl *LEIN* LE4 .... 126 E1
Cresswell Rd *BSTN/STPLFD* NG9 .. 62 F2
Cresta Gdns *ARN* NG5 .... 37 H5
The Crest *DERBYW* DE22 .... 43 J5
The Crestway *RLEIW/BBY* LE8 .. 136 D7
Crete Av *WGSTN* LE18 .... 137 J5
Crewe Cl *NOTTE* NG7 .... 4 A4
Crewe St *NORM/LIT* DE23 ..... 57 K6
Crewton Wy *DERBYSE* DE24 .. 58 D8
Cribb Cl *CFTN/RUD* NG11 ...... 50 F8
Crich Av *NORM/LIT* DE23 ...... 56 F5
Crich La *BPR/DUF* DE56 .... 17 L1
Crich Vw *ARN* NG5 .... 37 G5 ▣
  BPR/DUF DE56 .... 10 C7 ▣
Cricketers Ct *WBRGFD* NG2 ... 51 K6
Cricket La *LBORO* LE11 .... 103 H1
Cricklewood Rd *DERBYW* DE22 .. 56 F1
Criftin Rd *CALV/BJ* NG14 .... 39 L3
Cringle Ms *DERBYE* DE21 ...... 44 C5
Critchley St *ILK* DE7 .... 33 K6
Critchlow Rd *RLEIW/BAR* LE9 .. 135 H7
Critch's Flats
  EWD/SEL/PNX NG16 .... 34 D1 ▣
Crocus St *WBRGFD* NG2 .... 51 G5
Croft Av *HUCK/RAV* NG15 ...... 23 L1
  LEIS LE2 .... 137 G1
Croft Cl *BWSH/BRSTN* DE72 ... 60 A2
  DERBYE DE21 .... 59 K1
  ILK DE7 .... 46 D5
Croft Crs *EWD/SEL/PNX* NG16 .. 34 A2
Croft Dr *WGSTN* LE18 .... 137 M3
Croft End *DERBYE* DE21 .... 30 A7
Crofters Cl *LEIW* LE3 .... 123 L7
Crofters Ct *DERBYE* DE21 ..... 44 C5 ▣
The Crofters *LEIE* LE5 .... 126 E8
Croft Hill Rd *RLEIW/BAR* LE9 .. 141 C1
Croft La *DERBYE* DE21 .... 44 B4
Crofton Cl *BSTN/STPLFD* NG9 .. 63 H5
Crofton Rd *BSTN/STPLFD* NG9 .. 63 H5
Croft Rd *ARN* NG5 .... 25 K7
  COT/KEY/RAD NG12 .... 65 L3

Cott *COT/KEY/RAD* NG12 ...... 80 B4
  LEIN LE4 .... 119 C8
  RLEIW/BAR LE9 .... 134 E5
  RLEIW/BAR LE9 .... 141 K3
The Croft *BPR/DUF* DE56 ...... 10 C6
  BPR/DUF DE56 .... 18 A6
  BWSH/BRSTN DE72 .... 74 E1
  CDON/KEG DE74 .... 86 B5 ▣
  ILK DE7 .... 31 C6
  MELB/CHEL DE73 .... 82 E7 ▣
  NORM/LIT DE23 .... 57 H7
  RLEIW/BAR LE9 .... 129 H2
Croftway *COAL* LE67 .... 116 B7
Cromarty Cl *DERBYSE* DE24 ... 71 J3
  LEIN LE4 .... 126 B4 ▣
Cromarty Ct *WBRGFD* NG2 ..... 50 F5 ▣
Cromdale Cl *ARN* NG5 .... 26 A6
Cromer Cl *MCKLVR* DE3 .... 56 A6
Cromer Rd *MAPPK/POR/STA* NG3.. 5 M1
Cromer St *LEIS* LE2 .... 132 A4
Cromford Av *CARL* NG4 .... 38 B7
  WGSTN LE18 .... 137 L6
Cromford Cl
  EWD/SEL/PNX NG16 .... 20 E5 ▣
  LGEAT NG10 .... 75 L2
Cromford Dr *MCKLVR* DE3 .... 56 B3
Cromford Rd *DERBYE* DE21 ... 44 E7
  EWD/SEL/PNX NG16 .... 20 C2
  EWD/SEL/PNX NG16 .... 20 E5 ▣
  RIPLEY DE5 .... 11 H5
  RLEIW/BAR LE9 .... 142 B3
  WBRGFD NG2 .... 65 K1
Cromford St *LEIS* LE2 .... 7 L5
Cromore Cl *COAL* LE67 .... 109 C6 ▣
Crompton Rd *ILK* DE7 .... 47 M4
Crompton St *DERBY* DE1 .... 2 D5
Cromwell Av *ILK* DE7 .... 47 L2
  RDERBYSW DE65 .... 70 B5
Cromwell Crs *CARL* NG4 .... 26 F8
Cromwell Dr *RLBORO* LE12 ... 88 C6
Cromwell Rd *BSTN/STPLFD* NG9 .. 63 J1
  NORM/LIT DE23 .... 2 C9
  RLBORO LE12 .... 113 H7
  RLEIW/BBY LE8 .... 139 M7
Cromwell St *CARL* NG4 .... 38 C8
  EWD/SEL/PNX NG16 .... 22 A7 ▣
  NOTT NG7 .... 4 D5
Croome Cl *LBORO* LE11 .... 9 L8
Cropston Av *LBORO* LE11 .... 102 E5
Cropston Cl *WBRGFD* NG2 ..... 65 H3
Cropston Dr *COAL* LE67 .... 108 F7
Cropston Rd *GBY/RBY* LE6 .. 118 C5
  RLEINE/SYS LE7 .... 124 C1
Cropthorne Av *LEIE* LE5 ...... 132 D2
Cropton Cl *DERBYSE* DE24 .... 73 C1
Cropton Crs
  WOL/BIL/BRX NG8 .... 49 M1 ▣
Cropwell Gdns
  COT/KEY/RAD NG12 .... 53 L5
Cropwell Gn
  MAPPK/POR/STA NG3 .... 51 K1 ▣
Cropwell Rd *COT/KEY/RAD* NG12.. 53 L5
Crosby Rd *LBORO* LE11 .... 51 K6
Crosby St *DERBYW* DE22 .... 57 H3
Cross Cl *NORM/LIT* DE23 .... 57 G7
Crossdale Dr
  COT/KEY/RAD NG12 .... 80 C3
Crossdale Gv *DERBYE* DE21 ... 45 G4 ▣
Crossdale Wk *ARN* NG5 .... 24 C7
Crossfield Dr *ARN* NG5 .... 24 E6
Crossgate Dr *WBRGFD* NG2 ... 50 F6 ▣
Cross Gn *RLEINE/SYS* LE7 ... 119 J1
Cross Hedge *RLEINE/SYS* LE7 .. 113 J8
Cross Hedge Cl *LEIN* LE4 ..... 125 C3 ▣
Crosshill *COT/KEY/RAD* NG12 .. 67 L4
  RIPLEY DE5 .... 19 M1
Cross Hill *RLBORO* LE12 .... 98 A4 ▣
Crosshill Dr *ILK* DE7 .... 47 C2 ▣
Cross Hill La *LBORO* LE11 .... 8 F9
Cross Keys Gn *LEIE* LE5 .... 127 J8
Crosslands Meadow *CARL* NG4 .. 52 D3
Cross La *RIPLEY* DE5 .... 11 M8
  RLBORO LE12 .... 113 J7
Crossley Cl *RLBORO* LE12 ... 105 C8
Crossleys *RLEIW/BBY* LE8 .. 145 K8 ▣
Crossley St *ARN* NG5 .... 36 F5
  LEIE LE3 .... 124 A7 ▣
  RIPLEY DE5 .... 11 H6 ▣
Crossman St *ARN* NG5 .... 36 F5
Cross Rd *LEIS* LE2 .... 132 A5
Cross St *ARN* NG5 .... 25 J7
  BSTN/STPLFD NG9 .... 49 K8
  CARL NG4 .... 38 B7
  CARL NG4 .... 38 E8 ▣
  DERBYW DE22 .... 43 J8
  EWD/SEL/PNX NG16 .... 21 L5 ▣
  LBORO LE11 .... 9 L1 ▣
  LEIN LE4 .... 125 L6
  LEIS LE2 .... 132 E8
  LGEAT NG10 .... 62 A1
  LGEAT NG10 .... 62 C7
  RLBORO LE12 .... 94 E6
  RLEINE/SYS LE7 .... 120 F4
  RLEIW/BBY LE8 .... 135 M4
  RLEIW/BBY LE8 .... 136 F7 ▣
  WGSTN LE18 .... 138 B5 ▣
The Cross *RLEIW/BAR* LE9 ... 135 M4 ▣
The Crossways *LEIN* LE4 ...... 119 M8
The Crossway *LEIS* LE2 .... 137 K1
  LEIW LE3 .... 130 E7
Crosswood Cl *LBORO* LE11 .. 103 C4
Crowan Dr *WGSTN* LE18 ...... 138 A7 ▣
Crowborough Av
  WOL/BIL/BRX NG8 .... 49 J5 ▣
Crowcroft Wy *LGEAT* NG10 .. 61 M5
Crow Hill Rd *CARL* NG4 .... 38 D8 ▣
Crowhurst Dr *LEIW* LE3 .... 130 C7
Crow La *LEIW* LE3 .... 131 H4 ▣
Crowley Cl *WOL/BIL/BRX* NG8 .. 49 C1
Crown Cl *LGEAT* NG10 .... 61 L8 ▣
Crown Hills Av *LEIE* LE5 ...... 132 C2
Crown Hills Ri *LEIE* LE5 .... 132 C2
Crown Hill Wy *ILK* DE7 .... 31 M7 ▣
Crownland Dr
  MELB/CHEL DE73 .... 72 E5 ▣
Crown La *RLBORO* LE12 .... 113 H4
Crown Ms *DERBYW* DE22 .... 2 B7
Crown St *BPR/DUF* DE56 .... 29 J3

Crown Ter *BPR/DUF* DE56 ...... 17 K3 ▣
Crow Park Dr *CALV/BJ* NG14 .. 39 L5
Crowshaw St *DERBYSE* DE24 .. 57 M7 ▣
  DERBYSE DE24 .... 58 A7 ▣
Crowthorne Cl *ARN* NG5 .... 24 C5
Crowthorne Gdns *ARN* NG5 ... 24 C6 ▣
Croxall Cl *CFTN/RUD* NG11 ... 64 C3 ▣
Croxley Gdns
  EWD/SEL/PNX NG16 .... 35 H4
Croxton Rd *RLEINE/SYS* LE7 .. 121 L3
Croydon Rd *RLBORO* NG7 ...... 50 C2
Croyland Gn *LEIE* LE5 .... 133 J1
Crummock Cl
  BSTN/STPLFD NG9 .... 49 G7 ▣
Crusaders Cl *COAL* LE67 ..... 108 D2
Cuckmere Cl *DERBYW* DE22 .. 43 M2
Cufflin Cl *GBY/RBY* LE6 .... 123 H7
Cuffling Cl *LEIW* LE3 .... 130 E5 ▣
Cuffling Dr *LEIW* LE3 .... 130 E1 ▣
Cuillin Cl *ARN* NG5 .... 24 D5
  LGEAT NG10 .... 61 L6 ▣
Culham Av *LEIE* LE5 .... 126 B7
Culver Rd *LEIW* LE3 .... 125 C7
Culworth Cl *BPR/DUF* DE56 .. 18 B3 ▣
Culworth Dr *WGSTN* LE18 .... 138 C5
Cumberhills Rd *DERBYW* DE22.. 28 F6
Cumberland Av
  BSTN/STPLFD NG9 .... 63 H1
  DERBYE DE21 .... 58 C1
Cumberland Cl
  CFTN/RUD NG11 .... 65 C8 ▣
  EWD/SEL/PNX NG16 .... 13 C3 ▣
Cumberland Crs
  BWSH/BRSTN DE72 .... 59 M6
Cumberland Pl *NOTT* NG1 .... 4 F7
Cumberland Rd *LBORO* LE11 .. 8 E2
  WGSTN LE18 .... 137 J4
Cumberland St *LEI* LE1 .... 6 C8
Cumberwell Dr *RLEIW/BAR* LE9 .. 136 A6
Cumbrian Wy *RLBORO* LE12 .. 102 A4
Cummings St *NORM/LIT* DE23 .. 2 E9
The Cunnery *ASHB* LE65 .... 41 K5
Curborough Dr *DERBYSE* DE24 .. 73 C1
Curlew Cl *COAL* LE67 .... 108 F7
  DERBYSE DE24 .... 71 H3 ▣
  MAPPK/POR/STA NG3 .... 52 A2
  RLEINE/SYS LE7 .... 120 D3 ▣
Cursley Wy *BSTN/STPLFD* NG9 .. 63 G5
Curteys Cl *LEIW* LE3 .... 130 F6
Curtis Cl *RLEIW/BBY* LE8 ..... 136 D8
Curtis St *HUCK/RAV* NG15 .... 23 L1
Curzon Av *LEIN* LE4 .... 125 L1
  WGSTN LE18 .... 137 L6
Curzon Cl *DERBYW* DE22 ...... 43 C3
  RLEINE/SYS LE7 .... 121 H2
Curzon La *BPR/DUF* DE56 ...... 29 H4 ▣
  DERBYSE DE24 .... 58 E7
Curzon Pl *MAPPK/POR/STA* NG3 .. 5 J5
Curzon Rd *DERBYE* DE21 ...... 44 D8
  LEIS LE2 .... 131 H8
Curzon St *CARL* NG4 .... 38 E8
  CFTN/RUD NG11 .... 77 M6
  DERBY DE1 .... 2 D4
  DERBYW DE22 .... 2 C4
  LBORO LE11 .... 9 G3
  LEI LE1 .... 7 K2 ▣
  LGEAT NG10 .... 61 M5
  MAPPK/POR/STA NG3 .... 5 J5
Cutters Cl *RLEIW/BAR* LE9 .. 135 L8
The Cuttings *RLEINE/SYS* LE7 .. 133 K1
Cuttlebrook Cl
  NORM/LIT DE23 .... 71 J1 ▣
Cuxton Cl *WOL/BIL/BRX* NG8 .. 35 H6
Cycle Rd *NOTTE* NG7 .... 50 C3
Cygnet Cl *RLEINE/SYS* LE7 .. 120 D3
Cypress Cl *LBORO* LE11 .... 103 L8
Cypress Ct *HUCK/RAV* NG15 .. 22 F2
Cyprus Av *BSTN/STPLFD* NG9 .. 49 K8
Cyprus Dr *BSTN/STPLFD* NG9 .. 49 K8
Cyprus Rd *LEIS* LE2 .... 137 J1
  MAPPK/POR/STA NG3 .... 37 G7
Cyril Av *BSTN/STPLFD* NG9 ... 48 B7
  WOL/BIL/BRX NG8 .... 36 B7
Cyril Rd *WBRGFD* NG2 .... 51 L8
Cyril St *LEIW* LE3 .... 130 E7

D

Dabell Av *BLWL* NG6 .... 23 J7
Dabey Cl *COAL* LE67 .... 116 B7
Dagmar Gv *BSTN/STPLFD* NG9 .. 63 L1
  MAPPK/POR/STA NG3 .... 37 H6
Dahlia Dr *DERBYE* DE21 .... 45 C4
Dairy House Rd *NORM/LIT* DE23 .. 57 L6
Daisy Cl *COT/KEY/RAD* NG12 .. 67 J5
Daisy Farm Rd
  EWD/SEL/PNX NG16 .... 21 H7
Daisy Rd *MAPPK/POR/STA* NG3.. 37 L6
Dakeyne St *MAPPK/POR/STA* NG3.. 5 M6
Dakota Rd *CDON/KEG* DE74 .... 84 F7
Dakyn Rd *LEIE* LE5 .... 133 H1
Dalbeattie Cl *ARN* NG5 .... 25 M7
Dalby Av *RLEINE/SYS* LE7 ... 119 M7
  RLEINE/SYS LE7 .... 133 L2
Dalby Dr *GBY/RBY* LE6 .... 123 K4
Dalby Rd *RLEINE/SYS* LE7 ... 118 B3
Dalby Sq *WOL/BIL/BRX* NG8 .. 50 A4
Dale Acre *RLEIW/BBY* LE8 .... 143 K3
Daleacre Av *CDON/KEG* DE74 .. 85 K2 ▣
Dale Av *ALFN* DE55 .... 12 A1
  CARL NG4 .... 38 A8
  LGEAT NG10 .... 62 B6
  MAPPK/POR/STA NG3 .... 37 L5
  WGSTN LE18 .... 137 J3
Dale Brook *RDERBYSW* DE65 .. 68 C6 ▣
Dalebrook Crs *HUCK/RAV* NG15.. 23 G2
Dale Cl *BWSH/BRSTN* DE72 ... 61 H7
  HUCK/RAV NG15 .... 23 G1
  WBRGFD NG2 .... 51 M8
Dale Ct *BPR/DUF* DE56 .... 18 D7 ▣
Dale End La *RDERBYSW* DE65... 68 A5
Dale Farm Av
  MAPPK/POR/STA NG3 .... 51 L2
Dale Gv *WBRGFD* NG2 .... 51 K3
Dalehead Rd *CFTN/RUD* NG11 .. 64 B5

Dale La BSTN/STPLFD NG9 .... 63 J1
Dalemoor Gdns
WOL/BIL/BRX NG8 .... 35 M7
Dale Park Av BPR/DUF DE56 .... 18 E7
Dale Rd CARL NG4 .... 38 A8
COT/KEY/RAD NG12 .... 80 C4
DERBYE DE21 .... 59 K1
DERBYSE DE24 .... 59 G8
EWD/SEL/PNX NG16 .... 34 D2
ILK DE7 .... 46 A3
ILK DE7 .... 47 G5
NORM/LIT DE23 .... 57 K5
Daleside COT/KEY/RAD NG12 .... 67 K5
Daleside Rd WBRGFD NG2 .... 51 L4
Daleside Rd East WBRGFD NG2 .... 52 A3
The Dales RLEIW/BBY LE8 .... 143 G3
Dale St ILK DE7 .... 33 K8 1
LEIS LE2 .... 7 L6
WBRGFD NG2 .... 5 M8
Dale Vw ILK DE7 .... 47 J1
Dale View Gdns BPR/DUF DE56 .... 18 D7
Dale View Rd CARL NG4 .... 37 M8
Dalkeith Av DERBYSE DE24 .... 72 D2
Dalkeith Rd LEIN LE4 .... 126 B3
Dalkeith Ter NOTTE NG7 .... 4 A2
Dallas York Rd
BSTN/STPLFD NG9 .... 63 M1 2
Dalley Cl BSTN/STPLFD NG9 .... 48 C7
RLEINE/SYS LE7 .... 120 F5
Dalley La BPR/DUF DE56 .... 17 G1
Dallimore Rd ILK DE7 .... 47 H3
Dalness Ct DERBYSE DE24 .... 71 H4 5
Dalton Av DERBYW DE22 .... 57 G4
Dalton Cl BSTN/STPLFD NG9 ...... 62 C2 2
Daltons Cl EWD/SEL/PNX NG16 .... 20 E3
Danbury Dr LEIN LE4 .... 125 H5
Danbury Mt ARN NG5 .... 37 H5 1
Dandees Cl COAL LE67 .... 116 C6
Danebridge Crs DERBYE DE21 ...... 44 E6
Dane Cl MAPPK/POR/STA NG3 .... 5 J4
Dane Hl GBY/RBY LE6 .... 123 H7
Danehurst Av LEIW LE3 .... 130 F1
Danesby Crs RIPLEY DE5 .... 18 D6
Danesby Ri RIPLEY DE5 .... 18 E6
Danes Cl ARN NG5 .... 25 H7
Daneshill Rd LEIW LE3 .... 131 G2
Dane St LEIW LE3 .... 6 A6
Danethorpe V ARN NG5 .... 37 G3
Daniels Wy HUCK/RAV NG15 .... 23 J3
Dannah Crs RIPLEY DE5 .... 11 J6
Dannah St RIPLEY DE5 .... 11 J5
Dannett St LEIW LE3 .... 6 A5 1
Dan's La RLEIW/BAR LE9 .... 128 B8
Danver's La RLBORO LE12 .... 102 A3
Danvers Rd LEIW LE3 .... 131 G4
RLBORO LE12 .... 113 J6
Darby St NORM/LIT DE23 .... 2 D9
Darenth Dr LEIN LE4 .... 124 E4
Darfield Dr HEANOR DE75 .... 20 E5
Darien Wy LEIW LE3 .... 130 A5
Darker St LEI LE1 .... 6 E4 1
Darkey La BSTN/STPLFD NG9 .... 62 C2
Dark La BPR/DUF DE56 .... 29 L1
RLBORO LE12 .... 87 K5
Darley Abbey Dr
DERBYW DE22 .... 43 L5 2
Darley Av BSTN/STPLFD NG9 .... 62 C4
CARL NG4 .... 38 C6
NOTTE NG7 .... 36 C8
WGSTN LE18 .... 137 L6 1
Darley Dr ILK DE7 .... 32 C7 3
LGEAT NG10 .... 75 L2
RIPLEY DE5 .... 11 G4
Darley Gv DERBY DE1 .... 43 L8
DERBYW DE22 .... 43 L6
Darley La DERBY DE1 .... 2 E1
Darley Park Dr DERBYW DE22 .... 43 K6
Darley Park Rd DERBYW DE22 .... 43 K6
Darley Rd NOTTE NG7 .... 36 C8
RLEIW/BBY LE8 .... 136 E8
Darley Sq ILK DE7 .... 33 J2
Darley St DERBYW DE22 .... 43 L6
LEIS LE2 .... 7 L6
Darlington Rd LEIW LE3 .... 124 E7
Darlton Dr ARN NG5 .... 25 M8
Darnal Cl ARN NG5 .... 24 C8
Darnhall Crs WOL/BIL/BRX NG8 .... 35 H8
Darsway CDON/KEG DE74 .... 84 E3
Dart Cl LEIS LE2 .... 139 G2
Dartford Pl DERBYSE DE24 .... 72 E2
Dartford Rd LEIS LE2 .... 131 H6
Darvel Cl WOL/BIL/BRX NG8 .... 49 M1
Darwen Cl LEIW LE3 .... 124 F7
Darwin Av DERBYSE DE24 .... 72 B3
ILK DE7 .... 33 J8
Darwin Cl ARN NG5 .... 24 C7
LEIW LE3 .... 130 A6
Darwin Rd LGEAT NG10 .... 75 M2
MCKLVR DE3 .... 56 C4
Dashwood Rd LEIS LE2 .... 132 A4
Dashwood St NORM/LIT DE23 .... 2 F8 1
Datchet Cl NORM/LIT DE23 .... 56 E7
Dauphine Cl COAL LE67 .... 109 H6
Davenport Av LEIS LE2 .... 138 D1
Davenport Rd DERBYSE DE24 .... 58 A7
LEIE LE5 .... 132 F2 1
WGSTN LE18 .... 138 B6
Daventry Cl MCKLVR DE3 .... 56 A4
Davett Cl LEIE LE5 .... 132 F1 2
David Av LEIN LE4 .... 125 J2
David Gv BSTN/STPLFD NG9 .... 49 H6
David La BLWL NG6 .... 36 B4
David's Cl MELB/CHEL DE73 .... 72 C6
Davidson Cl ARN NG5 .... 26 A8 1
Davies Rd WBRGFD NG2 .... 51 L8
Davison Cl LEIE LE5 .... 132 E1
Davis Rd BSTN/STPLFD NG9 .... 62 F4
Davy Cl HUCK/RAV NG15 .... 15 M5
Dawlish Cl HUCK/RAV NG15 .... 23 H1
LEIE LE5 .... 133 H2
Dawlish Ct DERBYSE DE24 .... 59 G8
EWD/SEL/PNX NG16 .... 21 H4
Dawlish Dr ARN NG5 .... 36 F2
Dawn Cl HUCK/RAV NG15 .... 15 M6
Dawn Vw BSTN/STPLFD NG9 .... 48 B5 2
Dawsmere Cl DERBYE DE21 .... 44 B6 2
Dawson Cl EWD/SEL/PNX NG16 .... 21 L6
Dawson's Rd RLBORO LE12 .... 100 B3
Dawver Rd EWD/SEL/PNX NG16 .. 34 D2
Daybell Cl RLEIW/BBY LE8 .... 136 D6
Daybrook Av ARN NG5 .... 37 G4 1
Daybrook St ARN NG5 .... 37 G4
Daylesford Cl NORM/LIT DE23 .. 56 E7 5
Days La BPR/DUF DE56 .... 17 K4
Day St LEIN LE4 .... 125 L4 2
Dayton Cl DERBYE DE21 .... 59 G2
Deabill St CARL NG4 .... 52 E1
Deacon Cl DERBYE DE21 .... 44 C5 5
RLBORO LE12 .... 102 A4
Deacon Rd LEIN LE4 .... 119 H7
Deacon St LEIS LE2 .... 6 D9
Dead La EWD/SEL/PNX NG16 .... 34 B6
Deadman's La DERBYSE DE24 .... 58 B5
Deakins Pl NOTTE NG7 .... 50 C2
Dean Av MAPPK/POR/STA NG3 ...... 37 M4
Dean Cl NORM/LIT DE23 .... 56 E5
WOL/BIL/BRX NG8 .... 49 H2
Deancourt Rd LEIS LE2 .... 137 M1
Deanery Crs LEIN LE4 .... 119 H7
Deane St LBORO LE11 .... 8 D1
Dean Rd ARN NG5 .... 37 J2
LEIN LE4 .... 126 A6
Deanscourt COT/KEY/RAD NG12 .. 67 L4
Deans Cft BSTN/STPLFD NG9 .... 48 F6
Deans Dr BWSH/BRSTN DE72 .... 59 M5
Deanside Dr LBORO LE11 .... 103 H1
Dean's La RLBORO LE12 .... 110 F4
Dean St DERBYW DE22 .... 2 A7
EWD/SEL/PNX NG16 .... 21 G4
NOTT NG1 .... 5 K8
Debdale La COT/KEY/RAD NG12 .... 80 B3
Deborah Dr DERBYE DE21 .... 44 E8
Deddington La
BSTN/STPLFD NG9 .... 49 G5
Dee Cl DERBYSE DE24 .... 71 J4
Dee La RDERBYSW DE65 .... 68 B4
Deeming Dr RLBORO LE12 .... 112 D1
Deepdale EWD/SEL/PNX NG16 .... 12 D7
LEIE LE5 .... 132 D1
Deepdale Av BSTN/STPLFD NG9 ...... 62 B1
Deepdale Cl WBRGFD NG2 .... 52 A8
Deep Dale La DERBYSE DE24 .... 71 J5
Deepdale Rd BPR/DUF DE56 .... 17 M2
DERBYE DE21 .... 59 K4
LGEAT NG10 .... 75 L2 1
WOL/BIL/BRX NG8 .... 49 H3
Deepdene Cl
WOL/BIL/BRX NG8 .... 35 L5 2
Deepdene Wy
WOL/BIL/BRX NG8 .... 35 L5
Deep Furrow Av CARL NG4 .... 38 B7
The Deepway RLBORO LE12 .... 112 C2
Deerleap Dr ARN NG5 .... 25 G8
Deer Pk WOL/BIL/BRX NG8 .... 49 J3
Deer Park Dr ARN NG5 .... 24 F7
Deer Park Vw DERBYE DE21 .... 59 K1
Deers Acre LBORO LE11 .... 103 M1
De Ferrers Cl RLBORO LE12 .... 88 C6 1
Degge St DERBY DE1 .... 2 E5
Deighton Wy LBORO LE11 .... 103 G1 3
Deincourt Cl DERBYE DE21 .... 59 L1
Delamere Cl BWSH/BRSTN DE72 .. 61 H7
DERBYE DE21 .... 44 E6 3
Delaware Rd LEIE LE5 .... 133 J4
De Lisle Ct LBORO LE11 .... 102 F5 2
Dell Wy CFTN/RUD NG11 .... 64 D5
Dellwood Cl
MAPPK/POR/STA NG3 .... 38 A5 1
Delta St NOTTE NG7 .... 36 D6 1
Delven La CDON/KEG DE74 .... 84 E4 2
Delves Rd HEANOR DE75 .... 20 B7
Delville Av COT/KEY/RAD NG12 .... 80 C3
De Montfort Cl LBORO LE11 .... 103 G2 2
De Montfort Sq LEI LE1 .... 7 H8 1
De Montfort St LEI LE1 .... 7 G9
De Morgan Cl
EWD/SEL/PNX NG16 .... 13 L5
Denacre Av LGEAT NG10 .... 62 D6
WGSTN LE18 .... 137 L6
Denarth Av DERBYSE DE24 .... 72 C4
Denbigh St DERBYE DE21 .... 44 C8
Denby Common RIPLEY DE5 .... 19 K5
Denbydale WGSTN LE18 .... 138 D6
Denby La RIPLEY DE5 .... 18 F6
Denegate Av LEIN LE4 .... 119 K7
Denehurst Av WOL/BIL/BRX NG8 .. 36 A6
Denewood Av
BSTN/STPLFD NG9 .... 49 G5
Denewood Crs
WOL/BIL/BRX NG8 .... 35 J7
Denham Cl LEIW LE3 .... 130 A1 1
Denholme Rd WOL/BIL/BRX NG8 .. 49 H2
Denis Cl LEIW LE3 .... 130 F2
Denison Gdns DERBYE DE21 .... 58 F1
Denison St BSTN/STPLFD NG9 .... 49 J8
NOTTE NG7 .... 4 A4
Deniston Cl RLEIW/BAR LE9 .... 141 H8
Denman La RLEIW/BAR LE9 .... 135 H7
Denman Street Central
NOTTE NG7 .... 50 C2
Denman St East NOTTE NG7 .... 4 B5
Denman St West NOTTE NG7 .... 50 C2
Denmark Gv
MAPPK/POR/STA NG3 .... 37 H7
Denmark Rd LEIS LE2 .... 131 J7
Denmead Av WGSTN LE18 .... 138 A4
Dennett Cl MAPPK/POR/STA NG3 .. 5 L5
Dennis Av BSTN/STPLFD NG9 .... 49 J7
Dennis Cl NORM/LIT DE23 .... 56 C8
Dennis St CARL NG4 .... 38 E8 2
Denstone Dr DERBYSE DE24 .... 72 E3
Denstone Rd
MAPPK/POR/STA NG3 .... 5 M6
Dentdale Dr WOL/BIL/BRX NG8 ...... 48 F3
Denton Av LGEAT NG10 .... 61 L1 1
Denton Dr WBRGFD NG2 .... 65 H3
Denton St LEIW LE3 .... 130 F2
Denver Ct BSTN/STPLFD NG9 .... 48 C6
Denver Rd MCKLVR DE3 .... 56 B4
Depedale Av BWSH/BRSTN DE72 .. 60 A5
ILK DE7 .... 47 H2
Depot St NORM/LIT DE23 .... 2 F9
Deptford Crs BLWL NG6 .... 36 A1
Derby Gv NOTTE NG7 .... 4 B6
Derby La NORM/LIT DE23 .... 57 K7
Derby Rd BPR/DUF DE56 .... 18 C8 2
BPR/DUF DE56 .... 29 K2
BSTN/STPLFD NG9 .... 48 F7
BSTN/STPLFD NG9 .... 62 A1
BWSH/BRSTN DE72 .... 59 L5
BWSH/BRSTN DE72 .... 60 F3
BWSH/BRSTN DE72 .... 60 C7
BWSH/BRSTN DE72 .... 73 L4
CDON/KEG DE74 .... 86 A5
DERBYE DE21 .... 30 B2
DERBYE DE21 .... 45 J4
DERBYE DE21 .... 58 F3
EWD/SEL/PNX NG16 .... 21 J5
EWD/SEL/PNX NG16 .... 21 H4 2
HEANOR DE75 .... 20 B6
ILK DE7 .... 33 H8
LBORO LE11 .... 95 G8
LGEAT NG10 .... 61 M7
MELB/CHEL DE73 .... 72 D5
MELB/CHEL DE73 .... 82 E6
NOTTE NG7 .... 4 B7
NOTTE NG7 .... 49 L6
RDERBYSW DE65 .... 68 B5
RIPLEY DE5 .... 11 H6
RIPLEY DE5 .... 11 J2
RIPLEY DE5 .... 19 J1
RLBORO LE12 .... 94 D5
Derbyshire Av
BSTN/STPLFD NG9 .... 48 B3
ILK DE7 .... 32 C7
Derbyshire Cl ILK DE7 .... 32 C7 5
Derbyshire Dr
EWD/SEL/PNX NG16 .... 13 G3
ILK DE7 .... 47 J1
Derbyshire La HUCK/RAV NG15 .... 15 L8
Derby St ARN NG5 .... 25 K8 1
BSTN/STPLFD NG9 .... 49 K8
ILK DE7 .... 33 K7 2
NOTT NG1 .... 4 E6 1
Dereham Dr ARN NG5 .... 37 K1
Derrington Leys DERBYSE DE24 .... 73 H1
Derry Dr ARN NG5 .... 25 K5
Derry Hill Rd ARN NG5 .... 25 J6
Dersingham Rd LEIN LE4 .... 125 H5
Derventio Cl DERBY DE1 .... 43 L8 1
Derwent Av BPR/DUF DE56 .... 17 K7
BWSH/BRSTN DE72 .... 60 A4
DERBYW DE22 .... 43 L3
ILK DE7 .... 32 C7
ILK DE7 .... 33 H5
Derwent Cl BSTN/STPLFD NG9 .. 63 J4 2
DERBYW DE22 .... 43 L3 1
WBRGFD NG2 .... 52 A8
Derwent Ct BPR/DUF DE56 .... 17 M3 1
Derwent Crs ARN NG5 .... 37 L1 1
Derwent Dr DERBYSE DE24 .... 71 H5
HUCK/RAV NG15 .... 23 L3 2
LBORO LE11 .... 8 A8
Derwent Ri DERBYE DE21 .... 59 K3
Derwent Rd DERBYE DE21 .... 59 H4 1
RIPLEY DE5 .... 11 G6
RLBORO LE12 .... 105 H6 2
Derwent St BPR/DUF DE56 .... 17 J4
BWSH/BRSTN DE72 .... 60 E8
DERBY DE1 .... 3 G3
LEIS LE2 .... 7 L7
Derwent V BPR/DUF DE56 .... 17 K5 1
Derwent Vw BPR/DUF DE56 .... 17 K2
Derwent Wk LEIS LE2 .... 139 G2
Desford Cl ARN NG5 .... 36 E3
Desford La GBY/RBY LE6 .... 122 F8
GBY/RBY LE6 .... 128 F1
RLEIW/BAR LE9 .... 128 C2
Desford Rd GBY/RBY LE6 .... 129 H1
RLEIW/BAR LE9 .... 129 G7
RLEIW/BAR LE9 .... 134 C2
RLEIW/BAR LE9 .... 134 E4
RLEIW/BAR LE9 .... 134 D3
RLEIW/BAR LE9 .... 135 K2
RLEIW/BAR LE9 .... 135 M8 2
RLEIW/BAR LE9 .... 135 M7
Devana Av COAL LE67 .... 108 C7
Devana Rd LEIS LE2 .... 132 A4
Devas Gdns DERBYE DE21 .... 59 H2
Devenports Wy
RLEINE/SYS LE7 .... 133 M2
De Verdun Av RLBORO LE12 .... 100 F2
De Vere Gdns ARN NG5 .... 37 K2
Deveron Cl COAL LE67 .... 109 G6
Devon Circ ARN NG5 .... 25 H6
Devon Cl DERBYE DE21 .... 3 M1
EWD/SEL/PNX NG16 .... 21 M5 1
LGEAT NG10 .... 61 M2
Devon Dr ARN NG5 .... 37 G5
CFTN/RUD NG11 .... 65 H7
Devonia Rd LEIS LE2 .... 139 H3
Devonshire Av
BSTN/STPLFD NG9 .... 63 J1
BWSH/BRSTN DE72 .... 60 A5
DERBYW DE22 .... 43 K4
LGEAT NG10 .... 62 E7
RIPLEY DE5 .... 11 G5
WGSTN LE18 .... 137 L6
Devonshire Cl ILK DE7 .... 33 J2 1
Devonshire Crs ARN NG5 .... 36 F5
Devonshire Dr BPR/DUF DE56 .... 29 H5
BSTN/STPLFD NG9 .... 48 B5
EWD/SEL/PNX NG16 .... 21 K5 1
MCKLVR DE3 .... 56 C4
Devonshire La LBORO LE11 .... 9 H4
Devonshire Rd ARN NG5 .... 36 F5
LEIN LE4 .... 125 J6
WBRGFD NG2 .... 65 J1
Devonshire Sq LBORO LE11 .... 9 J4
Devonshire St LEI LE1 .... 6 E3
Devon St ILK DE7 .... 47 L2
MAPPK/POR/STA NG3 .... 51 K2 1
Devon Wy LEIE LE5 .... 132 D2 1
Dewberry La
COT/KEY/RAD NG12 .... 53 M5
Dewchurch Dr NORM/LIT DE23 .... 70 F2
Dexters Cl RLBORO LE12 .... 104 E8 1
Dexter St NORM/LIT DE23 .... 3 J9
The Dial COT/KEY/RAD NG12 .... 67 J6
Diamond Dr DERBYE DE21 .... 44 D4
Dickens Cl RLBORO LE12 .... 114 B3 1
Dickens Ct
EWD/SEL/PNX NG16 .... 21 M4 2
LEIW LE3 .... 130 E2 1
Dickens Sq NORM/LIT DE23 .... 57 K8
The Dicken RLEIW/BBY LE8 .... 136 D8
Dickinson St DERBYSE DE24 .... 58 B5
Dickinson Wy LEIN LE4 .... 120 D8
Dickson Dr CFTN/RUD NG11 .... 79 H1
Didcot Dr WOL/BIL/BRX NG8 .... 36 B6 2
Didsbury St LEIW LE3 .... 130 C4
Digby Av MAPPK/POR/STA NG3 .... 37 M4
Digby Cl LEIW LE3 .... 130 F3
Digby Hall Dr
MAPPK/POR/STA NG3 .... 38 A4
Digby St EWD/SEL/PNX NG16 .... 34 B1
ILK DE7 .... 33 L6
Dillon Ri LEIW LE3 .... 124 D7 1
Dillon Rd LEIW LE3 .... 124 D7
Dillon Wy LEIW LE3 .... 124 D6
Dimmingsdale Cl
RLEINE/SYS LE7 .... 118 C8 1
Dingley Av LEIN LE4 .... 126 A6
Dingley Link WGSTN LE18 .... 138 C4 1
Diseworth Cl
MELB/CHEL DE73 .... 72 E5 5
Diseworth Rd CDON/KEG DE74 .... 84 E6
Diseworth St LEIS LE2 .... 7 L7
Disney Cl RLEIW/BAR LE9 .... 140 B5
Disraeli Cl RLEIW/BBY LE8 .... 146 D7 5
Disraeli St LEIS LE2 .... 131 G8
RLBORO LE12 .... 112 E1
Distillery St CFTN/RUD NG11 .... 79 G1
Ditchling Av LEIW LE3 .... 130 E1
Dix Av ILK DE7 .... 31 K1
Dixie St EWD/SEL/PNX NG16 .... 12 F3
Dixon Dr LEIS LE2 .... 132 A4
Dobholes La ILK DE7 .... 31 J1
Dobney Av RLEINE/SYS LE7 .... 121 G2
Dockholm Rd LGEAT NG10 .... 62 A5
Dodburn Ct DERBYSE DE24 .... 71 H3
Dodgeford La RLBORO LE12 .... 100 D2
Dog And Bear La
HUCK/RAV NG15 .... 14 E2
Dog And Gun La
RLEIW/BBY LE8 .... 142 D2
Dogwood Av BLWL NG6 .... 23 K8
Dogwood Ct LEIS LE2 .... 132 E8
Doles La RDERBYSW DE65 .... 70 A4
Dolphin Cl DERBYE DE21 .... 59 L1
Dominion Rd LEIW LE3 .... 124 A7
Domont Cl RLBORO LE12 .... 101 M4
Donald Cl LEIN LE4 .... 126 D3
Donald Hawley Wy
BPR/DUF DE56 .... 29 K4
Donaldson Rd LEIN LE4 .... 125 L7
Donbas Cl BLWL NG6 .... 35 M3
Doncaster Av LGEAT NG10 .... 61 M1
Doncaster Gv LGEAT NG10 .... 62 D6
Doncaster Rd LEIN LE4 .... 125 M6
Doncaster Ter WBRGFD NG2 .... 51 G6 5
Donington Cl NORM/LIT DE23 .... 71 J2 5
Donington Dr NORM/LIT DE23 .... 71 J2
Donington La
BWSH/BRSTN DE72 .... 75 G7
CDON/KEG DE74 .... 75 G8
Donington Rd CFTN/RUD NG11 .... 64 C6
Donkey La CFTN/RUD NG11 .... 79 J4
Donner Crs ILK DE7 .... 33 J2
Donnett Cl LEIE LE5 .... 132 F1 5
Donnington St LEIS LE2 .... 7 L7
Dooland Dr
MAPPK/POR/STA NG3 .... 37 K6
Dorchester Av DERBYE DE21 .... 44 C8
Dorchester Cl RLEIW/BBY LE8 .... 143 G1
WGSTN LE18 .... 138 A7
Dorchester Gdns
WBRGFD NG2 .... 65 J4 1
Dorchester Rd
EWD/SEL/PNX NG16 .... 22 D8 5
LEIW LE3 .... 130 F3
Dore Rd LEIE LE5 .... 7 M9
Doris Rd ILK DE7 .... 33 L8
Dorket Cl ARN NG5 .... 25 L6 1
Dorket Dr WOL/BIL/BRX NG8 .... 50 A4
Dorking Rd DERBYW DE22 .... 56 F1
NOTTE NG7 .... 50 C1 1
Dormy Cl BSTN/STPLFD NG9 .... 49 G8
COT/KEY/RAD NG12 .... 53 M4
Dormy Ct BLWL NG6 .... 24 B8
Dornoch Av ARN NG5 .... 37 H5
Dorothy Av EWD/SEL/PNX NG16 .... 21 L4
HUCK/RAV NG15 .... 15 M6
LEIN LE4 .... 126 B1
LEIS LE2 .... 136 F4
LGEAT NG10 .... 61 M2
Dorothy Gv WOL/BIL/BRX NG8 .... 50 A1
Dorothy Rd LEIE LE5 .... 132 B2
Dorrien Av NORM/LIT DE23 .... 57 K8
Dorset Av LEIW LE3 .... 124 A6
WGSTN LE18 .... 137 K4
Dorset Gdns WBRGFD NG2 .... 65 G2
Dorset St DERBYE DE21 .... 3 L1
LEIN LE4 .... 125 L7
WOL/BIL/BRX NG8 .... 50 B2
Dorterry Crs ILK DE7 .... 47 L2
Double Rail Cl WGSTN LE18 .... 137 L6 2
Doudney Cl RLEIW/BAR LE9 .... 140 B6
Douglas Av CARL NG4 .... 52 B1
EWD/SEL/PNX NG16 .... 34 A2
HEANOR DE75 .... 20 A5
Douglas Cl
COT/KEY/RAD NG12 .... 53 K5 1
Douglas Crs CARL NG4 .... 52 C1
Douglas Rd LGEAT NG10 .... 61 M6
NOTTE NG7 .... 4 B6
Douglas St NORM/LIT DE23 .... 3 J9
NORM/LIT DE23 .... 57 M5
Douro Dr ARN NG5 .... 25 M6 5
Dove Cl BPR/DUF DE56 .... 18 E7 2
MCKLVR DE3 .... 56 E4 2
Dovecote RLBORO LE12 .... 102 A3
Dovecote Cl RLEIW/BAR LE9 .... 140 B8 5
Dovecote Dr BWSH/BRSTN DE72 .... 59 L5
WOL/BIL/BRX NG8 .... 49 J3 1
Dovecote La BSTN/STPLFD NG9 .... 63 K1
RLEIW/BAR LE9 .... 141 G2
Dovecote Rd
EWD/SEL/PNX NG16 .... 21 M5
Dovecote St RLBORO LE12 .... 94 E6
The Dovecote DERBYE DE21 .... 30 D1
Dovedale Av DERBYSE DE24 .... 59 G8
LGEAT NG10 .... 75 L1
RLEIW/BBY LE8 .... 136 F8
Dovedale Cir ILK DE7 .... 33 J2
Dovedale Cl RIPLEY DE5 .... 19 H1
Dovedale Ct LGEAT NG10 .... 75 M1
Dovedale Crs BPR/DUF DE56 .... 17 M2
Dovedale Ri DERBYW DE22 .... 43 H6
Dovedale Rd DERBYE DE21 .... 59 J4
LEIN LE4 .... 120 C8
LEIS LE2 .... 132 C6
MAPPK/POR/STA NG3 .... 52 A1
WBRGFD NG2 .... 65 L2
Dove La LGEAT NG10 .... 62 A7
Dovenby Rd CFTN/RUD NG11 .... 64 D4
Dover Beck Dr CALV/BJ NG14 .... 27 G3
Dover Cl RLBORO LE12 .... 113 H7 2
Doveridge Av CARL NG4 .... 38 E7
Doveridge Rd CARL NG4 .... 38 D7
Dove Ri LEIS LE2 .... 139 G1
RDERBYSW DE65 .... 68 A5 1
Dove Rd CDON/KEG DE74 .... 85 G7
COAL LE67 .... 108 E8
RIPLEY DE5 .... 11 G6
Dover St LEI LE1 .... 7 G7
NORM/LIT DE23 .... 57 G6 1
RLEIW/BBY LE8 .... 146 D7
Dove St BLWL NG6 .... 23 M8 5
Dower Cl DERBYW DE22 .... 43 L6 2
Dower House Gdns
RLBORO LE12 .... 112 E1 1
Downes Cl BLWL NG6 .... 23 L8 2
Downham Av LEIN LE4 .... 125 J5
Downham Cl ARN NG5 .... 37 L1
MCKLVR DE3 .... 56 C6 1
Downing Cl BLWL NG6 .... 23 M7
DERBYW DE22 .... 56 D1 5
Downing Dr LEIE LE5 .... 133 G4
Downing Rd DERBYE DE21 .... 3 M4
Downing St BLWL NG6 .... 23 M7
Downmeadow
BPR/DUF DE56 .... 10 C7 2
The Downs CFTN/RUD NG11 .... 64 E4
Down St LEIN LE4 .... 125 M6
Dowson St
MAPPK/POR/STA NG3 .... 51 K1 5
Doyle Cl LBORO LE11 .... 103 H1 2
Drage St DERBY DE1 .... 43 M8
Dragwell CDON/KEG DE74 .... 86 B5
Drakemyre Cl ARN NG5 .... 25 M6 5
Drake Rd CARL NG4 .... 52 F2
Draper St LEIS LE2 .... 132 A4
Draycott Cl HEANOR DE75 .... 20 A3 1
Draycott Dr MCKLVR DE3 .... 56 A4
Draycott Rd BWSH/BRSTN DE72 .... 60 A6
BWSH/BRSTN DE72 .... 61 G8
LGEAT NG10 .... 75 K2
Draymans Ct NOTTE NG7 .... 36 D6 2
Drayton Av DERBYW DE22 .... 56 D1 5
Drayton Rd LEIW LE3 .... 124 C8
Drayton St ARN NG5 .... 37 G5 5
Dresden Cl MCKLVR DE3 .... 56 A5
Drewry Ct DERBYW DE22 .... 2 C4
Drewry La DERBYW DE22 .... 2 B5
Dreyfus Cl DERBYE DE21 .... 59 K2 1
Dribdale RLEIW/BBY LE8 .... 145 L8
The Drift CFTN/RUD NG11 .... 64 C4
HUCK/RAV NG15 .... 15 M6
Drinkstone Rd LEIE LE5 .... 132 C3
The Drive BPR/DUF DE56 .... 16 D4
BSTN/STPLFD NG9 .... 63 J4
LEIN LE4 .... 125 L1
RLBORO LE12 .... 111 K6
RLEINE/SYS LE7 .... 127 K7
RLEIW/BBY LE8 .... 142 F3
RLEIW/BBY LE8 .... 146 F7 5
Drome Cl COAL LE67 .... 109 H6
Dronfield Pl ILK DE7 .... 33 J2 5
Dronfield St LEIS LE2 .... 7 M7
Drovers Wy RLEIW/BAR LE9 .... 135 M8
Drumcliff Rd LEIE LE5 .... 133 J1
Drummond Av CARL NG4 .... 38 F8 1
Drummond Dr
EWD/SEL/PNX NG16 .... 35 J3
Drummond Rd ILK DE7 .... 33 H6
LEIN LE4 .... 125 K4
RLEIW/BAR LE9 .... 135 L4
Drury Av DERBYE DE21 .... 59 H3
Drury La LEIS LE2 .... 138 D1
Dryden St LEI LE1 .... 7 G4
NORM/LIT DE23 .... 71 K1
NOTT NG1 .... 4 F4
Dry Pot La RLBORO LE12 .... 93 J5
Drysdale Cl BLWL NG6 .... 35 M2
Drysdale Rd MCKLVR DE3 .... 56 B4
Duchess St BLWL NG6 .... 23 M7
Dudleston Cl LEIE LE5 .... 132 E2 1
Dudley Av LEIE LE5 .... 133 G1
Dudley Cl LEIE LE5 .... 133 G1
Duesbury Cl DERBYSE DE24 .... 58 C8
Duffield Av WGSTN LE18 .... 137 M3
Duffield Bank BPR/DUF DE56 .... 29 L3
Duffield Cl LGEAT NG10 .... 75 L2
Duffield Rd BPR/DUF DE56 .... 29 M6
DERBYW DE22 .... 43 K6
DERBYW DE22 .... 43 L2
Duffield St LEIS LE2 .... 7 L6
Duke Cl BLWL NG6 .... 35 K2
Duke Crs EWD/SEL/PNX NG16 .... 22 A6
Dukeries La DERBYE DE21 .... 44 F5
Dukes Cl LEIN LE4 .... 120 D8
WGSTN LE18 .... 137 M4
Dukes Pl ILK DE7 .... 33 J3
NOTT NG1 .... 5 K7
Duke St ARN NG5 .... 25 H8
DERBY DE1 .... 2 F1
HUCK/RAV NG15 .... 15 M8
ILK DE7 .... 33 K4
LBORO LE11 .... 9 K1
LEI LE1 .... 6 F7
NOTTE NG7 .... 36 D7
Duke William Mt NOTTE NG7 .... 4 C8
Duluth Av DERBYE DE21 .... 44 E8
Dulverton Av DERBYSE DE24 .... 71 G5 1
Dulverton Cl LBORO LE11 .... 103 H7 1
WGSTN LE18 .... 138 B7 2
Dulverton Rd LEIW LE3 .... 131 G2
Dulverton V
WOL/BIL/BRX NG8 .... 35 L4 1

Dulwich Rd DERBYW DE22 ... 56 C1
NOTTE NG7 ... 50 C2
Dumbles Cl ILK DE7 ... 47 G1
Dumbles La RIPLEY DE5 ... 19 K5
The Dumbles CARL NG4 ... 26 F7
Dumbleton Av LEIW LE3 ... 131 G6
Dumps Rd COAL LE67 ... 108 C1
Dunbar Cl DERBYSE DE24 ... 71 J5
Dunbar Rd COAL LE67 ... 109 C7
LEIN LE4 ... 126 C5
Dunblane Av LEIN LE4 ... 126 B3
Dunblane Rd RLEIW/BAR LE9 ... 135 H8
Duncan Cl BPR/DUF DE56 ... 17 M1
Duncan Dr LEIS LE2 ... 131 H8
NORM/LIT LE23 ... 57 K7
Duncan Wy LBORO LE11 ... 103 G1
Duncombe Cl
MAPPK/POR/STA NG3 ... 5 L2
Duncroft Av CARL NG4 ... 38 D6
Dundas Cl NOTT NG1 ... 5 G4
Dundee Rd DERBYW LE8 ... 142 F1
Dundonald Rd LEIN LE4 ... 125 L6
Dunedin Cl MCKLVR DE3 ... 10 C5
Dungannon Rd CFTN/RUD NG11 ... 64 C7
Dungley Hl BPR/DUF DE56 ... 10 B5
Dunholme Av LBORO LE11 ... 102 F3
Dunholme Cl BLWL NG6 ... 23 M7
Dunholme Rd LEIN LE4 ... 126 C6
Dunire Cl LEIN LE4 ... 125 G4
Dunkery Ct DERBYE DE21 ... 44 E5
Dunkery Rd CFTN/RUD NG11 ... 64 D7
Dunkirk DERBYW DE22 ... 2 D5
Dunkirk Rd NOTTE NG7 ... 50 C6
Dunkirk St LEI LE1 ... 7 G8
Dunlin Rd LEIE LE5 ... 7 J3
Dunlop Av NOTTE NG7 ... 50 C3
Dunnicliffe La MELB/CHEL DE73 ... 82 E8
Dunoon Cl ARN NG5 ... 24 C5
DERBYSE DE24 ... 71 J4
Dunsby Cl CFTN/RUD NG11 ... 64 C6
Dunsford Dr
MAPPK/POR/STA NG3 ... 38 A1
Dunsil Dr WBRGFD NG2 ... 50 E7
Duns La LEIW LE3 ... 6 C7
Dunsmore Cl
BSTN/STPLFD NG9 ... 63 M3
LBORO LE11 ... 103 H7
Dunsmore Dr DERBYE DE21 ... 44 C5
Dunstall Av LEIW LE3 ... 130 B5
Dunstall Park Rd DERBYSE DE24 ... 58 B7
Dunstan St CARL NG4 ... 38 B4
Dunster Rd EWD/SEL/PNX NG16 ... 21 M5
RLBORO LE12 ... 113 H6
WBRGFD NG2 ... 65 L1
Dunster St LEIW LE3 ... 130 F2
Dunton St LEIW LE3 ... 6 B3
WGSTN LE18 ... 137 K6
Dunvegan Cl DERBYSE DE24 ... 71 H5
Dunvegan Dr ARN NG5 ... 24 D5
Dupont Gdns LEIW LE3 ... 124 B8
Durban Rd LEIN LE4 ... 119 G8
Durham Av DERBYE DE21 ... 58 C1
WBRGFD NG2 ... 51 K3
Durham Cl WBRGFD NG2 ... 51 K3
Durham Crs BLWL NG6 ... 36 A1
Durham Dr WGSTN LE18 ... 137 L3
Durham Rd LBORO LE11 ... 103 J1
Durham St ILK DE7 ... 33 K6
Durley Cl DERBYSE DE24 ... 59 G8
Durlston Cl WBRGFD NG2 ... 64 F2
Durnford Rd WGSTN LE18 ... 138 A4
Durnford St NOTTE NG7 ... 36 D5
Durrell Cl LBORO LE11 ... 103 G1
Durris Cl COAL LE67 ... 109 C6
Dursley Cl BLWL NG6 ... 35 M2
Durston Cl LEIE LE5 ... 133 H3
Durward Cl DERBYSE DE24 ... 58 A8
Duxbury Rd LEIE LE5 ... 126 C8
Dylan Thomas Rd ARN NG5 ... 24 F7
Dysart Wy LEI LE1 ... 7 H2

E

Eagle Cl ARN NG5 ... 25 L8
BSTN/STPLFD NG9 ... 49 H7
RLEIW/BAR LE9 ... 141 J3
Eagle Cl BLWL NG6 ... 24 B8
Eagle Rd ILK DE7 ... 47 K3
Eagle St BPR/DUF DE56 ... 10 C5
Ealing Cl DERBYW DE22 ... 56 E1
Ealing Rd LEIS LE2 ... 131 K6
Eamont Cl LEIS LE2 ... 137 H4
Eardley Cl DERBYE DE21 ... 58 F2
Eardley Rd ARN NG5 ... 36 C1
Earl Crs CARL NG4 ... 38 D4
Earl Dr EWD/SEL/PNX NG16 ... 22 A6
Earle Smith Cl RLEIW/BBY LE8 ... 136 D8
Earl Howe St LEIS LE2 ... 7 J8
Earl Howe Ter LEIS LE2 ... 6 B7
Earl Russell St LEIS LE2 ... 137 G1
Earls Cl LEIN LE4 ... 120 D8
WOL/BIL/BRX NG8 ... 49 G2
Earls Crs DERBYE DE21 ... 44 F5
Earlsfield Dr ARN NG5 ... 24 B6
Earl Shilton Rd RLEIW/BAR LE9 ... 134 A6
Earl St LEI LE1 ... 7 G4
Earls Wy LEIN LE4 ... 120 D8
Earlswood Cl
BWSH/BRSTN DE72 ... 61 H7
Earlswood Dr
COT/KEY/RAD NG12 ... 65 M4
MCKLVR DE3 ... 56 D3
Earlswood Rd LEIE LE5 ... 133 H4
East Acres COT/KEY/RAD NG12 ... 67 K3
East Av LEIS LE2 ... 132 A5
MCKLVR DE3 ... 56 B4
RLEINE/SYS LE7 ... 121 C3
RLEIW/BBY LE8 ... 136 D7
East Bond St LEI LE1 ... 6 E4
Eastbrae Rd NORM/LIT DE23 ... 57 J8
East Circus St NOTT NG1 ... 4 F7
Eastcliffe Av CARL NG4 ... 38 B4
East Cl COT/KEY/RAD NG12 ... 80 C5
DERBYW DE22 ... 43 J5

Eastcote Av BSTN/STPLFD NG9 ... 48 F5
Eastcourt Rd LEIS LE2 ... 138 A1
East Crs BPR/DUF DE56 ... 18 A7
BSTN/STPLFD NG9 ... 63 M2
East Croft Av NORM/LIT LE23 ... 71 H2
Eastdale Rd
MAPPK/POR/STA NG3 ... 52 A1
Eastern Bvd LEIW LE3 ... 131 J4
Eastfield Rd LEIN LE4 ... 120 D7
LEIW LE3 ... 130 F2
RIPLEY DE5 ... 11 L6
Eastglade Rd ARN NG5 ... 36 E1
East Gv NOTTE NG7 ... 36 E7
Eastham Cl MAPPK/POR/STA NG3 ... 5 L4
Eastham Rd ARN NG5 ... 38 A1
Eastholme Cft WBRGFD NG2 ... 52 B2
Easthorpe St CFTN/RUD NG11 ... 65 H8
East Lawn RDERBYSW DE65 ... 70 B5
Eastleigh Dr MCKLVR DE3 ... 56 C5
Eastleigh Rd LEIS LE2 ... 131 G4
East Link LEIW LE3 ... 130 B8
Eastmere Rd WGSTN LE18 ... 138 D4
Eastmoor Dr CARL NG4 ... 38 D7
East Nelson St HEANOR DE75 ... 20 C5
LEIN LE4 ... 125 L3
RLBORO LE12 ... 98 B3
East Service Rd DERBYE DE21 ... 58 F5
East St CFTN/RUD NG11 ... 77 M6
DERBY DE1 ... 2 F4
HEANOR DE75 ... 20 E7
ILK DE7 ... 33 K7
LEI LE1 ... 7 G7
LEIS LE2 ... 138 E1
LGEAT NG10 ... 62 D7
NOTT NG1 ... 5 J6
East Vw WBRGFD NG2 ... 65 H1
East View Rd BPR/DUF DE56 ... 10 C1
Eastway CDON/KEG DE74 ... 84 F4
Eastway Rd WGSTN LE18 ... 138 B3
Eastwold COT/KEY/RAD NG12 ... 67 L5
Eastwood Av NORM/LIT DE23 ... 57 G5
Eastwood Cl HUCK/RAV NG15 ... 23 J3
Eastwood Dr NORM/LIT DE23 ... 57 G5
Eastwood Rd
COT/KEY/RAD NG12 ... 53 L4
EWD/SEL/PNX NG16 ... 34 C1
LEIS LE2 ... 137 H2
Eastwood St BLWL NG6 ... 36 A2
Eaton Av ARN NG5 ... 25 L8
DERBYW DE22 ... 43 L2
ILK DE7 ... 47 H1
Eaton Bank BPR/DUF DE56 ... 29 L5
Eaton Cl BSTN/STPLFD NG9 ... 63 M1
DERBYW DE22 ... 43 L2
Eaton Ct BPR/DUF DE56 ... 29 J5
DERBY DE1 ... 2 B1
Eaton Grange Dr LGEAT NG10 ... 62 A1
Eaton Rd CDON/KEG DE74 ... 84 F4
Eaton St BSTN/STPLFD NG9 ... 49 L8
Eaton St MAPPK/POR/STA NG3 ... 37 K4
Ebchester Cl LEIS LE2 ... 137 G4
Ebchester Rd LEIS LE2 ... 137 G4
Ebenezer St
EWD/SEL/PNX NG16 ... 20 F4
ILK DE7 ... 33 K4
Ebers Gv MAPPK/POR/STA NG3 ... 37 G2
Ebers Rd MAPPK/POR/STA NG3 ... 37 G7
Ebury Rd ARN NG5 ... 36 F6
Ecclesbourne Av BPR/DUF DE56 ... 29 K4
Ecclesbourne Cl BPR/DUF DE56 ... 29 J4
Eckington Cl ILK DE7 ... 32 C7
Eckington Ter WBRGFD NG2 ... 51 G6
Ecton Cl ARN NG5 ... 24 D7
Edale Av DERBYSE DE24 ... 58 F8
MCKLVR DE3 ... 56 B5
NORM/LIT DE23 ... 57 J5
Edale Cl DERBYW DE22 ... 43 H6
HUCK/RAV NG15 ... 23 C1
LEIW LE3 ... 130 C4
LGEAT NG10 ... 75 M1
Edale Dr BPR/DUF DE56 ... 59 K4
Edale Ri BSTN/STPLFD NG9 ... 62 C3
Edale Rd WBRGFD NG2 ... 51 K2
Edale Sq ILK DE7 ... 33 J2
Eddleston Dr CFTN/RUD NG11 ... 64 A8
Eddystone Rd LEIE LE5 ... 127 J8
Edelin Rd LBORO LE11 ... 9 J8
Edenbridge Ct
WOL/BIL/BRX NG8 ... 49 H5
Eden Cl ARN NG5 ... 37 K1
LBORO LE11 ... 103 G2
LEIS LE2 ... 139 G1
Edenhall Cl LEIN LE4 ... 126 B4
LEIS LE2 ... 139 H3
Edenhall Gdns
CFTN/RUD NG11 ... 64 D5
Edenhurst Av LEIW LE3 ... 130 D8
Eden Rd DERBYE DE21 ... 58 F3
LEIS LE2 ... 139 G1
Edensor Dr BPR/DUF DE56 ... 18 A2
Edensor Sq DERBYW DE22 ... 2 C6
Edensor St LEIN LE4 ... 126 A4
Eden St DERBYSE DE24 ... 58 F7
Eden Wy LEIS LE2 ... 137 H5
Edern Cl ARN NG5 ... 24 E8
Edgbaston Cl LEIN LE4 ... 119 H8
Edgbaston Rd NORM/LIT DE23 ... 57 G7
Edgbaston Gdns
WOL/BIL/BRX NG8 ... 36 B7
Edgcote Cl LEIE LE5 ... 126 C7
Edge Hl MELB/CHEL DE73 ... 129 M4
Edgehill Cl RLEIW/BBY LE8 ... 139 M7
Edge Hill Ct LGEAT NG10 ... 76 B3
Edgehill Rd LEIN LE4 ... 126 C6
Edgelaw Ct DERBYSE DE24 ... 71 H4
Edgeley Rd RLEIW/BBY LE8 ... 143 K3
Edgewood Gv HUCK/RAV NG15 ... 23 H2
Edgewood Rd
EWD/SEL/PNX NG16 ... 34 D1
Edginton Cl ARN NG5 ... 24 D5
Edgware Rd BLWL NG6 ... 24 B8
DERBYW DE22 ... 56 D1
Edgwood Rd
COT/KEY/RAD NG12 ... 67 L5
Edginton St
MAPPK/POR/STA NG3 ... 37 K8
DERBYW DE22 ... 56 D1

Edinburgh Wy RLBORO LE12 ... 113 G6
Edingale Ct BSTN/STPLFD NG9 ... 48 F3
Edingley Av ARN NG5 ... 37 G3
Edingley Sq ARN NG5 ... 36 F4
Edith Av LEIW LE3 ... 130 D7
Edith Wood Cl DERBYSE DE24 ... 72 F2
Edlington Dr WOL/BIL/BRX NG8 ... 49 G4
Edmonds Cl ARN NG5 ... 24 E5
Edmonton Rd WBRGFD NG2 ... 65 H1
Edmonton Rd LEI LE1 ... 7 H3
Edmund Rd DERBYE DE21 ... 59 K4
Ednaston Av NORM/LIT DE23 ... 71 H2
Ednaston Rd NOTTE NG7 ... 50 B6
Edwald Rd COT/KEY/RAD NG12 ... 65 M4
Edwalton Cl
COT/KEY/RAD NG12 ... 65 M4
Edwalton Ct BLWL NG6 ... 36 B1
Edwalton Lodge Cl
COT/KEY/RAD NG12 ... 65 L4
Edward Dr DERBYE DE21 ... 58 E2
EWD/SEL/PNX NG16 ... 12 F3
LEIW LE3 ... 130 D7
WOL/BIL/BRX NG8 ... 36 B7
Edward Cl HUCK/RAV NG15 ... 23 H3
LEIS LE2 ... 139 G2
Edward Rd EWD/SEL/PNX NG16 ... 21 L5
EWD/SEL/PNX NG16 ... 35 G2
LEIS LE2 ... 131 M5
LGEAT NG10 ... 62 B7
RLEIW/BBY LE8 ... 145 K8
WBRGFD NG2 ... 51 K7
Edwards Crs BPR/DUF DE56 ... 10 C1
Edwards La ARN NG5 ... 37 G3
Edward St BPR/DUF DE56 ... 17 L2
BSTN/STPLFD NG9 ... 48 B8
DERBY DE1 ... 2 D1
EWD/SEL/PNX NG16 ... 20 F4
LBORO LE11 ... 8 F1
LEIE LE5 ... 7 L3
RLEINE/SYS LE7 ... 124 C1
Edwinstowe Dr ARN NG5 ... 37 G3
Edwinstowe Rd DERBYE DE21 ... 44 E6
Edwin St ARN NG5 ... 37 H1
Eelwood Rd HUCK/RAV NG15 ... 23 H3
Egerton Av LEIN LE4 ... 125 J5
Egerton Dr BSTN/STPLFD NG9 ... 48 B5
Egerton Rd ARN NG5 ... 37 H3
Egerton St
MAPPK/POR/STA NG3 ... 5 G2
Eggesford Rd DERBYSE DE24 ... 71 H5
Eggington Rd RDERBYSW DE65 ... 68 F6
RDERBYSW DE65 ... 68 C5
Egginton St LEIE LE5 ... 7 M8
Eglantine Cl LEIS LE2 ... 132 E8
Egling Cft CARL NG4 ... 52 D3
Egmanton Cl DERBYE DE21 ... 44 F6
Egreaves Av HEANOR DE75 ... 20 A6
Egypt Rd NOTTE NG7 ... 36 D6
Eider Cl RLEIW/BBY LE8 ... 142 C3
Eighth Av BSTN/STPLFD NG9 ... 64 A2
Eileen Av LEIN LE4 ... 125 J5
Eisele Cl BLWL NG6 ... 35 K1
Ekland Cl DERBYE DE21 ... 59 L1
Ekowe St NOTTE NG7 ... 36 D5
Eland Cl DERBYE DE21 ... 59 L1
Eland St NOTTE NG7 ... 36 D6
Elbow La LEI LE1 ... 6 L6
Elder Cl ARN NG5 ... 25 L6
Elder Gv HUCK/RAV NG15 ... 23 M3
Eldon Rd BSTN/STPLFD NG9 ... 63 G6
Eldon St LEI LE1 ... 7 G4
Eleanor Av ILK DE7 ... 47 L2
Eleanor Crs BSTN/STPLFD NG9 ... 48 D6
Electric Av WBRGFD NG2 ... 50 E8
Eley Cl ILK DE7 ... 47 L2
Elford Ri MAPPK/POR/STA NG3 ... 51 K2
Elgar Dr LGEAT NG10 ... 75 M2
Elgar Gdns
MAPPK/POR/STA NG3 ... 51 K1
Elgin Av LEIW LE3 ... 124 D7
NORM/LIT DE23 ... 56 E6
Eliot Cl LBORO LE11 ... 102 F1
LGEAT NG10 ... 75 M2
Eliot Dr ILK DE7 ... 47 H2
Eliot Rd NORM/LIT DE23 ... 56 F7
Elizabeth Cl DERBYE DE21 ... 58 F2
HUCK/RAV NG15 ... 23 J2
ILK DE7 ... 32 B7
Elizabeth Ct WGSTN LE18 ... 138 A5
Elizabeth Crs WGSTN LE18 ... 137 M3
Elizabeth Dr LEIN LE4 ... 120 C7
LEIS LE2 ... 139 G3
Elizabeth Gdns RLEIW/BBY LE8 ... 136 D8
Elizabeth Gv CARL NG4 ... 38 C5
Elizabeth Pk
EWD/SEL/PNX NG16 ... 12 D3
Elizabeth Rd RLEIW/BBY LE8 ... 145 K8
Elizabeth St LEIS LE2 ... 132 C2
Elkstone Cl DERBYE DE21 ... 44 F5
Ella Bank Rd HEANOR DE75 ... 20 D8
Ellaby Rd LBORO LE11 ... 103 H1
Elland Rd LEIW LE3 ... 129 M2
Ella Rd WBRGFD NG2 ... 51 K6
Ellastone Av ARN NG5 ... 25 K5
Ellastone Gdns DERBYSE DE24 ... 58 F8
Ellendale Rd DERBYE DE21 ... 44 F8
Ellerby Av CFTN/RUD NG11 ... 64 C5
Ellerslie Gv LGEAT NG10 ... 61 L2
Ellesmere Av DERBYSE DE24 ... 58 B6
Ellesmere Cl ARN NG5 ... 25 M8
Ellesmere Dr BSTN/STPLFD NG9 ... 48 A2
Ellesmere Pl LEIW LE3 ... 130 F5
Ellesmere Rd LEIE LE5 ... 130 F5
WBRGFD NG2 ... 65 K3
Ellington Rd ARN NG5 ... 25 K5
Elliot Cl LEIS LE2 ... 139 J5
RLEIW/BBY LE8 ... 146 E7
Elliott Dr LEIN LE4 ... 126 E1
LEIS LE2 ... 129 M4
Elliott St NOTTE NG7 ... 4 D6
Ellis Av HUCK/RAV NG15 ... 23 M1
LEIN LE4 ... 125 L6
Ellis Cl LEIW LE3 ... 123 M7
LGEAT NG10 ... 75 M1
RLBORO LE12 ... 104 D8

Ellis Ct MAPPK/POR/STA NG3 ... 5 J3
Ellis Dr LEIW LE3 ... 129 K4
Ellis Flds LEIS LE2 ... 139 J4
Ellis Gv BSTN/STPLFD NG9 ... 63 K2
Ellison Av WBRGFD NG2 ... 73 L8
Ellison Cl RLEIW/BAR LE9 ... 140 B4
WGSTN LE18 ... 137 K7
Ellis St RLEINE/SYS LE7 ... 124 B1
Ellsworth Ri ARN NG5 ... 36 D1
Ellwood Cl LEIE LE5 ... 132 F3
Ellwood Crs WOL/BIL/BRX NG8 ... 49 L2
Elm Av BPR/DUF DE56 ... 17 M5
BSTN/STPLFD NG9 ... 63 J1
BSTN/STPLFD NG9 ... 63 H5
CARL NG4 ... 38 D8
COT/KEY/RAD NG12 ... 80 D5
EWD/SEL/PNX NG16 ... 34 F1
HUCK/RAV NG15 ... 23 J2
LGEAT NG10 ... 47 M8
LGEAT NG10 ... 62 A6
RLBORO LE12 ... 88 D8
Elm Bank MAPPK/POR/STA NG3 ... 37 G7
Elmbridge ARN NG5 ... 24 F8
Elm Cl COT/KEY/RAD NG12 ... 80 D5
GBY/RBY LE6 ... 123 K5
RLBORO LE12 ... 113 J5
Elmcroft Av LEIE LE5 ... 126 F8
Elmdale Gdns WOL/BIL/BRX NG8 ... 35 M7
Elmdale St LEIN LE4 ... 125 L5
LGEAT NG10 ... 62 B7
Elm Dr CARL NG4 ... 38 D8
RDERBYSW DE65 ... 68 B5
Elmfield Av LEIN LE4 ... 119 K8
LEIS LE2 ... 132 A4
Elm Gv ARN NG5 ... 25 L7
DERBYE DE21 ... 58 F2
DERBYW DE22 ... 43 H2
Elmhurst Av
MAPPK/POR/STA NG3 ... 38 A5
Elmhurst Cl RLEIW/BAR LE9 ... 135 L8
Elmore Ct NOTTE NG7 ... 4 C4
Elms Av NORM/LIT DE23 ... 56 F5
RIPLEY DE5 ... 11 H7
Elms Cl CFTN/RUD NG11 ... 79 H1
LEIS LE2 ... 138 E3
RLBORO LE12 ... 97 H2
Elmsdale Gdns CALV/BJ NG14 ... 39 J3
Elms Dr NORM/LIT DE23 ... 56 F6
RLBORO LE12 ... 112 D2
Elmsfield Av HEANOR DE75 ... 20 E5
Elms Gdns CFTN/RUD NG11 ... 79 C1
Elms Gv LBORO LE11 ... 9 L5
RDERBYSW DE65 ... 69 C5
RLBORO LE12 ... 105 H6
Elmsham Av ARN NG5 ... 24 B6
Elmsleigh Av LEIS LE2 ... 132 B6
Elms Pk CFTN/RUD NG11 ... 79 H1
Elms Rd LEIS LE2 ... 132 A7
Elms St DERBY DE1 ... 43 K8
The Elms CARL NG4 ... 52 D1
EWD/SEL/PNX NG16 ... 22 D8
RLEIW/BBY LE8 ... 136 F7
RLEIW/BBY LE8 ... 143 J5
Elmsthorpe Av NOTTE NG7 ... 50 C5
Elmsthorpe Ri LEIW LE3 ... 130 E4
Elm St BWSH/BRSTN DE72 ... 59 M5
Elmswood Gdns ARN NG5 ... 37 H4
Elm Tree Av BPR/DUF DE56 ... 18 E8
LEIW LE3 ... 123 L7
WBRGFD NG2 ... 65 K3
Elmtree Av DERBYSE DE24 ... 57 M8
Elmtree Cl LEIE LE5 ... 127 G5
Elm Tree Rd RLEIW/BAR LE9 ... 142 A5
Elmwood Dr DERBYE DE21 ... 44 E4
Elmwood Rw WGSTN LE18 ... 137 L3
Elnor St EWD/SEL/PNX NG16 ... 21 C5
Elsadene Av LEIN LE4 ... 125 M4
Elsalene Dr GBY/RBY LE6 ... 123 G2
Elsdon Cl COAL LE67 ... 108 B2
Elsham Cl LEIS LE2 ... 130 B2
Elson St NOTTE NG7 ... 36 D7
Elston Flds LEIS LE2 ... 137 K1
Elston Gdns CFTN/RUD NG11 ... 64 C3
Elstree Av LEIE LE5 ... 127 J7
Elstree Dr WOL/BIL/BRX NG8 ... 49 L1
Elswick Cl ARN NG5 ... 24 F7
Elswick Dr BSTN/STPLFD NG9 ... 63 M3
Elsworthy Wk LEIW LE3 ... 130 B1
Elterwater Dr WBRGFD NG2 ... 52 A8
Eltham Cl WOL/BIL/BRX NG8 ... 35 K4
Eltham Dr WOL/BIL/BRX NG8 ... 35 L4
Eltham Rd WBRGFD NG2 ... 51 L8
Elton Cl BSTN/STPLFD NG9 ... 48 B7
Elton Rd ARN NG5 ... 36 F6
DERBYSE DE24 ... 57 M8
Elton Rd North ARN NG5 ... 36 E6
Elton Ter NOTTE NG7 ... 4 A1
Elvaston Dr LGEAT NG10 ... 75 K3
Elvaston La BWSH/BRSTN DE72 ... 59 J8
DERBYSE DE24 ... 58 F8
Elvaston Rd WOL/BIL/BRX NG8 ... 49 L2
Elvaston St BWSH/BRSTN DE72 ... 60 F8
Elveden Dr ILK DE7 ... 33 C3
Elwin Av WGSTN LE18 ... 138 B3
Embankment Cl
DERBYW DE22 ... 42 D8
Emberton Cl WGSTN LE18 ... 138 D4
Emerald Cl DERBYE DE21 ... 44 D5
Emerson Cl LEIN LE4 ... 124 E4
Emerson Sq NORM/LIT DE23 ... 71 K1
Emerys Rd CARL NG4 ... 38 F7
Emmanuel Av ARN NG5 ... 24 E6
MAPPK/POR/STA NG3 ... 5 K1
Emmas Williams Ct RIPLEY DE5 ... 11 H6
Emneth Cl MAPPK/POR/STA NG3 ... 37 K7
Emperor Wy RLEIW/BBY LE8 ... 142 D3
Empingham Cl
BSTN/STPLFD NG9 ... 62 F5
Empire Rd LEIW LE3 ... 6 A3
Empress Rd LBORO LE11 ... 9 M3
NORM/LIT DE23 ... 2 C8
Emsworth Cl ILK DE7 ... 33 H4
Ena Av WBRGFD NG2 ... 51 K2
Enderby Gdns ARN NG5 ... 25 J6
Enderby Rd RLEIW/BAR LE9 ... 134 E4
RLEIW/BBY LE8 ... 136 E7
Enderby Sq
BSTN/STPLFD NG9 ... 49 K7

Endsleigh Gdns
BSTN/STPLFD NG9 ... 49 K8
COT/KEY/RAD NG12 ... 65 L3
DERBYW DE22 ... 56 D1
Enfield Cl RDERBYSW DE65 ... 68 C5
Enfield Rd DERBYW DE22 ... 42 F8
Enfield St BSTN/STPLFD NG9 ... 63 L1
Engine La EWD/SEL/PNX NG16 ... 21 M3
England Crs HEANOR DE75 ... 20 E5
Englefield Rd LEIE LE5 ... 133 H2
Ennerdale Cl LEIS LE2 ... 139 H3
WBRGFD NG2 ... 52 A8
Ennerdale Rd ARN NG5 ... 37 H2
LGEAT NG10 ... 61 M5
RLBORO LE12 ... 105 H7
Ennis Cl DERBYE DE21 ... 45 G8
Ennismore Gdns
WOL/BIL/BRX NG8 ... 50 A1
Ennismore Ms
CFTN/RUD NG11 ... 65 G8
Enoch Stone Dr DERBYE DE21 ... 58 F3
Ensbury Gdns LEIE LE5 ... 132 B4
Enthorpe St WOL/BIL/BRX NG8 ... 49 M1
Epinal Wy LBORO LE11 ... 9 H8
LBORO LE11 ... 103 H2
Epperstone By-Pass
CALV/BJ NG14 ... 27 J2
Epperstone Rd WBRGFD NG2 ... 51 J7
Epping Cl DERBYW DE22 ... 56 C1
Epping Wy LEIS LE2 ... 137 G4
Epsom Rd BSTN/STPLFD NG9 ... 62 C4
LEIN LE4 ... 125 M5
Epworth Dr DERBYSE DE24 ... 72 E3
Equity Rd LEIS LE2 ... 6 A9
RLEIW/BAR LE9 ... 135 L4
Erdington Wy
BSTN/STPLFD NG9 ... 62 C4
Erdyngton Rd LEIW LE3 ... 130 D3
Erewash Dr ILK DE7 ... 47 L1
Erewash Gdns ARN NG5 ... 24 E7
Erewash Gv BSTN/STPLFD NG9 ... 62 D5
Erewash Sq ILK DE7 ... 47 L1
Erewash St ALFN DE55 ... 12 E1
LGEAT NG10 ... 62 C6
Eric Av HUCK/RAV NG15 ... 15 K6
Erith Cl WOL/BIL/BRX NG8 ... 35 H6
Erith Rd LEIS LE2 ... 131 H6
Ernee Cl LEIE LE5 ... 124 B8
Ernest Rd CARL NG4 ... 37 M7
Erskine Rd ARN NG5 ... 36 F6
Erskine St LEI LE1 ... 7 H4
Ervin's Lock WGSTN LE18 ... 137 L7
Ervin Wy RLEINE/SYS LE7 ... 121 F1
Esher Gv MAPPK/POR/STA NG3 ... 37 G6
Eskdale Cl LEIN LE4 ... 125 L5
LGEAT NG10 ... 75 M2
Eskdale Dr WBRGFD NG2 ... 52 A8
Eskdale Dr BSTN/STPLFD NG9 ... 62 E3
WOL/BIL/BRX NG8 ... 35 M7
Esk Hause Cl
COT/KEY/RAD NG12 ... 66 A3
Essex Rd LEIN LE4 ... 126 C5
WGSTN LE18 ... 137 K4
Essex St DERBYE DE21 ... 3 L1
EWD/SEL/PNX NG16 ... 21 K5
Estley Rd RLEIW/BAR LE9 ... 141 J8
Estoril Av WGSTN LE18 ... 138 D4
Estwic Av EWD/SEL/PNX NG16 ... 21 K4
Ethel Av HUCK/RAV NG15 ... 15 M6
MAPPK/POR/STA NG3 ... 37 L6
Ethel Rd LEIE LE5 ... 132 B1
WBRGFD NG2 ... 51 K8
Eton Cl LEIS LE2 ... 131 M7
Eton Ct ILK DE7 ... 32 B7
Eton Gv WOL/BIL/BRX NG8 ... 49 M3
Eton Rd WBRGFD NG2 ... 65 J2
Eton St DERBYSE DE24 ... 58 C6
Etruria Gdns DERBY DE1 ... 43 L8
Etta's Wy RDERBYSW DE65 ... 68 F3
Ettrick Dr DERBYSE DE24 ... 71 J5
Etwall La RDERBYSW DE65 ... 69 H2
Etwall Rd MCKLVR DE3 ... 55 L8
RDERBYSW DE65 ... 69 L8
Etwall St DERBYW DE22 ... 57 H2
Eucalyptus Av
CFTN/RUD NG11 ... 64 C6
Eugene Gdns WBRGFD NG2 ... 51 H5
Eugene St WBRGFD NG2 ... 51 H4
Eunice Av RLEIW/BAR LE9 ... 135 H8
Europa Wy CFTN/RUD NG11 ... 65 G4
Euston Dr DERBY DE1 ... 43 M8
Euston St LEIS LE2 ... 131 K6
Evans Av DERBYW DE22 ... 43 L2
Evans Rd BLWL NG6 ... 36 B4
Evanston Gdns DERBYE DE21 ... 58 F1
Evedon Wk ARN NG5 ... 24 F6
Evelyn Dr LEIW LE3 ... 131 G5
Evelyn Gv DERBYE DE21 ... 58 E2
Evelyn Rd LEIW LE3 ... 130 C5
Evelyn St BSTN/STPLFD NG9 ... 63 M3
WBRGFD NG2 ... 5 L8
Everard Wy RLEIW/BAR LE9 ... 136 C2
Everett Cl LEIN LE4 ... 126 E1
Evergreen Cl DERBYE DE21 ... 44 E4
Eversley Wk ARN NG5 ... 24 F7
Every St LEI LE1 ... 6 F6
Evesham Cl DERBYE DE21 ... 44 C6
Evesham Ct
BSTN/STPLFD NG9 ... 62 E6
Evesham Rd LEIW LE3 ... 131 G5
Evington Cl LEIE LE5 ... 132 C3
Evington Dr LEIE LE5 ... 132 C4
Evington La LEIE LE5 ... 132 D4
Evington Parks Rd LEIS LE2 ... 132 B4
Evington Pl LEIS LE2 ... 7 M9
Evington Rd LEIS LE2 ... 7 K9
Evington St LEIS LE2 ... 7 K8
Evington Valley Rd LEIE LE5 ... 132 B4
Ewart Rd NOTTE NG7 ... 36 E7
Ewe Lamb Cl BSTN/STPLFD NG9 ... 48 D6
Ewe Lamb La BSTN/STPLFD NG9 ... 48 D6
Ewell Rd WOL/BIL/BRX NG8 ... 49 J2
Exbourne Rd
WOL/BIL/BRX NG8 ... 35 K6
Exbury Gdns WBRGFD NG2 ... 64 F5
Excalibur Cl LEIW LE3 ... 129 L3
Excelsior Av DERBYSE DE24 ... 72 D1
Exchange Rd WBRGFD NG2 ... 51 K8

Exchange St *DERBY* DE1 .... 2 F4
Exchange Wk *NOTT* NG1 .... 5 H7
Exeter Cl *CARL* NG4 .... 38 D5
RLBORO LE12 .... 88 B6
Exeter Pl *DERBY* DE1 .... 3 G3
Exeter Rd *NOTTE* NG7 .... 36 E7
WBRGFD NG2 .... 65 K1 2
WGSTN LE18 .... 137 M4
Exmoor Av *LEIN* LE4 .... 125 H7
Exmoor Cl *LBORO* LE11 .... 103 H7
WGSTN LE18 .... 138 B6
Extension St *ILK* DE7 .... 33 K8 2
Exton Rd *ARN* NG5 .... 36 E4
LEIE LE5 .... 126 C8
Eyam Cl *BSTN/STPLFD* NG9 .... 49 G5
Eye Brook Cl *LBORO* LE11 .... 102 F5
Eynsford Cl *LEIS* LE2 .... 132 D7 1
Eyre's Gdn *ILK* DE7 .... 33 K5
Eyres La *CFTN/RUD* NG11 .... 77 L7
Eyre St *WBRGFD* NG2 .... 5 L7
The Eyrie *DERBYSE* DE24 .... 71 J5 4

F

Fabis Dr *CFTN/RUD* NG11 .... 64 C3
Factory La *BSTN/STPLFD* NG9 .... 63 J2 2
ILK DE7 .... 33 J5
Factory St *LBORO* LE11 .... 9 L4
RLBORO LE12 .... 101 M3
Failsworth Cl *CFTN/RUD* NG11 .... 64 C4
Fairbank Crs *ARN* NG5 .... 37 H5
Fairbourne Dr *MCKLVR* DE3 .... 56 B3
Fairbourne Rd *LEIW* LE3 .... 130 E6
Fairburn Cl *WOL/BIL/BRX* NG8 .... 49 G3
Faircroft Av *LGEAT* NG10 .... 61 M2 2
Fairdale Dr *EWD/SEL/PNX* NG16 .. 21 M5
Fairdene *NORM/LIT* DE23 .... 57 K5 1
Fairefield Crs *LEIW* LE3 .... 124 B5
Faire Rd *LEIW* LE3 .... 124 B6
Faires Cl *BWSH/BRSTN* DE72 .... 60 B6 3
Fairestone Av *LEIW* LE3 .... 124 A7
Faire St *DERBYW* DE22 .... 2 B8
Fairfax Cl *LEIN* LE4 .... 126 C5
Fairfax Rd *LEIN* LE4 .... 126 C5
NORM/LIT DE23 .... 2 C9
Fairfield Av
BWSH/BRSTN DE72 .... 60 A4 1
Fairfield Cl *CFTN/RUD* NG11 .... 64 F2 2
Fairfield Crs *LGEAT* NG10 .... 75 L3
Fairfield Rd *ILK* DE7 .... 19 G8
ILK DE7 .... 33 L6
LEIS LE2 .... 138 F1
NORM/LIT DE23 .... 57 J5
Fairfield St *LEIS* LE2 .... 7 M7
WGSTN LE18 .... 137 K5
Fairford Av *LEIE* LE5 .... 132 F4
Fairford Gdns *NORM/LIT* DE23 .. 70 E1 2
Fairham Av *CFTN/RUD* NG11 .... 77 M6
Fairham Cl *CFTN/RUD* NG11 .... 64 F7
Fairham Dr *WOL/BIL/BRX* NG8 .... 50 A3
Fairham Rd *COT/KEY/RAD* NG12 .. 80 B4
Fairhaven Rd *RLEINE/SYS* LE7 .... 118 C7
Fairholme Rd *LEIS* LE2 .... 137 L1
Fairisle Cl *CFTN/RUD* NG11 .... 64 E6
DERBYE DE21 .... 45 G4 2
Fairisle Wy *RLEIW/BBY* LE8 .... 143 K4
Fairland Crs *WBRGFD* NG2 .... 65 H3 2
Fairlawns *BPR/DUF* DE56 .... 29 H4
Fair Lea Cl *LGEAT* NG10 .... 76 B1
Fairlight Wy *ARN* NG5 .... 24 F8 3
Fairmaid Gv *CFTN/RUD* NG11 .... 64 C5
Fair Md *RLBORO* LE12 .... 113 J7
Fairmead Cl
MAPPK/POR/STA NG3 .... 37 K7
Fairmeadows Wy *LBORO* LE11 .... 103 L8
Fairmount Dr *LBORO* LE11 .... 8 C7
Fairnley Rd *WOL/BIL/BRX* NG8 .... 35 H7
Fairstone Hl *LEIS* LE2 .... 138 F3
Fairview Av *EWD/SEL/PNX* NG16 .. 13 K5
RLEIW/BBY LE8 .... 136 D8
Fairview Cl *BPR/DUF* DE56 .... 18 F8
NORM/LIT DE23 .... 56 E7
Fairview Ct *CFTN/RUD* NG11 .... 65 G5 1
Fairview Gra *BPR/DUF* DE56 .... 18 F8 2
Fairview Rd *ARN* NG5 .... 37 J3
Fairway *COT/KEY/RAD* NG12 .... 80 E5
RLEIW/BBY LE8 .... 146 F8
Fairway Cl *DERBYW* DE22 .... 43 H5
Fairway Crs *DERBYW* DE22 .... 43 H5
Fairway Dr *BLWL* NG6 .... 24 B8
BSTN/STPLFD NG9 .... 63 H1
Fairway Rd *RLBORO* LE12 .... 102 A4
Fairway Rd South
RLBORO LE12 .... 102 A6
The Fairway *CARL* NG4 .... 38 C4
LEIS LE2 .... 132 D7
LEIS LE2 .... 137 K1
RLEIW/BAR LE9 .... 129 K3
RLEIW/BBY LE8 .... 136 E8
Fairwood Dr *DERBYSE* DE24 .... 73 H1
Falaise Wy *RDERBYSW* DE65 .... 68 C5 2
Falcon Cl *LEIW* LE3 .... 129 J5
NOTTE NG7 .... 50 C3
RLEIW/BAR LE9 .... 141 J8
Falconer Crs *LEIW* LE3 .... 124 C7
Falcon Gv *NOTTE* NG7 .... 36 E6 1
Falcon Rd *RLEINE/SYS* LE7 .... 124 B1
Falcons Ri *BPR/DUF* DE56 .... 18 A2
Falcon St *LBORO* LE11 .... 9 M1
NOTTE NG7 .... 36 E6 2
Falcon Wy *DERBYSE* DE24 .... 71 J5
Falconwood Gdns
CFTN/RUD NG11 .... 64 A6 5
Faldo Cl *LEIN* LE4 .... 126 C2
Fallow Cl *CFTN/RUD* NG11 .... 64 C5
Fallowfield Rd *LEIE* LE5 .... 133 H3
Fallow Rd *DERBYE* DE21 .... 59 K1
Fall Rd *HEANOR* DE75 .... 20 C4
Falmouth Dr *WGSTN* LE18 .... 138 A6
Falmouth Rd *DERBYSE* DE24 .... 73 G2
LEIE LE5 .... 132 D3
Falston Rd *WOL/BIL/BRX* NG8 .... 49 L1
Faraday Rd *NOTTE* NG7 .... 50 C3
Far Cft *BWSH/BRSTN* DE72 .... 61 H7
Farfield Av *BSTN/STPLFD* NG9 .... 49 J7
Farfield Gv *BSTN/STPLFD* NG9 .... 49 J7 1
Far La *BWSH/BRSTN* DE72 .... 60 B2
RLBORO LE12 .... 95 H4
Far Laund *BPR/DUF* DE56 .... 17 M1
Farleigh Av *WGSTN* LE18 .... 138 A4
Farleigh Cl *RLEIW/BAR* LE9 .... 141 J8
Farley Rd *LEIS* LE2 .... 132 B7
NORM/LIT DE23 .... 57 H5
Farleys La *HUCK/RAV* NG15 .... 23 L2
Farley St *BLWL* NG6 .... 23 M8 6
Farley Wy *RLBORO* LE12 .... 104 D8
RLEIW/BAR LE9 .... 129 K1
Farm Av *HUCK/RAV* NG15 .... 23 H3
Farm Cl *BPR/DUF* DE56 .... 18 A3
BPR/DUF DE56 .... 18 E7 3
CFTN/RUD NG11 .... 64 C5
ILK DE7 .... 33 L7
LEIN LE4 .... 119 M8
LGEAT NG10 .... 76 C2 2
RIPLEY DE5 .... 10 F1
RLEIW/BAR LE9 .... 142 A1
WGSTN LE18 .... 137 K2
Farm Dr *DERBYSE* DE24 .... 72 E2
Farmers Cl *LEIW* LE3 .... 123 M7 1
Farmer St *CFTN/RUD* NG11 .... 79 J4
Farmhouse Rd *DERBYSE* DE24 .... 71 J5
Farmlands La *NORM/LIT* DE23 .... 70 F1
Farm Rd *ARN* NG5 .... 25 M8
BSTN/STPLFD NG9 .... 63 H2
Farm St *DERBYW* DE22 .... 2 C7 1
Farmway *LEIW* LE3 .... 130 C8
Farnah Green Rd *BPR/DUF* DE56 .. 17 H4
Farnborough Gdns
DERBYW DE22 .... 43 M3
Farnborough Rd
CFTN/RUD NG11 .... 64 C3 4
Farncombe La *DERBYE* DE21 .... 44 D4 2
Farndale *COAL* LE67 .... 108 B1
WGSTN LE18 .... 138 D5 3
Farndale Cl *LGEAT* NG10 .... 75 L2
Farndale Dr *LBORO* LE11 .... 103 K7
WOL/BIL/BRX NG8 .... 48 F3
Farndon Dr
BSTN/STPLFD NG9 .... 62 D4 1
RLEIW/BAR LE9 .... 140 A5
Far New Cl *LGEAT* NG10 .... 61 M2 3
Farneworth Rd *MCKLVR* DE3 .... 56 A5
Farnham Cl *MCKLVR* DE3 .... 56 A5
Farnham Rd *LBORO* LE11 .... 9 J9
Farnham St *LEIE* LE5 .... 7 L4
RLBORO LE12 .... 112 D1
Farningham Cl *DERBYE* DE21 .... 59 K2 2
Farnsfield Av *CALV/BJ* NG14 .... 39 L2
Farnway *DERBYW* DE22 .... 43 J6
Farnworth Cl *LEIN* LE4 .... 126 B4
Far Pastures Cl
COT/KEY/RAD NG12 .... 80 C5 2
Farrier Gdns *NORM/LIT* DE23 .... 56 E8 3
Farrier La *LEIN* LE4 .... 124 F3 1
Farriers Cft *ILK* DE7 .... 33 G4
Farriers Gn *CFTN/RUD* NG11 .... 64 A5
Farriers' Wy *RLEINE/SYS* LE7 .... 115 H8
Farringdon Cl *DERBYW* DE22 .... 56 D1 2
WOL/BIL/BRX NG8 .... 35 H4 2
Farringdon St *LEIE* LE5 .... 7 L2
Farr Wood Cl *GBY/RBY* LE6 .... 123 J4
Far Rye *WOL/BIL/BRX* NG8 .... 49 K1 2
Far St *CFTN/RUD* NG11 .... 79 J4
RLBORO LE12 .... 98 A3
Farthing Ct *LGEAT* NG10 .... 61 M8
Farthingdale Cl *RLEIW/BAR* LE9 .. 142 C4
The Farthings *RLBORO* LE12 .... 94 E6 3
Farwells Cl *BLWL* NG6 .... 36 A4
Fastnet Rd *LEIE* LE5 .... 127 J8
Faulconbridge Cl *BLWL* NG6 .... 35 M1
Faversham Cl *DERBYSE* DE24 .... 72 D2
LEIW LE3 .... 130 A1 3
Fayrhurst Rd *LEIS* LE2 .... 137 J1
Fearn Av *RIPLEY* DE5 .... 11 J6
Fearn Cha *CARL* NG4 .... 38 C8
Fearn Cl *BWSH/BRSTN* DE72 .... 61 L8
Fearnleigh Dr *BLWL* NG6 .... 36 B5
Fearon St *LBORO* LE11 .... 8 E2
Featherby Dr *LEIS* LE2 .... 136 E4
Featherstone Cl *CARL* NG4 .... 38 B4 1
Featherstone Dr *LEIS* LE2 .... 137 G5
Feature Rd *LEIN* LE4 .... 120 C7
RLEINE/SYS LE7 .... 120 C6
Federation St *RLEIW/BAR* LE9 .... 135 L5
Feldspar Cl *RLEIW/BAR* LE9 .... 135 M2 1
Felen Cl *ARN* NG5 .... 24 E8
Fellbarrow Cl *WBRGFD* NG2 .... 66 A2 4
Felley Wy *LEIW* LE3 .... 125 G7 1
Fellow Lands Wy
MELB/CHEL DE73 .... 72 E5
Fellows Rd *BSTN/STPLFD* NG9 .... 49 J8
Fellows Yd *COT/KEY/RAD* NG12 .... 66 C8
Fell Side *ARN* NG5 .... 37 L2
Fellside *BPR/DUF* DE56 .... 17 L3
DERBYE DE21 .... 59 K2
Fellside Cl *WBRGFD* NG2 .... 66 A1
Felly Mill La (North)
EWD/SEL/PNX NG16 .... 13 M5
Felly Mill La (South)
EWD/SEL/PNX NG16 .... 13 L6
Felstead Ct *BSTN/STPLFD* NG9 .. 49 G6 1
Felstead Rd *LEIN* LE4 .... 125 H3
WOL/BIL/BRX NG8 .... 49 M1
Felton Cl *BSTN/STPLFD* NG9 .... 62 F2
Felton Rd *WBRGFD* NG2 .... 51 H7
Fenchurch Cl *ARN* NG5 .... 24 E6 3
Fenchurch Wk *DERBYW* DE22 .... 56 F1
Fennel St *LBORO* LE11 .... 9 J2
Fenners Cl *LEIN* LE4 .... 119 G8 2
Fenroth Cl *BLWL* NG6 .... 23 K7 4
Fenton Cl *LEIS* LE2 .... 138 E4
Fenton Dr *BLWL* NG6 .... 24 A5
Fenton Rd *ARN* NG5 .... 36 D3
MCKLVR DE3 .... 56 A5
Fenwick Cl *WOL/BIL/BRX* NG8 .... 35 K5 1
Fenwick Rd *LEIS* LE2 .... 139 J3 1
WOL/BIL/BRX NG8 .... 35 K5
Fenwick St *DERBYSE* DE24 .... 58 B8
Fergus Cl *CFTN/RUD* NG11 .... 64 D7
Ferguson Cl
BSTN/STPLFD NG9 .... 63 G5 2
Fermain Cl *LEIE* LE5 .... 133 H2
Fern Av *ARN* NG5 .... 36 F6
Fern Cl *BSTN/STPLFD* NG9 .... 48 F8
LEIE LE5 .... 133 J2
Fern Crs *EWD/SEL/PNX* NG16 .... 21 J4 1
GBY/RBY LE6 .... 123 H3
Ferndale Cl *BSTN/STPLFD* NG9 .... 63 H5
Ferndale Dr *GBY/RBY* LE6 .... 123 H7
Ferndale Rd *LEIN* LE4 .... 126 C1
LEIS LE2 .... 137 M1
MAPPK/POR/STA NG3 .... 51 M1
Ferndene Dr *LGEAT* NG10 .... 61 L8
Ferndown Cl *LEIW* LE3 .... 130 A1
Ferneley Ri *RLEINE/SYS* LE7 .... 115 K3
Ferngill Cl *WBRGFD* NG2 .... 50 F6
Fernhill Ct *MELB/CHEL* DE73 .... 72 E4
Fernhurst Rd *LEIW* LE3 .... 130 D7
Fernie Cl *LEIS* LE2 .... 139 G3
Fernie Rd *LEIE* LE5 .... 126 B8
Fernilee Cl *ILK* DE7 .... 32 C7
Fernlea *RLEIW/BAR* LE9 .... 135 K6
Fern Lea Av *COT/KEY/RAD* NG12 .. 67 J5
Fernleigh Av
MAPPK/POR/STA NG3 .... 37 M5
Fernleys Cl *LEIN* LE4 .... 124 F4
Fern Ri *LEIE* LE5 .... 127 G6
Fernwood Cl *NORM/LIT* DE23 .... 57 G7 2
Fernwood Crs
WOL/BIL/BRX NG8 .... 49 G3
Fernwood Dr
COT/KEY/RAD NG12 .... 53 K3
Ferny Hollow Cl *ARN* NG5 .... 24 C7
Ferrars Ct *LEIW* LE3 .... 130 B6
Ferrers Cl *CDON/KEG* DE74 .... 84 E4
Ferrers Crs *BPR/DUF* DE56 .... 29 H4
Ferrers Ri *GBY/RBY* LE6 .... 123 J4
Ferrers Rd *COAL* LE67 .... 108 D3
Ferrers St *LEIS* LE2 .... 137 K2
Ferrers Wy *DERBYW* DE22 .... 43 J5
RIPLEY DE5 .... 11 G4
Ferriby Ter *WBRGFD* NG2 .... 51 G6 7
Ferrous Cl *LEIN* LE4 .... 126 A7
Festival Av *BWSH/BRSTN* DE72 .... 61 G8
LEIN LE4 .... 126 B1
Festival Dr *LBORO* LE11 .... 103 L1
Festival Rd *ILK* DE7 .... 47 G2 2
Festus Cl *MAPPK/POR/STA* NG3 .. 5 J3 1
Festus St *CARL* NG4 .... 38 E8 3
Field Av *RLBORO* LE12 .... 102 A1
Field Cl *BSTN/STPLFD* NG9 .... 62 F3
BWSH/BRSTN DE72 .... 59 M4
BWSH/BRSTN DE72 .... 61 K8
CARL NG4 .... 38 D5
COAL LE67 .... 100 A8
RDERBYSW DE65 .... 68 B5
RLEIW/BAR LE9 .... 136 A8
Field Ct *BPR/DUF* DE56 .... 18 E8
Field Court Rd *GBY/RBY* LE6 .... 123 K4
Field Crs *DERBYSE* DE24 .... 72 E2
Field Crest *RLBORO* LE12 .... 113 H7 3
Field Dr *DERBYSE* DE24 .... 72 E2
Field End Cl *RLBORO* LE12 .... 88 A6
Fieldfare Ct *NORM/LIT* DE23 .... 70 E1 3
Fieldgate Crs *LEIN* LE4 .... 119 J7
Fieldgate Dr *DERBYE* DE21 .... 44 D5
Field Head Wy *DERBYE* DE21 .... 44 F4 3
Field House Cl
WOL/BIL/BRX NG8 .... 49 H2 2
Fieldhouse Rd *LEIN* LE4 .... 125 M4 1
Fieldhurst Av *LEIW* LE3 .... 130 C7 2
Fielding Rd *LEIN* LE4 .... 119 K8
Field La *BPR/DUF* DE56 .... 17 K3
BSTN/STPLFD NG9 .... 62 E3
CALV/BJ NG14 .... 27 G3
DERBYE DE21 .... 44 E8
DERBYSE DE24 .... 72 F1
Fieldon Cl *ASHB* DE6 .... 41 K5 1
Field Ri *NORM/LIT* DE23 .... 57 G8
Field Rd *ILK* DE7 .... 33 K8
Field Rw *BPR/DUF* DE56 .... 17 K3
Fields Av *CFTN/RUD* NG11 .... 79 G2
Fields Farm Rd *LGEAT* NG10 .... 76 A2
Field St *RIPLEY* DE5 .... 11 M8
RLBORO LE12 .... 101 M3
Fieldsway Dr *DERBYE* DE21 .... 44 B5
Field Ter *RIPLEY* DE5 .... 11 H6 3
Field Vw *LEIN* LE4 .... 120 E8
Fieldway *CFTN/RUD* NG11 .... 64 F3
Fieldway Crs *RLEIW/BBY* LE8 .... 139 M6
Fiennes Crs *NOTTE* NG7 .... 4 C9
Fife St *DERBYSE* DE24 .... 58 C7
Fifth Av *BSTN/STPLFD* NG9 .... 64 B1
Filbert St *LEIS* LE2 .... 131 J4
Filbert St East *LEIS* LE2 .... 131 K4
Filey St *BLWL* NG6 .... 24 A7
Fincham Cl *DERBYE* DE21 .... 44 B6 3
Finch Cl *LEIW* LE3 .... 130 C2
NOTTE NG7 .... 50 D7
Finch Crs *MCKLVR* DE3 .... 56 A7
Finchley Av *DERBYW* DE22 .... 56 D1
Finchley Cl *CFTN/RUD* NG11 .... 64 A6
Finch Wy *RLEIW/BAR* LE9 .... 135 K8
Findern Cl *BPR/DUF* DE56 .... 17 M1
DERBYW DE22 .... 43 H6
Findern Gn
MAPPK/POR/STA NG3 .... 51 L1 1
Findern La *RDERBYSW* DE65 .... 69 L2
RDERBYSW DE65 .... 70 A8
Findern St *DERBYW* DE22 .... 57 H2 3
Fineshade Av *LEIW* LE3 .... 125 G7
Fingal Cl *CFTN/RUD* NG11 .... 64 D6
Finmere Cl *NORM/LIT* DE23 .... 56 E7
Finningley Dr *DERBYW* DE22 .... 43 J5 1
Finsbury Av *DERBYW* DE22 .... 56 F1
LBORO LE11 .... 9 L5
RLBORO LE12 .... 114 C4
WBRGFD NG2 .... 51 K3
Finsbury Park Cl
WBRGFD NG2 .... 65 G2 2
Finsbury Rd *ARN* NG5 .... 24 E5
BSTN/STPLFD NG9 .... 49 G4
LEIN LE4 .... 126 A6
Finson Cl *WGSTN* LE18 .... 138 B4
Fiona Dr *LEIE* LE5 .... 133 J2
RLEINE/SYS LE7 .... 133 K2
Firbank Ct *BSTN/STPLFD* NG9 .... 62 F2 1
Firbeck Rd *ARN* NG5 .... 25 L7 1
WOL/BIL/BRX NG8 .... 49 G3
Fir Cl *BLWL* NG6 .... 23 K8 1
Fircroft Av *WOL/BIL/BRX* NG8 .... 35 J7
Fircroft Dr *HUCK/RAV* NG15 .... 23 G2
Fir Dl *COT/KEY/RAD* NG12 .... 67 L4
Firecrest Wy *BLWL* NG6 .... 36 B4 3
Firestone *BPR/DUF* DE56 .... 17 H7
Firestone Cl *LEIW* LE3 .... 130 A1 6
Firfield Av *BWSH/BRSTN* DE72 .... 61 J7
LEIN LE4 .... 119 L8
Firs Av *BSTN/STPLFD* NG9 .... 49 K8
RIPLEY DE5 .... 11 H6
Firsby Rd *WOL/BIL/BRX* NG8 .... 35 K5
Firs Crs *DERBYW* DE22 .... 43 J2
Firs Rd *COT/KEY/RAD* NG12 .... 65 M2
Firs St *LGEAT* NG10 .... 75 L3
First Av *BLWL* NG6 .... 23 M8
BSTN/STPLFD NG9 .... 64 A1
BWSH/BRSTN DE72 .... 61 K2
CARL NG4 .... 38 D6
CARL NG4 .... 38 A7
CARL NG4 .... 52 C2
Firth Cl *ARN* NG5 .... 26 A6
Firth Dr *BSTN/STPLFD* NG9 .... 63 G5
Firth Wy *BLWL* NG6 .... 23 L7
Fir Tree Av *RLEIW/BBY* LE8 .... 143 J3
Fir Tree Cl *WGSTN* LE18 .... 138 A2
Firtree Gv *DERBYE* DE21 .... 44 F5
Fir Tree La *GBY/RBY* LE6 .... 123 J3
Fisher Av *ARN* NG5 .... 37 K2
Fisher Cl *RLBORO* LE12 .... 88 D5
RLBORO LE12 .... 114 B7
RLEIW/BAR LE9 .... 140 A5
Fisher Ct *ILK* DE7 .... 33 K3
Fisher Ga *NOTT* NG1 .... 5 K8
Fisher La *BPR/DUF* DE56 .... 29 J3
Fisher St *DERBYSE* DE24 .... 72 C1 1
NOTTE NG7 .... 36 D7
Fishley Cl *LEIW* LE3 .... 123 M8 2
Fish Pond Dr *NOTTE* NG7 .... 4 D9
Fishponds Cl *LEIW* LE3 .... 123 M7 2
Fishpond Wy *RLBORO* LE12 .... 111 L1 2
Fishpools *LEIW* LE3 .... 130 C8
Fishpool Wy *RLBORO* LE12 .... 105 J6
Fiskerton Wy *DERBYE* DE21 .... 44 F7
Fitzroy St *LEIW* LE3 .... 6 A6
Fitzwilliam Cl *LEIS* LE2 .... 139 H3
Five Acres *CFTN/RUD* NG11 .... 64 E3
Flagholme *COT/KEY/RAD* NG12 .... 67 K5
Flagshaw La *ASHB* DE6 .... 41 J2
Flake La *ILK* DE7 .... 47 J6 1
Flamborough Rd *LEIE* LE5 .... 127 H8
Flamingo Dr *RLEIW/BBY* LE8 .... 142 D3
Flamstead Av *CARL* NG4 .... 26 F8
HEANOR DE75 .... 19 M3
Flamstead La *RIPLEY* DE5 .... 19 H6
Flamstead Rd *ILK* DE7 .... 33 K6
Flamstead St *DERBYSE* DE24 .... 72 B1
Flamsteed Rd
WOL/BIL/BRX NG8 .... 35 H6
Flatholme Rd *LEIE* LE5 .... 127 J7
The Flat *BPR/DUF* DE56 .... 18 D7
Flatts La *EWD/SEL/PNX* NG16 .... 13 H4
The Flatts *BSTN/STPLFD* NG9 .... 62 F2 2
Flawforth Av *CFTN/RUD* NG11 .... 65 H8
Flawforth La
COT/KEY/RAD NG12 .... 65 L7
Flaxendale *COT/KEY/RAD* NG12 .... 67 L5
Flaxfield Cl *GBY/RBY* LE6 .... 123 K4 1
Flaxholme Av *BPR/DUF* DE56 .... 29 K6 1
Flaxland *RLEINE/SYS* LE7 .... 113 J8
Flaxland Crs *RLBORO* LE12 .... 114 A5
Flax Rd *LEIN* LE4 .... 125 M5
Flaxton Wy *ARN* NG5 .... 24 D8
Fleam Rd *CFTN/RUD* NG11 .... 64 C3
Fleckney Rd *RLEIW/BBY* LE8 .... 144 E5
RLEIW/BBY LE8 .... 146 B7
Fleeman Gv *WBRGFD* NG2 .... 51 L6
Fleet Cl *NOTTE* NG7 .... 50 B1
Fleet Crs *BPR/DUF* DE56 .... 17 K4 2
Fleet Pk *BPR/DUF* DE56 .... 17 L4
Fleet St *NORM/LIT* DE23 .... 57 L5
The Fleet *BPR/DUF* DE56 .... 17 K5
RLEIW/BAR LE9 .... 140 C4
Fleetway Cl
EWD/SEL/PNX NG16 .... 21 M6 1
Fleetwith Cl *WBRGFD* NG2 .... 66 A2 5
Fleetwood Rd *LEIS* LE2 .... 131 L6
Fleming Cl *EWD/SEL/PNX* NG16 .... 22 E7
LBORO LE11 .... 103 H1 1
Fleming Dr *CARL* NG4 .... 38 A8 2
Fleming Gdns *CFTN/RUD* NG11 .... 64 A6
Flesh Hovel La *RLBORO* LE12 .... 104 E6
Fletcher Ga *NOTT* NG1 .... 5 H7
Fletcher Rd *BSTN/STPLFD* NG9 .... 49 L8
RLEIW/BAR LE9 .... 140 C4 1
Fletchers Cl *RLEIW/BAR* LE9 ... 135 M8 3
Fletcher St *HEANOR* DE75 .... 20 C5
LGEAT NG10 .... 62 B7
RIPLEY DE5 .... 11 J5
Fletchers' Wy *RLEINE/SYS* LE7 .... 115 H8
Flewitt Gdns
MAPPK/POR/STA NG3 .... 5 M4
Flintham Dr *ARN* NG5 .... 36 F3
Flint St *DERBYSE* DE24 .... 72 B1
Flixton Rd *EWD/SEL/PNX* NG16 .... 22 D8
Flood St *BWSH/BRSTN* DE72 .... 60 A3
Flora St *LEIW* LE3 .... 6 A6
Florence Av *LGEAT* NG10 .... 62 D6
WGSTN LE18 .... 137 L6
Florence Crs *CARL* NG4 .... 38 F7 1
Florence Gv
MAPPK/POR/STA NG3 .... 37 L8 3
Florence Rd *CARL* NG4 .... 38 F6
LEIS LE2 .... 7 L5 1
MAPPK/POR/STA NG3 .... 37 L6
WBRGFD NG2 .... 51 L7
Florence St *HUCK/RAV* NG15 .... 23 L2
LEIS LE2 .... 131 J8 1
Florence Wragg Wy *LEIS* LE2 .... 139 J3
Florin Gdns *LGEAT* NG10 .... 61 M8
Flowers Cl *ARN* NG5 .... 37 M1
Floyd Cl *LEIN* LE4 .... 126 C2
Folkestone Dr *DERBYSE* DE24 .... 72 E2
Folkton Gdns
MAPPK/POR/STA NG3 .... 37 K6
Folly Br *RLEIW/BBY* LE8 .... 143 M8
Folly Rd *DERBYW* DE22 .... 43 M6
Folville Ri *LEIW* LE3 .... 130 E5
Fontwell Dr *LEIS* LE2 .... 136 F2
Forbes Cl *LEIW* LE3 .... 124 A8
LGEAT NG10 .... 76 C2
Ford Av *HEANOR* DE75 .... 20 A3
Ford Cl *LEIS* LE2 .... 137 G4
RIPLEY DE5 .... 11 G7
Fordham Gn *CFTN/RUD* NG11 .... 64 C7
Fordice Cl *COAL* LE67 .... 108 A8
Ford La *DERBYE* DE21 .... 44 A2
DERBYW DE22 .... 43 M2
Ford Ri *LEIS* LE2 .... 137 G4
Ford St *BPR/DUF* DE56 .... 17 K3
DERBY DE1 .... 2 D3
NOTTE NG7 .... 36 E6
Ford St North *NOTTE* NG7 .... 36 E6
The Ford *RLEIW/BBY* LE8 .... 137 G7
Fordview Cl *RLEIW/BBY* LE8 .... 139 L6
Fordwells Cl *NORM/LIT* DE23 .... 56 E7 4
Foredrift Cl *CFTN/RUD* NG11 .... 77 L6
Foremark Av *NORM/LIT* DE23 .... 57 J7
Forest Av *LEIN* LE4 .... 120 B7
Forest Cl *BPR/DUF* DE56 .... 17 M2
COT/KEY/RAD NG12 .... 67 J4
GBY/RBY LE6 .... 123 H4
Forest Dr *RLBORO* LE12 .... 114 A3
RLEIW/BAR LE9 .... 129 J3
Forester Cl *BSTN/STPLFD* NG9 .... 63 G3
Forester Gv *CARL* NG4 .... 38 B8
Forester Rd
MAPPK/POR/STA NG3 .... 37 L7
Foresters Cl *LEIW* LE3 .... 123 M7
Forester St *CARL* NG4 .... 38 E8
DERBY DE1 .... 2 D5
Foresters Wy *RIPLEY* DE5 .... 11 G5
Forest Ga *RLEINE/SYS* LE7 .... 124 B1
Forest Gv *NOTT* NG1 .... 4 F2
NOTTE NG7 .... 4 C3
Forest House La *LEIW* LE3 .... 129 K6
Forest La *RLBORO* LE12 .... 101 G3
Forest Ri *GBY/RBY* LE6 .... 123 H4
LEIS LE2 .... 139 G1
LEIW LE3 .... 129 K4
RLEINE/SYS LE7 .... 133 K2
Forest Rd *COAL* LE67 .... 108 B8
COAL LE67 .... 116 A7
LBORO LE11 .... 8 B9
LEIE LE5 .... 7 M2
RLBORO LE12 .... 111 M4
RLEIW/BAR LE9 .... 135 K2
Forest Rd East *NOTT* NG1 .... 4 E3
Forest Rd West *NOTTE* NG7 .... 4 C4
Forest St *RLBORO* LE12 .... 102 A4
Forest Vw *GBY/RBY* LE6 .... 123 H3
Forest View Dr *HUCK/RAV* NG15 .. 15 J8
Forge Cl *LEIW* LE3 .... 123 L7
RLBORO LE12 .... 94 E6 3
RLEIW/BBY LE8 .... 145 K7
Forge End *RLEINE/SYS* LE7 .... 119 J2
Forge Hl *BSTN/STPLFD* NG9 .... 63 H3
Forge Mill Gv *HUCK/RAV* NG15 .. 24 B2 1
The Forge *BSTN/STPLFD* NG9 .... 47 M2
Forman Rd *RLBORO* LE12 .... 101 M5
Forman St *DERBY* DE1 .... 2 D4
DERBYW DE22 .... 2 C4
NOTT NG1 .... 5 G6
Forrester Av
BWSH/BRSTN DE72 .... 83 K2 1
Forrester Cl *RLEIW/BAR* LE9 .... 142 B4
Forryan Cl *RLEIW/BAR* LE9 .... 142 B5
Forryans Cl *WGSTN* LE18 .... 138 C7
Forster St *NOTTE* NG7 .... 50 C1
Forsyth Cl *RLBORO* LE12 .... 102 F1 2
Forsythia Gdns *NOTTE* NG7 .... 50 C5 2
Forth Av *BSTN/STPLFD* NG9 .... 64 A1
Fort Rd *RLBORO* LE12 .... 113 H6
Forty Horse Cl *RIPLEY* DE5 .... 11 L5
Forum Cl *DERBYSE* DE24 .... 73 H2 3
Fosbrook Dr *CDON/KEG* DE74 .... 84 D3
Fosbrooke Dr *LGEAT* NG10 .... 76 B2
Fosse Cl *BWSH/BRSTN* DE72 .... 60 A6
RLEIW/BAR LE9 .... 136 B5
Fosse La *LEIW* LE3 .... 125 G8
Fosse Park Av *RLEIW/BAR* LE9 .... 136 D1
Fosse Road Central *LEIW* LE3 .... 131 G2
Fosse Rd North *LEIW* LE3 .... 131 G1
Fosse Rd South *LEIW* LE3 .... 130 F5
Foster Av *BSTN/STPLFD* NG9 .... 63 K1 6
Fosters Dr *ARN* NG5 .... 37 H3 2
Foston Ga *WGSTN* LE18 .... 138 C7
Foston La *RLEIW/BBY* LE8 .... 144 A4
Foston Rd *RLEIW/BBY* LE8 .... 145 G3
Foundry La *BPR/DUF* DE56 .... 17 K8
LEI LE1 .... 6 F2
RLEINE/SYS LE7 .... 120 D4 1
Foundry Sq *LEI* LE1 .... 7 G2 1
Fountains Av *LEIS* LE2 .... 137 H4
Fountains Cl *DERBYW* DE22 .... 43 L3 2
WBRGFD NG2 .... 65 M1
Fourth Av *BSTN/STPLFD* NG9 .... 64 A1
CARL NG4 .... 37 M7
Fowke St *RLEINE/SYS* LE7 .... 119 J1
Fowler Av *DERBYE* DE21 .... 59 H3
Fowler Cl *LEIN* LE4 .... 125 G3
Fowler St *BWSH/BRSTN* DE72 .... 60 F8
DERBYW DE22 .... 2 B2 1
MAPPK/POR/STA NG3 .... 37 H7
Fox Cl *DERBYSE* DE24 .... 71 H5
LGEAT NG10 .... 76 B2
Foxcote Dr *LBORO* LE11 .... 102 E5
Fox Covert *CARL* NG4 .... 52 D3
LBORO LE11 .... 103 M1 2
RLEIW/BBY LE8 .... 142 D2
Fox Covert La *CFTN/RUD* NG11 .... 63 M6
Foxcroft Cl *LEIW* LE3 .... 131 G7
Foxdell Wy *MELB/CHEL* DE73 .... 72 F5
Foxearth Av *CFTN/RUD* NG11 .... 64 D5
Foxes Wk *DERBYW* DE22 .... 43 J3 3
Foxfields Dr *DERBYE* DE21 .... 44 C5
Foxglove Cl *RLBORO* LE12 .... 113 K5 2
RLEINE/SYS LE7 .... 115 J8
RLEIW/BAR LE9 .... 135 L7
Foxglove Dr *DERBYE* DE21 .... 44 D4
Foxglove Rd *COAL* LE67 .... 108 E7 1
EWD/SEL/PNX NG16 .... 21 M7
LEIE LE5 .... 127 G5
Fox Gv *BLWL* NG6 .... 36 C4
Foxhall Rd *NOTTE* NG7 .... 36 E7
Fox Hl *COT/KEY/RAD* NG12 .... 67 J5
Foxhill Dr *LEIS* LE2 .... 136 E4
Foxhill Rd *CALV/BJ* NG14 .... 39 J2
CARL NG4 .... 38 A7

Foxhill Road Central *CARL* NG4 .... 37 M7
Foxhill Rd East *CARL* NG4 .... 38 B7
Foxhill Rd West *CARL* NG4 .... 37 M7
Foxhills *CDON/KEG* DE74 .... 86 A6
Foxholes Rd *LEIW* LE3 .... 130 A3
Foxhollies Gv *ARN* NG5 .... 36 F4
Fox Hollow *LEIS* LE2 .... 139 H3
RLEINE/SYS LE7 .... 115 H7 1
Foxhunter Dr *LEIS* LE2 .... 138 D1
Foxlands Av *DERBYW* DE22 .... 43 K5
Fox La *LEI* LE1 .... 6 F5 1
RLEIW/BAR LE9 .... 129 H1
Foxley Ct *DERBYE* DE21 .... 44 E5 5
Fox Meadow *HUCK/RAV* NG15 ...... 23 K2
Foxon St *LEIW* LE3 .... 6 B7
Foxon Wy *LEIW* LE3 .... 130 B6
Foxpond La *RLEIW/BBY* LE8 .... 139 J6
Fox Rd *CDON/KEG* DE74 .... 84 D3
WBRGFD NG2 .... 51 K6
Fox St *DERBY* DE1 .... 3 G1
LEI LE1 .... 7 H6
Foxton Cl *BLWL* NG6 .... 23 K7 5
ILK DE7 .... 33 G4 5
Foxton Lock Cl *WGSTN* LE18 .... 137 L7 2
Foxwood La *CALV/BJ* NG14 .... 26 E2
Foyle Av *DERBYE* DE21 .... 58 E3
Fradley Cl *BLWL* NG6 .... 24 A5
Frampton Av *LEIW* LE3 .... 130 F2
Frampton Gdns
NORM/LIT DE23 .... 70 D1 5
Frampton Rd *WOL/BIL/BRX* NG8 .. 35 L8
Frances Gv *HUCK/RAV* NG15 .... 15 M6
Frances St *EWD/SEL/PNX* NG16 .... 13 H6
Franche Rd *LEIW* LE3 .... 131 G1
Franchise St *DERBYW* DE22 .... 2 A6
Francis Av *LEIW* LE3 .... 130 D8
Francis Dr *LBORO* LE11 .... 103 G1
Francis Gv *BLWL* NG6 .... 36 C4
Francis Rd *CARL* NG4 .... 38 D7 1
Francis St *DERBYE* DE21 .... 3 L2
LEIS LE2 .... 132 B6
NOTTE NG7 .... 4 D4
Franklin Cl *ARN* NG5 .... 25 G7 4
Franklin Dr *COT/KEY/RAD* NG12 .... 66 B6
Franklin Rd *EWD/SEL/PNX* NG16 .. 12 E3
Franklin Wy *RLEIW/BBY* LE8 .... 142 D2
Franklyn Dr *DERBYSE* DE24 .... 72 E1
Franklyn Gdns
COT/KEY/RAD NG12 .... 80 C3 2
WOL/BIL/BRX NG8 .... 50 A1 1
Franklyn Rd *LEIS* LE2 .... 136 F2
Frankson Av *LEIW* LE3 .... 130 E6 1
Fraser Cl *LEI* LE1 .... 7 H3
Fraser Crs *CARL* NG4 .... 37 M6
Fraser Rd *CARL* NG4 .... 37 M6
WBRGFD NG2 .... 51 H6 4
Fraser Sq *CARL* NG4 .... 37 M6
Fraser St *HUCK/RAV* NG15 .... 15 H1
Frazer Cl *DERBYE* DE21 .... 59 J1
Freckingham St *NOTT* NG1 .... 5 K6
Freda Av *CARL* NG4 .... 38 B5
Freda Cl *CARL* NG4 .... 38 B4
Frederic Av *HEANOR* DE75 .... 20 D8
Frederick Av *CARL* NG4 .... 37 M8
CDON/KEG DE74 .... 86 A4
DERBYSE DE24 .... 72 D1
ILK DE7 .... 47 L2
Frederick Cl *RLEINE/SYS* LE7 .... 121 J1 1
Frederick Gv *NOTTE* NG7 .... 4 A9
Frederick Rd *BSTN/STPLFD* NG9 .. 48 B8
LEIE LE5 .... 7 L4
Frederick St *ALFN* DE55 .... 12 A2
DERBYW DE22 .... 57 H1 2
LBORO LE11 .... 9 G4
LGEAT NG10 .... 62 D8
WGSTN LE18 .... 138 B4
Fredscott Cl *LEIE* LE5 .... 127 J8
Freeboard Rd *LEIW* LE3 .... 130 D8
Freehold Rd *LEIN* LE4 .... 125 L2
Freehold St *DERBYW* DE22 .... 2 A6
LBORO LE11 .... 9 L2
LEI LE1 .... 7 K3
RLBORO LE12 .... 102 A4 1
RLBORO LE12 .... 112 F1
Freeland Cl
BSTN/STPLFD NG9 .... 62 D4 2
Free La *LEI* LE1 .... 6 F5
Freeman Av *NORM/LIT* DE23 .... 71 J1
Freeman Rd North *LEIE* LE5 .... 126 D8
Freemans Ter *CARL* NG4 .... 38 E7
Freeman's Wy *RLEINE/SYS* LE7 .. 115 H7
Freemantle Rd *LEIS* LE2 .... 132 C6
MCKLVR DE3 .... 56 C4 1
Freemantle Wk *ARN* NG5 .... 24 C7 2
Freeman Wy *RLBORO* LE12 .... 104 D8
Freemen's Common Rd
LEIS LE2 .... 131 K5
Freer Cl *RLEIW/BBY* LE8 .... 136 F7
WGSTN LE18 .... 138 C7
Freeschool La *LEI* LE1 .... 6 D5
Freesia Cl *MCKLVR* DE3 .... 56 C6 5
RLBORO LE12 .... 111 L1
Freeston Dr *BLWL* NG6 .... 23 K7
Freeth St *WBRGFD* NG2 .... 51 K5
Fremount Dr *WOL/BIL/BRX* NG8 .. 35 L8
French La *DERBYE* DE21 .... 30 D2
French Rd *LEIE* LE5 .... 126 C8
French St *ILK* DE7 .... 47 L1 3
NORM/LIT DE23 .... 57 J5
Frensham Cl *LEIS* LE2 .... 138 E3 1
Fresco Dr *NORM/LIT* DE23 .... 56 D8
Freshwater Cl *WGSTN* LE18 .... 138 A7
Fretwell St *NOTTE* NG7 .... 36 C8 1
Frewen Rd *RLEIW/BAR* LE9 .... 140 B7
Frewin St *LEIE* LE5 .... 126 C8 2
Friar Ct *WBRGFD* NG2 .... 50 F6 5
Friar Ga *DERBY* DE1 .... 2 D3
Friar Gate Ct *DERBY* DE1 .... 2 C3
Friar La *LEI* LE1 .... 6 D7
NOTT NG1 .... 4 F8
Friars Cswy *LEI* LE1 .... 6 C5
Friars Cl *DERBYW* DE22 .... 43 K5 3
Friars Ct *ILK* DE7 .... 47 G1
NOTTE NG7 .... 4 D9
Friar St *LGEAT* NG10 .... 62 B8
NOTTE NG7 .... 50 C5
Friary Av *DERBYSE* DE24 .... 72 C2
Friary St *DERBY* DE1 .... 2 C4
The Friary *NOTTE* NG7 .... 50 C5
Friday La *CARL* NG4 .... 38 D6
Friday St *LEI* LE1 .... 6 D3
Friesland Dr *BWSH/BRSTN* DE72 .. 61 K2
Frinton Av *LEIE* LE5 .... 133 H3
Frinton Rd *WOL/BIL/BRX* NG8 ...... 35 J6
Frisby Av *LGEAT* NG10 .... 76 C1
Frisby Rd *LEIE* LE5 .... 7 M1
Fritchley Cl *RLEIW/BAR* LE9 .... 135 J8
Frith Cl *LEIW* LE3 .... 124 A7
Frizams La *MELB/CHEL* DE73 .... 70 D8
Froanes Cl *RLEIW/BAR* LE9 .... 135 L3
Froggatt Cl *DERBYW* DE22 .... 43 L2
Frog Island *LEIW* LE3 .... 6 C2
Frogmore St *NOTT* NG1 .... 5 G3 2
Frolesworth Rd *LEIW* LE3 .... 130 C1
Frolesworth Wy *LEIW* LE3 .... 130 C1 1
Frome Av *LEIS* LE2 .... 139 H1
Front St *ARN* NG5 .... 25 K8
LEIN LE4 .... 125 M1
Frost Av *EWD/SEL/PNX* NG16 .... 20 E3
Fryar Rd *EWD/SEL/PNX* NG16 .... 21 K3
Fulbeck Av *LEIE* LE5 .... 133 H3
Fulbrook Rd *NORM/LIT* DE23 .... 56 E8
Fulford Rd *LEIW* LE3 .... 130 A2
Fulforth St *NOTT* NG1 .... 4 F4
Fulham Rd *DERBYW* DE22 .... 56 E2
Fuller Cl *RLEIW/BAR* LE9 .... 128 A3
Fuller St *CFTN/RUD* NG11 .... 79 G1
Fullhurst Av *LEIW* LE3 .... 130 F4
Full St *DERBY* DE1 .... 2 E2
Fullwood Av *ILK* DE7 .... 33 J6 2
Fullwood Cl
BSTN/STPLFD NG9 .... 63 G3 1
Fullwood St *ILK* DE7 .... 33 J6
Fulmar Cl *MCKLVR* DE3 .... 56 E4
Fulmar Rd *RLEINE/SYS* LE7 .... 124 B1 1
Fulwood Crs *WOL/BIL/BRX* NG8 .... 35 L6
Fulwood Dr *LGEAT* NG10 .... 61 L8
Furlong Av *ARN* NG5 .... 25 J7
Furlong Cl *BSTN/STPLFD* NG9 .... 48 B7
Furlongs Cl *RLEINE/SYS* LE7 ..... 121 G4 1
Furlong St *ARN* NG5 .... 25 J8
Furnace La *HEANOR* DE75 .... 20 A3
Furnace Rd *ILK* DE7 .... 33 M8
Furness Cl *WBRGFD* NG2 .... 51 L8 2
Furness Rd *BLWL* NG6 .... 36 A4
Furrow Cl *RLEINE/SYS* LE7 .... 119 J1
Furrows Cl *DERBYE* DE21 .... 45 G4 5
RLEIW/BAR LE9 .... 136 A8 1
Furzebrook Rd *CARL* NG4 .... 52 C1 1
Furze Gdns *MAPPK/POR/STA* NG3 .. 5 J2
Fylde Cl *BSTN/STPLFD* NG9 .... 62 C5

G

Gable Ct *MCKLVR* DE3 .... 56 C7 1
Gables Farm Dr *RLBORO* LE12 ...... 89 G6
Gables Lea *RLBORO* LE12 .... 94 F1
Gabor Cl *CFTN/RUD* NG11 .... 64 A7
Gabrielle Cl *BLWL* NG6 .... 36 B3
Gaddesby Av *LEIW* LE3 .... 131 G4
Gaddesby La *RLEINE/SYS* LE7 ...... 115 M7
Gadd St *NOTTE* NG7 .... 4 B4
Gadsby Cl *ILK* DE7 .... 47 L3
Gadsby Ri *BPR/DUF* DE56 .... 10 A5
Gadwall Crs *WBRGFD* NG2 .... 50 D5
Gainsborough Cl
BSTN/STPLFD NG9 .... 62 C1
DERBYE DE21 .... 44 F6 5
LGEAT NG10 .... 76 C2 3
Gainsborough Rd *LEIS* LE2 .... 131 M7
RLEIW/BBY LE8 .... 146 E6 1
Gainsford Cl *ARN* NG5 .... 36 D2
Gainsford Crs *ARN* NG5 .... 36 D2
Gairloch Cl *DERBYSE* DE24 .... 71 H5
Galahad Cl *LEIW* LE3 .... 129 L5
Gala Wy *ARN* NG5 .... 36 C1
Galby St *LEIE* LE5 .... 126 B8
Gale Cl *BSTN/STPLFD* NG9 .... 63 M1 4
Galena Dr *MAPPK/POR/STA* NG3 .. 37 L8
Gallards Hl *LEIW* LE3 .... 130 C3
Galleywood Dr *LEIN* LE4 .... 125 H5
Gallico Cl *LBORO* LE11 .... 103 H2
Gallimore Cl *LEIW* LE3 .... 124 C6
Gallows Inn Cl *ILK* DE7 .... 47 L2 1
Gallowtree Ga *LEI* LE1 .... 6 F5
Galsworthy Ct *LEIW* LE3 .... 130 E2 2
Galway Av *DERBYE* DE21 .... 58 F3
Galway Rd *ARN* NG5 .... 25 J7
LEIN LE4 .... 125 J2
NOTTE NG7 .... 4 B9
Gamble St *NOTTE* NG7 .... 4 C5
Gamble Wy *RLBORO* LE12 .... 104 D8 2
Gamel Rd *LEIE* LE5 .... 132 F2
Gamston Crs *ARN* NG5 .... 37 G4
Gamston Lings Bar Rd
COT/KEY/RAD NG12 .... 66 A5
Ganton Cl *MAPPK/POR/STA* NG3 .. 37 K6
Ganton Rd *LEIW* LE3 .... 130 A1
Garden Av *ILK* DE7 .... 47 K2
Garden City *CARL* NG4 .... 38 C7
Garden Cl *LEIS* LE2 .... 138 E2
Garden Crs *CDON/KEG* DE74 .... 84 F4
Gardendale Av *CFTN/RUD* NG11 .... 64 B7
Gardenfield Rd *LEIN* LE4 .... 126 D3
Gardenia Crs
MAPPK/POR/STA NG3 .... 37 M5
Gardenia Gv
MAPPK/POR/STA NG3 .... 37 M5
Garden Rd *COAL* LE67 .... 108 B5
EWD/SEL/PNX NG16 .... 21 L4
HUCK/RAV NG15 .... 15 K8
Gardens Ct *WBRGFD* NG2 .... 51 L8
The Gardens *RIPLEY* DE5 .... 11 H8
Garden St *DERBY* DE1 .... 2 D1
LEI LE1 .... 6 F3
LEIN LE4 .... 120 C8
NOTTE NG7 .... 4 B5
WGSTN LE18 .... 137 K6
Gardinia Cl *BSTN/STPLFD* NG9 .... 62 E5 4
Gardner Cl *LBORO* LE11 .... 103 G1 4
Garendon Av *RLBORO* LE12 .... 94 E7
Garendon Cl *RLBORO* LE12 .... 102 A4
Garendon Gn *LBORO* LE11 .... 8 B3
Garendon Rd *COAL* LE67 .... 108 F7
LBORO LE11 .... 8 B3
RLBORO LE12 .... 101 M4
Garendon St *LEIS* LE2 .... 7 K5
Garendon Wy *GBY/RBY* LE6 .... 123 J5
Garfield Av *BWSH/BRSTN* DE72 ...... 60 E8
Garfield Cl *BSTN/STPLFD* NG9 .... 48 C6
NORM/LIT DE23 .... 71 G1 2
Garfield Pk *RLEIW/BBY* LE8 .... 139 M6
Garfield Rd *COAL* LE67 .... 108 A8
NOTTE NG7 .... 4 A4
NOTTE NG7 .... 50 C1
Garfield St *LEIN* LE4 .... 125 L7
Garfit Rd *RLEIW/BAR* LE9 .... 129 J2
Garforth Cl *WOL/BIL/BRX* NG8 .. 36 C7 1
Garganey Cl *COAL* LE67 .... 108 E7
Garland *RLEINE/SYS* LE7 .... 113 J8
Garland Crs *LEIW* LE3 .... 124 F7
Garnet Ct *MAPPK/POR/STA* NG3 .... 5 M5
Garnet St *CARL* NG4 .... 38 D8 2
Garnett Av *HEANOR* DE75 .... 20 D5
Garnett Crs *LEIS* LE2 .... 137 G3
Garrett Gv *CFTN/RUD* NG11 .... 64 A5
Garrick St *DERBYSE* DE24 .... 58 E8
Garry Cl *DERBYSE* DE24 .... 71 H5
Garsdale *WGSTN* LE18 .... 138 D5 4
Garsdale Cl *WBRGFD* NG2 .... 66 A1
Garsdale Dr *CFTN/RUD* NG11 .... 64 E4
Garth Av *LEIN* LE4 .... 125 J3
Garth Crs *DERBYSE* DE24 .... 72 F1 2
Garthorpe Ct *DERBYE* DE21 .... 44 D5 5
Garton Cl *BLWL* NG6 .... 35 M2
BSTN/STPLFD NG9 .... 62 F2 5
Garton Rd *LBORO* LE11 .... 9 J5
Gartree Rd *LEIS* LE2 .... 133 G7
Gary Cl *NORM/LIT* DE23 .... 71 H2
Gascoigne Av *RLEINE/SYS* LE7 .... 121 J2
Gascoigne Dr *DERBYE* DE21 .... 59 H3
Gaskell Av *NORM/LIT* DE23 .... 57 J8
Gas La *WGSTN* LE18 .... 138 A5
Gasny Av *CDON/KEG* DE74 .... 84 F2
Gas St *LEI* LE1 .... 6 F2
LGEAT NG10 .... 62 A1
Gatcombe Cl
COT/KEY/RAD NG12 .... 53 L4
DERBYE DE21 .... 44 E5
Gatcombe Gv *LGEAT* NG10 .... 61 L4
Gate Brook Cl *RIPLEY* DE5 .... 11 M6 1
Gateford Cl *BSTN/STPLFD* NG9 .... 48 F5
Gateside Rd *WBRGFD* NG2 .... 50 E6
Gateway St *LEIS* LE2 .... 6 D8
Gatling St *NOTTE* NG7 .... 50 C2 2
Gaulby La *LEIS* LE2 .... 133 H7
Gaul St *BLWL* NG6 .... 23 M8
LEIS LE2 .... 6 A9
Gauntley St *NOTTE* NG7 .... 36 C7
Gautries Cl *ARN* NG5 .... 24 E7
Gavin Cl *LEIW* LE3 .... 130 A5
Gavin Dr *LBORO* LE11 .... 103 H1
Gawthorne St *NOTTE* NG7 .... 36 D6
Gayhurst Cl *LEIW* LE3 .... 130 D8
WGSTN LE18 .... 138 C5 5
Gayhurst Rd *BLWL* NG6 .... 36 C2
Gaynor Ct *WOL/BIL/BRX* NG8 .... 49 M1 5
Gayrigg Ct *BSTN/STPLFD* NG9 .... 62 F3 2
Gayton Av *LEIN* LE4 .... 126 A6
NORM/LIT DE23 .... 71 H1
Gayton Cl *WOL/BIL/BRX* NG8 .... 35 H7
Gayton Hts *RLEIW/BAR* LE9 .... 135 L3 1
Gayton Thorpe Cl
NORM/LIT DE23 .... 56 D8 5
Gaywood Cl *CFTN/RUD* NG11 ...... 64 D7 3
Geary Cl *RLEIW/BAR* LE9 .... 135 M8
Gedding Rd *LEIE* LE5 .... 132 C2
Geddington Cl *WGSTN* LE18 .... 138 C5 5
Gedge Wy *LEIS* LE2 .... 137 J1
Gedling Gv *ARN* NG5 .... 25 K8
NOTTE NG7 .... 4 D4
Gedling Rd *ARN* NG5 .... 25 K8
CARL NG4 .... 38 D7
Gedling St *NOTT* NG1 .... 5 K7
Gedney Av
MAPPK/POR/STA NG3 .... 37 K7
Gees Lock Cl *LEIS* LE2 .... 136 F3 1
Gelders Hall Rd *RLBORO* LE12 .... 101 L6
Gelert Av *LEIE* LE5 .... 133 H1
Gell Rd *BSTN/STPLFD* NG9 .... 62 E4
Gelscoe La *MELB/CHEL* DE73 .... 92 B6
Gema Cl *DERBYW* DE22 .... 43 L3
George Av *BSTN/STPLFD* NG9 .... 63 K3
LGEAT NG10 .... 62 D7
George Crs *ALFN* DE55 .... 12 A1
Georgeham Cl *WGSTN* LE18 .... 138 B6 2
George Hill Cl *RLEIW/BAR* LE9 .... 140 B4
George Mariott Cl
RLEIW/BAR LE9 .... 140 A6
George Rd *CARL* NG4 .... 38 C8
WBRGFD NG2 .... 51 J8
George's La *CALV/BJ* NG14 .... 26 A1
George St *ALFN* DE55 .... 12 B1
ARN NG5 .... 37 J1
BPR/DUF DE56 .... 17 K3
COAL LE67 .... 108 D3
DERBY DE1 .... 2 D3
EWD/SEL/PNX NG16 .... 20 F4
HUCK/RAV NG15 .... 15 L7
LBORO LE11 .... 8 E2
LEI LE1 .... 7 G3
MELB/CHEL DE73 .... 82 E8
NOTT NG1 .... 5 H6
RLEINE/SYS LE7 .... 124 B1
RLEIW/BAR LE9 .... 135 L4
George Yd *LBORO* LE11 .... 9 J3
Georgia Dr *ARN* NG5 .... 25 J5
Georgina Rd *BSTN/STPLFD* NG9 .... 63 K2
Gerard Cl *DERBYE* DE21 .... 59 K1 2
Gerard Ct *DERBY* DE1 .... 2 D5
Gerard Gv *RDERBYSW* DE65 .... 69 G3 2
Gerard St *DERBY* DE1 .... 2 D6
Gerrard Cl *ARN* NG5 .... 24 E5
Gerrard Crs *CDON/KEG* DE74 .... 86 B6
Gertrude Rd *BWSH/BRSTN* DE72 .. 60 E8
DERBYE DE21 .... 44 E7
WBRGFD NG2 .... 51 L7
Gervase Gdns *CFTN/RUD* NG11 .... 64 B5
Gervas Rd *LEIE* LE5 .... 127 G8
Ghost House La
BSTN/STPLFD NG9 .... 62 F2
Gibbons Av *BSTN/STPLFD* NG9 .... 48 B8
Gibbons Cl *LEIN* LE4 .... 125 L7
Gibbons St *NOTTE* NG7 .... 50 C7
Gibb St *LGEAT* NG10 .... 62 C8
Gibfield La *BPR/DUF* DE56 .... 17 K5 2
Gibson Cl *WGSTN* LE18 .... 138 B4 1
Gibson Rd *NOTTE* NG7 .... 36 E7 2
RLBORO LE12 .... 114 B3
Gibson's La *RMMWB* LE14 .... 99 M6
Gifford Cl *LEIE* LE5 .... 132 F4
Gilbert Av *CFTN/RUD* NG11 .... 77 M6 1
Gilbert Cl *DERBYE* DE21 .... 59 H3
LEIN LE4 .... 126 C3
Gilbert Crs *BPR/DUF* DE56 .... 29 J5
Gilbert Gdns
MAPPK/POR/STA NG3 .... 51 L1 2
Gilbert St *DERBYSE* DE24 .... 72 F2
Gilderdale Wy *DERBYE* DE21 .... 44 F4
Gilead St *BLWL* NG6 .... 23 M8
Giles Av *WBRGFD* NG2 .... 65 H1
Giles Cl *RLBORO* LE12 .... 112 F3
Gillam Butts *RLEIW/BBY* LE8 .... 143 J4
Gillamoor Ct *DERBYSE* DE24 .... 73 H1 5
Gillamore Dr *COAL* LE67 .... 108 E5
Gillbank Dr *GBY/RBY* LE6 .... 123 G7
Gillercomb Cl
COT/KEY/RAD NG12 .... 66 B3
Gilliver La *COT/KEY/RAD* NG12 .... 67 G6
Gilliver St *LEIS* LE2 .... 131 M7
Gillman Rd *LEIW* LE3 .... 124 E7
Gillott St *HEANOR* DE75 .... 20 E7
Gill St *EWD/SEL/PNX* NG16 .... 13 L1
NOTT NG1 .... 4 F4
Gilmorton Av *LEIS* LE2 .... 136 F2
Gilmorton Cl *LEIS* LE2 .... 136 F3
Gilmour Cl *LEIN* LE4 .... 124 F2
Gilpet Av *MAPPK/POR/STA* NG3 .... 37 K7
Gilstead Cl *RLEINE/SYS* LE7 .... 133 K3
Giltbrook Crs
EWD/SEL/PNX NG16 .... 22 A7
Gilt Hl *EWD/SEL/PNX* NG16 .... 22 B8
Giltway *EWD/SEL/PNX* NG16 .... 22 A8
Gimson Av *RLEIW/BAR* LE9 .... 142 B4
Gimson Cl *ILK* DE7 .... 33 G4 4
LEIE LE5 .... 126 E6
Gimson Rd *LEIW* LE3 .... 130 F2
Gin Close Wy
EWD/SEL/PNX NG16 .... 34 A1
Gipsy La *LEIE* LE5 .... 126 D6
LEIN LE4 .... 126 C5
RLEINE/SYS LE7 .... 113 G7
Gipsy Rd *LEIN* LE4 .... 125 M5
Girton Rd *ARN* NG5 .... 36 E4
Gisborne Cl *MCKLVR* DE3 .... 56 C3
Gisborne Crs *DERBYW* DE22 .... 43 K3
Gisborne Gn *DERBY* DE1 .... 2 B1
Gisborough Wy *RLBORO* LE12 .... 102 F2
Gisburn Cl *CFTN/RUD* NG11 .... 64 E3 1
Glade Av *WOL/BIL/BRX* NG8 .... 50 A2
Gladehill Rd *ARN* NG5 .... 25 G8
The Glade *CFTN/RUD* NG11 .... 64 C8
LEIW LE3 .... 130 D8
Gladstone Av
CFTN/RUD NG11 .... 77 M6 2
HEANOR DE75 .... 20 C5
LBORO LE11 .... 103 L2
Gladstone Cl *MELB/CHEL* DE73 .... 72 D4
Gladstone Dr
EWD/SEL/PNX NG16 .... 13 J8 1
Gladstone Rd *DERBYE* DE21 .... 59 J2
Gladstone St *BSTN/STPLFD* NG9 .... 63 J2
CARL NG4 .... 38 B8
EWD/SEL/PNX NG16 .... 21 G4 2
HEANOR DE75 .... 20 C5
LBORO LE11 .... 9 J1
LEI LE1 .... 7 G4
LGEAT NG10 .... 76 B1
NORM/LIT DE23 .... 57 J6
NOTTE NG7 .... 36 D7
RLBORO LE12 .... 94 E6
RLEINE/SYS LE7 .... 124 C1
RLEIW/BBY LE8 .... 145 K8
WGSTN LE18 .... 138 B4
Gladstone St East *ILK* DE7 .... 33 K8 3
Gladstone St West *ILK* DE7 .... 33 K8 3
Glaisdale Cl *LEIN* LE4 .... 125 G4
Glaisdale Dr East
WOL/BIL/BRX NG8 .... 49 J1
Glaisdale Dr West
WOL/BIL/BRX NG8 .... 49 H2
Glaisdale Pkwy
WOL/BIL/BRX NG8 .... 49 H2
Glaisdale Rd *WGSTN* LE18 .... 138 C6
Glamis Cl *DERBYE* DE21 .... 44 F5
RLBORO LE12 .... 113 G7
Glamis Rd *ARN* NG5 .... 36 E5
Glamorgan Av *WGSTN* LE18 .... 137 K5
Glanton Wy *ARN* NG5 .... 25 L5
Glapton La *CFTN/RUD* NG11 .... 64 B5
Glapton Rd *WBRGFD* NG2 .... 51 G6
Glaramara Cl *WBRGFD* NG2 .... 50 F6 3
Glasshouse Hl *RIPLEY* DE5 .... 11 M7
Glasshouse St *NOTT* NG1 .... 5 H5
Glastonbury Rd *DERBYSE* DE24 .... 59 G8
Glazebrook Rd *LEIW* LE3 .... 124 D6
Glazebrook Sq *LEIW* LE3 .... 124 E7 2
Gleadmoss La *DERBYE* DE21 .... 44 E6 5
Glebe Av *ILK* DE7 .... 31 K1
RIPLEY DE5 .... 11 G5
Glebe Cl *ASHB* DE6 .... 40 C6
LEIS LE2 .... 132 C8
LEIW LE3 .... 123 M7
RLBORO LE12 .... 113 H5
WGSTN LE18 .... 138 B4
Glebe Crs *ILK* DE7 .... 33 L8
ILK DE7 .... 45 M1
Glebe Dr *CALV/BJ* NG14 .... 39 H4
RLEIW/BBY LE8 .... 143 H4
Glebe Farm Cl *WBRGFD* NG2 .... 65 G3 3
Glebe Farm Vw *CARL* NG4 .... 38 D4
Glebeland Cl *RLEINE/SYS* LE7 .... 115 K2
Glebelands Rd *LEIN* LE4 .... 119 H7
The Glebelands
RLEIW/BBY LE8 .... 139 L7 1
Glebe La *COT/KEY/RAD* NG12 .... 53 K4
Glebe Ri *NORM/LIT* DE23 .... 57 G6
Glebe Rd *CARL* NG4 .... 38 A5
COAL LE67 .... 100 A7
EWD/SEL/PNX NG16 .... 35 G1
GBY/RBY LE6 .... 123 J4
LEIS LE2 .... 132 D8
RLEINE/SYS LE7 .... 121 J2
WBRGFD NG2 .... 51 K8
Glebe St *BSTN/STPLFD* NG9 .... 63 J1
HUCK/RAV NG15 .... 15 L7
LBORO LE11 .... 104 A2
LEIS LE2 .... 7 H7
The Glebe *EWD/SEL/PNX* NG16 .... 33 M3
Glebe Wy *RLEINE/SYS* LE7 .... 120 C4
Glen Av *BPR/DUF* DE56 .... 18 A8
EWD/SEL/PNX NG16 .... 21 M6
Glenbarr Av *LEIN* LE4 .... 6 B1
Glenborne Rd *WGSTN* LE18 .... 137 L3
Glenbrook *COT/KEY/RAD* NG12 .... 67 L4
Glenbrook Crs
WOL/BIL/BRX NG8 .... 35 L8
Glencairn Dr *WOL/BIL/BRX* NG8 .... 35 L7
Glencoe Av *LEIN* LE4 .... 126 A3
Glencoe Rd *CFTN/RUD* NG11 .... 64 D6
Glencoyne Rd
CFTN/RUD NG11 .... 64 C7 5
Glencroft Dr *DERBYSE* DE24 .... 71 H4
Glendale Av *LEIW* LE3 .... 123 M4
Glendale Cl *CARL* NG4 .... 38 B5
Glendale Ct *BSTN/STPLFD* NG9 .... 63 J4
Glendale Dr *DERBYE* DE21 .... 59 K2
Glendale Gdns *ARN* NG5 .... 25 K8 2
Glendon Dr *ARN* NG5 .... 36 E4
HUCK/RAV NG15 .... 23 L2
Glendon Rd *DERBYSE* DE24 .... 71 H4
ILK DE7 .... 47 G3
Glendon St *ILK* DE7 .... 31 L6
LEIN LE4 .... 125 M6
Glendower Cl *LEIE* LE5 .... 132 F1
Gleneagles Av *LEIN* LE4 .... 126 B3
Gleneagles Cl *MCKLVR* DE3 .... 56 D5 3
Gleneagles Ct
COT/KEY/RAD NG12 .... 66 A4 1
Gleneagles Dr *ARN* NG5 .... 25 M6
Glenfield Av
EWD/SEL/PNX NG16 .... 22 B8
Glenfield Crs *LEIW* LE3 .... 124 A7
MCKLVR DE3 .... 56 A5
Glenfield Frith Dr *LEIW* LE3 .... 124 A6
Glenfield La *RLEIW/BAR* LE9 .... 129 J1
Glenfield Rd *LEIW* LE3 .... 124 D8
LGEAT NG10 .... 76 B2
Glenfield Rd East *LEIW* LE3 .... 6 A6 2
Glenfields *RLBORO* LE12 .... 101 L4
Glenfrith Cl *LEIW* LE3 .... 124 D5
RLBORO LE12 .... 113 K6 2
Glenfrith Wy *LEIW* LE3 .... 124 D5
Glengarry Cl *LEIW* LE3 .... 124 E8 1
Glengarry Ct *LEIW* LE3 .... 124 D8
Glengarry Wy *DERBYSE* DE24 .... 71 H3
LEIW LE3 .... 124 D7
Glen Ga *WGSTN* LE18 .... 137 K5
Glen Helen *CARL* NG4 .... 52 D1
Glenhills Bvd *LEIS* LE2 .... 137 H2 1
Glenhills Wy *LEIS* LE2 .... 137 J2
Glenlivet Gdns *CFTN/RUD* NG11 .... 64 D6
Glenloch Dr *CFTN/RUD* NG11 .... 64 D7
Glenmore Av *RLBORO* LE12 .... 101 M4
Glenmore Dr *DERBYSE* DE24 .... 71 H3 5
Glenmore Rd *LEIN* LE4 .... 126 B4
WBRGFD NG2 .... 65 M1
Glenmoy Cl *NORM/LIT* DE23 .... 57 H8
Glenn Wy *BWSH/BRSTN* DE72 .... 74 C6
Glenorchy Ct *DERBYE* DE21 .... 44 F4 5
Glenorchy Crs *ARN* NG5 .... 24 C7 5
Glen Park Av *LEIW* LE3 .... 123 M5
Glen Parva Av *ARN* NG5 .... 25 J7 2
Glenridding Cl *WBRGFD* NG2 .... 66 B2 5
Glen Ri *LEIS* LE2 .... 136 F4
RLEIW/BBY LE8 .... 139 J5
Glen Rd *CALV/BJ* NG14 .... 39 J2
LEIS LE2 .... 139 G3
RLEIW/BBY LE8 .... 139 H8
Glenrothes Cl *LEIW* LE3 .... 130 A2 1
Glensford Gdns *ARN* NG5 .... 24 C6
Glenside *ARN* NG5 .... 37 M2
Glenside Rd *BSTN/STPLFD* NG9 .... 49 G5
Glen St *LEIN* LE4 .... 125 M6
The Glen *CFTN/RUD* NG11 .... 64 C6
Glentworth Rd *NOTTE* NG7 .... 50 C1
Glen Vw *BPR/DUF* DE56 .... 17 K5
Glenville Av *LEIS* LE2 .... 136 F5
LEIW LE3 .... 124 A5
Glen Vine *RIPLEY* DE5 .... 11 L6
Glen Wy *COAL* LE67 .... 108 E8
LEIS LE2 .... 139 G3
Glenwood Av *WOL/BIL/BRX* NG8 .... 49 H3
Glenwood Rd *MELB/CHEL* DE73 .... 72 E7
Glins Rd *ARN* NG5 .... 24 D7
Glossop St *DERBYSE* DE24 .... 57 M8
LEIS LE2 .... 7 M9
LEIS LE2 .... 132 A4
Gloster St *DERBYSE* DE24 .... 58 C5
Gloucester Av
BSTN/STPLFD NG9 .... 63 J2
EWD/SEL/PNX NG16 .... 35 K3
LGEAT NG10 .... 61 L3 1
NOTTE NG7 .... 50 C3 4
RLEINE/SYS LE7 .... 121 G3
Gloucester Crs *WGSTN* LE18 .... 137 K4
Glover Av *WOL/BIL/BRX* NG8 .... 49 H3
Goathland Cl *ARN* NG5 .... 24 F7 2
Goathland Rd *DERBYSE* DE24 .... 71 H5
Godber Rd *HUCK/RAV* NG15 .... 23 J2
Goddard Cl *RLEINE/SYS* LE7 .... 133 L2 1
Goddards Cl *LEIN* LE4 .... 124 F5
WGSTN LE18 .... 144 E4
Godfrey Cl *LEIN* LE4 .... 124 E1 1
Godfrey Dr *ILK* DE7 .... 47 G1
Godfrey St *CARL* NG4 .... 52 E1
HEANOR DE75 .... 20 C6
Godkin Dr *EWD/SEL/PNX* NG16 .... 20 E3
Godwin Av *WGSTN* LE18 .... 138 C5
Goldcrest Dr *DERBYE* DE21 .... 59 K1
Goldcrest Rd *BLWL* NG6 .... 35 M4
Golden Sq *RLBORO* LE12 .... 94 D7
Golden Va *ILK* DE7 .... 18 F8
ILK DE7 .... 30 F1
Goldhill *WGSTN* LE18 .... 137 L3
Goldhill Rd *LEIS* LE2 .... 132 B8
Golding Cl *LBORO* LE11 .... 102 F1
Gold La *DERBYW* DE22 .... 42 C7

Goldsmith St NOTT NG1...... 4 F5
Goldstone Ct DERBYE DE21 ... 59 J3 🔞
Goldswong Ter
  MAPPK/POR/STA NG3........ 5 H2
Golf Club Rd ILK DE7 .... 47 L6
Golf Course La LEIW LE3 .... 130 A2
Golf Course Rd
  COT/KEY/RAD NG12 .... 80 F5
Golf La BPR/DUF DE56 .... 29 J2
Golf Rd COT/KEY/RAD NG12 ... 53 L4
Goliath Rd COAL LE67......... 108 B5
Gonalston La CALV/BJ NG14 .... 24 M2
Goodale St NORM/LIT DE23 ... 57 L6
Goodall Crs HUCK/RAV NG15.... 24 A1
Goodall St NOTTE NG7 .... 4 A1
Goode's Av RLEINE/SYS LE7 ... 120 F5
Goode's La RLEINE/SYS LE7 ... 120 E4
Gooding Av LEIW LE3 .... 130 D3 🔞
Goodliffe St NOTTE NG7 .... 36 D7
Goodman Cl
  EWD/SEL/PNX NG16 .... 22 A7 🔞
Goodrington Rd
  DERBYE DE21 .... 45 G4 🔞
Goodsmoor Rd DERBYSE DE24 ... 71 J2
Goods Rd BPR/DUF DE56 ..... 17 J5
Goods Yd BPR/DUF DE56 ..... 17 K6 🔞
Goodwin Cl LGEAT NG10 ...... 61 L1
Goodwin Dr
  EWD/SEL/PNX NG16 .... 34 B1
Goodwin's La BPR/DUF DE56.... 17 L8
Goodwin's Rd NOTTE NG7 ..... 4 D4 🔞
Goodwood Av ARN NG5 .... 25 J7
Goodwood Crs ILK DE7 .... 47 H3
  LEIW LE3 .... 132 F3
Goodwood Dr
  BSTN/STPLFD NG9 .... 62 D5
  DERBYSE DE24 .... 73 G1
Goodwood Rd LEIW LE5 .... 132 F2
  WOL/BIL/BRX NG8 .... 49 H3
Goole Av ILK DE7 .... 47 H2
Goose Ga NOTT NG1 .... 5 J7
Goose La EWD/SEL/PNX NG16 ... 12 B7
Gopsall St LEIS LE2 .... 7 K8
Gordon Cl BSTN/STPLFD NG9 .... 63 H5 🔞
Gordon Ri
  MAPPK/POR/STA NG3........ 37 J5 🔞
Gordon Rd BWSH/BRSTN DE72 ... 59 M6
  CALV/BJ NG14............... 39 L2
  LBORO LE11 .... 104 A1
  MAPPK/POR/STA NG3........ 51 K1
  NORM/LIT DE23 .... 2 D8
  WBRGFD NG2 .... 51 K8
Gordon St ILK DE7 .... 33 K6
Gorham Ri RLEINE/BAR LE9 .... 141 H8
Gorman Ct ARN NG5 .... 25 M8 🔞
Gorse Cl EWD/SEL/PNX NG16 ... 21 M6
  LGEAT NG10 .... 61 M5 🔞
  NORM/LIT DE23 .... 70 F1
Gorse Ct ARN NG5 .... 36 C2 🔞
Gorse Hl LEIN LE4 .... 124 D2
  RLEINE/SYS LE7 .... 124 C2
Gorse La LEIS LE2 .... 139 H4
  RLEINE/SYS LE7 .... 120 D4
Gorse Rd COT/KEY/RAD NG12.... 80 B4
Gorsey Cl BPR/DUF DE56 ...... 17 J1 🔞
Gorsey Rd MAPPK/POR/STA NG3 ... 5 J1
Gorsty Cl LEIN LE4 .... 124 F4
Gorsty Leys RDERBYSW DE65 ... 70 B6 🔞
Goscote Hall Rd LEIN LE4 ...... 125 K1
Gosforth Rd DERBYSE DE24 .... 58 C8
Goshawk Cl RLEIW/BAR LE9 .... 141 J8 🔞
Goshawk Rd ILK DE7 .... 47 L4
Gosling St LEIS LE2 .... 6 D8
Gotham La CFTN/RUD NG11 .... 78 F8
Gotham Rd CFTN/RUD NG11 .... 86 F2
  RLBORO LE12 .... 88 C5
Gotham St LEIS LE2 .... 7 J8
Gothic Cl BLWL NG6 .... 36 C3
Gough Rd LEIE LE5 .... 132 C1
Goverton Sq BLWL NG6 .... 36 B2 🔞
Gowan Cl BSTN/STPLFD NG9 ... 63 G5 🔞
Gower St DERBY DE1 .... 2 E5
  LEI LE1 .... 7 G3
Goyden Cl ARN NG5 .... 24 E7
Grace Av BSTN/STPLFD NG9 ... 63 M2
Grace Crs HEANOR DE75 ...... 20 D6
Gracedieu La RLBORO LE12.... 100 D5
Grace Dieu Rd COAL LE67 ..... 100 B8
Gracedieu Rd LBORO LE11 ..... 8 A4
Grace Dr WOL/BIL/BRX NG8 .... 36 A2
Grace Rd LEIS LE2 .... 131 J7
  RLEIW/BAR LE9 .... 140 C7
Graham St ILK DE7 .... 33 K8
  LEIE LE5 .... 7 J4
  NOTTE NG7 .... 50 C2 🔞🔞
Grainger Av WBRGFD NG2 ..... 65 J4
Grainger St RIPLEY DE5 .... 19 L3
Grammer St RIPLEY DE5 .... 19 L3
Grampian Cl LEIS LE2 .... 131 K8
Grampian Dr ARN NG5 .... 25 K6
Grampian Wy DERBYSE DE24 ... 71 H4
  LGEAT NG10 .... 61 L7
Granary Cl LEIW LE3 .... 123 M8 🔞
  RLEIW/BBY LE8 .... 146 E8
Granby Pl LEI LE1 .... 6 F6
Granby St LEIS LE2 .... 131 H8
  ILK DE7 .... 33 J5
  LBORO LE11 .... 9 H3
  LEI LE1 .... 6 F6
Grandfield Av
  COT/KEY/RAD NG12 .... 53 K3
Grandfield Crs
  COT/KEY/RAD NG12 .... 53 K3
Grandfield St HEANOR DE75 ... 20 A3
Grandstand Rd DERBYE DE21 ... 2 A1
Grange Av BSTN/STPLFD NG9.... 63 K1
  DERBYSE DE72 .... 61 H7
  CFTN/RUD NG11 .... 64 D7
  LEIW LE3 .... 129 L4
  NORM/LIT DE23 .... 57 J8

RLEINE/SYS LE7 .... 115 K7
Grange Cl CARL NG4 .... 27 G8
  CFTN/RUD NG11 .... 50 F7
  GBY/RBY LE6 .... 123 H7
  LEIW LE3 .... 123 M7
  MELB/CHEL DE73 .... 82 F7
  RLEIW/BBY LE8 .... 139 M6
Grange Ct CFTN/RUD NG11.... 65 G5
Grange Crs CARL NG4 .... 53 L4
Grange Dr CDON/KEG DE74 ... 84 E4
  LEIS LE2 .... 136 F4
  LGEAT NG10 .... 62 D7
  RLEIW/BBY LE8 .... 136 D7
Grange Farm Cl
  BSTN/STPLFD NG9 .... 62 E6
  CDON/KEG DE74 .... 85 G2
Grangefields Dr
  RLEINE/SYS LE7 .... 119 K1
Grange La LEIS LE2 .... 6 D8
  RLBORO LE12 .... 113 H7
  RLEINE/SYS LE7 .... 133 J3
Grangelea Gdns
  BSTN/STPLFD NG9 .... 48 F8
Grange Pk WBRGFD NG2 ...... 66 A2
Grange Rd ARN NG5 .... 37 J3
  BLWL NG6 .... 36 B4
  COT/KEY/RAD NG12 .... 65 L3
  DERBYSE DE24 .... 72 F2
  LGEAT NG10 .... 62 D7
  RLBORO LE12 .... 101 L4
  WGSTN LE18 .... 138 B3
Grange St LBORO LE11 .... 9 G1
  NORM/LIT DE23 .... 3 H9
  NORM/LIT DE23 .... 57 M5
The Grange HEANOR DE75 .... 20 A7
Grange Vw EWD/SEL/PNX NG16 ... 21 K4
Grange View Rd CARL NG4 .... 38 B5
Grangeway Rd WGSTN LE18.... 138 A3
Grangewood Av ILK DE7 .... 33 K8 🔞
Grangewood Dr BPR/DUF DE56 .. 17 L8
Grangewood Rd
  WOL/BIL/BRX NG8 .... 49 G4
Granite Cl RLEIW/BAR LE9 ..... 135 L3
Granite Wy RLBORO LE12 ...... 113 H3
Grannis Dr WOL/BIL/BRX NG8 ... 35 L7
Grant Av DERBYE DE21 .... 58 F2 🔞
Grantham Av DERBYE DE21 .... 44 C6
  RLEINE/BAR LE9 .... 141 H7 🔞
Grantham Cl
  EWD/SEL/PNX NG16 .... 22 A8 🔞
Grantham Rd
  COT/KEY/RAD NG12 .... 53 G6
  LEIE LE5 .... 127 G7
  WBRGFD NG2 .... 51 K8
Granton Av CFTN/RUD NG11.... 64 D7
Grant St NOTTE NG7 .... 4 B5
Granville Av LEIS LE2 .... 138 D1
  LGEAT NG10 .... 62 B6
Granville Cl BPR/DUF DE56 .... 29 J4
Granville Crs
  COT/KEY/RAD NG12 .... 53 J5
  WGSTN LE18 .... 137 M2
Granville Rd LEI LE1 .... 131 M4
  WGSTN LE18 .... 138 A2
Granville St DERBY DE1 .... 2 A4
  LBORO LE11 .... 9 G3
Grape St LEI LE1 .... 6 D4 🔞
Grasmere COAL LE67 .... 108 F5
Grasmere Av DERBYE DE21 .... 59 J1
Grasmere Cl HUCK/RAV NG15 ... 15 K7
  RLBORO LE12 .... 105 H7
Grasmere Crs DERBYSE DE24 ... 71 J3
Grasmere Gdns CFTN/RUD NG11 ... 77 M5
Grasmere Rd BSTN/STPLFD NG9 ... 49 H7
  LBORO LE11 .... 103 K8
  LGEAT NG10 .... 61 M5
  WGSTN LE18 .... 138 D4
Grasmere St LEIS LE2 .... 7 J8
  LGEAT NG10 .... 61 M2 🔞
Grass Acres LEIW LE3 .... 130 C8
Grasshoime Dr LBORO LE11 ... 102 E4
Grassingdale Cl CARL NG4 .... 38 B5
Grassington Cl LEIS LE2 ...... 125 G3
Grassington Dr WGSTN LE18 ... 138 C6 🔞
Grassington Rd
  WOL/BIL/BRX NG8 .... 50 B1
Grassmere COT/KEY/RAD NG12.... 67 L4
Grass St ILK DE7 .... 33 J5
Grassthorpe Cl DERBY DE21 .... 44 F6 🔞
Grassy La BSTN/STPLFD NG9 ... 63 L2
  MCKLVR DE3 .... 55 L8
Gravel Pit La DERBYE DE21 .... 59 J5
Gravel St LEI LE1 .... 6 E4 🔞
Graylands Rd WOL/BIL/BRX NG8 ... 49 J1
Grayling St NORM/LIT DE23 .... 3 H9
Grays Ct RLEIW/BAR LE9 ...... 135 L4
Graystones Cl WBRGFD NG2 ... 66 A2
Gray St LBORO LE12 .... 9 J6
  LEIS LE2 .... 6 C8
Grayswood Dr LEIN LE4 .... 118 E3
Grazingfield CFTN/RUD NG11 ... 64 E3
Greasley Av
  EWD/SEL/PNX NG16 .... 22 A5 🔞
Greasley St BLWL NG6 .... 35 M1
Great Arler Rd LEIS LE2 .... 131 L7
Great Central Rd LBORO LE11 ... 9 L4
Great Central St LEIW LE3 .... 6 C4
Great Freeman St
  MAPPK/POR/STA NG3........ 5 H4
Great Hoggett Dr
  BSTN/STPLFD NG9 .... 62 E1
Great Meadow Rd LEIN LE4 ... 124 F5
The Great Northern Cl
  WBRGFD NG2 .... 5 K9
Great Northern Rd DERBY DE1 ... 2 A4
  EWD/SEL/PNX NG16 .... 21 M5 🔞
Great Northern Wy CARL NG4 ... 52 F1
Creatorex Av DERBYSE DE24 ... 72 F2 🔞
Greaves Cl ARN NG5 .... 37 M2
  WOL/BIL/BRX NG8 .... 35 H6
Greaves St RIPLEY DE5 .... 19 L3
Grebe Cl RLBORO LE12 .... 105 J7
Grebe Wy RLEIW/BBY LE8 ..... 146 D7
Greedon Ri RLBORO LE12 ..... 114 A3
Greek St NOTTE NG7 .... 4 C6 🔞
Green Acre COT/KEY/RAD NG12 ... 65 M3
  WOL/BIL/BRX NG8 .... 48 F2 🔞
Greenacre Av HEANOR DE75 .... 20 E4

Greenacre Dr LEIE LE5 .... 132 E3
Greenacres NORM/LIT DE23 ... 56 F7 🔞
Greenacres
  EWD/SEL/PNX NG16 .... 22 A5
Green Av CARL NG4 .... 38 E8
  MELB/CHEL DE73 .... 72 E6
Greenbank CARL NG4.......... 52 B1
  DERBYE DE21 .... 59 H3 🔞
Greenbank Dr LEIS LE2 .... 138 F2
Greenbank Rd LEIE LE5 .... 127 H6
Greenburn Cl NORM/LIT DE23 ... 71 G1
  WBRGFD NG2 .... 66 A1
Green Cl COT/KEY/RAD NG12 ... 80 D3
  HUCK/RAV NG15 .... 24 A2 🔞
Greenclose La LBORO LE11 ..... 9 H3
Greencoat Rd LEIW LE3 .... 124 C8
Green Crs EWD/SEL/PNX NG16... 13 J1
Greencroft CFTN/RUD NG11 .... 64 D4
Greendale Gdns
  WOL/BIL/BRX NG8 .... 35 M7
Greendale Rd ARN NG5 .... 37 K1
  LEIS LE2 .... 136 F4
  MAPPK/POR/STA NG3........ 52 A1
Green Farm Rd
  EWD/SEL/PNX NG16 .... 13 H1
Greenfield Gv CARL NG4 ...... 38 A7
Greenfields EWD/SEL/PNX NG16 ... 20 E3
  RLEIW/BBY LE8 .... 136 D8 🔞
Greenfields Av
  NORM/LIT DE23 .... 56 F8 🔞
Greenfields Dr COAL LE67 ..... 108 E6
  COT/KEY/RAD NG12 .... 67 K5 🔞
Greenfield St NOTTE NG7 ..... 50 B6
Greenfinch Cl DERBYE DE21 ... 59 K1 🔞
Greenford Cl WOL/BIL/BRX NG8 .. 35 J4 🔞
Greengate La LEIN LE4 .... 119 J8
Greengates Av
  MAPPK/POR/STA NG3........ 37 K4 🔞
Green Hl RLBORO LE12 .... 94 E6
Greenhill Av RIPLEY DE5 ...... 11 J7
Greenhill Cl RLEIW/BAR LE9 ... 135 K8
Greenhill Crs CARL NG4 .... 52 C1
Greenhill Ri CARL NG4 .... 38 C8
Green Hill Ri RLBORO LE12 .... 94 E5
Greenhill Rd CARL NG4 .... 52 C1
  COAL LE67 .... 108 F6
  LEIS LE2 .... 131 M6
Greenhills Av
  EWD/SEL/PNX NG16 .... 21 L4 🔞
Greenhills Rd
  EWD/SEL/PNX NG16 .... 21 K4
Greenhithe Rd LEIS LE2 ...... 131 H6
Greenland Av DERBYW DE22 ... 56 F2
  LEIE LE5 .... 126 E7
Greenland Crs
  BSTN/STPLFD NG9 .... 63 G3
Greenland Dr LEIE LE5 .... 126 E7
Green La BPR/DUF DE56 ...... 17 K3
  BWSH/BRSTN DE72 .... 60 A2
  CARL NG4 .... 26 F6
  CDON/KEG DE74 .... 92 F1
  CFTN/RUD NG11 .... 64 D6
  COAL LE67 .... 108 C4
  DERBY DE1 .... 2 E5
  DERBYSE DE24 .... 59 C7
  ILK DE7 .... 33 L8
  RDERBYSW DE65 .... 69 K3
  RLBORO LE12 .... 106 D6
  RLEIW/BBY LE8 .... 143 K3
Green Lane Cl LEIE LE5 .... 132 D1
Green Lane Rd LEIE LE5 ...... 126 D7
Green Leys WBRGFD NG2 ..... 65 G6
Green Pk DERBYW DE22 ...... 56 E1 🔞
Green Platt COT/KEY/RAD NG12 ... 67 J5
Green Rd RLEIW/BAR LE9 ..... 141 J8
Greenside Cl LGEAT NG10 ..... 62 C8
Greenside Cl MCKLVR DE3 .... 56 A5
Greenside PI RLEIW/BBY LE18 ... 137 K2 🔞
Greens La EWD/SEL/PNX NG16 ... 34 C1
Green St CFTN/RUD NG11 ...... 77 K2
  WBRGFD NG2 .... 51 H6
Greensward RLEINE/SYS LE7 ... 115 J7
The Green ASHB DE6 .... 41 G6
  BSTN/STPLFD NG9 .... 63 J3 🔞
  BWSH/BRSTN DE72 .... 73 M8 🔞
  CALV/BJ NG14.............. 27 K5
  CDON/KEG DE74 .... 84 E4
  CDON/KEG DE74 .... 92 F2
  COAL LE67 .... 100 B8
  COAL LE67 .... 116 B7
  COT/KEY/RAD NG12 .... 53 J4
  DERBYW DE22 .... 43 H6
  MCKLVR DE3 .... 56 B6
  RDERBYSW DE65 .... 70 B6
  RLBORO LE12 .... 88 C6
  RLBORO LE12 .... 94 A4
  RLBORO LE12 .... 94 E6
  RLEINE/SYS LE7 .... 115 K2
  RLEIW/BAR LE9 .... 135 H8
Green Wk LEIW LE3 .... 130 C2
Green Wy RDERBYSW DE65 ... 70 B5 🔞
Greenway RLEIW/BBY LE8 .... 146 E7 🔞
Greenway Cl BWSH/BRSTN DE72... 59 M4
  COT/KEY/RAD NG12 .... 53 J7
  RLEINE/SYS LE7 .... 119 J1
The Greenway DERBYSE DE24 ... 73 H2 🔞
  LEIN LE4 .... 125 L5
  LGEAT NG10 .... 61 M1
Greenwich Av BLWL NG6 ...... 36 A3
Greenwich Cl
  RLEIW/BAR LE9 .... 135 M7 🔞
Greenwich Dr North
  DERBYW DE22 .... 56 F2
Greenwich Dr South
  DERBYW DE22 .... 56 E2
Greenwich Park Cl
  WBRGFD NG2 .... 65 G2 🔞
Greenwood Av DERBYE DE21 ... 44 D7
  HUCK/RAV NG15 .... 15 K7
  ILK DE7 .... 33 L8
  MAPPK/POR/STA NG3........ 52 B2
Greenwood Cl DERBYSE DE24 ... 72 B2 🔞
Greenwood Crs CARL NG4 .... 52 B1
Greenwood Gdns
  CFTN/RUD NG11 .... 79 H1
Greenwood Rd CARL NG4 .... 52 B2

LEIE LE5 .... 132 D1
  MAPPK/POR/STA NG3........ 52 A2
Greenwood V HUCK/RAV NG15 ... 15 J7
Greetwell Cl
  WOL/BIL/BRX NG8 .... 49 L1 🔞
Gregg Av HEANOR DE75 .... 20 C5
Gregory Av BWSH/BRSTN DE72 ... 61 G7
  EWD/SEL/PNX NG16 .... 20 E4
  MAPPK/POR/STA NG3........ 37 L5
  NOTTE NG7 .... 4 A9
Gregory Bvd NOTTE NG7 ...... 4 B2
Gregory Cl BSTN/STPLFD NG9 ... 48 D6
  LEIN LE4 .... 120 E8
Gregory Ct BSTN/STPLFD NG9 ... 62 F3 🔞
Gregorys Cl LEIW LE3 .... 130 B6 🔞
Gregorys Wy BPR/DUF DE56 ... 18 A2
Gregson Cl LEIN LE4 .... 126 B2 🔞
Gregson Gdns
  BSTN/STPLFD NG9 .... 62 F6 🔞
Gregson Rd BSTN/STPLFD NG9 ... 62 F5
Grendon Cl BPR/DUF DE56 .... 17 M1 🔞
  WGSTN LE18 .... 138 C4 🔞
Grenfell Av NORM/LIT DE23 ... 71 J1
Grenfell Rd LEIS LE2 .... 132 C8
Grenville Dr BSTN/STPLFD NG9 ... 48 C7
  ILK DE7 .... 33 K4
Grenville Ri ARN NG5 .... 25 K6 🔞
Grenville Rd BSTN/STPLFD NG9 ... 63 M3
Grenvoir Dr RIPLEY DE5 ...... 11 L6 🔞
Gresham Cl WBRGFD NG2 .... 51 G8
Gresham Gdns ARN NG5 ..... 37 L2 🔞
  WBRGFD NG2 .... 51 H8
Gresham Rd DERBYSE DE24 ... 58 A7
Gresley Cl LEIN LE4 .... 125 G3
  RLEINE/SYS LE7 .... 133 K1
Gresley Dr WBRGFD NG2 ..... 51 K4
Gresley Rd ILK DE7 .... 33 K6 🔞
Cressy Rd CFTN/RUD NG11 .... 64 D5 🔞
Gretna Wy LEIE LE5 .... 127 J8 🔞
Gretton Rd
  MAPPK/POR/STA NG3........ 37 L3
Grey Cl GBY/RBY LE6 .... 123 K4
Grey Crs GBY/RBY LE6 .... 117 H6
Greyfriar Ga NOTT NG1 .... 5 G9
Grey Friars LEI LE1 .... 6 E6 🔞
Greyhound St NOTT NG1 ..... 5 H7 🔞
Greylag Wy RLEIW/BBY LE8 ... 142 D3
Greyland Paddock
  GBY/RBY LE6 .... 123 K4
Greys Dr GBY/RBY LE6 .... 123 J5
Greys Rd ARN NG5 .... 37 K3
Greystoke Cl WOL/BIL/BRX NG8 ... 49 G1
Greystoke Dr WOL/BIL/BRX NG8 ... 48 F5
Greystone Av LEIE LE5 .... 132 F1
Grey St DERBYW DE22 .... 2 D6
  EWD/SEL/PNX NG16 .... 21 L6
Greythorn Dr WBRGFD NG2 ... 65 H3
Grierson Av ARN NG5 .... 24 F7
Griffin Cl DERBYSE DE24 ...... 58 D8
  LEIN LE4 .... 126 D2
  RLBORO LE12 .... 101 L4
Griffon Rd ILK DE7 .... 47 K3
Griffs Hollow CARL NG4 ...... 38 C8
Griggs Rd LBORO LE11 .... 103 M7
Grimes Ga CDON/KEG DE74.... 85 G8
Grimshaw Av DERBYSE DE24 ... 58 F8
Grimston Cl LEIN LE4 .... 126 E3 🔞
Grimston Rd NOTTE NG7 ..... 50 C1
Grindlow Rd DERBYE DE21 .... 44 E7
Grindon Crs BLWL NG6........ 24 A5
Grindslow Av ILK DE7 .... 32 C7 🔞
Grinsbrook NOTTE NG7 .... 50 C3 🔞
Gripps Common
  COT/KEY/RAD NG12 .... 67 K6
Grisedale Cl LEIS LE2 .... 131 J4 🔞
Grisedale Dr
  BSTN/STPLFD NG9 .... 62 E3 🔞
Gritley Ms WBRGFD NG2 ...... 50 F5
Grizedale Gv RLEIW/BAR LE9 ... 135 K6
Groby La GBY/RBY LE6 .... 117 H8
Groby Rd GBY/RBY LE6 .... 123 H6
  LEIW LE3 .... 123 M4
  LEIW LE3 .... 124 E6
  RLEINE/SYS LE7 .... 124 A2
Grocot Rd LEIE LE5 .... 132 E4
Groome Av HEANOR DE75 .... 20 A3 🔞
Grosvenor Av
  BWSH/BRSTN DE72 .... 61 K7
  LGEAT NG10 .... 75 L3
  MAPPK/POR/STA NG3........ 37 C6 🔞
Grosvenor Cl WGSTN LE18..... 137 H6
Grosvenor Crs LEIS LE2 ...... 132 D8
Grosvenor Dr NORM/LIT DE23 ... 70 E1
Grosvenor Rd
  EWD/SEL/PNX NG16 .... 21 K5 🔞
  RIPLEY DE5 .... 11 H6
Grosvenor St DERBYSE DE24 ... 58 A6
  LEI LE1 .... 7 G3 🔞
Grouville Dr ARN NG5 .... 37 L2
Grove Av BSTN/STPLFD NG9 ... 63 J1
  NOTTE NG7 .... 4 C3
Grovebury Dr NORM/LIT DE23 ... 71 G2
Grovebury Rd LEIN LE4 .... 125 J4
Grove Cl BWSH/BRSTN DE72 ... 73 K3
  CALV/BJ NG14.............. 39 K2
Grove Ct RIPLEY DE5 .... 11 K7
Grove La RLBORO LE12 .... 105 H8
Grove Pk RDERBYSW DE65 ... 68 C5
Grover Av MAPPK/POR/STA NG3 ... 37 L4
Grove Rd COAL LE67 .... 108 C3
  LBORO LE11 .... 7 L4
  LEIE LE5 .... 127 L5
  NOTTE NG7 .... 50 D4
  RLEIW/BBY LE8 .... 142 D1
Groveside Crs CFTN/RUD NG11 ... 64 A4
Groves Nook
  MELB/CHEL DE73 .... 72 C6 🔞
Grove St BSTN/STPLFD NG9 ... 63 L2
  NORM/LIT DE23 .... 57 K8
The Grove BWSH/BRSTN DE72 ... 61 K7
  MCKLVR DE3 .... 56 C5
  NOTTE NG7 .... 4 B3
Grove Wy RLEIW/BAR LE9 ..... 136 D2
Grundy St NOTTE NG7 .... 36 C8
Guild Cl RLEINE/SYS LE7 ...... 118 D4

LEIE LE5 .... 132 D1
  MAPPK/POR/STA NG3........ 52 A2
Guildford Dr WGSTN LE18 .... 137 M2
Guildford Rd LEIS LE2 .... 132 C6
Guildford Wy LBORO LE11 .... 103 G7 🔞
Guildhall La LEICE LE1 .... 6 D6
Guildford St LEIS LE2 .... 7 J6 🔞
Guinea Cl LGEAT NG10 .... 61 L8
Guinevere Wy LEIW LE3 ...... 129 L5
Gullet La RLEIW/BAR LE9 ..... 129 G2
Gumley Sq RLEIW/BAR LE9 ... 135 M4 🔞
Gunhills La BPR/DUF DE56 .... 28 C1
Gunn Cl BLWL NG6 .... 23 L8 🔞
Gunnersbury Wy
  WOL/BIL/BRX NG8 .... 35 J4 🔞
Gunthorpe Cl ARN NG5 .... 36 F4 🔞
Gunthorpe Dr ARN NG5 .... 37 G4 🔞
Gunthorpe Rd CARL NG4 ..... 38 B4
  LEIW LE3 .... 130 B3
Gurnall Rd LEIN LE4 .... 124 E3
Gurney Av NORM/LIT DE23 ... 71 H1
Gurney Crs RLEIW/BAR LE9 ... 142 A1
Guthlaxton Gap
  RLEIW/BAR LE9 .... 141 J3
Guthlaxton St LEIS LE2 .... 7 K7
Guthlaxton Wy WGSTN LE18 ... 138 C7
Guthridge Crs LEIW LE3 ...... 130 F4
Gutteridge St COAL LE67 ..... 108 A6
Guy Cl BSTN/STPLFD NG9 .... 62 C1
Gwenbrook Av
  BSTN/STPLFD NG9 .... 63 J2
Gwenbrook Rd
  BSTN/STPLFD NG9 .... 63 H2
Gwencole Av LEIW LE3 .... 130 E7
Gwencole Crs LEIW LE3 ...... 130 E8
Gwendolen Rd LEIE LE5 ...... 132 B2
Gwendolin Av LEIN LE4 ...... 119 M8
Gwendoline Dr RLEIW/BBY LE8 ... 143 H3
Gynsill La RLEINE/SYS LE7 .... 124 C2
Gypsum Wy CFTN/RUD NG11 ... 77 L8
Gypsy La BWSH/BRSTN DE72 ... 60 C7

H

Hackett Rd LEIW LE3 .... 124 D7
Hackworth Cl
  EWD/SEL/PNX NG16 .... 21 M4
Hadbury Rd ARN NG5 .... 36 D5
Haddenham Rd LEIW LE3 ..... 131 G5
Haddon Cl CARL NG4 .... 38 B5
  DERBYW DE22 .... 43 H4
  ILK DE7 .... 32 C7 🔞
  RLEINE/SYS LE7 .... 120 D4
Haddon Crs BSTN/STPLFD NG9 ... 63 J5
Haddon Dr DERBYE DE21 ..... 59 K3
  DERBYW DE22 .... 56 C4
  MCKLVR DE3 .... 56 C4
Haddon Nurseries ILK DE7 .... 33 J4 🔞
Haddon Rd WBRGFD NG2 ..... 65 K1
Haddon St ARN NG5 .... 37 G5
  ILK DE7 .... 33 J4
  LEIS LE2 .... 7 M5
  NORM/LIT DE23 .... 57 J6
Haddon Wy
  COT/KEY/RAD NG12 .... 53 L3 🔞
  LGEAT NG10 .... 75 K3
  RLBORO LE12 .... 111 L1
Hades La RLBORO LE12 .... 99 G1
Hadleigh Cl BSTN/STPLFD NG9 ... 62 C5
Hadley St ILK DE7 .... 47 L2
Hadrian Cl RLEINE/SYS LE7 ... 120 C5
Hadley St ILK DE7 .... 47 L2
Hadrian Cl RLEINE/SYS LE7 ... 120 C5
Hadrian Gdns ARN NG5 ...... 24 E5
Hadrian Rd LEIN LE4 .... 120 C8
  LEIN LE4 .... 125 H2
Hadstock Cl LGEAT NG10 ..... 61 M3 🔞
Hagg La CALV/BJ NG14 .... 27 M1
  ILK DE7 .... 46 B3
Hag La BPR/DUF DE56 .... 16 A5
Hagley Cl
  MAPPK/POR/STA NG3........ 51 L1 🔞
Haig St DERBYSE DE24 .... 58 D7
Hailey Av LBORO LE11 .... 103 G2
Haileybury Crs WBRGFD NG2 ... 65 K3
Haileybury Rd WBRGFD NG2 ... 65 K3
Hailsham Cl MCKLVR DE3 .... 56 B4 🔞
Haines Cl DERBYSE DE24 ..... 71 K3
Haise Ct BLWL NG6 .... 35 K2
Halberton Dr WBRGFD NG2 ... 65 H3
Halcroft Ri WGSTN LE18 ...... 138 B6
Hales Cl COT/KEY/RAD NG12 ... 67 J4
Haley Cl EWD/SEL/PNX NG16 ... 34 B1
The Half Cft RLEINE/SYS LE7 ... 120 E3 🔞
Half Moon Crs LEIS LE2 ...... 139 G1
Halford Cl WGSTN LE18 ...... 139 M7
  RLEIW/BBY LE8 .... 142 D1
Halford Rd RLEIW/BBY LE8 ... 146 D7
Halford St LEI LE1 .... 6 F6
  RLEINE/SYS LE7 .... 120 E4
Halifax Cl RDERBYSW DE65 ... 68 C5
Halifax Ct WOL/BIL/BRX NG8 ... 35 H5 🔞
Halifax Dr LEIN LE4 .... 125 J4
Halifax Pl NOTT NG1 .... 5 J8 🔞
Halkin St LEIN LE4 .... 125 M6
Hallam Av LEIN LE4 .... 119 K8
Hallam Crs East LEIW LE3 .... 130 D5
Hallam Flds CDON/KEG DE74 ... 84 F5
Hallam Fields Rd ILK DE7 ..... 47 L3
Hallamford Rd RLBORO LE12 ... 93 K8
Hallam Rd BSTN/STPLFD NG9 ... 63 K1 🔞
Hallam's La ARN NG5 .... 25 K8
Hallam Wy ILK DE7 .... 32 B7
Hallaton St LEIS LE2 .... 131 J8
Hallaton St LEIS LE2 .... 131 J8
Hall Cl COT/KEY/RAD NG12 ... 53 J4
  LEIS LE2 .... 136 F4
  RLBORO LE12 .... 114 B7 🔞
  RLEINE/BBY LE8 .... 146 D6
Hall Cft ILK DE7 .... 32 C8
Hall Cft BSTN/STPLFD NG9 ... 63 K2 🔞
  RLBORO LE12 .... 101 M3
Hallcroft Av RLEINE/BBY LE8 ... 143 J4
Hallcroft Rd ILK DE7 .... 33 K7 🔞
Hall Dr BSTN/STPLFD NG9 .... 63 H2
  CFTN/RUD NG11 .... 77 L6
  LEIS LE2 .... 138 F1
  LGEAT NG10 .... 61 M1

RLBORO LE12 97 L8
WOL/BIL/BRX NG8 49 J4
Hall Dyke DERBYE DE21 59 J2
Halley Cl LEIN LE4 124 E1
Hall Farm Cl CDON/KEG DE74 84 E4
COT/KEY/RAD NG12 66 C6 1
RLEINE/SYS LE7 121 K2
Hall Farm Rd BPR/DUF DE56 29 J5
RLEINE/SYS LE7 118 F5
Hallfields COT/KEY/RAD NG12 65 M4
Hallfields La RLEINE/SYS LE7 119 J2
Hall Gdns BSTN/STPLFD NG9 48 F8
RLBORO LE12 88 D7
RLEIW/BBY LE8 139 M7
Hall Ga CDON/KEG DE74 93 G1
COAL LE67 109 G7
Hallgate Cl DERBYE DE21 45 G4
Hallington Dr HEANOR DE75 20 B6
Hall La ASHB DE6 40 E1
BPR/DUF DE56 10 A4
COAL LE67 108 D3
EWD/SEL/PNX NG16 13 H8
LEIS LE2 131 G8
Hall Leys RLBORO LE12 112 E2
Hall Leys La MELB/CHEL DE73 83 H6
Hall Park Cl NORM/LIT DE23 56 F6
Hall Rd EWD/SEL/PNX NG16 21 G3
RLEINE/SYS LE7 127 K7
Halls Brook RLBORO LE12 88 C5
Halls La EWD/SEL/PNX NG16 21 L7
Halls Rd BSTN/STPLFD NG9 62 B1 1
Hall St ARN NG5 37 H4
DERBYSE DE24 58 E8
Hall View Dr WOL/BIL/BRX NG8 49 H1
Hall Wk RLEIW/BAR LE9 135 M3
Halsbury St LEIS LE2 132 B4
Halstead Cl BSTN/STPLFD NG9 63 G3 2
WOL/BIL/BRX NG8 35 M4
Halstead Rd RLBORO LE12 113 H6
RLEINE/SYS LE7 113 G6
Halstead St LEIE LE5 132 B1
Halstock Dr DERBYSE DE24 59 G7
Halter Slade WGSTN LE18 138 C6 5
Hambledon Crs LBORO LE11 103 K7
Hambledon Dr
DERBYSE DE24 71 H5 3
WOL/BIL/BRX NG8 49 M2
Hamble Rd LEIS LE2 139 G1
Hambleton Cl LEIW LE3 129 K5 3
LGEAT NG10 61 L6 4
Hamblin Crs DERBYSE DE24 71 K3
Hambling Cl BLWL NG6 23 L8
Hamelin Rd LEIW LE3 130 D3
Hamilford Cl LEIE LE5 127 J6 4
Hamilton Cl ARN NG5 26 A6 2
BSTN/STPLFD NG9 62 D5
MCKLVR DE3 56 D4 1
Hamilton Dr COT/KEY/RAD NG12 53 K3
NOTTE NG7 4 E9
Hamilton La RLEINE/SYS LE7 127 J4
Hamilton Rd ARN NG5 36 F7
COAL LE67 109 G7
DERBYE DE21 59 K1
LGEAT NG10 62 B7
NORM/LIT DE23 2 C9
Hamilton St LEIS LE2 7 K9
Hamilton Wy LEIE LE5 126 F5
The Hamlet HEANOR DE75 20 C5 5
Hammercliffe Rd LEIE LE5 7 M1 1
Hammersmith RIPLEY DE5 11 H4
Hammersmith Cl
EWD/SEL/PNX NG16 35 J3 1
Hampden Gv BSTN/STPLFD NG9 63 J1
Hampden Rd LEIN LE4 126 C5
Hampden St
EWD/SEL/PNX NG16 21 M7
NORM/LIT DE23 57 L7 2
NOTT NG1 4 F4
Hampshire Ct
EWD/SEL/PNX NG16 12 F3
Hampshire Dr LGEAT NG10 61 M2
Hampshire Rd DERBYE DE21 44 A7
LEIS LE2 131 H8
Hampstead Cl
RLEIW/BAR LE9 135 M7 3
Hampstead Dr DERBYW DE22 56 E1
Hampstead Rd
MAPPK/POR/STA NG3 37 J6 1
Hampton Cl BSTN/STPLFD NG9 62 C4
DERBYE DE21 59 K2
ILK DE7 32 B8
WGSTN LE18 137 H6 2
WGSTN LE18 138 C5 6
Hampton Ct HEANOR DE75 20 B5 4
Hampton Rd WBRGFD NG2 65 J1
Hanbury Rd DERBYE DE21 58 C1
LEIE LE5 133 H3 1
Hand Av LEIW LE3 130 C4
Handel St DERBYSE DE24 58 A7
MAPPK/POR/STA NG3 5 L6
Handford St DERBYW DE22 57 H2
Handley St LEIS LE2 131 J8
Hand's Rd HEANOR DE75 20 D6
Handyside St DERBY DE1 2 E1
Hanford Wy LBORO LE11 103 M2
Hanger Bank
BWSH/BRSTN DE72 73 M7
Hankin Av EWD/SEL/PNX NG16 13 L5
Hankin St HUCK/RAV NG15 24 A1
Hanley Av BSTN/STPLFD NG9 48 F7
Hanley St NOTT NG1 4 F6 1
Hannah Crs CFTN/RUD NG11 50 F8
Hanover Cl LEIE LE5 126 F6
Hanover Dr RLBORO LE12 114 B4
Hanover Sq DERBYW DE22 56 E1
Hansen Ct WGSTN LE18 137 L5
Hanslope Crs WOL/BIL/BRX NG8 35 H8
Hanslynn BWSH/BRSTN DE72 73 K3 1
Hanson Crs HUCK/RAV NG15 15 L8
Hanstubbin Rd
EWD/SEL/PNX NG16 13 K1
Hanwell Wy DERBYW DE22 56 F1
Hanworth Gdns ARN NG5 25 H7
Haramead Rd LEI LE1 7 K3
Harberton Cl ARN NG5 25 J6 2
Harborough Rd LEIS LE2 138 F2
RLEIW/BBY LE8 146 F7
Harby Dr WOL/BIL/BRX NG8 50 A3
Harcourt Cl RLEINE/SYS LE7 120 E3
Harcourt Crs WOL/BIL/BRX NG8 35 K4
Harcourt Pl CDON/KEG DE74 84 F3
Harcourt Rd NOTTE NG7 36 E7
RLEIW/BBY LE8 146 D7
WGSTN LE18 138 C6
Harcourt St BSTN/STPLFD NG9 63 J1
DERBY DE1 2 D6
Hardacre Cl MELB/CHEL DE73 82 E7 4
Hardhurst Rd DERBYSE DE24 72 F2
Hardie Crs LEIW LE3 130 B5
Harding St LEI LE1 6 C3
Hardstaff Rd WBRGFD NG2 51 L2
Hardwick Av DERBYW DE22 43 H4
ILK DE7 32 C7
Hardwick Cl RIPLEY DE5 11 G4
Hardwick Ct LEIW LE3 131 G4 1
Hardwick Crs RLEINE/SYS LE7 120 D4
Hardwick Dr MCKLVR DE3 56 C5
Hardwicke Rd
BSTN/STPLFD NG9 63 G4 1
RLEIW/BAR LE9 135 K7
Hardwick Gv NOTTE NG7 4 B8
WBRGFD NG2 51 K6 1
Hardwick Pl ILK DE7 47 G2 3
Hardwick Rd ARN NG5 37 G4
LEIE LE5 133 H3
NOTTE NG7 4 C9
Hardwick St DERBYSE DE24 58 A7
Hardwood Cl BLWL NG6 23 K8 2
Hardy Barn HEANOR DE75 20 E7
Hardy Cl EWD/SEL/PNX NG16 22 D8
LGEAT NG10 76 B1
Hardy Crs RIPLEY DE5 11 M7
Hardy's Av LEIN LE4 126 A3
Hardy's Dr CARL NG4 38 D6
Hardy St EWD/SEL/PNX NG16 22 D8
NOTTE NG7 4 C3
Harebell Cl DERBYE DE21 44 E4
LEIE LE5 126 F5
Harecroft Crs RLEIW/BAR LE9 140 C7
Harefield RLBORO LE12 88 C4
Harefield Av LEIW LE3 130 F7
Harene Crs LEIW LE3 129 J5
Harepit Cl DERBYSE DE24 72 E2 1
Harewood Av BLWL NG6 36 B2
Harewood Cl BPR/DUF DE56 18 B2 3
COT/KEY/RAD NG12 53 L4
LGEAT NG10 61 M3 7
Harewood Rd DERBYW DE22 43 H4
Harewood St LEIE LE5 126 B8
Hargrave Av
BWSH/BRSTN DE72 60 A2 2
Harkstead Rd ARN NG5 24 F6
Harland Cl RLEIW/BAR LE9 142 B4 1
Harlaxton Dr LGEAT NG10 62 E6
NOTTE NG7 4 B8
Harlaxton St LEIW LE3 130 F5
Harlech Cl DERBYE DE21 59 L2 1
ILK DE7 33 G4 5
LBORO LE11 103 J2
Harlech Ri BSTN/STPLFD NG9 62 F3
Harlequin Cl
COT/KEY/RAD NG12 53 M4 1
Harlequin Ct
EWD/SEL/PNX NG16 21 H4 3
Harlequin Wy
RLEIW/BBY LE8 142 D3 1
Harlesden Av DERBYW DE22 42 E8
Harley Cl RLBORO LE12 101 M5 1
Harley St NOTTE NG7 4 A9
NOTTE NG7 50 D4 7
Harlow Cl DERBYSE DE24 72 D3 1
Harlow Ct ILK DE7 32 B8
Harlow Gv CARL NG4 38 C5 5
Harmston Ri ARN NG5 36 D3
Harold Av EWD/SEL/PNX NG16 20 F3
Harolds La RLEIW/BAR LE9 135 M2
Harold St LEIS LE2 131 J7
WBRGFD NG2 5 M7
Harpenden Sq
WOL/BIL/BRX NG8 35 M4 1
Harpswell Cl DERBYW DE22 43 J5 2
Harpur Av NORM/LIT DE23 56 F8
Harrier Cl RLEIW/BAR LE9 141 J8
Harrier Gv HUCK/RAV NG15 23 J3
Harrier Rd BPR/DUF DE56 18 A2
Harrier Wy DERBYSE DE24 71 J4
Harriet St NORM/LIT DE23 2 F8
Harriett St BSTN/STPLFD NG9 48 B7
Harriman Cl RLBORO LE12 101 M3 1
Harrimans Dr
BWSH/BRSTN DE72 61 K7
Harrimans La NOTTE NG7 50 B7
Harringay Gdns
DERBYW DE22 57 G1 2
Harrington Av
BWSH/BRSTN DE72 60 A5
Harrington Cl CARL NG4 38 F6
RLBORO LE12 112 E1 2
Harrington Dr NOTTE NG7 4 B8
Harrington Rd
NORM/LIT DE23 57 G6 2
RLBORO LE12 102 A4
WGSTN LE18 138 C4
Harrington St
BWSH/BRSTN DE72 60 F8 1
DERBYSE DE24 72 C1 2
LEIN LE4 7 L1
LGEAT NG10 75 M2
NORM/LIT DE23 57 L7
Harringworth Rd LEIE LE5 132 F3
Harris Av RIPLEY DE5 11 G5
Harris Cl RIPLEY DE5 11 G6
WOL/BIL/BRX NG8 49 K2
Harrison Cl LEIW LE3 124 A7
RLEIW/BBY LE8 142 E2 2
WGSTN LE18 137 M6
Harrison Rd BSTN/STPLFD NG9 48 B7
LEIN LE4 126 A5
Harrison St DERBYW DE22 2 A7
LEIN LE4 120 C7 1
Harris Rd BSTN/STPLFD NG9 63 G2
LEIN LE4 124 F4
Harrogate Crs DERBYE DE21 44 B6
Harrogate Rd LEIN LE4 126 A6
MAPPK/POR/STA NG3 52 A2
Harrogate St CARL NG4 38 D8 3
Harrogate Wy WGSTN LE18 138 C6
Harrowby Rd NOTTE NG7 4 B8
Harrow Cl LEIW LE3 129 K6
Harrowden Ri LEIE LE5 132 E1
Harrow Dr ILK DE7 47 L3
Harrow Gdns WOL/BIL/BRX NG8 50 A3
Harrowgate Dr LEIN LE4 119 K7
Harrow Rd HUCK/RAV NG15 23 H2
LEIW LE3 131 G3
WBRGFD NG2 65 J2
WOL/BIL/BRX NG8 49 M3
Harrow St DERBYSE DE24 58 C5
Hart Av LGEAT NG10 61 L2
Hart Cl RLEIW/BBY LE8 142 D2
Hartcroft Rd ARN NG5 36 F1
Hartfield Rd LEIE LE5 127 H7
Hartford Cl WBRGFD NG2 51 H5 3
Hartington Av HUCK/RAV NG15 23 G1
CARL NG4 38 B6
Hartington Cl ILK DE7 32 C7 8
Hartington Pl ILK DE7 33 J2 6
Hartington Rd ARN NG5 37 G4
LEIS LE2 7 L5
Hartington St NORM/LIT DE23 2 F7
Hartington Wy MCKLVR DE3 56 B5
Hartland Dr NORM/LIT DE23 71 H1
Hartley Dr BSTN/STPLFD NG9 63 M1
Hartley Rd NOTTE NG7 4 A4
NOTTE NG7 50 C1
Hartness Rd CFTN/RUD NG11 64 A6
Hartopp Cl RLEINE/SYS LE7 133 L2
Hartopp Rd LEIS LE2 131 M5
Hart Rd LEIS LE2 7 L4
Hartshay Hl RIPLEY DE5 11 G4
Hartshorn Cl LEIN LE4 126 D1
Hartshorne Rd NORM/LIT DE23 71 G2
Hartside Cl WBRGFD NG2 52 A8 3
Hartside Gdns LGEAT NG10 61 L7 2
Hart St NOTTE NG7 4 A9
Hartwell St MAPPK/POR/STA NG3 5 J3
Hartwood Dr BSTN/STPLFD NG9 48 B6
Harvard Cl LEIS LE2 138 F1
Harvest Cl ARN NG5 24 D7
LEIN LE4 124 F4
RLEIW/BAR LE9 142 B1 1
Harvester Cl LEIW LE3 129 K6
Harvest Wy DERBYE DE21 45 G4
Harvey Cl CFTN/RUD NG11 79 H2
Harvey Cft BSTN/STPLFD NG9 48 A3 1
Harvey Rd CDON/KEG DE74 84 F5
DERBYSE DE24 58 E8
Harwich Cl BLWL NG6 23 L7 2
Harwill Crs WOL/BIL/BRX NG8 35 M5
Harwin Rd LEIE LE5 132 F3
Harwood Cl ARN NG5 25 M7
Hasgill Cl DERBYE DE21 45 G4 7
Haskell Cl LEIW LE3 130 B5
Haslam's La DERBYW DE22 43 L5
Haslam St NOTTE NG7 4 F9
Haslemere Ct NORM/LIT DE23 3 H9 1
Haslemere Rd LGEAT NG10 61 M7
WOL/BIL/BRX NG8 36 B7
Haslyn Wk COAL LE67 108 F7
Hassal Rd LEIW LE3 124 C7
Hassock La North HEANOR DE75 20 F8
HEANOR DE75 32 F1
Hassock La South HEANOR DE75 33 G1
Hassocks La BSTN/STPLFD NG9 49 M8
Hassop Rd DERBYE DE21 44 E7
Hastings Av COAL LE67 108 E3
Hastings Rd LEIE LE5 126 B7
RLBORO LE12 111 K7
RLEIW/BAR LE9 129 J3
Hastings St CARL NG4 38 A8
CDON/KEG DE74 84 F5
LBORO LE11 9 G3
NORM/LIT DE23 57 L6
The Hastings LEIW LE3 130 B6
Haswell Rd BLWL NG6 35 M2
Hatchmere Cl DERBYE DE21 44 E6
Hatfield Av LGEAT NG10 61 M3
Hatfield Dr WBRGFD NG2 65 G3 4
Hatfield Rd DERBYSE DE24 72 D2
MAPPK/POR/STA NG3 37 G5
Hathaway Av LEIW LE3 130 D6
Hatherleigh Cl
MAPPK/POR/STA NG3 38 A1 3
Hatherleigh Rd LEIE LE5 132 D4
Hathern Cl LGEAT NG10 76 B2 1
NORM/LIT DE23 71 J2
Hathern Dr RLBORO LE12 102 D1
Hathern Gn BSTN/STPLFD NG9 49 L7
Hathern Rd RLBORO LE12 94 B4
RLBORO LE12 102 B1
Hathersage Av LGEAT NG10 75 K2
NORM/LIT DE23 57 J7
Hatley Cl WBRGFD NG2 50 F6 7
Hat Rd LEIW LE3 130 C8
Hattern Av LEIN LE4 125 H3
Hatton Ct MELB/CHEL DE73 82 E8 1
Hatton Crofts LGEAT NG10 76 A1 3
Hatton Gdns WOL/BIL/BRX NG8 35 J4
Haulton Dr CDON/KEG DE74 84 E3
Havelock Rd NORM/LIT DE23 57 K7
Havelock St ILK DE7 33 K8 6
LBORO LE11 8 E2
LEIS LE2 6 D9
RIPLEY DE5 11 H5
Haven Baulk Av NORM/LIT DE23 56 C8
Haven Baulk La MCKLVR DE3 56 B8
Haven Cl LEIW LE3 129 K5
RLBORO LE12 100 F1 1
WBRGFD NG2 65 H2
Haven Ct DERBYSE DE24 73 H1
Havencrest Dr LEIE LE5 126 F8
Havenwood Ri CFTN/RUD NG11 64 B7
Haverhill Crs ARN NG5 24 B6
Haversham Cl BLWL NG6 36 B5 2
Hawarden Av LEIE LE5 126 D8
Hawarden Ter NOTTE NG7 4 A2
Hawcliffe Rd RLBORO LE12 113 G4
Hawk Cl RLEIW/BAR LE9 141 J8 3
Hawker Rd LEIS LE2 139 H3
Hawkesbury Rd LEIS LE2 131 J8
Hawkes Hl LEIS LE2 137 K2
Hawke St DERBYW DE22 57 G2
Hawkhurst Dr
WOL/BIL/BRX NG8 49 H5 3
Hawk Ridge Gdns
MAPPK/POR/STA NG3 5 L5
Hawksdale Cl
MELB/CHEL DE73 72 E5 4
Hawkshead Av DERBYE DE21 44 B6
Hawkshead Cl
COT/KEY/RAD NG12 66 B2 4
Hawksley Gdns CFTN/RUD NG11 64 A5
Hawksley Rd NOTTE NG7 4 B2
Hawkswood Cl
BSTN/STPLFD NG9 62 F3 4
Hawksworth Av ARN NG5 37 H3 3
Hawksworth Rd
WBRGFD NG2 51 K6 2
Hawksworth St
MAPPK/POR/STA NG3 5 M6
Hawley Cl RLBORO LE12 88 D6
Hawthorn Av
BWSH/BRSTN DE72 61 K7
COT/KEY/RAD NG12 67 K5 2
DERBYSE DE24 58 E8 1
HUCK/RAV NG15 23 K1
RIPLEY DE5 11 H7
RLEINE/SYS LE7 119 M7
Hawthorn Cl CALV/BJ NG14 27 G3
COAL LE67 108 C6
COT/KEY/RAD NG12 65 M3 1
COT/KEY/RAD NG12 80 C5
LEIW LE3 129 J5
RDERBYSW DE65 68 B6
Hawthorn Crs ARN NG5 25 L6
RDERBYSW DE65 70 B5 3
Hawthorn Dr RLEIW/BBY LE8 142 F1 1
Hawthorne Av
BSTN/STPLFD NG9 62 B1
BWSH/BRSTN DE72 59 M4
LGEAT NG10 62 A8
LGEAT NG10 76 A1
RLBORO LE12 94 E6
Hawthorne Cl BPR/DUF DE56 18 D5 2
Hawthorne Dr LEIE LE5 132 E4
Hawthorne St LEIW LE3 130 F1
Hawthorn Gv BSTN/STPLFD NG9 63 M1
LEIS LE2 132 F8 1
Hawthorn Ri
EWD/SEL/PNX NG16 33 M3
GBY/RBY LE6 123 K4
Hawthorn Rd CDON/KEG DE74 84 F2
RLBORO LE12 113 J6
The Hawthorns COAL LE67 116 C7 3
DERBYE DE21 30 B7 1
RLEIW/BBY LE8 143 J3 1
Hawthorn St DERBYSE DE24 58 A7
Hawton Crs WOL/BIL/BRX NG8 50 A3
Hawton Spinney
WOL/BIL/BRX NG8 50 A3 2
Hawtrey Gdns DERBYSE DE24 72 E1 1
Haybarn Cl RLEIW/BAR LE9 142 B1
Haybrooke Rd RLBORO LE12 114 B3
Hayden Av LEIS LE2 139 H3
Hayden Cl LEIN LE4 125 J4
Hayden La HUCK/RAV NG15 15 M5
Haydn Av ARN NG5 36 F5
Haydn Rd ARN NG5 36 E5
DERBYE DE21 44 D7
Haydock Cl
EWD/SEL/PNX NG16 22 C8 3
Haydock Park Rd
DERBYSE DE24 58 C7
Haydon Rd LBORO LE11 8 D3
Hayes Av BWSH/BRSTN DE72 60 F8
NORM/LIT DE23 57 H7
Hayes Cl COAL LE67 108 D3
ILK DE7 32 C7 9
Hayes Crs ALFN DE55 11 K1
Hayes Rd COT/KEY/RAD NG12 80 B4
WGSTN LE18 138 C4
The Hayes RDERBYSW DE65 70 A6
Hayes Wood Rd ILK DE7 31 M6
Hayfield Cl BPR/DUF DE56 17 M2 2
LEIW LE3 123 M7
Hayhill RLBORO LE12 113 L2
Hayhill La RLBORO LE12 113 K1
Hayles Cl ARN NG5 36 F1 3
Hayley Cft BPR/DUF DE56 29 K6
Hayling Cl ILK DE7 33 G4 6
Hayling Crs LEIE LE5 126 E7
Hayling Dr BLWL NG6 36 B5
Haymarket LEI LE1 6 F5
Haynes Av BSTN/STPLFD NG9 48 A2
Haynes Cl CFTN/RUD NG11 64 D4
Haynes Rd LEIE LE5 126 C8
Hays Cl ILK DE7 33 H5 1
Hayward Av LBORO LE11 9 M7
Haywood Cl DERBYSE DE24 72 E2 2
LEIE LE5 132 E3
Haywood Rd
MAPPK/POR/STA NG3 37 K5
Haywood St WBRGFD NG2 5 L7
Hayworth Rd LGEAT NG10 61 M2
Hazel Av NORM/LIT DE23 71 H1
Hazelbank Av
MAPPK/POR/STA NG3 37 K6
Hazelbank Rd RLEIW/BBY LE8 143 K3
Hazel Cl HEANOR DE75 20 B6
LEIN LE4 119 M7 1
RDERBYSW DE65 70 C5 1
RLEIW/BAR LE9 142 A1
Hazeldene Cl BPR/DUF DE56 29 J2
Hazeldene Rd LEIE LE5 127 H5
Hazel Dr DERBYE DE21 59 L1
EWD/SEL/PNX NG16 34 F1
LEIW LE3 136 D1
Hazel Gv BPR/DUF DE56 29 J4 1
HUCK/RAV NG15 23 L2
MAPPK/POR/STA NG3 37 L3
Hazelhead Rd RLEINE/SYS LE7 124 B1
Hazel Hill Crs ARN NG5 24 F8
Hazel Mdw HUCK/RAV NG15 23 L2
Hazelmere NOTTE NG7 50 C3 3
Hazelnut Cl LEIE LE5 132 F3
Hazelrigg Cl CDON/KEG DE74 84 D3
Hazel Rd LBORO LE11 103 L7
Hazel St BLWL NG6 23 M7 3
LEIS LE2 131 K4
Hazeltree Cl RIPLEY DE5 11 G7
Hazel Wy HUCK/RAV NG15 15 M5
Hazelwood
COT/KEY/RAD NG12 67 L4 1
Hazelwood Cl
EWD/SEL/PNX NG16 21 M5
Hazelwood Dr HUCK/RAV NG15 23 G1
Hazelwood Hl BPR/DUF DE56 16 F7
Hazelwood Rd BPR/DUF DE56 17 G8
DERBYE DE21 44 D7 3
LEIE LE5 132 B4
NOTTE NG7 36 C8
WGSTN LE18 137 L7
Heacham Dr LEIN LE4 124 F4
Headingley Ct
NORM/LIT DE23 57 G7 3
Headingley Gdns
WOL/BIL/BRX NG8 36 B7 2
Headingly Cl LEIN LE4 119 G8 3
Headland Rd LEIE LE5 132 E4
The Headlands RLEINE/SYS LE7 115 J7
Headley Rd LEIW LE3 130 D8
Heafield Dr CDON/KEG DE74 86 B5
Heage La RDERBYSW DE65 55 G8
Heage Rd RIPLEY DE5 10 F6
Healey Cl WBRGFD NG2 51 G5 3
Healey St WGSTN LE18 137 K6
Healy Cl LEIN LE4 125 H3
Heanor Gate Rd HEANOR DE75 20 B7
Heanor Rd HEANOR DE75 20 B4
ILK DE7 19 L8
ILK DE7 33 J4
RIPLEY DE5 11 M8
RIPLEY DE5 19 L4
Heanor St LEI LE1 6 D3
Heard Crs BSTN/STPLFD NG9 49 K7
Heards Cl WGSTN LE18 138 C7
Heath Av NORM/LIT DE23 57 G5
RLEINE/SYS LE7 120 D4
RLEIW/BAR LE9 136 C5
Heathbrook Dr GBY/RBY LE6 123 H7
Heathcoat St LBORO LE11 9 G3
NOTT NG1 5 J7
Heathcote Cl DERBYSE DE24 73 G2 2
Heathcote Dr RLBORO LE12 114 C3 1
Heathcott Rd LEIS LE2 131 K8
Heath Ct DERBYSE DE24 71 J4 3
Heatherbrook Rd LEIN LE4 124 D2
Heather Cl DERBYSE DE24 71 H5 4
EWD/SEL/PNX NG16 21 M6
MAPPK/POR/STA NG3 5 K1
Heather Ct HEANOR DE75 20 F6 2
Heather Crs
BWSH/BRSTN DE72 61 K8 1
NORM/LIT DE23 71 G1
Heather Cft WBRGFD NG2 65 G3
Heatherley Dr BLWL NG6 36 D3
Heathermead Cl DERBYE DE21 44 D6
Heather Ri BSTN/STPLFD NG9 49 J6
Heather Rd CARL NG4 38 B6
LEIS LE2 131 L7
Heathervale CFTN/RUD NG11 64 F1
Heather Wy RLEIW/BBY LE8 143 K4
Heathfield COAL LE67 100 B7
Heathfield Av ILK DE7 33 L7
Heathfield Gv BSTN/STPLFD NG9 63 G4
Heathfield Rd ARN NG5 36 D3
WGSTN LE18 138 B2 1
Heath Gdns BWSH/BRSTN DE72 61 L7
Heathgate Cl LEIN LE4 119 K7
Heath La RDERBYSW DE65 70 B7
Heathley Cl LEIW LE3 129 K5
Heathrington Gdns ARN NG5 24 D6
Heath Rd RIPLEY DE5 11 J6
The Heath
EWD/SEL/PNX NG16 21 L7 3
Heaton Cl
MAPPK/POR/STA NG3 37 K6 3
Heawood Wy LEIW LE3 130 B6
Heays Cl LEIW LE3 124 C7
Hebden Cl LEIS LE2 137 G5
NORM/LIT DE23 70 D1
Hebrides Cl DERBYSE DE24 71 H4 11
Heckington Dr
WOL/BIL/BRX NG8 49 M2
Hector Rd COAL LE67 108 B5
Hedderley Wk
MAPPK/POR/STA NG3 5 J4
Heddington Cl WGSTN LE18 137 L2 1
Heddington Wy WGSTN LE18 137 L2
Hedgebank Ct DERBYE DE21 45 G4 8
Hedge Rd COAL LE67 108 A8
Hedgerow Gdns
DERBYE DE21 45 G4 9
Hedgerow La RLEIW/BAR LE9 129 G2
Hedges Dr ILK DE7 47 K3
Hedingham Wy MCKLVR DE3 56 A7
Hedley St NOTTE NG7 36 E7 3
Hefford Gdns LEIN LE4 125 H3
Heigham Cl DERBYSE DE24 72 B4
Heighton Crs RLEIW/BAR LE9 142 A1
Helena Crs LEIN LE4 125 J3
Helen Cl BSTN/STPLFD NG9 63 H1 1
Hellebore Cl ARN NG5 24 C8 3
Helm Cl BLWL NG6 23 K8
Helmsdale Cl COAL LE67 109 G7 1
Helmsdale Gdns ARN NG5 24 D6 2
Helmsley Rd LEIS LE2 137 K2
Helston Cl DERBYSE DE24 72 F1 3
WGSTN LE18 138 A6
Helston Dr WOL/BIL/BRX NG8 35 J6
Helvellyn Cl WBRGFD NG2 51 G5
Helvellyn Wy LGEAT NG10 61 M5 2
Hemington Hl CDON/KEG DE74 85 H3
Hemington La CDON/KEG DE74 85 J2
Hemington Rd LEIE LE5 133 H4
Hemingway Cl CARL NG4 38 B8 1
EWD/SEL/PNX NG16 22 A6
Hemlock Av BSTN/STPLFD NG9 48 C7
LGEAT NG10 62 B6
Hemlock Cl DERBYE DE21 44 E4
RLEIW/BAR LE9 135 K6
Hemlock Gdns BLWL NG6 23 K8
Hemlock La ILK DE7 47 H2 3
Hempshill La BLWL NG6 35 K1
Hemsby Gdns BLWL NG6 23 L7
Hemscott Cl BLWL NG6 23 K7 6
Hemsley Dr
EWD/SEL/PNX NG16 21 H4 4

Hemswell Cl
MAPPK/POR/STA NG3 51 L2
Hendon Ri MAPPK/POR/STA NG3 37 K7
Hendon Wy DERBYW DE22 56 F1
Henley Cl CARL NG4 52 E1
Henley Crs LEIW LE3 130 D6
Henley Gdns
BSTN/STPLFD NG9 48 C6 5
Henley Ri ARN NG5 36 E4
Henley Rd LEIW LE3 131 G1
Henley Wy ILK DE7 32 B7
Henray Av LEIS LE2 137 G5
Henrietta St BLWL NG6 36 A1
Henry Cl LEIW LE3 129 K5 1
Henry Rd BSTN/STPLFD NG9 63 L1
NOTTE NG7 50 C4 1
WBRGFD NG2 51 J7
Henry St ARN NG5 25 J5
DERBY DE1 2 D1
HUCK/RAV NG15 23 M1
RIPLEY DE5 11 H5
WBRGFD NG2 5 M7
Henshaw Av ILK DE7 47 H2 4
Henshaw Pl ILK DE7 33 J3
Henshaw St LEIS LE2 6 E8
Henson Cl LEIN LE4 125 K1
Henson's La COAL LE67 100 B7
Henton Rd LEIW LE3 131 G2
Hepple Dr BLWL NG6 23 K8 3
Herald Cl BSTN/STPLFD NG9 49 M8
Herbert Av LEIN LE4 125 M5
Herbert Cl RLEIW/BBY LE8 136 D8 4
Herbert Rd ARN NG5 36 E6
Herbert St LBORO LE11 103 M2
Herdsmans Cl
RLEIW/BAR LE9 136 A8 2
Hereford Rd ARN NG5 37 J2
CARL NG4 38 D5 2
DERBYE DE21 44 B7
LEIS LE2 131 H8
MAPPK/POR/STA NG3 51 M2
Hereward Dr RLEINE/SYS LE7 133 K2
Herle Av LEIW LE3 130 D5
Hermitage Av ALFN DE55 12 A2
BWSH/BRSTN DE72 60 A5
Hermitage Cl LEIS LE2 138 E2 2
Hermitage Ct DERBYE DE21 44 F6
Hermitage Rd COAL LE67 108 B4
LBORO LE11 102 F5
LEIN LE4 125 L2 1
Hermitage Wk ILK DE7 47 K1
NOTTE NG7 4 D9
Hermon St NOTTE NG7 4 C6
Heron Cl RLBORO LE12 113 K5
RLEIW/BBY LE8 139 M6
Heron Dr NOTTE NG7 50 C3 2
Herongate Rd LEIE LE5 126 D7
Heron Rd LEIE LE5 7 M3
RLBORO LE12 105 J7
Herons Ct WBRGFD NG2 66 A3
Heronswood Dr
DERBYE DE21 59 H1 1
Heron Wy COAL LE67 108 D7
MCKLVR DE3 56 E5
RLEINE/SYS LE7 120 D3 2
RLEIW/BAR LE9 136 B5
Herrick Cl RLBORO LE12 113 M4
RLEIW/BAR LE9 135 L4
Herrick Dr RLEINE/SYS LE7 133 K2
Herrick Rd LBORO LE11 9 H7
LEIS LE2 131 L7
RLBORO LE12 111 K5
Herricks Av LEIN LE4 126 D2
Herrick Wy WGSTN LE18 138 C6
Herriot Wy LBORO LE11 103 H2
Herschell St LEIS LE2 132 A4
Hervey Gn CFTN/RUD NG11 64 C5
Hervey Woods COAL LE67 108 B2
Hesketh Av LEIS LE2 137 G4
Hesketh Cl LEIS LE2 137 G4
Heskey Cl MAPPK/POR/STA NG3 5 H3
Heslington Av
WOL/BIL/BRX NG8 36 C7 2
Hetley Rd BSTN/STPLFD NG9 49 K8
Hewes Cl LEIS LE2 136 F4
Hewett Cl RLEIW/BBY LE8 139 L7
Hewitt Dr RLEIW/BAR LE9 129 K3
Hexham Av ILK DE7 47 L3
Hexham Cl WBRGFD NG2 65 L1 1
Hextall Rd LEIE LE5 132 E4
Heybridge Rd LEIE LE5 126 D7
Heybrook Av RLEIW/BBY LE8 136 E8
Heydon Cl BPR/DUF DE56 17 M1 5
Heyford Ct HEANOR DE75 20 E6 2
Heyford Rd LEIW LE3 130 B3
Hey St LGEAT NG10 75 M3
Heythrop Cl LEIS LE2 139 H3 6
Heyworth Rd LEIW LE3 131 G6
Heyworth St DERBYW DE22 57 G1
Hickings La BSTN/STPLFD NG9 48 C7
Hickleton Cl RIPLEY DE5 11 G6
Hickling Cl DERBYSE DE24 72 B4 2
Hickling Ct LBORO LE11 8 F3
Hickling Dr RLBORO LE12 114 B3
Hickling Rd
MAPPK/POR/STA NG3 37 L5
Hickling Wy COT/KEY/RAD NG12 67 L6
Hickton Dr BSTN/STPLFD NG9 62 F6
Hickton Rd ALFN DE55 11 K1
Hidcote Rd LEIS LE2 138 E3
Higgs Cl LEIE LE5 132 E2
High Bank RIPLEY DE5 19 K5
Highbank Dr CFTN/RUD NG11 64 C8
Highbridge RLBORO LE12 114 A4
Highbury Av BLWL NG6 36 A2
Highbury Cl DERBYW DE22 56 D1 3
WOL/BIL/BRX NG8 35 H4
Highbury Rd BLWL NG6 36 A1
COT/KEY/RAD NG12 80 C3
LEIN LE4 126 A7
High Church St NOTTE NG7 36 D6
Highclere Dr CARL NG4 38 D7
Highcliffe Rd LEIN LE4 126 E4
MAPPK/POR/STA NG3 51 L2
Highcroft MAPPK/POR/STA NG3 37 K3
Highcroft Av LEIS LE2 139 G3
Highcroft Cl LGEAT NG10 76 C2
Highcroft Dr WOL/BIL/BRX NG8 48 F2
Highcroft Rd LEIS LE2 139 H4
Highcross St LEI LE1 6 D5
LEIW LE3 6 C4
High Cross St NOTT NG1 5 J6 5
High Edge Dr BPR/DUF DE56 10 C7
Higher Gn RLEIW/BBY LE8 139 M7
Highfield Cl HEANOR DE75 19 M2
RLBORO LE12 102 A2
Highfield Crs WGSTN LE18 138 B3
Highfield Dr CARL NG4 37 M7
EWD/SEL/PNX NG16 35 K3 1
ILK DE7 46 F2
WGSTN LE18 138 B3
Highfield Gdns DERBYW DE22 43 K7
Highfield Gv WBRGFD NG2 51 K8
Highfield La DERBYE DE21 58 C2
Highfield Rd ALFN DE55 11 H1
BPR/DUF DE56 17 K5
BPR/DUF DE56 18 D7
BSTN/STPLFD NG9 62 E4 2
COT/KEY/RAD NG12 80 C3
DERBYE DE21 30 A8
DERBYW DE22 43 K8
EWD/SEL/PNX NG16 35 J3
GBY/RBY LE6 123 J5
NORM/LIT DE23 57 G8 1
NOTTE NG7 50 B6
WBRGFD NG2 51 K8
Highfields RIPLEY DE5 11 M7 1
RLBORO LE12 105 H7
Highfields Dr LBORO LE11 8 B7
Highfields Rd RLBORO LE12 113 H6
Highfield St LEIS LE2 7 J9
LGEAT NG10 62 A6
RLEINE/SYS LE7 124 C1
RLEIW/BAR LE9 140 B4 1
RLEIW/BAR LE9 140 B4
RLEIW/BBY LE8 145 J7
Highfield Wy RIPLEY DE5 11 G7
Highgate WGSTN LE18 137 L3
Highgate Av LEIN LE4 119 J7
Highgate Cl CARL NG4 38 A5 2
Highgate Dr ILK DE7 33 G4
WGSTN LE18 137 M2
Highgate Rd RLBORO LE12 114 C4 1
High Gv BPR/DUF DE56 18 B3
Highgrove Av BSTN/STPLFD NG9 63 H1
Highgrove Crs LEIS LE2 136 F2
Highgrove Dr MELB/CHEL DE73 72 D5
Highgrove Gdns
COT/KEY/RAD NG12 65 L4 1
High Hazles Cl CARL NG4 38 C4
High Hazles Rd
COT/KEY/RAD NG12 67 K3
High Holborn ILK DE7 33 J4 3
High Holborn Rd RIPLEY DE5 11 L6
Highland Av LEIW LE3 129 J5
High Lane Central ILK DE7 32 D6
High La East ILK DE7 32 F7
High La West ILK DE7 32 B7
High Leys Rd HUCK/RAV NG15 23 K2
High Meadow
COT/KEY/RAD NG12 66 C6
RLBORO LE12 94 E6
High Meadow Cl RIPLEY DE5 11 H7 2
Highmeres Rd LEIN LE4 126 D4
High Pavement
BPR/DUF DE56 17 L4 1
NOTT NG1 5 J8
High Rd BSTN/STPLFD NG9 49 L8
BSTN/STPLFD NG9 62 E6
High Spania
EWD/SEL/PNX NG16 22 D8
High St ALFN DE55 12 B2
ARN NG5 25 K8
BPR/DUF DE56 17 L3
BPR/DUF DE56 18 E7
BSTN/STPLFD NG9 48 C8 1
CDON/KEG DE74 84 E5
CDON/KEG DE74 86 A5
CFTN/RUD NG11 65 C8
CFTN/RUD NG11 79 G1 4
COAL LE67 108 A6
EWD/SEL/PNX NG16 13 H6
EWD/SEL/PNX NG16 34 D1
HEANOR DE75 20 A3
HEANOR DE75 20 C5
HUCK/RAV NG15 15 M8
ILK DE7 33 K7 4
LBORO LE11 9 J3
LEI LE1 6 E5
LEIE LE5 132 F5
LEIS LE2 138 E1 1
LGEAT NG10 62 C7
MELB/CHEL DE73 72 E6 3
MELB/CHEL DE73 82 E8
NOTT NG1 5 H7
RIPLEY DE5 11 H6
RIPLEY DE5 11 M7
RLBORO LE12 105 H8
RLBORO LE12 114 A4
RLEINE/SYS LE7 120 E3
RLEIW/BAR LE9 135 M4
RLEIW/BBY LE8 136 D8
RLEIW/BBY LE8 139 L7
RLEIW/BBY LE8 145 K7
High Street Av ARN NG5 25 J8
Highhurst St NOTTE NG7 4 C6
High View Cl
COT/KEY/RAD NG12 80 D4
Highway Rd LEIE LE5 132 C5
LEIN LE4 120 D7
Highwood Av BPR/DUF DE56 17 M6
WOL/BIL/BRX NG8 35 K7
High Wood Bank BPR/DUF DE56 18 A6
Highwray Gv CFTN/RUD NG11 64 B6
Hilary Cl BPR/DUF DE56 18 C2
WOL/BIL/BRX NG8 49 H4
Hilary Crs COAL LE67 108 E4
GBY/RBY LE6 123 H4
Hilcot Dr WOL/BIL/BRX NG8 35 M6
Hilders Rd LEIW LE3 130 E1
Hilderstone Cl DERBYSE DE24 73 H1
Hildyard Rd LEIN LE4 125 L6
Hillary Pl ILK DE7 46 F2
LEIW LE3 130 E5
Hillberry RIPLEY DE5 11 K6
Hillberry Cl RLEIW/BAR LE9 135 L7
Hill Brow DERBY DE1 2 E5
Hill Cl DERBYE DE21 59 J3
EWD/SEL/PNX NG16 22 A6
ILK DE7 31 L6
WBRGFD NG2 65 M1
Hillcrest Av RLEIW/BBY LE8 146 D6
Hillcrest Cl EWD/SEL/PNX NG16 35 E1
Hillcrest Dr BPR/DUF DE56 18 E7
HUCK/RAV NG15 23 H1
RIPLEY DE5 11 M7
Hillcreste Dr
MELB/CHEL DE73 72 D4 1
Hillcrest Gdns CALV/BJ NG14 39 J2
Hill Crest Gv ARN NG5 36 F4
Hill Crest Rd DERBYE DE21 44 B8
Hillcrest Rd COT/KEY/RAD NG12 80 C3
WGSTN LE18 137 M2
Hillcrest Vw CARL NG4 37 L6
Hillcroft Cl LEIN LE4 120 C7
Hill Croft Dr BWSH/BRSTN DE72 60 A3
Hillcroft Rd LEIE LE5 132 C2 1
Hill Cross Av NORM/LIT DE23 57 G8
Hill Cross Dr NORM/LIT DE23 56 F8
Hill Farm Ct
COT/KEY/RAD NG12 65 L5 1
Hill Fld LEIS LE2 139 J3
Hillfield Gdns ARN NG5 24 C6 5
Hillfield Rd BSTN/STPLFD NG9 48 D7
Hillingdon Av
EWD/SEL/PNX NG16 35 H4
Hillington Ri ARN NG5 25 G8
Hill La COAL LE67 116 A6
RLEIW/BBY LE8 142 E4
Hill Lane Cl COAL LE67 116 A5
Hill Ri BSTN/STPLFD NG9 48 A3
LEIN LE4 119 L7
LEIN LE4 126 D2
RLBORO LE12 111 K6
Hillrise Av LEIW LE3 130 E7
Hill Rise Cl NORM/LIT DE23 57 H8
Hill Rd BLWL NG6 24 C3
BSTN/STPLFD NG9 62 F5
CFTN/RUD NG11 77 M8
HEANOR DE75 20 B6
Hillsborough Cl LEIS LE2 137 G5 1
Hillsborough Crs LEIS LE2 137 G5
Hillsborough Rd LEIS LE2 137 G5
Hillsford Cl WOL/BIL/BRX NG8 49 L1
Hill Side NOTTE NG7 50 B4
Hillside CDON/KEG DE74 86 A6
COAL LE67 116 B6
EWD/SEL/PNX NG16 20 E4
RDERBYSW DE65 70 B5
Hillside Av DERBYE DE21 58 E2
MAPPK/POR/STA NG3 50 C2
WGSTN LE18 138 B6
Hillside Crs BSTN/STPLFD NG9 49 J6
DERBYE DE21 59 J3
Hillside Dr CALV/BJ NG14 39 K2
LGEAT NG10 61 M7
Hillside Gv LGEAT NG10 61 L1
Hillside Ri BPR/DUF DE56 17 K5
Hillside Rd BSTN/STPLFD NG9 49 H7
BSTN/STPLFD NG9 62 F4
COT/KEY/RAD NG12 53 L4
DERBYE DE21 59 J3
Hills Rd ARN NG5 37 J3
BWSH/BRSTN DE72 60 F7
Hill St LEI LE1 7 G4
RIPLEY DE5 11 H4
RLEIW/BAR LE9 141 G3
Hillsway MELB/CHEL DE73 72 D4
NORM/LIT DE23 56 F6
Hill Syke CALV/BJ NG14 27 L5
The Hill DERBYW DE22 43 L6 3
Hill Top CDON/KEG DE74 84 E6
DERBYE DE21 44 B5
Hilltop La ASHB DE6 54 B2
BPR/DUF DE56 18 C5
Hill Top Rd ALFN DE55 12 A2
LBORO LE11 8 D9
Hilltop Rd LEIN LE4 126 F4
Hill Vw BPR/DUF DE56 29 H4 1
Hill View Cl ILK DE7 18 F8 3
Hill View Dr RLEIW/BAR LE9 142 B4
Hill View Gv DERBYE DE21 59 J2 1
Hill View Rd BSTN/STPLFD NG9 62 E5
Hillview Rd
MAPPK/POR/STA NG3 37 L6
Hill Wy LEIS LE2 139 G3
Hilton Cl LGEAT NG10 75 K3
MCKLVR DE3 56 B6
Hilton Crs WBRGFD NG2 65 M2
Hilton Rd MAPPK/POR/STA NG3 37 L5
RDERBYSW DE65 68 E8
RDERBYSW DE65 68 F3
Hinchin Brook NOTTE NG7 50 C3
Hinckley Rd LEIW LE3 130 A3
RLEIW/BAR LE9 128 F7
RLEIW/BAR LE9 134 C2
RLEIW/BAR LE9 140 A6
RLEIW/BAR LE9 140 A7
Hind Av BWSH/BRSTN DE72 61 G8
Hind Cl RLEIW/BBY LE8 142 E1 2
Hindoostan Av WGSTN LE18 137 J4
Hindscarth Crs MCKLVR DE3 56 C6 6
Hinks Av RLEINE/SYS LE7 127 K7
Hinsley Cl ARN NG5 25 M7
Hipwell Crs LEIN LE4 125 J4
Hirst Crs WOL/BIL/BRX NG8 49 J3
Hixon's La ILK DE7 46 F6
Hoare Rd BSTN/STPLFD NG9 62 F5
Hoball Cl LEIW LE3 124 C7
Hobart Cl MCKLVR DE3 56 D5
WBRGFD NG2 51 G6 6
Hobart Dr BSTN/STPLFD NG9 48 D6
Hobart St LEIS LE2 7 J7
Hobby Cl RLEIW/BAR LE9 141 J8
Hob Hl BPR/DUF DE56 16 F7
Hobill Cl LEIW LE3 129 M5
RLEIW/BAR LE9 135 J7
Hobkirk Dr DERBYSE DE24 71 J5
Hobsic Cl EWD/SEL/PNX NG16 13 H7
Hobson Dr ILK DE7 47 J1
Hobson Rd LEIN LE4 125 J4
Hoby Rd RLEINE/SYS LE7 115 M2
Hoby St LEIW LE3 6 A4
Hockerwood CFTN/RUD NG11 64 C3 5
Hockley NOTT NG1 5 K7
Hockley Farm Rd LEIW LE3 130 A3
Hodge Beck Cl DERBYSE DE24 73 G1
Hodgkin Cl CFTN/RUD NG11 64 A6 1
Hodgkinson St CARL NG4 52 E1 3
Hodgson Cl LEIW LE3 124 E6 1
Hodson Cl RLEIW/BBY LE8 142 D1 1
Hodson Ct LBORO LE11 9 J6
Hodthorpe Cl DERBYE DE21 44 E6 5
Hoefield Crs BLWL NG6 35 L1
Hoe Hill Vw COT/KEY/RAD NG12 66 B6
Hoewood Rd BLWL NG6 23 L8
Hogarth Cl BSTN/STPLFD NG9 62 C1 1
Hogarth Rd COAL LE67 108 D2
LEIN LE4 119 G6
Hogarth St
MAPPK/POR/STA NG3 51 K1
Hogbarn La HEANOR DE75 20 B2
Hoggetts Cl
BSTN/STPLFD NG9 62 F1 1
Hogg La COT/KEY/RAD NG12 53 J4
Holbeck Rd HUCK/RAV NG15 15 L6
WOL/BIL/BRX NG8 50 A1
Holbein Cl LBORO LE11 9 M2
Holborn Av WBRGFD NG2 51 K3
Holborn Dr DERBYW DE22 42 E8
Holborn Vw RIPLEY DE5 11 L7
Holbourne Cl RLBORO LE12 105 G8
Holbrook LEIS LE2 139 J3
Holbrook Rd BPR/DUF DE56 17 K5
DERBYSE DE24 72 F1
LEIS LE2 132 C8
Holbrook St HEANOR DE75 20 E5
Holbrook Vw BPR/DUF DE56 18 E7 4
Holby Cl ARN NG5 24 D7 5
Holcombe Cl COAL LE67 108 C1
WOL/BIL/BRX NG8 35 M5
Holcombe St NORM/LIT DE23 57 M6
Holdale Rd
MAPPK/POR/STA NG3 51 M1
Holden Av BWSH/BRSTN DE72 73 L7
Holden Cl RLEIW/BBY LE8 142 E2 3
Holden Crs EWD/SEL/PNX NG16 35 G1
Holden Gdns
BSTN/STPLFD NG9 62 C1 2
Holden Rd BSTN/STPLFD NG9 49 J8
Holden St LEIN LE4 125 L5
NOTTE NG7 4 C5
Holderness Cl DERBYSE DE24 71 H5
Holderness Rd LEIN LE4 125 H2
Holgate CFTN/RUD NG11 64 A5
Holgate Cl RLEINE/SYS LE7 118 C8
Holgate Rd WBRGFD NG2 51 G6 6
Holkham Av BSTN/STPLFD NG9 63 G2
LEIN LE4 126 B6
Holkham Cl ARN NG5 37 L1
ILK DE7 33 G4 7
Holland Cl CFTN/RUD NG11 77 M6 3
Holland Meadow LGEAT NG10 76 B2 2
Holland Rd LEIS LE2 7 K4
Holland St NOTTE NG7 4 A2
Holland Wy RLEIW/BAR LE9 135 M7
Holles Crs NOTTE NG7 4 D9
Holliers Wy RLEIW/BAR LE9 141 G3
Hollies Cl RLEIW/BAR LE9 134 E4
Hollies Dr COT/KEY/RAD NG12 65 L3
Hollies Rd DERBYW DE22 43 H4
The Hollies BWSH/BRSTN DE72 61 L2
Hollies Wy RLEINE/SYS LE7 133 K3
Hollington Cl DERBYE DE21 44 C8 1
Hollington Rd LEIE LE5 132 B3
WOL/BIL/BRX NG8 49 L1
Hollingworth Av LGEAT NG10 61 M4
Hollins Rd LEIW LE3 130 C3
Hollinwell Av WOL/BIL/BRX NG8 50 A2
Hollinwell Cl LEIW LE3 130 A2 2
Hollinwell Ct
COT/KEY/RAD NG12 65 M4 2
Hollis Meadow RLBORO LE12 88 C4
Hollis St DERBYSE DE24 58 E7
NOTTE NG7 36 E6
Holloway Rd BPR/DUF DE56 29 H3
DERBYSE DE24 72 D1
Hollow Brooks DERBYE DE21 30 A8 1
Hollowood Av NORM/LIT DE23 57 G7
Hollow Rd RLEINE/SYS LE7 124 B1
Hollow Station
RLEIW/BBY LE8 146 E7 2
The Hollows CFTN/RUD NG11 64 E3
LGEAT NG10 62 E7 1
Hollow Stone NOTT NG1 5 K8 1
The Hollow CDON/KEG DE74 84 F3
LEIE LE5 132 F5 2
MCKLVR DE3 56 B6
NORM/LIT DE23 56 F6
Hollowtree Rd LEIE LE5 127 G5
Holly Av BWSH/BRSTN DE72 61 K6
CARL NG4 38 B8
CFTN/RUD NG11 50 F7
MAPPK/POR/STA NG3 37 L8 6
RIPLEY DE5 11 H7
Holly Bank Cl LEIE LE5 127 G5
Hollybrook Cl LEIN LE4 126 E1
Hollybrook Gv
EWD/SEL/PNX NG16 22 F8 1
Hollybrook Wy NORM/LIT DE23 70 D1
Hollybush Cl LEIE LE5 127 H8
RLEINE/SYS LE7 120 D3 3
Holly Bush La BPR/DUF DE56 29 L1 1
Holly Cl BWSH/BRSTN DE72 60 E8
HUCK/RAV NG15 23 M2 4
Holly Ct BSTN/STPLFD NG9 49 G7
LEIS LE2 132 E8
MCKLVR DE3 56 B6 3
Hollycroft WBRGFD NG2 65 L3 2
Hollydale Rd
MAPPK/POR/STA NG3 51 M1
Hollydene Cl HUCK/RAV NG15 22 F2
Hollydene Crs BLWL NG6 35 M3
Holly Gdns
MAPPK/POR/STA NG3 37 K8
Hollygate La
COT/KEY/RAD NG12 67 M2
Holly Gv RLEIW/BBY LE8 136 F7
Holly Hayes Rd COAL LE67 108 D3
Holly Hill Rd
EWD/SEL/PNX NG16 13 K1
Holly House La BPR/DUF DE56 17 G3
Holly La BSTN/STPLFD NG9 63 J2
Hollymoor Dr MELB/CHEL DE73 72 C5
Holly Rd EWD/SEL/PNX NG16 22 E8
Holly Tree Av LEIN LE4 119 L7
Hollytree Cl LBORO LE11 103 L8
RLBORO LE12 97 G5
Hollywell Av RIPLEY DE5 11 M8
Holm Av DERBYE DE21 29 M8
Holmdale Rd RLEINE/SYS LE7 120 E4
Holmden Av WGSTN LE18 137 M5
Holme Av RLBORO LE12 88 C4
Holme Cl CALV/BJ NG14 27 H3
ILK DE7 33 H5
Holme Cft ILK DE7 32 C8
Holme Dr LEIS LE2 132 F8
Holmefield Crs ILK DE7 33 L7
Holme Gv WBRGFD NG2 51 M5
Holme La COT/KEY/RAD NG12 53 H4
DERBYE DE21 59 G5
Holme Rd WBRGFD NG2 51 L6
Holmes Cl
EWD/SEL/PNX NG16 20 E4 4
GBY/RBY LE6 123 J4
Holmesfield Dr HEANOR DE75 20 E7
MCKLVR DE3 56 D5 4
Holmes Rd BWSH/BRSTN DE72 61 H7
Holmes St HEANOR DE75 20 B5
NORM/LIT DE23 2 E9
Holme St WBRGFD NG2 51 J5
Holmewood Crs ARN NG5 36 E1
Holmewood Dr
EWD/SEL/PNX NG16 21 M7 1
RLEIW/BAR LE9 129 K3
Holmfield NORM/LIT DE23 57 J8
Holmfield Av LBORO LE11 103 K1
LEIS LE2 132 B5
Holmfield Av East LEIW LE3 130 A4
Holmfield Av West LEIW LE3 130 A4
Holmfield Rd BSTN/STPLFD NG9 63 G4
LEIS LE2 132 A5
Holmleigh Gdns
RLEINE/SYS LE7 133 K3
Holmoak Cl DERBYE DE21 44 F4 10
Holmsfield COT/KEY/RAD NG12 80 C5
Holmwood Dr LEIW LE3 124 C6
Holroyd Av WBRGFD NG2 51 K3 5
Holt Av DERBYSE DE24 73 G1
Holt Crs RLEIW/BAR LE9 134 E4
Holt Dr LBORO LE11 8 F8
RLEIW/BAR LE9 129 K3
Holtlands Dr DERBYSE DE24 72 D2
Holt Ri RLBORO LE12 102 A6
Holt Rd LEIN LE4 125 L2
Holts Cl LEIS LE2 136 F3
Holy Bones LEI LE1 6 C5 2
Holyhead Dr DERBYE DE21 44 F5
Holyoake Dr LGEAT NG10 62 D8
Holyoake Rd
MAPPK/POR/STA NG3 38 A4 1
Holyoake St RLEIW/BAR LE9 135 L5
Holyrood Cl DERBYE DE21 59 K2
Holyrood Dr RLEIW/BBY LE8 143 H3
Holywell Dr LBORO LE11 8 A8
Holywell Rd ILK DE7 33 G4
LEIS LE2 137 G1
Holywell Wy LBORO LE11 103 G5
Home Cl ARN NG5 25 H7
RLEIW/BBY LE8 136 F7
RLEIW/BBY LE8 146 E7 5
The Home Cft BSTN/STPLFD NG9 48 F8
Home Dr WBRGFD NG2 65 J3 1
Homefarm Cl
BWSH/BRSTN DE72 60 A2
Home Farm Cl CFTN/RUD NG11 77 L6
LEIN LE4 125 G4
RLBORO LE12 111 M4
Home Farm Dr DERBYW DE22 43 L3
Homefield Av ARN NG5 25 L6
Homefield La RLEINE/SYS LE7 119 K1
Homefield Rd RLBORO LE12 114 A3
WOL/BIL/BRX NG8 36 B8
Homemead Av LEIN LE4 125 H5
Homer Dr RLEIW/BAR LE9 135 L7
Homestead
EWD/SEL/PNX NG16 20 E3 2
Homestead Cl RLBORO LE12 114 B7
Homestead Dr WGSTN LE18 138 B6
Homestead Rd COAL LE67 100 B7
The Homestead
RLBORO LE12 113 J4 1
Homestone Gdns LEIE LE5 133 J1 3
Homestone Ri LEIE LE5 133 J1 4
Homeway Cl RLBORO LE12 102 A4
Homeway Rd LEIE LE5 132 C4
Honeybourne Cl LEIS LE2 138 E2 5
Honeycomb Cl RLEIW/BAR LE9 135 L7
Honeycroft Cl BPR/DUF DE56 17 M5 3
Honeyfield Dr RIPLEY DE5 11 K7
Honeysuckle Cl COAL LE67 108 E7 2
Honeysuckle Gv BLWL NG6 35 M3
Honeysuckle Rd LEIE LE5 127 G5 1
Honeysuckle Wy
RLBORO LE12 111 L1 3
Honeywood Dr
MAPPK/POR/STA NG3 37 L8
Honingham Cl ARN NG5 37 K2
Honingham Rd ILK DE7 33 G4
Honister Cl CFTN/RUD NG11 64 B8 1
WBRGFD NG2 52 A8 1
Honiton Cl BSTN/STPLFD NG9 62 E5 3
WGSTN LE18 138 A6
Honiton Rd WOL/BIL/BRX NG8 35 J6
Hood St ARN NG5 37 H5
Hooley Cl LGEAT NG10 75 M1
Hooley St EWD/SEL/PNX NG16 13 K1
Hooton Rd CARL NG4 38 A8
Hooton St MAPPK/POR/STA NG3 51 K2
Hope Av MCKLVR DE3 56 B5
Hope Cl WBRGFD NG2 50 F5
Hopedale Cl NOTTE NG7 50 C2 11
Hope Dr NOTTE NG7 4 E9
Hopefield Rd LEIW LE3 131 G5
Hope St BSTN/STPLFD NG9 49 J8
DERBY DE1 3 G5
ILK DE7 33 K8 7
MELB/CHEL DE73 82 D8
Hopetoun St NORM/LIT DE23 57 L7
Hopewell Cl COT/KEY/RAD NG12 53 L2

Hopewell Wk *ILK* DE7 .... 33 K2
Hopping Hl *BPR/DUF* DE56 ..... 17 K7
Hoppner Cl *LEIN* LE3 .... 119 H6 🔟
Hopton Cl *DERBYE* DE21 ...... 44 E6
Hopwell Rd *BWSH/BRSTN* DE72 .. 60 E6
Hopwood Cl *LEIN* LE4 .... 124 F4 🔟
Hopyard Cl *LEIS* LE2 .... 136 F3
Horace Av *BSTN/STPLFD* NG9 .... 48 A8
Hornbeam Cl *DERBYE* DE21 ...... 44 C5 🔟
   LEIS LE2 .... 132 E8
   RLBORO LE12 .... 103 L8 🔟
   RLEIW/BAR LE9 .... 135 L7
Horncastle Rd *DERBYE* DE21 .... 44 B6
Hornchurch Rd
   WOL/BIL/BRX NG8 .... 35 H8
Horndean Av *WGSTN* LE18 .... 138 A4
Hornecroft *RLEINE/SYS* LE7 .. 119 J1
Hornsby Wk *ARN* NG5 .... 24 C7
Hornsea Rd *DERBYE* DE21 ...... 44 B6
Horridge St *ILK* DE7 .... 33 K3 🔟
Horsefair St *LEI* LE1 .... 6 E6 🔟
Horsendale Av
   EWD/SEL/PNX NG16 .... 35 K3
Horseshoe Cl *RLEIW/BAR* LE9 .. 142 B3
The Horse Shoes
   CDON/KEG DE74 .... 85 G3
Horsewell La *WGSTN* LE18 .... 138 B7
Horsham Dr *ARN* NG5 .... 24 D7
Horsley Crs *BPR/DUF* DE56 .... 18 A8 🔟
   EWD/SEL/PNX NG16 .... 20 E4
Horsley La *DERBYE* DE21 ...... 30 C3
Horsley Rd *DERBYE* DE21 ...... 30 D1
Horston Rd *LEIE* LE5 .... 132 C4
Horton St *NORM/LIT* DE23 ...... 3 J9
Horwood Av *NORM/LIT* DE23 .. 57 H5
Horwood Cl *WGSTN* LE18 .... 138 C3
Hoselett Field Rd *LGEAT* NG10 .. 76 C2
Hoskins Cl *WGSTN* LE18 ...... 138 C7 🔟
Hospital Cl *LEIE* LE5 .... 132 C1
Hospital La *MCKLVR* DE3 ...... 55 M8
   RLEIW/BBY LE9 .... 137 C8
Hospital Wy *LBORO* LE11 .... 8 D2
Hotel St *COAL* LE67 .... 108 B6
   LEI LE1 .... 6 E6
Hoten Rd *WBRGFD* NG2 .... 51 K4
Hotoft Rd *LEIE* LE5 .... 126 F7
Hoton Rd *RLBORO* LE12 .... 98 A4
Hotspur Cl *BLWL* NG6 .... 36 C2
Houghton Av *ILK* DE7 .... 33 G4 🔟
Houghton Cl
   EWD/SEL/PNX NG16 .... 35 J3
Houghton Ct *DERBYE* DE21 ...... 44 D5
Houghton La *LEIS* LE2 .... 133 L6
Houghton St *LEIE* LE5 .... 126 B8
Houlditch Rd *LEIS* LE2 .... 131 M7
Houldsworth Ri *ARN* NG5 ...... 25 J5
Hoult St *DERBYE* DE22 .... 57 H3
Hound Rd *WBRGFD* NG2 .... 51 J7
Hounds Ga *NOTT* NG1 .... 5 G8 🔟
Hounslow Gdns *WBRGFD* NG2 .. 51 G5
Houseman Gdns *WBRGFD* NG2 .. 51 G5
Houston Ct *ARN* NG5 .... 24 C6 🔟
Hove Rd *ARN* NG5 .... 36 C2
Hoveton Cl *DERBYSE* DE24 .... 72 B4
Howard Cl *LBORO* LE11 .... 103 G2
   LGEAT NG10 .... 62 C6 🔟
Howard Rd *LEIS* LE2 .... 131 L6
   LEIS LE2 .... 136 F5
Howard St *LBORO* LE11 .... 103 M2
   NORM/LIT DE23 .... 2 D9
   NOTT NG1 .... 5 H6
Howarth Cl *LGEAT* NG10 .... 61 L8
Howbeck Rd *ARN* NG5 .... 26 A7
Howden Cl *LBORO* LE11 .... 102 F4
   MCKLVR DE3 .... 56 A6
Howden Rd *BLWL* NG6 .... 24 A5 🔟
   LEIS LE2 .... 137 G3
Howdon Rd *LEIS* LE2 .... 138 F4
Howe Cl *RLEIW/BAR* LE9 ...... 140 A6
Howe Ct *COAL* LE67 .... 108 B2
Howe La *RLEINE/SYS* LE7 .... 119 J1
Howell-Jones Rd
   BSTN/STPLFD NG9 .... 62 F4
Howells Cl *ARN* NG5 .... 25 G7 🔟
Howe Rd *COAL* LE67 .... 108 B2
   LBORO LE11 .... 9 J9
Howe St *DERBYW* DE22 .... 57 H2
Howick Dr *BLWL* NG6 .... 23 K7
Howitt St *HEANOR* DE75 ...... 20 D5
   LGEAT NG10 .... 62 C8 🔟
Howth Cl *DERBYE* DE21 .... 58 E3
Hoylake Cl *LEIE* LE5 .... 132 C5
Hoylake Ct *MCKLVR* DE3 ...... 56 A4
Hoylake Crs *WOL/BIL/BRX* NG8 .. 35 H8
Hoylake Dr *MCKLVR* DE3 ...... 56 A4
Hoyland Av *NOTTE* NG7 .... 50 C5
Hoyland Ct *BPR/DUF* DE56 .... 18 C2 🔟
Hubbard Cl *RLEIW/BBY* LE8 .. 142 E2
Hubert Shaw Cl
   DERBYSE DE24 .... 72 C3 🔟
Hubert St *NOTT* NG7 .... 4 B3
Huckerby Rd *ILK* DE7 .... 33 G5 🔟
Hucklow Cl *DERBYE* DE21 ...... 44 E1 🔟🔟
Hucknall La *WOL/BIL/BRX* NG8 .. 35 H5 🔟
Hucknall La *CARL* NG4 .... 38 C5
Hucknall La *BLWL* NG6 .... 24 A7
Hucknall Rd *ARN* NG5 .... 36 F4
   BLWL NG6 .... 24 B7
   HUCK/RAV NG15 .... 15 H3
Hudson Cl *LEIW* LE3 .... 124 E7
Hudson Rd *RLBORO* LE12 .... 114 A3 🔟
Hudson St *LBORO* LE11 .... 9 L2
   MAPPK/POR/STA NG3 ...... 51 K1 🔟
Hufton's Ct *HEANOR* DE75 .... 20 E8
Huggett Cl *LEIN* LE4 .... 126 C3
Hughenden Dr *LEIS* LE2 ...... 131 J6
Hulland St *DERBYW* DE22 .... 3 J7
Hulland Vw *DERBYW* DE22 .... 43 H6
Humber Cl *DERBYSE* DE24 .... 73 C1 🔟
   LEIE LE5 .... 126 F6
   WBRGFD NG2 .... 51 J7
Humber Rd *BSTN/STPLFD* NG9 .. 49 L8
   LGEAT NG10 .... 62 A6
Humber Rd South
   BSTN/STPLFD NG9 .... 63 M1 🔟
   BSTN/STPLFD NG9 .... 64 A1 🔟
Humberstone Dr *LEIE* LE5 .... 126 D7

Humberstone Ga *LEI* LE1 .... 6 F5
Humberstone La *LEIN* LE4 .... 126 D2
Humberstone Rd *LEIE* LE5 .... 7 L3
Humberston Rd
   WOL/BIL/BRX NG8 .... 49 G4
   RLEINE/SYS LE7 .... 114 E6
Humble La *RLBORO* LE12 .... 114 B7
Humes Cl *RLEIW/BBY* LE8 .... 142 D3
Hume St *LBORO* LE11 .... 9 L3
Humphrey Cl *DERBYW* DE22 ...... 9 K7
Humphries Cl *LEIE* LE5 .... 132 E2
Huncote Rd *RLEIW/BAR* LE9 .. 135 J8
   RLEIW/BAR LE9 .... 140 F2
   RLEIW/BAR LE9 .... 140 C5
Hungarton Bvd *LEIE* LE5 ...... 126 F7
Hungarton Dr *RLEINE/SYS* LE7 .. 121 G4
Hungary La *RLBORO* LE12 ...... 94 F1
Hungerhill La *CARL* NG4 .... 26 E5
Hungerhill Rd
   MAPPK/POR/STA NG3 .... 5 K1
Hungerton St *NOTTE* NG7 .... 50 D4 🔟
Hunston Cl *WOL/BIL/BRX* NG8 .. 35 L8
Hunt Av *HEANOR* DE75 .... 20 C5
Hunter Dr *BPR/DUF* DE56 ...... 18 D7
Hunter Rd *ARN* NG5 .... 38 A1
   BPR/DUF, DE56 .... 18 B2
   LEIN LE4 .... 125 L6
Hunters Cl *CFTN/RUD* NG11 .. 64 F1 🔟
Hunters Cft *DERBYSE* DE24 .. 71 J5 🔟
Hunters Wy *LEIS* LE2 .... 139 H2
   LEIW LE3 .... 129 K5
Huntingdon Cl *RLBORO* LE12 .. 97 L8 🔟
Huntingdon Ct
   MELB/CHEL DE73 .... 82 F7
   NOTT NG7 .... 4 D7
Huntingdon Dr *CDON/KEG* DE74 .. 84 E3
Huntingdon Gn *DERBYE* DE21 .... 3 K2
Huntingdon Rd *LEIN* LE4 ...... 126 B5
Huntingdon St *NOTT* NG1 .... 5 H4
Huntingdon Wk *LGEAT* NG10 .. 61 M2 🔟
Huntingdon Wy
   BSTN/STPLFD NG9 .... 62 D5 🔟
The Huntings *RLEIW/BAR* LE9 .. 129 G2
Huntley Av *DERBYE* DE21 ...... 59 L1
Huntly Cl *CFTN/RUD* NG11 .... 64 D6 🔟
Hunts Cl *GBY/RBY* LE6 .... 122 A7
Huntsmans Cl *COAL* LE67 .... 116 C7
   RLBORO LE12 .... 104 F8
Huntsman's Di *RLEINE/SYS* LE7 .. 115 H7
Huntsmans Wy *LEIN* LE4 ...... 126 B4
Huntspill Rd *RDERBYSW* DE65 .. 68 C5 🔟
Hurcomb St
   MAPPK/POR/STA NG3 ...... 37 K8 🔟
Hurley Ct *ILK* DE7 .... 32 C7
Hursley Cl *LEIS* LE2 .... 139 C2
Hurst Dr *ILK* DE7 .... 46 A1
Hurst Ri *LEIE* LE5 .... 132 E2
Hurstwood Rd *LBORO* LE11 .. 102 F4
Hurts Cft *DERBYSE* DE24 ...... 63 H3
Hurts Yd *NOTT* NG1 .... 5 G6 🔟
   NOTT NG1 .... 5 G7 🔟
Huss's La *LGEAT* NG10 .... 62 D8
Huston Cl *RLEIW/BAR* LE9 .. 113 K1
Hutchinson St *LEIS* LE2 .... 7 J6
Hutton Cl *BSTN/STPLFD* NG9 .. 49 H6
Hutton Ct *DERBYSE* DE24 ...... 72 C1
   WBRGFD NG2 .... 51 K3
Huxley Cl *WOL/BIL/BRX* NG8 .. 35 H8
Hyam's La *CDON/KEG* DE74 .. 95 H1
Hyde Cl *CFTN/RUD* NG11 ...... 64 D3
   LEIS LE2 .... 139 G4
   RLEIW/BAR LE9 .... 135 M7
Hyde Park Cl *WBRGFD* NG2 .. 65 G2 🔟
Hyde Park Rd *DERBYW* DE22 .. 56 E1
Hylion Rd *LEIS* LE2 .... 137 L1
Hyson St *NOTTE* NG7 .... 4 B2

I

Ian Gv *CARL* NG4 .... 38 C7
Ibbetson Av *RLEIW* LE3 ...... 124 A8
Ibsley Cl *DERBYSE* DE24... ...... 73 G1
Ibsley Wy *LEIS* LE2 .... 137 H4
Ickworth Cl *LEIE* LE5 .... 126 C7 🔟
Iffley Cl *LEIW* LE3 .... 132 E1 🔟
Ilam Sq *ILK* DE7 .... 33 J2
Ilford Cl *ILK* DE7 .... 33 H4
Ilford Rd *DERBYW* DE22 ...... 56 E2
Iliffe Av *LEIS* LE2 .... 138 D2
Iliffe Rd *LEIN* LE4 .... 126 C6
Iliffes Cl *RLBORO* LE12 ...... 105 J7
Ilkeston Rd *BSTN/STPLFD* NG9 .. 47 M2
   HEANOR DE75 .... 20 D7
   ILK DE7 .... 31 J5
   ILK DE7 .... 47 K4
   NOTT NG1 .... 4 D6 🔟
   NOTTE NG7 .... 4 C6
Illingworth Rd *LEIE* LE5 ...... 132 E1
Ilmington Cl *LEIW* LE3 .... 124 A6
Imperial Av *BSTN/STPLFD* NG9 .. 63 J1 🔟
   CARL NG4 .... 38 C6
   LEIW LE3 .... 130 F4
Imperial Ct *DERBYW* DE22 .... 43 H2
Imperial Rd *BLWL* NG6 .... 36 B1
   BSTN/STPLFD NG9 .... 63 J1
   RLEIW/BBY LE8 .... 146 D7
Inchwood Cl
   BSTN/STPLFD NG9 .... 62 D5 🔟
Incinerator Rd *WBRGFD* NG2 .. 51 J5
Independent St *NOTTE* NG7 ..... 4 B4
Industrial St *NORM/LIT* DE23 .. 2 E9 🔟
Infirmary Cl *LEIS* LE2 .... 6 E9
Infirmary Rd *LEI* LE1 .... 6 E8
Infirmary Sq *LEIS* LE2 .... 6 E8 🔟
Ingarsby Dr *LEIE* LE5 .... 133 G4
Ingham Dr *MCKLVR* DE3 ...... 56 B7
Ingham Gv *NOTTE* NG7 .... 50 C4
Ingham Rd *LGEAT* NG10 .... 62 A5
Ingleberry Rd *RLBORO* LE12 .. 102 B8
Ingleborough Gdns
   LGEAT NG10 .... 61 L7 🔟
Ingleby Av *NORM/LIT* DE23 .. 57 K8
Ingleby Cl *COT/KEY/RAD* NG12 .. 47 H7 🔟
   WOL/BIL/BRX NG8 .... 48 F3 🔟
Ingleby Rd *LGEAT* NG10 ...... 75 K2

   WGSTN LE18 .... 138 A4
Ingle Cl *DERBYE* DE21 .... 59 J2
Ingledew Cl *DERBYE* DE21 .... 44 C6
Ingle Dr *GBY/RBY* LE6 .... 123 G7
Inglefield Rd *ILK* DE7 .... 47 K1
Ingle's Channel
   BPR/DUF DE56 .... 18 D8 🔟
Ingle St *LEIW* LE3 .... 124 F8
Inglewood Rd *MCKLVR* DE3 .. 56 B3
Inglewood Rd *CFTN/RUD* NG11 .. 64 C6
Ingliston Cl *DERBYSE* DE24 .. 73 H1 🔟
Ingold Av *LEIN* LE4 .... 125 H4 🔟
Ingram Rd *BLWL* NG6 .... 36 B1
Ingrams Wy *WGSTN* LE18 .... 138 C7
Inham Circ *BSTN/STPLFD* NG9 .. 63 G1 🔟
Inham Cl *BSTN/STPLFD* NG9 .. 62 E2
Inham Rd *BSTN/STPLFD* NG9 .. 62 E2
Inkerman Rd
   EWD/SEL/PNX NG16 .... 13 K2
Inkerman St
   EWD/SEL/PNX NG16 .... 13 K2
The Inleys *RLBORO* LE12 .... 102 B4
Innes Cl *CARL* NG4 .... 38 A8
Inn La *BPR/DUF* DE56 .... 42 F1
Instow Dr *NORM/LIT* DE23 .... 71 H2
Instow Ri *MAPPK/POR/STA* NG3 .... 5 K4
Intake Rd *COT/KEY/RAD* NG12 .. 80 B4
Inveraray Cl *DERBYSE* DE24 .. 71 H4
Invergary Cl *LEIN* LE4 .... 126 B3 🔟
Invernia Cl *NORM/LIT* DE23 .. 71 J2 🔟
Iona Cl *DERBYSE* DE24 .... 71 J3
   LEIN LE4 .... 124 F4
Iona Dr *BSTN/STPLFD* NG9 .. 48 B4
Iona Rd *RLEINE/SYS* LE7 .... 120 D3
Iona Wy *RLEIW/BAR* LE9 .... 143 K4
Ipswich Circ
   MAPPK/POR/STA NG3 ...... 51 L2
Ipswich Cl *LEIN* LE4 .... 124 E1
Ireland Av *BSTN/STPLFD* NG9 .. 63 L2
Ireland Rd *BSTN/STPLFD* NG9 .. 63 L2 🔟
Iremonger Rd *WBRGFD* NG2 .. 51 H5
Ireton Av *LEIN* LE4 .... 126 D5
Ireton Gv *BSTN/STPLFD* NG9 .. 63 H5
Ireton Rd *LEIN* LE4 .... 126 C6
Ireton St *BSTN/STPLFD* NG9 .. 63 J1
   NOTTE NG7 .... 4 D5
Iris Av *LEIN* LE4 .... 119 M7
   LEIS LE2 .... 139 H3
Iris Cl *RLBORO* LE12 .... 113 K5
Irlam St *WGSTN* LE18 .... 137 K7
Irmington Gdns *LEIE* LE5 .... 133 G1
Iron Ga *DERBY* DE1 .... 2 E3
Ironworks Rd *LEIN* LE4 ...... 126 A7
Irvine Cl *DERBYSE* DE24 ...... 71 H4
Irving Pl *DERBYSE* DE24 ...... 58 D8
Irwin Av *LBORO* LE11 .... 103 G1
Irwin Dr *BLWL* NG6 .... 35 K2
Isaac's La *BSTN/STPLFD* NG9 .. 48 B8
Isabella St *NOTT* NG1 .... 5 G9
Isis Cl *LEIS* LE2 .... 139 H1
Islay Cl *ARN* NG5 .... 25 K6 🔟
   BSTN/STPLFD NG9 .... 48 B5
Islay Rd *DERBYSE* DE24 ...... 71 J3
Isleworth Dr *DERBYW* DE22 .. 56 D1
Islington St *LEIS* LE2 .... 131 K5
Ismay Rd *DERBYE* DE21 ...... 58 D1
Ivanhoe Cl *ARN* NG5 .... 37 H3
Ivanhoe St *LEIW* LE3 .... 131 G1
Ivanhoe St *WGSTN* LE18 .... 137 K5 🔟
Ivatt Cl *RLEINE/SYS* LE7 .... 133 L2
Ivatt Dr *WBRGFD* NG2 .... 51 K4
Ives Cl *WBRGFD* NG2 .... 65 G3
Iveshead La *RLBORO* LE12 .. 101 M7
Iveshead Rd *RLBORO* LE12 .. 101 L8
Ivybridge Cl *DERBYE* DE21 .. 45 G4 🔟
Ivychurch Crs *LEIE* LE5 ...... 127 J6
Ivy Cl *EWD/SEL/PNX* NG16 .. 22 D6
Ivy Ct *RDERBYSW* DE65 ...... 68 B6
Ivydale Rd *LEIN* LE4 .... 126 D1
Ivy Gv *CARL* NG4 .... 38 B8
   RIPLEY DE5 .... 11 H6
Ivy La *EWD/SEL/PNX* NG16 .. 21 J5
Ivy Rd *LEIW* LE3 .... 131 G4
Ivy Sq *NORM/LIT* DE23 .... 3 J9

J

Jacklin Dr *LEIN* LE4 .... 126 B2
Jacksdale Cl *DERBYW* DE22 .. 43 H6
Jackson Av *ILK* DE7 .... 33 J6
   LGEAT NG10 .... 61 L1
   MCKLVR DE3 .... 56 E5
Jackson Cl *LEIS* LE2 .... 139 H2
Jackson's La *RLEIW/BAR* LE9 .. 135 L4
   BPR/DUF DE56 .... 10 B8
   BPR/DUF DE56 .... 17 J8
   RDERBYSW DE65 .... 69 G5
Jackson St *COAL* LE67 .... 108 A7
   DERBYW DE22 .... 2 B5 🔟
   LEIN LE4 .... 125 M4
Jacob Ct *RLEIW/BAR* LE9 .... 135 L4
Jacqueline Rd *COAL* LE67 .... 116 D7
Jacquemart Cl *COAL* LE67 .. 109 H6
Jacques Cl *RLEIW/BAR* LE9 .. 135 L4 🔟
James Av *LBORO* LE11 .... 103 G5
James Cl *DERBY* DE1 .... 2 A3
James Gavin Wy *LEIS* LE2 .. 139 J3
James St *ARN* NG5 .... 25 J7
   COAL LE67 .... 108 A7
   EWD/SEL/PNX NG16 .... 34 D1
   RLEINE/SYS LE7 .... 118 B8
   RLEIW/BAR LE9 .... 140 B4
   RLEIW/BBY LE8 .... 136 E7
Jamesway *RLEIW/BAR* LE9 .. 142 B3
Janes Wy *COAL* LE67 .... 108 A7
Japonica Cl *LBORO* LE11 .... 103 L8 🔟
Japonica Dr *BLWL* NG6 .... 36 B1
Jardine Ri *BWSH/BRSTN* DE72 .. 60 F8 🔟
The Jardines *BSTN/STPLFD* NG9... 49 G6 🔟
Jarrett Cl *RLEIW/BAR* LE9 .. 135 L4
Jarrom St *LEIS* LE2 .... 131 J4
Jarrow Gdns *ARN* NG5 .... 24 D5 🔟
Jarvey's La *DERBYW* DE22 .. 42 C7
Jarvis Rd *DERBYSE* DE24 ...... 71 J3
Jarvis St *LEI* LE1 .... 6 C5
Jarvis Wy *COAL* LE67 .... 108 C2

Jasmine Cl *BSTN/STPLFD* NG9 .. 49 H6
Jasmine Cl *CFTN/RUD* NG11 .. 64 A6 🔟
   LBORO LE11 .... 103 L8 🔟
   LEIE LE5 .... 126 F4
Jasmine Ct *RLEIW/BAR* LE9 .. 135 K6
   WGSTN LE18 .... 137 K5
Jasmine Rd *ARN* NG5 .... 36 C4 🔟
Jasper Cl *COT/KEY/RAD* NG12 .. 53 J5 🔟
Jawbone La *MELB/CHEL* DE73 .. 83 G7
Jayne Cl *CARL* NG4 .... 38 C6
   WOL/BIL/BRX NG8 .... 49 J1 🔟
Jean Dr *LEIN* LE4 .... 125 H6
Jedburgh Cl *DERBYSE* DE24 .. 71 J5 🔟
   MAPPK/POR/STA NG3 .... 5 K4
Jeffares Cl *CDON/KEG* DE74 .. 86 A4 🔟
Jefferson Pl *DERBYSE* DE24 .. 58 D8 🔟
Jellicoe Rd *LEIE* LE5 .... 132 C1
Jemison Cl *NORM/LIT* DE23 .. 56 C8 🔟
Jenned Rd *ARN* NG5 .... 25 L5
Jenner St *ARN* NG5 .... 36 F7
Jenness Av *ARN* NG5 .... 24 C6 🔟
Jennett Cl *LEIE* LE5 .... 133 C1
Jennison St *BLWL* NG6 .... 24 A8
Jenny Burton Wy
   HUCK/RAV NG15 .... 24 A2
Jenny's Ct *BPR/DUF* DE56 .... 18 A2 🔟
Jeremy Cl *LEIE* LE5 .... 125 M5
Jermyn Dr *ARN* NG5 .... 24 E6
Jermyn St *LEIE* LE5 .... 125 M5
Jersey Gdns
   MAPPK/POR/STA NG3 .... 5 M4
Jersey Rd *LEIN* LE4 .... 125 H3
Jesmond Rd *BLWL* NG6 .... 36 B1
Jesop Dr *DERBYSE* DE24 ...... 71 J5 🔟
Jessons Cl *LEIN* LE4 .... 126 B4
Jessop Av *EWD/SEL/PNX* NG16 .. 12 C4 🔟
Jessop Cl *LEIW* LE3 .... 124 E7
Jessop's La *CARL* NG4 .... 38 D4
Jessop St *RIPLEY* DE5 .... 11 L8
Jetcott Av *LBORO* LE11 ...... 103 L8
Joan Av *HEANOR* DE75 .... 20 C5
Jodrell Av *BPR/DUF* DE56 .... 18 B3
Joe Moore's La *RLBORO* LE12 .. 111 H8
John Berrysford Cl
   DERBYE DE21 .... 58 D2
John Bold Av *RLEIW/BAR* LE9 .. 140 C4
John F Kennedy Gdns
   DERBYE DE21 .... 59 G1 🔟
John Lombe Dr *DERBY* DE1 .. 43 L8
John O'gaunts Wy
   BPR/DUF DE56 .... 18 B2
John Phillips Cl *LBORO* LE11 .... 8 C3
John Port Cl *RDERBYSW* DE65 .. 69 G3 🔟
Johns Av *RLBORO* LE12 .... 113 J6
John's Lee Cl *LEIE* LE5 .... 8 E9
Johnson Av *DERBYSE* DE24 .. 58 C8
   HUCK/RAV NG15 .... 23 M2
Johnson Cl *RLEIW/BBY* LE8 .. 136 D8
Johnson Dr *HEANOR* DE75 .... 20 D5
Johnson Ri *RLEIW/BAR* LE9 .. 140 C5 🔟
   NOTTE NG7 .... 50 C3
Johnson St *LEI* LE1 .... 6 C5 🔟
Johns Rd *COT/KEY/RAD* NG12 .. 53 L4
John St *COAL* LE67 .... 100 B8
   DERBY DE1 .... 3 H6
   HEANOR DE75 .... 20 B5
   ILK DE7 .... 33 K6
   NOTTE NG7 .... 36 D6
   RLEIW/BAR LE9 .... 135 M5
Jolly Farmers La *RLBORO* LE12 .. 101 L7
Jonathan Cl *GBY/RBY* LE6 .. 123 J8
Jordan Av *WGSTN* LE18 ...... 137 L6 🔟
Jordan Cl *LEIW* LE3 .... 124 A7
Joseph St *BPR/DUF* DE56 .... 17 K3
   NORM/LIT DE23 .... 57 L6
Journeyman's Gn
   GBY/RBY LE6 .... 123 H7 🔟
Jowett Cl *LEIW* LE3 .... 124 E6
Joyce Av *ARN* NG5 .... 37 H3
   BSTN/STPLFD NG9 .... 62 C4
Joyce Cl *ARN* NG5 .... 37 H3
Joyce Rd *LEIW* LE3 .... 124 F7 🔟
Jubalton Cl *DERBYSE* DE24 .. 72 C1 🔟
Jubilee Av *RIPLEY* DE5 .... 11 G6
   RLBORO LE12 .... 114 B2
Jubilee Cl *MELB/CHEL* DE73 .. 82 F8
Jubilee Ct *BPR/DUF* DE56 .... 17 L5
Jubilee Dr *LBORO* LE11 ...... 103 L1
   LEIN LE4 .... 124 A8
Jubilee Gdns *LEIE* LE5 .... 126 B7
Jubilee Rd *ARN* NG5 .... 37 J1
   DERBYSE DE24 .... 72 C3
   LEI LE1 .... 6 F3
Jubilee St *EWD/SEL/PNX* NG16 .. 22 C8 🔟
   WBRGFD NG2 .... 51 K3 🔟
Judges St *LBORO* LE11 .... 9 M4
Judith Dr *LEIE* LE5 .... 132 F3
   RLEIW/BBY LE8 .... 143 K3
Judson Av *BSTN/STPLFD* NG9 .. 62 D1
Julian Cl *ILK* DE7 .... 47 L1
Julian Rd *LEIS* LE2 .... 137 C5
   WBRGFD NG2 .... 51 M7
Julie Av *HEANOR* DE75 .... 20 F6
Junction Rd *LEI* LE1 .... 7 G2
   LGEAT NG10 .... 76 C1 🔟
   WGSTN LE18 .... 138 B4
June Av *LEIN* LE4 .... 126 C2
Junior St *LEI* LE1 .... 6 D4
Juniper Cl *CFTN/RUD* NG11 .. 64 A6
   LEIW LE3 .... 129 K5
Juniper Ct
   EWD/SEL/PNX NG16 .... 22 A7 🔟
Juniper Wy *RLBORO* LE12 .. 111 L1
Juno Cl *LEIW* LE3 .... 124 A8
Jupiter Cl *LEIS* LE2 .... 139 K8
Jura Av *RIPLEY* DE5 .... 11 H5
Jury St *DERBY* DE1 .... 2 D3

K

Kamloops Crs *LEI* LE1 .... 7 G3
Kappler Cl *CARL* NG4 .... 38 E8
Karen Ri *ARN* NG5 .... 25 L6

Kashmir Rd *LEIE* LE1 .... 7 J2
Kate St *LEIW* LE3 .... 6 A6
Katherine Dr *BSTN/STPLFD* NG9 .. 62 B4 🔟
Kayes Wk *NOTT* NG1 .... 5 J8 🔟
Kay Rd *LEIW* LE3 .... 124 D7
Keats Av *HEANOR* DE75 ...... 56 F6
Keats Cl *ARN* NG5 .... 25 H8
   LEIW/SEL/PNX NG16 .... 34 F1 🔟
   LGEAT NG10 .... 75 M2
   RLEIW/BAR LE9 .... 135 L4
Keats Dr *HUCK/RAV* NG15 .... 23 H1
Keays Wy *RLEINE/SYS* LE7 .. 127 K7
Keble Cl *DERBY* DE1 .... 3 H8
Keble Dr *RLEINE/SYS* LE7 .. 120 F4
Keble Rd *LEIS* LE2 .... 131 L6
Kedleston Av *LEIN* LE4 ...... 125 L2
Kedleston Cl
   BSTN/STPLFD NG9 .... 63 G2 🔟
   DERBYE DE22 .... 43 H6
   LGEAT NG10 .... 75 L3
   RIPLEY DE5 .... 11 G4
Kedleston Dr *ILK* DE7 .... 33 H4
Kedleston Old Rd
   DERBYW DE22 .... 43 H7 🔟
Kedleston Rd *DERBY* DE1 .... 43 K8 🔟
   DERBYW DE22 .... 28 B8
   DERBYW DE22 .... 43 H7
   LEIE LE5 .... 132 B3
Keeling Cl *DERBY* DE1 .... 2 C1
Keenan Cl *LEIS* LE2 .... 136 F2
Keepers Cl *BLWL* NG6 .... 24 C3
Keepers' Cft *RLEINE/SYS* LE7 .. 115 J8
The Keep *RLBORO* LE12 ...... 88 D7
   RLEIW/BAR LE9 .... 129 H2
Kegworth Av *LEIE* LE5 .... 132 D2
   NORM/LIT DE23 .... 71 G1 🔟
Kegworth La *RLBORO* LE12 ... 93 M3
Kegworth Rd *CFTN/RUD* NG11 ... 77 K6
   CFTN/RUD NG11 .... 77 L6 🔟
   NOTTE NG7 .... 86 D2
Keightley Rd *LEIW* LE3 ...... 124 C6
Kelbrook Cl *LEIN* LE4 .... 125 G3
Keldholme La *DERBYE* DE24 .. 59 G8 🔟
Kelfield Cl *BLWL* NG6 .... 36 C3
Kelham Gn
   MAPPK/POR/STA NG3 ...... 51 K1 🔟
Kelham Wy
   EWD/SEL/PNX NG16 .... 21 J4 🔟
Kelling Cl *ARN* NG5 .... 36 E1
Kelmarsh Av *WGSTN* LE18 .. 138 B5
Kelmoor Rd *DERBYSE* DE24 .. 72 B4
Kelsey Cl *BSTN/STPLFD* NG9 .. 63 J4
Kelso Ct *COAL* LE67 .... 100 B7
Kelso Gdns *WBRGFD* NG2 .... 50 F5 🔟
Kelso Gn *LEIS* LE2 .... 139 H1
Kelstern Cl *WOL/BIL/BRX* NG8 .. 35 M4
Kelvedon Dr *NORM/LIT* DE23 .. 70 E1 🔟
Kelvedon Gdns
   MAPPK/POR/STA NG3 .... 5 L4
Kelvin Cl *BSTN/STPLFD* NG9 .. 62 A2
Kelvin Rd *MAPPK/POR/STA* NG3 .. 37 L8
Kelvon Cl *LEIW* LE3 .... 124 B6
Kemble Pl *DERBYSE* DE24 .. 58 D8 🔟
Kemmel Rd *BLWL* NG6 .... 36 B2 🔟
Kemp Rd *LEIW* LE3 .... 124 C6
Kempsey Cl *ARN* NG5 .... 24 C7 🔟
Kempson Rd *LEIS* LE2 .... 131 J7
Kempton Cl
   EWD/SEL/PNX NG16 .... 22 C8 🔟
Kempton Dr *ARN* NG5 .... 25 L6
Kempton Park Rd
   DERBYSE DE24 .... 58 B7
Kendal Av *HUCK/RAV* NG15 .. 15 K7 🔟
Kendal Ct *WBRGFD* NG2 ...... 51 M7
Kendal Dr *BSTN/STPLFD* NG9 .. 49 H7
Kendall's Av *RLEIW/BAR* LE9 .. 141 G3
Kendal Rd *LEIN* LE4 .... 126 B4
   RLBORO LE12 .... 114 B5
Kendon Av *NORM/LIT* DE23 .. 71 J1
Kendray Cl *BPR/DUF* DE56 .. 18 B2 🔟
Kendrick Dr *LEIS* LE2 .... 138 F2
Kenia Cl *CARL* NG4 .... 38 E8
Kenilworth Av *LBORO* LE11 .. 103 G3
   NORM/LIT DE23 .... 57 K7
Kenilworth Cl *RLBORO* LE12 .. 113 G6 🔟
   RLEIW/BAR LE9 .... 141 J7 🔟
Kenilworth Ct
   BSTN/STPLFD NG9 .... 49 L7
Kenilworth Dr *ILK* DE7 .... 47 G2
   LEIS LE2 .... 138 D2
Kenilworth Rd
   BSTN/STPLFD NG9 .... 49 L8
   NOTTE NG7 .... 4 E9
   RIPLEY DE5 .... 11 G6 🔟
   WGSTN LE18 .... 137 K4
Kenmore Crs *COAL* LE67 .... 109 H6
Kenmore Gdns
   MAPPK/POR/STA NG3 .... 5 K4
Kennedy Av *LGEAT* NG10 .... 76 A2
Kennedy Cl *ARN* NG5 .... 25 H8
   DERBYE DE21 .... 44 E8 🔟
Kennedy Wy *LEIS* LE2 .... 129 L5
Kennel La *HUCK/RAV* NG15 .. 14 E6
Kenneth Gamble Ct
   WGSTN LE18 .... 137 M3 🔟
Kenneth Rd *ARN* NG5 .... 25 K5
Kennington Rd
   WOL/BIL/BRX NG8 .... 50 B2
Kenny Cl *RLEIW/BBY* LE8 .. 142 E1 🔟
Kenrick Rd
   MAPPK/POR/STA NG3 ...... 37 L5 🔟
Kenrick St *CARL* NG4 .... 38 E8 🔟
Kensal Rd *DERBYSE* DE24 .. 72 B4
Kensington Av *HEANOR* DE75 .. 20 A6
   LBORO LE11 .... 103 G2
Kensington Cl
   BSTN/STPLFD NG9 .... 62 E6 🔟
   LEIS LE2 .... 139 G4 🔟
   LEIS LE2 .... 137 H6
Kensington Dr *WGSTN* LE18 .. 138 B2
Kensington Gdns *CARL* NG4 .. 38 C8
   ILK DE7 .... 33 K8

Kensington Park Cl
  WBRGFD NG2 .... 65 C2
Kensington Rd LGEAT NG10 ... 61 M3
Kensington St DERBYW DE22... 2 C4
  ILK DE7 .... 47 K1
  LEIW LE4 .... 125 L6
Kenslow Av NOTTE NG7 .... 36 C8
  EWD/SEL/PNX NG16 .... 12 F3
Kent Av BSTN/STPLFD NG9 .... 63 K3
  EWD/SEL/PNX NG16 .... 12 F3
Kent Crs WGSTN LE18 .... 137 K5
Kent Dr LEIS LE2 .... 139 G2
Kentish Ct DERBY DE1 .... 43 M8
Kentmere Cl WBRGFD NG2 .... 52 A8
Kenton Av EWD/SEL/PNX NG16 .... 11 M7
  WGSTN LE18 .... 138 A6
Kent Rd HUCK/RAV NG15 .... 22 A6
  MAPPK/POR/STA NG3 .... 37 L5
  LEIE LE5 .... 7 J4
  NOTT NG1 .... 5 J6
Kentwood Rd WBRGFD NG2 .... 51 K3
Kenwood Rd LEIS LE2 .... 132 A8
Kenyon Rd NOTTE NG7 .... 50 B4
Kepple Ga RIPLEY DE5 .... 11 K7
Kepston Cl LEIS LE2 .... 137 H5
Kercey Rd RLBORO LE12 .... 104 D8
Kernan Dr LBORO LE11 .... 95 K8
Kernel Cl NORM/LIT DE23 .... 56 E7
Kerrial Rd LEIW LE3 .... 124 C8
Kerry Dr ILK DE7 .... 31 K1
Kerrysdale Av LEIN LE4 .... 126 B5
Kerry St DERBYE DE21 .... 44 B8
Kerry's Yd BPR/DUF DE56 .... 18 D7
Kersall Ct BLWL NG6 .... 36 B1
Kersall Dr BLWL NG6 .... 36 B2
Kersall Gdns HUCK/RAV NG15 ... 15 M8
Kershope Dr DERBYE DE21 .... 44 F4
Kertley RLEIW/BBY LE8 .... 145 K7
Kestrel Av CARL NG4 .... 37 M6
  ILK DE7 .... 47 K3
  LEIE LE5 .... 7 M3
  LEIW LE3 .... 129 J5
  RLEINE/SYS LE7 .... 120 D3
  RLEIW/BAR LE9 .... 141 J8
Kestrel Hts EWD/SEL/PNX NG16 ... 12 D4
Kestrel La RLBORO LE12 .... 113 K5
Kestrels Cft DERBYE DE24 .... 71 H4
Keswick Av LBORO LE11 .... 8 A8
  NORM/LIT DE23 .... 71 J1
Keswick Cl BSTN/STPLFD NG9 ... 49 H7
  ILK DE7 .... 47 H2
  LEIN LE4 .... 119 M7
  WBRGFD NG2 .... 52 A8
Keswick Ct LGEAT NG10 .... 61 M5
Keswick Rd RLEIW/BBY LE8 .... 136 E8
Keswick St WBRGFD NG2 .... 5 L7
Kett St BLWL NG6 .... 35 M1
Kevern Cl WGSTN LE18 .... 138 A6
Keverne Cl WOL/BIL/BRX NG8 ... 35 M5
Kevin Cl DERBYE DE21 .... 44 F7
Kevin Rd WOL/BIL/BRX NG8 ... 49 H5
Kew Cl CFTN/RUD NG11 .... 65 C4
Kew Crs DERBYE DE75 .... 20 F6
Kew Dr LEIS LE2 .... 139 C4
  WGSTN LE18 .... 137 M2
Kew Gdns DERBYW DE22 .... 56 F2
  WOL/BIL/BRX NG8 .... 35 J4
Keyham Cl LEIS LE2 .... 126 F6
Keyham La LEIE LE5 .... 127 G6
Keyham La East
  RLEINE/SYS LE7 .... 127 M5
Keyham La West LEIE LE5... 127 H6
Keyhaven Cl DERBYE DE21 .... 44 B7
Keynsham Cl DERBYSE DE24 ... 58 C7
Keys Cl BLWL NG6 .... 23 L8
Keys St DERBY DE1 .... 3 G2
Key St MAPPK/POR/STA NG3 ... 51 K2
Keythorpe St LEIS LE2 .... 7 K5
Keyworth La
  COT/KEY/RAD NG12 .... 79 K6
Keyworth Rd CARL NG4 .... 38 B4
  COT/KEY/RAD NG12 .... 91 C2
Kibworth Cl ARN NG5 .... 36 D3
  DERBYE DE21 .... 44 F7
Kibworth Rd RLEIW/BBY LE8 ... 145 K8
  RLEIW/BBY LE8 .... 145 J3
  RLEIW/BBY LE8 .... 147 G5
  RLEIW/BBY LE8 .... 147 G3
  RLEIW/BBY LE8 .... 147 J5
Kiddier Av ARN NG5 .... 25 M8
Kielder Cl RLEIW/BAR LE9 ... 135 K5
Kilbourne Rd ARN NG5 .... 25 M7
Kilbourne Rd RLBORO LE12 ... 114 A5
Kilbourn St MAPPK/POR/STA NG3 .. 5 J6
Kilburn Av LEIS LE2 .... 138 D1
Kilburn Cl BSTN/STPLFD NG9 ... 48 F5
Kilburn Dr ILK DE7 .... 33 H4
Kilburn La BPR/DUF DE56 .... 18 B4
Kilburn Rd BPR/DUF DE56 .... 17 M3
  BPR/DUF DE56 .... 18 A3
Kilby Av LEIN LE4 .... 125 L2
  MAPPK/POR/STA NG3 .... 51 L1
Kilby Dr WGSTN LE18 .... 138 C6
Kilby Rd RLEIW/BBY LE8 .... 145 G3
Kildare Rd DERBYE DE21 .... 58 F3
  MAPPK/POR/STA NG3 .... 37 K7
Kildare St LEI LE1 .... 6 F5
Kildonan Cl WOL/BIL/BRX NG8 ... 35 L5
Killerton Gn CFTN/RUD NG11 ... 64 D8
Killerton Park Dr
  CFTN/RUD NG11 .... 64 F3
Killingworth Av DERBYSE DE24 71 K3
Kilisick Rd ARN NG5 .... 25 M7
Killis La BPR/DUF DE56 .... 18 B7
Kilmelford Cl LEIN LE4 .... 126 D3
Kiln Av LEIN LE4 .... 126 D1
Kiln Cl ILK DE7 .... 32 C6
Kiln Cft RDERBYSW DE65 .... 69 C3
Kilnsey Ct NORM/LIT DE23 ... 70 D1
Kilnwood Cl
  MAPPK/POR/STA NG3 .... 51 L1
Kilsby Rd CFTN/RUD NG11 ... 64 D5
Kilverstone Av LEIE LE5 .... 133 H4
Kilverton Cl
  WOL/BIL/BRX NG8 .... 50 A3
Kilvington Rd ARN NG5 .... 25 M8
Kilworth Dr LEIE LE5 .... 132 C4

Kimber Cl WOL/BIL/BRX NG8 ... 49 H1
Kimberley Cl
  EWD/SEL/PNX NG16 .... 34 D2
Kimberley Rd
  BWSH/BRSTN DE72 .... 59 M5
  EWD/SEL/PNX NG16 .... 34 F2
  LEIS LE2 .... 7 M9
  LEIS LE2 .... 132 A4
  WBRGFD NG2 .... 51 J3
Kimberley St RLEIW/BBY LE8 ... 146 D7
Kimbolton Av NOTTE NG7 .... 4 A6
Kincaple Rd LEIN LE4 .... 126 B3
Kinchley La RLEINE/SYS LE7 ... 112 F6
Kincraig Rd LEIN LE4 .... 126 B3
Kinder Cl RLEIW/BBY LE8 ... 142 E2
Kindlewood Dr
  BSTN/STPLFD NG9 .... 62 F6
King Alfred St DERBYW DE22 ... 2 C7
King Charles St NOTT NG1 .... 4 F8
Kingcup Cl LEIE LE3 .... 129 K5
King Edward Av
  RLEIW/BAR LE9 .... 136 A7
King Edward Rd LBORO LE11 ... 9 M5
  LEIE LE5 .... 126 D8
King Edward St
  HUCK/RAV NG15 .... 23 M1
  LGEAT NG10 .... 61 M1
  NOTT NG1 .... 5 J6
Kingfisher Av LEIE LE5 .... 7 M3
Kingfisher Cl
  RLEINE/SYS LE7 .... 63 M2
  LEIW LE3 .... 129 J5
  MCKLVR DE3 .... 55 M8
  RLBORO LE12 .... 105 J7
  RLEINE/SYS LE7 .... 120 D3
  RLEIW/BBY LE8 .... 139 M6
Kingfisher Rd RLBORO LE12 ... 113 K5
Kingfishers Ct
  COT/KEY/RAD NG12 .... 66 A3
Kingfisher Wy LBORO LE11... 9 G5
King George Av ILK DE7 .... 33 J7
King George Rd LBORO LE11 ... 104 B4
King John's Rd COAL LE67 .... 108 D1
Kinglake Pl NG2 .... 51 G5
King Richard's Hl COAL LE67 ... 108 E1
King Richards Rd LEIE LE3 ... 6 C7
Kingrove Av BSTN/STPLFD NG9 ... 63 H1
Kingsbridge Av
  MAPPK/POR/STA NG3 .... 38 A1
Kingsbridge Cl
  RLEIW/BAR LE9 .... 135 L7
Kingsbridge Crs LEIN LE4 ... 118 F8
Kingsbridge Wy
  BSTN/STPLFD NG9 .... 63 G1
Kings Brook Rd RLBORO LE12 ... 97 H1
Kingsbury Av LEIS LE5 .... 133 G3
Kingsbury Dr WOL/BIL/BRX NG8 .. 35 L7
Kingsbury Rd DERBYW DE22 ... 56 E1
Kingsclere Av DERBYE DE21 ... 44 F5
Kingscliffe Crs LEIE LE5 .... 133 H3
Kings Cl HEANOR DE75 .... 20 A6
Kings Cft DERBYW DE22 .... 43 K3
Kingsdale Cl LGEAT NG10 ... 75 L2
Kingsdown Mt
  WOL/BIL/BRX NG8 .... 49 J5
Kings Dr EWD/SEL/PNX NG16 ... 13 J8
  LEIW LE3 .... 129 L4
  MCKLVR DE3 .... 56 F5
  WGSTN LE18 .... 138 A4
Kingsfield Rd RLEIW/BAR LE9 ... 142 A5
Kingsford Av NOTTE NG7 .... 50 C1
Kings Ga CDON/KEG DE74 ... 85 K3
Kingsgate Av LEIN LE4 .... 119 K7
Kingsland Ct DERBYE DE21 ... 44 D5
Kingsley Cl RLEIW/BAR LE9 ... 135 L6
Kingsley Crs LGEAT NG10 ... 75 M3
Kingsley Dr CARL NG4 .... 38 E8
Kingsley Rd DERBYW DE22 ... 43 H4
  WBRGFD NG2 .... 51 J3
Kingsley St DERBYSE DE24 ... 71 K2
  LEIS LE2 .... 131 L7
Kingsmead Av
  BSTN/STPLFD NG9 .... 48 B5
King's Mead Cl DERBY DE1 ... 2 D1
King's Meadow Rd
  WBRGFD NG2 .... 50 E5
Kingsmead Rd LEIS LE2 .... 138 A1
Kings Moor ARN NG5 .... 24 C8
Kingsmuir Rd MCKLVR DE3 ... 56 A4
Kings Newton St LEIS LE2 ... 7 L8
King's Pl NOTT NG1 .... 5 J7
Kings Rd LGEAT NG10 .... 61 M1
  RLBORO LE12 .... 101 M5
Kingsthorpe Cl LEIN LE4 ... 125 K4
  MAPPK/POR/STA NG3 .... 37 K6
Kingston Av ILK DE7 .... 47 L3
  WGSTN LE18 .... 137 M3
Kingston Ct ILK DE7 .... 32 B7
Kingston La CDON/KEG DE74 ... 86 D4
Kingston Rd LEIS LE2 .... 132 A4
  WBRGFD NG2 .... 65 J1
Kingston St DERBY DE1 .... 43 K8
King St BPR/DUF DE56 .... 17 K4
  BPR/DUF DE56 .... 29 J3
  BSTN/STPLFD NG9 .... 63 L1
  COAL LE67 .... 108 B7
  DERBY DE1 .... 2 D1
  EWD/SEL/PNX NG16 .... 21 K5
  LBORO LE11 .... 9 L5
  LEI LE1 .... 6 F7
  LEIS LE2 .... 138 F2
  LGEAT NG10 .... 62 D7
  NOTT NG1 .... 5 G7
  RLBORO LE12 .... 106 D7
  RLBORO LE12 .... 114 A4
  RLEINE/SYS LE7 .... 127 H1
  RLEIW/BAR LE9 .... 135 M4
  RLEIW/BBY LE8 .... 136 D8
Kings Wk LEIW LE3 .... 129 L5
Kings Wy GBY/RBY LE6 .... 123 K5
Kingsway COT/KEY/RAD NG12 .. 53 J5
  DERBYW DE22 .... 56 F1
  HEANOR DE75 .... 20 B5

ILK DE7 .... 47 L2
  LEIW LE3 .... 130 E8
Kingsway Crs BPR/DUF DE56 ... 18 E7
Kingsway Gdns
  HUCK/RAV NG15 .... 23 J3
Kingsway North LEIW LE3 ... 130 C5
Kingsway Park Cl DERBYW DE22.. 57 G2
Kingsway Rd HUCK/RAV NG15 ... 23 J3
  LEIE LE5 .... 132 C5
Kingswell Rd ARN NG5 .... 25 K8
Kingswood Av BPR/DUF DE56 ... 18 A1
  LEIW LE3 .... 130 F5
  RLBORO LE12 .... 102 E2
Kingswood Rd WBRGFD NG2 ... 65 H2
  WOL/BIL/BRX NG8 .... 49 M2
King William St
  EWD/SEL/PNX NG16 .... 12 D3
King Williams Wy
  RLEINE/SYS LE7 .... 118 C8
Kinlet Rd LEIN LE4 .... 36 E1
Kinley Rd LEIN LE4 .... 125 J3
Kinoulton La
  COT/KEY/RAD NG12 .... 81 M7
Kinross Av DERBYE DE21... 44 A7
  LEIS LE2 .... 133 J1
Kinross Crs LBORO LE11 ... 103 H2
  WOL/BIL/BRX NG8 .... 49 L1
Kinsdale Dr LEIS LE2 .... 133 K1
Kintore Dr DERBYE DE21 ... 44 F5
Kintyre Dr DERBYSE DE24 ... 71 H4
  LEIN LE4 .... 126 A3
Kiplin Dr RLEIW/BAR LE9 ... 135 L5
Kipling Cl CFTN/RUD NG11 ... 64 A7
Kipling Dr MCKLVR DE3 ... 56 B6
Kipling Gv LEIE LE5 .... 124 E5
Kipps St NOTT NG1 .... 5 J6
  RLBORO LE12 .... 113 H7
  RLEIW/BAR LE9 .... 140 B7
Kirby Cl EWD/SEL/PNX NG16 ... 21 L4
  RLBORO LE12 .... 113 H7
  RLEIW/BAR LE9 .... 140 B7
Kirby Dr CDON/KEG DE74 ... 86 A6
Kirby La LEIW LE3 .... 128 K4
Kirby Rd EWD/SEL/PNX NG16 ... 21 L4
  GBY/RBY LE6 .... 123 K8
  LEIW LE3 .... 123 L7
  LEIW LE3 .... 131 G2
Kirk Av CDON/KEG DE74 ... 86 B5
Kirkbride Ct
  BSTN/STPLFD NG9 .... 62 F3
Kirkby Av ILK DE7 .... 47 K1
Kirkby Gdns WBRGFD NG2 ... 51 H5
Kirk Cl BSTN/STPLFD NG9 ... 48 F3
  RIPLEY DE5 .... 11 G7
Kirk Dale Av DERBYE DE21 ... 59 K4
Kirkdale Cl WOL/BIL/BRX NG8 ... 48 F3
Kirkdale Gdns LGEAT NG10 ... 75 M1
Kirkdale Rd LGEAT NG10 ... 75 M1
  WGSTN LE18 .... 137 K5
Kirkewhite Av LGEAT NG10 ... 62 B8
Kirkfell Cl WBRGFD NG2 ... 66 A2
Kirkfield Dr BWSH/BRSTN DE72 ... 61 H7
Kirkfield Rd RLEIW/BBY LE8 ... 143 K3
Kirkham Cl HEANOR DE75 ... 20 B6
Kirkham Dr BSTN/STPLFD NG9.. 62 D5
Kirkhill RLBORO LE12 .... 102 A4
Kirkhill Cl COAL LE67 .... 109 C6
Kirkistown Cl DERBYSE DE24 .. 73 G1
Kirkland Cl BSTN/STPLFD NG9 ... 62 C1
Kirkland Dr BSTN/STPLFD NG9 ... 62 C1
Kirkland Rd LEIW LE3 .... 130 D7
Kirkland Wy DERBYSE DE24 ... 71 H4
Kirk La CFTN/RUD NG11 ... 65 H8
  RLEIW/BAR LE9 .... 136 A4
Kirkley Gdns ARN NG5 .... 25 L7
Kirk Ley Av North
  DERBYE DE21 .... 59 J3
Kirk Ley Av South
  DERBYE DE21 .... 59 J3
Kirkman Rd HEANOR DE75 ... 20 A3
Kirk Rd MAPPK/POR/STA NG3 ... 37 L5
Kirk's La BPR/DUF DE56 ... 18 A4
Kirkstead Cl DERBYE DE21 ... 44 F6
Kirkstead Gdns NOTTE NG7 ... 4 A1
Kirkstead St NOTT NG7 ... 4 A1
Kirkstone Cl LEIE LE5 .... 124 B6
Kirkstone Ct LGEAT NG10 ... 61 M5
Kirkstone Dr LBORO LE11 ... 8 A9
  WBRGFD NG2 .... 52 A8
Kirk St DERBY DE1 .... 43 L7
Kirkwall Crs LEIE LE5 .... 127 J8
Kirloe Av LEIW LE3 .... 129 K4
Kirtle Cl WOL/BIL/BRX NG8 ... 35 M8
Kirtley Dr WBRGFD NG2 .... 50 E5
Kirton Av LGEAT NG10 .... 62 B8
Kirton Rd COAL LE67 .... 109 H6
Kitchener Av NORM/LIT DE23.. 57 K8
Kitchener Rd LEIE LE5 .... 132 C2
  RLEINE/SYS LE7 .... 118 C8
Kite Cl RLEIW/BAR LE9 ... 141 J7
Kitson Av EWD/SEL/PNX NG16.. 13 C3
Kittiwake Ms NOTTE NG7 ... 50 C3
Kiwi Cl HUCK/RAV NG15 .... 23 H2
Knapp Av EWD/SEL/PNX NG16.. 21 K6
Kneesall Cl HUCK/RAV NG15 ... 15 M8
Kneeton Cl ARN NG5 .... 37 C3
  CARL NG4 .... 38 B3
Kneeton V ARN NG5 .... 37 C3
Knight Cl LEIN LE4 .... 120 D8
Knighton Av NOTTE NG7 ... 50 C1
Knighton Church Rd LEIS LE2 .. 132 A8
Knighton Dr LEIS LE2 .... 132 A7
Knighton Fields Rd East
  LEIS LE2 .... 131 K7
Knighton Grange Rd LEIS LE2 ... 132 C7
Knighton Junction La LEIS LE2 .. 131 L6
Knighton La LEIS LE2 .... 131 J1
Knighton La East LEIS LE2 ... 131 L1
Knighton Park Rd LEIS LE2 ... 132 A5
Knighton Ri LEIS LE2 .... 132 D6
Knighton Rd ARN NG5 .... 37 H2
  LEIS LE2 .... 131 M7
Knightsbridge DERBYW DE22 ... 56 E1
Knightsbridge Dr
  WBRGFD NG2 .... 65 G3
  WOL/BIL/BRX NG8 .... 35 J4
Knightsbridge Gdns
  HUCK/RAV NG15 .... 15 K5
Knightsbridge Rd WGSTN LE18 .. 137 H6

Knights Cl DERBYSE DE24 ... 71 J5
  RLEIW/BAR LE9 .... 140 B4
  WBRGFD NG2 .... 65 G4
Knight's Crs RLEINE/SYS LE7 ... 119 J1
Knight's Garth COAL LE67 ... 108 D2
Knights Rd LEIN LE4 .... 125 G1
Knight St CARL NG4 .... 52 D1
Knightthorpe Rd LBORO LE11 ... 8 A2
Knightwood Dr ARN NG5 ... 24 F2
Knipton Dr LBORO LE11... 102 F4
Kniveton Pk ILK DE7 .... 33 H8
Knole Rd WOL/BIL/BRX NG8 ... 49 J2
Knoll Av HUCK/RAV NG15 ... 23 H2
Knoll Cl NORM/LIT DE23 ... 56 E7
Knollgate Cl LEIN LE4 .... 119 J7
Knowl Av BPR/DUF DE56 ... 17 J1
Knowle Hl EWD/SEL/PNX NG16 .. 34 E2
Knowle La EWD/SEL/PNX NG16 .. 34 E3
Knowle Pk EWD/SEL/PNX NG16.. 34 E2
Knowles Rd LEIN LE4 .... 124 C8
Krebs Cl CFTN/RUD NG11 ... 64 A6
Krefeld Wy LEIN LE4 .... 124 E4
Kyle Gv DERBYE DE21 ... 44 F4
Kyle Vw ARN NG5 .... 24 E6
Kyme St NOTTE NG7 .... 4 B5
Kynance Cl DERBYSE DE24 ... 73 G2
Kynance Gdns CFTN/RUD NG11 .. 64 F2

L

Laburnam Cl RLBORO LE12 ... 111 K3
Laburnam Wy RLBORO LE12... 111 L3
Laburnum Av
  COT/KEY/RAD NG12 .... 80 E5
  LGEAT NG10 .... 62 D3
  RLBORO LE12 .... 94 E6
Laburnum Crs DERBYW DE22... 43 H2
Laburnum Gv BSTN/STPLFD NG9 .. 63 M2
  DERBYW DE22 .... 56 E2
Laburnum Rd LEIS LE5 .... 127 G6
Laburnum St
  MAPPK/POR/STA NG3 .... 5 J1
Lace Rd BSTN/STPLFD NG9 ... 49 K8
Lace St NOTTE NG7 .... 50 B6
Lacey Av HUCK/RAV NG15 ... 23 H2
Lacey Cl ILK DE7 .... 33 G4
Lacey Ct RLBORO LE12 .... 101 M4
Lacey Fields Rd HEANOR DE75 .. 20 E6
Ladbroke Gdns DERBYW DE22 .. 56 D1
Ladbroke Gv RLEIW/BBY LE8 ... 143 K3
Ladbrooke Crs BLWL NG6 ... 36 A4
Ladybank Ri MCKLVR DE3 ... 56 A6
Ladybank Rd MCKLVR DE3 ... 56 A6
Lady Bay Av WBRGFD NG2 ... 51 K6
Lady Bay Br WBRGFD NG2 ... 51 J5
Lady Bay Rd WBRGFD NG2 ... 51 L6
Ladybower Rd DERBYE DE21 ... 59 K3
  LBORO LE11 .... 102 F4
Ladybridge Cl
  BSTN/STPLFD NG9 .... 63 J4
Ladycroft Av HUCK/RAV NG15 .. 15 L8
Ladycroft Paddock
  DERBYW DE22 .... 43 J5
Lady Ga CDON/KEG DE74 ... 93 G2
Lady La RIPLEY DE5 .... 19 H6
Lady Lea Hl DERBYE DE21 ... 30 E2
Lady Lea Rd ILK DE7 .... 30 E1
Ladylea Rd LGEAT NG10 ... 75 L3
Lady Leys RLEIW/BAR LE9 ... 142 B4
Lady Mantle Cl
  MELB/CHEL DE73 .... 72 C5
Ladysmith Rd
  BWSH/BRSTN DE72 .... 59 M5
  RLEIW/BAR LE9 .... 129 H1
  WGSTN LE18 .... 137 J4
Ladysmith St WBRGFD NG2 ... 51 L3
Ladysmock Gdns WBRGFD NG2 .. 51 H5
Ladywood Av CFTN/RUD DE56... 17 M2
Ladywood Rd ILK DE7 .... 46 D3
  ILK DE7 .... 47 H2
Laithwaite Cl LEIN LE4 ... 124 F1
Lake Av HEANOR DE75 .... 20 A3
Lake Dr NORM/LIT DE23 ... 57 K7
Lakeland Av HUCK/RAV NG15 ... 24 A2
Lakeside Av LGEAT NG10 ... 76 A3
Lakeside Ct RLEINE/SYS LE7 ... 133 J3
Lakeside Crs LGEAT NG10 ... 76 A2
Lakeside Dr NORM/LIT DE23 ... 56 D8
Lake St NOTTE NG7 .... 4 B3
Lake View Rd HUCK/RAV NG15 .. 14 D1
Lamartine St
  MAPPK/POR/STA NG3 .... 5 K5
Lamb Close Dr
  EWD/SEL/PNX NG16 .... 21 L3
Lamb Crs RIPLEY DE5 .... 11 K6
Lambert Av RLBORO LE12 ... 101 M4
Lambert Gdns
  WOL/BIL/BRX NG8 .... 36 A7
Lambert Rd LEIN LE4 .... 124 D2
Lambert St NOTT NG7 .... 36 C8
Lambeth Rd ARN NG5 .... 24 E5
Lambhouse La BPR/DUF DE56 ... 16 C2
Lambie Cl WOL/BIL/BRX NG8 ... 50 A2
Lambley Av
  MAPPK/POR/STA NG3 .... 37 M4
Lambley Bridle Rd
  CALV/BJ NG14 .... 39 H1
Lambley Dr DERBYW DE22 ... 43 C5
Lambley La CARL NG4 .... 38 D4
Lambley La CALV/BJ NG14 ... 27 L7
Lamborne Rd LEIS LE2 .... 137 L1
Lambourn Ct DERBYSE DE24 .. 43 L4
Lambourn Dr DERBYW DE22 ... 43 M2
Lambourne Dr
  WOL/BIL/BRX NG8 .... 49 K2
Lambourne Rd LEIN LE4 ... 119 M7
Lambrook Cl MCKLVR DE3 ... 56 A5
Lambton Cl ILK DE7 .... 33 J4
Lamcote Gdns
  COT/KEY/RAD NG12 .... 53 H4
Lamcote Gv WBRGFD NG2 ... 51 H6
Lamcote Ms
  COT/KEY/RAD NG12 .... 53 J4
Lamcote St WBRGFD NG2 ... 51 H6
Lamen Rd LEIW LE3 .... 124 C6

Laming Gap La
  COT/KEY/RAD NG12 .... 81 H3
Lamins La ARN NG5 .... 25 H3
Lammas Gdns WBRGFD NG2 ... 51 H5
Lamorna Gv CFTN/RUD NG11 ... 64 F1
Lampad Cl MELB/CHEL DE73 ... 82 E7
Lampeter Cl DERBYE DE21 ... 44 F5
Lamplands
  COT/KEY/RAD NG12 .... 67 J4
Lamplighters RLEIW/BBY LE8 ... 145 K8
Lamport Cl LBORO LE11 ... 103 C3
  WGSTN LE18 .... 138 D5
Lanark Cl WOL/BIL/BRX NG8 ... 50 A4
Lanark St DERBYE DE21 ... 44 C8
Lancashire St LEIN LE4 ... 125 M4
Lancaster Av BSTN/STPLFD NG9 .. 62 C1
  LGEAT NG10 .... 61 L3
Lancaster Cl COAL LE67 ... 109 H6
Lancaster Ct GBY/RBY LE6 ... 123 J5
Lancaster Dr
  RDERBYSW DE65 .... 68 C5
Lancaster Rd BLWL NG6 ... 24 C3
  HUCK/RAV NG15 .... 23 H3
  LEI LE1 .... 131 L4
  MAPPK/POR/STA NG3 .... 37 L8
Lancaster St LEIE LE5 .... 132 B1
Lancaster Wk DERBYE DE21 ... 59 L1
Lancaster Wy WGSTN LE18 ... 137 J6
  WOL/BIL/BRX NG8 .... 35 H5
Lancelot Cl LEIW LE3 .... 129 L5
Lancelot Dr EWD/SEL/PNX NG16 .. 22 D4
Lancelyn Gdns WBRGFD NG2 ... 65 J3
Lancing Av LEIW LE3 .... 130 E1
Lancing La RLBORO LE12 ... 114 B3
Landcroft Crs ARN NG5 ... 36 E1
Landcroft La RLBORO LE12 ... 87 H6
Lander La BPR/DUF DE56 ... 17 L3
Landmere Cl ILK DE7 .... 33 G4
Landmere Gdns
  MAPPK/POR/STA NG3 .... 37 K6
Landmere La CFTN/RUD NG11 ... 64 F1
  WBRGFD NG2 .... 65 H5
Landscape Dr LEIS LE5 ... 133 G3
Landsdowne Rd LEIS LE2 ... 131 J7
Landsdown Gv LGEAT NG10 ... 62 D6
Landseer Rd LEIS LE2 .... 131 M6
Lane Cl LEIE LE5 .... 124 A7
Laneham Av ARN NG5 .... 25 L8
Lanesborough Cl
  RLEINE/SYS LE7 .... 118 F4
Lanesborough Ct LBORO LE11 ... 9 H6
Lanesborough Rd LEIN LE4 ... 125 M3
Lanes Cl RLBORO LE12 ... 114 B3
Laneshaw Av LBORO LE11 ... 102 F5
Lanes Hill Gv RLEIW/BAR LE9 ... 140 C6
Laneside Av BSTN/STPLFD NG9 .. 62 C5
The Lane EWD/SEL/PNX NG16 ... 34 C3
Laneward Cl ILK DE7 .... 33 G3
Langar Cl ARN NG5 .... 37 G3
Langbank Av ARN NG5 .... 24 C6
Langdale Av LBORO LE11 ... 145 K7
Langdale La LBORO LE11 ... 8 A8
Langdale Dr DERBYE DE21 ... 44 B5
  LGEAT NG10 .... 75 L1
Langdale Rd LEIN LE4 .... 120 D8
  MAPPK/POR/STA NG3 .... 52 A1
Langdon Cl LGEAT NG10 ... 61 L6
Langdown Cl BLWL NG6 ... 23 L7
Langford Rd ARN NG5 ... 25 M8
  MCKLVR DE3 .... 56 B4
Langham Av
  MAPPK/POR/STA NG3 .... 51 L3
Langham Dr CALV/BJ NG14 ... 39 K2
Langham Rd LEIN LE4 .... 135 M7
Langham Rd LEIN LE4 ... 126 D4
The Langhill LEIE LE5 ... 132 D1
Langholm Rd LEIE LE5 ... 133 J1
Langley Av ARN NG5 .... 37 K1
  ILK DE7 .... 33 H2
  LEIN LE4 .... 125 K4
Langley Cl RLEIW/BAR LE9 ... 135 H7
Langley Dr CDON/KEG DE74 ... 86 A5
Langley Rd DERBYE DE21 ... 59 J4
Langley St DERBYW DE22 ... 57 H2
Langsett Dr MELB/CHEL DE73 ... 72 E5
Langstrath Dr
  COT/KEY/RAD NG12 .... 66 A3
Langstrath Rd CFTN/RUD NG11 .. 64 C6
Langton Cl CARL NG4 .... 52 C1
  COAL LE67 .... 108 C1
Langton Hollow
  EWD/SEL/PNX NG16 .... 13 H1
Langton Rd RLEIW/BBY LE8 ... 146 F6
  WGSTN LE18 .... 138 B6
Langton St LEI LE1 .... 6 F4
Langtry Gv NOTTE NG7 ... 36 E6
Lanscombe Park Rd
  DERBYW DE22 .... 43 J6
Lansdown Cl BSTN/STPLFD NG9 .. 62 F3
Lansdowne Av
  DERBYSE DE24 .... 72 D2
  RLBORO LE12 .... 102 A2
Lansdowne Dr LBORO LE11 ... 9 H8
  WBRGFD NG2 .... 65 H3
Lansdowne Gv WGSTN LE18 ... 137 L7
Lansdowne Rd BLWL NG6 ... 36 C3
  RLBORO LE12 .... 101 M2
Lansing Cl CFTN/RUD NG11 ... 64 D7
Lansing Gdns DERBYE DE21 ... 58 F1
Lantern La RLBORO LE12 ... 88 D5
Lanthwaite Cl
  CFTN/RUD NG11 .... 64 D6
Lanthwaite Rd CFTN/RUD NG11 .. 64 C6
The Lant RLBORO LE12 ... 102 A3
Lapford Cl MAPPK/POR/STA NG3.. 38 B1
Lapwing Cl DERBYSE DE24 ... 71 J5
  LEIN LE4 .... 124 F1
Lapwing Ct RLEIW/BAR LE9 ... 135 L8
Larch Av RIPLEY DE5 .... 11 H6
Larch Cl ARN NG5 .... 25 L5
  DERBYW DE22 .... 43 H4
  HUCK/RAV NG15 .... 23 M2
Larch Crs BSTN/STPLFD NG9 ... 49 H8
  EWD/SEL/PNX NG16 .... 21 J5
Larchdene Av WOL/BIL/BRX NG8.. 49 H4
Larch Dr LGEAT NG10 ... 47 M8
Larch Gv LEIS LE2 .... 130 A4
Larch Rd BPR/DUF DE56 ... 18 F8

Larch St *LEIE* LE5 .... 7 M2
Larch Wy *COT/KEY/RAD* NG12 ...... 80 E5
Larchwood Av *GBY/RBY* LE6 .. 123 K4
Larchwood Cl *LEIS* LE2 .... 131 L8
Larges St *DERBY* DE1 .... 2 B3
Largs Cl *ARN* NG5 .... 24 C6
Lark Cl *BSTN/STPLFD* NG9 .... 62 E2
  LEIW LE3 .... 129 K5
  NORM/LIT DE23 .... 71 G1
Larkdale St *NOTTE* NG7 .... 4 C4
Larkfield Rd
  EWD/SEL/PNX NG16 .... 21 M2
Larkhill Crs *DERBYSE* DE24 .... 71 K3
Larkland's Av *ILK* DE7 .... 33 L8
Lark Ri *RLBORO* LE12 .... 111 K1
Larkspur Av *ARN* NG5 .... 25 J5
Larkspur Cl *LEIN* LE4 .... 119 H7
Larkspur Ct *DERBYE* DE21 .... 44 E4
Larkswood *RLEIW/BBY* LE8.. 146 F7
Larwood Gv *ARN* NG5 .... 37 G3
Lascelles Av *CARL* NG4 .... 38 B5
Lashley Gdns *DERBYE* DE21 .... 44 D5
Lastingham Cl *LEIS* LE2 .... 137 L1
Latham St *BLWL* NG6 .... 23 M8
Lathbury Cl *DERBYE* DE21 .... 44 B6
Lathkill Av *DERBYSE* DE24 .... 59 C8
  ILK DE7 .... 33 J2
Lathkill Cl *BLWL* NG6 .... 23 M8
  ILK DE7 .... 32 C7
Lathkilldale Crs *LGEAT* NG10 ...... 75 L2
Lathkill Dr *RIPLEY* DE5 .... 19 H1
Lathkill Rd *DERBYE* DE21 .... 44 D7
Latimer Cl *BLWL* NG6 .... 36 A1
  NORM/LIT DE23 .... 56 C8
  RLEIW/BBY LE8 .... 142 E1
Latimer Ct *RLEINE/SYS* LE7 .. 124 B2
Latimer Dr *BSTN/STPLFD* NG9 .... 48 F1
Latimer Rd *RLEINE/SYS* LE7 .... 118 D4
Latimer St *DERBYE* DE21 .... 72 B1
  LEIW LE3 .... 6 A8
  RLEINE/SYS LE7 .... 124 C2
Latrigg Cl *MCKLVR* DE3 .... 56 C6
Lauder Cl *DERBYSE* DE24 .... 71 J5
Laughton Av *WBRGFD* NG2 ..... 65 H3
Laughton Crs *HUCK/RAV* NG15 ..... 23 J3
Launceston Crs *CFTN/RUD* NG11.. 64 E3
Launceston Dr *COAL* LE67 .... 108 A8
Launceston Rd *DERBYSE* DE24 .... 72 F2
  WGSTN LE18 .... 138 A7
Laund Av *BPR/DUF* DE56 .... 17 M1
Laund Cl *BPR/DUF* DE56 .... 17 M2
Launde Rd *COAL* LE67 .... 116 C7
  LEIS LE2 .... 133 G8
Launder St *WBRGFD* NG2 .... 51 G5
Laund Hl *BPR/DUF* DE56 .... 17 L2
Laundon Cl *GBY/RBY* LE6 .... 123 K5
Laundon Wy *GBY/RBY* LE6 .... 123 J6
  RLEIW/BBY LE8 .... 142 E2
Laundry La *LEIN* LE4 .... 125 M5
Laurel Av *COT/KEY/RAD* NG12 .... 80 D5
  RIPLEY DE5 .... 11 H6
Laurel Cl *LEIW* LE3 .... 124 C7
  RLBORO LE12 .... 113 J5
Laurel Crs *EWD/SEL/PNX* NG16 .. 34 F1
  ILK DE7 .... 31 K2
  LGEAT NG10 .... 62 A8
Laurel Dr *LEIS* LE2 .... 139 H4
  RLEIW/BBY LE8 .... 143 J3
Laurel Rw *CARL* NG4 .... 38 A7
  LEIE LE5 .... 7 M8
  RLBORO LE12 .... 111 L1
  RLEIW/BBY LE8 .... 136 F8
The Laurels *DERBYE* DE21 .. 122 C1
Laureston Dr *LEIS* LE2 .... 132 B5
Laurie Pl *DERBYSE* DE24 .... 58 C8
Lavender Cl *RLBORO* LE12 .. 111 L1
  RLEIW/BBY LE8 .... 136 E7
Lavender Crs *CARL* NG4 .... 38 B6
Lavender Gdns *HEANOR* DE75 .. 20 F6
Lavender Gv *BSTN/STPLFD* NG9.. 63 M2
Lavender Rd *LEIW* LE3 .... 131 G4
Lavender Rw *DERBYW* DE22 ...... 43 K6
Laver Cl *ARN* NG5 .... 25 M8
Laverick Rd *EWD/SEL/PNX* NG16.. 12 E3
Laverstock Rd *WGSTN* LE18 .... 138 A7
Laverstoke Ct *DERBYW* DE22 .... 2 B5
Lawdon Rd *ARN* NG5 .... 25 L6
Lawford Rd *LEIS* LE2 .... 137 H3
Lawley Av *BSTN/STPLFD* NG9.. 49 L6
Lawn Av *DERBYW* DE22 .... 43 H5
  LEIN LE4 .... 119 M8
  RDERBYSW DE65 .... 69 G2
Lawn Cl *HEANOR* DE75 .... 20 D5
Lawn Heads Av *NORM/LIT* DE23 .. 57 G5
Lawnlea Cl *NORM/LIT* DE23 .... 71 J2
Lawn Mill Rd
  EWD/SEL/PNX NG16 .... 22 B8
Lawnside *DERBYE* DE21 .... 59 K2
The Lawns
  BWSH/BRSTN DE72 .... 73 M7
Lawnswood Cl
  NORM/LIT DE23 .... 57 G7
Lawnwood Rd *GBY/RBY* LE6.. 123 H4
Lawrence Av *BWSH/BRSTN* DE72.. 61 H7
  CARL NG4 .... 52 C2
  DERBYE DE21 .... 44 F8
  EWD/SEL/PNX NG16 .... 21 K5
  EWD/SEL/PNX NG16 .... 34 A2
  RIPLEY DE5 .... 11 C7
Lawrence Cl *COT/KEY/RAD* NG12.. 67 K4
  LEIN LE4 .... 119 C6
Lawrence Dr
  EWD/SEL/PNX NG16 .... 13 H7
Lawrence Pk
  EWD/SEL/PNX NG16 .... 13 M4
Lawrence St *BSTN/STPLFD* NG9 .. 62 B1
  LGEAT NG10 .... 48 A8
  LGEAT NG10 .... 62 B7
  NORM/LIT DE23 .... 57 K7
Lawrence Wy *LBORO* LE11 .... 95 C8
  WBRGFD NG2 .... 50 E5
Lawson Av *LGEAT* NG10 .... 62 C8
Lawson St *NOTTE* NG7 .... 4 C3
Law St *LEIN* LE4 .... 125 L6
Lawton Dr *BLWL* NG6 .... 24 A6
Lawyers La *LEIS* LE2 .... 138 E2

Laxford Cl *LEIN* LE4 .... 125 C5
Laxton Av *BLWL* NG6 .... 36 B2
Laxton Cl *LEIN* LE4 .... 119 M7
  WGSTN LE18 .... 138 D5
Laxton Dr *HUCK/RAV* NG15 .... 23 J3
Layton Av *LEIE* LE5 .... 126 C8
Leabrook Cl *CFTN/RUD* NG11 ..... 64 A4
Lea Cl *DERBYW* DE22 .... 43 J4
  LEIE LE5 .... 120 B8
Leacroft Rd *NORM/LIT* DE23...... 57 M6
  WOL/BIL/BRX NG8 .... 36 B7
Lea Dr *DERBYE* DE21 .... 58 D1
  MCKLVR DE3 .... 56 C4
Leafe Cl *BSTN/STPLFD* NG9 .... 63 G5
Leafenden Cl *DERBYW* DE22 ...... 43 L5
Leafgreen Cl *NORM/LIT* DE23 .... 71 G1
Leafield Gn *CFTN/RUD* NG11...... 64 C5
Leafy La *HEANOR* DE75 .... 20 D6
Leahurst Gdns *WBRGFD* NG2 .. 65 M1
Leahurst Rd *WBRGFD* NG2 .... 65 M2
Leake La *RLBORO* LE12 .... 96 B4
Leake Rd *CFTN/RUD* NG11 .... 77 M6
  CFTN/RUD NG11 .... 88 B1
  RLBORO LE12 .... 88 F6
Leake St *DERBYE* DE22 .... 57 H2
Lea La *RLEIW/BBY* LE8 .... 116 D3
  EWD/SEL/PNX NG16 .... 13 K1
Leamington Cl *NORM/LIT* DE23 .. 57 H6
Leamington Dr
  BSTN/STPLFD NG9 .... 63 G3
  RLEIW/BBY LE8 .... 142 F1
Leamington St *RIPLEY* DE5 .... 11 J5
Leander Cl *CFTN/RUD* NG11 .... 64 F1
  NORM/LIT DE23 .... 57 H8
Leaper St *DERBY* DE1 .... 2 B1
Leas Cl *RLEINE/SYS* LE7 .... 133 K1
Leas Gn *BWSH/BRSTN* DE72 ...... 73 L7
The Leas *CALV/BJ* NG14 .... 39 M2
The Lea *RLEIW/BBY* LE8 .... 146 F7
Leawood Gdns *DERBYSE* DE24 .. 18 B3
Leche Cft *BPR/DUF* DE56 .... 18 B3
Lechlade Cl *ILK* DE7 .... 32 B7
Lechlade Rd *ARN* NG5 .... 36 E1
Leckhampton Rd *LEIW* LE11 .. 103 G3
Leconfield Rd *LBORO* LE11 .... 103 G1
Ledbury Cha *DERBYSE* DE24 ...... 71 H5
Ledbury Cl *LEIS* LE2 .... 139 H5
Ledbury Gn *LEIN* LE4 .... 125 H2
Ledbury Rd *LBORO* LE11 .... 103 K8
Ledbury V *WOL/BIL/BRX* NG8 .. 35 M7
Ledo Av *RIPLEY* DE5 .... 11 H5
Ledwell Dr *LEIW* LE3 .... 124 A6
Lee Cl *RLEIW/BAR* LE9 .... 140 C4
Lee Crs *ILK* DE7 .... 33 M7
Leeds Pl *DERBY* DE1 .... 3 J6
Lee Farm Cl *MELB/CHEL* DE73 .. 72 D6
Lee La *HEANOR* DE75 .... 20 F6
Leen Cl *BLWL* NG6 .... 24 D3
Leen Dr *BLWL* NG6 .... 24 A6
  HUCK/RAV NG15 .... 15 M7
Leen Ga *NOTTE* NG7 .... 50 C5
Leen Mills La *HUCK/RAV* NG15 .. 15 M6
Leen Pl *NOTTE* NG7 .... 50 C2
Leen Valley Wy *HUCK/RAV* NG15 .. 24 A2
Lee Ri *GBY/RBY* LE6 .... 123 H7
Lee Rd *CALV/BJ* NG14 .... 39 L2
Lees Barn Rd
  COT/KEY/RAD NG12 .... 53 H5
Lees Crs *COAL* LE67 .... 108 C2
Lees Hill St *WBRGFD* NG2 .... 5 H7
Leeson St *LEIS* LE2 .... 131 J8
Lees Rd *MAPPK/POR/STA* NG3 .... 37 L6
The Lees *DERBYSE* DE24 .... 73 H2
Lee St *LEI* LE1 .... 7 G4
Leeway *DERBYE* DE21 .... 59 H3
Legion Wy *LEIW* LE3 .... 130 B7
Leicester Cl *RLBORO* LE12......... 118 B1
  RLEIW/BAR LE9 .... 128 B4
  RLEIW/BAR LE9 .... 135 M4
Leicester Rd *COAL* LE67 .... 108 D3
  COAL LE67 .... 116 D6
  GBY/RBY LE6 .... 123 M4
  LBORO LE11 .... 9 K5
  LEIN LE4 .... 119 H7
  LEIS LE2 .... 136 F5
  LEIS LE2 .... 138 E1
  LEIS LE2 .... 124 B5
  RLBORO LE12 .... 102 A5
  RLBORO LE12 .... 112 E2
  RLEINE/SYS LE7 .... 118 E4
  RLEINE/SYS LE7 .... 124 C1
  RLEIW/BAR LE9 .... 136 A7
  RLEIW/BAR LE9 .... 140 C8
  RLEIW/BAR LE9 .... 141 H6
  RLEIW/BBY LE8 .... 136 F6
  RLEIW/BBY LE8 .... 143 K3
  RLEIW/BBY LE8 .... 145 K6
  RLEIW/BBY LE8 .... 146 B2
  WGSTN LE18 .... 138 A2
Leicestershire Round
  COAL LE67 .... 116 E6
  GBY/RBY LE6 .... 117 J7
Leicestershire Wy
  RLBORO LE12 .... 114 A7
Leicester St *DERBYW* DE22 .... 2 A7
  LEIE LE5 .... 132 B1
  LGEAT NG10 .... 62 B7
Leigh Rd *BSTN/STPLFD* NG9 .... 62 D4
Leighton Av *LBORO* LE11 .... 102 F4
Leighton St
  MAPPK/POR/STA NG3 .... 51 K1
Leire St *LEIN* LE4 .... 125 M5
Leiston Gdns *ARN* NG5 .... 24 E7
Leivers Av *ARN* NG5 .... 25 K7
Leivers Cl *RLBORO* LE12 .... 88 B6
Lema Cl *BLWL* NG6 .... 24 B7
Leman St *DERBYE* DE22 .... 2 B7
Lemontree La *RLBORO* LE12 .. 103 L8
Lemyngton St *LBORO* LE11 .... 9 J2
Lena Dr *GBY/RBY* LE6 .... 123 G2
Lendrum Ct *CALV/BJ* NG14 ...... 39 K3
Leniscar Av *HEANOR* DE75 .... 20 A3
Lennox St *NOTT* NG1 .... 5 K6
Lens Rd *DERBYW* DE22 .... 43 G5
Lenton Av *COT/KEY/RAD* NG12.. 66 A6
  DERBYE DE21 .... 58 D1

  .... 4 C8
Lenton Bvd *NOTTE* NG7 .... 4 A9
Lenton La *NOTTE* NG7 .... 50 D8
Lenton Mnr *NOTTE* NG7 .... 50 C4
Lenton Rd *NOTTE* NG7 .... 4 C9
  NOTTE NG7 .... 50 E4
Lenton St *LGEAT* NG10 .... 62 A1
Leominster Dr *DERBYE* DE21 .... 45 G5
Leonard Av *ARN* NG5 .... 36 F5
Leonard Cl *NORM/LIT* DE23...... 2 F7
Leonard St *BLWL* NG6 .... 35 M2
  NORM/LIT DE23 .... 3 G7
Leopold Cl *RLEIW/BBY* LE8 .... 143 H3
Leopold Rd *LEIS* LE2 .... 131 L6
Leopold St *DERBY* DE1 .... 2 F6
  LBORO LE11 .... 8 F2
  LGEAT NG10 .... 62 B7
  LGEAT NG10 .... 137 K5
Leroy Wallace Av *NOTTE* NG7...... 4 A5
Lerwick Cl *CFTN/RUD* NG11 .... 64 E6
Leslie Av *BSTN/STPLFD* NG9 ...... 63 K2
  EWD/SEL/PNX NG16 .... 34 D2
Leslie Cl *LBORO* LE11 .... 103 H1
  NORM/LIT DE23 .... 56 C7
Leslie Rd *NOTTE* NG7 .... 36 E7
Letchworth Crs
  BSTN/STPLFD NG9 .... 63 G3
Letchworth Rd *LEIW* LE5 .... 130 E1
Letcombe Rd *CFTN/RUD* NG11.... 64 C4
Lethbridge Cl *LEI* LE1 .... 7 G3
Leven Cl *DERBYSE* DE24 .... 71 K5
Levens Cl *WBRGFD* NG2 .... 66 A2
Leveret Cl *MELB/CHEL* DE73 .... 72 F5
Leveret Dr *RLEIW/BBY* LE8 .... 142 D2
Leveric Rd *LEIE* LE5 .... 126 C7
Lewcote La *ILK* DE7 .... 32 E6
Lewett Cl *LEIN* LE4 .... 125 H3
Lewin Br *RLEINE/SYS* LE7 .... 120 E1
Lewindon Ct *ARN* NG5 .... 37 J3
Lewis Cl *LEIN* LE4 .... 124 F5
  MAPPK/POR/STA NG3 .... 5 J4
Lewisher Rd *LEIN* LE4 .... 126 C4
Lewis Rd *LBORO* LE11 .... 103 H2
Lewis St *NORM/LIT* DE23 .... 57 K6
Lewiston Rd *DERBYE* DE21 .... 58 F2
Lewis Wy *RLEIW/BBY* LE8 .... 143 K4
Lexham St *LEIN* LE4 .... 125 M5
Lexington Rd *DERBYE* DE21...... 58 F2
Leybourne Dr *ARN* NG5 .... 36 C1
Leybury Wy *RLEINE/SYS* LE7 .. 127 K8
Leycroft Rd *LEIN* LE4 .... 126 A1
Leyland Cl *BSTN/STPLFD* NG9 .. 62 D5
Leyland Rd *LEIW* LE3 .... 130 D8
Leyland Rd *DERBYW* DE22 .... 43 J8
Leys Cl *LEIS* LE2 .... 139 C1
Leys Ct *BPR/DUF* DE56 .... 18 B3
Leysdale Cl *LEIN* LE4 .... 124 F4
Leys Dr *LEIS* LE2 .... 138 E3
Leys Field Gdns
  MELB/CHEL DE73................... 72 E5
Leysland Av *RLEIW/BBY* LE8 .. 143 G3
The Leys *CFTN/RUD* NG11 .... 64 B5
  COT/KEY/RAD NG12 .... 66 D8
  DERBYE DE21 .... 30 B5
  RLEIW/BBY LE8 .... 143 G4
  RLEIW/BBY LE8 .... 146 E6
Ley St *LEIE* LE5 .... 38 E8
Leyton Crs *BSTN/STPLFD* NG9 .. 63 M2
Leytonstone Dr *DERBYW* DE22 .. 56 F2
Liberty Rd *LEIE* LE5 .... 130 B1
Lichfield Av *BSTN/STPLFD* NG9 .. 141 H7
Lichfield Cl *BSTN/STPLFD* NG9 .. 62 F2
Lichfield Dr *DERBYSE* DE24...... 58 E8
  RLEIW/BBY LE8 .... 142 F1
Lichfield Rd *WBRGFD* NG2......... 51 L3
Lichfield St *LEI* LE1 .... 6 E3
Liddell Gv *WOL/BIL/BRX* NG8 .... 49 K2
Liddington St *NOTTE* NG7 .... 36 D6
Lidgate Cl *MCKLVR* DE3 .... 56 A6
Lidster Cl *LEIE* LE5 .... 127 G6
  DERBYE DE22 .... 72 E1
  LEIE LE5 .... 127 G6
Lilac Cl *COT/KEY/RAD* NG12 ..... 80 E5
  DERBYSE DE24 .... 72 E1
  LBORO LE11 .... 103 L8
Lilac Crs *BSTN/STPLFD* NG9 ...... 63 M2
Lilac Gv *BSTN/STPLFD* NG9 .... 63 M2
  HEANOR DE75 .... 20 C6
Lilac Ms *ILK* DE7 .... 33 H4
Lilleker Ri *ARN* NG5 .... 25 J6
Lilleshall Wy *LBORO* LE11 .... 102 F2
Lilley Rd *DERBYSE* DE24 .... 72 F1
Lillingstone Cl *COAL* LE67 .. 116 C6
Lillington Rd *BLWL* NG6 .... 35 M1
Lily Av *CARL* NG4 .... 38 B6
Lily Bank *COAL* LE67 .... 100 A6
Lily Gv *BSTN/STPLFD* NG9 .... 63 M2
Limber Crs *LEIW* LE3 .... 130 C4
Lime Av *BPR/DUF* DE56 .... 29 J3
  DERBY DE1 .... 2 D7
  DERBYE DE21 .... 44 B5
  EWD/SEL/PNX NG16 .... 21 C5
  GBY/RBY LE6 .... 123 J6
  RIPLEY DE5 .... 11 H6
Lime Cl *COT/KEY/RAD* NG12 ..... 53 K4
  EWD/SEL/PNX NG16 .... 34 E1
  RLEINE/SYS LE7 .... 120 F4
Lime Crs *BPR/DUF* DE56 .... 17 M5
Limedale Av *DERBYE* DE21...... 44 F8
Lime Dr *RLEINE/SYS* LE7 .... 120 F5
Lime Gv *BSTN/STPLFD* NG9 .... 62 B2
  BWSH/BRSTN DE72 .... 60 D8
  DERBYE DE21 .... 58 F1
  LGEAT NG10 .... 61 M1
  LGEAT NG10 .... 62 B7
  RLEIW/BAR LE9 .... 129 H2
  RLEIW/BBY LE8 .... 136 F7
Lime Grove Av
  BSTN/STPLFD NG9 .... 63 J2
Lime Grove Cl *LEIN* LE4 .... 125 C3
Limehurst Av *LBORO* LE11......... 9 H1
Limehurst Rd *LEIE* LE5 .... 127 H6
Lime Kilns *WGSTN* LE18 .... 138 C7

Lime La *ARN* NG5 .... 25 K3
  DERBYE DE21 .... 44 F1
  DERBYE DE21 .... 45 K2
Limerick Rd *DERBYE* DE21...... 58 F3
Limes Av *MELB/CHEL* DE73 .... 56 B6
The Limes *RIPLEY* DE5 .... 11 C6
  ILK DE7 .... 32 C4
  ILK DE7 .... 33 K8
Lime Ter *LGEAT* NG10 .... 62 B7
Lime Tree Av *RLEINE/SYS* LE7 .. 119 L7
  WOL/BIL/BRX NG8 .... 36 A4
  WOL/BIL/BRX NG8 .... 49 L4
Limetree Cl *COT/KEY/RAD* NG12 .. 80 D5
Limetree Ri *ILK* DE7 .... 47 C1
Lime Tree Rd *HUCK/RAV* NG15 .. 23 M3
  RLEIW/BAR LE9 .... 136 B5
Lime Wk *NORM/LIT* DE23 .... 57 H6
Limmen Gdns
  MAPPK/POR/STA NG3 .... 5 M4
Limpenny St *NOTTE* NG7 .... 4 B4
Linacres Dr *MELB/CHEL* DE73 .. 72 E5
Linacres Rd *LEIW* LE3 .... 130 C4
Linby Av *HUCK/RAV* NG15 .... 15 M8
Linby Cl *ARN* NG5 .... 37 H2
  CARL NG4 .... 38 C5
Linby Dr *WOL/BIL/BRX* NG8 .... 35 H5
Linby Gv *HUCK/RAV* NG15 .... 15 M7
Linby La *HUCK/RAV* NG15 .... 15 M4
Linby Rd *HUCK/RAV* NG15 .... 15 M7
Linby St *BLWL* NG6 .... 24 A7
Linby Wk *HUCK/RAV* NG15 .... 15 L6
Lincoln Av *DERBYSE* DE24 .... 58 E7
  LGEAT NG10 .... 61 C3
Lincoln Circ *NOTTE* NG7 .... 4 C8
Lincoln Cl *BSTN/STPLFD* NG9 .. 48 C6
Lincoln Dr *RLEINE/SYS* LE7 .. 121 G5
  RLEIW/BBY LE8 .... 142 F1
  WGSTN LE18 .... 138 C7
Lincoln Gn *MELB/CHEL* DE73 .. 72 D5
Lincoln Gv *COT/KEY/RAD* NG12 .. 53 K4
Lincoln St *BLWL* NG6 .... 36 C4
  LEIS LE2 .... 7 J7
  NOTT NG1 .... 5 H6
Lindale Dr *WBRGFD* NG2 .... 66 A1
Lindbridge Rd
  WOL/BIL/BRX NG8 .... 35 K5
Linden Av *DERBYSE* DE24 .... 58 F2
  RLEIW/BBY LE8 .... 143 G3
Linden Cl *BPR/DUF* DE56 .... 18 F7
Linden Dr *LEIE* LE5 .... 132 C4
Linden Farm Dr *RLEIW/BBY* LE8.. 143 H3
Linden Gv *BSTN/STPLFD* NG9 .. 62 C1
  BSTN/STPLFD NG9 .... 63 L2
  CARL NG4 .... 38 F6
  LGEAT NG10 .... 47 L8
  RLBORO LE12 .... 113 J6
Linden La *RLEIW/BAR* LE9 .... 129 K3
Linden Rd *LBORO* LE11 .... 9 H1
Linden St *LEIE* LE5 .... 132 C2
  MAPPK/POR/STA NG3 .... 5 J1
Linden Wy *COAL* LE67 .... 108 A5
Lindfield Cl *WOL/BIL/BRX* NG8 .. 35 L5
Lindfield Rd *LEIW* LE3 .... 130 E1
  WOL/BIL/BRX NG8 .... 35 K5
Lindford Cl *DERBYE* DE21 .... 44 D3
Lindisfarne Cl
  DERBYSE DE24 .... 71 H4
Lindisfarne Dr *RLBORO* LE12 .. 102 E2
Lindisfarne Rd *RLEINE/SYS* LE7 .. 120 D4
Lindley St *EWD/SEL/PNX* NG16 .. 13 H1
  EWD/SEL/PNX NG16 .... 21 M3
Lindon Dr *DERBYSE* DE24 .... 71 H5
Lindrick Cl *MCKLVR* DE3 .... 56 D6
Lindrick Dr *LEIE* LE5 .... 132 C5
Lindsay Rd *LEIW* LE3 .... 130 F6
Lindsey Cl *DERBYE* DE21 .... 58 C1
Lindum Cl *RLEINE/SYS* LE7 .. 120 D5
Lindum Gv *WBRGFD* NG2 .... 51 K4
Lindum Rd *BLWL* NG6 .... 36 B4
Linford Cl *WGSTN* LE18 .... 138 C5
Linford Ct *BSTN/STPLFD* NG9 .. 48 F3
Linford Crs *COAL* LE67 .... 108 F6
  COAL LE67 .... 116 C7
Linford Rd *LBORO* LE11 .... 103 J7
Linford St *LEIN* LE4 .... 125 L4
Ling Av *LBORO* LE11 .... 104 A7
Ling Crs *CFTN/RUD* NG11 .... 65 H8
Ling Dl *RLEINE/SYS* LE7 .... 115 J8
Lingdale Cl *LBORO* LE11 .... 9 J2
Lingford Ri *MCKLVR* DE3 .... 56 A4
Lingford *COT/KEY/RAD* NG12 .... 67 L4
Lingford St *HUCK/RAV* NG15 .... 23 M1
Ling Rd *LBORO* LE11 .... 9 K9
Lings Ln *COT/KEY/RAD* NG12 .... 80 C7
Lingwood La *CALV/BJ* NG14 .... 26 F5
Linkfield Av *RLBORO* LE12 .... 113 J6
Linkfield Rd *RLBORO* LE12...... 113 J6
Linkin Rd *BSTN/STPLFD* NG9 .. 63 C1
Linkmel Cl *WBRGFD* NG2 .... 50 E6
Linkmel Rd *WBRGFD* NG2 .... 66 A1
Linkmel Rd
  EWD/SEL/PNX NG16 .... 21 H4
Link Ri *COAL* LE67 .... 116 D7
Link Rd *LEIS* LE2 .... 132 C8
  RLEINE/SYS LE7 .... 118 B8
  RLEINE/SYS LE7 .... 121 H2
Links Cl *DERBYSE* DE24 .... 71 K3
Linksfield Ct *CFTN/RUD* NG11 .. 65 G5
Links Rd *RLEIW/BAR* LE9 .... 129 G3
  RLEIW/BBY LE8 .... 146 F7
Linkway Gdns *LEIW* LE3 .... 131 C2
Linley Av *RLBORO* LE12 .... 102 A5
Linley Gn *RLEIW/BAR* LE9 .... 129 K3
Linnet Cl *DERBYE* DE21 .... 59 K1
Linnet Hl *RLMCLVR* DE3 .... 56 A8
Linnett Cl *RLEIW/BAR* LE9 .... 135 L8
Linney Rd *LEIN* LE4 .... 125 C4
Linsdale Cl *WOL/BIL/BRX* NG8 .. 48 F2
Linsdale Gdns *CARL* NG4 .... 38 B3
Lintlaw Cl *LEIN* LE4 .... 126 A3
Linton Ri *MAPPK/POR/STA* NG3 .... 5 L1
Linton St *LEIS* LE2 .... 132 A4
Linwood Crs
  EWD/SEL/PNX NG16 .... 21 K6
Linwood La *LEIS* LE2 .... 137 L5
Lion Cl *WOL/BIL/BRX* NG8 .... 36 A5
Lipton Rd *LEIN* LE4 .... 124 E1

Liskeard Dr *DERBYW* DE22 .... 43 H3
Lisle St *LBORO* LE11 .... 103 L2
Lismore Cl *NOTTE* NG7 .... 50 D8
Lismore Ct *DERBYSE* DE24 .... 71 H4
Lissett Av *ILK* DE7 .... 33 J3
Liston Dr *DERBYE* DE21 .... 43 K7
Listowel Crs *CFTN/RUD* NG11 .. 64 C7
Litchen Cl *ILK* DE7 .... 33 K5
Litchfield Cl *LGEAT* NG10 .... 62 E8
Litchfield Ri *ARN* NG5 .... 25 J5
Litchurch La *DERBYSE* DE24 .... 58 A5
Litchurch St *DERBY* DE1 .... 3 H7
  NORM/LIT DE23 .... 3 G7
Litelmede *LEIE* LE5 .... 126 C8
Little Av *LEIN* LE4 .... 125 M4
Little Bridge St *DERBY* DE1...... 2 C2
Little Dl *WGSTN* LE18 .... 138 C7
Littledale Cl *DERBYE* DE21 .... 45 G4
Little Dunmow Rd *LEIE* LE5 .... 126 D7
The Littlefare *LEIW* LE3 .... 130 B5
Littlegarth *WGSTN* LE18 .... 137 K3
Little Glen Rd *LEIS* LE2 .... 137 G6
Littlegreen Rd *ARN* NG5 .... 37 K3
Little Hallam Hl *ILK* DE7 .... 47 J2
Little Hallam La *ILK* DE7 .... 47 K1
Little Haw La *RLBORO* LE12...... 101 L4
Little Hayes *WBRGFD* NG2 .... 65 G3
Little Holme St *LEIW* LE3 .... 6 B7
Littlejohn Rd *LEIS* LE2 .... 137 H3
Little La *COT/KEY/RAD* NG12.... 66 C4
  EWD/SEL/PNX NG16 .... 34 E2
Little Lane *ARN* NG5 .... 25 J2
Little Lincoln
  COT/KEY/RAD NG12 .... 90 A5
Little London La
  COT/KEY/RAD NG12 .... 90 A4
Little Longstone Cl
  MCKLVR DE3 .... 56 D5
Little Lunnon *CFTN/RUD* NG11.. 77 J2
Little Masons Cl *LEIW* LE3 .... 130 B6
Little Meadow
  COT/KEY/RAD NG12 .... 67 L5
Little Meadow Rd
  MELB/CHEL DE73 .... 72 E5
Littlemeer Cl *LEIW* LE3 .... 130 B6
Little Moor La *LBORO* LE11...... 9 M4
Littlemore Cl *LEIE* LE5 .... 132 D1
Little Oak Wood Dr *BLWL* NG6 .. 24 B5
Littleover La *NORM/LIT* DE23 .. 57 H7
Littleover La *NORM/LIT* DE23 .. 57 H7
Little Ox *CARL* NG4 .... 52 D3
Little Tennis St *WBRGFD* NG2 .. 51 L4
Little Tennis St South
  WBRGFD NG2 .... 51 L5
Littleton St *LEIE* LE5 .... 6 B2
The Littleway *LEIE* LE5 .... 132 D1
Littlewell La *ILK* DE7 .... 47 K6
Little Woodbury Dr
  NORM/LIT DE23 .... 70 D1
Little Wood Cl *LEIN* LE4 .... 125 G3
Litton Cl *ARN* NG5 .... 37 J5
  BPR/DUF DE56 .... 17 M2
  ILK DE7 .... 33 J3
Litton Dr *DERBYE* DE21 .... 59 K4
Liverpool St *DERBYE* DE21 .... 44 C7
  MAPPK/POR/STA NG3 .... 5 L2
Liversage Pl *DERBY* DE1 .... 3 G6
Liversage Rd *DERBY* DE1 .... 3 H6
Liversage St *DERBY* DE1 .... 3 G6
Livesey Dr *RLEIW/BAR* LE9 .... 140 A8
Livingstone Rd *NORM/LIT* DE23.. 57 J6
Livingstone St *HUCK/RAV* NG15 .. 15 J1
  LEIW LE3 .... 131 G3
Lianberis Gv *WOL/BIL/BRX* NG8 .. 36 A6
Limekiln Ct *BLWL* NG6 .... 23 L7
Lloyd St *ARN* NG5 .... 37 G5
Lobbs Wood Cl *LEIE* LE5 .... 126 F7
Lobelia Cl *MAPPK/POR/STA* NG3 .. 5 K1
  RLEIW/BAR LE9 .... 135 K7
Lochinvar Cl *DERBYE* DE21 .... 59 K3
Lock Cl *ILK* DE7 .... 47 C1
Locke Av *LEIN* LE4 .... 126 B2
Lockerbie Av *LEIN* LE4 .... 126 A3
Lockerbie St *CARL* NG4 .... 52 D1
Lockhouse Cl *LEIS* LE2 .... 136 F3
Lockington Cl
  MELB/CHEL DE73 .... 72 D5
Lockington Rd *CDON/KEG* DE74.. 85 H2
Lock La *LGEAT* NG10 .... 61 M2
  LGEAT NG10 .... 75 M3
Lockley Cl *GBY/RBY* LE6 .... 123 H7
Locko Rd *DERBYE* DE21 .... 45 J8
Locksley La *CFTN/RUD* NG11 .... 64 C3
The Locks *LBORO* LE11 .... 103 K1
Lockton Av *HEANOR* DE75......... 20 C7
Lockwood Cl *ARN* NG5 .... 24 F6
  BSTN/STPLFD NG9 .... 63 A3
Lockwood Rd *DERBYW* DE22 .... 43 H3
Lodge Cl *ARN* NG5 .... 25 J5
  BPR/DUF DE56 .... 29 J4
  LEIN LE4 .... 126 D1
  RDERBYSW DE65 .... 69 G3
  RLBORO LE12 .... 105 H8
  RLEINE/SYS LE7 .... 121 G3
  RLEIW/BAR LE9 .... 135 H7
  RLEIW/BBY LE8 .... 146 D5
  WOL/BIL/BRX NG8 .... 36 B7
Lodge Dr *BPR/DUF* DE56 .... 17 J2
Lodge Farm La *ARN* NG5 .... 25 J6
Lodge Farm Rd *LEIE* LE5 .... 133 G2
Lodge La *ASHB* DE6 .... 41 L3
  DERBY DE1 .... 2 D1
  DERBYE DE21 .... 59 H4
  DERBYW DE22 .... 42 A7
  EWD/SEL/PNX NG16 .... 20 C1
  RLEINE/SYS LE7 .... 118 B4
Lodge Rd *EWD/SEL/PNX* NG16.... 12 C1
  ILK DE7 .... 32 C4
  LBORO LE11 .... 76 A2
Lodge St *BWSH/BRSTN* DE72 .... 60 E8
Lodge Wy *MCKLVR* DE3 .... 56 B5
Lodgewood Av *LEIN* LE4 .... 119 K8
Lodgewood Cl *BLWL* NG6 .... 35 L1
Lodore Cl *WBRGFD* NG2 .... 66 A1
Logan Av *LEIS* LE2 .... 137 C1
Logan St *BLWL* NG6 .... 36 D1
Lois Av *NOTTE* NG7 .... 50 D4

Lombard Cl *NOTTE* NG7 .... 4 A8
Lombard St *DERBYW* DE22 .... 56 D1 9
Lombardy Ri *LEIE* LE5 .... 7 M2
Lomond Av *DERBYSE* DE24 .... 71 K5
Lomond Crs *LEIN* LE4 .... 125 G5
London La *RLBORO* LE12 .... 91 H8
RLBORO LE12 .... 97 M4
London Rd *BWSH/BRSTN* DE72 .... 74 D6
CDON/KEG DE74 .... 86 B6
CDON/KEG DE74 .... 94 C1
COAL LE67 .... 108 C6
COAL LE67 .... 116 B7
COT/KEY/RAD NG12 .... 91 G4
DERBY DE1 .... 2 F5
DERBYSE DE24 .... 58 D6
LEI LE1 .... 7 H8
LEIS LE2 .... 132 A5
LEIS LE2 .... 139 J5
RLBORO LE12 .... 99 J2
RLEIW/BBY LE8 .... 139 M8
WBRGFD NG2 .... 51 H4
London St *LEIE* LE5 .... 132 B1
Longacre *ARN* NG5 .... 37 K3
Long Acre *HUCK/RAV* NG15 .... 15 H8
Longbeck Av
MAPPK/POR/STA NG3 .... 37 L6
Long Bridge La *DERBYSE* DE24 .... 58 B7
Longbridge La *HEANOR* DE75 .... 20 B4
Longcliffe Gdns *LBORO* LE11 .... 102 E8
Longcliffe Rd *LEIE* LE5 .... 7 M2
RLBORO LE12 .... 101 L4
Longcliff Rd *COAL* LE67 .... 108 F7
Long Cl *RLBORO* LE12 .... 104 D8 3
Long Cft *BWSH/BRSTN* DE72 .... 73 L7
Longdale Rd *ARN* NG5 .... 37 H1
Longden Cl *BSTN/STPLFD* NG9 .... 48 D5
Longden St *NOTT* NG1 .... 5 L6
Longfellow Rd *LEIS* LE2 .... 131 L7 1
Longfellows Cl *ARN* NG5 .... 24 F7 3
Longfield Crs *ILK* DE7 .... 47 K2
Longfield La *ILK* DE7 .... 47 K2
Longford Cl *DERBYW* DE22 .... 43 H5
WGSTN LE18 .... 138 A7 3
Longford Crs *BLWL* NG6 .... 24 A5
Longford St *DERBYW* DE22 .... 43 H7
Long Furlong *RLBORO* LE12 .... 113 H7
Long Furrow *RLEINE/SYS* LE7 .. 115 J8 2
Longgrey *RLEIW/BBY* LE8 .... 145 J6
Longhade Furlong
RLEINE/SYS LE7 .... 118 D8 1
Long Hill Ri *HUCK/RAV* NG15 .... 23 K1
Longhurst Cl *LEIN* LE4 .... 126 C2
Longlands Dr *WBRGFD* NG2 .... 66 B2
Longlands La *RDERBYSW* DE65 .... 70 A6
Longlands Rd *BSTN/STPLFD* NG9 .. 63 M4
Long La *BSTN/STPLFD* NG9 .... 63 H5
CDON/KEG DE74 .... 86 B1
COAL LE67 .... 108 C5
EWD/SEL/PNX NG16 .... 22 F5
ILK DE7 .... 33 H1
LEI LE1 .... 6 D4
Longleat Cl *LEIE* LE5 .... 126 B7
Longleat Crs *BSTN/STPLFD* NG9 .... 63 G3
Longley La *DERBYE* DE21 .... 59 H1
Longmead Cl *ARN* NG5 .... 37 G1
Longmead Dr *ARN* NG5 .... 37 G1
Long Meadow *WGSTN* LE18 .... 138 C7
Long Meadow Hl *CALV/BJ* NG14 .... 27 L5
Long Mere La *CDON/KEG* DE74 .... 92 F5
Longmoor Gdns *LGEAT* NG10 ... 61 M5 4
Longmoor La
BWSH/BRSTN DE72 .... 61 J6
LGEAT NG10 .... 61 M4
Longmoor Rd *LGEAT* NG10 .... 61 L5
Longore Sq *WOL/BIL/BRX* NG8 .... 50 B3
Longridge Rd *ARN* NG5 .... 37 K3
Long Rw *BPR/DUF* DE56 .... 17 K3
BWSH/BRSTN DE72 .... 74 F5
NOTT NG1 .... 5 G7 2
Long Rw West *NOTT* NG1 .... 5 G7
Longstock Cl *DERBYE* DE21 .... 44 C6 2
Longstone Gn *LEIE* LE5 .... 127 J8 2
Longstone Ri *BPR/DUF* DE56 ... 17 M1 4
Long St *RLBORO* LE12 .... 100 F1
RLEIW/BAR LE9 .... 140 C4
WGSTN LE18 .... 138 A5
Longthorpe Cl
NORM/LIT DE23 .... 56 E8 6
Longwall Av *WBRGFD* NG2 .... 50 E6
Longwalls La *BPR/DUF* DE56 .... 17 G2
Lonscale Cl *WBRGFD* NG2 .... 66 A2
Lonsdale Dr *BSTN/STPLFD* NG9 .... 62 C5
Lonsdale Pl *DERBYW* DE22 .... 57 H3
Lonsdale Rd *LEIN* LE4 .... 126 C1
NOTTE NG7 .... 50 C1 2
Lonsdale St *LEIS* LE2 .... 7 L8
Loom Cl *BPR/DUF* DE56 .... 18 A2
Lord Byron St *LEIS* LE2 .... 131 L7
Lord Haddon Rd *ILK* DE7 .... 33 J6
Lord Nelson St *WBRGFD* NG2 .... 51 K3 3
Lords Av *LEIN* LE4 .... 119 G8
Lords Cl *COAL* LE67 .... 108 E8
Lord St *DERBYSE* DE24 .... 72 B1
WBRGFD NG2 .... 5 M7
Lorimer Av *CARL* NG4 .... 38 D4
Lorne Cl *MAPPK/POR/STA* NG3 .... 5 H2
Lorne Gv *COT/KEY/RAD* NG12 .... 53 K4
Lorne Rd *LEIS* LE2 .... 131 L6
Lorne St *DERBYW* DE22 .... 2 C8
Lorraine Cl *DERBYSE* DE24 .... 72 C4 1
Lorraine Rd *LEIS* LE2 .... 131 H8
Lorrimer Rd *LEIS* LE2 .... 131 J7
Lorrimer Wy *LBORO* LE11 .... 103 G2 4
Lortas Rd *NOTTE* NG7 .... 36 D5
Loscoe-denby La *RIPLEY* DE5 .... 19 M3
Loscoe Gra *HEANOR* DE75 .... 20 A4
Loscoe Mount Rd *ARN* NG5 .... 37 G5 7
Loscoe Rd *ARN* NG5 .... 37 G6
DERBYE DE21 .... 44 E6
HEANOR DE75 .... 20 B4
Loseby La *LEI* LE1 .... 6 E6
Lothair Rd *LEIS* LE2 .... 131 J6
Lothian Pl *CDON/KEG* DE74 .... 84 E4 3
DERBYE DE21 .... 44 B8
Lothian Rd *COT/KEY/RAD* NG12 .... 66 A6
Lothlorien Cl *NORM/LIT* DE23 .... 56 F8 2
Lotus Cl *MAPPK/POR/STA* NG3 .... 5 M1
Loudon St *NORM/LIT* DE23 .... 2 F8
Loudoun Pl *CDON/KEG* DE74 .... 84 E3 1
Loughborough Av *WBRGFD* NG2 .. 51 K3
Loughborough Rd
CFTN/RUD NG11 .... 65 H6
CFTN/RUD NG11 .... 79 J8
COAL LE67 .... 100 B8
COAL LE67 .... 108 D1
LBORO LE11 .... 104 B7
LEIN LE4 .... 125 L1
RLBORO LE12 .... 94 E7
RLBORO LE12 .... 96 C1
RLBORO LE12 .... 96 D8
RLBORO LE12 .... 97 G3
RLBORO LE12 .... 102 A3
RLBORO LE12 .... 104 C8
RLBORO LE12 .... 104 F1
RLBORO LE12 .... 105 J1
RLBORO LE12 .... 112 D1
RLEINE/SYS LE7 .... 113 K7
WBRGFD NG2 .... 51 J8
WBRGFD NG2 .... 65 J3 3
WBRGFD NG2 .... 65 J1 2
Loughrigg Cl *WBRGFD* NG2 .... 50 F6 8
Louis Av *BSTN/STPLFD* NG9 .... 49 J8
Louise Av *CARL* NG4 .... 38 E7
GBY/RBY LE6 .... 123 K5
Lound Rd *RLEIW/BAR* LE9 .... 140 B7
Lousie Greaves La *DERBYE* DE21 .. 59 J1
Louvain Rd *NORM/LIT* DE23 .... 57 G4
Lovelace Wy *RLEIW/BBY* LE8 .... 145 K8
Lovell Cl *BLWL* NG6 .... 35 K2
Lowater St *CARL* NG4 .... 37 M8
Lowcroft Dr *LEIS* LE2 .... 139 G3
Lowdham La *CALV/BJ* NG14 .... 27 H3
Lowdham Rd *CALV/BJ* NG14 .... 27 L2
CARL NG4 .... 38 A4
Lowdham St
MAPPK/POR/STA NG3 .... 5 L6
Lower Bagthorpe
EWD/SEL/PNX NG16 .... 13 J4
Lower Beauvale
EWD/SEL/PNX NG16 .... 21 L4
Lower Bloomsgrove Rd
ILK DE7 .... 33 K5 2
Lower Brook St *LGEAT* NG10 .... 62 C8
Lower Brown St *LEI* LE1 .... 6 E7
Lower Chapel St *ILK* DE7 .... 33 K6
Lower Church St
RLEINE/SYS LE7 .... 120 F3
Lower Clara Mount Rd
HEANOR DE75 .... 20 E6
Lower Ct *BSTN/STPLFD* NG9 .... 49 L8
Lower Dale Rd *NORM/LIT* DE23 .... 57 K5
Lower Dunstead Rd
EWD/SEL/PNX NG16 .... 20 E4
Lower Eldon St *WBRGFD* NG2 .... 5 M8
Lower Eley St *DERBY* DE1 .... 2 D7
Lower Free La *LEI* LE1 .... 6 F5 3
Lower Gladstone St
HEANOR DE75 .... 20 C5 6
LBORO LE11 .... 9 J1 1
Lower Granby St *ILK* DE7 .... 33 K5 3
Lower Gn *LBORO* LE11 .... 103 H7
RDERBYSW DE65 .... 70 B6
Lower Hall Cl *BPR/DUF* DE56 .... 30 A1 1
Lower Hastings St *LEI* LE1 .... 7 G9
Lower Holme *RLBORO* LE12 .... 94 F4
Lower Keyham La *LEIE* LE5 .... 126 F6 1
Lower Lee St *LEI* LE1 .... 6 F4
Lower Maples *HEANOR* DE75 .... 20 E7 1
Lower Middleton St *ILK* DE7 .... 33 L6
Lower Nelson St *HEANOR* DE75 .... 20 B5
Lower Orchard St
BSTN/STPLFD NG9 .... 48 B8 1
Lower Park St
BSTN/STPLFD NG9 .... 62 A1 1
Lower Parliament St *NOTT* NG1 .... 5 K7
Lower Regent St
BSTN/STPLFD NG9 .... 63 L1
Lower Rd *BSTN/STPLFD* NG9 .... 49 M8
DERBYW DE22 .... 42 C7
Lower Stanton Rd *ILK* DE7 .... 47 K1
Lower Whitworth Rd *ILK* DE7 ... 47 K1 2
Lower Willow St *LEI* LE1 .... 7 G2
Lowes Hl *RIPLEY* DE5 .... 11 H4
Lowes La *MELB/CHEL* DE73 .... 72 B6
Lowe St *DERBYSE* DE24 .... 58 C8
Loweswater Cl *RLBORO* LE12 .. 105 H6 3
Loweswater Ct *WBRGFD* NG2 ... 52 A8 6
Loweswater Dr *LBORO* LE11 .... 103 G6
Lowick Dr *WGSTN* LE18 .... 138 C5
Lowland Av *LEIW* LE3 .... 129 L5
Lowlands Dr
COT/KEY/RAD NG12 .... 80 D3
Lowlands Lea *HEANOR* DE75 .... 20 D5
Lowlands Rd *BPR/DUF* DE56 .... 17 M3
Low's La *ILK* DE7 .... 47 L5
Lowther Wy *LBORO* LE11 .... 9 K9
Low Wood Rd *BLWL* NG6 .... 35 K2
Low Woods La *RLBORO* LE12 .... 100 E4
Loxley Cl *DERBYE* DE21 .... 44 F5
Loxley Rd *LEIW* LE3 .... 124 A6
Loxton Ct *MCKLVR* DE3 .... 56 A4
Loyne Cl *DERBYSE* DE24 .... 71 K5
Lubbesthorpe Bridle Rd
LEIW LE3 .... 130 C6
Lubbesthorpe Rd *LEIW* LE3 .... 130 C8
Lubbesthorpe Wy *LEIW* LE3 .... 130 B7
RLEIW/BAR LE9 .... 136 C2
Lucas La *RDERBYSW* DE65 .... 68 C5
Luccombe Dr *DERBYSE* DE24 .... 73 H2
Lucerne Cl *CFTN/RUD* NG11 .... 64 F1 3
Lucerne Rd *DERBYE* DE21 .... 45 G4
Lucknow Av
MAPPK/POR/STA NG3 .... 37 H7
Lucknow Ct
MAPPK/POR/STA NG3 .... 37 H7 1
Lucknow Dr
MAPPK/POR/STA NG3 .... 37 H7
Lucknow Rd
MAPPK/POR/STA NG3 .... 37 H7
Ludford Rd *BLWL* NG6 .... 24 A7
Ludgate Cl *ARN* NG5 .... 24 E5
LEIN LE4 .... 119 J7 2
Ludgate Wk *DERBYW* DE22 .... 56 C2
Ludham Av *BLWL* NG6 .... 23 M6
Ludlam Av
EWD/SEL/PNX NG16 .... 21 L8 1
Ludlam Cl *RLEIW/BBY* LE8 .... 143 G3 1
Ludlow Cl *BSTN/STPLFD* NG9 .... 49 H6 3
DERBYE DE21 .... 59 K2 3
LBORO LE11 .... 103 G7
LEIS LE2 .... 139 G2
Ludlow Hill Rd *WBRGFD* NG2 .... 65 K2
Lulworth Cl *LEIE* LE5 .... 132 E3 1
NORM/LIT DE23 .... 71 H1 3
WBRGFD NG2 .... 65 G2 6
WGSTN LE18 .... 138 B8
Lulworth Ct
EWD/SEL/PNX NG16 .... 22 D8 4
Lumb La *BPR/DUF* DE56 .... 16 F5
BPR/DUF DE56 .... 16 A5
BPR/DUF DE56 .... 17 G4
Lundie Cl *DERBYSE* DE24 .... 71 H5
Lune Cl *BSTN/STPLFD* NG9 .... 63 J4 4
Lunsford Rd *LEIE* LE5 .... 126 B7
Lupin Cl *DERBYE* DE21 .... 45 G4 12
MAPPK/POR/STA NG3 .... 5 J2
Luther Cl *MAPPK/POR/STA* NG3 .... 5 M2
Luther St *LEIW* LE3 .... 131 G3
Luton Cl *WOL/BIL/BRX* NG8 .... 36 B6
Lutterell Ct *WBRGFD* NG2 .... 65 H2
Lutterell Wy *WBRGFD* NG2 .... 66 A2
Lutterworth Rd *LEIS* LE2 .... 137 G2
RLEIW/BBY LE8 .... 142 E1
Lyall Cl *LBORO* LE11 .... 103 H1
Lybster Ms *WBRGFD* NG2 .... 50 F5 7
Lychgate Cl *DERBYE* DE21 .... 44 B5 1
Lydall Rd *LEIS* LE2 .... 137 H3
Lydford Rd *LEIN* LE4 .... 126 C5
Lydia Gdns *EWD/SEL/PNX* NG16 .... 21 J6
Lydney Pk *WBRGFD* NG2 .... 64 F2
Lydstep Cl *DERBYE* DE21 .... 45 G5
Lyle Cl *EWD/SEL/PNX* NG16 .... 22 C8
LEIN LE4 .... 126 C2
Lyme Pk *CFTN/RUD* NG11 .... 64 F2
Lymington Gdns
MAPPK/POR/STA NG3 .... 51 K1
Lymington Rd *LEIE* LE5 .... 127 H7
Lymn Av *CARL* NG4 .... 38 D5
Lyncombe Gdns
COT/KEY/RAD NG12 .... 80 D3
Lyncote Rd *LEIW* LE3 .... 130 F7
Lyncroft Av *RIPLEY* DE5 .... 11 J5
Lyncroft Leys *LEIE* LE5 .... 127 K8
Lyndale Cl *LEIN* LE4 .... 126 C1
Lyndale Dr *RIPLEY* DE5 .... 11 L7
Lyndale Rd *BSTN/STPLFD* NG9 .... 48 E7
LEIW LE3 .... 130 D7
Lynden Av *LGEAT* NG10 .... 76 B1
Lyndhurst Gdns *WBRGFD* NG2 .. 65 H3 6
Lyndhurst Gv *DERBYE* DE21 .... 58 E2
Lyndhurst Rd *LEIS* LE2 .... 138 E1 2
WBRGFD NG2 .... 51 L3 4
Lyndhurst St *NORM/LIT* DE23 .... 2 E9
Lyndon Dr *LEIS* LE2 .... 138 D1
Lyngate Av *LEIN* LE4 .... 119 L7
Lynholme Rd *LEIS* LE2 .... 137 M1
Lynmouth Cl *LEIW* LE3 .... 124 A8
Lynmouth Crs *NOTTE* NG7 .... 36 C8
Lynmouth Dr *ILK* DE7 .... 33 H4
WGSTN LE18 .... 137 L2
Lynmouth Rd *LEIE* LE5 .... 127 H7
Lynncroft *EWD/SEL/PNX* NG16 .... 21 L5
Lynstead Dr *HUCK/RAV* NG15 .... 23 G2
Lynton Cl *RIPLEY* DE5 .... 11 H4 1
Lynton Gdns *ARN* NG5 .... 25 L7
Lynton Rd *BSTN/STPLFD* NG9 .... 63 G1
Lynton St *DERBYW* DE22 .... 2 B6
Lynwood Rd *DERBYSE* DE24 .... 71 K3
Lyon Cl *WGSTN* LE18 .... 137 L3
Lyons Cl *CFTN/RUD* NG11 .... 64 F7 1
Lytham Cl *DERBYE* DE21 .... 44 B6 4
Lytham Dr *COT/KEY/RAD* NG12 .... 66 A4
Lytham Gdns *ARN* NG5 .... 24 E6
Lytham Rd *LEIS* LE2 .... 131 L6
Lythe Cl *CFTN/RUD* NG11 .... 64 E2
Lyttelton St *DERBYW* DE22 .... 56 F2
Lytton Cl *MAPPK/POR/STA* NG3 .... 5 L5
Lytton Rd *LEIS* LE2 .... 131 M6

M

Mabel Gv *WBRGFD* NG2 .... 51 L7
Mabel St *WBRGFD* NG2 .... 51 H5
Mablowe Fld *WGSTN* LE18 .... 138 C7
Macaulay Rd *RLEINE/SYS* LE7 .... 119 J1
Macaulay St *DERBYSE* DE24 .... 71 L2
LEIS LE2 .... 131 K6
Macdonald Rd *LEIN* LE4 .... 125 L6
Macdonald Sq *ILK* DE7 .... 47 H2 5
Mackenzie St *DERBYW* DE22 .... 57 G1
Mackenzie Wy *LEI* LE1 .... 7 H3 1
Mackinley Av *BSTN/STPLFD* NG9 .. 48 C6
Macklin St *DERBY* DE1 .... 2 D4
Mackworth Rd *DERBYW* DE22 .... 2 A1
Maclaren Gdns
CFTN/RUD NG11 .... 79 H2 1
Maclean Av *LBORO* LE11 .... 103 G1
Maclean Rd *CARL* NG4 .... 38 A8 3
Macready Pl *DERBYSE* DE24 .... 58 D8 4
Madeley Ct *MCKLVR* DE3 .... 56 B6 4
Madeley St *NORM/LIT* DE23 .... 57 L5
Madeline Rd *LEIN* LE4 .... 125 G1
Madison Av *DERBYE* DE21 .... 44 C8
Madras Rd *LEI* LE1 .... 7 J4
Mafeking St *WBRGFD* NG2 .... 51 L3
Magdala Rd
MAPPK/POR/STA NG3 .... 37 G7
Magna Rd *WGSTN* LE18 .... 137 L6
Magnolia Av *RLBORO* LE12 .... 103 L8
Magnolia Cl *LEIS* LE2 .... 137 G2
LEIW LE3 .... 129 J5 2
Magnolia Ct *BSTN/STPLFD* NG9 .... 49 H6
Magnolia Gv *HUCK/RAV* NG15 .... 23 M3
Magnus Rd *LEIN* LE4 .... 126 A5
Magson Cl *MAPPK/POR/STA* NG3 .... 5 M5
Maiden La *NOTT* NG1 .... 5 K7
Maidens Dl *ARN* NG5 .... 25 H7
Maiden St *RLEINE/SYS* LE7 .... 120 D4
Maidenwell Av *LEIE* LE5 .... 127 G6
Maid Marian Wy *NOTT* NG1 .... 5 G9 2
Maidstone Dr *BSTN/STPLFD* NG9 .. 49 H5
DERBYSE DE24 .... 72 D2
Maidstone Rd *LEIS* LE2 .... 7 J7
Maidwell Cl *BPR/DUF* DE56 .... 17 M2
WGSTN LE18 .... 138 D5
Main Av *DERBYW* DE22 .... 43 K2
Maine Dr *DERBYE* DE21 .... 58 E1
Main Rd *ALFN* DE55 .... 12 E1
BSTN/STPLFD NG9 .... 64 A1
BWSH/BRSTN DE72 .... 73 L1
CARL NG4 .... 38 D6
CFTN/RUD NG11 .... 50 F8
COT/KEY/RAD NG12 .... 53 J4
COT/KEY/RAD NG12 .... 66 C8
COT/KEY/RAD NG12 .... 67 J3
EWD/SEL/PNX NG16 .... 12 F3
EWD/SEL/PNX NG16 .... 13 J4
EWD/SEL/PNX NG16 .... 13 G4
EWD/SEL/PNX NG16 .... 22 D6
ILK DE7 .... 31 K4
RIPLEY DE5 .... 10 E4
RIPLEY DE5 .... 10 F2
Mainside Crs
EWD/SEL/PNX NG16 .... 13 L6
Main St *BLWL* NG6 .... 24 A8
BWSH/BRSTN DE72 .... 61 H8
BWSH/BRSTN DE72 .... 74 B1
BWSH/BRSTN DE72 .... 83 J3
CALV/BJ NG14 .... 26 F3
CALV/BJ NG14 .... 27 K1
CALV/BJ NG14 .... 39 L2
CARL NG4 .... 26 F8
CDON/KEG DE74 .... 85 H3
CDON/KEG DE74 .... 85 K2
CFTN/RUD NG11 .... 79 J7
CFTN/RUD NG11 .... 79 J4
COAL LE67 .... 100 B7
COAL LE67 .... 116 B6
COT/KEY/RAD NG12 .... 80 C6
COT/KEY/RAD NG12 .... 90 A4
EWD/SEL/PNX NG16 .... 13 H6
EWD/SEL/PNX NG16 .... 21 K6
EWD/SEL/PNX NG16 .... 22 A5
EWD/SEL/PNX NG16 .... 34 D1
EWD/SEL/PNX NG16 .... 34 A2
GBY/RBY LE6 .... 117 H6
GBY/RBY LE6 .... 123 G7
HUCK/RAV NG15 .... 15 L4
ILK DE7 .... 18 F8
ILK DE7 .... 32 C4
ILK DE7 .... 47 K7
LEIE LE5 .... 126 E7
LEIE LE5 .... 132 F4
LEIW LE3 .... 123 M6
LEIW LE3 .... 130 D5
LGEAT NG10 .... 62 C8
MELB/CHEL DE73 .... 83 G6
RDERBYSW DE65 .... 68 F3
RDERBYSW DE65 .... 68 A5
RDERBYSW DE65 .... 70 B6
RLBORO LE12 .... 86 E8
RLBORO LE12 .... 87 K6
RLBORO LE12 .... 88 D6
RLBORO LE12 .... 89 G6
RLBORO LE12 .... 91 G8
RLBORO LE12 .... 93 M3
RLBORO LE12 .... 94 F4
RLBORO LE12 .... 95 H4
RLBORO LE12 .... 96 A6
RLBORO LE12 .... 97 H2
RLBORO LE12 .... 100 A3
RLBORO LE12 .... 104 A8
RLBORO LE12 .... 111 K5
RLBORO LE12 .... 111 M8
RLBORO LE12 .... 114 A7
RLEINE/SYS LE7 .... 115 G5
RLEINE/SYS LE7 .... 121 G7
RLEINE/SYS LE7 .... 121 K2
RLEINE/SYS LE7 .... 127 K7
RLEINE/SYS LE7 .... 133 K3
RLEIW/BAR LE9 .... 128 A1
RLEIW/BAR LE9 .... 129 H2
RLEIW/BAR LE9 .... 134 E4
RLEIW/BAR LE9 .... 135 H8
RLEIW/BAR LE9 .... 141 J8
RLEIW/BAR LE9 .... 142 B5
RLEIW/BBY LE8 .... 139 M7
RLEIW/BBY LE8 .... 143 K4
RLEIW/BBY LE8 .... 145 K8
RLEIW/BBY LE8 .... 146 E5
RLEIW/BBY LE8 .... 147 L2
WBRGFD NG2 .... 52 A8
WGSTN LE18 .... 144 D4
WOL/BIL/BRX NG8 .... 34 F6
Maitland *RLBORO* LE12 .... 113 J6 2
Maitland Av *ARN* NG5 .... 37 K3
Maitland Rd *ARN* NG5 .... 37 K3
Major St *NOTT* NG1 .... 5 G4 1
Makeney Rd *BPR/DUF* DE56 .... 18 A8
BPR/DUF DE56 .... 29 K5
Malabar Rd *LEI* LE1 .... 7 J4
Malbon Cl *MAPPK/POR/STA* NG3 .. 37 J7
Malcolm Gv *NORM/LIT* DE23 .... 56 C7 2
Malcolm St *NORM/LIT* DE23 .... 57 M5
Maldon Cl *BSTN/STPLFD* NG9 .... 62 F3 6
Malham Cl *LEIN* LE4 .... 124 F4
Malham Rd *NORM/LIT* DE23 .... 70 D1 7
Malham Wy *LEIS* LE2 .... 139 H2
Malin Cl *DERBYSE* DE24 .... 72 F2
Malin Hl *NOTT* NG1 .... 5 K8
Malkin Av *COT/KEY/RAD* NG12 .... 53 L3
Mallard Av *GBY/RBY* LE6 .... 123 J4
Mallard Ct *BSTN/STPLFD* NG9 ... 63 M2 2
Mallard Dr *RLEINE/SYS* LE7 .... 120 D3
Mallard Rd *CARL* NG4 .... 52 F1
RLBORO LE12 .... 113 K5
Mallard Wk *MCKLVR* DE3 .... 56 A8
Mallard Wy *LEIW* LE3 .... 129 J5
Malling Av *RLEIW/BAR* LE9 .... 141 H8
Malling Cl *RLEINE/SYS* LE7 .... 119 M6
Mallory Pl *LEIE* LE5 .... 126 C7
Mallow Cl *LEIE* LE5 .... 127 G4
Malmesbury Rd
MAPPK/POR/STA NG3 .... 37 L3
Maltby Cl *DERBYW* DE22 .... 43 K5 4
WOL/BIL/BRX NG8 .... 35 M5
Maltby Rd *MAPPK/POR/STA* NG3 .. 37 L3
Malt Cottages *NOTTE* NG7 .... 36 D6 3
Malthouse Cl
EWD/SEL/PNX NG16 .... 21 K6 3
Malting Cl *CFTN/RUD* NG11 .... 79 G1 6
The Maltings
BWSH/BRSTN DE72 .... 74 E6 2
LEIW LE3 .... 123 M6
Maltmill La *NOTT* NG1 .... 5 H8
Malton Dr *LEIS* LE2 .... 139 G1
Malton Pl *DERBYE* DE21 .... 44 B6
Malton Rd *NOTTE* NG7 .... 36 D5
Malt St *CFTN/RUD* NG11 .... 77 M6
Malvern Av *RLBORO* LE12 .... 102 A5
Malvern Cl
MAPPK/POR/STA NG3 .... 37 J6 2
MCKLVR DE3 .... 56 B4 3
Malvern Crs *RLEIW/BAR* LE9 .... 142 B4
WBRGFD NG2 .... 65 K2
Malvern Gdns *LGEAT* NG10 .... 61 L7 4
Malvern Rd *LEIS* LE2 .... 132 B5 1
WBRGFD NG2 .... 65 J2
Malvern Wy *DERBYE* DE21 .... 44 B6
Mammoth St *COAL* LE67 .... 108 B6
Manchester St *DERBYW* DE22 .... 57 H1
LGEAT NG10 .... 76 B1
Mandalay St *BLWL* NG6 .... 36 B3
Mandarin Wy *RLEIW/BBY* LE8 .... 142 D3
Mandervell Rd *LEIS* LE2 .... 138 D2
Mandora La *LEIS* LE2 .... 7 J9 1
Manesty Crs *CFTN/RUD* NG11 .... 64 C8
Manifold Dr *DERBYSE* DE24 .... 58 F7
Manifold Gdns *WBRGFD* NG2 .... 51 G5
Manitoba Rd *LEI* LE1 .... 7 G3
Manly Cl *ARN* NG5 .... 24 C7
Mann Cl *LEIW* LE3 .... 130 B5 2
Manners Av *ILK* DE7 .... 33 H6
Manners Rd *ILK* DE7 .... 33 J6
LEIS LE2 .... 131 J8
Manners St *ILK* DE7 .... 47 L1 4
Manning St *MAPPK/POR/STA* NG3 .. 5 J1
Manning Vw *ILK* DE7 .... 33 K5
Mannion Crs *LGEAT* NG10 .... 75 M2
Manns Leys *COT/KEY/RAD* NG12 .. 67 J5
Mann St *NOTTE* NG7 .... 36 D7 3
Manor Av *BSTN/STPLFD* NG9 .... 48 B7
BSTN/STPLFD NG9 .... 63 J4
BSTN/STPLFD NG9 .... 63 K1 3
DERBYW DE22 .... 57 G4
Manor Brook Cl
RLEIW/BAR LE9 .... 140 C4 3
Manor Cl *COT/KEY/RAD* NG12 .... 65 M4
LEIS LE2 .... 132 F7
RLBORO LE12 .... 89 G6
Manor Ct *BWSH/BRSTN* DE72 .... 61 H7
CARL NG4 .... 38 D7
RLEIW/BBY LE8 .... 137 G7
Manor Crs *CARL* NG4 .... 38 D7
Manor Cft *RIPLEY* DE5 .... 11 H3
Manor Dr *LBORO* LE11 .... 103 M7
LEIN LE4 .... 124 E2
RLBORO LE12 .... 114 A5
Manor Farm Cl *CFTN/RUD* NG11 .. 79 J4
Manor Farm La *CFTN/RUD* NG11 .. 64 C6
Manor Farm Meadow
RLBORO LE12 .... 88 C6 2
Manor Farm Rd
BWSH/BRSTN DE72 .... 73 M7
Manor Farm Wy *LEIW* LE3 .... 123 M8
Manor Fields Dr *ILK* DE7 .... 33 H8
Manor Gdns *LEIW* LE3 .... 124 A7
RLBORO LE12 .... 101 M3 2
Manor Green Ct *CARL* NG4 .... 38 D7 2
Manor Green Wk *CARL* NG4 .... 38 D7 3
Manor House Dr
COT/KEY/RAD NG12 .... 90 B4 1
Manor House Gdns *LEIE* LE5 .... 126 F7 1
Manor House Rd *LGEAT* NG10 .... 62 D8
Manorleigh *BWSH/BRSTN* DE72 .... 61 J7
Manor Pk *BWSH/BRSTN* DE72 .... 59 L6
CFTN/RUD NG11 .... 64 F8
Manor Park Wy
DERBYW DE22 .... 56 F4 1
Manor Rd *BPR/DUF* DE56 .... 17 K4
BWSH/BRSTN DE72 .... 59 L6
CARL NG4 .... 38 D7
CFTN/RUD NG11 .... 77 J1
COT/KEY/RAD NG12 .... 80 C4
EWD/SEL/PNX NG16 .... 21 K6
ILK DE7 .... 33 J6
LBORO LE11 .... 103 M7 1
LEIN LE4 .... 126 B1
LEIS LE2 .... 132 D7
MELB/CHEL DE73 .... 72 D6
NORM/LIT DE23 .... 57 G5 2
RLBORO LE12 .... 88 D4
RLEIW/BAR LE9 .... 140 B7 2
RLEIW/BAR LE9 .... 142 B3
RLEIW/BBY LE8 .... 145 L8
Manor Road Extension
LEIS LE2 .... 132 F8
Manor St *WBRGFD* NG2 .... 51 K4
WGSTN LE18 .... 137 M5
Manorwood Rd
COT/KEY/RAD NG12 .... 67 K5 3
Mansell Cl *EWD/SEL/PNX* NG16 .... 21 M6
Mansfield Av *RLBORO* LE12 .... 112 E1
Mansfield Gv *NOTT* NG1 .... 4 F4
Mansfield Rd *ARN* NG5 .... 25 J6
ARN NG5 .... 37 H3
DERBY DE1 .... 2 F1
DERBYE DE21 .... 44 C4 2
EWD/SEL/PNX NG16 .... 13 M4
EWD/SEL/PNX NG16 .... 21 J2
HEANOR DE75 .... 20 D5
HUCK/RAV NG15 .... 14 D2
NOTT NG1 .... 4 F1
Mansfield Road Arch Hl
ARN NG5 .... 25 J5
Mansfields Cft
RDERBYSW DE65 .... 68 F3 2
Mansfield St *ARN* NG5 .... 37 G5
DERBY DE1 .... 43 L8
LEI LE1 .... 6 E4
RLBORO LE12 .... 112 E1
Manston Cl *LEIN* LE4 .... 126 E2
Manthorpe Crs *ARN* NG5 .... 37 K4 2
Mantle La *COAL* LE67 .... 108 A5
Mantle Rd *LEIW* LE3 .... 6 A4
Manton Crs *BSTN/STPLFD* NG9 .... 49 K7
Manvers Av *RIPLEY* DE5 .... 11 J6 1
Manvers Gv *COT/KEY/RAD* NG12 .. 53 K4

Manvers Rd WBRGFD NG2 .... 65 K1
Manvers St CARL NG4 .... 52 E1
  NOTT NG1 .... 5 L7
  RIPLEY DE5 .... 11 J6
  WBRGFD NG2 .... 5 M9
Manville Cl BSTN/STPLFD NG9 .... 48 F4 🔟
  WOL/BIL/BRX NG8 .... 50 A1 ②
Maori Av HUCK/RAV NG15 .... 23 H3
Maple Av BSTN/STPLFD NG9 .... 63 M2 ⑦
  LEIW LE3 .... 130 A4
  LGEAT NG10 .... 47 M8
  NORM/LIT DE23 .... 71 H1
  RIPLEY DE5 .... 11 G7
  RLEIW/BBY LE8 .... 142 F1
Maplebeck Ct DERBY DE1 .... 2 F1
  DERBY DE1 .... 43 L8 ⑧
Maplebeck Rd ARN NG5 .... 25 L8
Maple Cl COT/KEY/RAD NG12 .... 53 K5
  COT/KEY/RAD NG12 .... 80 E5
  RLBORO LE12 .... 88 B7
Mapledene Crs
  WOL/BIL/BRX NG8 .... 49 G4
Maple Dr BPR/DUF DE56 .... 17 M5
  CARL NG4 .... 38 F5
  DERBYSE DE24 .... 72 E1
  EWD/SEL/PNX NG16 .... 34 F1
  HUCK/RAV NG15 .... 23 J3
  MELB/CHEL DE73 .... 72 D5
Maple Gdns HEANOR DE75 .... 20 B6 ②
Maple Gv BWSH/BRSTN DE72 .... 61 K7
  DERBYW DE22 .... 43 H2
Maple Rd LBORO LE11 .... 103 M7
  LEIN LE4 .... 126 B1
Maple Rd North LBORO LE11 .... 103 M7
Maple Rd South LBORO LE11 .... 103 M8
Maples St NOTTE NG7 .... 4 B2
Maplestead Av
  CFTN/RUD NG11 .... 64 F1 ④
Mapleton Av DERBYE DE21 .... 44 D6
Mapleton Rd BWSH/BRSTN DE72 .... 60 D7
  WGSTN LE18 .... 138 A4
Mapletree Wk RLEIW/BAR LE9 .... 136 A8
Maplewell Dr LEIN LE4 .... 124 E1
Maplewell Rd RLBORO LE12 .... 111 J8
Maplin Rd LEIE LE5 .... 127 J6
Mapperley Crs
  MAPPK/POR/STA NG3 .... 37 J5 ⑤
Mapperley Hall
  MAPPK/POR/STA NG3 .... 37 H6 ①
Mapperley Hall Dr
  MAPPK/POR/STA NG3 .... 37 J6 ③
Mapperley La ILK DE7 .... 32 C5
Mapperley Orch ARN NG5 .... 26 A8
Mapperley Plns
  MAPPK/POR/STA NG3 .... 26 A8
Mapperley Ri ARN NG5 .... 37 J4 ①
  MAPPK/POR/STA NG3 .... 37 J5
Mapperley Rd
  MAPPK/POR/STA NG3 .... 5 G2
Mapperley St ARN NG5 .... 37 G5
Marble St LEI LE1 .... 6 E7 ②
March Cl ARN NG5 .... 24 C8
Marchesi Cl HUCK/RAV NG15 .... 23 J3 ③
Marchington Cl DERBYW DE22 .... 43 J6
Marchwood Cl
  WOL/BIL/BRX NG8 .... 50 B2
Marcus Ct RLEINE/SYS LE7 .... 120 C5
Mardale Cl WBRGFD NG2 .... 66 A2
Mardale Wy LBORO LE11 .... 103 H7
Maree Cl DERBYSE DE24 .... 71 J3
Marefield Cl RLEINE/SYS LE7 .... 133 L2
Marfitt St LEIN LE4 .... 125 M5
Marfleet Cl MCKLVR DE3 .... 56 A4
Margaret Anne Rd LEIS LE2 .... 138 F3 ⑧
Margaret Av DERBYE DE21 .... 58 C2
  ILK DE7 .... 33 K7
  LGEAT NG10 .... 61 M3
Margaret Ct LEIN LE4 .... 120 C7
Margaret Crs CARL NG4 .... 38 C5 ⑦
  WGSTN LE18 .... 137 M4
Margaret Rd LEIE LE5 .... 132 C2
Margaret's Ct
  BSTN/STPLFD NG9 .... 48 E7 ②
Margaret St COAL LE67 .... 108 A6
  DERBY DE1 .... 43 L8 ⑧
Margreave Rd DERBYE DE21 .... 44 D8
Marham Cl WBRGFD NG2 .... 5 M9 ①
Marhill Rd CARL NG4 .... 38 D8
Marie Gdns HUCK/RAV NG15 .... 23 L2 ③
Marigold Cl DERBYE DE21 .... 44 F4
Marigold La RLBORO LE12 .... 113 J5
Marigold Wy RLEIW/BAR LE9 .... 135 K7
Marina Av BSTN/STPLFD NG9 .... 63 K2
Marina Dr DERBYE DE21 .... 59 H2
  DERBYSE DE24 .... 72 C2
  GBY/RBY LE6 .... 123 L4
Marina Rd HEANOR DE75 .... 19 M7
  LEIE LE5 .... 132 B3
Marion's Wy RLEIW/BAR LE9 .... 141 H3
Maris Cl CFTN/RUD NG11 .... 64 A5
Maris Dr CALV/BJ NG14 .... 39 J4
Marjorie Rd DERBYE DE21 .... 44 C7
Marjorie St LEIN LE4 .... 125 L6
Markeaton La DERBYW DE22 .... 42 F7
Markeaton St DERBYW DE22 .... 2 A1
Market Head BPR/DUF DE56 .... 17 K4
Market Pl ALFN DE55 .... 12 C1
  BPR/DUF DE56 .... 17 L4 ⑧
  COAL LE67 .... 108 D2
  EWD/SEL/PNX NG16 .... 12 C3
  HEANOR DE75 .... 20 C6
  ILK DE7 .... 33 K7 ⑧
  LBORO LE11 .... 9 J3
  LEI LE1 .... 6 E6
  LGEAT NG10 .... 62 C7
  MELB/CHEL DE73 .... 82 F8 ⑧
  RIPLEY DE5 .... 11 M7
  RIPLEY DE5 .... 19 M1
  RLBORO LE12 .... 101 M3 ⑧
  RLBORO LE12 .... 113 J4
Market Pl South LEI LE1 .... 6 E6
Market St BWSH/BRSTN DE72 .... 60 E8
  COAL LE67 .... 108 A5
  HEANOR DE75 .... 20 C5
  ILK DE7 .... 33 K7
  LBORO LE11 .... 9 H3
  LEI LE1 .... 6 E6
  NOTT NG1 .... 5 G6
Markfield La COAL LE67 .... 116 E7
  COAL LE67 .... 122 A6
  GBY/RBY LE6 .... 117 G6
Markfield Rd COAL LE67 .... 122 C3
  GBY/RBY LE6 .... 122 F5
  GBY/RBY LE6 .... 123 J3
Markham Ct DERBYE DE21 .... 44 D5 ⑦
Markham Crs ARN NG5 .... 37 G3
Markham Rd BSTN/STPLFD NG9 .... 49 H6
Markham St HUCK/RAV NG15 .... 15 H1
Markland LEIS LE2 .... 137 G3
Mark's Cl NORM/LIT DE23 .... 71 H1
Mark St LGEAT NG10 .... 62 A2
Marlborough Dr BPR/DUF DE56 .... 18 A2
Marlborough Rd ARN NG5 .... 37 H2
  BSTN/STPLFD NG9 .... 49 K8
  BWSH/BRSTN DE72 .... 61 H8
  DERBYSE DE24 .... 57 M8
  LGEAT NG10 .... 62 D7
Marlborough Sq COAL LE67 .... 108 A6 ①
Marlborough St LEI LE1 .... 6 F7
  NOTTE NG7 .... 50 C6
Marldon Cl WOL/BIL/BRX NG8 .... 49 G2 ②
Marle Pit HI RLBORO LE12 .... 86 E7
Marl Flds RLBORO LE12 .... 113 K6
Marlow Av BLWL NG6 .... 36 C5
Marlow Crs ILK DE7 .... 32 B7
Marlow Rd RLEIW/BAR LE9 .... 131 H5
Marl Rd COT/KEY/RAD NG12 .... 53 M4
Marlwood COT/KEY/RAD NG12 .... 67 L5
Marmion Rd
  MAPPK/POR/STA NG3 .... 51 L1
Marnham Dr
  MAPPK/POR/STA NG3 .... 37 J6
Maromme Sq WGSTN LE18 .... 138 B4 ②
Marquis St LEI LE1 .... 6 F8 ②
Marriott Av BSTN/STPLFD NG9 .... 62 E2
Marriott Cl BSTN/STPLFD NG9 .... 62 E2
Marriott Dr RLEIW/BBY LE8 .... 146 F7
Marriott Rd LEIS LE2 .... 137 J2
Marsden Av RLEINE/SYS LE7 .... 121 H2
Marsden Cl BPR/DUF DE56 .... 29 J4 ③
Marsden La LEIS LE2 .... 136 F1
Marsden St DERBYSE DE24 .... 58 C8 ①
Marshall Av BSTN/STPLFD NG9 .... 48 E7
Marshall Hill Dr
  MAPPK/POR/STA NG3 .... 37 M6
Marshall Rd CARL NG4 .... 37 L6
Marshall St ARN NG5 .... 37 G5 ⑧
  HEANOR DE75 .... 20 D5
  LEIW LE3 .... 6 A2
Marsh Av RLEIW/BBY LE8 .... 146 F6
Marshaw Cl MCKLVR DE3 .... 56 C6
Marsh Cl LEIN LE4 .... 126 C2
Marsh Dr BPR/DUF DE56 .... 17 M2
Marshgreen Cl DERBYSE DE24 .... 73 H2 ⑦
Marsh La BPR/DUF DE56 .... 17 M2
Marsh Lane Crs
  BPR/DUF DE56 .... 17 M3 ③
Marsh Rd RLBORO LE12 .... 113 J6
Marston Brook
  RDERBYSW DE65 .... 68 C6 ⑧
Marston Cl BPR/DUF DE56 .... 18 A1
  LEIS LE2 .... 138 E4 ①
  NORM/LIT DE23 .... 71 H2
Marston Crs RLEIW/BBY LE8 .... 143 J4
Marston Dr GBY/RBY LE6 .... 123 K4
Marston Rd LEIN LE4 .... 126 C5
  MAPPK/POR/STA NG3 .... 37 M8
  RLEIW/BAR LE9 .... 140 F2
Marstown Av WGSTN LE18 .... 137 K5
Martin Av LEIS LE2 .... 138 F2
  LEIW LE3 .... 129 K4
  RLBORO LE12 .... 105 H8
  RLBORO LE12 .... 113 H6
Martin Cl BLWL NG6 .... 23 K7
  COAL LE67 .... 108 B1
  LEIN LE4 .... 125 M7 ②
  RLEIW/BAR LE9 .... 140 B6
Martindale Cl LBORO LE11 .... 8 B8
  LEIS LE2 .... 131 J4 ②
  WBRGFD NG2 .... 52 A8 ⑦
Martindale Ct BPR/DUF DE56 .... 18 B2 ③
Martin Dr DERBYE DE21 .... 44 E7
  RLEINE/SYS LE7 .... 120 C3
Martinmass Cl NOTTE NG7 .... 50 C5
Martinshaw La GBY/RBY LE6 .... 123 J4
Martins HI CARL NG4 .... 38 C8
Martin St LEIN LE4 .... 125 M7
Martival LEIE LE5 .... 126 C8
Marton Rd BLWL NG6 .... 24 A6
  BSTN/STPLFD NG9 .... 63 G4
Marvin Cl LEIW LE3 .... 124 F8
Marvin Rd BSTN/STPLFD NG9 .... 63 K1 ②
Marwell Cl LEIN LE4 .... 125 K3
Marwood Crs CARL NG4 .... 38 A5
Marwood Rd CARL NG4 .... 38 A6
  LEIN LE4 .... 125 H3
Marydene Ct LEIE LE5 .... 133 G4
Marydene Dr LEIE LE5 .... 133 G4
Maryland Ct BSTN/STPLFD NG9 .... 48 C5
Maryland Rd DERBYE DE21 .... 58 F1
Marylebone Crs DERBYW DE22 .... 56 D2
Mary Rd EWD/SEL/PNX NG16 .... 21 M6
  LEIW LE3 .... 124 F7
Mary's Cl RLBORO LE12 .... 98 A4
Masefield Av NORM/LIT DE23 .... 57 J8
  RLEIW/BAR LE9 .... 135 L5
Masonic Pl NOTT NG1 .... 4 F6
Mason Rd ILK DE7 .... 33 H5
Masons Cl RLEIW/BAR LE9 .... 135 M8 ②
Massey Cl CALV/BJ NG14 .... 39 J4 ①
Massey Gdns
  MAPPK/POR/STA NG3 .... 5 M3
Matlock Av RLEIW/BBY LE8 .... 137 L6 ②
Matlock Ct NOTT NG1 .... 5 G5
Matlock Rd BPR/DUF DE56 .... 17 K2
  DERBYE DE21 .... 44 D6
Matlock St CARL NG4 .... 38 D8
  LEIS LE2 .... 7 L5
Matthew St DERBYSE DE24 .... 72 D1
Matthew Wy NORM/LIT DE23 .... 56 C8 ⑨
Mattingly Rd BLWL NG6 .... 35 L1
Matts Cl LEIS LE2 .... 137 H2
Maud St NOTTE NG7 .... 36 E6

Maun Av NOTTE NG7 .... 50 B1
Maura Cl RLEIW/BBY LE8 .... 142 D2 ③
Maurice Dr
  MAPPK/POR/STA NG3 .... 37 J5
  RLEIW/BBY LE8 .... 143 H4
Mavis Av LEIW LE3 .... 131 G5
Mawby Cl RLEIW/BBY LE8 .... 142 E2
Maws La EWD/SEL/PNX NG16 .... 22 C8
Max Rd DERBYE DE21 .... 44 C7
Maxtoke Rd NOTTE NG7 .... 4 C9
Maxwell Av DERBYW DE22 .... 43 H7
Maxwell Cl NOTTE NG7 .... 4 B9
Maxwell Dr RLEIW/BBY LE8 .... 102 F1
Maxwell St BWSH/BRSTN DE72 .... 61 K7
  LGEAT NG10 .... 62 C8
May Av WOL/BIL/BRX NG8 .... 49 J5
May Ct ARN NG5 .... 36 F6 ①
Maycroft Gdns
  MAPPK/POR/STA NG3 .... 37 L8
Maydene Cl CFTN/RUD NG11 .... 64 B6
Mayes Ri BLWL NG6 .... 24 C3 ①
Mayfair Crs DERBYW DE22 .... 56 C1
Mayfield Av BPR/DUF DE56 .... 18 E7
  CALV/BJ NG14 .... 39 K2
  HEANOR DE75 .... 20 C6
Mayfield Dr BSTN/STPLFD NG9 .... 48 D5
  LBORO LE11 .... 9 H7
  WGSTN LE18 .... 138 B3 ③
Mayfield Gv LGEAT NG10 .... 62 C6
Mayfield Rd CARL NG4 .... 37 M8
  DERBYE DE21 .... 44 C8
  LEIS LE2 .... 132 A4
Mayflower Cl COAL LE67 .... 116 C7
Mayflower Ct WBRGFD NG2 .... 51 L8
Mayflower Rd
  EWD/SEL/PNX NG16 .... 21 M7
  LEIE LE5 .... 133 G1
Maylands BWSH/BRSTN DE72 .... 59 M6 ②
Maylands Av BWSH/BRSTN DE72 .... 61 J7
Maynard Rd LEIS LE2 .... 7 K5
Mayns La RLEIW/BBY LE8 .... 146 B1
Mayo Cl LBORO LE11 .... 103 K8
Mayo Rd ARN NG5 .... 36 F6
Mayor's Wk LEI LE1 .... 131 L4
Maypole CFTN/RUD NG11 .... 64 C4
Maypole La NORM/LIT DE23 .... 56 C8
Maypole Yd NOTT NG1 .... 5 H6
Mays Av MAPPK/POR/STA NG3 .... 52 B1
Mays Cl MAPPK/POR/STA NG3 .... 52 A1 ①
Mays Farm Dr RLEIW/BAR LE9 .... 140 B4
May St DERBYW DE22 .... 2 C1
  ILK DE7 .... 33 J2
Maythorn Cl
  CFTN/RUD NG11 .... 65 G4 ①
Maytree Cl DERBYE DE21 .... 45 G4 ⑬
  LEIW LE3 .... 129 J4
Maytree Dr LEIW LE3 .... 129 J4
May Tree La RLBORO LE12 .... 111 M3
Mccarthy Cl COAL LE67 .... 108 C2 ③
Mc Carthy Rd RLBORO LE12 .... 101 L3
Mc Dowell Wy RLEIW/BAR LE9 .... 135 M8
Mcintosh Rd CARL NG4 .... 38 B4
Mcneil Gv BWSH/BRSTN DE72 .... 60 E8 ①
Mcvicker Cl LEIE LE5 .... 132 F1
Mead Cl DERBYSE DE24 .... 71 K3
Meadfoot Rd BLWL NG6 .... 35 M3
Meadhurst Rd LEIW LE3 .... 130 E2
Meadow LBORO LE11 .... 103 M1
  RIPLEY DE5 .... 11 M7
Meadowbank Ct
  EWD/SEL/PNX NG16 .... 21 H4 ②
Meadowbank Wy
  EWD/SEL/PNX NG16 .... 21 H4
Meadowbrook Rd
  RLEIW/BBY LE8 .... 146 D7
Meadow Cl BWSH/BRSTN DE72 .... 60 E8
  BWSH/BRSTN DE72 .... 61 J8
  DERBYE DE21 .... 59 J3
  EWD/SEL/PNX NG16 .... 21 K3 ②
  GBY/RBY LE6 .... 123 H7
  HUCK/RAV NG15 .... 23 H2 ①
  ILK DE7 .... 33 J2
  RDERBYSW DE65 .... 70 B5 ①
  RLBORO LE12 .... 105 J7 ③
  RLEIW/BAR LE9 .... 140 B4
  WBRGFD NG2 .... 51 J6 ①
Meadow Cottages CARL NG4 .... 38 D8
Meadow Ct BPR/DUF DE56 .... 17 K3
  BPR/DUF DE56 .... 18 E3 ②
  BWSH/BRSTN DE72 .... 74 B1
  RLEIW/BAR LE9 .... 135 L6
Meadow Court Rd
  GBY/RBY LE6 .... 123 K4 ②
Meadowcourt Rd LEIS LE2 .... 132 D8
Meadow Crs CDON/KEG DE74 .... 84 F5
Meadowcroft Cl LEIW LE3 .... 125 M8 ②
Meadow Dr COT/KEY/RAD NG12 .... 80 E4
Meadow Edge
  RLEIW/BAR LE9 .... 135 L5 ①
Meadow End CFTN/RUD NG11 .... 77 M6
Meadow Gdns
  BSTN/STPLFD NG9 .... 63 J3 ②
  LEIS LE2 .... 137 K2
Meadowgrass Cl
  NORM/LIT DE23 .... 70 F1
Meadow Gv WBRGFD NG2 .... 51 J5 ②
Meadow HI RLEIW/BBY LE8 .... 139 L7 ③
Meadow La BSTN/STPLFD NG9 .... 63 J3
  BSTN/STPLFD NG9 .... 63 K4 ①
  CALV/BJ NG14 .... 39 K3
  COAL LE67 .... 108 E6
  COAL LE67 .... 116 C6
  DERBY DE1 .... 3 H3
  DERBYE DE21 .... 58 D2
  DERBYSE DE24 .... 58 D6
  LBORO LE11 .... 9 K1
  LEIN LE4 .... 119 M7
  LGEAT NG10 .... 76 E1
  RLBORO LE12 .... 95 M7
  RLEINE/SYS LE7 .... 120 C3
  WBRGFD NG2 .... 51 J5
  WBRGFD NG2 .... 51 K4 ②
Meadowlark Gv DERBYE DE21 .... 44 E6
Meadow Nook DERBYE DE21 .... 44 F4 ⑦
Meadow Ri EWD/SEL/PNX NG16 .... 35 K1
Meadow Rd BSTN/STPLFD NG9 .... 63 M2
  CARL NG4 .... 52 D1

  DERBY DE1 .... 3 G3
  EWD/SEL/PNX NG16 .... 34 A2
  RIPLEY DE5 .... 11 H6
  RLBORO LE12 .... 111 L6
  RLBORO LE12 .... 113 H8
Meadows Wy WBRGFD NG2 .... 51 H5 ⑤
Meadowsweet Rd LEIE LE5 .... 127 G6 ⑧
Meadow V BPR/DUF DE56 .... 29 H4
Meadowvale Crs
  CFTN/RUD NG11 .... 64 C6
Meadow Vw GBY/RBY LE6 .... 122 A8
  LEIS LE2 .... 138 F2 ⑧
Meadow View Cl
  DERBYE DE21 .... 44 F4 ⑭
Meadow Wy WBRGFD NG2 .... 51 H5 ⑤
  MELB/CHEL DE73 .... 72 D6
  WGSTN LE18 .... 138 D4
The Meads LEIW LE3 .... 130 C2
Meadvale Rd LEIS LE2 .... 132 A8
The Meadway LEIN LE4 .... 130 E1
  RLEINE/SYS LE7 .... 119 L7
  RLEINE/SYS LE7 .... 120 D5
Meadwell Rd LEIW LE3 .... 130 B3
Mear Dr BWSH/BRSTN DE72 .... 59 M6
The Mease RDERBYSW DE65 .... 68 C7
Meath Av DERBYE DE21 .... 58 F3
Medawar Cl CFTN/RUD NG11 .... 64 A6
Meden Cl CFTN/RUD NG11 .... 64 A6
Medhurst Cl RLEIW/BBY LE8 .... 142 E2 ⑧
Medina Cl DERBYSE DE24 .... 73 H2
Medina Dr COT/KEY/RAD NG12 .... 66 B6
Medina Rd LEIW LE3 .... 6 A1
Medway Cl BSTN/STPLFD NG9 .... 62 F2
Medway Dr DERBYW DE22 .... 43 L2
Medway St LEIS LE2 .... 7 L8
  WOL/BIL/BRX NG8 .... 50 B2
Meeks Rd ARN NG5 .... 25 M7
Meerbrook Cl DERBYE DE21 .... 44 E6
Meerbrook Pl ILK DE7 .... 47 G2 ④
Meer Rd BSTN/STPLFD NG9 .... 62 E2
Meeting House Cl RLBORO LE12 .... 88 D6
Meeting St RLBORO LE12 .... 112 D2
Megaloughton La DERBYE DE21 .... 59 G4
Melba Wy RLEINE/SYS LE7 .... 119 M6
Melbourn Cl BPR/DUF DE56 .... 29 J5
Melbourne Cl BPR/DUF DE56 .... 17 L5 ①
  MCKLVR DE3 .... 56 D4
  RLEINE/SYS LE7 .... 146 D7 ⑧
Melbourne Rd
  BSTN/STPLFD NG9 .... 48 C5
  LEIS LE2 .... 7 L8
  WBRGFD NG2 .... 51 K6 ②
  WOL/BIL/BRX NG8 .... 36 A6
Melbourne St COAL LE67 .... 108 A6
  DERBY DE1 .... 2 F7
  EWD/SEL/PNX NG16 .... 13 M1
  LEIS LE2 .... 7 K5
Melbreak Av LBORO LE11 .... 103 J7
Melbreak Cl MCKLVR DE3 .... 56 C4
Melbury Rd WOL/BIL/BRX NG8 .... 35 H7
Melcroft Av LEIW LE3 .... 130 F2 ①
Meldreth Rd
  WOL/BIL/BRX NG8 .... 35 J8 ①
Melford Hall Dr WBRGFD NG2 .... 65 G3
Melford Rd WOL/BIL/BRX NG8 .... 35 H7
Melford St LEIE LE5 .... 126 D8
Melfort Cl DERBYSE DE24 .... 71 K5
Melksham Rd ARN NG5 .... 25 G7
Melland Pl LEIS LE2 .... 137 J2
Mellbreak Cl WBRGFD NG2 .... 66 A1
Mellier Cl RLEIW/BAR LE9 .... 135 L5
Mellor Rd LEIE LE5 .... 130 E2
Mellor's La BPR/DUF DE56 .... 30 A1
Mellors Rd WBRGFD NG2 .... 65 K2
Mellor St DERBYSE DE24 .... 72 C1
Melrose Av ARN NG5 .... 37 G4 ③
  BSTN/STPLFD NG9 .... 63 L2
Melrose Cl DERBYSE DE24 .... 71 J5
Melrose Gdns WBRGFD NG2 .... 65 H3 ⑦
Melrose Rd COAL LE67 .... 100 B8
Melrose St ARN NG5 .... 37 G5 ⑧
  LEIE LE5 .... 125 M6
Melton Av LEIN LE4 .... 126 A2
  MELB/CHEL DE73 .... 82 E7
  NORM/LIT DE23 .... 71 G1
Melton Ct ALFN DE55 .... 12 A1
  LGEAT NG10 .... 61 L2
Melton Dr RLEIW/BAR LE9 .... 141 J7
Melton Gdns
  COT/KEY/RAD NG12 .... 65 L3
Melton Gv WBRGFD NG2 .... 51 J8
Melton La RLBORO LE12 .... 86 F5
Melton Rd COT/KEY/RAD NG12 .... 65 L6
  COT/KEY/RAD NG12 .... 81 L8
  COT/KEY/RAD NG12 .... 81 J5
  LEIN LE4 .... 126 A3
  RLBORO LE12 .... 96 D2
  RLBORO LE12 .... 96 B2
  RLBORO LE12 .... 98 B8
  RLBORO LE12 .... 105 H8
  RLEINE/SYS LE7 .... 115 K7
  RLEINE/SYS LE7 .... 120 C6
  RLEIW/BBY LE8 .... 147 M3
  RMMWB LE14 .... 91 L1
  WBRGFD NG2 .... 51 J8
Melton St LEI LE1 .... 7 H9
Melville Cl LBORO LE11 .... 102 F1 ⑧
  RDERBYSW DE65 .... 68 F4 ⑧
Melville Gdns
  MAPPK/POR/STA NG3 .... 5 H9
Melville St NOTT NG1 .... 5 H9
Memorial Rd DERBYW DE22 .... 43 G5
Memorial Sq COAL LE67 .... 108 A6 ⑧
Memory La LEI LE1 .... 7 G2
Mendip Av LEIN LE4 .... 125 G6
Mendip Cl LGEAT NG10 .... 61 L6 ⑧
  RLBORO LE12 .... 102 A4
Mendip Ct DERBY DE1 .... 44 C5
Menin Rd DERBYW DE22 .... 43 G5
Mennecy Cl RLEIW/BBY LE8 .... 143 H4

Mensa Cl LEIS LE2 .... 7 L6
Mensing Av COT/KEY/RAD NG12 .... 67 J4
Menzies Rd LEIN LE4 .... 125 J5
Mercaston La DERBYW DE22 .... 28 A8
Mercaston Rd DERBYE DE21 .... 44 B7
Merchant Av DERBYE DE21 .... 59 H3
Merchant St DERBY NG6 .... 2 A2
  DERBYW DE22 .... 2 A2
Mercia Dr LEIS LE2 .... 138 D1
Mercia Ms DERBYE DE21 .... 59 H3 ⑧
Mercury Cl BLWL NG6 .... 36 C2 ⑧
  LEIS LE2 .... 7 K7
Mere Beck BWSH/BRSTN DE72 .... 74 B1
Mere Cl LEIE LE5 .... 7 M4
  RLBORO LE12 .... 113 J7
Meredith Cl WBRGFD NG2 .... 50 F6 ⑧
Meredith Ct BSTN/STPLFD NG9 .... 48 C5
Meredith Rd LEIE LE5 .... 130 F6
Meregill Cl ARN NG5 .... 24 D6 ⑧
Mere La RLEINE/SYS LE7 .... 121 K2
  RLEIW/BBY LE8 .... 139 H5
Mere Rd LEIE LE5 .... 7 M8
  LEIS LE2 .... 1 M7
  LEIS LE2 .... 147 J2
  WGSTN LE18 .... 138 C4
The Mere RLEIW/BBY LE8 .... 139 J7
Merevale Av CFTN/RUD NG11 .... 64 D3
Mereway Rd NORM/LIT DE23 .... 79 H2
Mereworth Cl LEIE LE5 .... 126 B7 ⑧
Merganster Wy COAL LE67 .... 108 E7
Meriac Cl ARN NG5 .... 24 D7 ⑧
Meriden Av BSTN/STPLFD NG9 .... 49 L7
Meridian Cl ILK DE7 .... 33 J3
Meridian East LEIW LE3 .... 130 B7
Meridian North LEIW LE3 .... 130 B7
Meridian South LEIW LE3 .... 136 B1
Meridian Wy LEIW LE3 .... 130 B8
Meridian West LEIW LE3 .... 130 B8
Merlin Cl CFTN/RUD NG11 .... 129 L5
  LEIS LE2 .... 129 L5
  RLEIW/BAR LE9 .... 141 J8 ⑧
Merlin Dr HUCK/RAV NG15 .... 23 H3
Merlin Gn DERBYSE DE24 .... 71 H3 ⑧
Merlin Wy ILK DE7 .... 47 L4
  MCKLVR DE3 .... 55 M8
Merridale Rd NORM/LIT DE23 .... 57 G8
Merrill Wy DERBYSE DE24 .... 72 A2
Merrivale Ct
  MAPPK/POR/STA NG3 .... 37 G7
Merrybower Cl
  DERBYSE DE24 .... 71 G4 ⑧
Mersey St BLWL NG6 .... 23 M8
Merthull Rd LEIE LE5 .... 133 G1
Merthyr Ct DERBYE DE21 .... 44 F5 ⑦
Merton Av LEIW LE3 .... 131 G2
  RLEINE/SYS LE7 .... 120 F4
Merton Cl ARN NG5 .... 25 M6
  RLEIW/BAR LE9 .... 141 H8
Merton Ct BSTN/STPLFD NG9 .... 48 C6
  RLEIW/BBY LE8 .... 146 D6
Mervyn Rd LEIE LE5 .... 132 B3
Messenger Cl LBORO LE11 .... 95 J3
Metcalf Cl RLEIW/BAR LE9 .... 140 B5 ①
Metcalfe Cl DERBYSE DE24 .... 58 F7
Metcalf Rd EWD/SEL/PNX NG16 .... 21 M4
Methuen Av LEIN LE4 .... 120 C7
Mettham St NOTTE NG7 .... 4 A9 ⑧
Meynell Cl LEIS LE2 .... 139 G3
Meynell Ct DERBYE DE22 .... 43 G5
Meynell Gv NOTTE NG7 .... 36 E7 ⑧
Meynell Rd LEIE LE5 .... 126 B8
  LGEAT NG10 .... 76 B2
Meynell St NORM/LIT DE23 .... 57 K5
Michael Cl RLEINE/SYS LE7 .... 121 J1
Michael Ramsey Ct LEIS LE2 .... 137 G4 ⑧
Michelle Cl DERBYSE DE24 .... 71 G4 ⑧
Michigan Cl DERBYE DE21 .... 59 G2
Mickleborough Av
  MAPPK/POR/STA NG3 .... 37 K7
Mickleborough Wy
  CFTN/RUD NG11 .... 65 G4
Micklebring Cl RIPLEY DE5 .... 11 G6 ③
Micklecroft Gdns
  NORM/LIT DE23 .... 56 C8 ⑧
Mickleden Cl WBRGFD NG2 .... 66 A1
Mickleden Gn COAL LE67 .... 108 E5
Mickledon Cl LGEAT NG10 .... 61 M7 ③
Mickleross Cl MCKLVR DE3 .... 56 B3 ①
Mickleton Dr LEIE LE5 .... 132 F4
Middle Av CARL NG4 .... 38 A7
  LBORO LE11 .... 103 K1
Middlebeck Av ARN NG5 .... 26 A7 ⑧
Middlebeck Cl MELB/CHEL DE73 .... 72 D6
Middlebeck Dr ARN NG5 .... 26 A7
Middlebrook Rd
  EWD/SEL/PNX NG16 .... 13 L3
Middledale Rd CARL NG4 .... 52 A1
Middlefell Wy CFTN/RUD NG11 .... 64 A6
Middlefield Rd RLEINE/SYS LE7 .... 114 B8
Middle Furlong Ms
  WBRGFD NG2 .... 50 F5 ⑧
Middle HI NOTT NG1 .... 5 H7
Middle La BSTN/STPLFD NG9 .... 63 J2 ⑧
Middle Nook
  WOL/BIL/BRX NG8 .... 49 J2 ⑧
Middle Orch RLBORO LE12 .... 114 A6 ⑧
Middlesex Rd LEIS LE2 .... 131 H8
Middleton Av NORM/LIT DE23 .... 57 G5
  RIPLEY DE5 .... 19 M2
Middleton Bvd
  WOL/BIL/BRX NG8 .... 50 A3
Middleton Cl
  EWD/SEL/PNX NG16 .... 35 G1 ①
  RLEIW/BAR LE9 .... 140 C5
  WGSTN LE18 .... 138 D4 ②
Middleton Crs
  BSTN/STPLFD NG9 .... 49 J6
Middleton Dr NORM/LIT DE23 .... 57 G5 ③
Middleton Pl LBORO LE11 .... 9 H7
Middleton Rd ILK DE7 .... 47 L2
Middleton St BSTN/STPLFD NG9 .... 49 J8
  EWD/SEL/PNX NG16 .... 34 A3 ⑧
  ILK DE7 .... 33 L6
  LEIS LE2 .... 131 G8
Midhurst Av LEIW LE3 .... 130 D7 ⑧
Midhurst Cl BSTN/STPLFD NG9 .... 63 J3

Midhurst Wy CFTN/RUD NG11 64 C5
Midlame Gdns BLWL NG6 23 K8 4
Midland Av BSTN/STPLFD NG9 62 A2
CARL NG4 38 E8 10
NOTTE NG7 50 C4
Midland Crs CARL NG4 38 D8
Midland Gv CARL NG4 38 E7
Midland Pl DERBY DE1 3 J6
Midland Rd CARL NG4 38 D8
DERBY DE1 3 H7
EWD/SEL/PNX NG16 21 K5
HEANOR DE75 20 C5
Midland St LEI LE1 7 H5
LGEAT NG10 62 C7 1
Midshires Wy BPR/DUF DE56 17 G1
CDON/KEG DE74 76 A8
COT/KEY/RAD NG12 90 A4
ILK DE7 45 M3
ILK DE7 45 K1
RLBORO LE12 88 E5
Midway DERBYW DE22 43 J5 3
Midway Rd LEIE LE5 132 B5
The Midway NOTTE NG7 50 C7
Mikado Rd LGEAT NG10 76 A2
Milbank Cl DERBYW DE22 56 C1 2
Milburn Gdns DERBYE DE21 44 F4 15
Milbury Cl DERBYE DE21 44 D5
Mildenhall Crs ARN NG5 25 G7
Mildenhall Rd LBORO LE11 103 G3
Mile Ash La DERBYW DE22 43 K6
Mile End Rd CARL NG4 52 C2
Milestone Cl RLEIW/BBY LE8 147 G7 1
Milford Av LGEAT NG10 61 M4
Milford Cl BLWL NG6 23 L7
RLEIW/BAR LE9 135 L7 3
Milford Dr ILK DE7 33 H4
MAPPK/POR/STA NG3 38 A8
Milford Rd BPR/DUF DE56 29 J3
LEIS LE2 131 M7
Milford St DERBY DE1 43 K8
Mill Acre Cl ILK DE7 33 G5
Millbank Av BPR/DUF DE56 17 M5 3
Millbank Cl ILK DE7 33 H4 7
Millbeck Av WOL/BIL/BRX NG8 49 G3 2
Millbeck Cl WBRGFD NG2 66 A1
Millbrook Cl LEIN LE4 125 K4
Mill Cl BPR/DUF DE56 18 E7 6
BWSH/BRSTN DE72 60 A6
LEIN LE4 125 M1
RDERBYSW DE65 70 B5
RLBORO LE12 102 A2
RLEIW/BAR LE9 140 C7
WGSTN LE18 137 K7
The Mill Cl BLWL NG6 36 C4
Mill Crs ARN NG5 25 J7
Mill Cft MCKLVR DE3 56 B3
Milldale Cl CFTN/RUD NG11 64 A5
RIPLEY DE5 19 H1 1
Milldale Ct BPR/DUF DE56 17 M4 1
Milldale Rd DERBYE DE21 59 K4
LGEAT NG10 75 M1
Mill Dr GBY/RBY LE6 123 H8
Millennium Wy East BLWL NG6 35 L3
Millennium Wy West
EWD/SEL/PNX NG16 35 L3
Miller Cl LEIN LE4 126 C2 1
Miller Hives Cl
COT/KEY/RAD NG12 67 J4
Millers Br COT/KEY/RAD NG12 67 J5
Millers Cl LEIW LE3 123 L7
RLEINE/SYS LE7 120 E5
Millers Ct NOTTE NG7 50 C1 3
Millersdale Av ILK DE7 33 J2 7
LEIE LE5 133 H2
Millersdale Cl BPR/DUF DE56 17 M2
Miller's La RLBORO LE12 89 G6
Millfield BWSH/BRSTN DE72 74 F5
Mill Field Cl CALV/BJ NG14 39 J4
Millfield Cl ILK DE7 33 G4 10
RLEINE/SYS LE7 124 B2
Millfield Crs LEIW LE3 136 D1
Millfield Rd EWD/SEL/PNX NG16 22 C8
ILK DE7 33 L8
Mill Fleam RDERBYSW DE65 68 C6 6
Mill Hl DERBYSE DE24 73 G3
RLEIW/BAR LE9 135 K2
Mill Hill Cl RLEIW/BBY LE8 136 D8
Mill Hill La BWSH/BRSTN DE72 61 J6
COAL LE67 116 B6
LEIS LE2 7 J9
NORM/LIT DE23 2 D8
Mill Hill Rd NORM/LIT DE23 2 D8 2
Millhouse Ct
BWSH/BRSTN DE72 60 F8 5
Millicent Gv WBRGFD NG2 51 K7 2
Millicent Rd WBRGFD NG2 51 J7
Milligan Rd LEIS LE2 137 J1
Mill La BPR/DUF DE56 17 M4
CARL NG4 26 F8
CDON/KEG DE74 86 B5
COT/KEY/RAD NG12 67 J3
EWD/SEL/PNX NG16 34 A6
LBORO LE11 9 L1
LEIN LE4 120 B7
LEIS LE2 6 C8
LGEAT NG10 61 M1
MCKLVR DE3 56 B3
RDERBYSW DE65 68 A5
RIPLEY DE5 11 M7
RLBORO LE12 88 D7
RLBORO LE12 91 H7
RLBORO LE12 92 F8
RLBORO LE12 94 A4
RLBORO LE12 113 G1
RLEIW/BAR LE9 134 B8
RLEIW/BAR LE9 135 M4
RLEIW/BBY LE8 137 J8
RLEIW/BBY LE8 146 D8
Mill Meadow Wy
RDERBYSW DE65 68 F3
Mill Moor Cl MELB/CHEL DE73 72 C5 2
Millom Pl DERBYE DE21 44 B6
Mill Rd BSTN/STPLFD NG9 48 B7
EWD/SEL/PNX NG16 21 M4
HEANOR DE75 20 E7
RLBORO LE12 111 K6
RLEINE/SYS LE7 115 K6
RLEINE/SYS LE7 118 F4
Mills Armston Rd RLBORO LE12 112 E2
Mills Cl BWSH/BRSTN DE72 60 E8
The Mills RLBORO LE12 112 E2
Millstone La LEI LE1 6 E7
RLEINE/SYS LE7 121 G2
Mill St BLWL NG6 36 B4 4
BPR/DUF DE56 17 K3
DERBY DE1 2 B2
ILK DE7 33 K6
LEI LE1 6 F8
Mill Vw RLEIW/BAR LE9 135 H8
Mill View Cl WBRGFD NG2 51 K3 3
Millwood Cl LEIN LE4 125 J2
Milner Av BWSH/BRSTN DE72 60 E8
RIPLEY DE5 11 M7
Milner Cl RLBORO LE12 114 A5
Milner Rd ARN NG5 37 G5
LGEAT NG10 62 B7
Milnhay Rd EWD/SEL/PNX NG16 21 G5
Milnroy Rd LEIE LE5 133 J1
Milton Av ILK DE7 33 J3
Milton Cl WGSTN LE18 138 C5
Milton Ct ARN NG5 25 M8
Milton Crs BSTN/STPLFD NG9 63 H5
LEIN LE4 124 F5
Milton Gdns LEIS LE2 138 E2 5
Milton Ri HUCK/RAV NG15 23 H2
Milton Rd ILK DE7 33 J3
MCKLVR DE3 56 A4
Milton St DERBYW DE22 57 H3
ILK DE7 33 K3
LGEAT NG10 62 B8
NOTT NG1 5 H5
RLEIW/BAR LE9 135 L6
Milverton Av LEIN LE4 125 H6
Milverton Cl WGSTN LE18 138 A3
Milverton Dr WGSTN LE18 138 A3
Milverton Rd ARN NG5 25 G7
Milward Rd HEANOR DE75 20 A5
Mimosa Cl CFTN/RUD NG11 64 A6 3
RLBORO LE12 111 L1 5
Mimosa Crs NORM/LIT DE23 71 J2
Minehead St LEIW LE3 130 F2
Minerva St BLWL NG6 23 M7
Minster Cl HUCK/RAV NG15 15 M7
Minster Crs LEIN LE4 125 H6
Minster Gdns
EWD/SEL/PNX NG16 21 M6 5
Minster Rd DERBYE DE21 44 C5
Mint Gv LGEAT NG10 61 L8
Minton Cl BSTN/STPLFD NG9 62 F6 4
Minton Rd CDON/KEG DE74 84 D3
Mint Rd LEIS LE2 6 B9
Minver Crs WOL/BIL/BRX NG8 35 M6
Misk Hollows HUCK/RAV NG15 15 K7
Misk Vw EWD/SEL/PNX NG16 21 M5 2
Mission St
MAPPK/POR/STA NG3 37 J5 5
Misterton Cl DERBYW DE22 43 J5 4
Mitchell Av EWD/SEL/PNX NG16 20 E3
Mitchell Cl BLWL NG6 35 K1
Mitchell Dr LBORO LE11 103 G1
Mitchell Rd RLEIW/BAR LE9 135 L4
Mitchell St LGEAT NG10 62 C8
Mitchell Ter ILK DE7 47 L2
Moat Cl RLEIW/BAR LE9 134 D4
Moat Rd LBORO LE11 103 J7
LEIE LE5 132 B2
Moat St WGSTN LE18 138 A5
The Moat CDON/KEG DE74 84 F3 1
Modbury Av LEIN LE4 125 J3 2
Moira Cl DERBYE DE21 44 E8 2
Moira Dl CDON/KEG DE74 85 G4
Moira St LBORO LE11 9 K4
LEIN LE4 125 M6
MELB/CHEL DE73 82 E8 2
Molineux St NORM/LIT DE23 57 M5
Mollington Sq BLWL NG6 35 M3 3
Molyneux Dr RLBORO LE12 114 B6
Monal Cl RLEIW/BBY LE8 142 D3 2
Monarch Dr DERBYE DE21 45 H4
Monarch Wy HEANOR DE75 20 B5
LBORO LE11 103 L1
Monar Cl LEIN LE4 126 B3
Mona Rd WBRGFD NG2 51 L6
Mona St BSTN/STPLFD NG9 63 L1
Monckton Cl LEI LE1 7 H2 1
Moncrieff Crs DERBYE DE21 44 E7
Mondello Dr DERBYSE DE24 73 G1
Monica Rd LEIW LE3 130 D8
Monks Cl DERBYSE DE24 71 G5
ILK DE7 33 L7
Monks Crs LEIN LE4 119 G7
Monk's La CFTN/RUD NG11 77 L6
Monks Meadow RLBORO LE12 88 D5
Monk St DERBYW DE22 2 C5
Monksway CFTN/RUD NG11 64 E3
Monkton Cl ILK DE7 33 H4 3
Monkton Dr WOL/BIL/BRX NG8 35 J8
Monmouth Cl
WOL/BIL/BRX NG8 48 F3 5
Monmouth Dr LEIS LE2 137 G5
Monmouth St DERBYE DE21 3 L1
Monroe Wk ARN NG5 24 E8 1
Monsaldale Cl LGEAT NG10 75 M1
Monsal Dr DERBYE DE21 59 K4
Monsall Av ILK DE7 33 J2 3
Monsall St NOTTE NG7 36 D6
Monsarrat Wy LBORO LE11 103 H1 5
Monsell Dr ARN NG5 25 J6
LEIS LE2 137 G2
Montague Av RLEINE/SYS LE7 120 F5
Montague Dr LBORO LE11 103 G7
Montague Rd HUCK/RAV NG15 15 L7
LEIS LE2 131 M5
RLEIW/BAR LE9 141 K8
Montague St BLWL NG6 24 A8
BSTN/STPLFD NG9 49 J8
Monteith Pl CDON/KEG DE74 84 F3 2
Montford Ms CDON/KEG DE74 84 F3 3
Montfort Crs ARN NG5 37 H3
Montfort St NOTTE NG7 4 C6
Montgomery Cl
BSTN/STPLFD NG9 63 G5 4
RDERBYSW DE65 68 C5 4
Montgomery St NOTTE NG7 4 D4 2
Montpelier DERBYW DE22 29 H8
Montpelier Rd NOTTE NG7 50 C6
Montreal Rd LEI LE1 7 H2
Montrose Cl DERBYSE DE24 71 J3
Montrose Ct
BSTN/STPLFD NG9 48 C6 6
Montrose Rd LEIS LE2 137 G2
Montrose Rd South LEIS LE2 137 G2
Montsoreau Wy
RLBORO LE12 113 H7 4
Monument Hl
EWD/SEL/PNX NG16 12 D4
Monument La
EWD/SEL/PNX NG16 12 C5
Monyash Cl DERBYE DE21 44 E7
ILK DE7 33 J4
Monyash Wy BPR/DUF DE56 17 M2
Moon Cl LEIS LE2 7 J7 1
Moor Br BLWL NG6 24 B5
Moorbridge La
BSTN/STPLFD NG9 48 A6
Moor Dr DERBYSE DE24 72 E2
Moore Av CDON/KEG DE74 86 B4
Moore Cl RLBORO LE12 88 D5
WBRGFD NG2 51 M6
Moore Ga BSTN/STPLFD NG9 63 L1 2
Moor End DERBYE DE21 59 J2 2
Moore Rd MAPPK/POR/STA NG3 37 L5
Moores Av LGEAT NG10 48 A8
Moores Cl WGSTN LE18 137 J5
Moores La RLEIW/BAR LE9 135 M4
Moores Rd LEIN LE4 125 M5
Moore St NORM/LIT DE23 2 E8
Moor Farm Inn La
BSTN/STPLFD NG9 48 E5
Moorfield Ct
BSTN/STPLFD NG9 48 C6 7
Moorfield Crs LGEAT NG10 61 M2
Moorfield Pl RLBORO LE12 101 M3
Moorfield Rd BPR/DUF DE56 18 A8
Moorfields LEIE LE5 127 H7
Moorfields Av
EWD/SEL/PNX NG16 21 K4
Moorgate DERBYW DE22 56 C1 3
Moorgate Av LEIN LE4 119 K7
Moorgate St LEIN LE4 125 L7
NOTTE NG7 4 C5
Moorgreen EWD/SEL/PNX NG16 22 A4
Moorgreen Dr
WOL/BIL/BRX NG8 35 H5
Moorhead Av DERBYSE DE24 72 D2 3
Moorhouse Rd
WOL/BIL/BRX NG8 49 J1
The Moorings WBRGFD NG2 50 D5
Moorland Av BSTN/STPLFD NG9 62 B1
Moorland Rd MCKLVR DE3 56 B4
RLEINE/SYS LE7 120 C3 1
Moorlands Cl LGEAT NG10 61 M5
Moor La ASHB DE6 41 K5
BSTN/STPLFD NG9 48 F5
BWSH/BRSTN DE72 46 A8
BWSH/BRSTN DE72 73 M7
CFTN/RUD NG11 77 M6
CFTN/RUD NG11 78 B6
CFTN/RUD NG11 79 H7
CFTN/RUD NG11 79 G1
CFTN/RUD NG11 79 J5
DERBYE DE21 30 B6
DERBYSE DE24 71 M6
DERBYSE DE24 72 A1
ILK DE7 46 D5
LBORO LE11 9 K3
LBORO LE11 104 B4
MELB/CHEL DE73 71 M8
MELB/CHEL DE73 92 A4
RLBORO LE12 95 G3
Moorpool Crs BPR/DUF DE56 18 A8 2
Moor Ri BPR/DUF DE56 18 A7
Moor Rd BLWL NG6 24 C2
EWD/SEL/PNX NG16 13 J7
ILK DE7 44 D1
WOL/BIL/BRX NG8 35 H6
Moorsholm Dr
WOL/BIL/BRX NG8 49 H3
Moorside Crs DERBYSE DE24 71 K3
Moorside La BPR/DUF DE56 18 A7
Moor St CARL NG4 38 E8
DERBYE DE21 59 J2
The Moor EWD/SEL/PNX NG16 13 H7
Moorway ILK DE7 44 C3
Moorway Cft NORM/LIT DE23 56 F8 5
Moorway La NORM/LIT DE23 70 E2
Moray Ct EWD/SEL/PNX NG16 22 D8 5
Morban Rd LEIS LE2 136 F1
Morcote Rd LEIW LE3 130 C3
Morden Cl WOL/BIL/BRX NG8 35 H7
Morden Rd EWD/SEL/PNX NG16 22 A7
Morefern Dr DERBYE DE21 44 D5
Moreland St WBRGFD NG2 51 K4
Morello Av CARL NG4 38 D8
Moreton Dl RLBORO LE12 114 B3
Moreton Rd CFTN/RUD NG11 64 C8
Morgan Ms CFTN/RUD NG11 64 B5 2
Morgans Orch RLBORO LE12 105 H7
Morkinshire La
COT/KEY/RAD NG12 67 J3
Morland Av LEIS LE2 132 C7
Morledge DERBY DE1 2 F4
Morledge St LEIE LE5 7 H5
Morleston St NORM/LIT DE23 3 G8
Morley Almshouses La ILK DE7 30 F8
Morley Av MAPPK/POR/STA NG3 37 J5
Morley Cl BPR/DUF DE56 18 C1
Morley Dr ILK DE7 33 H4
Morleyfields Cl RIPLEY DE5 11 K6
Morley Gdns DERBYE DE21 44 F7
Morley La ILK DE7 30 D7
ILK DE7 45 M1
RLBORO LE12 101 L6
Morley Rd DERBYE DE21 44 E8
LEIE LE5 7 M5
MAPPK/POR/STA NG3 37 L7
RLEIW/BAR LE9 140 C8
Morley St ARN NG5 37 H1
DERBYW DE22 57 G1
LBORO LE11 104 A2
Morlich Dr DERBYSE DE24 71 H3
Morningside Cl
DERBYSE DE24 72 B3 1
Mornington Cl LGEAT NG10 61 M1
Mornington Crs
DERBYW DE22 56 F1 2
EWD/SEL/PNX NG16 35 H4 3
WOL/BIL/BRX NG8 35 H4
Mornington St LEIE LE5 126 B8
Morpeth Av LEIN LE4 125 H2
Morpeth Dr LEIS LE2 139 H3 7
Morpeth Gdns DERBYE DE21 44 B5 2
Morrell Bank ARN NG5 36 D1
Morrell Wood Dr
BPR/DUF DE56 18 C2 3
Morris Av BSTN/STPLFD NG9 62 F6 5
Morris Cl LBORO LE11 9 M3
LEIW LE3 130 B5
Morrison Ct RLEIW/BBY LE8 146 E7
Morris Rd LEIS LE2 131 L6
WOL/BIL/BRX NG8 35 H6
Morris St CARL NG4 38 E8
Mortiboys Wy
RLEIW/BAR LE9 140 B5 2
Mortimer Pl LEIW LE3 130 F6 2
Mortimer St DERBYSE DE24 57 M8
Mortimer Wy LBORO LE11 102 F1
LEIW LE3 130 E6 2
Mortoft Rd LEIN LE4 125 M4 3
Morval Rd WOL/BIL/BRX NG8 35 J8
Morven Av HUCK/RAV NG15 23 M1
The Morwoods LEIS LE2 138 E2
Moscow La RLBORO LE12 101 L6
Mosedale Cl DERBYSE DE24 58 D7 1
Moseley St RIPLEY DE5 11 H5
Moses La ILK DE7 31 J8
Mosley St HUCK/RAV NG15 23 L1
NOTTE NG7 36 D7
Moss Cl ARN NG5 25 G7 6
Mosscroft Av CFTN/RUD NG11 64 B6 3
Mossdale COAL LE67 108 C1
Mossdale Cl LEIS LE2 131 J4
Mossdale Rd ARN NG5 37 G2
LEIW LE3 130 C7
Moss Dr BSTN/STPLFD NG9 48 F8
Mosse Wy LEIS LE2 139 G1
Mossgate LEIW LE3 124 E8
Moss La RIPLEY DE5 11 H4
Moss Rd HUCK/RAV NG15 15 K8
ILK DE7 33 J8
Moss Side CFTN/RUD NG11 64 E4
Moss St DERBYW DE22 2 A7
Mosswood Crs ARN NG5 24 F8
Mostyn Av NORM/LIT DE23 57 H6
RLEINE/SYS LE7 121 G3
Mostyn St LEIW LE3 130 F2
Mottisford Rd LEIN LE4 125 K3
Mottistone Cl DERBYSE DE24 73 H2 3
Mottram Rd BSTN/STPLFD NG9 63 G1
Moult Av DERBYE DE21 59 J3
Moulton Cl BPR/DUF DE56 18 B2 6
Mountain Rd LEIN LE4 126 E3
Mount Av LEIE LE5 132 B1 4
Mountbatten Cl
DERBYSE DE24 72 C3 5
Mountbatten Gv CARL NG4 38 C5 5
Mountbatten Wy
BSTN/STPLFD NG9 62 F5
Mount Carmel St NORM/LIT DE23 2 D8
Mountcastle Rd LEIW LE3 131 G5
Mountfield Av LGEAT NG10 61 L3
Mountfield Dr ARN NG5 24 E8
Mountfields Dr LBORO LE11 8 D6
Mountfield Wy
DERBYSE DE24 73 H3 1
Mountford Cl DERBYE DE21 44 F5 5
Mount Grace Rd LBORO LE11 102 F2
Mount Hooton Rd NOTTE NG7 4 C2
Mount Pleasant ALFN DE55 12 B2
BLWL NG6 36 B5
CARL NG4 38 C8
CDON/KEG DE74 84 F4 2
COT/KEY/RAD NG12 53 J4 2
COT/KEY/RAD NG12 80 D4
ILK DE7 33 J3
LEIS LE2 139 H3
RIPLEY DE5 11 H5
Mount Pleasant Dr
BPR/DUF DE56 17 J2
Mount Rd LEIE LE5 7 L4
LEIS LE2 138 F2 2
RLEIW/BAR LE9 142 B4
Mountsorrel Dr WBRGFD NG2 65 M1
Mountsorrel La RLBORO LE12 113 L4
Mount St BSTN/STPLFD NG9 48 C8
BWSH/BRSTN DE72 61 K8
DERBY DE1 2 E7
HEANOR DE75 20 C6 2
NOTT NG1 4 F7
NOTTE NG7 36 D6
The Mount ARN NG5 25 H6
BSTN/STPLFD NG9 62 B1
MAPPK/POR/STA NG3 37 M5
RLEINE/SYS LE7 127 K7
Mowbray Dr RLEINE/SYS LE7 121 G3
Mowbray Gdns
DERBYSE DE24 58 A7 2
WBRGFD NG2 65 K2 2
Mowbray Ri ARN NG5 25 K7
Mowbray St DERBYSE DE24 58 A7
Mowmacre Hl LEIN LE4 125 J2
Mowsley End WGSTN LE18 138 B5 3
Moy Av DERBYSE DE24 71 K5
Moyne Gdns MELB/CHEL DE73 72 E7
Moyra Dr ARN NG5 25 G8
Muckle Gate La RLBORO LE12 106 D6
Mudpie La WBRGFD NG2 52 A6
Muir Av COT/KEY/RAD NG12 66 B7
Muirfield Cl LEIW LE3 130 A1 2
Muirfield Dr MCKLVR DE3 56 D6
Muirfield Rd ARN NG5 24 E6
Mulberries Ct DERBYW DE22 43 J3 6
Mulberry Av LEIW LE3 130 A1
Mulberry Cl BPR/DUF DE56 17 M4 2
WBRGFD NG2 64 F2
Mulberry Gv HUCK/RAV NG15 23 M3 2
Mulberry Ms RIPLEY DE5 19 G1 1
Mulberry Wy RDERBYSW DE65 68 C5
Mull Ct DERBYSE DE24 71 H4 14
Mullion Pl DERBYSE DE24 72 F2
Mull Wy RLEIW/BBY LE8 143 K4
Mundella Rd WBRGFD NG2 51 H6
Mundella St LEIS LE2 132 A4 1
Mundy Cl DERBY DE1 2 B1
RLBORO LE12 97 K8
Mundy's Dr HEANOR DE75 20 D7
Mundy St DERBY DE1 2 B1
HEANOR DE75 20 C6
ILK DE7 33 K5 4
Munford Circ
WOL/BIL/BRX NG8 35 M4 2
Munks Av HUCK/RAV NG15 15 K8
Munnings Cl LEIN LE4 7 J1 1
Muntjack Rd RLEIW/BBY LE8 142 D2
Murby Crs BLWL NG6 23 M7
Murby Wy LEIW LE3 130 A6
Murden Wy BSTN/STPLFD NG9 63 M1
Murdoch Ri LBORO LE11 103 H1
Muriel Rd BSTN/STPLFD NG9 49 K8
LEIW LE3 131 G2
Muriel St BLWL NG6 23 M8
Murrayfield Rd LEIW LE3 130 A2
Murray Rd MCKLVR DE3 56 D3
Murray St DERBYSE DE24 58 D7 2
LEIS LE2 7 K5
Muscovey Rd COAL LE67 108 E7 5
Museum Sq LEI LE1 7 G8 2
Musgrove Cl LEIW LE3 6 A7
Mushill La RLBORO LE12 98 B2
Muskham Av ILK DE7 33 K4
Muskham St WBRGFD NG2 51 H6 5
Musson Rd LEIW LE3 124 C8
Musters Crs WBRGFD NG2 65 K2 2
Musters Cft CARL NG4 52 D4
Musters Rd CFTN/RUD NG11 78 F1
HUCK/RAV NG15 15 H1
WBRGFD NG2 51 J7
Muston Cl
MAPPK/POR/STA NG3 37 K6 4
Muswell Rd DERBYW DE22 56 C2
Myers Cl DERBYSE DE24 71 K3
Myrtle Av BSTN/STPLFD NG9 62 C1
LGEAT NG10 76 A1
NOTTE NG7 36 F7 5
RLEINE/SYS LE7 119 M6
Myrtle Gv BSTN/STPLFD NG9 49 L8
Myrtle Rd CARL NG4 38 A7
LEIS LE2 7 M9 3
Myrtus Cl CFTN/RUD NG11 64 A5

N

Nabbs La HUCK/RAV NG15 23 J2
Nagle Gv LEIN LE4 126 B2
Nailers Wy BPR/DUF DE56 18 A2
Nairn Av DERBYE DE21 44 B8
Nairn Cl ARN NG5 25 M6 5
DERBYSE DE24 71 H4
Namur Cl DERBYW DE22 57 G4
Namur Rd WGSTN LE18 137 J4
Nanhill Dr RLBORO LE12 111 L7
Nanpantan Rd LBORO LE11 8 B9
RLBORO LE12 110 D2
Nansen Rd LEIE LE5 132 C3
Nansen St BLWL NG6 36 A1
Naomi Crs BLWL NG6 24 A6
Napier Cl MCKLVR DE3 56 C3 1
Napier St DERBYW DE22 57 G2 1
Narborough Rd LEIW LE3 6 B8
LEIW LE3 131 G4
RLEIW/BAR LE9 135 H8
RLEIW/BAR LE9 142 A2
Narborough Rd North LEIW LE3 6 B7
Narborough Rd South
LEIW LE3 136 D1
RLEIW/BAR LE9 136 C2
Narrow Boat Cl WGSTN LE18 137 L7 3
Narrow La EWD/SEL/PNX NG16 22 D6
LEIS LE2 137 G1
RLBORO LE12 94 E6
RLBORO LE12 98 B4
Naseby Cl ARN NG5 36 D3
WGSTN LE18 138 C5 7
Naseby Dr LBORO LE11 102 E5
LGEAT NG10 76 B2
Naseby Rd BPR/DUF DE56 18 B3
LEIN LE4 126 C5
Naseby Wy RLEIW/BBY LE8 139 M7
Nathaniel Rd LGEAT NG10 62 C8
Nathans La COT/KEY/RAD NG12 52 D8
Navigation St LEI LE1 6 F2
Navigation Wy LBORO LE11 103 L2
The Navins RLBORO LE12 113 J5
Naworth Cl BLWL NG6 36 B2
Naylor Av CFTN/RUD NG11 77 M6
LBORO LE11 104 B5
Naylor Rd RLEINE/SYS LE7 121 G2
Neal Av LEIW LE3 130 C5
Neal Ct EWD/SEL/PNX NG16 20 E4 5
Neale St LGEAT NG10 62 C8
Near Meadow LGEAT NG10 76 C2
Nearsby Dr WBRGFD NG2 65 M1
Nearwood Dr DERBYE DE21 44 C4 3
Necton St RLEINE/SYS LE7 120 E4
Nedham St LEIE LE5 7 K4
Needham Av LEIS LE2 136 E4
Needham Cl LEIS LE2 139 J3 2
Needham Rd ARN NG5 25 L7
Needham St RIPLEY DE5 11 M8
Need Wood Av
BSTN/STPLFD NG9 48 B5 6
Needwood Wy
RLEIW/BAR LE9 135 K5 1
Neeps Cft CALV/BJ NG14 27 L1
Neighwood Cl
BSTN/STPLFD NG9 62 C5
Neilson St DERBYSE DE24 58 D8
Nell Gwyn Crs ARN NG5 25 G6
Nelot Wy LEIE LE5 132 F2 2
Nelper Crs ILK DE7 47 L2
Nelson Cl MCKLVR DE3 56 C4
RLBORO LE12 102 B3
Nelson Flds COAL LE67 108 E6
Nelson Rd ARN NG5 25 J8
BLWL NG6 24 A8
BSTN/STPLFD NG9 63 L3
Nelson St DERBY DE1 3 J7 2
ILK DE7 33 K3

LEI LE1 .... 7 H8
LGEAT NG10 .... 62 B9
NOTT NG1 .... 5 K7
RLEINE/SYS LE7 .... 120 F4
Nene CI HUCK/RAV NG15 ...... 23 J4
Nene Dr LEIS LE2 .... 139 G2
Nene Wy COAL LE67 .... 108 E8
RDERBYSW DE65 .... 68 B7
Neptune CI LEIS LE2 .... 7 L6
Nesfield CI DERBYSE DE24 ... 59 G8
Nesfield Ct ILK DE7 .... 33 J6
Nesfield Rd ILK DE7 .... 33 J6
Ness Wk DERBYW DE22 .... 43 J4
Neston Dr BLWL NG6 .... 35 M3
Neston Gdns LEIS LE2 .... 137 K1
Neston Rd LEIS LE2 .... 137 K1
Nether CI BPR/DUF DE56 ..... 29 H2
EWD/SEL/PNX NG16 .... 21 K3
MAPPK/POR/STA NG3 .... 51 L1
Netherclose Rd
NORM/LIT DE23 .... 57 L6
Netherfield La CDON/KEG DE74 ... 75 J8
Netherfield Rd LGEAT NG10 ... 61 M2
LGEAT NG10 .... 75 M3
RLEINE/SYS LE7 .... 118 B8
Nether Field Wy LEIW LE3 ... 130 B6
Nethergate LEIN LE4 .... 125 M1
Netherhall La LEIN LE4 ...... 125 M1
Netherhall Rd LEIE LE5 ...... 127 G7
Netherhall Rd LEIE LE5 ...... 127 G7
Nether La BPR/DUF DE56 ..... 16 E7
BPR/DUF DE56 .... 30 B1
Nether Pasture CARL NG4 .... 52 E1
Netherside Dr MELB/CHEL DE73 ... 72 E5
Nether St BSTN/STPLFD NG9 ... 63 L1
Netherwood Ct
DERBYW DE22 .... 43 G4
Nettlecliff Wk ARN NG5 .... 24 C7
Nettlefold Crs MELB/CHEL DE73 ... 82 F6
Netton CI WGSTN LE18 .... 138 A7
Nevanthon Rd LEIW LE3 ..... 130 F2
Neville CI RLBORO LE12 ..... 101 L3
Neville Dr COAL LE67 .... 108 E6
COAL LE67 .... 116 B7
Neville Rd CALV/BJ NG14 .... 26 D1
LEIW LE3 .... 130 F2
Neville Smith CI RLEIW/BAR LE9 ... 140 B8
Nevinson Av NORM/LIT DE23 ... 71 H1
Nevinson Dr NORM/LIT DE23 ... 57 H8
Nevis CI DERBYSE DE24 .... 71 H5
Newall Dr BSTN/STPLFD NG9 ... 63 G5
Newark CI ARN NG5 .... 36 D2
RLBORO LE12 .... 101 K4
Newark Crs DERBYSE NG2 ..... 5 M8
Newarke CI LEIS LE2 .... 6 C8
Newarke St LEI LE1 .... 6 D7
The Newarke LEIS LE2 .... 6 C7
Newark Rd DERBYE DE21 ...... 44 B5
LEIN LE4 .... 120 C8
Newark St WBRGFD NG2 .... 5 M8
New Ashby Rd LBORO LE11 ... 8 A5
LBORO LE11 .... 103 G5
New Av RLEINE/SYS LE7 ..... 115 K6
Newbery Av LGEAT NG10 ...... 76 D1
Newbold Av BWSH/BRSTN DE72 ... 60 A6
Newbold CI MELB/CHEL DE73 ... 72 D5
RLBORO LE12 .... 114 B3
Newbold Dr CDON/KEG DE74 ... 84 F2
Newbon CI LBORO LE11 .... 8 C3
New Bond St LEI LE1 .... 6 E5
Newborough Rd
DERBYSE DE24 .... 73 G1
New Breck Rd BPR/DUF DE56 ... 17 L4
New Brickyard La
CDON/KEG DE74 .... 86 B6
Newbridge CI ILK DE7 .... 32 B7
Newbridge Crs DERBYSE 72 C3
New Bridge Rd LEIS LE2 ..... 136 F5
New Bridge St LEIS LE2 ..... 131 J4
Newbury CI
MAPPK/POR/STA NG3 .... 37 L3
WGSTN LE18 .... 138 A6
Newbury Dr
EWD/SEL/PNX NG16 .... 35 H4
Newbury St DERBYSE DE24 ... 58 C7
Newby CI RLEIW/BBY LE8 ..... 136 D7
Newby Gdns LEIS LE2 .... 139 H3
Newcastle Av
BSTN/STPLFD NG9 .... 63 K1
CARL NG4 .... 38 C6
Newcastle Circ NOTTE NG7 ... 4 C8
Newcastle Dr NOTTE NG7 ...... 4 C7
Newcastle Farm Dr
WOL/BIL/BRX NG8 .... 36 B6
Newcastle St BLWL NG6 ...... 24 A8
NOTT NG1 .... 5 H6
Newcastle Ter NOTTE NG7 .... 4 A8
Newcombe Dr ARN NG5 .... 26 A8
Newcombe Rd LEIW LE3 ..... 130 F5
New Derby Rd
EWD/SEL/PNX NG16 .... 21 H5
Newdigate Rd
EWD/SEL/PNX NG16 .... 22 E8
Newdigate St
EWD/SEL/PNX NG16 .... 34 E1
ILK DE7 .... 32 A7
ILK DE7 .... 47 L1
NORM/LIT DE23 .... 57 K7
NOTTE NG7 .... 4 C5
New Eaton Rd
BSTN/STPLFD NG9 .... 62 B2
New Farm La
EWD/SEL/PNX NG16 .... 35 G1
Newfield Rd ARN NG5 .... 36 D4
New Fields Av LEIW LE3 ..... 130 F5
New Fields Sq LEIW LE3 ..... 130 F6
New Forest CI WGSTN LE18 ... 138 B7
Newgate CI CARL NG4 .... 38 C8
MELB/CHEL DE73 .... 72 F5
Newgate End WGSTN LE18 ... 138 A4
Newhall Gv WBRGFD NG2 ..... 51 K6
Newham Av HEANOR DE75 .... 11 G6
Newham CI HEANOR DE75 .... 20 E6
LEIN LE4 .... 126 E2
Newhaven Rd DERBYE DE21 ... 58 F1
LEIE LE5 .... 133 H4
New Henry St LEIW LE3 .... 6 C3
Newholm Dr CFTN/RUD NG11 ... 64 E2

Newington St LEIN LE4 ...... 125 M5
New Inn La DERBYE DE21 ..... 30 A8
New King St LBORO LE11 .... 9 L4
Newland CI BSTN/STPLFD NG9 ... 62 E5
WOL/BIL/BRX NG8 .... 50 A2
Newlands CI
COT/KEY/RAD NG12 .... 66 A3
Newlands Dr ALFN DE55 .... 12 A2
CARL NG4 .... 38 D6
HEANOR DE75 .... 20 C4
Newlands Rd ALFN DE55 ...... 12 A3
Newland St DERBY DE1 .... 2 D4
New La RLBORO LE12 .... 105 K3
New Lawn Rd ILK DE7 .... 33 J7
Newlyn Dr NORM/LIT DE23 ... 57 K7
WOL/BIL/BRX NG8 .... 36 B7
Newlyn Gdns WOL/BIL/BRX NG8 ... 36 A7
Newlyn Pde LEIE LE5 .... 127 H6
Newmanleys Rd
EWD/SEL/PNX NG16 .... 21 J7
Newmanleys Rd (South)
EWD/SEL/PNX NG16 .... 21 J6
Newmarket Ct DERBYSE DE24 ... 58 C6
Newmarket Dr DERBYSE DE24 ... 58 C7
Newmarket Rd BLWL NG6 .... 35 M1
Newmarket St LEIS LE2 ..... 131 M7
Newmarket Wy
BSTN/STPLFD NG9 .... 62 D5
New Mount CI
NORM/LIT DE23 .... 71 H2
New Park Rd LEIS LE2 .... 131 J7
New Parks Bvd LEIW LE3 ... 124 C8
LEIW LE3 .... 130 B2
New Parks Crs LEIW LE3 .... 124 E7
New Park St LEIW LE3 .... 6 B7
New Parks Wy LEIW LE3 .... 130 C1
LEIW LE3 .... 124 C8
New Pingle St LEIW LE3 .... 6 C3
Newpool Bank LEIS LE2 ..... 139 J3
Newport Ct DERBYSE DE24 ... 73 G2
Newport Dr
WOL/BIL/BRX NG8 .... 36 B6
Newport PI LEI LE1 .... 7 G7
Newport St LEIW LE3 .... 131 G1
Newquay Av NOTTE NG7 .... 36 C8
Newquay Dr LEIW LE3 .... 124 A6
Newquay PI DERBYSE DE24 ... 73 G2
New BPR/DUF DE56 .... 10 B8
BPR/DUF DE56 .... 17 K4
BSTN/STPLFD NG9 .... 48 B6
CFTN/RUD NG11 .... 77 K1
COT/KEY/RAD NG12 .... 53 K4
DERBYW DE22 .... 43 L6
EWD/SEL/PNX NG16 .... 12 D4
EWD/SEL/PNX NG16 .... 22 B3
LEI LE1 .... 6 E4
NOTT NG1 .... 50 B1
RDERBYSW DE65 .... 68 C5
RIPLEY DE5 .... 12 B5
RLEIW/BAR LE9 .... 140 B5
RLEIW/BBY LE8 .... 146 F7
New Romney CI LEIE LE5 ... 127 J7
The Newry WGSTN LE18 .... 137 K2
New Star Rd LEIN LE4 .... 126 D4
Newstead Av
COT/KEY/RAD NG12 .... 53 L3
DERBYE DE21 .... 58 D1
LEIW LE3 .... 125 G6
MAPPK/POR/STA NG3 .... 38 A5
RLEINE/SYS LE7 .... 133 L3
WGSTN LE18 .... 138 A3
Newstead Dr WBRGFD NG2 ... 51 M8
Newstead Gv NOTT NG1 .... 4 F3
Newstead Rd LEIS LE2 .... 132 A7
LGEAT NG10 .... 61 M4
Newstead Rd North ILK DE7 ... 33 H4
Newstead Rd South ILK DE7 ... 33 H4
Newstead St ARN NG5 .... 37 C4
Newstead Ter HUCK/RAV NG15 ... 15 L7
Newstead Wy
WOL/BIL/BRX NG8 .... 35 H5
New St ARN NG5 .... 36 F7
BWSH/BRSTN DE72 .... 60 E8
BWSH/BRSTN DE72 .... 60 A3
CDON/KEG DE74 .... 86 B4
COAL LE67 .... 108 B7
DERBY DE1 .... 3 H5
DERBYE DE21 .... 30 A7
LBORO LE11 .... 9 H4
LEI LE1 .... 6 E6
LEIS LE2 .... 138 E1
LGEAT NG10 .... 62 C7
RIPLEY DE5 .... 11 J6
RLBORO LE12 .... 105 H8
RLEINE/SYS LE7 .... 121 J2
RLEIW/BBY LE8 .... 136 F6
RLEIW/BBY LE8 .... 143 K3
New Ter LGEAT NG10 .... 61 M1
Newthorpe Common
EWD/SEL/PNX NG16 .... 21 L7
Newthorpe St WBRGFD NG2 ... 51 H5
Newton Av COT/KEY/RAD NG12 ... 53 L3
Newton CI ARN NG5 .... 37 M1
LBORO LE11 .... 103 H1
RLBORO LE12 .... 105 J7
Newtondale CI
WOL/BIL/BRX NG8 .... 36 B6
Newton Dr BSTN/STPLFD NG9 ... 62 C1
WBRGFD NG2 .... 65 G3
Newton La RLEIW/BBY LE8 ... 139 K8
WGSTN LE18 .... 138 D6
Newton Rd CARL NG4 .... 38 B4
Newton's La
EWD/SEL/PNX NG16 .... 33 M4
Newton St LEIW LE3 .... 6 B3
Newton's Wk DERBYW DE22 ... 43 J7
Newtown Linford La
GBY/RBY LE6 .... 123 J2
Newtown St LEI LE1 .... 6 F9
New Tythe St LGEAT NG10 ... 62 D8
New Vale Rd CARL NG4 .... 52 B2
New Wk LEI LE1 .... 7 H8
RLBORO LE12 .... 101 M3
RLEIW/BAR LE9 .... 140 B8
New Way Rd LEIE LE5 .... 132 B5
New Zealand La BPR/DUF DE56 ... 29 J5
RLEINE/SYS LE7 .... 121 G1

New Zealand Sq
DERBYW DE22 .... 57 G2
Nicholas CI DERBYE DE21 ..... 59 J1
Nicholas Dr GBY/RBY LE6 ... 123 H7
Nicholas Rd BSTN/STPLFD NG9 ... 49 H6
Nichols CI LEIE LE5 .... 7 H5
Nicker HI COT/KEY/RAD NG12 ... 80 E4
Nicklaus Rd LEIN LE4 .... 126 B2
Nicola Gdns NORM/LIT DE23 ... 71 H3
Nicolson Rd LBORO LE11 .... 103 G7
Nidderdale CI DERBYE DE24 ... 49 G3
Nidderdale CI WOL/BIL/BRX NG8 ... 49 G4
Nidderdale Rd WGSTN LE18 ... 138 D5
Nightingale Av RLBORO LE12 ... 94 E6
Nightingale CI
EWD/SEL/PNX NG16 .... 13 M1
RIPLEY DE5 .... 11 H6
Nightingale Crs
EWD/SEL/PNX NG16 .... 13 M1
Nightingale Rd DERBYE DE24 ... 58 D8
Nile St NOTT NG1 .... 5 K6
Nilsson Rd BSTN/STPLFD NG9 ... 62 F4
Nine Acre Gdns BLWL NG6 ... 23 K7
Nine Acres CDON/KEG DE74 ... 86 A5
Nixon Ri HUCK/RAV NG15 ..... 23 H2
Nobel Rd CFTN/RUD NG11 .... 64 A7
Noble St LEIW LE3 .... 131 G2
Nock Verges RLEIW/BAR LE9 ... 140 B5
Noel St DERBYW DE22 .... 57 H1
EWD/SEL/PNX NG16 .... 34 E1
LEIS LE2 .... 131 H4
NOTTE NG7 .... 4 C7
NOTTE NG7 .... 36 D7
No Man's La ILK DE7 .... 46 F7
Nook CI GBY/RBY LE6 .... 123 G6
Nook End Rd HEANOR DE75 ... 20 B6
Nook St LEIW LE3 .... 124 F8
The Nook BPR/DUF DE56 ..... 18 A8
BSTN/STPLFD NG9 .... 63 J3
HEANOR DE75 .... 20 A3
RLBORO LE12 .... 88 C6
RLEINE/SYS LE7 .... 121 H2
RLEIW/BAR LE9 .... 135 L4
RLEIW/BAR LE9 .... 142 B5
RLEIW/BBY LE8 .... 136 D8
RLEIW/BBY LE8 .... 139 L8
WOL/BIL/BRX NG8 .... 49 J3
Nooning La BWSH/BRSTN DE72 ... 60 C8
Norbett CI BSTN/STPLFD NG9 ... 62 F4
Norbett Rd ARN NG5 .... 25 L7
Norbreck CI WOL/BIL/BRX NG8 ... 35 M6
Norburn Crs BLWL NG6 .... 36 D4
Norbury Av LEIN LE4 .... 126 A6
Norbury CI DERBYW DE22 .... 43 H6
Norbury Crs NORM/LIT DE23 ... 71 G2
Norbury Wy BPR/DUF DE56 ... 18 A1
LGEAT NG10 .... 61 L1
Nordean Rd ARN NG5 .... 37 L3
Norfolk Av LEIN LE4 .... 126 A5
Norfolk CI HUCK/RAV NG15 ... 23 H2
Norfolk PI NOTT NG1 .... 5 G6
Norfolk Rd LGEAT NG10 .... 62 D6
WGSTN LE18 .... 137 K4
Norfolk St LEIW LE3 .... 6 A1
NORM/LIT DE23 .... 3 G9
Norfolk Wk LGEAT NG10 ...... 61 M2
Norland CI MAPPK/POR/STA NG3 ... 5 L2
Norman Av NORM/LIT DE23 ... 57 J8
Normanby Rd
WOL/BIL/BRX NG8 .... 49 C4
Norman CI BSTN/STPLFD NG9 ... 63 G2
MAPPK/POR/STA NG3 .... 5 H3
Norman Ct LEIS LE2 .... 139 H4
Norman Crs ILK DE7 .... 33 H4
Norman Dr EWD/SEL/PNX NG16 ... 21 M5
HUCK/RAV NG15 .... 23 J3
Normandy CI LEIW LE3 ...... 124 A8
Normandy Rd RDERBYSW DE65 ... 68 C5
Norman St LEIN LE4 .... 120 B7
MAPPK/POR/STA NG3 .... 37 L7
RIPLEY DE5 .... 11 J6
Norman St CARL NG4 .... 52 E1
EWD/SEL/PNX NG16 .... 22 D8
ILK DE7 .... 33 J4
LEIS LE2 .... 6 C8
Normanton CI RLEIW/BAR LE9 ... 134 E4
Normanton La
COT/KEY/RAD NG12 .... 80 D3
NORM/LIT DE23 .... 57 G6
RLBORO LE12 .... 95 L5
Normanton Rd DERBY DE1 ..... 2 F2
LEIE LE5 .... 7 M9
LEIS LE2 .... 132 B3
NORM/LIT DE23 .... 2 E9
Norris CI LEIN LE4 .... 124 E4
Northacre Rd DERBYE DE21 ... 44 F5
Northage CI RLBORO LE12 ... 112 E3
Northall Av BLWL NG6 .... 35 M1
Northam Dr RIPLEY DE5 .... 11 G5
Northampton St LEI LE1 .... 7 G6
North Av COAL LE67 .... 108 B8
DERBYW DE22 .... 43 L4
LEIS LE2 .... 132 A5
LGEAT NG10 .... 61 L1
MCKLVR DE3 .... 56 C4
North Bridge PI LEIW LE3 ...... 6 B3
North Church St NOTT NG1 ..... 4 E7
North Circus St NOTT NG1 ..... 4 E7
Northcliffe Av
MAPPK/POR/STA NG3 .... 37 M5
North CI MCKLVR DE3 .... 56 C4
Northcote Rd LEIS LE2 ...... 131 M7
Northcote St LGEAT NG10 ... 62 C8
Northdale Rd LEIE LE5 ...... 133 J4
Northdene Rd LEIS LE2 ...... 137 M2
Northdown Dr
BSTN/STPLFD NG9 .... 62 F3
WGSTN LE18 .... 138 D6
Northdown Rd
WOL/BIL/BRX NG8 .... 50 A1
North Dr BSTN/STPLFD NG9 ... 63 J1
North End CI LEIS LE2 .... 137 K1
Northern Dr BSTN/STPLFD NG9 ... 48 B4

Northern Rd HEANOR DE75 ... 20 B5
Northfield BPR/DUF DE56 ..... 18 D5
DERBYSE DE24 .... 71 H4
Northfield Av ILK DE7 .... 33 J5
LEIN LE4 .... 119 L7
LGEAT NG10 .... 75 L3
WGSTN LE18 .... 137 M3
Northfield Crs
BSTN/STPLFD NG9 .... 62 E3
Northfield Dr COAL LE67 .... 108 E6
Northfield Rd BSTN/STPLFD NG9 ... 62 E1
LEIN LE4 .... 126 C6
RLEIW/BBY LE8 .... 136 F6
Northfields LGEAT NG10 ...... 75 M3
RLEINE/SYS LE7 .... 120 F3
Northfields Wy RLBORO LE12 ... 88 C4
Northfold Rd LEIS LE2 .... 132 A8
North Ga NOTTE NG7 .... 36 D6
Northgate St ILK DE7 .... 33 J6
North Hill Av HUCK/RAV NG15 ... 15 K7
North Hill Crs HUCK/RAV NG15 ... 15 K8
North La BPR/DUF DE56 .... 17 J8
Northmead Dr DERBYW DE22 ... 56 F4
Northolme Av BLWL NG6 ...... 24 A8
Northolt Dr WOL/BIL/BRX NG8 ... 35 H4
North Pde DERBY DE1 .... 43 L8
LBORO LE11 .... 103 M1
LGEAT NG10 .... 76 A1
NOTTE NG7 .... 4 C7
WBRGFD NG2 .... 65 J1
North Rw DERBYW DE22 ...... 43 L6
North Sherwood St NOTT NG1 ... 4 F2
North St ALFN DE55 .... 12 B1
BSTN/STPLFD NG9 .... 63 J1
COAL LE67 .... 108 C2
DERBY DE1 .... 43 K8
EWD/SEL/PNX NG16 .... 20 F4
ILK DE7 .... 33 K6
MELB/CHEL DE73 .... 82 E8
NORM/LIT DE23 .... 57 G5
RLBORO LE12 .... 105 H7
RLEINE/SYS LE7 .... 119 J1
RLEINE/SYS LE7 .... 120 E3
WBRGFD NG2 .... 5 L7
WGSTN LE18 .... 138 B4
Northumberland Av
LEIN LE4 .... 126 A5
Northumberland CI
MAPPK/POR/STA NG3 .... 5 J4
Northumberland Rd
WGSTN LE18 .... 137 K4
Northumberland St LEI LE1 ... 6 D5
NORM/LIT DE23 .... 2 D9
Northwold Av WBRGFD NG2 ... 65 H1
Northwood Av DERBYE DE21 ... 44 C8
Northwood Crs ARN NG5 ...... 37 C1
Northwood Dr RLBORO LE12 ... 102 A1
Northwood Rd ARN NG5 .... 37 C1
Northwood St
BSTN/STPLFD NG9 .... 48 B7
Norton St LEI LE1 .... 6 E8
NOTTE NG7 .... 4 A4
Norwich CI RLBORO LE12 ... 101 L5
Norwich Gdns BLWL NG6 .... 23 M6
Norwich Rd LEIN LE4 .... 125 H4
Norwich St DERBYE DE21 .... 44 B8
Norwood CI DERBYW DE22 ... 56 E2
Norwood Rd LEIE LE5 .... 132 C4
NOTTE NG7 .... 50 C2
Notintone St WBRGFD NG2 ... 5 M8
Nottingham La ALFN DE55 ... 12 C2
RMMWB LE14 .... 99 M1
Nottingham Rd ARN NG5 ...... 37 J1
BLWL NG6 .... 36 C4
BPR/DUF DE56 .... 17 L4
BSTN/STPLFD NG9 .... 48 B3
BSTN/STPLFD NG9 .... 48 D1
BSTN/STPLFD NG9 .... 48 D2
BSTN/STPLFD NG9 .... 62 F6
BWSH/BRSTN DE72 .... 59 M6
CALV/BJ NG14 .... 39 M1
CALV/BJ NG14 .... 39 H5
CARL NG4 .... 26 B5
CDON/KEG DE74 .... 86 B4
CFTN/RUD NG11 .... 77 M6
CFTN/RUD NG11 .... 89 J2
COT/KEY/RAD NG12 .... 53 H5
COT/KEY/RAD NG12 .... 80 C5
DERBY DE1 .... 2 F2
DERBYE DE21 .... 3 K2
DERBYE DE21 .... 58 E2
DERBYE DE21 .... 59 K4
EWD/SEL/PNX NG16 .... 13 J1
EWD/SEL/PNX NG16 .... 21 M6
EWD/SEL/PNX NG16 .... 34 E1
EWD/SEL/PNX NG16 .... 35 H2
HUCK/RAV NG15 .... 24 A2
ILK DE7 .... 33 K8
LBORO LE11 .... 9 K2
LEIE LE5 .... 132 B1
LGEAT NG10 .... 76 A5
NOTTE NG7 .... 36 D5
RIPLEY DE5 .... 11 J6
RLBORO LE12 .... 89 H5
RLBORO LE12 .... 104 B1
RLBORO LE12 .... 105 H7
RLBORO LE12 .... 105 H1
RMMWB LE14 .... 91 M2
Nuart Rd BSTN/STPLFD NG9 ... 49 K8
Nugent Gdns
MAPPK/POR/STA NG3 .... 5 L3
Nugent St LEI LE1 .... 6 A4
Nunsfield Dr DERBYSE DE24 ... 58 F8
Nun's St DERBY DE1 .... 2 B2
The Nurseries
EWD/SEL/PNX NG16 .... 21 L5
BWSH/BRSTN DE72 .... 61 K2
Nursery Av BSTN/STPLFD NG9 ... 63 G2
ILK DE7 .... 32 C8
Nursery CI BWSH/BRSTN DE72 ... 59 M6
COT/KEY/RAD NG12 .... 53 M4
HUCK/RAV NG15 .... 23 J3
LEIN LE4 .... 126 B1
RLBORO LE12 .... 102 A1
RLEINE/SYS LE7 .... 121 J2
RLEIW/BAR LE9 .... 134 E5

Nursery Dr CARL NG4 .... 38 B7
Nursery End LBORO LE11 .... 103 H7
Nursery Gv LBORO LE11 ..... 105 J7
Nursery Hollow ILK DE7 .... 47 J1
LEIS LE2 .... 138 B3
Nursery La BLWL NG6 .... 36 C3
RLBORO LE12 .... 112 E1
Nursery Rd ARN NG5 .... 25 K8
COT/KEY/RAD NG12 .... 53 M4
LEIE LE5 .... 127 H8
Nutbrook Crs ILK DE7 .... 47 H3
Nutbrook Trail ILK DE7 .... 33 G4
ILK DE7 .... 47 H3
Nutfield Rd LEIW LE3 .... 131 G4
Nuthall Cir ILK DE7 .... 47 G3
Nuthall Gdns WOL/BIL/BRX NG8 ... 36 B7
Nuthall Gv LEIS LE2 .... 136 F5
Nuthall Rd WOL/BIL/BRX NG8 ... 35 M4
Nutkin CI LBORO LE11 .... 8 F7
Nutwood CI DERBYW DE22 ... 43 L4

O

Oadby Hill Dr LEIS LE2 .... 138 D1
Oadby Ri NORM/LIT DE23 .... 71 J1
Oadby Rd WGSTN LE18 ...... 138 C4
Oak Acres BSTN/STPLFD NG9 ... 62 E2
Oak Apple Crs ILK DE7 .... 47 J1
Oak Av COT/KEY/RAD NG12 ... 53 J5
EWD/SEL/PNX NG16 .... 20 F2
LGEAT NG10 .... 47 L8
RIPLEY DE5 .... 11 H8
Oak CI BPR/DUF DE56 .... 29 J5
BWSH/BRSTN DE72 .... 60 A2
COAL LE67 .... 108 E7
DERBYW DE22 .... 43 J3
RLBORO LE12 .... 111 L1
Oak Crs NORM/LIT DE23 ...... 56 F7
RLBORO LE12 .... 88 B7
Oakcroft Av RLEIW/BAR LE9 ... 129 J3
Oakdale CI LEIW LE5 .... 130 A1
Oakdale Dr BSTN/STPLFD NG9 ... 62 E3
Oakdale Gdns DERBYE DE21 ... 44 F4
Oakdale Rd ARN NG5 .... 25 M7
CARL NG4 .... 52 E1
MAPPK/POR/STA NG3 .... 51 M1
Oakdene Rd LEIS LE2 .... 137 L1
Oak Dr DERBYSE DE24 .... 72 E1
EWD/SEL/PNX NG16 .... 21 J5
EWD/SEL/PNX NG16 .... 34 F1
MCKLVR DE3 .... 56 C4
RDERBYSW DE65 .... 68 F2
RLEINE/SYS LE7 .... 120 F5
Oakenshaw CI LEIN LE4 ...... 125 J2
Oakfield Av COAL LE67 .... 116 B7
LEIN LE4 .... 119 K8
LEIW LE3 .... 124 B5
Oakfield CI RLEIW/BBY LE8 ... 139 M6
WOL/BIL/BRX NG8 .... 49 C4
Oakfield Ct ILK DE7 .... 31 L5
Oakfield Crs RLEIW/BBY LE8 ... 137 C8
Oakfield Dr LGEAT NG10 ...... 61 M4
Oakfield Rd BSTN/STPLFD NG9 ... 48 B8
HUCK/RAV NG15 .... 23 M1
LEIS LE2 .... 132 A4
WOL/BIL/BRX NG8 .... 49 C4
Oakfields Rd WBRGFD NG2 ... 51 L6
Oak Flatt BSTN/STPLFD NG9 ... 62 C2
Oakford CI WOL/BIL/BRX NG8 ... 35 L5
Oak Gv HUCK/RAV NG15 ...... 23 M3
Oakham CI ARN NG5 .... 24 D8
DERBYE DE21 .... 44 B6
LBORO LE11 .... 103 J1
Oakham Dr COAL LE67 ...... 109 G5
Oakham Rd WBRGFD NG2 .... 65 H5
Oakham Wy ILK DE7 .... 33 H4
Oakhurst CI BPR/DUF DE56 ... 17 H1
Oakhurst Ct LBORO LE11 .... 103 G3
Oakington CI ARN NG5 .... 36 F2
Oakland Av LEIN LE4 .... 125 M2
LGEAT NG10 .... 76 A2
Oakland Ct BSTN/STPLFD NG9 ... 48 E1
Oakland Crs ALFN DE55 .... 12 B2
Oakland Rd LEIS LE2 .... 131 L6
Oaklands Av HEANOR DE75 ... 20 E5
LBORO LE11 .... 8 E6
NORM/LIT DE23 .... 71 G2
Oaklands CI RIPLEY DE5 ...... 19 H6
Oaklands Rd RDERBYSW DE65 ... 69 G3
Oakland St NOTTE NG7 .... 36 C8
Oaklands Wy MELB/CHEL DE73 ... 82 F7
Oakland Ter LGEAT NG10 ..... 76 A2
Oakleigh Av DERBYE DE21 ... 58 D1
MAPPK/POR/STA NG3 .... 38 A5
WGSTN LE18 .... 137 J6
Oakleigh St BLWL NG6 .... 36 B3
Oakley Av RLBORO LE12 ..... 101 M3
Oakley CI RLBORO LE12 ..... 101 M2
Oakley Dr LBORO LE11 .... 8 B5
RLBORO LE12 .... 94 B5
Oakley Ms BLWL NG6 .... 35 K1
Oakley Rd LEIE LE5 .... 126 B8
RLBORO LE12 .... 101 J6
RLBORO LE12 .... 93 M8
RLBORO LE12 .... 101 M2
Oakley's Rd LGEAT NG10 ..... 76 C1
Oak Lodge Dr
EWD/SEL/PNX NG16 .... 22 D8
Oakmead Av WOL/BIL/BRX NG8 ... 35 K7
Oakmeadow Wy GBY/RBY LE6 ... 123 J5
Oakmere CI COT/KEY/RAD NG12 ... 66 A3
Oakover Dr DERBYW DE22 ..... 43 J7
Oak Pool Gdns LEIS LE2 ..... 137 H4
Oakridge CI LEIE LE5 .... 127 G4
Oak Rd BWSH/BRSTN DE72 ... 141 M1
RLEIW/BAR LE9 .... 141 M1
Oaks Dr RLEIW/BBY LE8 ..... 133 G2
Oakside Crs LEIE LE5 .... 133 G2
Oakside Wy DERBYE DE21 ... 44 F5
Oaks Rd COAL LE67 .... 108 C1
RLEIW/BBY LE8 .... 139 M7
The Oaks DERBYE DE21 ...... 30 A7
Oak St LEIE LE5 .... 7 M2
NORM/LIT DE23 .... 57 L5
Oaks Wy LEIS LE2 .... 132 D7

Oakthorpe Av LEIW LE3 130 F3
Oak Tree Av COT/KEY/RAD NG12 53 K3
Oaktree Av DERBYSE DE24 57 M8
Oaktree Cl GBY/RBY LE6 123 J4
HUCK/RAV NG15 23 H3 1
LEIE LE5 127 G5 2
RLEIW/BBY LE8 146 F6 1
Oak Tree Cl WBRGFD NG2 51 L7
Oak Tree Ct BWSH/BRSTN DE72 60 A6
Oak Tree Dr CARL NG4 38 E5
Oakwell Crs ILK DE7 33 J7
Oakwell Dr ILK DE7 33 J7
Oakwood Av WGSTN LE18 138 B3 4
Oakwood Cl DERBYSE DE24 71 H5 5
LEIW LE3 129 K5 5
Oakwood Dr DERBYE DE21 44 F5
LBORO LE11 102 F6
WOL/BIL/BRX NG8 36 A8
The Oasis LEIW LE3 123 M7
Oban Rd BSTN/STPLFD NG9 63 G1
Oban St LEIW LE3 131 G1
Occupation Rd BLWL NG6 35 M2
HUCK/RAV NG15 23 L2
Ocean Cl LEIE LE5 127 G8
Ocean Rd LEIE LE5 133 G1
Ockerby St BLWL NG6 36 A1
Odam Cl LEIW LE3 130 D5
Odesa Dr BLWL NG6 35 M3
Offerton Av NORM/LIT DE23 57 J7
Offranville Cl LEIN LE4 126 D1
Ogle Dr NOTTE NG7 4 E8
Ogle St HUCK/RAV NG15 15 L8
Ogwen Cl LEIE LE5 133 H1
Okehampton Av LEIE LE5 132 D4
Okehampton Crs
MAPPK/POR/STA NG3 38 A1
Oldacres CALV/BJ NG14 27 H3 2
Old Ashby Rd LBORO LE11 102 F5
Old Barn Cl DERBYE DE21 30 A7 5
Old Brickyard
MAPPK/POR/STA NG3 37 L8
Old Bull Farm Cl RLBORO LE12 86 E5
Oldbury Cl CFTN/RUD NG11 64 B8 2
DERBYE DE21 44 D5
Old Chapel La
EWD/SEL/PNX NG16 13 L5
Old Chester Rd DERBY DE1 43 L7 1
Old Church Cl DERBYW DE22 43 G2
Old Church St LEIS LE2 137 G1
NOTTE NG7 50 C5
Old Coach Rd WOL/BIL/BRX NG8 49 L2
Old Coppice Side HEANOR DE75 20 C8
Old Derby Rd
EWD/SEL/PNX NG16 21 H4 7
Old Dr BSTN/STPLFD NG9 49 H7
Old Epperstone Rd
CALV/BJ NG14 27 M3
Oldershaw Av CDON/KEG DE74 86 A5
Oldershaw Rd RLBORO LE12 88 D6
Old Farm Rd ARN NG5 24 D7
Old Field Cl RLEIW/BBY LE8 143 G3 2
Oldfield La RDERBYSW DE65 68 D7
RLBORO LE12 113 K7
Old Gate Av
BWSH/BRSTN DE72 83 J2 1
Old Gate Rd RLEINE/SYS LE7 115 K2
Old Hall Av BPR/DUF DE56 29 H4
DERBYSE DE24 58 F8
NORM/LIT DE23 56 F6
Old Hall Cl GBY/RBY LE6 123 K5
LEIN LE4 120 C7 2
Old Hall Dr
MAPPK/POR/STA NG3 37 H6
Old Hall Rd NORM/LIT DE23 57 G6
Old Hartshay Hl RIPLEY DE5 11 G5
Oldknow St NOTTE NG7 4 A3
Old La DERBYW DE22 43 L5
Old Lenton St NOTT NG1 5 J6 6
Old Main Rd CALV/BJ NG14 39 M2
RLBORO LE12 89 H6
Old Manor Cl CALV/BJ NG14 27 H3
Old Mansfield Rd DERBYE DE21 44 A6
Old Melton Rd
COT/KEY/RAD NG12 80 C1
Old Mill Cl BLWL NG6 24 B4
BPR/DUF DE56 29 J4
BSTN/STPLFD NG9 62 E5 6
NOTTE NG7 4 B5
Old Mill La LEI LE1 6 C4
Old Milton St LEI LE1 7 G3 2
Oldoak Rd CFTN/RUD NG11 64 D5
Old Park Cl CFTN/RUD NG11 86 D1
The Old Pk COT/KEY/RAD NG12 67 K3
Old Parsonage La RLBORO LE12 97 G6
Old Pit La ILK DE7 31 L1
The Old Pond HEANOR DE75 20 E7
Old Rectory Cl RLBORO LE12 88 C6
Old Rd BPR/DUF DE56 10 B7
COT/KEY/RAD NG12 65 H6
WBRGFD NG2 65 J4
Old School Cl CFTN/RUD NG11 64 C7 6
Old School La
EWD/SEL/PNX NG16 34 A2
Old School Ms
BWSH/BRSTN DE72 73 M7 2
Old Station Cl COAL LE67 108 B6
RLBORO LE12 101 M5
Old St NOTT NG1 5 H5 1
Old Tollerton Rd WBRGFD NG2 52 A8
Old Vicarage Cl
NORM/LIT DE23 57 G6 5
Old Vicarage La
DERBYW DE22 43 G2 1
Old Wy RLBORO LE12 94 E6
Olga Rd MAPPK/POR/STA NG3 51 K1
Olive Av LGEAT NG10 62 B6
Olive Gv CALV/BJ NG14 39 K2
Oliver Cl HEANOR DE75 20 F5
NOTTE NG7 4 D4
Oliver Rd ILK DE7 47 G2
LBORO LE11 9 J7
LEIN LE4 126 B5
Oliver St LEIS LE2 131 J7 2
NOTTE NG7 4 D4
Olive St DERBYW DE22 2 A6
Olivier St NORM/LIT DE23 57 M6
Ollerton Rd ARN NG5 25 J8
Olphin St LEIN LE4 125 L7
Olton Av BSTN/STPLFD NG9 49 K7
Olton Rd MCKLVR DE3 56 A3
Olympic Cl LEIW LE3 124 B7
Olympus Ct HUCK/RAV NG15 23 H4
Onchan Av CARL NG4 52 C1
Onchan Dr CARL NG4 52 C1
One Barrow La RLBORO LE12 109 J1
Onslow Rd MCKLVR DE3 56 B3
Onslow St LEIS LE2 7 L9 2
Ontario Cl LEI LE1 7 G3
Opal Cl DERBYE DE21 44 E5
Openacre EWD/SEL/PNX NG16 12 D3
Openwoodgate BPR/DUF DE56 18 A3
Openwood Rd BPR/DUF DE56 18 B4
Orange Gdns WBRGFD NG2 51 H5
Orange St WGSTN LE18 137 K7
Orby Cl MAPPK/POR/STA NG3 51 K1
Orchard Av CARL NG4 38 C8
CDON/KEG DE74 84 E4
LEIS LE2 136 F5
Orchard Cl BPR/DUF DE56 17 M7
BWSH/BRSTN DE72 60 A3
BWSH/BRSTN DE72 61 J7
CALV/BJ NG14 39 K2
CDON/KEG DE74 93 G2
CFTN/RUD NG11 64 A5
COT/KEY/RAD NG12 53 J4 5
COT/KEY/RAD NG12 66 B6
DERBYSE DE24 73 G3 1
ILK DE7 32 B8
ILK DE7 44 B3 1
LEIS LE2 138 E3
MELB/CHEL DE73 82 E8 5
NORM/LIT DE23 57 G8
RIPLEY DE5 11 L8
RLBORO LE12 88 B7
RLBORO LE12 95 G2
RLBORO LE12 100 A3
RLBORO LE12 101 M4
Orchard Ct DERBYE DE21 59 J2
Orchard Crs BSTN/STPLFD NG9 63 G2
Orchard Est RLBORO LE12 112 D1
Orchard Gdns LEIN LE4 126 D1
Orchard Gv ARN NG5 37 G1
Orchard La RLEIW/BBY LE8 139 M8
RLEIW/BBY LE8 143 K4
Orchard Ri CARL NG4 26 F8
HEANOR DE75 20 D5 5
Orchard Rd ALFN DE55 12 A1
LEIN LE4 119 M8
RLEIW/BAR LE9 141 J8
Orchards Dr WGSTN LE18 137 M5
Orchardson Av LEI LE1 7 J1
The Orchards CARL NG4 38 E6
DERBYW DE22 43 H4 1
LEIE LE5 127 J8
Orchard St BSTN/STPLFD NG9 48 B8
CFTN/RUD NG11 77 L6
DERBY DE1 2 D2 1
EWD/SEL/PNX NG16 20 F4 5
EWD/SEL/PNX NG16 21 L6 1
EWD/SEL/PNX NG16 34 D1
HUCK/RAV NG15 23 L1
ILK DE7 33 K8
LBORO LE11 9 H2
LEI LE1 6 F3
LGEAT NG10 62 C8 6
MCKLVR DE3 56 B6
RLEIW/BBY LE8 145 K8
The Orchard BPR/DUF DE56 17 L3 2
GBY/RBY LE6 123 J4
ILK DE7 31 H1 1
ILK DE7 47 K6
RIPLEY DE5 11 M6
RLBORO LE12 106 D7
RLEIW/BAR LE9 140 C5
Orchard Vw RLBORO LE12 113 H7
Orchard Wy LGEAT NG10 61 L4
MELB/CHEL DE73 72 D5
RLBORO LE12 98 B4
RLEINE/SYS LE7 121 G4
Orchid Cl CFTN/RUD NG11 65 G3
LEIE LE5 127 G5 3
RLBORO LE12 113 K5 4
RLEIW/BAR LE9 135 L6
Ordish Av DERBYE DE21 58 D2
Oregon Wy DERBYE DE21 59 G2
Orford Av CFTN/RUD NG11 64 D4
COT/KEY/RAD NG12 53 J4
Oriel Dr RLEINE/SYS LE7 120 F4
Orion Cl WOL/BIL/BRX NG8 35 J8
Orion Dr WOL/BIL/BRX NG8 35 J8
Orkney Cl DERBYSE DE24 71 H4
Orkney Wy RLEIW/BBY LE8 143 K4
Orlando Dr CARL NG4 38 D7
Orlando Rd LEIS LE2 131 M5 1
Orly Av CDON/KEG DE74 84 E5
Orme Cl LEIN LE4 124 E4
Ormen Gn LEIW LE3 130 B1
Ormonde St
EWD/SEL/PNX NG16 20 F3
Ormonde Ter
EWD/SEL/PNX NG16 20 F3
Ormskirk Ri DERBYE DE21 59 K3
Ornsay Cl ARN NG5 24 C5
Oronsay Rd LEIN LE4 124 F4
Orpean Wy BSTN/STPLFD NG9 62 C5
Orpine Rd LEIE LE5 126 F5
Orsett Cl LEIE LE5 126 D7
Orson Dr WGSTN LE18 137 M4
Orson St LEIE LE5 132 B2
Orston Av ARN NG5 25 L8
Orston Dr WOL/BIL/BRX NG8 50 A3
Orston Gn WOL/BIL/BRX NG8 50 B4 1
Orston Rd East WBRGFD NG2 51 K6 6
Orston Rd West WBRGFD NG2 51 J6 2
Orton Av BSTN/STPLFD NG9 63 G1
Orton Cl RLEINE/SYS LE7 115 K6
Orton Rd LEIN LE4 125 J4
Orton Wy BPR/DUF DE56 17 M1
Ortzen St NOTTE NG7 4 B4
Orville Rd ARN NG5 36 C2
Orwell Cl LBORO LE11 103 H1
Orwell Dr LEIN LE4 124 E3 1
Osborne Av ARN NG5 37 G4 5
Osborne Cl LGEAT NG10 61 M3 6
Osborne Gv ARN NG5 37 G5
Osborne Rd LBORO LE11 103 G1
LEIE LE5 132 B2
Osborne St DERBY DE1 3 J8 1
NOTTE NG7 50 C1
Osbourne Cl
EWD/SEL/PNX NG16 22 F8
Osgood Rd ARN NG5 38 A2
Osier Rd WBRGFD NG2 51 G6
The Osiers CDON/KEG DE74 86 C5
LBORO LE11 103 L8
LEIW LE3 130 D8
RLEINE/SYS LE7 113 G6
Osler Dr HUCK/RAV NG15 14 E1
Osman Cl WBRGFD NG2 50 F6 10
Osmaston Cl LGEAT NG10 75 K2
Osmaston Park Rd
DERBYSE DE24 58 A8
Osmaston Rd DERBY DE1 2 F5
DERBYSE DE24 58 A6
DERBYSE DE24 72 B1
LEIE LE5 7 M9
NORM/LIT DE23 3 G7
Osmaston St LGEAT NG10 62 A2
NOTTE NG7 50 D4 12
Osprey Cl CFTN/RUD NG11 64 A6
DERBYSE DE24 71 J5
RLEIW/BAR LE9 141 J8
Osprey Rd LEIN LE4 124 E1
Ossington Cl NOTT NG1 5 G4
Ossington St NOTTE NG7 4 B4
Osterley Cl LBORO LE11 103 G3
Osterley Gv WOL/BIL/BRX NG8 35 H5
Osterly Gn DERBYW DE22 56 E2
Oswestry Cl DERBYE DE21 44 F4 17
Oswin Rd LEIW LE3 130 D2 1
Ottawa Rd LEI LE1 7 H4
Otterburn Dr DERBYW DE22 43 G5
Otter La RLBORO LE12 113 K5
Otter St DERBY DE1 43 L8
Otter Wy RLEIW/BBY LE8 142 D2
Oulton Cl ARN NG5 37 K1
DERBYSE DE24 72 B3
Oundle Dr ILK DE7 33 L8
WOL/BIL/BRX NG8 50 A4
Ousebridge Crs CARL NG4 38 E7 2
Ouse Bridge Dr CARL NG4 38 E7
Outfields Dr RLEINE/SYS LE7 118 D5
Outram St RIPLEY DE5 11 H5
Outram Wy DERBYSE DE24 71 J5
Outwood Cl LEIW LE3 130 B2
Outwoods Av LBORO LE11 8 F8
Outwoods Dr LBORO LE11 8 F9
Outwoods Rd LBORO LE11 103 K7
Oval Ct NORM/LIT DE23 57 G7
Oval Gdns WOL/BIL/BRX NG8 36 B7 4
The Oval COAL LE67 108 E8
LEI LE1 7 H9
RLEIW/BAR LE9 140 C5
WGSTN LE18 138 D3
Overdale Av LEIW LE3 123 M5
Overdale Cl LEIW LE3 123 L5
LGEAT NG10 75 K1
Overdale Rd BLWL NG6 36 A4
LEIN LE4 126 D1 1
LEIS LE2 138 A1
Overfield Cl GBY/RBY LE6 123 H6 1
RLEIW/BAR LE9 135 L8 4
Overing Cl LEIN LE4 125 L4 3
Over La BPR/DUF DE56 16 E5
BPR/DUF DE56 18 C2
Overpark Av LEIW LE3 130 D3
Overseal Rd LEIW LE3 124 C7
Overstone Cl BPR/DUF DE56 18 B3 6
Overstrand Cl ARN NG5 37 K1
Overton Rd LEIE LE5 126 B8
Owen Av LGEAT NG10 76 E1
Owen Cl LEIN LE4 126 C2 2
LEIW LE3 130 B6
Owen St COAL LE67 108 A6
Owers Av HEANOR DE75 20 D8
Owlers La DERBYW DE22 57 G5
Owlston Cl
EWD/SEL/PNX NG16 21 K4 1
Owlswick Cl NORM/LIT DE23 56 F7
Owsthorpe Cl ARN NG5 24 E7 5
Owston Dr WGSTN LE18 137 M4
Owthorpe Gv ARN NG5 36 F5 5
Owthorpe Rd
COT/KEY/RAD NG12 67 K5
Oxborough Rd ARN NG5 25 G8 1
Oxbow Cl WBRGFD NG2 51 G6 10
Oxbury Rd EWD/SEL/PNX NG16 22 D7
Oxclose La ARN NG5 36 F1
Oxendale Cl WBRGFD NG2 66 A1 2
Oxendon St LEIS LE2 7 K7
Oxendon Wk LEIS LE2 7 K7
Oxengate ARN NG5 36 F1
Oxenhope Cl NORM/LIT DE23 56 C8 7
Oxford Ct RLEINE/SYS LE7 121 G3
Oxford Dr WGSTN LE18 137 K4
Oxford Rd LEIS LE2 131 M5
WBRGFD NG2 51 L8
Oxford St CARL NG4 38 C6
COAL LE67 108 C6
DERBY DE1 3 H7
DERBYE DE21 59 J2
EWD/SEL/PNX NG16 21 K5 7
ILK DE7 33 K8 5
LBORO LE11 8 F2
LEI LE1 6 E7
LGEAT NG10 62 B7
NOTT NG1 4 E7
RIPLEY DE5 11 H6 6
RLBORO LE12 101 M5
RLEINE/SYS LE7 121 G3
Oxley Cl RLBORO LE12 101 L4
Oxon Wy LEIE LE5 132 E2
Oxted Ri LEIS LE2 138 E4
Oxton Av ARN NG5 37 G3
Oxwich Ct DERBYE DE21 44 F5 9
Ozier Holt CARL NG4 52 C3
LGEAT NG10 76 A1

P

Packer Av LEIW LE3 129 M3
Packe St LBORO LE11 9 H3
Pack Horse La LBORO LE11 9 K4
Packhorse Rd LEIS LE2 137 H4
Pack Horse Rd MELB/CHEL DE73 82 F6
Packington Hl CDON/KEG DE74 86 A5
Packman Dr CFTN/RUD NG11 65 H7
Packwood Rd LEIN LE4 125 J3
Paddock Cl BLWL NG6 35 M2 1
CDON/KEG DE74 84 D4
COT/KEY/RAD NG12 53 J5
LEIS LE2 138 C2
RLBORO LE12 112 E2
RLEINE/SYS LE7 119 J2
RLEIW/BBY LE8 143 J3
Paddock Cft DERBYE DE21 44 D5 6
The Paddocks
COT/KEY/RAD NG12 65 M4
EWD/SEL/PNX NG16 34 F2
LGEAT NG10 61 L2
RLBORO LE12 94 F1 1
RLEIW/BAR LE9 136 A8
Paddock St WGSTN LE18 138 B5
Paddocks Vw LGEAT NG10 61 L7
The Paddock BPR/DUF DE56 30 A1
BSTN/STPLFD NG9 63 H5
BWSH/BRSTN DE72 60 A3
COAL LE67 116 C6
DERBYSE DE24 73 H3 2
RLBORO LE12 101 M4 1
RLEIW/BBY LE8 146 F7
Paddock Vw RLEINE/SYS LE7 120 D4 2
Paddy's La RMMWB LE14 99 L6
Padgate Cl RLEINE/SYS LE7 133 K1 1
Padge Rd BSTN/STPLFD NG9 63 M1
Padley Cl DERBYW DE22 43 L2 1
RIPLEY DE5 11 G4
Padleys La CALV/BJ NG14 39 J2
Padstow Cl DERBYSE DE24 71 H4 16
Padstow Rd ARN NG5 36 D1
DERBYSE DE24 73 G2
LEIN LE4 126 C5
Padwell La RLEINE/SYS LE7 133 L3
Page La CDON/KEG DE74 93 G2
Paget Av LEIN LE4 119 M7
Paget Ct RLEIW/BBY LE8 146 E7 4
Paget Crs CFTN/RUD NG11 65 G7
Paget Rd LEIW LE3 131 G1
Paget St LBORO LE11 8 F2
LEIS LE2 137 G1
RLEIW/BBY LE8 146 E7 5
Paigle Rd LEIS LE2 137 G1
Paignton Cl
WOL/BIL/BRX NG8 35 M5 5
Painter St LEI LE1 7 G1
Paisley Gv BSTN/STPLFD NG9 63 G6 1
Palatine Gv NORM/LIT DE23 56 D8
Palatine St NOTTE NG7 4 E9
NOTTE NG7 50 F4 2
Palfreyman La LEIS LE2 139 J3 4
Palin Gdns COT/KEY/RAD NG12 53 L4
Palin St NOTTE NG7 4 A3
Palladium Dr NORM/LIT DE23 70 E1 5
Pall Ml ILK DE7 44 C3
Palm Cl NORM/LIT DE23 56 E6
Palmer Av HUCK/RAV NG15 15 L7
LBORO LE11 103 K2
Palmer Crs CARL NG4 38 B8
Palmer Dr BSTN/STPLFD NG9 62 B2
Palmer Rd BSTN/STPLFD NG9 62 F5
Palmerston Bvd WGSTN LE18 138 A1
Palmerston Cl RLEIW/BBY LE8 146 D7
Palmerston Ct
MELB/CHEL DE73 82 F8 5
Palmerston Gdns
MAPPK/POR/STA NG3 5 H4 1
Palmerston St
EWD/SEL/PNX NG16 13 G3
EWD/SEL/PNX NG16 13 K5
NORM/LIT DE23 57 J6
Palmerston Wy LEIS LE2 138 A1
Palmer St LEIN LE4 125 L4
Palm St NOTTE NG7 36 D6 4
Pamela Pl LEIN LE4 125 J3
Pankhurst Rd LEIN LE4 124 E1
Pantain Rd LBORO LE11 8 D9
LBORO LE11 103 J7
Paper Mill Cl RLEINE/SYS LE7 124 B1
The Parade LEIS LE2 138 E1
Paramore Cl RLEIW/BBY LE8 142 E2
Parcel Ter DERBYW DE22 57 H2
Pares Wy BWSH/BRSTN DE72 60 A2
Park Av ARN NG5 37 J2
CALV/BJ NG14 26 F3
CALV/BJ NG14 39 J3
CARL NG4 38 D7
CDON/KEG DE74 84 D4
COAL LE67 116 C6
COT/KEY/RAD NG12 80 D3
EWD/SEL/PNX NG16 21 J4 3
EWD/SEL/PNX NG16 33 M2
EWD/SEL/PNX NG16 34 E2
HUCK/RAV NG15 15 K8
ILK DE7 33 K7
ILK DE7 46 A1 1
LBORO LE11 9 J8
LEIS LE2 131 J7
MAPPK/POR/STA NG3 37 H7
RIPLEY DE5 11 K6
RLBORO LE12 102 A5
WBRGFD NG2 51 K7
Park Av East
COT/KEY/RAD NG12 80 B4
Park Av West
COT/KEY/RAD NG12 80 B4
Park Cl BPR/DUF DE56 18 E7
DERBYE DE21 29 M7
ILK DE7 47 K7
MAPPK/POR/STA NG3 37 J5
RLBORO LE12 101 M3
RLEIW/BAR LE9 142 B5
WBRGFD NG2 65 G2
Park Crs BPR/DUF DE56 10 C7
EWD/SEL/PNX NG16 21 K3
ILK DE7 33 L7
LEIS LE2 139 G3
WOL/BIL/BRX NG8 49 G3 4
Parkcroft Rd WBRGFD NG2 65 K1
Parkdale Rd LEIN LE4 126 D1
MAPPK/POR/STA NG3 52 A1
Park Dr ALFN DE55 11 K1
HUCK/RAV NG15 23 L2
ILK DE7 33 K8
LEIW LE3 123 M7
LEIW LE3 130 A4
LGEAT NG10 61 L4
NORM/LIT DE23 57 G6
NOTTE NG7 4 D8
Parker Cl ARN NG5 26 A7 6
DERBY DE1 2 C1
Parker Dr LEIN LE4 125 J5
Parker Gdns BSTN/STPLFD NG9 48 D7
Parkers Flds RLBORO LE12 104 E8 2
Parker St DERBY DE1 43 K8
HUCK/RAV NG15 15 M8
Park Farm Dr DERBYW DE22 43 H5
Parkfield Cl GBY/RBY LE6 123 H7 5
Parkfields Dr DERBYW DE22 43 J7 5
Parkgate HUCK/RAV NG15 15 M6 2
Park Gv DERBYW DE22 43 J7
Park Hall La ILK DE7 32 B5
Park Hall Rd RIPLEY DE5 18 E4
Parkham Rd
EWD/SEL/PNX NG16 22 D8 5
Park Hl EWD/SEL/PNX NG16 33 M2
Parkhill LEIS LE2 131 H7 1
Park Hill Av LEIS LE2 131 H8
Park Hill Dr LEIS LE2 131 H8
NORM/LIT DE23 57 K8
Park Hill La RLEINE/SYS LE7 106 E8
Parkhouse Cl LEIN LE4 125 L2
Park House Gates
MAPPK/POR/STA NG3 37 H6 2
Parkland Cl CFTN/RUD NG11 64 A4
Parkland Dr LEIS LE2 138 E1
Parklands Av GBY/RBY LE6 123 H4
Parklands Cl ARN NG5 24 F6 3
Parklands Dr LBORO LE11 103 L7
MELB/CHEL DE73 72 E7 1
Park La BLWL NG6 36 C3
BPR/DUF DE56 10 D7
BWSH/BRSTN DE72 83 J3 1
CALV/BJ NG14 27 K7
CDON/KEG DE74 84 B4
DERBYW DE22 43 K3
LEIS LE2 132 B5
NORM/LIT DE23 57 G6
RLBORO LE12 94 F1
Park Leys Ct DERBYE DE21 59 J3
Park Ravine NOTTE NG7 4 D9
Park Ri LEIW LE3 130 C2
RLBORO LE12 101 M4
Park Rd ARN NG5 37 J2
BLWL NG6 24 C3
BPR/DUF DE56 10 C7
BPR/DUF DE56 17 L5
BPR/DUF DE56 29 J4
BSTN/STPLFD NG9 48 E7
BSTN/STPLFD NG9 63 J1
CARL NG4 38 D7
COAL LE67 108 B6
COT/KEY/RAD NG12 53 K3
COT/KEY/RAD NG12 80 D3
DERBYE DE21 59 H2
GBY/RBY LE6 123 G8
HUCK/RAV NG15 15 K8
ILK DE7 33 K8
LBORO LE11 9 J6
LBORO LE11 103 L7
LEIN LE4 125 K1
MCKLVR DE3 56 B5
NOTTE NG7 50 D4
RIPLEY DE5 11 J6
RLBORO LE12 114 A3
RLEINE/SYS LE7 124 B1
RLEIW/BAR LE9 135 M8
RLEIW/BAR LE9 140 B8
RLEIW/BAR LE9 142 B5
RLEIW/BBY LE8 136 E7
WGSTN LE18 137 K7
Park Rd North
BSTN/STPLFD NG9 63 J1
Park Rw NOTT NG1 4 F8
Parks Cl COAL LE67 108 C2
Park Side BPR/DUF DE56 17 L4
Parkside BPR/DUF DE56 10 C7
COT/KEY/RAD NG12 80 D3
GBY/RBY LE6 123 K3
WOL/BIL/BRX NG8 49 K6 1
Parkside Av LGEAT NG10 61 M7
Parkside Cl EWD/SEL/PNX NG16 12 D3
LEIN LE4 124 E1
Parkside Dr EWD/SEL/PNX NG16 12 D3
LGEAT NG10 61 M7
Parkside Gdns North
WOL/BIL/BRX NG8 49 J4
Parkside Gdns South
WOL/BIL/BRX NG8 49 J5
Parkside Ri WOL/BIL/BRX NG8 49 J5
Parkside Rd DERBYE DE21 58 E2
Parkstone Cl WBRGFD NG2 64 F2
Parkstone Ct MCKLVR DE3 56 A5
Parkstone Rd LEIE LE5 127 H7
RLEINE/SYS LE7 120 F2
Park St BSTN/STPLFD NG9 62 A1
BSTN/STPLFD NG9 63 J1
BWSH/BRSTN DE72 61 K7
DERBY DE1 3 J6
HEANOR DE75 20 B5
LBORO LE11 9 J5
LEI LE1 6 F7
LGEAT NG10 62 A6
NOTTE NG7 4 A8
RIPLEY DE5 11 J6
RLEIW/BBY LE8 145 K7
Park Ter COT/KEY/RAD NG12 80 D2
NOTT NG1 4 E7
The Park COT/KEY/RAD NG12 67 K3
EWD/SEL/PNX NG16 12 C4
Park Vale Rd LEIS LE2 7 M7
Park Va NOTTE NG7 4 E8
Park Vw ALFN DE55 12 B2
BWSH/BRSTN DE72 73 M8
DERBYE DE21 30 A7
HEANOR DE75 20 B6
LEIW LE3 130 C1 2
MAPPK/POR/STA NG3 37 J5
Park View Cl DERBYW DE22 43 K3

Parkview Rd *ARN* NG5 .... 24 D8
Parkway *MELB/CHEL* DE73 ..... 72 D6
Park Wy *RDERBYSW* DE65 .... 69 G2
The Parkway *LEIE* LE5 .... 126 F8
Parkwood Ct *BLWL* NG6 .... 36 C2 🔟
Parkyn Rd *ARN* NG5 .... 37 H1
Parkyns St *CFTN/RUD* NG11 .. 79 C1 🔽
Parliament Cl *DERBYW* DE22 .. 2 A6
Parliament St *DERBYW* DE22 .. 2 B6
  LEIS LE2 .... 6 E9
  NOTT NG1 .... 4 F6 🔽
Parlour Cl *WGSTN* LE18 .... 138 A5
Parr Ga *BSTN/STPLFD* NG9 ..... 62 E2
Parr La *CALV/BJ* NG14 .... 27 L2
The Parrs *BSTN/STPLFD* NG9 ... 63 M1
Parry Wy *ARN* NG5 .... 25 M7
Parsons Dr *LEIS* LE2 .... 136 E4
  RLBORO LE12 .... 114 C3
Parsons Gv *RIPLEY* DE5 .... 19 H5
Parsons Meadow *CARL* NG4 ..... 52 C3
Parsonwood HI *COAL* LE67 ..... 108 C2
Partridge Cl *RLBORO* LE12 ... 113 K5 🔽
  RLEINE/SYS LE7 .... 120 D3 🔽
Partridge Rd *LEIE* LE5 .... 126 D2
Partridge Wy *MCKLVR* DE3 ..... 56 E4
Parvian Rd *WGSTN* LE18 .... 137 L2
Pasley Cl *LEIS* LE2 .... 137 H3 🔽
Pasley Rd *LEIS* LE2 .... 137 H3
Pasteur Av *RIPLEY* DE5 .... 11 H5
Pasture Cl *WBRGFD* NG2 .... 52 C3
Pasture La *CFTN/RUD* NG11 ... 78 D2
  LEI LE1 .... 6 D3
  LGEAT NG10 .... 76 E3
  RLBORO LE12 .... 94 E1
  RLBORO LE12 .... 94 F5
Pasture Rd *BSTN/STPLFD* NG9 .. 48 B6
Pastures Av *CFTN/RUD* NG11 .. 64 B7
Pastures HI *NORM/LIT* DE23 ... 56 E7
The Pastures *BPR/DUF* DE56 ... 29 J3
  EWD/SEL/PNX NG16 .... 21 M7 🔽
  RLBORO LE12 .... 113 J1
  RLEINE/SYS LE7 .... 120 C4
  RLEIW/BAR LE9 .... 135 L6
Pateley Rd *ARN* NG5 .... 37 L3
Paterson Av *DERBYE* DE21 ..... 58 E1
Paterson Cl *LEIE* LE4 .... 124 E1 🔽
Paterson Dr *RLBORO* LE12 ..... 111 K6
Paterson Pl *NORM/LIT* DE23 ... 101 M2
Patmore Sq *NORM/LIT* DE23 ... 57 K8 🔽
Paton Rd *ARN* NG5 .... 36 C2
Paton St *LEIS* LE2 .... 6 A9
Patricia Dr *ARN* NG5 .... 25 L6
Patrick Rd *WBRGFD* NG2 .... 51 J7
Patterdale Cl *WBRGFD* NG2 .... 66 A1
Patterdale Dr *RLBORO* LE11 ... 103 C6
Patterdale Rd *ARN* NG5 .... 37 K2
  LEIN LE4 .... 126 C1 🔽
Patterson Rd *NOTTE* NG7 ...... 4 B2 🔽
Paudy La *RLBORO* LE12 .... 106 A6
  RMMWB LE14 .... 107 H1
Paul Dr *LEIE* LE4 .... 126 D3
Pauline Av *LEIN* LE4 .... 125 M3
Pavilion Cl *WBRGFD* NG2 ...... 51 H6 🔽
Pavilion Rd *ARN* NG5 .... 24 F6
  ILK DE7 .... 33 J2
  NORM/LIT DE23 .... 57 G7
  WBRGFD NG2 .... 51 J6 🔽
Pawley Cl *RLEIW/BAR* LE8 ..... 142 E2
Pawley Gdns *LEIS* LE2 .... 137 H3
Paxton Cl *MCKLVR* DE3 .... 56 A6
Paxton Gdns
  MAPPK/POR/STA NG3 .... 5 L5
Payne Rd *BSTN/STPLFD* NG9 .... 62 E4
Payne St *DERBYW* DE22 .... 57 H1 🔽
  LEIN LE4 .... 125 M4
Peach Av *EWD/SEL/PNX* NG16 .. 13 K1
Peache Wy *BSTN/STPLFD* NG9 .. 48 F8
Peachey St *NOTT* NG1 .... 5 H3 🔽
Peach St *DERBYW* DE22 .... 57 H2
  HEANOR DE75 .... 20 B6
Peacock Cl *CFTN/RUD* NG11 ... 78 F1
Peacock Crs *CFTN/RUD* NG11 .. 64 C5
Peacock Dr *RLEIW/BBY* LE8 .. 142 D2
Peacock La *LEI* LE1 .... 6 D6
Peacock Pl *ILK* DE7 .... 33 H3
Peacroft Cl *RDERBYSW* DE65 .. 68 B5
Peacroft La *RDERBYSW* DE65 .. 68 B6
Peak Av *ALFN* DE55 .... 11 M1
Peakdale *WGSTN* LE18 .... 138 D6
Peakdale Cl *LGEAT* NG10 ...... 75 L1
  RIPLEY DE5 .... 19 H1 🔽
Peak Dr *DERBYSE* DE24 .... 57 L8
Peake Rd *LEIE* LE4 .... 126 B6
Pearce Dr *WOL/BIL/BRX* NG8 .. 49 M1
Pearl Cl *DERBYE* DE21 .... 44 E5
Pearmain Dr
  MAPPK/POR/STA NG3 .... 37 K8
Pearson Av *BSTN/STPLFD* NG9 . 62 F2
Pearson St *CARL* NG4 .... 52 E1
  NOTTE NG7 .... 36 D5 🔽
Pear Tree Av *RIPLEY* DE5 ..... 11 G7
Peartree Av *RLBORO* LE12 .... 102 B4 🔽
Peartree Cl *CDON/KEG* DE74 .. 84 E4 🔽
  LEIW LE3 .... 123 M8
  RLEINE/SYS LE7 .... 124 B2
Pear Tree Crs *NORM/LIT* DE23 . 57 L7
Pear Tree La *RLBORO* LE12 ... 102 F1
Peartree Orch
  CFTN/RUD NG11 .... 65 G8 🔽
Pear Tree Rd *NORM/LIT* DE23 . 57 L7 🔽
Pear Tree St *NORM/LIT* DE23 . 57 L7
Peary Cl *ARN* NG5 .... 36 D1
Peasehill Rd *RIPLEY* DE5 ..... 11 J7
Peashill Rd *RLBORO* LE12 ..... 114 C4
Peas Hill Rd
  MAPPK/POR/STA NG3 .... 5 J3
Peatburn Av *HEANOR* DE75 ..... 20 A6
Peatfield Rd *BSTN/STPLFD* NG9 . 48 B6
Peatling Rd *RLEIW/BBY* LE8 .. 143 L5
Peckham Gdns *DERBYW* DE22 ... 56 E2 🔽
Peckleton Common
  RLEIW/BAR LE9 .... 128 A8
Peckleton La *RLEIW/BAR* LE8 . 128 C7
Pedlars Cl *LEIS* LE2 .... 124 F4
Pedley St *ILK* DE7 .... 33 K8
Pedmore Va *ARN* NG5 .... 24 E8
Peebles Cl *DERBYSE* DE24 ..... 71 J5 🔽

Peebles Wy *LEIN* LE4 .... 126 B4
Peel Cl *RLEIW/BBY* LE8 .... 146 D7
Peel Dr *LBORO* LE11 .... 9 L2
Peel St *DERBYW* DE22 .... 57 H1
  EWD/SEL/PNX NG16 .... 20 F4
  LGEAT NG10 .... 62 C7
  NOTT NG1 .... 4 F4
Peel Vls *MAPPK/POR/STA* NG3 . 37 J5 🔽
Peers Cl *DERBYE* DE21 .... 44 F5
Peet St *DERBYW* DE22 .... 2 B5
Peewit Cl *LEIN* LE4 .... 136 E4 🔽
Pegasus Cl *LEIS* LE2 .... 7 K6
Pegasus Wy *RDERBYSW* DE65 .. 68 C5
Peggs La *RLEINE/SYS* LE7 ..... 121 K2
Pegwell Cl *NORM/LIT* DE23 ... 57 H8
Peldar Pl *COAL* LE67 .... 108 F7
Peldon Cl *LEIN* LE4 .... 125 H5
Pelham Av *ARN* NG5 .... 36 F7
  ILK DE7 .... 33 J6 🔽
Pelham Crs *BSTN/STPLFD* NG9 . 49 M8
  NOTTE NG7 .... 4 B7
Pelham Rd *ARN* NG5 .... 36 F7
Pelham St *DERBYW* DE22 .... 2 C6
  ILK DE7 .... 33 J6 🔽
  LEI LE1 .... 6 E8
  LEIS LE2 .... 138 E1
  NOTT NG1 .... 5 H7
Pelham Wy *LEI* LE1 .... 6 E8
Pell Cl *RLBORO* LE12 .... 105 J7
Pells Cl *RLEIW/BBY* LE8 ...... 145 K7
Pemberton St *NOTT* NG1 .... 5 K8 🔽
Pembrey Cl
  BSTN/STPLFD NG9 .... 48 B5 🔽
Pembridge Cl *BLWL* NG6 .... 36 B5 🔽
Pembroke Av *RLEINE/SYS* LE7 . 120 F5
  WGSTN LE18 .... 137 K5 🔽
Pembroke St *DERBYE* DE21 ..... 44 B7 🔽
  DERBYE DE21 .... 44 B8 🔽
  LEIS LE2 .... 7 L2
Pembury Cl *RLEIW/BBY* LE8 .. 139 M6 🔽
Pembury Rd
  WOL/BIL/BRX NG8 .... 49 J2 🔽
Penallton Cl *DERBYSE* DE24 .. 72 C1
Penarth Gdns
  MAPPK/POR/STA NG3 .... 37 J4
Penarth Ri *ARN* NG5 .... 37 J4
Pen Cl *WGSTN* LE18 .... 137 J3
Penclose Rd *RLEIW/BBY* LE8 .. 145 J7
Pendene Rd *LEIS* LE2 .... 132 A6
Pendennis Cl *CARL* NG4 .... 38 F6 🔽
  DERBYE DE21 .... 72 F1 🔽
Pendine Cl *ARN* NG5 .... 25 H6
Pendlebury Dr *LEIS* LE2 ...... 131 L8
Pendle Crs
  MAPPK/POR/STA NG3 .... 37 K6
Pendleside Wy *NORM/LIT* DE23 . 56 C8
Pendock La *COT/KEY/RAD* NG12 . 79 K5
Pendragon Wy *LEIW* LE3 .... 129 K5
Penfold Cl *RLEIW/BBY* LE8 .. 140 B7
Penfold Dr *RLEIW/BBY* LE8 .. 143 H4
Penge Rd *DERBYW* DE22 .... 42 E8 🔽
Penhale Dr *HUCK/RAV* NG15 ... 23 G2
Penhale Rd *RLEIW/BAR* LE9 ... 130 D7 🔽
Penhaligon's Cl
  MELB/CHEL DE73 .... 72 D6 🔽
Penhurst Cl *CFTN/RUD* NG11 .. 64 E3 🔽
Pen La *COT/KEY/RAD* NG12 .... 91 H3
Penllech Cl *ARN* NG5 .... 24 E8
Penman Wy *RLEIW/BAR* LE9 .... 136 C2
Pennant Cl *LEIW* LE3 .... 124 B8
Pennant Rd *BLWL* NG6 .... 36 B5
Pennine Vw *BPR/DUF* DE56 ..... 10 C7
Penn La *MELB/CHEL* DE73 ...... 82 E8
Penn St *BPR/DUF* DE56 .... 17 L3
Pennycress Cl
  NORM/LIT DE23 .... 56 E8 🔽
Pennyfields Bvd *LGEAT* NG10 . 61 L8
Pennyfoot St *NOTT* NG1 .... 5 L8
Penny Long La *DERBYW* DE22 .. 43 J7
Penrhyn Av *NORM/LIT* DE23 ... 57 H7
Penrhyn Cl *MAPPK/POR/STA* NG3 . 5 J4
Penrhyn Crs *BSTN/STPLFD* NG9 . 62 F3
Penrith Av *COT/KEY/RAD* NG12 . 53 L3
  RLBORO LE12 .... 101 K5
Penrith Crs *WOL/BIL/BRX* NG8 . 36 A5
Penrith Pl *DERBYE* DE21 ...... 44 B5 🔽
Penrith Rd *LEIN* LE4 .... 126 A5
Penryn Dr *WGSTN* LE18 .... 138 A6 🔽
Penshore Cl *CFTN/RUD* NG11 .. 64 B6
Pensilva Cl *WGSTN* LE18 ...... 138 A6
Pentewen Cl *DERBYW* DE22 .... 43 J5
Pentland Av *RLBORO* LE12 .... 102 B5
Pentland Cl *DERBYE* DE21 ..... 58 F5
Pentland Gdns *LGEAT* NG10 ... 61 L6
Pentrich Rd *RIPLEY* DE5 ...... 11 H5
Pentridge Cl *WGSTN* LE18 .... 138 A7 🔽
Pentridge Dr *ILK* DE7 .... 33 G4
Pentwood Av *ARN* NG5 .... 25 K5
Penzance Av *WGSTN* LE18 ...... 138 A6
Penzance Rd *DERBYSE* DE24 ... 72 F2 🔽
Peppercorn Cl *LEIN* LE4 ...... 125 G4
Pepper La *ILK* DE7 .... 47 J6
Pepper's Cl *RLBORO* LE12 ..... 113 H3
Peppers Dr *CDON/KEG* DE74 ... 85 M5
Percival Av *ARN* NG5 .... 37 G5
Percival Rd *LEIE* LE5 .... 126 B8
Percy Rd *LEIS* LE2 .... 131 J8
Percy St *BLWL* NG6 .... 36 B4
  DERBYW DE22 .... 2 B7
  EWD/SEL/PNX NG16 .... 21 L5
  ILK DE7 .... 33 K8 🔽
  LEIW LE3 .... 130 E7
Percy Wood Cl
  RDERBYSW DE65 .... 68 A5 🔽
Peregrine Dr *DERBYSE* DE24 .. 71 H3 🔽
  NOTTE NG7 .... 50 C3 🔽
Peregrine Ri *LEIN* LE4 .... 124 E1 🔽

Peregrine Rd *RLEIW/BAR* LE9 . 141 J8
Perivale Cl *HUCK/RAV* NG16 .. 35 H4
Perkyn Rd *LEIE* LE5 .... 133 G1
Perlethorpe Av *CARL* NG4 ..... 38 B5
  5 M8
Perlethorpe Cl *CARL* NG4 .... 38 C5 🔽
Perlethorpe Dr *CARL* NG4 ..... 38 B5
  HUCK/RAV NG15 .... 15 M8
Perran Av *COAL* LE67 .... 108 C5
Perry Cl *RLBORO* LE12 .... 111 K5
Perry Gdns *ARN* NG5 .... 36 F4
Perry Gv *LBORO* LE11 .... 9 J3
Perry Rd *ARN* NG5 .... 36 D4
Perseverance St *LEIN* LE4 ... 125 L2
Perth Av *LEIW* LE3 .... 124 E8
Perth Cl *MCKLVR* DE3 .... 56 C3
Perth Dr *BSTN/STPLFD* NG9 ... 48 C6
Perth St *DERBYE* DE21 .... 44 B6
  NOTT NG1 .... 5 H5
Peterborough St
  DERBYE DE21 .... 44 C7 🔽
Peterlee Pl *DERBYSE* DE24 ... 72 E5 🔽
Peters Cl *ARN* NG5 .... 38 A1
  EWD/SEL/PNX NG16 .... 22 A5
  RLEIW/BAR LE9 .... 140 A5
Peters Dr *LEIE* LE5 .... 126 F8
Petersfield Cl *RLEIW/BAR* LE9 141 G3
Petersfield Cl *ARN* NG5 ..... 24 D8 🔽
Petersfield Rd *COAL* LE67 ... 108 E4
Petersgate *LGEAT* NG10 .... 61 L6
Petersgate Cl *LGEAT* NG10 .. 61 L5 🔽
Petersham Dr *DERBYSE* DE24 .. 73 G1
Petersham Ms *NOTTE* NG7 .... 50 D4 🔟
Petersham Rd *LGEAT* NG10 ... 61 L5
Petty Close La *ASHB* DE6 ..... 41 G5
Petunia Cl *LEIW* LE3 .... 129 K5 🔽
Petworth Av *BSTN/STPLFD* NG9 . 62 D4
Petworth Dr *ARN* NG5 .... 36 D3
  LBORO LE11 .... 103 G2
  LEIW LE3 .... 130 F1
Pevensey Av *LEIE* LE5 .... 133 H4
Pevensey Rd *LBORO* LE11 ...... 103 J2
Peverel Rd *LEIW* LE3 .... 130 E5
Peveril Av *RLEIW/BRSTN* DE72 . 60 A5
Peveril Cl *ALFN* DE55 .... 11 M1
Peveril Ct *RIPLEY* DE5 .... 11 G6
Peveril Crs *ILK* DE7 .... 32 C7
  LGEAT NG10 .... 75 K2
Peveril Dr *ALFN* DE55 .... 12 A1
  ILK DE7 .... 33 H5
  NOTTE NG7 .... 4 E9
  WBRGFD NG2 .... 65 J4
Peveril St *BSTN/STPLFD* NG9 . 49 K7
  HUCK/RAV NG15 .... 15 L7
  NOTTE NG7 .... 4 B3
Pheasant Field Dr
  DERBYE DE21 .... 59 L1 🔽
Philip Av *EWD/SEL/PNX* NG16 . 35 G1
  EWD/SEL/PNX NG16 .... 21 L9
Philip Gv *CARL* NG4 .... 38 C5
Philips Cft *BPR/DUF* DE56 .... 29 J3
Phillip Dr *WGSTN* LE18 .... 137 J6
Phillips Crs *LEIN* LE4 .... 124 E1
Phipps Cl *RLEIW/BBY* LE8 .... 142 E1
Phoenix Av *CARL* NG4 .... 38 C5
Phoenix Cl *DERBYW* DE22 ..... 50 F5 🔽
Phoenix Dr *RLBORO* LE12 ...... 114 B5
Phoenix St *DERBYE* DE1 .... 2 F2
Phyllis Gv *LGEAT* NG10 .... 62 D8
Piccadilly *BLWL* NG6 .... 36 B1
Piccaver Ri *LEIW* LE3 .... 130 B1
Pickard La *BPR/DUF* DE56 ..... 10 B6
Pickering Av
  EWD/SEL/PNX NG16 .... 21 K5
Pickering Cl *LEIN* LE4 ...... 126 B6 🔽
Pickering Ri *DERBYE* DE21 ... 44 A6
Pick St *RLBORO* LE12 .... 101 M3
Pickwell Cl *LEIE* LE5 .... 124 C7
Pieris Dr *CFTN/RUD* NG11 ..... 64 A6
Pierrepont Av *CARL* NG4 ..... 38 C6 🔽
Pierrepont Rd *WBRGFD* NG2 ... 51 L7
Piers Rd *LEIW* LE3 .... 124 A6
Pilcher Ga *NOTT* NG1 .... 5 J7 🔽
Pilgrims Wy *DERBYE* DE24 ..... 71 G5
Pilkington Rd *LEIW* LE3 ...... 130 C4
  MAPPK/POR/STA NG3 .... 37 L6
Pilkington St *BLWL* NG6 ..... 23 M8 🔽
Pilsley Cl *BPR/DUF* DE56 .... 18 A1 🔽
Pimlico *DERBYW* DE22 .... 56 F1 🔽
  ILK DE7 .... 33 J7
Pimlico Av *BSTN/STPLFD* NG9 . 48 F4
Pimm's Rd *ASHB* DE6 .... 41 L7
Pimpernel Cl *RLEIW/BAR* LE9 . 135 K6
Pinchom's Hill Rd
  BPR/DUF DE56 .... 17 M4
Pindar Rd *LEIW* LE3 .... 124 F7
Pinder St *WBRGFD* NG2 .... 5 K8
Pine Av *EWD/SEL/PNX* NG16 ... 20 E4
Pine Cl *DERBYE* DE21 .... 58 F3
  ILK DE7 .... 31 K2
  RDERBYSW DE65 .... 68 F3
  RIPLEY DE5 .... 11 H6
  RLBORO LE12 .... 88 B7
  RLBORO LE12 .... 103 L8
Pinecroft Ct *DERBYE* DE21 ... 44 F6
Pine Dr *RLEINE/SYS* LE7 ...... 120 F5
Pine Gv *HUCK/RAV* NG15 .... 23 M3
Pine Hill Cl *ARN* NG5 .... 25 M6
Pinehurst Av *HUCK/RAV* NG15 . 23 G2 🔽
Pinehurst Cl *LEIW* LE3 ...... 130 A1 🔽
Pine Rd *LEIW* LE3 .... 124 A7
Pine Tree Av *GBY/RBY* LE6 ... 123 K5
  LEIE LE5 .... 126 E8
Pine Tree Cl *LEIS* LE2 .... 138 F3
Pine Tree Gv *LEIW* LE3 .... 129 J5
Pinewood *RIPLEY* DE5 .... 11 M8
Pinewood Av *ARN* NG5 .... 25 M6
  LEIN LE4 .... 126 C2
Pinewood Cl *LEIN* LE4 .... 124 D2
  RLEIW/BBY LE8 .... 143 J3
Pinewood Dr *COAL* LE67 .... 122 C1
Pinewood Gdns
  CFTN/RUD NG11 .... 64 B7
Pinewood Rd *BPR/DUF* DE56 ... 17 J1

Pinfold *LEIW* LE3 .... 130 C8
Pinfold Cl *CALV/BJ* NG14 .... 27 G3
  COT/KEY/RAD NG12 .... 67 K4
Pinfold Crs *CALV/BJ* NG14 ... 27 G3
Pinfold Ga *LBORO* LE11 .... 9 K5
Pinfold La *BSTN/STPLFD* NG9 . 48 C8
Pinfold Rd *EWD/SEL/PNX* NG16 . 22 C4
  LEIN LE4 .... 126 A1
The Pinfold *BPR/DUF* DE56 ... 18 A2 🔽
  BWSH/BRSTN DE72 .... 73 K3
  COAL LE67 .... 116 C7
Pingle *DERBYW* DE22 .... 43 J3
Pingle Crs *ARN* NG5 .... 24 D7
  BPR/DUF DE56 .... 17 K2
Pingle La *BPR/DUF* DE56 ...... 10 D5
  BPR/DUF DE56 .... 17 K2
  RLEIW/BAR LE9 .... 134 C8
Pingle St *LEIW* LE3 .... 6 C3
The Pingle *DERBYE* DE21 ...... 59 J3
  LGEAT NG10 .... 62 B7 🔽
  RLBORO LE12 .... 112 C2
Pingreaves Dr
  MELB/CHEL DE73 .... 72 E5 🔽
Pintail Cl *RLEIW/BAR* LE9 ... 52 F2
  RLEIW/BBY LE8 .... 142 C3
Piper Cl *HUCK/RAV* NG15 ..... 15 M5 🔽
  LBORO LE11 .... 8 E8
  LEIW LE3 .... 124 E8
  RLBORO LE12 .... 94 A5
  RLBORO LE12 .... 101 M1
Piper Dr *RLBORO* LE12 .... 94 A4
Piper Wy *LEIW* LE3 .... 124 E8
Pippin Cl *MAPPK/POR/STA* NG3 . 37 K8
Pippin HI *RIPLEY* DE5 .... 19 J6
Pitcairn Cl *WBRGFD* NG2 ...... 51 G6
Pitchens Cl *LEIN* LE4 .... 124 D2 🔽
Pit Close La *MELB/CHEL* DE73 . 72 E6 🔽
Pithouse La *RLBORO* LE12 ..... 87 J6
Pit La *HEANOR* DE75 .... 32 F1
  RIPLEY DE5 .... 11 L8
Pits Av *LEIW* LE3 .... 130 C8
Pitsford Dr *LBORO* LE11 ...... 102 E5
Pittar St *DERBYW* DE22 .... 2 C7
Pitton Cl *WGSTN* LE18 .... 138 A7
Plackett Cl *BSTN/STPLFD* NG9 . 48 D7
  BWSH/BRSTN DE72 .... 61 H7
Plain Ga *RLEINE/SYS* LE7 ..... 113 G7
Plaintree Ct
  MAPPK/POR/STA NG3 .... 5 K5
Plaintree St
  MAPPK/POR/STA NG3 .... 5 K5
Plantain Gdns
  NORM/LIT DE23 .... 71 G2 🔽
Plantation Av *LEIE* LE5 ...... 137 G1
Plantation Cl *ARN* NG5 ...... 24 F6 🔽
Plantation Rd
  COT/KEY/RAD NG12 .... 80 B4
  WOL/BIL/BRX NG8 .... 48 F3
Plantation Side *NOTTE* NG7 .. 36 C8
The Plantations *LGEAT* NG10 . 61 L7 🔽
The Plantation *RLEIW/BBY* LE8 . 143 J3
Plant La *LGEAT* NG10 .... 75 L3
Platt La *COT/KEY/RAD* NG12 .. 80 E1
Platts Av *HEANOR* DE75 ...... 20 A6 🔽
Platts La *RLBORO* LE12 .... 114 A8
Player Cl *LEIE* LE4 .... 126 B2 🔽
Player St *NOTTE* NG7 .... 4 C5
Plaza Gdns *BLWL* NG6 .... 36 D3 🔽
Pleasant Cl *LBORO* LE11 ...... 9 G2
  LEIW LE3 .... 129 K5
Pleasant Pl *CDON/KEG* DE74 .. 86 B5
Pleasant Rw *NOTTE* NG7 .... 4 A2
Plimsoll St *DERBYW* DE22 .... 57 L1 🔽
Plough Cl *RLBORO* LE12 ...... 113 H7 🔽
Ploughfield Cl
  NORM/LIT DE23 .... 70 F1 🔽
Plough Ga *DERBYW* DE22 ...... 43 K5 🔽
Plough La *NOTT* NG1 .... 5 L8
Ploughman Av *CALV/BJ* NG14 .. 27 H3 🔽
Ploughmans Dr
  RLBORO LE12 .... 102 A2 🔽
Ploughman's Lea
  RLEINE/SYS LE7 .... 115 H8
Plover Crs *LEIN* LE4 .... 124 F1
Plowman Cl *LEIW* LE3 .... 124 A6 🔽
Plowman St
  BSTN/STPLFD NG9 .... 62 B1 🔽
Plowright St
  MAPPK/POR/STA NG3 .... 5 H1
Plumb Rd *HUCK/RAV* NG15 ...... 15 K8
Plumptre Cl
  EWD/SEL/PNX NG16 .... 21 K6 🔽
Plumptre Pl *NOTT* NG1 .... 5 J8 🔽
Plumptre Rd
  EWD/SEL/PNX NG16 .... 20 F2
Plumptre Sq *NOTT* NG1 .... 5 K8 🔽
Plumptre Wy
  EWD/SEL/PNX NG16 .... 21 K6
Plumtree Cl *LBORO* LE11 ..... 103 K1
Plumtree Rd
  COT/KEY/RAD NG12 .... 67 J4
Plumtree Wy *RLEINE/SYS* LE7 . 120 F5
Plungar Cl *WOL/BIL/BRX* NG8 . 49 M1 🔽
Pluto Cl *LEIS* LE2 .... 7 K6
Plymouth Cl *LEIE* LE5 .... 132 D4
Plymstock Cl *LEIW* LE3 .... 130 F1
Poachers Cl *LEIW* LE3 .... 123 M7 🔽
Poachers Pl *LEIS* LE2 .... 139 H3 🔽
Pochin's Bridge Rd
  WGSTN LE18 .... 137 L3
Pochins Cl *WGSTN* LE18 .... 138 A6
Pochin St *RLEIW/BAR* LE9 ... 141 G3
Pochin Wy *RLBORO* LE12 .... 114 B3
Pocket End *LBORO* LE11 .... 103 H7
Pocklingtons Wk *LEI* LE1 .... 6 E6
Podder La *MAPPK/POR/STA* NG3 . 38 A1
The Point *MAPPK/POR/STA* NG3 . 37 M7
Polaris Cl *LEIS* LE2 .... 7 M8
Polden Cl *RLBORO* LE12 .... 102 A5

Pole's Rd *ASHB* DE6 .... 41 L7
Pollard Rd *LEIW* LE3 .... 130 C4
Pollards Oaks
  BWSH/BRSTN DE72 .... 59 M6 🔽
Polly Bott's Lane or Lea La
  COAL 116 E3
Polperro Wy *HUCK/RAV* NG15 .. 23 G2
Pomeroy Dr *LEIS* LE2 .... 138 D2
Pond Hills La *ARN* NG5 .... 25 K6
Pond Rd *BPR/DUF* DE56 .... 18 A8
Pond St *RLBORO* LE12 .... 106 D8
Ponsonby Ter *DERBY* DE1 ..... 2 B4
Pontefract St *DERBYSE*
Pontypool Cl *DERBYE* DE21 ... 44 F5 🔟
Pool Cl *DERBYSE* DE24 .... 73 G3
Poole Meadow *CARL* NG4 .... 52 D3
Poole St *DERBYSE* DE24 ...... 72 C1 🔽
Pool Rd *LEIW* LE3 .... 130 F1
Pope Crs *RLEIW/BAR* LE9 ..... 135 L4
Pope St *LEIS* LE2 .... 131 L7
Popham St *NOTT* NG1 .... 5 J8
Poplar Av *ARN* NG5 .... 36 E6
  COAL LE67 .... 116 E7
  DERBYE DE21 .... 59 J2
  LEIN LE4 .... 119 J7
  LGEAT NG10 .... 47 L8
  RIPLEY DE5 .... 11 H7
  RLBORO LE12 .... 88 B7
  RLEIW/BBY LE8 .... 143 J4
Poplar Cl *CARL* NG4 .... 52 B1
  DERBYSE DE24 .... 58 F8 🔽
Poplar Crs *EWD/SEL/PNX* NG16 . 34 C1
Poplar HI *RLBORO* LE12 .... 105 L3
Poplar Nook *DERBYW* DE22 ... 43 L3 🔽
Poplar Rd *BWSH/BRSTN* DE72 .. 61 K6
  LBORO LE11 .... 103 M7
  RLEIW/BAR LE9 .... 141 M1
Poplar Rw *DERBYW* DE22 ...... 43 L6 🔽
Poplars Av *CALV/BJ* NG14 .... 39 L2
Poplars Cl *COT/KEY/RAD* NG12 . 80 D3
  GBY/RBY LE6 .... 123 J6
The Poplars *BSTN/STPLFD* NG9 . 49 K8
  LEIE LE5 .... 130 E8
Poplar St *NOTT* NG1 .... 5 K8
  WBRGFD NG2 .... 65 K1
Poplar Wy *ILK* DE7 .... 47 H2
The Poppins *LEIE* LE4 .... 124 F1
Poppy Cl *RLBORO* LE12 .... 111 L1
  WGSTN LE18 .... 137 K3
Porchester Rd
  MAPPK/POR/STA NG3 .... 37 L8
Porlock Cl *LGEAT* NG10 ...... 61 L7 🔽
  RLBORO LE12 .... 102 A5
Porlock St *LEIN* LE4 .... 130 F2
Portage Cl
  COT/KEY/RAD NG12 .... 53 J5
Port Arthur Rd *WBRGFD* NG2 . 51 L3 🔽
Portcullis Rd *LEIE* LE5 ...... 127 J6
Porter Cl *CFTN/RUD* NG11 ... 64 A7 🔽
Porterhouse Rd *RIPLEY* DE5 .. 11 K6
Porter Rd *NORM/LIT* DE23 ..... 57 J5
Porter's La *DERBYE* DE21 ..... 44 D4
  RDERBYSW DE65 .... 70 B5
Portgate *WGSTN* LE18 .... 138 C6 🔽
Porthcawl Pl *DERBYE* DE21 .. 45 G5 🔽
Portico Rd *NORM/LIT* DE23 ... 70 E1
Portinscale Cl *WBRGFD* NG2 .. 66 A2
Portishead Rd *LEIE* LE5 ...... 126 C7
Portland Cl *MCKLVR* DE3 ...... 56 B5
Portland Ct *ARN* NG5 .... 36 F2
Portland Crs
  BSTN/STPLFD NG9 .... 62 C1 🔽
Portland Gra *BSTN/STPLFD* NG9 . 62 E6
  CARL NG4 .... 38 A5 🔽
  EWD/SEL/PNX NG16 .... 21 M7 🔽
  ILK DE7 .... 33 K4
  LGEAT NG10 .... 75 L3
  NOTTE NG7 .... 4 D5
  RLEIW/BAR LE9 .... 129 J2
  WBRGFD NG2 .... 65 K1
Portland Rd *ARN* NG5 .... 37 J1
  BSTN/STPLFD NG9 .... 49 L8 🔽
  DERBYE DE21 .... 57 L7
  RDERBYSW DE65 .... 68 F3
  RLEIW/BAR LE9 .... 142 B4
Portloc Dr *WGSTN* LE18 .... 138 A7
Portman Cha *DERBYSE* DE24 ... 71 H5
Portman St *LEIN* LE4 .... 125 M5
Portmore Cl *LEIN* LE4 .... 125 G5
Portreath Dr *DERBYW* DE22 ... 43 J4
Portree Dr *ARN* NG5 .... 24 D5
Portsdown Rd *LEIS* LE2 .... 138 B1
Portsmouth Rd *LEIN* LE4 ..... 125 L6
Port Wy *DERBYE* DE21 .... 30 B3
Portway Cl *DERBYW* DE22 .... 43 L3 🔽
The Portwey *LEIE* LE5 .... 126 C7
Postern St *NOTT* NG1 .... 4 F7
Post Office La *RLEIW/BBY* LE8 . 139 K8
Post Rd *RLEINE/SYS* LE7 ...... 120 C6
Posy La *BWSH/BRSTN* DE72 .... 73 L8
Potato Pit La *ILK* DE7 .... 46 E6
Pott Acre *RLBORO* LE12 ...... 113 K6 🔽
Potters Cl *ARN* NG5 .... 24 E8
Potters La *RLBORO* LE12 ...... 88 C7
Potter St *DERBYE* DE21 .... 59 H3
  LEI LE1 .... 7 G4 🔽
  MELB/CHEL DE73 .... 82 F8
Potterton Rd *LEIE* LE4 ...... 125 H3
Pottery Cl *BPR/DUF* DE56 ..... 18 A2
Pottery La *RIPLEY* DE5 .... 19 G4
Pougher Cl *RLEIW/BAR* LE9 ... 140 C8
Poulteney Dr *RLBORO* LE12 ... 112 C1
Poulter Cl *NOTTE* NG7 .... 36 B8
Poulton Dr *WBRGFD* NG2 .... 51 K4
Poultry AV *NOTT* NG1 .... 5 H7 🔽
Powell St *NORM/LIT* DE23 ..... 57 J5
Powis St *BLWL* NG6 .... 23 M8 🔽
Powtrell Pl *ILK* DE7 .... 47 M1
Powys Av *LEIS* LE2 .... 132 C6
Poynings Av *LEIW* LE3 .... 130 E1
Poynter Cl *HEANOR* DE75 ..... 20 A6 🔽
Poyser Av *DERBYE* DE21 .... 44 E8
Poyser La *ASHB* DE6 .... 41 L6
Prebend St *LEIS* LE2 .... 7 H8
Premier Rd *NOTTE* NG7 .... 36 F7

Prendwick Gdns ARN NG5 24 F7 4
Prescot Cl MCKLVR DE3 56 A6
Presents La RLBORO LE12 100 F1
Prestbury Cl DERBYE DE21 44 F6 10
Prestbury Rd LBORO LE11 102 F3
Preston Cl RLBORO LE12 114 A5
Preston Ri LEIE LE5 127 G6
Prestwick Cl
WOL/BIL/BRX NG8 35 H5 8
Prestwold La RLBORO LE12 97 H8
Prestwold Rd LEIE LE5 126 B7
Prestwood Dr
WOL/BIL/BRX NG8 35 M8
Pretoria Cl LEIN LE4 119 G8 4
Pretoria Rd RLEIW/BAR LE9 129 H1
Previn Gdns
MAPPK/POR/STA NG3 51 K1
Price Wy LEIN LE4 120 D8
Pride Pkwy DERBYSE DE24 3 L6
Priestland Av DERBYE DE21 59 H3
Priestley Rd LEIW LE3 130 E3
Priest Meadow
RLEIW/BBY LE8 145 K7 1
Primary Cl BPR/DUF DE56 17 L3 3
Prime Pkwy DERBY DE1 3 G1
Primerose Wy RLEINE/SYS LE7 121 J1
Primrose Av
EWD/SEL/PNX NG16 13 K5 2
Primrose Cl DERBYE DE21 44 D4
MAPPK/POR/STA NG3 5 K2
RLEIW/BAR LE9 135 L7
Primrose Crs CARL NG4 38 D8 4
Primrose Dr ILK DE7 31 G7
Primrose Hl ILK DE7 33 J4 5
LEIS LE2 138 D1
Primrose Ri EWD/SEL/PNX NG16 21 L7
Primrose St CARL NG4 38 D8
ILK DE7 33 J4 2
Primrose Wy RLEIW/BAR LE9 129 K1
Primula Cl CFTN/RUD NG11 64 A5
Primula Wy NORM/LIT DE23 71 H3
Prince Albert Dr LEIW LE3 124 A8
Prince Charles Av DERBYW DE22 42 F8
DERBYW DE22 56 D2
Prince Dr LEIS LE2 139 G2
Prince Edward Crs
COT/KEY/RAD NG12 53 H5
Princes Cl RLEINE/SYS LE7 124 C1
Princes Dr NORM/LIT DE23 56 F5
Princess Av BSTN/STPLFD NG9 63 L1
LEIS LE2 139 G3
Princess Cl CARL NG4 38 C5
Princess Dr BWSH/BRSTN DE72 59 L6
LGEAT NG10 61 M3 2
RLEIW/BAR LE9 129 H3
Princess Road Backways
LEI LE1 6 F8 3
Princess Rd East LEI LE1 7 G9
Princess Rd West LEI LE1 6 F8
Princess St LBORO LE11 9 J5
LGEAT NG10 62 B7
RLEIW/BAR LE9 136 A7
Princes St EWD/SEL/PNX NG16 21 K4
NORM/LIT DE23 57 L6
Prince St COAL LE67 108 B7
ILK DE7 33 J3
LGEAT NG10 62 B7
Prince William Rd LBORO LE11 103 L1
Prioridge COT/KEY/RAD NG12 67 L5
Prior Rd ARN NG5 37 H1
Priors Barn Cl
BWSH/BRSTN DE72 60 A5
Priorway Av BWSH/BRSTN DE72 60 A5
Priorway Gdns
BWSH/BRSTN DE72 60 A6 3
Priory Av COT/KEY/RAD NG12 66 A6
Priory Circ COT/KEY/RAD NG12 66 A6
Priory Cl COAL LE67 100 A7
ILK DE7 47 G1 1
MELB/CHEL DE73 72 E6
RLEINE/SYS LE7 120 D4
Priory Crs CARL NG4 38 D6 2
LEIW LE3 130 C2
Priory Gdns DERBYE DE21 44 D4
Priory La COAL LE67 116 B4
GBY/RBY LE6 117 G1
Priory Ms NOTTE NG7 50 C5
Priory Rd CARL NG4 38 D6
EWD/SEL/PNX NG16 21 K6
HUCK/RAV NG15 15 J8
LBORO LE11 103 J7
WBRGFD NG2 51 L7
Priory St NOTTE NG7 50 C5
Priory Wk LEIW LE3 129 L4
Pritchard Dr BSTN/STPLFD NG9 62 C1
Pritchett Dr NORM/LIT DE23 56 C7
Private Rd ARN NG5 37 H5
CALV/BJ NG14 26 F2
HUCK/RAV NG15 15 J8
MAPPK/POR/STA NG3 37 G5
Prize Cl CFTN/RUD NG11 64 A6 10
Proctor's Park Rd
RLBORO LE12 105 G8
Progress Wy LEIN LE4 126 E4
Prospect Dr BPR/DUF DE56 17 K5
Prospect Hl LEIE LE5 7 M5
Prospect Pl NOTTE NG7 50 D4 14
Prospect Rd CARL NG4 37 L6
HEANOR DE75 20 E7 2
LEIE LE5 132 B1
RIPLEY DE5 18 E6
RLEIW/BBY LE8 146 D7
Prospect St NOTTE NG7 50 C1
Providence Pl ILK DE7 33 J6 5
Providence Rd
EWD/SEL/PNX NG16 12 E3
Providence St RIPLEY DE5 11 J7
Provident St NORM/LIT DE23 2 D9
Pryor Rd RLBORO LE12 114 B3
Pudding Bag La RLBORO LE12 101 K7
Pulborough Cl ARN NG5 36 D3 2
Pulborough Gdns
NORM/LIT DE23 70 E1 6
Pulford Dr RLEINE/SYS LE7 133 K1
Pullman Rd DERBYE DE21 58 D3
WBRGFD NG2 51 K3 10
WGSTN LE18 137 M5
Pulteney Av LBORO LE11 103 M7
Pulteney Rd LBORO LE11 103 M7
Purbeck Av RLBORO LE12 102 B4
Purbeck Cl LGEAT NG10 61 L7 7
WGSTN LE18 138 B7
Purbeck Dr WBRGFD NG2 65 G2
Purcell Rd LEIN LE4 125 L7
Purchase Av HEANOR DE75 20 A5
Purdy Meadow LGEAT NG10 75 K2
Purley Ri RLBORO LE12 102 A5
Purley Rd LEIN LE4 126 A6
Putney Cl DERBYW DE22 56 C2
Putney Rd West LEIS LE2 131 J5
Pyatt St WBRGFD NG2 51 H6
Pybus St DERBYW DE22 57 H1
Pye Hill Rd EWD/SEL/PNX NG16 12 E3
Pygall Av CFTN/RUD NG11 77 L6
Pykestone Cl DERBYE DE21 44 D5
Pym Leys LGEAT NG10 75 K2 1
Pymm Ley Cl GBY/RBY LE6 123 K4
Pymm Ley La GBY/RBY LE6 123 K5
Pym St MAPPK/POR/STA NG3 51 K1
Pytchley Cl BPR/DUF DE56 18 B3 7
LEIN LE4 125 J2
Pytchley Dr LBORO LE11 103 K7

Q

The Quadrangle
HUCK/RAV NG15 15 H1 1
Quaker Rd RLBORO LE12 114 A6
Quantock Cl ARN NG5 24 F5
DERBYSE DE24 71 H5
Quantock Ri RLBORO LE12 102 A5
Quantock Rd LGEAT NG10 61 L6
Quarndon Hts DERBYW DE22 43 G5 2
Quarndon Vw DERBYW DE22 43 G5 3
Quarn Dr DERBYW DE22 43 G4
Quarn St DERBY DE1 2 B1
Quarn Wy DERBY DE1 2 C1
Quarry Av BLWL NG6 35 M1
Quarry Dl HUCK/RAV NG15 15 K6
Quarry Hl ILK DE7 47 K7
Quarry Hill Rd ILK DE7 47 K2
Quarry La HUCK/RAV NG15 15 M3
RLEIW/BAR LE9 135 L3
Quarry Rd BPR/DUF DE56 17 K5 3
ILK DE7 30 F6
Quayside Cl WBRGFD NG2 51 J6
Quebec Rd LEI LE1 7 H4
Queen Elizabeth Wy ILK DE7 47 G2
Queen Mary Ct DERBYW DE22 43 K8
Queen Mary St LEI LE1 6 F2
Queen's Av CARL NG4 38 C5
HEANOR DE75 20 B5
ILK DE7 46 A1 2
ILK DE7 47 L2
Queensberry St BLWL NG6 36 C3 4
Queen's Bower Rd ARN NG5 25 G7
Queen's Bridge Rd
WBRGFD NG2 51 G4 5
Queensbury Av WBRGFD NG2 65 H4
Queensbury Cha
NORM/LIT DE23 56 E8 3
Queen's Dr BPR/DUF DE56 17 J2
BSTN/STPLFD NG9 63 L1
EWD/SEL/PNX NG16 13 J8
EWD/SEL/PNX NG16 34 F1
ILK DE7 33 J8
LEIW LE3 129 L4
LGEAT NG10 61 M3
NORM/LIT DE23 57 G5
NOTTE NG7 50 E8
RLEIW/BAR LE9 136 B5
WBRGFD NG2 50 F5
WGSTN LE18 137 M5
Queensferry Gdns
DERBYSE DE24 72 B3
Queensferry Pde LEIS LE2 137 G4 4
Queensgate Dr LEIN LE4 119 J7
Queens Gv WBRGFD NG2 51 G4 10
Queensland Cl MCKLVR DE3 56 C3 2
Queensmead Cl GBY/RBY LE6 123 J5
Queens Park Wy LEIS LE2 137 H5
Queens Rd BSTN/STPLFD NG9 63 L2
CDON/KEG DE74 86 B4 2
COT/KEY/RAD NG12 53 K3
LBORO LE11 9 L1
LEIS LE2 131 M6
RLEIW/BBY LE8 136 E8
WBRGFD NG2 51 H4
Queens Rd East
BSTN/STPLFD NG9 49 M8
Queens Rd North
EWD/SEL/PNX NG16 21 K5
Queens Rd South
EWD/SEL/PNX NG16 21 K6
Queens Rd West
BSTN/STPLFD NG9 63 J3
Queen's Sq
EWD/SEL/PNX NG16 21 K5 3
Queen St ARN NG5 25 L6 3
BPR/DUF DE56 17 L4
COAL LE67 108 B7
COAL LE67 116 B7
DERBY DE1 2 E2
EWD/SEL/PNX NG16 12 C3
EWD/SEL/PNX NG16 21 G4
HUCK/RAV NG15 15 K7 2
ILK DE7 33 J7 1
LBORO LE11 9 L4 1
LEI LE1 7 G5
LEIS LE2 138 F2 3
LGEAT NG10 62 B8
NOTT NG1 5 G6
RIPLEY DE5 11 K8
RLBORO LE12 102 A3
RLEINE/SYS LE7 121 G8
Queensview Dr RIPLEY DE5 11 L8
Queen's Wk WBRGFD NG2 50 F6 11
Queensway CDON/KEG DE74 84 D3
DERBYW DE22 43 H8
MELB/CHEL DE73 82 F7
Quemby Cl LEIN LE4 125 L5
Quenby Crs RLEINE/SYS LE7 121 G4
Quenby La RIPLEY DE5 11 J6
Quenby St LEIE LE5 126 B8
Queniborough Rd LEIN LE4 126 A6
RLEINE/SYS LE7 121 H7
RLEINE/SYS LE7 121 J2
Querneby Av
MAPPK/POR/STA NG3 37 J5 8
Querneby Rd
MAPPK/POR/STA NG3 37 J5
Quick Cl MELB/CHEL DE73 82 E8 4
Quick Hill Rd DERBYSE DE24 71 G5
Quickthorns LEIS LE2 132 F8
Quillings Wy
BWSH/BRSTN DE72 60 B6 4
Quiney Wy LEIS LE2 139 G1
Quinton Cl CFTN/RUD NG11 64 E2 3
Quinton Ri LEIS LE2 138 E2
Quorn Av LEIS LE2 139 G3
Quorn Cl BSTN/STPLFD NG9 63 J4 5
LBORO LE11 9 M7
Quorn Crs COAL LE67 108 F7
Quorndon Crs LGEAT NG10 76 B2
Quorndon Ri GBY/RBY LE6 123 J5 1
Quorn Gv ARN NG5 36 E4
Quorn Pk RLBORO LE12 105 M6
Quorn Ri NORM/LIT DE23 71 J1
Quorn Rd ARN NG5 36 E5
LEIE LE5 126 B8

R

Rabown Av NORM/LIT DE23 57 H7
Racecourse Rd WBRGFD NG2 51 M3 1
Radbourne La ASHB DE6 56 A2
DERBYW DE22 42 D8
Radbourne Rd WBRGFD NG2 51 K4 3
Radbourne St DERBYW DE22 57 G1
Radburn Ct BSTN/STPLFD NG9 48 C6
Radcliffe Av DERBYE DE21 44 D8
Radcliffe Dr DERBYW DE22 57 H4
Radcliffe Gdns CARL NG4 38 B7
Radcliffe Mt WBRGFD NG2 51 K6 7
Radcliffe Rd COT/KEY/RAD NG12 52 C7
WBRGFD NG2 51 J6
Radcliffe St WBRGFD NG2 51 H6
Radcot Lawns LEIS LE2 137 H4
Radford Bvd NOTTE NG7 50 C1
Radford Bridge Rd
WOL/BIL/BRX NG8 50 A1 3
Radford Crs CARL NG4 38 C5 11
Radford Dr LEIW LE3 130 A4
Radford Rd ILK DE7 31 K1
NOTTE NG7 4 B2
NOTTE NG7 36 D6
Radford St DERBYSE DE24 58 D8
Radiant Rd LEIE LE5 127 G8
Radley Sq BLWL NG6 36 B2 4
Radmarsh Rd NOTTE NG7 50 C4
Rad Mdw LGEAT NG10 76 A1 3
Radmoor Rd LBORO LE11 8 F4
Radnor Ct RLEIW/BAR LE9 135 K5
Radnor Dr RLBORO LE12 101 M2
Radnor Rd WGSTN LE18 137 L5
Radnor St DERBYE DE21 44 B8
Radstock Gdns DERBYE DE21 44 C5 3
Radstock Rd
MAPPK/POR/STA NG3 37 L8
Radstone Cl DERBYE DE21 44 F5 11
Radway Dr CFTN/RUD NG11 64 E2
Raeburn Dr BSTN/STPLFD NG9 62 C5
Raeburn Rd LEIS LE2 131 M6 2
Ragdale Rd BLWL NG6 23 M7
LEIN LE4 126 B6 3
Raglan Av DERBYW DE22 57 G2 3
Raglan Cl MAPPK/POR/STA NG3 5 J2
Raglan Dr CARL NG4 38 F6 3
Raglan St EWD/SEL/PNX NG16 21 L6
Raibank Gdns ARN NG5 37 J3
Railway St WGSTN LE18 137 K7
Railway Ter DERBY DE1 3 J6
LBORO LE11 104 A2
Raine Wy LEIS LE2 139 H4
Rainham Gdns CFTN/RUD NG11 78 F1
DERBYSE DE24 72 E2
Rainier Dr DERBYE DE21 58 E1 2
Rainsford Crs LEIN LE4 125 J4
Raithby Cl ARN NG5 36 E1
Raleigh Cl CFTN/RUD NG11 64 A6 11
ILK DE7 33 K4 1
Raleigh St DERBYW DE22 57 G2 4
NOTTE NG7 4 D5
Ralf Cl WBRGFD NG2 65 J3
Ralph Cl LBORO LE11 103 H7
Ramblers Cl CARL NG4 52 C2
Ramblers Dr DERBYE DE21 45 G4
Ramsbury Rd WGSTN LE18 137 L2
Ramsdale Crs ARN NG5 37 H5
Ramsdale Rd CARL NG4 38 C6
Ramsdean Av WGSTN LE18 138 A4
Ramsdean Cl DERBYE DE21 44 B7
Ramsey Cl BSTN/STPLFD NG9 48 C5
Ramsey Dr ARN NG5 38 A1
Ramsey Gdns LEIE LE5 127 J6 3
Ramsey Wy LEIE LE5 127 J6 2
Ramson Cl LEIE LE5 127 G5
Ranby Wk MAPPK/POR/STA NG3 51 K1
Rancliffe Av COT/KEY/RAD NG12 80 B3
Rancliffe Crs LEIW LE3 130 E3
Randal St NOTTE NG7 4 A1 3
NOTTE NG7 36 C8
Randles Cl RLEINE/SYS LE7 133 L3
Randolph Rd NORM/LIT DE23 57 K7
Ranelagh Gdns DERBYW DE22 42 F8 1
Ranelagh Gv WOL/BIL/BRX NG8 49 L2
Rangemore Cl MCKLVR DE3 56 C3
Ranmere Rd WOL/BIL/BRX NG8 35 L8
Ranmoor Rd CARL NG4 38 D6
Ranmore Cl BSTN/STPLFD NG9 48 F5
Rannerdale Cl WBRGFD NG2 66 A1 3
Rannoch Cl DERBYE DE21 59 K2 4
DERBYW DE22 43 J4 3
LEIN LE4 125 G4
Rannoch Ri ARN NG5 25 K6
Rannock Gdns
COT/KEY/RAD NG12 80 D4
Ranskill Gdns ARN NG5 24 E7
Ransom Dr
MAPPK/POR/STA NG3 37 J6
Ransom Rd
MAPPK/POR/STA NG3 37 J6
Ranson Rd BSTN/STPLFD NG9 63 G6
Ranton Wy LEIW LE3 125 G7
Ranworth Cl DERBYSE DE24 72 B4
Ratby La COAL LE67 116 C8
GBY/RBY LE6 123 J8
LEIW LE3 129 L2
RLEIW/BAR LE9 129 J1
Ratby Meadow La
RLEIW/BAR LE9 136 C4
Ratby Rd GBY/RBY LE6 123 J4
Ratcliffe Ct LEIS LE2 132 B7
Ratcliffe Dr RLEIW/BAR LE9 135 H8
Ratcliffe La CDON/KEG DE74 75 M8
Ratcliffe Rd LBORO LE11 104 A2
LEIS LE2 132 A7
RLBORO LE12 114 B4
RLEINE/SYS LE7 115 K3
Ratcliffe St EWD/SEL/PNX NG16 21 K5
LEIN LE4 125 M5 3
Rathgar Cl WOL/BIL/BRX NG8 49 H3
Rathmines Cl NOTTE NG7 50 C4 3
Raven Av ARN NG5 36 F3
Raven Cl ALFN DE55 12 A1 2
Ravenhill Cl
BSTN/STPLFD NG9 62 F3 7
Ravenhurst Rd LEIW LE3 130 D7
Raven Oak Cl BPR/DUF DE56 17 L5
Raven Rd LEIW LE3 130 C4 3
Ravensbridge Dr LEIN LE4 125 H7
Ravens Ct ARN NG5 36 F2
Ravenscourt Rd DERBYW DE22 56 F1
Ravenscroft Dr DERBYE DE21 58 D1
Ravensdale Av LGEAT NG10 61 M5
Ravensdale Dr
WOL/BIL/BRX NG8 49 G4
Ravensdale Rd DERBYW DE22 43 G4
Ravensmore Rd ARN NG5 36 F5
Ravensthorpe Dr
LBORO LE11 102 F5 3
Ravensthorpe Rd WGSTN LE18 138 B5
Raven St DERBYW DE22 2 A7
Ravenswood Rd ARN NG5 25 K8
Ravensworth Rd BLWL NG6 23 M7
Rawdon Cl CDON/KEG DE74 84 E3 2
Rawdon St NORM/LIT DE23 57 K5
Raw Dykes Rd LEIS LE2 131 J5
Rawlings Ct LEIS LE2 139 J3
Rawlins Cl RLBORO LE12 111 L6
Rawlinson Av NORM/LIT DE23 57 L8
Rawson Gn BPR/DUF DE56 18 D6
Rawson St EWD/SEL/PNX NG16 13 L1
LEI LE1 6 F8
NOTTE NG7 36 D6
RLEIW/BAR LE9 135 M4
Rayleigh Gn LEIE LE5 127 J6
Rayleigh Wy LEIE LE5 127 J6 2
Raymede Cl ARN NG5 36 D1 1
Raymede Dr ARN NG5 36 C1
Raymond Av LBORO LE11 103 H1 7
Raymond Rd LEIW LE3 131 G4
Rayneham Rd ILK DE7 33 G3
Rayner Rd LEIN LE4 126 C4
Raynesway DERBYE DE21 58 F3
DERBYSE DE24 58 F8 2
Raynesway Park Dr
DERBYE DE21 58 E6
Raynford Av BSTN/STPLFD NG9 63 G3
Raynham Dr LBORO LE11 103 G2
Ray's Av HEANOR DE75 20 C6
Ray St HEANOR DE75 20 C6
Read Av BSTN/STPLFD NG9 63 L1
Reader St DERBYE DE21 59 J2
Readman Rd BSTN/STPLFD NG9 62 E4
Rearsby Cl WOL/BIL/BRX NG8 49 H2 3
Rearsby Rd LEIN LE4 126 A6 1
RLEINE/SYS LE7 115 K3
RLEINE/SYS LE7 121 J1
Recreation Rd LGEAT NG10 61 M1
Recreation St
EWD/SEL/PNX NG16 13 M1
LGEAT NG10 62 D7
Recreation Ter
BSTN/STPLFD NG9 62 B1 3
Rectory Av WOL/BIL/BRX NG8 49 J3
The Rectory Dr CARL NG4 38 D5
Rectory Gdns
BWSH/BRSTN DE72 73 L8
LEIS LE2 132 F5
WOL/BIL/BRX NG8 49 K3
Rectory La ILK DE7 44 B3
RLEINE/SYS LE7 118 F5
RLEIW/BBY LE8 146 E6
Rectory Pl CFTN/RUD NG11 77 J1 1
LBORO LE11 9 J2
RLBORO LE12 98 A4 2
Rectory Rd BWSH/BRSTN DE72 61 J7
CARL NG4 52 C2 3
COAL LE67 116 C6
COT/KEY/RAD NG12 67 J4
LBORO LE11 9 K1
RLEINE/SYS LE7 119 M5
WBRGFD NG2 51 K8
Reculver Cl NORM/LIT DE23 57 H8
Redbourne Dr
WOL/BIL/BRX NG8 50 A1
Redbridge Dr
EWD/SEL/PNX NG16 35 H4
Redbury Cl DERBY DE1 2 A5
Redcar Cl CARL NG4 38 C5
Redcar Gdns DERBYE DE21 44 B6
Redcar Rd LEIN LE4 125 M5
Redcliffe Rd
MAPPK/POR/STA NG3 37 G7
Redfern Av RIPLEY DE5 11 J5
Redfield Rd NOTTE NG7 50 C7
Redfield Wy NOTTE NG7 50 C6 3
Red Hl LEIN LE4 125 K2
Red Hill Av RLEIW/BAR LE9 135 L7
Red Hill Cl LEIN LE4 120 C7 3
Redhill Ct BPR/DUF DE56 17 M5 3
Redhill La COAL LE67 108 A2
Red Hill La LEIN LE4 120 D7
Redhill Lodge Dr ARN NG5 25 H6
Redhill Rd ARN NG5 25 J6
Red Hill Wy LEIN LE4 125 H2
Red House Cl LEIS LE2 137 G3 1
Red House Gdns LEIS LE2 137 G3 2
Red House Ri LEIS LE2 137 G3
Red House Rd LEIS LE2 137 G3
Redland Av CARL NG4 38 D7
Redland Cl BSTN/STPLFD NG9 63 G3 3
DERBYSE DE24 71 K3 3
ILK DE7 33 K5
Redland Dr BSTN/STPLFD NG9 63 G4
Redland Gv CARL NG4 38 C7
Red La BPR/DUF DE56 29 M1
EWD/SEL/PNX NG16 13 J6
Redmarle Rd LEIW LE3 130 E4
Redmays Dr CALV/BJ NG14 39 M1
Redmile Rd WOL/BIL/BRX NG8 36 A5
Redmires Cl LBORO LE11 102 F4
Redmires Dr MELB/CHEL DE73 72 E5
Redmoor Cl RIPLEY DE5 11 M6
Redoubt St NOTTE NG7 50 C2 12
Redpath Cl LEI LE1 7 J2
Redruth Av WGSTN LE18 138 A7
Redruth Cl WOL/BIL/BRX NG8 49 G1
Redruth Pl DERBYSE DE24 73 G2 5
Redshaw St DERBYW DE22 43 J8
Redstart Cl DERBYE DE21 59 K1
Redway Cft MELB/CHEL DE73 82 E7 6
Redwing Cft NORM/LIT DE23 57 H8 2
Redwood WBRGFD NG2 65 G1 2
Redwood Av WOL/BIL/BRX NG8 49 H4
Redwood Crs
BSTN/STPLFD NG9 63 L2 3
Redwood Rd DERBYSE DE24 71 J4
LBORO LE11 103 L8
Reedman Rd LGEAT NG10 75 M3
Reedpool Cl RLEIW/BBY LE8 143 K3
Rees Gdns ARN NG5 24 E6
Rees Gv LEIN LE4 126 B2 3
Reeth Cl LEIN LE4 125 G4
Reeves Cl RLEIW/BBY LE8 142 D2 4
Reeves Rd NORM/LIT DE23 57 M6
Regatta Wy WBRGFD NG2 52 A7
Regency Cl NORM/LIT DE23 57 H8
WGSTN LE18 137 H6
Regent Cl WGSTN LE18 137 M4
Regent Ct EWD/SEL/PNX NG16 12 D3
Regent Rd LEI LE1 6 F8
RLEIW/BBY LE8 143 K3
Regents Park Cl WBRGFD NG2 65 G2
Regent St BSTN/STPLFD NG9 49 L8
DERBY DE1 3 H7 2
EWD/SEL/PNX NG16 20 F4 4
EWD/SEL/PNX NG16 34 D1
ILK DE7 33 K8 10
LBORO LE11 9 G2
LEI LE1 7 H8
LEIS LE2 138 E1
LGEAT NG10 62 A2
LGEAT NG10 62 B7
NOTT NG1 4 E7
NOTTE NG7 36 E6
RLEINE/SYS LE7 115 K3
RLEIW/BAR LE9 136 A7
Regents Wk LEIW LE3 129 L4
Regina Cl COT/KEY/RAD NG12 53 J5 4
Reginald Rd North
DERBYE DE21 44 D8
Reginald Rd South
DERBYE DE21 58 D1
Reginald St NORM/LIT DE23 3 G9
Regis Cl DERBYE DE21 44 F5
Reid Gdns
EWD/SEL/PNX NG16 34 F1 2
Reigate Cl BSTN/STPLFD NG9 63 J5 1
Reigate Dr BSTN/STPLFD NG9 63 J5
DERBYW DE22 42 D8
Reigate Rd NOTTE NG7 36 D5
Rempstone Dr BLWL NG6 36 B2
Rempstone Rd RLBORO LE12 88 B7
RLBORO LE12 95 L1
RLBORO LE12 97 L3
Renals St NORM/LIT DE23 2 E8
Renals Wy CALV/BJ NG14 26 D1
Rendell Rd LEIN LE4 125 M6
Rendell St LBORO LE11 103 M2
Renfrew Dr WOL/BIL/BRX NG8 49 J3
Renfrew Rd LEIE LE5 127 J7 1
Renfrew St DERBYE DE21 44 C8
Renishaw Dr LEIE LE5 132 C5
Renning End RLBORO LE12 113 J7
Repington Rw LEIS LE2 137 K2
Repton Av NORM/LIT DE23 57 J7
Repton Dr ILK DE7 33 M8 2
Repton Rd BLWL NG6 36 B1
LGEAT NG10 75 K3
WBRGFD NG2 65 J2
WGSTN LE18 137 M3
Repton St LEIW LE3 6 B3
Reservoir Rd RLEINE/SYS LE7 118 B4
Retford Cl DERBYE DE21 44 B5 3
Retford Rd ARN NG5 36 E4
The Retreat LEIE LE5 132 D2
RLBORO LE12 105 H7 2
Revell Cl RLBORO LE12 112 F1 1
Revelstoke Av ARN NG5 24 B6 2
Revelstoke Wy ARN NG5 24 B6
Revena Cl CARL NG4 52 C1
Revesby Gdns
WOL/BIL/BRX NG8 36 A8
Revesby Rd ARN NG5 37 K2
Revill Cl ILK DE7 33 G5
Revill Crs BSTN/STPLFD NG9 48 D7
Reydon Dr WOL/BIL/BRX NG8 36 B6
Reynolds Av RIPLEY DE5 11 K6
Reynolds Dr WOL/BIL/BRX NG8 49 K2
Reynolds Pl LEIW LE3 130 E5
Rhyl Crs CARL NG4 38 D5
Ribble Av LEIS LE2 139 H1
Ribble Dr RLBORO LE12 113 H1
Ribblesdale ILK DE7 47 G2 3
Ribblesdale Cl DERBYW DE22 43 G5 4
Ribblesdale Rd ARN NG5 37 G2
LGEAT NG10 75 L2
Riber Cl ILK DE7 32 C7
LGEAT NG10 76 B2
Riber Crs ARN NG5 36 D2
Richard 111 Rd LEIW LE3 6 B5
Richard Cl LEIW LE3 130 A4
Richardson Cl
CFTN/RUD NG11 64 A6 12

RLEIW/BAR LE9 .... 140 B6
Richardson Dr ILK DE7 .... 31 K1
Richardsons La ALFN DE55 .. 12 B2
Richardson DERBYW DE22 .. 57 H1
Richborough Pl
WOL/BIL/BRX NC8 .... 49 H5
Richey Cl ARN NC5 .... 25 M8
Richmond Av
BWSH/BRSTN DE72 .... 61 L7
EWD/SEL/PNX NG16 .... 21 M5
ILK DE7 .... 33 K3
LGEAT NG10 .... 61 L3
MAPPK/POR/STA NG3 ... 37 K8
NORM/LIT DE23 .... 57 G7
Richmond Cl ILK DE7 .... 32 B7
LEIS LE2 .... 131 J7
NORM/LIT DE23 .... 56 E8
RLEIW/BAR LE9 .... 142 A5
Richmond Dr BPR/DUF DE56 .. 29 H2
BSTN/STPLFD NG9 .... 63 J2
COT/KEY/RAD NG12 ..... 53 K3
MAPPK/POR/STA NG3 ... 37 H5
WGSTN LE18 .... 137 J6
Richmond Gdns ARN NC5 ... 25 J6
Richmond Rd DERBYE DE21 .. 58 D1
LEIS LE2 .... 131 J6
NORM/LIT DE23 .... 57 L6
WBRGFD NG2 .... 51 K6
Richmond St LEIS LE2 .... 6 D8
Richmond Ter
COT/KEY/RAD NG12 ..... 53 K4
Richmond Wy LEIS LE2 .... 139 G4
Rick St NOTT NG1 .... 5 J6
Riddings DERBYW DE22 ...... 43 J3
Riddings La ASHB DE6 ...... 40 F5
Riddings St DERBYW DE22 .... 2 C7
Riddington Rd LEIW LE3 .... 130 D6
RLEIW/BAR LE9 .... 142 A1
Ridgedale Vw RIPLEY DE5 ... 11 H5
Ridge La COT/KEY/RAD NG12 .. 53 L2
Ridgemere Cl RLEINE/SYS LE7 . 121 H3
Ridgemere La RLEINE/SYS LE7 . 121 J4
Ridge Wy LEIS LE2 .... 138 F4
Ridgeway ARN NC5 .... 24 D8
HEANOR DE75 .... 20 D7
MELB/CHEL DE73 ...... 72 E7
RLEIW/BAR LE9 .... 142 A1
Ridgeway Av NORM/LIT DE23 .. 71 G1
Ridgeway Dr ILK DE7 .... 46 F2
LEIN LE4 .... 126 D1
Ridgeway St
MAPPK/POR/STA NG3 ... 5 M3
The Ridgeway RLEINE/SYS LE7 . 118 F2
Ridgewood Ct DERBYE DE21 .. 44 C5
Ridgewood Dr
BSTN/STPLFD NG9 ...... 63 G3
Ridgmont Wk
CFTN/RUD NG11 .... 64 B7
Ridgway Cl WBRGFD NG2 .... 66 A2
Ridgway Rd LEIS LE2 .... 132 B7
Riding Bank MELB/CHEL DE73 . 82 C8
The Ridings BWSH/BRSTN DE72 . 60 A1
CALV/BJ NG14 .... 39 L2
COT/KEY/RAD NG12 ..... 80 E4
RLEINE/SYS LE7 .... 112 F3
RLEINE/SYS LE7 .... 121 J2
The Riding LEIN LE4 .... 124 F1
Ridley Cl RLEINE/SYS LE7 .... 118 C5
RLEIW/BBY LE8 .... 142 E1
Ridley St LEIW LE3 .... 6 A8
Ridsdale Rd ARN NC5 .... 37 G2
Rifle St NOTTE NG7 .... 50 C2
Rigga La BPR/DUF DE56 .... 29 L6
Rigley Av ILK DE7 .... 33 K6
Rigley Dr ARN NC5 .... 24 C8
Rigsby Ct MCKLVR DE3 ...... 56 A4
Riley Cl RLEIW/BAR LE9 .... 140 B6
Riley La RIPLEY DE5 .... 10 F1
Rimsdale Cl DERBYSE DE24.... 71 J4
Ringers Cl LEIS LE2 .... 132 E7
Ringer's Spinney LEIS LE2 ... 132 F7
Ring Fence RLBORO LE12 .... 101 M5
Ring Leas COT/KEY/RAD NG12 .. 67 K5
Ring Rd LEIS LE2 .... 138 A1
Ringstead Cl WBRGFD NG2 ... 65 G7
The Ringway RLEINE/SYS LE7 .. 121 J1
Ringwood Cl WGSTN LE18 ... 138 A6
Ringwood Crs
WOL/BIL/BRX NC8 .... 50 A2
Ringwood Rd LEIS LE5 ...... 127 J6
RLBORO LE12 .... 101 M2
Ripley Rd BPR/DUF DE56 .... 10 D6
BPR/DUF DE56 .... 10 A2
Ripon Crs DERBYE DE21 ...... 44 C7
Ripon Dr RLEIW/BBY LE8 .... 142 F1
Ripon Rd MAPPK/POR/STA NG3 .. 5 M4
Ripon St LEIS LE2 .... 132 A4
Riseborough Wk BLWL NG6 ... 23 M6
Risegate COT/KEY/RAD NG12 .. 67 K4
Risegate Gdns
COT/KEY/RAD NG12 ..... 67 K4
Riseholme Av WOL/BIL/BRX NC8 .. 49 G4
Rise Park Rd ARN NC5 ...... 24 B6
The Rise ARN NC5 .... 37 H4
DERBYW DE22 .... 43 J5
RLEINE/SYS LE7 .... 119 L1
RLEIW/BAR LE9 .... 135 L5
Risley Dr WBRGFD NG2 ...... 50 F5
Risley La BWSH/BRSTN DE72 .. 61 H5
Riste's Pl NOTT NG1 .... 5 J7
Riston Cl LEIS LE2 .... 138 F4
Ritchie Cl COT/KEY/RAD NG12 .. 67 L5
Ritson Cl MAPPK/POR/STA NG3 . 5 K4
Rivenhall Cl NORM/LIT DE23 .. 56 D8
Riverdale Rd BSTN/STPLFD NG9 . 63 H5
Rivergreen CFTN/RUD NG11 ... 64 C5
Rivergreen Cl
BSTN/STPLFD NG9 .... 49 G5
Rivergreen Crs
BSTN/STPLFD NG9 .... 49 G5
River Rd CARL NG4 .... 52 C3
Riverdale Cl LEIN LE4 ..... 125 M1
Riverside Cl RLEIW/BBY LE8 . 139 M6
Riverside Dr LEIS LE2 ..... 136 F1
Riverside Rd BSTN/STPLFD NG9 . 3 L6
DERBYSE DE24 .... 3 L6
Riverside Wy RLEIW/BAR LE9 . 136 A8

WBRGFD NG2 .... 50 F6
Rivers St LEIW LE3 .... 6 B5
River St DERBY DE1 .... 2 E1
River Vw BPR/DUF DE56 .... 17 K8
RLBORO LE12 .... 113 J1
WBRGFD NG2 .... 51 H6
Rivets Meadow Cl LEIW LE3 .. 130 B6
Rivington Dr LBORO LE11 .... 102 F5
Rivington Rd
BSTN/STPLFD NG9 .... 62 C5
Road No 1 CARL NG4 ...... 52 D2
Road No 2 CARL NG4 ...... 52 D2
Road No 3 CARL NG4 ...... 52 D2
Road No 4 CARL NG4 ...... 53 G3
Road No 5 CARL NG4 ...... 52 F2
Road No 7 CARL NG4 ...... 52 D1
Road No 8 CARL NG4 ...... 52 D1
Robbie Burns Rd ARN NG5 .. 25 G7
Robert Hall St LEIN LE4 .... 125 K4
Robertsbridge Av LEIN LE4... 125 J4
Roberts Cl CDON/KEG DE74 .. 86 A6
Robert's La HUCK/RAV NG15.. 15 J8
Robertson Cl RLEIW/BAR LE9 . 140 B5
Roberts St ILK DE7 .... 47 L1
WBRGFD NG2 .... 5 M7
Robert St DERBY DE1 .... 3 G2
Robey Cl HUCK/RAV NG15... 15 M6
Robey Dr EWD/SEL/PNX NG16 . 21 K4
Robey Ter NOTTE NG7 ...... 4 A1
Robina Dr
EWD/SEL/PNX NG16 ..... 21 M7
Robin Cl LEIS LE2 .... 131 J3
Robin Croft Rd DERBYW DE22 . 43 J3
Robinet Rd BSTN/STPLFD NG9 . 63 K2
Robinettes La
EWD/SEL/PNX NG16 ..... 34 B6
Robin Hood Cl
EWD/SEL/PNX NG16 ..... 21 K6
Robin Hood Dr HUCK/RAV NG15 . 23 J3
Robin Hood Rd ARN NC5 .... 25 G7
Robin Hood St
MAPPK/POR/STA NG3 ... 5 L6
Robin Hood Wy BLWL NG6 .. 24 C2
BSTN/STPLFD NG9 ...... 48 E5
EWD/SEL/PNX NG16 ..... 34 D2
HUCK/RAV NG15 .... 24 A4
NOTT NG1 .... 4 F9
WBRGFD NG2 .... 50 F6
Robina Cl DERBYE DE21 .... 45 G4
Robinia Cl WBRGFD NG2 .... 65 K2
Robin Rd COAL LE67 .... 108 D7
DERBYW DE22 .... 43 K8
Robinscross
BWSH/BRSTN DE72 ...... 59 M6
Robinson Gdns
CFTN/RUD NG11 .... 64 A6
LEIE LE5 .... 132 C1
MAPPK/POR/STA NG3 ... 37 K4
Robinson Wy COAL LE67 .... 116 D7
Robin's Wood Rd
WOL/BIL/BRX NC8 ...... 35 M8
Roborough Gn LEIE LE5 ..... 133 J1
Robotham Cl RLEIW/BAR LE9 . 135 J8
RLEIW/BAR LE9 .... 135M8
Robson Cl DERBYSE DE24 .... 58 E8
Roby Lea CDON/KEG DE74 ... 84 D3
Rochdale Crs COAL LE67 .... 109 H6
Roche Cl ARN NC5 .... 38 A1
LEIS LE2 .... 137 G3
Rochester Av CARL NG4 .... 38 E8
Rochester Cl DERBYSE DE24... 72 E2
LGEAT NG10 .... 61 L8
RLBORO LE12 .... 113 J7
RLEIW/BBY LE8 .... 146 D5
Rochester Ct
EWD/SEL/PNX NG16 ..... 35 K1
Rochester Wk
CFTN/RUD NG11 .... 64 D6
Rochford Ct COT/KEY/RAD NG12.. 66 A3
Rochley Cl DERBYE DE21..... 44 D4
Rockbourne Cl DERBYSE DE24.. 73 H1
Rockbridge Rd LEIS LE2 .... 139 H3
Rock Ct BLWL NG6 .... 36 B4
Rock Dr NOTTE NG7 .... 50 E4
NOTTE NG7 .... 50 E4
The Rockery DERBYE DE21 ... 30 C3
Rockford Ct
BSTN/STPLFD NG9 .... 48 C6
Rockford Rd ARN NC5 ...... 36 D4
Rockhill Dr RLBORO LE12 .... 113 H7
Rockhouse Rd DERBYSE DE24.. 72 E1
Rockingham Cl DERBYW DE22.. 43 L3
LEIE LE5 .... 132 F1
RLBORO LE12 .... 101 L5
RLEIW/BBY LE8 .... 142 F1
Rockingham Rd LBORO LE11 .. 103 J1
Rockland Ri COAL LE67 ..... 108 D1
Rockley Av COT/KEY/RAD NG12.. 53 K3
EWD/SEL/PNX NG16 ..... 21 L6
Rockley Cl HUCK/RAV NG15... 23 J1
Rockley Rd LEIN LE4 ...... 125 C6
Rock St BLWL NG6 .... 23M7
Rockwood Crs HUCK/RAV NG15.. 23 H1
Rockwood Wk
HUCK/RAV NG15 .... 23 J1
Roden St MAPPK/POR/STA NG3 . 5 L6
Rodney Cl RDERBYSW DE65.. 68 C5
Rodney Rd WBRGFD NG2 .... 65 L1
Rodney Wy ILK DE7 .... 33 K3
Rodsley Crs NORM/LIT DE23 .. 71 H2
Rodwell Cl WOL/BIL/BRX NC8.. 49M1
Roebuck Cl ARN NC5 ...... 24 F6
RLEIW/BBY LE8 .... 142 D2
Roecliff Cl COAL LE67 ...... 116 C7
Roecliffe WBRGFD NG2 ...... 65 H5
Roecliffe Rd RLBORO LE12 ... 117 L2
Roe Farm La DERBYE DE21 ... 44 C8
Roehampton Dr
BSTN/STPLFD NG9 .... 48 B5
DERBYW DE22 .... 57 L2
LEIS LE4 .... 137 M2
Roe Hl CALV/BJ NG14 ...... 27 G2
Roe La CALV/BJ NG14 ...... 27 G2
Roesta Cl RLBORO LE12 .... 100 F1
Roe Wk NORM/LIT DE23 .... 57 L6

Rogerstone Rd LEIE LE5 .... 133 H3
Roker Cl WOL/BIL/BRX NC8 .. 35 L6
Roland Av CFTN/RUD NG11... 50 F8
EWD/SEL/PNX NG16 ..... 35 J5
Rolleston Crs
EWD/SEL/PNX NG16 ..... 22 D6
Rolleston Dr ARN NC5 ...... 25 L8
EWD/SEL/PNX NG16 ..... 21 L7
NOTTE NG7 .... 4 B8
Rolleston Rd WGSTN LE18.... 137 M4
Rolleston St LEIE LE5 ...... 132 B1
Roman Dr BLWL NG6 ...... 36 D3
Roman Hl WGSTN LE18 ..... 138 C7
Roman Rd DERBY DE1 ...... 43 M8
LEIN LE4 .... 125 L2
Romans Ct BLWL NG6 ...... 36 C5
Romans Crs COAL LE67 ..... 109 H6
The Romans RLBORO LE12 ... 113 J6
Roman St LEIS LE2 .... 6 A8
Roman Wy BWSH/BRSTN DE72 . 60 A6
RLEINE/SYS LE7 .... 119 C5
Romilay Cl BSTN/STPLFD NG9 . 49 L7
Romney Av EWD/SEL/PNX NG16 .. 49 H5
Romsley Cl MCKLVR DE3 .... 56 B3
Romway Av LEIE LE5 ...... 132 C5
Romway Cl RLBORO LE12.... 102 A4
Romway Rd LEIE LE5 ...... 132 C5
Rona Cl DERBYSE DE24 ..... 71 J3
Rona Ct BLWL NG6 .... 36 C2
Rona Gdns LEIE LE5 ...... 127 J8
Ronald Cl NORM/LIT DE23 ... 56 C8
Ronald Cl NOTTE NG7 ...... 4 B5
Ronald West Ct LBORO LE11 .. 8 B9
The Roods RLEINE/SYS LE7 ... 119 J1
Rookery GBY/RBY LE6 ...... 123 K4
Rookery Cl RLEIW/BBY LE8 .. 146 F7
Rookery Gdns ARN NC5 .... 25 K7
Rookery La GBY/RBY LE6 ... 123 J4
LEIN LE4 .... 126 B1
The Rookery RLBORO LE12 ... 105 G7
Rookwood Cl
BSTN/STPLFD NG9 .... 63 J1
Roosa Cl BLWL NG6 .... 35 K1
Roosevelt Av DERBYE DE21 .. 58 F1
LGEAT NG10 .... 76 A2
Roper Av HEANOR DE75 ..... 20 D7
Ropewalk CDON/KEG DE74 ... 86 A5
Rope Wk RLBORO LE12 ..... 88 B6
The Ropewalk ILK DE7 ..... 31 M6
ILK DE7 .... 33 L6
NOTT NG1 .... 4 E7
Ropsley Crs WBRGFD NG2 ... 51 L7
Rosamond's Ride
NORM/LIT DE23 .... 57 H7
Rosamund Av LEIW LE3 .... 130 D7
Roscoe Av ARN NC5 ...... 25 J5
Roseacre BSTN/STPLFD NG9 .. 63 L2
Rose Acre Cl LEIE LE5 ...... 127 K8
Rose Ash La ARN NC5 ..... 24 F7
Rose Av BWSH/BRSTN DE72 .. 60 A6
ILK DE7 .... 33 J5
Rosebank Dr ARN NC5 ..... 25 M6
Rosebank Rd RLEIW/BBY LE8 . 143 K3
Rosebarn Wy LEIE LE5 ..... 127 H6
Roseberry Ct DERBYE DE21 .. 44 F6
Roseberry Gdns
HUCK/RAV NG15 .... 24 A1
Roseberry Av RLEIW/BBY LE8 . 146 D7
WBRGFD NG2 .... 51 J6
Rosebery Rd RLEINE/SYS LE7 . 118 F8
Rosebery St BLWL NG6 ..... 36 C4
LBORO LE11 .... 8 E2
LEIE LE5 .... 132 B1
Rose Cl MAPPK/POR/STA NG3 .. 5 J1
Rose Ct LGEAT NG10 ...... 61 M7
Rose Crs LEIW LE3 .... 129 K5
Rosecroft Dr ARN NC5 ..... 37 G1
Rosedale Cl LEIS LE2 ...... 126 B5
Rosedale Av DERBYSE DE24 .. 72 E1
LEIN LE4 .... 126 B5
Rosedale Cl LGEAT NG10 .... 75 M1
Rosedale Dr WOL/BIL/BRX NC8 . 48 F3
Rosedale Rd
MAPPK/POR/STA NG3 ... 52 A1
WGSTN LE18 .... 138 D5
Rosedene Av LEIN LE4 ..... 126 C1
Rosedene Cl RLEIW/BAR LE9 . 129 K3
Rose Farm Cl LEIE LE5 ..... 130 D3
Rosegarth Wk BLWL NG6 ... 36 B3
Rose Gv BSTN/STPLFD NG9 .. 63M2
COT/KEY/RAD NG12 ..... 80 D3
Rosegrove Av ARN NC5 ..... 25 K6
Roseheath Cl NORM/LIT DE23 . 71 J2
Rose Hl COT/KEY/RAD NG12 .. 80 C4
Rosehill LBORO LE11 ...... 103 G3
Rose Hill St NORM/LIT DE23 .. 2 F9
Roseland Cl COT/KEY/RAD NG12 .. 80 B5
Roseleigh Av
MAPPK/POR/STA NG3 ... 37 M5
Rosemary Crs COAL LE67 .... 108 E3
Rosemary Dr DERBYSE DE24 .. 72 E2
Rosemead Dr LEIS LE2 ..... 138 E3
Rosemoor La DERBYE DE21 .. 44 F6
Rosemount Ct DERBYW DE22 . 43 G4
Roseneath Av ARN NC5 .... 24 C6
LEIN LE4 .... 126 C4
Rosengrave St DERBY DE1 ... 2 D6
Rose St LEIN LE4 .... 125 K5
Rose Tree La LEIN LE4 ..... 119 L7
Rosetta Rd NOTTE NG7 ..... 36 D6
NOTTE NG7 .... 36 D5
Rosette Ct DERBYE DE21 .... 45 G4
Rosewall Ct ARN NC5 ...... 25 M8
Roseway LEIN LE4 .... 126 B4
Rosewood Cl DERBYSE DE24 .. 59 G8
Rosewood Crs HEANOR DE75.. 20 F5
Rosewood Gdns WBRGFD NG2 . 65 G4
Roslyn Av CARL NG4 ...... 38 C6
Roslyn St LEIS LE2 .... 7 M8
Rossell Dr BSTN/STPLFD NG9 . 62 C2
Rossendale Cl DERBYE DE21 .. 33 J3
Rossett Cl WBRGFD NG2 .... 66 B1
Rossett Dr LEIN LE4 ...... 125 H5
Rossetti Av RLEIW/BAR LE9 .. 135 L4
Rosshill Crs LEIE LE5 ...... 127 J8
Rossington Dr NORM/LIT DE23 . 70 D1
Rossington Rd WBRGFD NG2 . 51 K2

Ross La CARL NG4 .... 27 C8
Rosslyn Av RLBORO LE12.... 113 C6
RLEINE/SYS LE7 .... 113 G7
Rosslyn Dr WOL/BIL/BRX NC8 . 35 L5
Rosslyn Gdns DERBYSE DE24 . 72 E1
Rosslyn Rd COAL LE67 ..... 108 D3
Ross' Wk LEIE LE5 .... 125 L7
LEIN LE4 .... 125 L6
Rosthwaite Cl WBRGFD NG2 . 66 A2
Rothbury Av
BSTN/STPLFD NG9 .... 48 B5
Rothbury Pl DERBYE DE21 ... 44 C6
Rotherby Av LEIN LE4 ..... 126 B6
Rothesay Av NOTTE NG7 .... 4 A6
Rothesay Cl DERBYSE DE24 .. 71 J3
Rothley Av
MAPPK/POR/STA NG3 ... 51 K2
Rothley Rd RLBORO LE12 .... 113 J5
LEIN LE4 .... 125 L6
Rothwell Cl CFTN/RUD NG11 . 64 E3
Rothwell La BPR/DUF DE56 .. 17 M3
Rothwell Rd HUCK/RAV NG15 . 23 J2
Rough Heanor Rd MCKLVR DE3 . 56 E4
Roughs Wood La
HUCK/RAV NG15 .... 23 H3
Roughton Cl MCKLVR DE3 ... 56 B2
Roughton St LEIN LE4 ..... 125 M5
Roulstone Crs RLEIW/BBY LE8 . 146 C2
Roundhay Rd LEIW LE3 .... 131 C5
Roundhill RLEIW/BAR LE9 ... 129 J2
Roundhill Cl RLEINE/SYS LE7 . 120 D5
Roundhill Rd LEIE LE5 ..... 132 B4
Roundhill Wy LBORO LE11 .. 102 F4
The Roundway LEIN LE4 .... 126 D2
Roundwood Rd ARN NC5 ... 25 C8
Routh Av CDON/KEG DE74 ... 84 F5
Rowan Av BSTN/STPLFD NG9 . 48 C6
COAL LE67 .... 108 F7
RIPLEY DE5 .... 11 H7
RLBORO LE12 .... 94 E5
Rowanberry Av LEIW LE3 ... 130 A1
Rowan Cl DERBYSE DE24 .... 58 F2
DERBYSE DE24 .... 71 H4
ILK DE7 .... 47 K2
Rowan Crs EWD/SEL/PNX NG16 . 34 F1
LGEAT NG10 .... 76 A2
Rowan Dr BPR/DUF DE56 ... 18 F7
CFTN/RUD NG11 .... 64 E3
COT/KEY/RAD NG12 ..... 80 E5
EWD/SEL/PNX NG16 ..... 13 H1
Rowan Gdns BLWL NG6 .... 23 K8
Rowan Park NORM/LIT DE23 . 57 H8
The Rowans RLEIW/BBY LE8 . 143 J3
Rowan St LEIW LE3 ...... 131 G1
Rowan Wy LBORO LE11 .... 102 F4
Rowditch Av DERBYW DE22 .. 57 H4
Rowditch Pl DERBYW DE22 .. 57 H3
Rowe Gdns BLWL NG6 ..... 36 B1
Rowe Leyes Furlong
RLBORO LE12 .... 113 K6
Rowe Leys Furlong
RLBORO LE12 .... 113 K6
Rowena Cl DERBYSE DE24 ... 58 D8
Rowena Ct RLBORO LE12 ... 113 J7
Rowland Av
MAPPK/POR/STA NG3 ... 37 L5
Rowland St DERBYSE DE24 ... 72 C1
Rowlanson Cl LEIN LE4 .... 119 H6
Rowlatts Hill Rd LEIE LE5 ... 132 C5
Rowley Fields Av LEIW LE3 .. 130 F6
Rowley Gdns NORM/LIT DE23 . 57 G8
Rowley La NORM/LIT DE23 ... 57 C8
Rowsley Av LEIE LE5 ...... 132 B3
LGEAT NG10 .... 75 L2
NORM/LIT DE23 .... 57 H7
Rowsley St LEIE LE5 ...... 132 B3
Roxburgh Av DERBYE DE21 .. 44 C8
Roxton Ct
EWD/SEL/PNX NG16 ..... 22 D8
Royal Av LGEAT NG10 ..... 62 B6
Royal Cl BWSH/BRSTN DE72 .. 59M6
Royal East St LEI LE1 ...... 6 F3
Royal Ga BPR/DUF DE56 .... 18 B4
Royal Gv DERBYE DE21 ..... 45 H4
Royal Hill Rd DERBYE DE21 .. 59 H1
Royal Ms BSTN/STPLFD NG9 . 63 C4
Royal Rd LEIS LE2 .... 125M5
Royal Wy DERBYSE DE24 .... 58 C4
LBORO LE11 .... 103 L1
Roy Av BSTN/STPLFD NG9 ... 63M5
Royce Av HUCK/RAV NG15 ... 23 J3
Royce Cl LEIW LE3 .... 130 A5
Roy Cl RLEIW/BAR LE9 ..... 136 A7
Roydale Cl LBORO LE11 .... 103 J1
Royden Cl LEIN LE4 ...... 125 C6
Roydon Cl MCKLVR DE3 .... 56 A3
Royland Rd LBORO LE11 .... 9 H5
Royston Cl LEIS LE2 ...... 137 H5
WBRGFD NG2 .... 50 F6
Royston Dr BPR/DUF DE56 .. 18 B2
Ruby Paddocks
EWD/SEL/PNX NG16 ..... 34 D2
Ruby St LEIW LE4 .... 131 G1
Ruddington La CFTN/RUD NG11 . 64 F7
Rudge Cl WOL/BIL/BRX NC8 .. 49 K2
Ruding Rd LEIS LE2 ...... 131 G5
Rudkin Cl RLEIW/BBY LE8 ... 142 F2
Rudyard Av DERBYE DE21 ... 59 L1
Rudyard Cl LBORO LE11 .... 102 F5
Ruffles Av MAPPK/POR/STA NG3 . 37M2
Rufford Av BSTN/STPLFD NG9 . 48 E7
CARL NG4 .... 38 B5
Rufford Cl HUCK/RAV NG15 .. 24 A1
LBORO LE11 .... 102 F2
Rufford Rd ARN NC5 ...... 37 G4
CFTN/RUD NG11 .... 65 H8
LGEAT NG10 .... 75M3
Rufford St LEIE LE5 ...... 132 C1
Rufford Wy WBRGFD NG2 ... 65M1
Ruffstone Cl BPR/DUF DE56 .. 18 F8
Rugby Cl WBRGFD NG2 .... 50 A2
Rugby Rd LEIW LE3 .... 6 B5
Rugby Ter NOTTE NG7 ..... 4 A1
Rugeley Av LGEAT NG10 ... 62 D8
Ruislip Cl EWD/SEL/PNX NG16 . 22 C8
Rumsey Cl COAL LE67 ..... 100 A7
RLBORO LE12 .... 112 C1

Rumsey Dr RLEIW/BBY LE8 . 136 D7
Runcie Cl COT/KEY/RAD NG12 . 67 K8
Runcorn Cl LEIS LE2 ...... 137 G4
Runcorn Rd LEIS LE2 ...... 137 H4
Runswick Dr ARN NC5 ..... 25 K7
WOL/BIL/BRX NC8 ...... 49 L2
Runton Dr ARN NC5 ...... 25 K8
Rupert Brooke Rd LBORO LE11 . 8 A2
Rupert Crs RLEINE/SYS LE7 .. 121 J1
Rupert Law Cl RLBORO LE12 . 104 D8
Rupert Rd DERBYE DE21 .... 44 E8
Rupert St ILK DE7 .... 33 L6
LEI LE1 .... 6 F7
Rupert Wy RLEIW/BBY LE8 . 139 M7
Rushcliffe Av CARL NG4 .... 38 D7
COT/KEY/RAD NG12 ..... 53 K4
DERBYE DE21 .... 58 D1
Rushcliffe Ct BLWL NG6 .... 36 B1
Rushcliffe Gdns DERBYSE DE21 . 58 D1
Rushcliffe Gv RLBORO LE12 .. 88 C3
Rushcliffe Ri ARN NC5 ..... 37 H2
Rushcliffe Rd HUCK/RAV NG15 . 23 J2
Rushdale Av NORM/LIT DE23 . 71 H1
The Rushes CFTN/RUD NG11 . 77 M6
COAL LE67 .... 116 C6
LBORO LE11 .... 9 H2
Rushey Cl LEIN LE4 ...... 126 A3
Rushey La RLEINE/SYS LE7 .. 112 F5
Rushford Dr LEIN LE4 ..... 126 B6
WOL/BIL/BRX NC8 ...... 49 G3
Rush Leys LGEAT NG10 .... 76 B2
LGEAT NG10 .... 76 B3
Rushmere Wk LEIW LE3 ... 129 L5
Rushton Dr LEIS LE2 ...... 136 F3
Rushworth Av WBRGFD NG2 . 51 J7
Rushworth Cl
MAPPK/POR/STA NG3 ... 5 L2
Rushy Cl WOL/BIL/BRX NC8 .. 49 H2
Rushy La LGEAT NG10 ..... 60 B8
Ruskin Av BSTN/STPLFD NG9 . 63 H3
LGEAT NG10 .... 75M2
RLEINE/SYS LE7 .... 121 G5
Ruskington Dr WGSTN LE18 . 138 B2
Ruskin Rd DERBYW DE22 ... 43 K8
Ruskin Wy NORM/LIT DE23 .. 56 F7
Russ Cl RLBORO LE12 ..... 104 D8
Russell Av WOL/BIL/BRX NC8 . 49 K2
Russell Crs WOL/BIL/BRX NC8 . 49 K2
Russell Dr WOL/BIL/BRX NC8 . 49 J2
Russell Gdns
BSTN/STPLFD NG9 .... 63 G5
Russell Rd NOTTE NG7 ..... 36 D7
Russell Sq LEI LE1 .... 7 G2
Russell St DERBYSE DE24 .... 58 A6
LBORO LE11 .... 9 L3
LGEAT NG10 .... 62 B6
NOTTE NG7 .... 4 C4
Russet Av CARL NG4 ...... 38 C4
Russet Cl DERBYE DE21 .... 44 F6
Russley Rd BSTN/STPLFD NG9 . 48 E7
Ruth Dr ARN NC5 .... 25 L8
Rutherford Ri DERBYE DE21 .. 44 D5
Rutherford Rd LEIN LE4 .... 124 E3
Ruthwell Gdns ARN NC5 ... 24 E8
Rutland Av BSTN/STPLFD NG9 . 62 E5
BWSH/BRSTN DE72 ...... 60 E6
LEIS LE2 .... 131 J6
RIPLEY DE5 .... 11 K8
WGSTN LE18 .... 137 M4
Rutland Cl LEIN LE4 ...... 129 L4
Rutland Dr LEIN LE4 ...... 120 C8
MCKLVR DE3 .... 56 B4
Rutland Gv LGEAT NG10 .... 62 A2
Rutland Rd CARL NG4 ..... 38 C7
EWD/SEL/PNX NG16 ..... 12 F3
WBRGFD NG2 .... 50 D2
Rutland St ILK DE7 .... 33 K6
LBORO LE11 .... 9 L4
LEI LE1 .... 7 G6
NORM/LIT DE23 .... 57 L6
NOTT NG1 .... 4 F8
Rutland Ter ILK DE7 ...... 33 K5
Ryal Cl BWSH/BRSTN DE72 .. 60 A2
Ryan Cl DERBYSE DE24 ..... 71 J4
Rycroft Rd CDON/KEG DE74 .. 75 H8
Rydal Av LBORO LE11 ..... 8 A8
Rydal Cl DERBYW DE22 .... 43 J3
Rydal Dr BSTN/STPLFD NG9 .. 62 D8
HUCK/RAV NG15 .... 15 K7
Rydale Rd ARN NC5 ...... 37 G2
Rydal Gv WBRGFD NG2 .... 65 K3
Rydal Gv BLWL NG6 ...... 36 C4
Rydal St LEIS LE2 .... 6 C9
Ryde Av LEIS LE2 .... 132 B8
Ryder Rd LEIW LE3 ...... 130 A1
Rye Butts MELB/CHEL DE73 .. 72 C6
Rye Cl DERBYE DE21 ...... 44 C4
LEIS LE2 .... 137 J3
Ryecroft St BSTN/STPLFD NG9 . 48 C7
Ryedale Gdns NORM/LIT DE23 . 71 G3
Ryegate Crs LEIN LE4 ..... 119 K7
Ryegrass Cl BPR/DUF DE56 .. 18 B3
Ryegrass Rd DERBYE DE21 .. 45 G5
Ryehill Cl WBRGFD NG2 .... 51 H5
Ryehill St WBRGFD NG2 .... 51 H5
Ryeholm Cl RLBORO LE12 ... 88 D4
Ryeland Gdns WBRGFD NG2 . 51 G5
Ryemere Cl EWD/SEL/PNX NG16 . 21 J5
Rye St NOTTE NG7 .... 36 D6
Rykneld Cl NORM/LIT DE23 .. 70 C1
Rykneld Dr NORM/LIT DE23 .. 56 C8
Rykneld Rd NORM/LIT DE23 .. 70 C2
Rykneld Wy NORM/LIT DE23 . 70 C1
Rykneld Hl RIPLEY DE5 .... 70 C1
Ryknield Rd BPR/DUF DE56 .. 18 F8
Rylands Cl DERBYSE DE24 ... 58 B6
Rymill Dr DERBYE DE21 .... 44 D6
Ryton Sq WOL/BIL/BRX NC8 .. 35 M7

S

Sacheverell Wy GBY/RBY LE6... 123 J6

Sacheverel Rd LEIW LE3 130 B1
Sacheverel St DERBY DE1 2 E6
Sackville Gdns LEIS LE2 132 A7
Sackville St NORM/LIT DE23 57 K7
Saddington Rd RLEIW/BBY LE8 145 L8
Saddlers Cl LEIW LE3 123 M7
RLEINE/SYS LE7 115 H8
Saddlers Yd COT/KEY/RAD NG12 66 C8
Sadler Ga DERBY DE1 2 E3
Sadlers Wls RLBORO LE12 100 F1
Saffron Dr DERBYE DE21 44 E6
Saffron Gdns WBRGFD NG2 50 F5
Saffron Hill Rd LEIS LE2 131 J7 3
Saffron La LEIS LE2 131 J6
LEIS LE2 137 J3
WGSTN LE18 137 J3
Saffron Rd WGSTN LE18 137 J4
Saffron Wy LEIS LE2 137 J1
Sage Rd LEIS LE2 6 B9
St Agnes Av DERBYW DE22 43 H3
St Aidan's Av
RLEINE/SYS LE7 120 D5 1
St Albans Ms BLWL NG6 36 B1 3
St Albans Rd ARN NG5 25 H8
BLWL NG6 24 C3
BLWL NG6 24 B8
DERBYW DE22 57 G4
LEIS LE2 7 K9
St Albans St ARN NG5 37 G4
St Alkmund's Cl
BPR/DUF DE56 29 J3 1
St Alkmunds Wy
BPR/DUF DE56 29 J3 2
DERBY DE1 2 F2
St Andrew Cl CFTN/RUD NG11 77 M6
St Andrews Cl BLWL NG6 24 A8 1
COAL LE67 100 B7 1
RLBORO LE12 97 L8
St Andrew's Dr ILK DE7 33 J7 2
LEIS LE2 132 C6
St Andrew's Ri CDON/KEG DE74 86 A6
St Andrews Rd LEIS LE2 131 J8
NOTT NG1 4 F1
St Andrews Vw DERBYE DE21 44 C7
St Anne Dr LEIS LE2 137 H1
St Annes Cl RLEINE/SYS LE7 121 G5
St Anne's La CDON/KEG DE74 84 F4 3
RLBORO LE12 94 F1
St Ann's Hl
MAPPK/POR/STA NG3 5 J2 1
St Ann's Hill Rd
MAPPK/POR/STA NG3 5 G3
St Ann's St NOTT NG1 5 H5 2
St Ann's Va
MAPPK/POR/STA NG3 5 M2 1
St Ann's Wy
MAPPK/POR/STA NG3 5 G3
St Ann's Well Rd
MAPPK/POR/STA NG3 5 J5
St Augustine Rd LEIW LE3 6 B6
St Augustines Cl NOTTE NG7 36 E6 4
St Augustine St NORM/LIT DE23 57 K6
St Austell Dr CFTN/RUD NG11 64 F2
St Austell Rd LEIE LE5 127 J8
St Austins Ct CARL NG4 38 D7 4
St Austins Dr CARL NG4 38 D7
St Barnabas Rd LEIE LE5 132 B1
St Bartholomew's Rd
MAPPK/POR/STA NG3 37 K8
St Bernards Av LEIN LE4 125 M4
St Bernard's Cl RLBORO LE12 101 L5
St Bernard's Rd COAL LE67 108 E3
St Bernard St LEIN LE4 125 M5
St Botolph Rd RLBORO LE12 101 M4
St Bride's Wk DERBYW DE22 56 F1 4
Saintbury Rd LEIW LE3 124 B6
St Catherines St
COT/KEY/RAD NG12 53 J5 5
St Cecilia Gdns
MAPPK/POR/STA NG3 5 J3
St Chad's Rd
MAPPK/POR/STA NG3 5 M6
NORM/LIT DE23 2 B9
St Christopher St
WBRGFD NG2 51 K3 11
St Clare's Cl NORM/LIT DE23 57 H5
St Clares Ct COAL LE67 108 C7 1
St Columba Wy
RLEINE/SYS LE7 120 D3
St Crispin's Wy RLEINE/SYS LE7 120 C6
St Cuthbert's Av
RLEIW/BBY LE8 139 M7
St Cuthbert's Rd DERBYW DE22 57 G4
MAPPK/POR/STA NG3 5 M5
St David's Cl DERBYW DE22 57 H4
LEIS LE2 132 C6
LEIW LE3 129 K5
St Davids Ct COAL LE67 109 G6
St David's Crs COAL LE67 109 G5
St Davids Rd LEIW LE3 130 A1
St Denys Rd LEIE LE5 132 F3
St Dunstan Rd LEIW LE3 131 G1 2
St Edmund's Cl DERBYW DE22 43 K3
St Edward's Rd CDON/KEG DE74 84 F5
St Ervan Rd CFTN/RUD NG11 64 F1
St Faiths Cl COAL LE67 108 A8
St Georges Dr
BSTN/STPLFD NG9 62 D5 6
WBRGFD NG2 51 G5 7
St George's Pl BPR/DUF DE56 17 K3 4
St George St LEI LE1 7 H5 1
St Georges Wy LEI LE1 7 G7
St Giles Rd NORM/LIT DE23 57 K6
St Gregory's Dr RLBORO LE12 114 B4
St Helens Cl LEIN LE4 125 G6
St Helen's Crs BSTN/STPLFD NG9 48 A3
CALV/BJ NG14 39 K3
St Helens Dr LEIN LE4 125 H7
St Helen's Gv CALV/BJ NG14 39 J4
St Helen's Rd WBRGFD NG2 65 K1
St Helen's St DERBY DE1 2 D2
NOTTE NG7 4 D6
NOTTE NG7 4 D6 2
St Hildas Cl RLEINE/SYS LE7 121 G5
St Hugh's Cl DERBYW DE22 43 K5 6
St Ives COAL LE67 108 F7
St Ives Rd LEIN LE4 126 C5
WGSTN LE18 138 A6
St James Av ILK DE7 33 L8
St James Cl BPR/DUF DE56 18 B3 9
LEIS LE2 139 G4 2
RLEIW/BAR LE9 135 H8
St James Ct LGEAT NG10 61 M4 1
St James' Dr
EWD/SEL/PNX NG16 13 J7
St James Rd LEIS LE2 132 A4
NORM/LIT DE23 57 K6
RLBORO LE12 101 M4
St James's St
BSTN/STPLFD NG9 62 A1 2
DERBY DE1 2 E4
St James's Ter NOTT NG1 4 F8
St James St LEI LE1 7 G4
NORM/LIT DE23 57 L6
St Johns RLEIW/BAR LE9 136 C4
St John's Av DERBYE DE21 58 F2
RLEINE/SYS LE7 121 G5
St John's Cl DERBYW DE22 43 J4 2
EWD/SEL/PNX NG16 13 H6
RIPLEY DE5 11 K5
St John's Crs HUCK/RAV NG15 24 A2
St John's Dr BPR/DUF DE56 18 E7 7
St John's Rd BPR/DUF DE56 17 L3 4
CFTN/RUD NG11 65 G8 4
ILK DE7 31 K2
ILK DE7 33 L8
LEIS LE2 132 A5
St John's St LGEAT NG10 62 B8
St John's Ter DERBY DE1 2 B2
St John St LEI LE1 6 E3
St Jude's Av
MAPPK/POR/STA NG3 37 H5
St Laurence Ct LGEAT NG10 76 C1 2
St Lawrence Bvd
COT/KEY/RAD NG12 53 H5
St Lawrence Cl HEANOR DE75 20 D5 4
St Leonards Cl RLBORO LE12 97 L8 2
St Leonard's Dr
WOL/BIL/BRX NG8 49 K3
St Leonards Rd LEIS LE2 131 M5
St Leven Cl WOL/BIL/BRX NG8 35 H7 1
St Luke's Cl RLEINE/SYS LE7 133 K3
WBRGFD NG2 65 M2 1
St Luke's St MAPPK/POR/STA NG3 5 L6
St Luke's Wy CALV/BJ NG14 39 K7
St Margarets Av
WOL/BIL/BRX NG8 36 A7
St Margaret's St LEI LE1 6 E3 3
St Margaret's Wy LEI LE1 6 E3
LEIN LE4 125 J6
St Mark's Rd DERBYE DE21 44 B8
St Marks St LEI LE1 7 G2
NOTT NG1 5 J5
St Martins LEI LE1 6 E6
St Martin's Rd
WOL/BIL/BRX NG8 35 J7
St Mary's Av
BWSH/BRSTN DE72 60 E8 2
CARL NG4 38 C5
LEIE LE5 127 G7
LEIW LE3 130 A4
St Mary's Cl ARN NG5 25 K6
BSTN/STPLFD NG9 63 H6
DERBYSE DE24 72 E1 3
LBORO LE11 8 F2
RLBORO LE12 97 L8
St Mary's Ct DERBY DE1 2 E1
LEIW LE3 130 A4
St Mary's Crs CFTN/RUD NG11 65 G8
RLBORO LE12 88 C4
St Mary's Ga DERBY DE1 2 E3
NOTT NG1 5 J7 2
St Mary's Pl NOTT NG1 5 J7 3
St Marys Rd LEIS LE2 131 M5 2
RLBORO LE12 114 A3
St Mary St ILK DE7 33 J7
St Marys Wk
EWD/SEL/PNX NG16 12 F4
St Mary's Wy HUCK/RAV NG15 15 L7
St Marys Wharf Rd DERBY DE1 43 M8
St Matthew's Wk
DERBYW DE22 43 K5 7
St Matthews Wy LEI LE1 7 G3
St Matthias Rd
MAPPK/POR/STA NG3 5 M4
St Mawes Av CFTN/RUD NG11 64 F1
St Mawes Cl DERBYW DE22 43 H3
St Mellion NORM/LIT DE23 56 D6 3
St Mellion Cl LEIN LE4 118 F8
St Michael's Av CARL NG4 38 C5
LEIN LE4 125 M4
WOL/BIL/BRX NG8 35 H7
St Michael's Cl BPR/DUF DE56 30 A1 2
COAL LE67 116 B6
DERBYSE DE24 59 G8 5
St Michael's La DERBY DE1 2 E2
St Michael's Sq
BSTN/STPLFD NG9 48 F7 2
St Michaels Vw
DERBYSE DE24 59 G8 6
St Nicholas Cir LEI LE1 6 C6
St Nicholas Cl ARN NG5 25 J8
DERBYW DE22 43 H5 2
St Nicholas Pl LEI LE1 6 D6
St Nicholas St NOTT NG1 5 G8 2
St Norbert Dr ILK DE7 47 H2
St Olaves Cl LBORO LE11 102 F2 2
St Oswalds Rd LEIW LE3 124 D8
St Pancras Wy DERBY DE1 43 M8 6
St Patrick's Rd HUCK/RAV NG15 15 K8
EWD/SEL/PNX NG16 34 F1
St Paul's Av NOTTE NG7 4 A1
St Pauls Cl LEIS LE2 139 H1
St Paul's Dr RLEINE/SYS LE7 120 E5
St Pauls Rd LEIW LE3 131 G1 3
St Paul's St WOL/BIL/BRX NG8 50 B2 3
St Paul's Ter NOTTE NG7 4 A1
St Peters Av RLBORO LE12 94 E6
St Peters Church Wk NOTT NG1 5 H8
St Peter's Churchyard
DERBY DE1 2 E4
St Peter's Cl BPR/DUF DE56 17 L3 5
LEIW LE3 123 M7
St Peter's Crs
CFTN/RUD NG11 65 G8 5
St Peters Cft BPR/DUF DE56 17 L3 6
St Peters Dr RLEIW/BBY LE8 136 D7
St Peter's Ga NOTT NG1 5 H7
St Peters La LEI LE1 6 D5
St Peters Rd LEIS LE2 7 K8
MELB/CHEL DE73 72 E7
St Peter's St DERBY DE1 2 F4
NOTTE NG7 50 C2
RLEINE/SYS LE7 120 E4
St Philips Rd LEIE LE5 132 B4
RLBORO LE12 97 L8
St Quentin Cl NORM/LIT DE23 57 G4 1
St Ronan's Av BPR/DUF DE56 29 J4
St Saviour's Gdns WBRGFD NG2 51 H5
St Saviour's Hl LEIE LE5 7 M5 1
St Saviours Rd COAL LE67 108 A7
LEIE LE5 7 M4
LEIE LE5 132 B2
St Stephen's Av
WBRGFD NG2 51 K3 12
St Stephens Cl
BWSH/BRSTN DE72 59 M6
NORM/LIT DE23 71 H1 4
St Stephens Rd LEIS LE2 7 L9
WBRGFD NG2 5 M8
WBRGFD NG2 51 K3 13
St Swithin's Cl DERBYW DE22 57 H4
St Swithin's Rd LEIE LE5 133 H2
St Thomas Rd NORM/LIT DE23 57 L7
WGSTN LE18 137 J6
St Vincent Cl LGEAT NG10 76 C1
St Vincents Cl COAL LE67 108 A8
St Werburgh's Vw
DERBYE DE21 59 H2 1
St Wilfrid's Cl RLEIW/BBY LE8 146 E6
St Wilfrid's Rd ILK DE7 32 C8
St Winefride Rd RLBORO LE12 101 M4
St Wolstan's Cl WGSTN LE18 138 B4
St Wystan's Rd DERBYW DE22 57 G4
Salamander Cl CARL NG4 38 B6
Salcey Dr BSTN/STPLFD NG9 48 B5
Salcombe Circ ARN NG5 25 H6
Salcombe Cl
EWD/SEL/PNX NG16 22 A6
WGSTN LE18 138 A6 5
Salcombe Crs
CFTN/RUD NG11 65 H7 1
Salcombe Dr ARN NG5 25 H6
LEIW LE3 124 A6
Salcombe Rd ARN NG5 36 D4
Sale St NORM/LIT DE23 57 M5
Salford Gdns
MAPPK/POR/STA NG3 5 K5
Salisbury Av LEI LE1 7 J9
RLBORO LE12 88 D6
RLEIW/BAR LE9 141 G3
Salisbury Cl RLEIW/BBY LE8 142 F1
Salisbury Dr BPR/DUF DE56 18 B2 7
Salisbury La MELB/CHEL DE73 82 F8 4
Salisbury Rd LEI LE1 131 M4
Salisbury Sq NOTTE NG7 50 C3 10
Salisbury St BSTN/STPLFD NG9 49 M8
LBORO LE11 9 L2
LGEAT NG10 62 C8 7
NORM/LIT DE23 2 E8 2
NOTTE NG7 50 C3
Salkeld Rd LEIS LE2 137 G5
Sallywood Cl DERBYSE DE24 71 H5 6
Salmon Cl BLWL NG6 23 K8
Salop St ARN NG5 25 H8
Saltash Cl WGSTN LE18 138 A6 6
Saltburn Cl DERBYE DE21 44 A6
Saltburn Rd WOL/BIL/BRX NG8 35 L8
Saltcoates Av LEIN LE4 126 A3
Salter Cl CDON/KEG DE74 84 D3
Salterford Rd HUCK/RAV NG15 23 J2
Saltersford Rd LEIE LE5 126 D8
Saltersgate Dr LEIN LE4 119 L7 2
Saltford Cl CARL NG4 38 D5
Salthouse Ct
BSTN/STPLFD NG9 49 L8 3
Salthouse La BSTN/STPLFD NG9 49 L7
Saltney Wy CFTN/RUD NG11 64 E4
Salt's Cl RLEIW/BAR LE9 135 M5
Samantha Ct DERBYE DE21 44 F6 12
Samphire Cl LEIE LE5 127 H5 2
Samson Ct CFTN/RUD NG11 64 F7
Samson Rd COAL LE67 108 B4
LEIW LE3 124 F8
Samuel Ct RIPLEY DE5 11 H7 4
Samuel St LEI LE1 7 J5
Sancroft Av DERBYE DE21 59 J1
Sancroft Rd DERBYE DE21 59 K1
Sandacre St LEI LE1 6 E4
Sandale Cl WBRGFD NG2 66 A1
Sandalwood Cl
DERBYSE DE24 59 G8 7
Sandalwood Rd LBORO LE11 8 C9
Sandays Cl WBRGFD NG2 51 G6
Sandbach Cl DERBYE DE21 44 E6 6
Sandbed La BPR/DUF DE56 18 A5
Sandby Ct BSTN/STPLFD NG9 63 G2
Sanderson Cl RLEIW/BBY LE8 142 E1
Sanderson Rd DERBYE DE21 58 F1 3
Sanders Rd RLBORO LE12 112 D2
Sandfield Cl DERBYE DE21 44 F7 2
LEIN LE4 126 C2
Sandfield Rd ARN NG5 37 K1
BSTN/STPLFD NG9 62 C5 3
NOTTE NG7 4 A7
Sandford Av LGEAT NG10 62 C8 8
Sandford Brook
RDERBYSW DE65 68 C6 7
Sandford Cl LEIE LE5 132 E1 2
Sandford Rd
MAPPK/POR/STA NG3 37 K5
RLEINE/SYS LE7 120 E4
Sandgate BSTN/STPLFD NG9 49 H6 4
Sandgate Av LEIN LE4 119 K7
Sandgate Cl DERBYSE DE24 72 F2 2
Sandham Bridge Rd
RLEINE/SYS LE7 118 D4
Sandham La RIPLEY DE5 11 G6
Sandhill Dr RLEIW/BAR LE9 136 B6
Sandhill Rd EWD/SEL/PNX NG16 13 M4
Sandhills Av LEIE LE5 126 F4
Sandhills Cl RLBORO LE12 100 F1 3
The Sandhills RLBORO LE12 112 C1
Sandhole La RLBORO LE12 101 H6
Sandhurst Cl LEIW LE3 130 F1
Sandhurst Dr BSTN/STPLFD NG9 62 F5
CFTN/RUD NG11 78 F1
Sandhurst Rd BLWL NG6 23 M6
LEIW LE3 124 F8
Sandhurst St LEIS LE2 138 E1
Sandiacre Dr LEIN LE4 120 D7
Sandiacre Rd BSTN/STPLFD NG9 62 A1
Sandon St NOTTE NG7 36 E6
Sandown Av MCKLVR DE3 56 A4
Sandown Rd BSTN/STPLFD NG9 62 D4
DERBYSE DE24 58 B7
LEIS LE2 132 B6
LEIW LE3 124 A6
WGSTN LE18 138 B3 5
Sandpiper Cl LEIE LE5 7 L3
Sandpiper Wy NOTTE NG7 50 C3 11
Sandringham Av LEIN LE4 125 M4
WBRGFD NG2 51 J7 2
Sandringham Crs
WOL/BIL/BRX NG8 49 G2 3
Sandringham Dr
BSTN/STPLFD NG9 49 G6
DERBYE DE21 59 K3
Sandringham Pl ILK DE7 47 H2 6
Sandringham Ri RLBORO LE12 101 K5
Sandringham Rd COAL LE67 108 D7
DERBYE DE21 44 C6
LGEAT NG10 61 M3 10
WBRGFD NG2 51 K3 14
WGSTN LE18 137 J6 2
Sands Cl CARL NG4 52 C2
Sandside COT/KEY/RAD NG12 67 K5
Sandula Rd NOTTE NG7 36 D5
Sandwell Cl LGEAT NG10 75 L1
Sandyford Cl BLWL NG6 36 A4 3
Sandyhill Cl MELB/CHEL DE73 72 E5
Sandy La BSTN/STPLFD NG9 49 H6
COT/KEY/RAD NG12 52 F5
DERBYE DE21 30 D3
HUCK/RAV NG15 15 L8
Sandypits La RDERBYSW DE65 69 G3
Sandy Ri WGSTN LE18 138 C3
Sanger Cl CFTN/RUD NG11 64 A7
Sankey Dr BLWL NG6 23 L8
Santolina Dr DERBYE DE21 44 D5 10
Sanvey Ga LEI LE1 6 D4
Sanvey La LEIS LE2 136 F1
Sapcote Rd RLEIW/BAR LE9 140 C5
Sapele Cl CARL NG4 38 E5 2
Sapperton Cl NORM/LIT DE23 71 H2 3
Sargent Gdns
MAPPK/POR/STA NG3 51 K1
Sarson St RLBORO LE12 112 D1
Saskatoon Cl
COT/KEY/RAD NG12 53 J5 6
Saunby Cl ARN NG5 25 M8
Saundersfoot Wy DERBYE DE21 44 F5
Saunderson Rd LEIN LE4 125 H3
Saunton Cl COT/KEY/RAD NG12 66 A3
Savage's Rd CFTN/RUD NG11 65 G7
Save Penny La BPR/DUF DE56 29 L2
Savernake Rd LEIN LE4 125 G6
Saville Cl BSTN/STPLFD NG9 48 C7 1
Saville Rd ARN NG5 37 K2
RLEIW/BBY LE8 143 G1
Saville St LEIE LE5 132 C1
Sawbrook RLEIW/BBY LE8 145 L8
Sawday St LEIS LE2 131 J4
Sawley Rd BWSH/BRSTN DE72 60 F8
BWSH/BRSTN DE72 61 J8
Sawley St LEIS LE2 132 B4
Sawmand Cl LGEAT NG10 76 A1 5
Saxby St LEIS LE2 7 J8
Saxelby Gdns BLWL NG6 23 M7 4
Saxon Dl LEIS LE2 137 G5
Saxondale Av MCKLVR DE3 56 A3 1
Saxondale Dr BLWL NG6 36 B2
Saxondale Rd WGSTN LE18 138 C7 5
Saxons Ri GBY/RBY LE6 123 G6
Saxon St LEIS LE2 6 A8
Saxon Wy COT/KEY/RAD NG12 67 L6
Saxton Av HEANOR DE75 20 D5
Saxton Cl BSTN/STPLFD NG9 63 M1 6
Scafell Wy CFTN/RUD NG11 64 B8
Scalborough Cl RLEIW/BBY LE8 143 G3
Scalby Cl EWD/SEL/PNX NG16 21 H5
Scalford Dr WOL/BIL/BRX NG8 50 A4
Scalpay Cl LEIN LE4 124 F4
Scarborough Av ILK DE7 33 H7
Scarborough Ri DERBYE DE21 44 B6
Scarborough Rd LEIN LE4 126 A5
Scarborough St
MAPPK/POR/STA NG3 5 K6
Scarcliffe Cl DERBYSE DE24 72 C4
Scarfell Cl WBRGFD NG2 66 A2
Scargill Av EWD/SEL/PNX NG16 21 M6
Scargill Cl EWD/SEL/PNX NG16 21 M6
Scargill Rd ILK DE7 32 C7
Scargill Wk
EWD/SEL/PNX NG16 21 K4 2
Scarrington Rd WBRGFD NG2 51 K6 8
Scarsdale Av DERBYW DE22 43 G4
NORM/LIT DE23 57 G5
Scarsdale Rd BPR/DUF DE56 29 J4 4
Sceptre St ARN NG5 37 G5
Schofield Rd LBORO LE11 103 G4
School Cl RLEIW/BAR LE9 141 G4
WBRGFD NG2 51 H6 8
School Crs RLEIW/BAR LE9 141 J8 5
School Cft ALFN DE55 12 B1
Schoolgate WGSTN LE18 137 K3
School Gn RLBORO LE12 88 C6
School Hl RLBORO LE12 105 L3
School House Cl
RLEINE/SYS LE7 124 B2 2
Schoolhouse Hl BPR/DUF DE56 10 B6
School La BPR/DUF DE56 10 B5
BSTN/STPLFD NG9 63 G3
CDON/KEG DE74 84 E3
COAL LE67 108 B1
LEIE LE5 132 F5
LEIN LE4 125 L1
LGEAT NG10 47 K8
MELB/CHEL DE73 72 E6
RIPLEY DE5 11 G6
RLBORO LE12 97 H2
RLBORO LE12 100 F1
RLBORO LE12 111 M5
RLBORO LE12 112 E2
RLEINE/SYS LE7 121 H7
RLEINE/SYS LE7 121 K2
RLEIW/BAR LE9 135 M8
RLEIW/BAR LE9 135 H8
School Rd EWD/SEL/PNX NG16 13 L3
RLEIW/BBY LE8 146 E7 6
School Sq ILK DE7 32 C8 2
School St LBORO LE11 9 K3
RLEINE/SYS LE7 119 K1
RLEINE/SYS LE7 120 F3
RLEIW/BBY LE8 145 K8
School Wk BLWL NG6 24 C3
RLEIW/BBY LE8 146 E7
The Scotches BPR/DUF DE56 17 K2
Scotland Rd ARN NG5 36 D5
Scotlands Dr COAL LE67 108 B7
Scotlands Rd COAL LE67 108 B7
Scotland Wy RLEIW/BBY LE8 143 K4
Scotswood Crs LEIS LE2 137 G4
Scott Av BSTN/STPLFD NG9 63 K1
Scott Cl BLWL NG6 35 K2
Scott Ct LEIS LE2 131 L7
Scott Dr BPR/DUF DE56 18 C2
Scott St LEIS LE2 131 L7
NORM/LIT DE23 57 K6
Scraptoft La LEIE LE5 126 E8
Scraptoft Ms LEIE LE5 126 E8
Scraptoft Ri LEIE LE5 127 K7
Scrimshire La
COT/KEY/RAD NG12 67 J4
Script Dr BLWL NG6 36 C3 5
Scrivelsby Gdns
BSTN/STPLFD NG9 63 H3
Scrivener Cl RLEINE/SYS LE7 133 L2
Scudamore Rd LEIW LE3 129 M2
Seaburn Rd BSTN/STPLFD NG9 62 C4
Seacole Cl LEIW LE3 130 B5
Seaford Av WOL/BIL/BRX NG8 49 M2
Seaford Rd LEIS LE2 137 H2
Seaford Wy ILK DE7 33 K2
Seagrave Cl COAL LE67 109 G6
DERBYE DE21 44 F7
Seagrave Dr LEIS LE2 138 D1
Seagrave Rd RLBORO LE12 106 C8
RLBORO LE12 114 A3
RLEINE/SYS LE7 115 J2
WOL/BIL/BRX NG8 35 H6
Seale St DERBY DE1 43 M8 7
Seals Cl RLBORO LE12 97 L8
Seamer Rd
EWD/SEL/PNX NG16 22 D8 8
Searl St DERBY DE1 2 C2
Seascale Cl DERBYE DE21 44 B6
Seatallan Cl WBRGFD NG2 66 A1 4
Seathwaite Cl
COT/KEY/RAD NG12 66 A3
Seatoller Cl WBRGFD NG2 66 A2
Seaton Cl MCKLVR DE3 56 A4 4
Seaton Crs WOL/BIL/BRX NG8 35 L6
Seaton Ri LEIE LE5 127 J6
Seaton Rd WGSTN LE18 138 A6
Second Av BLWL NG6 23 M8
BSTN/STPLFD NG9 50 B8
BWSH/BRSTN DE72 61 J3
CARL NG4 38 D6
CARL NG4 38 A7
MELB/CHEL DE73 72 E7
Seddons Cl LEIN LE4 125 H3
Sedgebrook Cl BLWL NG6 36 A3
DERBYE DE21 44 D5 11
Sedgebrook Rd LEIE LE5 133 H3
Sedgefield Dr RLEINE/SYS LE7 120 C4
RLEINE/SYS LE7 133 K1
Sedgeley Rd
COT/KEY/RAD NG12 66 B7
Sedgewood Gv
CFTN/RUD NG11 64 C4 1
Sedgley Av WBRGFD NG2 51 K2
Sedgwick St
EWD/SEL/PNX NG16 12 F4
EWD/SEL/PNX NG16 20 F4
Sedley Av EWD/SEL/PNX NG16 35 G1
Seely Rd NOTTE NG7 4 B6
Sefton Av BSTN/STPLFD NG9 48 C7
Sefton Dr MAPPK/POR/STA NG3 37 H6
Sefton Rd DERBYE DE21 58 D1
Segrave Rd LEIW LE3 130 F5
Seine La RLEIW/BAR LE9 135 K3
Selborne St DERBYSE DE24 58 B5 2
Selbourne St LBORO LE11 9 L3
Selbury Dr LEIS LE2 138 D2
Selby Av LEIE LE5 127 H6
Selby Cl BSTN/STPLFD NG9 62 C4
Selby La COT/KEY/RAD NG12 80 D5
Selby Rd WBRGFD NG2 65 K2
Selhurst St NOTTE NG7 4 A1
Selina Cl CDON/KEG DE74 84 E3 3
Selina St MELB/CHEL DE73 82 E8
Selkirk Rd LEIN LE4 126 B4
Selkirk St DERBYE DE21 44 C8
Sellars Av CFTN/RUD NG11 79 G1
Seller's Wood Dr BLWL NG6 35 L1
Seller's Wood Dr West
BLWL NG6 23 J8
Selside Ct BSTN/STPLFD NG9 62 E3
Selston Dr WOL/BIL/BRX NG8 50 A3
Selston Rd EWD/SEL/PNX NG16 12 F3
Selvester Dr RLBORO LE12 112 F2
Selworthy Cl DERBYE DE21 44 E5 6
Selwyn Cl BLWL NG6 36 C2
Selwyn St DERBYW DE22 57 G1 4
Sence Crs RLEIW/BBY LE8 139 L7
Serina Av NORM/LIT DE23 57 H7 1
Serlby Ri MAPPK/POR/STA NG3 51 K1
Serlby Rd EWD/SEL/PNX NG16 21 L4
Seton Cl LBORO LE11 103 G1 5
The Settlement
BWSH/BRSTN DE72 60 A2
Sevenlands Dr DERBYSE DE24 73 G3
Sevenoaks Av DERBYW DE22 56 D2
Seven Oaks Crs
BSTN/STPLFD NG9 48 F6
Seven Oaks Rd ILK DE7 47 L6
Seventh Av BSTN/STPLFD NG9 64 A2
Severals BSTN/STPLFD NG9 48 D8
Severnale Cl DERBYW DE22 43 M2

Severn Cl RLEIW/BAR LE9 .... 142 B4
Severn St LBORO LE11 .... 139 H2
Severn Rd DERBYSE DE24 .... 58 D7
  LEIS LE2 .... 7 K8
Seward St LBORO LE11 .... 8 F4
Sextant Rd LEIE LE5 .... 127 C8
Seymour Cl DERBYSE DE22 .... 57 G2
  LBORO LE11 .... 102 F2
Seymour Rd
  EWD/SEL/PNX NG16 .... 21 K6
  HUCK/RAV NG15 .... 23 J2
  LEIS LE2 .... 131 M5
  LEIS LE2 .... 131 M6
  RLBORO LE12 .... 105 K1
  WBRGFD NG2 .... 51 M7
Seymour St LEIS LE2 .... 7 J8
  MAPPK/POR/STA NG3 .... 5 M5
Seymour Wy LEIW LE3 .... 129 K5
Shackerdale Rd WGSTN LE18 .... 137 M2
Shacklecross Cl
  BWSH/BRSTN DE72 .... 60 A6
Shackleton Cl
  WOL/BIL/BRX NG8 .... 35 H5
Shackleton St LEI LE1 .... 7 G2
Shacklock Cl ARN NG5 .... 24 E5
Shadrack Cl RLEIW/BAR LE9 .... 140 B8
Shady Gv RDERBYSW DE65 .... 68 A5
Shady La BSTN/STPLFD NG9 .... 63 H6
  LEIS LE2 .... 132 F6
Shaef Cl RDERBYSW DE65 .... 68 C5
Shaeffer Ct LEIN LE4 .... 124 F5
Shaftesbury Av CALV/BJ NG14 .... 39 L2
  LEIN LE4 .... 125 L5
  LGEAT NG10 .... 61 L2
  LGEAT NG10 .... 75 M3
Shaftesbury Crs NORM/LIT DE23 .... 57 M6
Shaftesbury Rd LEIW LE3 .... 131 G3
Shaftesbury St
  NORM/LIT DE23 .... 58 A6
  NOTTE NG7 .... 36 E6
Shaftesbury St South
  NORM/LIT DE23 .... 57 M7
Shakespear Cl CDON/KEG DE74 .... 93 M2
Shakespeare Cl CARL NG4 .... 52 C2
  CDON/KEG DE74 .... 92 F2
  LEIW LE3 .... 130 C6
Shakespeare Dr LEIW LE3 .... 130 D6
Shakespeare Rd
  EWD/SEL/PNX NG16 .... 34 A2
Shakespeare St
  DERBYSE DE24 .... 71 L2
  LBORO LE11 .... 9 H2
  LEIS LE2 .... 131 K7
  LGEAT NG10 .... 62 A6
  NOTT NG1 .... 4 F5
Shakespeare Vls NOTT NG1 .... 5 G5
Shaldon Cl ARN NG5 .... 24 D6
Shaldon Dr NORM/LIT DE23 .... 57 H6
Shalfleet Dr DERBYSE DE24 .... 73 G2
Shamrock St NORM/LIT DE23 .... 57 J6
Shangton Rd RLEIW/BBY LE8 .... 147 M4
Shanklin Av LEIS LE2 .... 132 B8
Shanklin Dr
  BSTN/STPLFD NG9 .... 48 B8
  LEIS LE2 .... 132 B8
Shanklin Gdns LEIS LE2 .... 132 B8
Shannon Cl NORM/LIT DE23 .... 71 H1
Shanti Margh LEIN LE4 .... 126 A5
Shanwell Cl
  WOL/BIL/BRX NG8 .... 35 H5
Shardlow Rd BWSH/BRSTN DE72 .... 73 M8
  DERBYSE DE24 .... 72 F1
  WGSTN LE18 .... 138 A4
Sharmon Crs LEIW LE3 .... 130 B1
Sharnford Rd RLEIW/BAR LE9 .... 140 C8
Sharnford Wy
  BSTN/STPLFD NG9 .... 48 F3
Sharp Cl ILK DE7 .... 47 G1
  LGEAT NG10 .... 76 A1
Sharpe Wy RLEIW/BAR LE9 .... 135 M8
Sharphill Rd COT/KEY/RAD NG12 .... 65 M3
Sharpland LEIS LE2 .... 137 G2
Sharpley Av COAL LE67 .... 108 E6
Sharpley Dr LEIN LE4 .... 124 E1
  RLBORO LE12 .... 88 D4
Sharpley Rd LBORO LE11 .... 102 F5
Sharply Hl GBY/RBY LE6 .... 134 F3
Sharrard Cl EWD/SEL/PNX NG16 .... 13 L5
Shaw Cl RLEIW/BBY LE8 .... 142 D1
Shaw Crs HUCK/RAV NG15 .... 23 J4
Shawcroft Av ALFN DE55 .... 12 A2
Shaw La BPR/DUF DE56 .... 17 M8
Shaw St ALFN DE55 .... 11 J1
  CFTN/RUD NG11 .... 79 G1
  DERBYW DE22 .... 2 A2
Shaw St East ILK DE7 .... 47 L1
Shaw St West ILK DE7 .... 47 L1
Shaw's Yd BPR/DUF DE56 .... 18 D7
Shaw Wood Cl GBY/RBY LE6 .... 123 J4
Shearer Cl LEIN LE4 .... 126 C3
Shearing Hl CARL NG4 .... 38 E6
Shearing Hl CARL NG4 .... 38 E6
Shearsby Rd WGSTN LE18 .... 138 B5
Sheene Rd LEIN LE4 .... 124 E3
Sheepcote RLEINE/SYS LE7 .... 113 M4
Sheepfold La CFTN/RUD NG11 .... 79 G1
Sheffield Pl DERBY DE1 .... 3 J6
Sheffield St LEIW LE3 .... 131 H4
Shelby Cl NOTTE NG7 .... 50 C5
Sheldon Cl LBORO LE11 .... 102 F1
  LGEAT NG10 .... 61 M4
Sheldon Rd HEANOR DE75 .... 20 A2
Sheldon St LEIE LE5 .... 7 J4
Shelford Cl BSTN/STPLFD NG9 .... 63 H3
  MCKLVR DE3 .... 56 A4
Shelford Crs CALV/BJ NG14 .... 39 L2
Shelford Ri
  MAPPK/POR/STA NG3 .... 51 L1
Shelford Rd CARL NG4 .... 38 A4
  COT/KEY/RAD NG12 .... 53 J2
Shellduck Cl RLEIW/BBY LE8 .... 142 D3
Shelley Av CFTN/RUD NG11 .... 64 C4
Shelley Cl EWD/SEL/PNX NG16 .... 21 M8
  HUCK/RAV NG15 .... 23 H1
Shelley Dr DERBYSE DE24 .... 71 L2
Shelley Rd ARN NG5 .... 25 H8
  RLEIW/BAR LE9 .... 135 L5

Shelley St LBORO LE11 .... 103 H2
  LEIS LE2 .... 131 L7
Shelmorey Cl DERBYSE DE24 .... 72 B2
Shelt Hl CALV/BJ NG14 .... 27 H2
Shelthorpe Av LBORO LE11 .... 9 K8
Shelthorpe Rd LBORO LE11 .... 9 K8
Shelton Av HUCK/RAV NG15 .... 24 B8
Shelton Dr DERBYSE DE24 .... 72 D4
Shelton Gdns CFTN/RUD NG11 .... 64 F8
Shelton St MAPPK/POR/STA NG3 .... 5 J4
Shenfield Gdns BLWL NG6 .... 24 B6
Shenington Wy
  DERBYSE DE21 .... 44 F5
Shenley Rd WGSTN LE18 .... 138 C3
Shenton Cl LEIN LE4 .... 126 E1
  RLEIW/BBY LE8 .... 136 D8
  WGSTN LE18 .... 138 A4
Shepard Cl BLWL NG6 .... 35 K1
Shepherd Cl LEIW LE3 .... 129 H4
Shepherds Cl LBORO LE11 .... 8 B8
  RLBORO LE12 .... 95 G2
  RLBORO LE12 .... 102 A2
  WOL/BIL/BRX NG8 .... 35 L8
Shepherd St NORM/LIT DE23 .... 57 G6
Shepherds Wood Dr
  WOL/BIL/BRX NG8 .... 36 A8
Shepshed Rd RLBORO LE12 .... 94 C7
Shepton Cl ILK DE7 .... 33 H4
Shepton Crs WOL/BIL/BRX NG8 .... 35 M6
Sherard Rd LEIE LE5 .... 7 L4
Sheraton Dr WOL/BIL/BRX NG8 .... 49 J4
Sherborne Av WGSTN LE18 .... 138 A7
Sherborne Rd WBRGFD NG2 .... 65 K2
  WOL/BIL/BRX NG8 .... 35 L6
Sherbourne Dr
  BPR/DUF DE56 .... 18 B2
Sherbrook Av ARN NG5 .... 37 H1
Sherbrooke Rd ARN NG5 .... 36 F6
Sherbrook Rd ARN NG5 .... 37 G1
Sherbrook Ter ARN NG5 .... 37 H1
Sherford Cl WGSTN LE18 .... 138 A5
Sheridan Cl RLEIW/BAR LE9 .... 135 L5
Sheridan Ct
  BSTN/STPLFD NG9 .... 48 D6
Sheridan St DERBYSE DE24 .... 71 K2
  LEIS LE2 .... 131 L3
Sheriff's Lea BSTN/STPLFD NG9 .... 62 C5
Sheriffs Wy WBRGFD NG2 .... 51 G4
Sheringham Ct ARN NG5 .... 37 K1
Sheringham Rd LEIN LE4 .... 125 H5
Sherloyd Cl LEIN LE4 .... 126 D3
Sherman Dr BSTN/STPLFD NG9 .... 63 G5
Sherrard Dr DERBYSE DE24 .... 114 A6
Sherrard Wy LEIW LE3 .... 130 B6
Sherrington Cl
  CFTN/RUD NG11 .... 64 A7
Sherston Cl DERBYSE DE21 .... 44 F1
Sherwin Cl MAPPK/POR/STA NG3 .... 5 H4
Sherwin Gv NOTTE NG7 .... 50 C4
Sherwin Rd BSTN/STPLFD NG9 .... 48 D6
  NOTTE NG7 .... 50 C4
Sherwin St DERBYW DE22 .... 43 J7
Sherwood Av
  BWSH/BRSTN DE72 .... 60 A5
  DERBYE DE21 .... 44 D8
  NORM/LIT DE23 .... 71 J2
Sherwood Ri
  EWD/SEL/PNX NG16 .... 21 K6
  NOTTE NG7 .... 36 F7
Sherwood St DERBYW DE22 .... 2 B7
  HUCK/RAV NG15 .... 24 A1
  LEIE LE5 .... 132 C1
Sherwood V ARN NG5 .... 37 J4
Sherwood Wk HUCK/RAV NG15 .... 15 L5
Shetland Cl DERBYE DE21 .... 44 A8
Shetland Rd LEIN LE4 .... 126 A5
Shetland Wy RLEIW/BBY LE8 .... 143 K4
Shield Crs LEIS LE2 .... 137 G5
Shields Crs CDON/KEG DE74 .... 84 D4
Shilling Wy LGEAT NG10 .... 61 L8
Shipley Common La ILK DE7 .... 33 G3
Shipley La ILK DE7 .... 32 D4
Shipley Ri CARL NG4 .... 38 C8
Shipley Rd LEIE LE5 .... 132 B3
  WOL/BIL/BRX NG8 .... 35 K5
Shipstone St ILK DE7 .... 47 M1
  NOTTE NG7 .... 36 D7
Shipston Hl LEIS LE2 .... 138 E3
Shipton Cl WGSTN LE18 .... 138 D5
Shireoaks BPR/DUF DE56 .... 17 H2
Shireoaks Cl NORM/LIT DE23 .... 57 G8
Shires La LEI LE1 .... 6 D5
Shirley Av LEIS LE2 .... 132 B7
Shirley Cl CDON/KEG DE74 .... 84 E3
Shirley Crs BWSH/BRSTN DE72 .... 61 H7
Shirley Dr ARN NG5 .... 25 M8
  RLEINE/SYS LE7 .... 120 F2
Shirley Pk BWSH/BRSTN DE72 .... 73 M8
  LEIS LE2 .... 132 B7
  MAPPK/POR/STA NG3 .... 37 G7
  RIPLEY DE5 .... 11 H6
Shirley St LEIN LE4 .... 125 L5
  LGEAT NG10 .... 75 L3
Shirreffs Cl RLBORO LE12 .... 105 J7
Shop La BPR/DUF DE56 .... 10 A5
Shop Stones BWSH/BRSTN DE72 .... 60 A2
Shoreswood Cl ARN NG5 .... 24 F7
Short Av DERBYW DE22 .... 43 K2
Short Cl RLEIW/BBY LE8 .... 145 K8
Shortcross Av ARN NG5 .... 37 K3
Short Hl NOTT NG1 .... 5 K8
Short Lands BPR/DUF DE56 .... 17 L3
Short La CDON/KEG DE74 .... 84 C3
Shortridge La RLEIW/BAR LE9 .... 135 M4
Short St BPR/DUF DE56 .... 17 M3
  LEI LE1 .... 6 E4
Shortwood Av HUCK/RAV NG15 .... 23 K2
Shortwood Cl NOTT NG1 .... 5 K5
Shorwell Gdns DERBYSE DE24 .... 73 G2
Shorwell Rd CARL NG4 .... 38 A8
Shottens Cl LEIN LE4 .... 124 F5
Shottery Av LEIW LE3 .... 130 D6
Shotton Dr ARN NG5 .... 25 L1
Shoulbard RLEIW/BBY LE8 .... 145 J7

Shrewsbury Av LEIS LE2 .... 137 L1
Shrewsbury Cl DERBYE DE21 .... 45 G5
Shrewsbury Rd WBRGFD NG2 .... 51 L3
Shrimpton Ct
  CFTN/RUD NG11 .... 79 H1
Shropshire Av DERBYE DE21 .... 44 C8
  EWD/SEL/PNX NG16 .... 13 G3
Shropshire Rd LEIS LE2 .... 131 H8
Shuttleworth La
  RLEIW/BAR LE9 .... 142 B6
Sibson Dr CDON/KEG DE74 .... 85 M5
Sibson Rd LEIN LE4 .... 119 L8
Sibton La LEIS LE2 .... 138 E3
Sickleholm Dr LEIE LE5 .... 132 C5
Siddals La DERBYW DE22 .... 43 K3
Siddals Rd DERBY DE1 .... 3 H4
Siddons St DERBYSE DE24 .... 58 E8
Side Ley CDON/KEG DE74 .... 86 A4
The Sidings DERBYE DE24 .... 58 E3
Sidlaw Ri ARN NG5 .... 24 F6
Sidmouth Av LEIE LE5 .... 132 E3
Sidmouth Cl
  COT/KEY/RAD NG12 .... 80 C3
  DERBYSE DE24 .... 59 G8
  LEIS LE2 .... 132 B8
Sidney Rd BSTN/STPLFD NG9 .... 49 J8
  LEIS LE2 .... 132 B8
Sidney St DERBY DE1 .... 3 H8
  EWD/SEL/PNX NG16 .... 34 D1
  LGEAT NG10 .... 76 D1
Sidwell Dr LEIE LE5 .... 132 C2
Sidwell St LEIE LE5 .... 7 M6
Silbury Cl CFTN/RUD NG11 .... 64 B8
Silbury Rd LEIN LE4 .... 125 G6
Sileby Rd RLBORO LE12 .... 105 H8
  RLBORO LE12 .... 113 J4
Silsden Ri LEIS LE2 .... 137 H4
Silver Birch Cl BLWL NG6 .... 35 M3
Silver Birches RLBORO LE12 .... 112 D1
Silverbirch Wy RLBORO LE12 .... 111 L1
Silverburn Dr DERBYSE DE21 .... 44 E5
Silverdale BSTN/STPLFD NG9 .... 62 C2
Silverdale Dr LEIN LE4 .... 126 D1
Silverdale Rd NOTTE NG7 .... 36 B5
Silver Hill Cl
  WOL/BIL/BRX NG8 .... 35 H5
Silverhill Rd DERBYE DE21 .... 59 J4
Silver Hill Rd NORM/LIT DE23 .... 2 E9
Silverhow Cl WBRGFD NG2 .... 66 A2
Silver La BWSH/BRSTN DE72 .... 73 K2
Silverstone Dr LEIN LE4 .... 126 B2
Silver St COAL LE67 .... 108 C3
  LEI LE1 .... 6 E5
Silverton Dr DERBYSE DE24 .... 71 G5
Silverton Rd LBORO LE11 .... 103 K7
  LEIS LE2 .... 139 G1
Silverwood Cl LEIE LE5 .... 133 G2
Silverwood Rd
  BSTN/STPLFD NG9 .... 63 J1
Silvey Gv DERBYE DE21 .... 59 H3
Simcoe Leys MELB/CHEL DE73 .... 72 D5
Simmins Crs LEIS LE2 .... 137 H3
Simon Fields Cl ILK DE7 .... 31 L5
Simons Cl WGSTN LE18 .... 138 C7
Simons Ct BSTN/STPLFD NG9 .... 49 H6
Simpson Cl RLEINE/SYS LE7 .... 120 C5
Sims Av DERBY DE1 .... 2 A3
Sinclair Cl DERBYSE DE24 .... 71 J3
  HEANOR DE75 .... 20 B7
Sinfin Av DERBYSE DE24 .... 72 B3
Sinfin Fields Crs
  DERBYSE DE24 .... 72 B2
Sinfin La DERBYSE DE24 .... 71 K2
  NORM/LIT DE23 .... 57 L8
Sinfin Moor La DERBYSE DE24 .... 71 L5
  MELB/CHEL DE73 .... 72 B5
Sir Frank Whittle Rd
  DERBYE DE21 .... 44 A8
Sir John Robinson Wy ARN NG5 .... 25 J8
Siskin Dr DERBYSE DE24 .... 71 H3
Siskin Hl LEIS LE2 .... 138 E3
Sisley Av BSTN/STPLFD NG9 .... 62 C1
Sister's La BWSH/BRSTN DE72 .... 60 A2
Sitwell Cl DERBYE DE21 .... 59 H5
Sitwell Dr BPR/DUF DE56 .... 18 E8
Sitwell St DERBY DE1 .... 2 F5
  DERBYE DE21 .... 59 J3
Sitwell Wk LEIE LE5 .... 132 D5
Six Hills La RMMWB LE14 .... 99 L8
Six Hills Rd RLBORO LE12 .... 106 A3
  RMMWB LE14 .... 107 M2
Sixth Av DERBYSE DE21 .... 44 A2
Skampton Rd LEIE LE5 .... 132 F3
Skeavington's La ILK DE7 .... 33 J2
Skelton Dr LEIS LE2 .... 137 L1
Skelwith Cl
  COT/KEY/RAD NG12 .... 66 A2
Sketchley Cl LEIE LE5 .... 133 H1
Sketchley St
  MAPPK/POR/STA NG3 .... 5 M3
  MAPPK/POR/STA NG3 .... 51 K1
Skevington Av LBORO LE11 .... 8 C3
Skiddaw Cl WBRGFD NG2 .... 66 A2
Skiddaw Dr MCKLVR DE3 .... 56 C6
Skinner's La COAL LE67 .... 108 D2
Skipton Circ
  MAPPK/POR/STA NG3 .... 5 M3
Skipton Cl ILK DE7 .... 33 H4
Skipworth St LEIS LE2 .... 7 L9
Skye Wy RLEIW/BBY LE8 .... 143 K4
Skylark Av RLBORO LE12 .... 113 K6
Skylark Dr BLWL NG6 .... 36 B3
Skylark Wy DERBYSE DE24 .... 71 H3
Slack La ALFN DE55 .... 11 M2
  BPR/DUF DE56 .... 10 A4
  DERBYW DE22 .... 43 K5
  DERBYW DE22 .... 57 H2
  HEANOR DE75 .... 20 C7
  RIPLEY DE5 .... 11 H6
Slack Rd BLWL NG6 .... 35 L1
Slade Cl ILK DE7 .... 32 D4
Slade Gn ILK DE7 .... 47 K2
The Slade Greens LEIS LE2 .... 137 G3
Slade Lands Dr
  MELB/CHEL DE73 .... 72 E5
Slade Rd BSTN/STPLFD NG9 .... 62 F2
Slaidburn Av CFTN/RUD NG11 .... 64 C1
Slaidburn Cl MCKLVR DE3 .... 56 C6
Slaney Cl DERBYSE DE24 .... 58 C8
Slash La RLBORO LE12 .... 113 K3

Slate Brook Cl GBY/RBY LE6 .... 123 K4
Slater Av DERBYE DE21 .... 123 M7
Slater Av DERBYSE DE22 .... 2 A3
Slater St LEIW LE3 .... 6 C2
Slate St LEIS LE2 .... 1 H7
Sledmere Cl DERBYSE DE24 .... 59 G8
Sleepy La MELB/CHEL DE73 .... 82 F6
Slindon Cft DERBYSE DE24 .... 73 H1
Sloan Dr BSTN/STPLFD NG9 .... 48 E7
Sloane Cl RLEIW/BAR LE9 .... 135 L4
Sloane Ct CFTN/RUD NG11 .... 65 G4
Sloane Rd DERBYSE DE22 .... 56 E1
Smalley Cl EWD/SEL/PNX NG16 .... 13 L5
Smalley Dr DERBYSE DE24 .... 44 F4
Smalley Mill Rd ILK DE7 .... 30 F3
Small Meer Cl
  MELB/CHEL DE73 .... 72 D6
Small's Cft CALV/BJ NG14 .... 27 G3
Smart Cl LEIW LE3 .... 130 B5
Smeath Rd EWD/SEL/PNX NG16 .... 13 L5
Smedley Av ILK DE7 .... 33 L8
Smedley Cl
  WOL/BIL/BRX NG8 .... 35 M5
Smedley's Av LGEAT NG10 .... 61 M2
Smedmore Rd LEIE LE5 .... 126 B7
Smeeton Rd RLEIW/BBY LE8 .... 146 E8
Smeeton St HEANOR DE75 .... 20 F6
Smith Av LEIE LE5 .... 126 D1
  MELB/CHEL DE73 .... 82 F7
  RIPLEY DE5 .... 11 M6
Smith Crs COAL LE67 .... 109 C7
Smith Dorrien Rd LEIE LE5 .... 126 C8
Smith Dr EWD/SEL/PNX NG16 .... 20 E4
Smith Rd BSTN/STPLFD NG9 .... 48 B3
Smithson Dr
  WOL/BIL/BRX NG8 .... 49 J3
Smithurst Rd
  EWD/SEL/PNX NG16 .... 21 M7
Smith Wy RLEIW/BAR LE9 .... 136 C3
Smithy Cl CFTN/RUD NG11 .... 64 B5
Smithy La ARN NG5 .... 25 K7
Smithy Farm Dr
  RLEIW/BBY LE8 .... 140 K5
Smithy La RLBORO LE12 .... 93 L5
Smithy Rw NOTT NG1 .... 5 G7
Smithy Wy RLBORO LE12 .... 102 A3
Smore Slade Hills LEIS LE2 .... 139 J3
Snake La BPR/DUF DE56 .... 29 H4
Snape Wood Rd BLWL NG6 .... 23 K8
Snarrow's Rd RLBORO LE12 .... 100 C5
Sneinton Bvd WBRGFD NG2 .... 51 K3
Sneinton Dl
  MAPPK/POR/STA NG3 .... 51 L2
  WBRGFD NG2 .... 51 K3
Sneinton Hermitage
  WBRGFD NG2 .... 5 L9
Sneinton Hollows WBRGFD NG2 .... 51 K3
Sneinton Rd WBRGFD NG2 .... 5 L7
Snell's Nook La LBORO LE11 .... 102 E6
Snelsmoor La MELB/CHEL DE73 .... 72 F5
Snelston Crs NORM/LIT DE23 .... 57 G5
Snowberry Av BPR/DUF DE56 .... 17 M5
Snowdens End WGSTN LE18 .... 138 C6
Snowdon Cl ARN NG5 .... 24 F6
  RLBORO LE12 .... 102 A5
Snowdrop Cl RLEIW/BAR LE9 .... 135 K7
Snow Hl LEIW LE3 .... 125 G6
Soarbank Cl
  EWD/SEL/PNX NG16 .... 22 C8
Soar La LEIW LE3 .... 6 B4
  RLBORO LE12 .... 86 D7
Soar Rd RLBORO LE12 .... 112 F1
  RLEINE/SYS LE7 .... 120 B6
Soar Valley Wy RLEIW/BAR LE9 .... 136 D3
Sobers Gdns ARN NG5 .... 37 M1
Society Pl NORM/LIT DE23 .... 2 D9
Softwood Cl BLWL NG6 .... 23 K8
Soloman Rd
  EWD/SEL/PNX NG16 .... 33 M5
Somerby Ct
  BSTN/STPLFD NG9 .... 48 F3
Somerby Dr LEIS LE2 .... 139 G2
Somerby Rd RLEINE/SYS LE7 .... 133 K1
Somerby Wy DERBYE DE21 .... 44 D5
Somerfield Wy LEIW LE3 .... 129 K5
Somersal Ct DERBYSE DE24 .... 72 C4
Somersby Rd ARN NG5 .... 37 L2
Somerset Av LEIN LE4 .... 125 H5
Somerset Cl LGEAT NG10 .... 62 E7
  RLBORO LE12 .... 97 K8
Somerset Dr LEIW LE3 .... 125 M8
Somerset St DERBYE DE21 .... 44 B8
Somers Rd LEIE LE5 .... 133 G1
Somerton Av CFTN/RUD NG11 .... 64 E5
Somerville Rd LEIW LE3 .... 130 F6
Somme Rd DERBYW DE22 .... 42 F4
Sonning Wy LEIS LE2 .... 136 F5
Sopers Rd RLEIW/BAR LE9 .... 141 G4
Sophie Rd NOTTE NG7 .... 4 B2
Sorrel Rd LEIE LE5 .... 127 G5
Sorrel Wy RLEIW/BAR LE9 .... 135 K6
Soudan Dr WBRGFD NG2 .... 50 F6
South Albion St LEI LE1 .... 7 G7
Southampton St LEI LE1 .... 7 G5
South Av COT/KEY/RAD NG12 .... 53 M3
  DERBYE DE21 .... 59 J3
  DERBYW DE22 .... 43 L4
  LEIW LE3 .... 129 M4
  MELB/CHEL DE73 .... 72 D4
  NORM/LIT DE23 .... 57 H6
  WGSTN LE18 .... 138 A5
South Brae Cl NORM/LIT DE23 .... 57 H8
Southchurch Dr
  CFTN/RUD NG11 .... 64 C7
  CFTN/RUD NG11 .... 64 C7
South Church Ga LEI LE1 .... 6 D3
Southcliffe Rd CARL NG4 .... 38 B8
Southcroft WGSTN LE18 .... 71 H7
Southdale Gn CARL NG4 .... 38 B8
Southdale Rd CARL NG4 .... 38 B8
South Devon Av
  MAPPK/POR/STA NG3 .... 37 M5
Southdown Cl DERBYSE DE24 .... 71 G5
Southdown Dr LEIN LE4 .... 126 C2
Southdown Rd LBORO LE11 .... 103 L3

  LEIE LE5 .... 132 B1
South Dr DERBY DE1 .... 43 K8
  DERBYE DE21 .... 58 E2
  LEIE LE5 .... 126 E7
  MCKLVR DE3 .... 56 C5
  MELB/CHEL DE73 .... 72 D4
  RLEIW/BAR LE9 .... 140 C6
Southernhay Cl LEIS LE2 .... 132 A6
Southernhay Rd LEIS LE2 .... 132 A6
Southey Cl LEIN LE4 .... 7 J1
Southey St NOTTE NG7 .... 4 C3
Southfield Av RLEINE/SYS LE7 .... 120 F4
Southfield Cl LEIE LE5 .... 127 K8
  LEIS LE2 .... 136 E4
Southfield Rd LBORO LE11 .... 9 J4
  WOL/BIL/BRX NG8 .... 50 B1
Southfields Av DERBYSE DE21 .... 138 C1
Southfields Dr LEIS LE2 .... 137 K2
  WGSTN LE18 .... 137 K2
Southgate Cl MCKLVR DE3 .... 56 A4
Southgates U/P LEI LE1 .... 6 D6
Southglade Rd ARN NG5 .... 36 C1
South Kingsmead Rd
  LEIS LE2 .... 138 A1
South Knighton Rd LEIS LE2 .... 132 B8
Southland Rd LEIS LE2 .... 138 B1
Southlea Rd CARL NG4 .... 38 B8
Southmeads Cl LEIS LE2 .... 132 D8
Southmead Rd LEIS LE2 .... 132 E7
Southmead Wy
  DERBYW DE22 .... 56 F4
South Pde NOTT NG1 .... 5 G7
South Pl RIPLEY DE5 .... 11 H6
  NOTTE NG7 .... 4 D9
South Sherwood St NOTT NG1 .... 5 G4
Southside ARN NG5 .... 26 A8
South Snape Cl BLWL NG6 .... 23 K8
South St ALFN DE55 .... 11 J1
  ALFN DE55 .... 12 A2
  BWSH/BRSTN DE72 .... 60 E8
  DERBY DE1 .... 2 B3
  EWD/SEL/PNX NG16 .... 21 J5
  EWD/SEL/PNX NG16 .... 22 A7
  HUCK/RAV NG15 .... 15 L8
  ILK DE7 .... 33 J7
  LBORO LE11 .... 9 J4
  LEIS LE2 .... 138 E1
  LGEAT NG10 .... 62 C8
  MELB/CHEL DE73 .... 82 E8
  RLBORO LE12 .... 105 H8
Southview Dr LEIE LE5 .... 132 D5
South View Rd CARL NG4 .... 38 B5
Southwark Cl DERBYSE DE22 .... 56 F2
Southway RLEIW/BBY LE8 .... 142 F1
South Wy RLEIW/BBY LE8 .... 146 F6
Southwell Cl RLBORO LE12 .... 88 C6
Southwell Ri
  EWD/SEL/PNX NG16 .... 21 M8
Southwell Rd NOTT NG1 .... 5 K7
Southwold Dr
  WOL/BIL/BRX NG8 .... 50 A2
Southwood St DERBYSE DE24 .... 58 C7
Sovereign Gv LGEAT NG10 .... 61 M8
Sovereign Wy DERBYE DE21 .... 45 H4
  HEANOR DE75 .... 20 B6
Sowbrook La ILK DE7 .... 47 J4
Sowter Rd DERBY DE1 .... 2 F2
Sowters La RLBORO LE12 .... 105 L1
Spa Dr RLEIW/BAR LE9 .... 140 B7
Spa La DERBY DE1 .... 2 D7
  WGSTN LE18 .... 138 B5
Spalding Rd
  MAPPK/POR/STA NG3 .... 51 K2
Spalding St LEIE LE5 .... 132 C1
Spaniel Rw NOTT NG1 .... 5 G8
Sparkenhoe RLEIW/BAR LE9 .... 141 G4
Sparkenhoe St LEIS LE2 .... 7 J7
  ILK DE7 .... 47 L2
Sparrow Cl DERBYSE DE24 .... 71 H3
Sparrow Hl LBORO LE11 .... 9 K2
Spean Dr WOL/BIL/BRX NG8 .... 35 M8
Speeds Pingle LBORO LE11 .... 9 H8
Speedwell Cl DERBYE DE21 .... 45 G4
  RLEIW/BAR LE9 .... 135 K6
Speedwell Dr LEIE LE5 .... 126 F4
Speedwell Rd RLBORO LE12 .... 113 K6
Speers Rd LEIW LE3 .... 124 C7
Spenbeck Dr DERBYW DE22 .... 43 L2
Spencefield Dr LEIE LE5 .... 132 F4
Spencefield La LEIS LE2 .... 133 G4
Spencer Av BPR/DUF DE56 .... 17 M3
  DERBYSE DE24 .... 72 B3
  LEIN LE4 .... 120 C8
  LGEAT NG10 .... 47 M8
  MAPPK/POR/STA NG3 .... 38 A2
Spencer Cl CFTN/RUD NG11 .... 64 F8
Spencer Crs BSTN/STPLFD NG9 .... 62 D4
Spencer Dr EWD/SEL/PNX NG16 .... 35 G1
Spencer Rd BPR/DUF DE56 .... 17 L3
Spencer St DERBYSE DE24 .... 58 E7
  ILK DE7 .... 31 K5
  LEIS LE2 .... 138 E1
Spence St LEIE LE5 .... 126 B8
Spendlow Gdns LEIS LE2 .... 137 J3
Sperry Cl EWD/SEL/PNX NG16 .... 13 K1
Spey Cl HUCK/RAV NG15 .... 23 H4
Spiers Cl RLEIW/BAR LE9 .... 135 M8
Spinde Gdns BLWL NG6 .... 23 L8
Spindle La CALV/BJ NG14 .... 26 B2
Spindle Rd RLBORO LE12 .... 111 L1
Spindletree Dr DERBYE DE21 .... 44 C5
Spindle Vw CALV/BJ NG14 .... 26 D1
Spinners Wy BPR/DUF DE56 .... 18 A1
Spinney Av RLEIW/BAR LE9 .... 143 J3
Spinney Cl
  COT/KEY/RAD NG12 .... 67 K5
  DERBYSE DE21 .... 43 L5
  GBY/RBY LE6 .... 123 J5
  LEIS LE2 .... 136 E4
  RLEINE/SYS LE7 .... 120 C4
  WBRGFD NG2 .... 65 A5
Spinney Crs BSTN/STPLFD NG9 .... 62 D4
Spinney Dr GBY/RBY LE6 .... 122 M4
  LGEAT NG10 .... 62 A5
  RLBORO LE12 .... 112 D2

Spinney Halt RLEIW/BBY LE8 ...... 136 C8
Spinney HI MELB/CHEL DE73 ...... 82 E8
Spinney Hill Dr LBORO LE11 ...... 8 A7
Spinney Hill Rd LEIE LE5 ...... 7 M3
Spinney Ri BSTN/STPLFD NG9 ...... 62 C4
  LEIN LE4 ...... 119 K8
Spinney Rd COT/KEY/RAD NG12 ...... 80 B4
  DERBYE DE21 ...... 44 D8
  DERBYW DE22 ...... 2 B8
  ILK DE7 ...... 47 J1
  LGEAT NG10 ...... 62 A5
Spinneyside GBY/RBY LE6 ...... 123 J5 [5]
The Spinney ARN NG5 ...... 37 J3
  BLWL NG6 ...... 24 C2
  BPR/DUF DE56 ...... 17 L1
  BWSH/BRSTN DE72 ...... 60 A6
  CALV/BJ NG14 ...... 39 M2
  CDON/KEG DE74 ...... 84 E3 [5]
Spinney Wy RLEIW/BAR LE9 ...... 135 K5
Spittal CDON/KEG DE74 ...... 84 E5
Spondon St ARN NG5 ...... 37 G5 [10]
Sponne Ri WGSTN LE18 ...... 137 J3
Spooneley Wood Ct
  NORM/LIT DE23 ...... 56 D8 [5]
Sports Field La RLEIW/BAR LE9 ...... 135 H7
Sports Rd LEIE LE3 ...... 124 A7
Spray Cl CARL NG4 ...... 52 C2
Spridgeon Cl LGEAT NG10 ...... 61 M5 [5]
Springbrook Dr
  RLEINE/SYS LE7 ...... 133 K1
  BWSH/BRSTN DE72 ...... 60 A6
  GBY/RBY LE6 ...... 123 H7 [6]
Springclose LEIS LE2 ...... 137 H2 [5]
Spring Cl RLBORO LE12 ...... 102 A5
Springdale Ct MCKLVR DE3 ...... 56 C6 [10]
Spring Dale Gdns
  BSTN/STPLFD NG9 ...... 48 B5 [5]
Springdale Rd LEIN LE4 ...... 126 C1
  COAL LE67 ...... 100 C7
  NORM/LIT DE23 ...... 56 F5
Springfield Av
  EWD/SEL/PNX NG16 ...... 21 L5 [2]
  HEANOR DE75 ...... 19 M2
  LGEAT NG10 ...... 61 L4
  LGEAT NG10 ...... 62 D7
Springfield Cl LBORO LE11 ...... 103 J1 [5]
Spring Field Cl LEIW LE3 ...... 123 M8
Springfield Cl RLBORO LE12 ...... 97 K8
  RLEIW/BBY LE8 ...... 146 F8 [10]
Springfield Crs RLEIW/BBY LE8 ...... 146 E8 [5]
Springfield Dr BPR/DUF DE56 ...... 29 H4 [2]
  EWD/SEL/PNX NG16 ...... 35 K1
Springfield Gdn ILK DE7 ...... 33 K5
Springfield Rd ARN NG5 ...... 25 J6
  DERBYE DE21 ...... 58 F2
  HUCK/RAV NG15 ...... 23 H1
  LEIS LE2 ...... 132 A6
  MELB/CHEL DE73 ...... 72 C5
  RDERBYSW DE65 ...... 68 F4
  RLBORO LE12 ...... 101 L4
  RLBORO LE12 ...... 114 B3
Springfields WBRGFD NG2 ...... 65 H1
Springfield St NOTTE NG7 ...... 36 D6
Springfield Ter RIPLEY DE5 ...... 11 J6 [3]
Springfield Vw RIPLEY DE5 ...... 11 H5
Spring Gdns DERBYE DE21 ...... 44 D8
Spring Garden Ter ILK DE7 ...... 33 K5 [3]
Spring Gn CFTN/RUD NG11 ...... 64 C8
Spring HI EWD/SEL/PNX NG16 ...... 34 D2
Springhill Cl BLWL NG6 ...... 23 M6
Springhill Wy RIPLEY DE5 ...... 11 L7
Spring Hollow BPR/DUF DE56 ...... 17 K8
Spring La CARL NG4 ...... 38 D2
  HEANOR DE75 ...... 20 C6 [3]
  RLBORO LE12 ...... 94 B5
  RLBORO LE12 ...... 101 M5
  WGSTN LE18 ...... 138 B4 [5]
Spring Meadow
  COT/KEY/RAD NG12 ...... 67 L4
Spring Moor WBRGFD NG2 ...... 52 B2 [2]
Spring Rd ALFN DE55 ...... 12 C1
  BLWL NG6 ...... 24 A8
Spring St DERBYW DE22 ...... 2 C6
  HUCK/RAV NG15 ...... 15 L7
The Spring LGEAT NG10 ...... 76 B2
Springway Cl LEIE LE5 ...... 133 J2 [5]
Springwell Cl RLEIW/BBY LE8 ...... 143 J5 [3]
Springwell Dr RLEIW/BBY LE8 ...... 143 H3
Springwell La RLEIW/BBY LE8 ...... 142 D4
Springwood Dr DERBYE DE21 ...... 44 E5
Springwood Gdns ARN NG5 ...... 37 K4
Spruce Av EWD/SEL/PNX NG16 ...... 13 V1 [2]
  LBORO LE11 ...... 103 L8
Spruce Gv HUCK/RAV NG15 ...... 23 M2
Sprydon Wk CFTN/RUD NG11 ...... 64 E3
Squares Rd ARN NG5 ...... 24 F1
The Square BLWL NG6 ...... 24 C3
  CFTN/RUD NG11 ...... 77 M6
  COT/KEY/RAD NG12 ...... 80 C5
  DERBYW DE22 ...... 43 G1
  MCKLVR DE3 ...... 56 B6
  RLEIW/BAR LE9 ...... 142 A1
  RLEIW/BBY LE8 ...... 143 K4
  RLEIW/BBY LE8 ...... 145 H1
Squires Av BLWL NG6 ...... 24 D8
Squire's Ride RLEINE/SYS LE7 ...... 115 H7
Squires Wy NORM/LIT DE23 ...... 70 E1
  WBRGFD NG2 ...... 65 H1 [2]
Squirrel Cl RLEIW/BAR LE9 ...... 135 L8
Squirrel's Cnr RLEINE/SYS LE7 ...... 115 J7
Squirrel Wy LBORO LE11 ...... 8 F7
Stable Cl RLEIW/BBY LE8 ...... 136 A8 [3]
Stables St DERBYW DE22 ...... 57 H2
Stacey Av ARN NG5 ...... 24 D8
Stackley Rd RLEIW/BBY LE8 ...... 139 M6
Stadium Pl LEIN LE4 ...... 125 J5
Stadon Rd RLEINE/SYS LE7 ...... 124 B1
Stafford Cl ILK DE7 ...... 31 K1
Stafford Ct BLWL NG6 ...... 35 K2
Stafford Dr WGSTN LE18 ...... 137 K5
Stafford Leys LEIW LE3 ...... 129 K4
Staffords Acre CDON/KEG DE74 ...... 86 A5

Stafford St DERBY DE1 ...... 2 C4
  LEIN LE4 ...... 126 A4
Stagsden Crs WOL/BIL/BRX NG8 ...... 49 G2
Staindale WGSTN LE18 ...... 138 D5
Staindale Dr WOL/BIL/BRX NG8 ...... 36 B6
Staines Cl MCKLVR DE3 ...... 56 A5 [5]
Stainforth Av RLEIW/BAR LE9 ...... 135 K5
Stainsborough Rd
  HUCK/RAV NG15 ...... 23 G1
  ILK DE7 ...... 31 J1
Stainsby Av HEANOR DE75 ...... 20 C6
Stainsby Rd LEIS LE2 ...... 123 J5 [3]
Stainsdale Gn COAL LE67 ...... 108 E5
Staker La MCKLVR DE3 ...... 70 B1
Stamford Cl LEIW LE3 ...... 123M7
Stamford Dr COAL LE67 ...... 109 G5 [3]
  GBY/RBY LE6 ...... 123 K5
  RLEINE/SYS LE7 ...... 118 D4
Stamford Rd RLEIW/BAR LE9 ...... 129 J3
  WBRGFD NG2 ...... 65 L1
Stamford St DERBYSE DE24 ...... 72 B1 [3]
  EWD/SEL/PNX NG16 ...... 22 A6
  EWD/SEL/PNX NG16 ...... 34 A3
  GBY/RBY LE6 ...... 122 F6
  GBY/RBY LE6 ...... 123 G6 [3]
  HEANOR DE75 ...... 20 C5 [3]
  ILK DE7 ...... 33 J6
  LEI LE1 ...... 6 F7
  LEIW LE3 ...... 123M7
Stanage Gn MCKLVR DE3 ...... 56 D6 [3]
Stanage Rd RLBORO LE12 ...... 114 C3
Stanbrig WGSTN LE18 ...... 138 C7 [2]
Stancliffe Av BLWL NG6 ...... 24 A8
Stancliff Rd LEIN LE4 ...... 126 D2
Standard HI NOTT NG1 ...... 4 F4
Standhill Av CARL NG4 ...... 37M7
Standhill Rd
  MAPPK/POR/STA NG3 ...... 37 L6
Stanesby Ri CFTN/RUD NG11 ...... 64 C6
Stanfell Rd LEIS LE2 ...... 131M7
Stanford Gdns
  COT/KEY/RAD NG12 ...... 53 K3
Stanford HI LBORO LE11 ...... 103M1
Stanford Rd RLBORO LE12 ...... 95 J5
Stanford St NOTT NG1 ...... 5 G8
Stanhome Dr WBRGFD NG2 ...... 65 H3
Stanhome Sq WBRGFD NG2 ...... 65 H3 [3]
Stanhope Crs ARN NG5 ...... 25 J7
  CALV/BJ NG14 ...... 39 K8
Stanhope Rd ARN NG5 ...... 25 J7
  CARL NG4 ...... 38 B3
  MCKLVR DE3 ...... 56 C4
  WGSTN LE18 ...... 138 C6
Stanhope St ILK DE7 ...... 47 L1 [2]
  LEIE LE5 ...... 132 B2
  LGEAT NG10 ...... 62 B7
  NORM/LIT DE23 ...... 57 K6
  NOTT NG1 ...... 5 K7
Stanier Dr LEIN LE4 ...... 126 E3
Stanier Wy DERBYE DE21 ...... 58 E4
Staniland Cl
  BSTN/STPLFD NG9 ...... 63 G5 [3]
Stanley Cl RIPLEY DE5 ...... 11 J5
Stanley Cl DERBYW DE22 ...... 43 K7
  ILK DE7 ...... 33 J8
Stanley Dr BSTN/STPLFD NG9 ...... 48 E7
  LEIE LE5 ...... 126 E7
Stanley Pl NOTT NG1 ...... 4 F6
Stanley Rd DERBYSE DE24 ...... 58 E2
  DERBYE DE24 ...... 72 C1
  LEIS LE2 ...... 132 A4
  MAPPK/POR/STA NG3 ...... 37 L5
  NOTTE NG7 ...... 36 E7
  WBRGFD NG2 ...... 65 K1
Stanley St DERBYW DE22 ...... 57 H2
  ILK DE7 ...... 33 K8
  LBORO LE11 ...... 9 J6
  LGEAT NG10 ...... 62 C8 [3]
Stanmore Cl WOL/BIL/BRX NG8 .... 35 J4
Stanmore Gdns ARN NG5 ...... 37 K1 [3]
Stansfield St NOTTE NG7 ...... 50 C2
Stanstead Av ARN NG5 ...... 24 B6
  COT/KEY/RAD NG12 ...... 66 B7
Stanstead Rd MCKLVR DE3 ...... 56 A3
Stanthorne Cl CFTN/RUD NG11 .... 64 E3
Stanton Av RLEIW/BBY LE8 ...... 140 E1
  RLEIW/BAR LE9 ...... 140 D3
Stanton Ga ILK DE7 ...... 48 A6
Stanton La COT/KEY/RAD NG12 .... 80 F5
  RLEIW/BAR LE9 ...... 140 E1
  RLEIW/BAR LE9 ...... 140 D3
  RLEIW/BBY LE8 ...... 140 B7
Stanton Rd ILK DE7 ...... 47 K1
  LGEAT NG10 ...... 62 B7
  RLEIW/BAR LE9 ...... 140 B7
Stanton Rw LEIS LE2 ...... 137 K1
Stanton St NORM/LIT DE23 ...... 57 K6
Stanway Cl
  MAPPK/POR/STA NG3 ...... 52 A1
Stanwick Cl WOL/BIL/BRX NG8 .... 35 J7
Stanyon Cl RLEIW/BBY LE8 ...... 143 J5 [3]
Stapleford La BSTN/STPLFD NG9.. 62 D4
Stapleford Rd
  BSTN/STPLFD NG9 ...... 48 A3
  LEIN LE4 ...... 125 H3
Staplehurst Av LEIW LE3 ...... 130 C7
Staplehurst Dr ARN NG5 ...... 36 E3
Stapleton Rd ILK DE7 ...... 33 J3
Starch La LGEAT NG10 ...... 47 M8
Starcross St MCKLVR DE3 ...... 56 A4
Starkie Av CDON/KEG DE74 ...... 84 D4
Starmer Cl RLEIW/BAR LE9 ...... 142 C4
Starthe Bank HEANOR DE75 ...... 20 D5
Starth Wood Rd
  HUCK/RAV NG15 ...... 23 H3
Statham St DERBYW DE22 ...... 43 J8
Stathern Wk ARN NG5 ...... 24 F8
Station Ap BPR/DUF DE56 ...... 29 K3 [3]
  DERBY DE1 ...... 3 H4
Station Av CARL NG4 ...... 38 E6
  HUCK/RAV NG15 ...... 15 K1
  LBORO LE11 ...... 9 J5
Station Cl MELB/CHEL DE73 ...... 72 D6
  RLEIW/BAR LE9 ...... 129 J3
Station Dr RLEIW/BAR LE9 ...... 129 J3
Station La EWD/SEL/PNX NG16 .... 12 C4
  RIPLEY DE5 ...... 19M1
  RLEINE/SYS LE7 ...... 127 K8
Station Rd BLWL NG6 ...... 36 A1

BPR/DUF DE56 ...... 29 K3 [3]
BSTN/STPLFD NG9 ...... 63 L2 [3]
BWSH/BRSTN DE72 ...... 59M6
BWSH/BRSTN DE72 ...... 60 F8
CALV/BJ NG14 ...... 39 K4
CARL NG4 ...... 38 D8
CDON/KEG DE74 ...... 84 F2
CDON/KEG DE74 ...... 85 G2
CDON/KEG DE74 ...... 86 B4
CDON/KEG DE74 ...... 86 E4
COT/KEY/RAD NG12 ...... 80 C1
COT/KEY/RAD NG12 ...... 91 G2
DERBYE DE21 ...... 30 A8
DERBYE DE21 ...... 59 H4
EWD/SEL/PNX NG16 ...... 20 F5
EWD/SEL/PNX NG16 ...... 34 D1 [3]
EWD/SEL/PNX NG16 ...... 34 A2
GBY/RBY LE6 ...... 123 G7
HUCK/RAV NG15 ...... 15M8
HUCK/RAV NG15 ...... 15 J1
ILK DE7 ...... 32 A7
ILK DE7 ...... 33 K6
ILK DE7 ...... 44 B3
ILK DE7 ...... 46 A1
LEIN LE4 ...... 125 K2
LEIW LE3 ...... 124 A6
HEANOR DE75 ...... 20 C5 [2]
ILK DE7 ...... 33 J6
LEIN LE4 ...... 125 K2
LEIE LE3 ...... 124 A6
LGEAT NG10 ...... 61M2
LGEAT NG10 ...... 62 D7
MCKLVR DE3 ...... 56 B4
MELB/CHEL DE73 ...... 72 D6
MELB/CHEL DE73 ...... 82 F7
RIPLEY DE5 ...... 18 F4
RLBORO LE12 ...... 88 B6
RLBORO LE12 ...... 112 E1
RLEINE/SYS LE7 ...... 115 L4
RLEINE/SYS LE7 ...... 118 E4
RLEINE/SYS LE7 ...... 120 E4
RLEINE/SYS LE7 ...... 127 L8
RLEIW/BAR LE9 ...... 128 H2
RLEIW/BAR LE9 ...... 129 A2
RLEIW/BAR LE9 ...... 136 A8
RLEIW/BAR LE9 ...... 140 A4
RLEIW/BAR LE9 ...... 141 G3
RLEIW/BBY LE8 ...... 145 L1
RLEIW/BBY LE8 ...... 145 L1
RMMWB LE14 ...... 91 L8
WGSTN LE18 ...... 137M5
Station St ILK DE7 ...... 33 L6
  LBORO LE11 ...... 8 F7
  LEI LE1 ...... 7 H7
  LGEAT NG10 ...... 62 D8
  RLEIW/BBY LE8 ...... 146 E7 [2]
  RLEIW/BBY LE8 ...... 146 E7 [2]
  WGSTN LE18 ...... 137 K5
Station Ter COT/KEY/RAD NG12 .... 53 K4
  HUCK/RAV NG15 ...... 15M8
Staunton Av NORM/LIT DE23 ...... 71 J1
Staunton Cl CDON/KEG DE74 ...... 84 E3
Staunton Dr ARN NG5 ...... 37 G3
Staveley Cl DERBYSE DE24 ...... 72 C4
  RLBORO LE12 ...... 114 B5
  WGSTN LE18 ...... 138 C5 [3]
Staveley Rd LEIE LE5 ...... 132 B4
Staverton Dr MCKLVR DE3 ...... 56 B3 [3]
Staverton Rd WOL/BIL/BRX NG8 .. 35 J8
Staythorpe Rd LEIN LE4 ...... 126 E2
Steadfold Cl BLWL NG6 ...... 35 M1 [3]
Steadman Av
  RLEIW/BAR LE9 ...... 142 C4 [10]
Steads Cl CARL NG4 ...... 38 D8
Steam Mill La RIPLEY DE5 ...... 11 L7
Stebbings Rd LEIS LE2 ...... 137 H2 [3]
Steedman Av
  MAPPK/POR/STA NG3 ...... 37 L3
Steele Cl LEIE LE5 ...... 132 E2
Steeles Wy CARL NG4 ...... 26 F8
Steeple Cl DERBYE DE21 ...... 44 C5
  WGSTN LE18 ...... 138 C5 [3]
Steeple Rw LBORO LE11 ...... 9 J2
Steinbeck Rd CARL NG4 ...... 38 A8
Steins La LEIE LE5 ...... 126 F7
Stella Cl COT/KEY/RAD NG12 ...... 66 B7
Stella Gv COT/KEY/RAD NG12 ...... 66 B7
Stenor Cl RLEIW/BBY LE8 ...... 145 J7
Stenson Av NORM/LIT DE23 ...... 71 J1
Stenson Ct RIPLEY DE5 ...... 11 K6
Stenson Rd COAL LE67 ...... 108 B5
  DERBYSE DE24 ...... 71 H3
  LEIW LE3 ...... 124 E6
  NORM/LIT DE23 ...... 57 J7 [2]
Stephenson Ct LEIW LE3 ...... 124 A5
Stephenson Dr LEIW LE3 ...... 125 G8
Stephensons Wy DERBYE DE21 .... 58 E4
Stephenson Wy COAL LE67 ...... 108 A4
  GBY/RBY LE6 ...... 123 J4 [3]
Stepney Cl WOL/BIL/BRX NG8 .... 35 K6 [2]
Stepping Cl DERBYW DE22 ...... 57 H2
Stepping La DERBYW DE22 ...... 57 H2
Sterndale Rd LGEAT NG10 ...... 75M1
Stevenage Cl DERBYSE DE24 ...... 72 D2
Steven Cl BSTN/STPLFD NG9 ...... 62 D3
Stevenholme Crs ARN NG5 ...... 36 E1
Stevens Cl RLEIW/BAR LE9 ...... 140 C5 [2]
Stevens La BWSH/BRSTN DE72 .... 61 H7
Stevenson Av
  BWSH/BRSTN DE72 ...... 60 F7
Stevenson Gdns
  CFTN/RUD NG11 ...... 79 H1
  RLEIW/BAR LE9 ...... 142 B3
Stevenson Pl NORM/LIT DE23 ...... 56 F7
Stevens Rd LGEAT NG10 ...... 61 L2
Stevenstone Cl LEIS LE2 ...... 139 H2 [3]
Stewart Av RLEIW/BAR LE9 ...... 135 L6
Stewart Cl DERBYSE DE24 ...... 59 J1
Stewart Dr LBORO LE11 ...... 103 G1
Stewart St ALFN DE55 ...... 12 B2
Steyning Crs LEIW LE3 ...... 124 B6
Stiles Rd DERBYSE DE24 ...... 58 F8
The Stiles RLEINE/SYS LE7 ...... 120 F3
Stinsford Cl ARN NG5 ...... 25 G7
Stinson Wy COAL LE67 ...... 108 B2
Stirland St RIPLEY DE5 ...... 11M6
Stirling Av LBORO LE11 ...... 8 A1
Stirling Cl DERBYE DE21 ...... 44 A7 [3]
  RLBORO LE12 ...... 104 D3 [3]
  RLEINE/SYS LE7 ...... 113 G7
Stirling Dr RLEINE/SYS LE7 ...... 133 K1

Stirling Gdns
  BSTN/STPLFD NG9 ...... 62 F5 [2]
Stirling Gv CFTN/RUD NG11 ...... 64 D7
Stockbrook Rd DERBYW DE22 ...... 57 H4
Stockbrook St DERBYW DE22 ...... 2 B6
Stockdale Cl ARN NG5 ...... 24 E5
Stocker Av DERBYE DE24 ...... 59 G8
Stockgill Cl WBRGFD NG2 ...... 66 A1
Stockhill Circ BLWL NG6 ...... 36 A4
Stockhill La BLWL NG6 ...... 36 B4 [3]
Stocking La RLBORO LE12 ...... 88 B3
Stockland Rd LEIS LE2 ...... 137 J3
Stocks Rd EWD/SEL/PNX NG16 .... 22 C8
  RLEINE/SYS LE7 ...... 127 K7
Stockton Rd LEIN LE4 ...... 126 B6
Stock Well BLWL NG6 ...... 35M1
Stockwell Rd LEIS LE2 ...... 138 A1
The Stockwell RLBORO LE12 ...... 98 A4 [3]
Stoddard Dr HEANOR DE75 ...... 20 D5
Stoke Cl BPR/DUF DE56 ...... 18 B3
Stoke Ferry La
  COT/KEY/RAD NG12 ...... 39 L6
Stoke La CALV/BJ NG14 ...... 39 K4
  CARL NG4 ...... 38 F6
Stokes Dr LEIW LE3 ...... 124 F7
Stolle Cl ARN NG5 ...... 26 A8
Stoneacre ARN NG5 ...... 24 F7
Stonebow Cl RLBORO LE12 ...... 102 F1
Stonebridge Dr RLBORO LE12 ...... 88 D3
  RLEINE/SYS LE7 ...... 127 K7
Stonebridge La SLEIE LE5 ...... 132 B1
Stonechat Cl MCKLVR DE3 ...... 56 E4
Stone Cl DERBYE DE21 ...... 59 J1
  LEIN LE4 ...... 124 E1
Stonecroft RLEIW/BBY LE8 ...... 143 C4
Stonehaven Cl ARN NG5 ...... 25 M6 [3]
  COAL LE67 ...... 109 G6
Stonehaven Rd LEIN LE4 ...... 126 B3
Stonehill CDON/KEG DE74 ...... 84 F5 [3]
Stonehill Av LEIN LE4 ...... 119 L7
Stone Hill Rd NORM/LIT DE23 ...... 2 C9
Stonehills CDON/KEG DE74 ...... 86 A5 [3]
Stonehurst La RLBORO LE12 ...... 95 H4
Stonehurst Rd LEIW LE3 ...... 130 D7
Stoneleigh St NOTTE NG7 ...... 4 D5
Stoneleigh Wy LEIW LE3 ...... 124 F7
Stone Mdw LGEAT NG10 ...... 76 C2 [3]
Stonepit Cl
  MAPPK/POR/STA NG3 ...... 37 K6 [3]
Stonesby Av WGSTN LE18 ...... 137 J2
Stonesby Cl DERBYSE DE24 ...... 44 D5
Stoneycroft Rd BLWL NG6 ...... 36 C2 [3]
Stoney Cross DERBYE DE21 ...... 59 J4
Stoney Flatts Crs
  DERBYE DE21 ...... 44 E7 [3]
Stoneygate Av LEIS LE2 ...... 132 A6
Stoneygate Rd LEIS LE2 ...... 132 B5
Stoney Houghton Gdns
  BLWL NG6 ...... 23 K7 [2]
  DERBYE DE21 ...... 59 J2
  EWD/SEL/PNX NG16 ...... 21 G1
Stoney La BSTN/STPLFD NG9 ...... 47M2
Stoney St NOTT NG1 ...... 5 J7
Stoneywell Rd LEIN LE4 ...... 119 K4
Stonyhurst Ct DERBYSE DE24 ...... 72 C4 [2]
Stony La BPR/DUF DE56 ...... 30 A1
Stoodley Pike Gdns
  DERBYW DE22 ...... 43 G5 [3]
Stoop La RLBORO LE12 ...... 112 E1
Stoppard Cl ILK DE7 ...... 33 H5
Storer Cl RLBORO LE12 ...... 114 B4
Storer Rd LBORO LE11 ...... 8 E2
Stores La RLEIW/BBY LE8 ...... 145 K8 [3]
Stores Rd DERBYE DE21 ...... 43M8
Storey Av CARL NG4 ...... 38 C5
Storey St LEIW LE3 ...... 6 B2
Stornaway Rd LEIE LE5 ...... 127 H8
Stornoway Cl
  DERBYSE DE24 ...... 71 H4 [18]
Storth Av HUCK/RAV NG15 ...... 23 L1
Story Gdns HUCK/RAV NG15 ...... 24 A2
Stotfield Rd WOL/BIL/BRX NG8 .... 48 F2
Stoughton Av LEIS LE2 ...... 132 B6
Stoughton Cl LEIS LE2 ...... 138 F1
Stoughton Dr LEIS LE2 ...... 132 D5
Stoughton Dr North LEIS LE2 ...... 132 B4
Stoughton Dr South LEIS LE2 ...... 132 D6
Stoughton La LEIS LE2 ...... 133 H6
Stoughton Rd LEIS LE2 ...... 132 B6
  LEIS LE2 ...... 138 E1
  RLEINE/SYS LE7 ...... 133 J4
Stoughton St LEIS LE2 ...... 7 K7
Stoughton St South LEIS LE2 ...... 7 K7
Stour Cl LEIS LE2 ...... 131 H4
  RDERBYSW DE65 ...... 68 C7 [3]
Stourdale Cl LGEAT NG10 ...... 75 L1
Stourport Dr MELB/CHEL DE73 .... 72 E4
Stowe Av WBRGFD NG2 ...... 65 H2
Stowmarket Dr DERBYE DE21 ...... 44 B6
Strachan Cl DERBYE DE21 ...... 113 K6
Strancliffe La RLBORO LE12 ...... 105 C3
Strand DERBY DE1 ...... 2 E3
The Strand BSTN/STPLFD NG9 .... 63 H6
Strasbourg Dr LEIN LE4 ...... 124 F4
Stratford Cl CARL NG4 ...... 52 C2
Stratford Rd DERBYE DE21 ...... 44 B5
  LEIW LE3 ...... 125 K7
  WBRGFD NG2 ...... 51 K7 [3]
Stratford St ILK DE7 ...... 33 K3
Strathaven Ct DERBYE DE21 ...... 59 J2
Strathaven Rd LEIN LE4 ...... 126 B3
Strathglen Cl
  EWD/SEL/PNX NG16 ...... 22 C8 [3]
Strathmore Av DERBYSE DE24 ...... 72 C4
Strathmore Cl COAL LE67 ...... 109 G7
  HUCK/RAV NG15 ...... 23 J2 [3]
Stratmore Rd ARN NG5 ...... 25 M6 [3]
Streatham Rd DERBYW DE22 ...... 56 E1
Street La RIPLEY DE5 ...... 11 C7
Strelley Av RIPLEY DE5 ...... 11 L7
Strelley Rd WOL/BIL/BRX NG8 .... 35 J7
Strelley St BLWL NG6 ...... 23M8
Stretton Cl MCKLVR DE3 ...... 56 B6 [3]
Stretton Dr COAL LE67 ...... 109 C6
Stretton Hall Dr LEIS LE2 ...... 139 K4

Stretton Rd LEIW LE3 ...... 131 G2
  RLEIW/BBY LE8 ...... 139 M5
Striding Edge Cl LGEAT NG10 .... 61 K7
Stripes Vw CALV/BJ NG14 ...... 26 D1 [3]
Stroma Cl DERBYSE DE24 ...... 71 K3 [3]
Stroma Ct WBRGFD NG2 ...... 51 G5
Stroud Rd LEIE LE5 ...... 126 B8 [3]
Strudwick Wy RLEIW/BBY LE8 .... 136 E7
Strutt St BPR/DUF DE56 ...... 17 K4
  DERBYE DE23 ...... 2 F9
Stuart Cl ARN NG5 ...... 25M7
Stuart Rd LEIS LE2 ...... 137 G4
Stuart St DERBY DE1 ...... 2 F2
  LEIS LE2 ...... 131 H4
  RLEIW/BBY LE8 ...... 146 E7
Stubbs Rd LEIN LE4 ...... 7 J1
Studbrook Cl CDON/KEG DE74 .... 84 D4
Studland Wy WBRGFD NG2 ...... 65 G2
Sturdee Cl LEIS LE2 ...... 137 H4
Sturdee Gn LEIS LE2 ...... 137 G3
Sturdee Rd LEIS LE2 ...... 137 H3
Sturgeon Av CFTN/RUD NG11 .... 64 D3
Sturges La BWSH/BRSTN DE72 .... 73 K3
Sturrock Cl RLEINE/SYS LE7 ...... 133 K1
Sturton St NOTTE NG7 ...... 36 E7
Styon Rd LEIW LE3 ...... 124 C6
Styring St BSTN/STPLFD NG9 .... 63 K1
Sudbury Av ILK DE7 ...... 33 L8
  LGEAT NG10 ...... 47 L8
Sudbury Cl DERBYE DE21 ...... 2 F9
Sudbury Ms
  EWD/SEL/PNX NG16 ...... 21 J6 [3]
Sudbury St DERBY DE1 ...... 2 A4
Sudeley Av LEIN LE4 ...... 125 J5
Suez St NOTTE NG7 ...... 36 D6
Suffolk Av BSTN/STPLFD NG9 .... 64 A3
  DERBYE DE21 ...... 44 C8
  HUCK/RAV NG15 ...... 23 G2 [3]
Suffolk Cl WGSTN LE18 ...... 137 L4
Suffolk St LEIS LE2 ...... 132 C2
Sulgrave Rd LEIE LE5 ...... 126 B8
Sulleys Fld DERBYW DE22 ...... 29 H8 [3]
Sullington Rd RLBORO LE12 ...... 101M5
Sullivan Cl MAPPK/POR/STA NG3.. 37 K8
Sumburgh Rd CFTN/RUD NG11 .... 64 D6
Summerbrook Ct
  DERBYW DE22 ...... 2 C6 [2]
Summerfields Wy ILK DE7 ...... 33 G4
Summerfields Wy South
  ILK DE7 ...... 33 H5
Summerlea Rd LEIE LE5 ...... 133 G1
Summer Leys La WBRGFD NG2 .... 51 H4
Summerpool Rd LBORO LE11 ...... 95 K8
Summer Wy COT/KEY/RAD NG12.. 53 J3
Summer Wood Ct
  NORM/LIT DE23 ...... 57 H8
Summerwood La
  CFTN/RUD NG11 ...... 64 B8
Sunart Cl DERBYSE DE24 ...... 71 K5
Sunbourne Ct NOTTE NG7 ...... 4 B4
Sunbury Gdns ARN NG5 ...... 25 L6
Sunbury Gn LEIE LE5 ...... 127 J8
Sunbury Ri RLEIW/BBY LE8 ...... 143 G3
Sunderland Gv
  WOL/BIL/BRX NG8 ...... 35 H5 [12]
Sundew Cl DERBYSE DE21 ...... 59 K3
Sundew Rd LEIE LE5 ...... 127 G5
Sundown Av NORM/LIT DE23 ...... 71 H1
Sunlea Crs BSTN/STPLFD NG9 .... 62 D2
Sunnindale Dr
  COT/KEY/RAD NG12 ...... 66 B6
Sunningdale Av DERBYE DE21 .... 59 H2
  HEANOR DE75 ...... 20 D7
Sunningdale Dr CALV/BJ NG14 .... 27 G2
  ILK DE7 ...... 46 F2
Sunningdale Rd LEIW LE3 ...... 129M3
Sunninghill Cl ILK DE7 ...... 32 B7 [3]
Sunninghill Dr CFTN/RUD NG11 .. 64 C4
Sunny Bank Gdns
  BPR/DUF DE56 ...... 17 K5 [3]
Sunnycroft Rd LEIW LE3 ...... 130 E2
Sunnydale Rd
  MAPPK/POR/STA NG3 ...... 51M1
Sunnyfield Cl LEIE LE5 ...... 133 G2
Sunny Gv DERBYE DE21 ...... 58 E2
Sunny HI BPR/DUF DE56 ...... 17 K8
Sunnyhill Av NORM/LIT DE23 ...... 71 J1
Sunnyhill Rd LBORO LE11 ...... 8 E9
Sunny Side LEIS LE2 ...... 139 G3 [3]
Sunnyside
  BSTN/STPLFD NG9 ...... 63 G2 [3]
Sunrise Av ARN NG5 ...... 25 G2
  ARN NG5 ...... 36 D2
Sun St DERBYW DE22 ...... 2 C6
Sun Wy LEIW LE3 ...... 130 B4
Surbiton Cl DERBYW DE22 ...... 56 E1 [3]
Surbiton Ct ILK DE7 ...... 32 B7
Surbiton Sq WOL/BIL/BRX NG8 .... 35M4
Surfleet Cl WOL/BIL/BRX NG8 ..... 49 G4
Surgey's La ARN NG5 ...... 25 L6
Surrey St DERBYW DE22 ...... 57 H1
  LEIN LE4 ...... 125M6
Susan Av LEIE LE5 ...... 132 F3
Susan Cl HUCK/RAV NG15 ...... 15M6
Susan Dr BLWL NG6 ...... 36 B3
Sussex Circ DERBYE DE21 ...... 44 C7
Sussex Rd WGSTN LE18 ...... 137 K4
Sussex St LEIE LE5 ...... 7 J4
Sussex Wy LGEAT NG10 ...... 61M2
Sutherland Wy
  RLEINE/SYS LE7 ...... 118 C8
Sutherland Dr WBRGFD NG2 ...... 65 L3
Sutherland Rd
  MAPPK/POR/STA NG3 ...... 37 M1 [3]
  NORM/LIT DE23 ...... 57 K7
Sutherland St LEIN LE4 ...... 7 J4
Suthers Rd CDON/KEG DE74 ...... 86 A5
Sutton Av LEIN LE4 ...... 126 A6
  MELB/CHEL DE73 ...... 72 C5
Sutton Cl DERBYW DE22 ...... 57 G1
  LEIS LE2 ...... 138 F4
  RLBORO LE12 ...... 95 G2
  RLBORO LE12 ...... 112 D2
Sutton Ct EWD/SEL/PNX NG16 .... 21 K5
  RLEIW/BAR LE9 ...... 141 D7 [3]
Sutton Dr DERBYSE DE24 ...... 72 C3

Sutton Gdns *CFTN/RUD* NG11 ... 79 G1
Sutton La *RDERBYSW* DE65 ... 68 A4
    RDERBYSW DE65 ... 68 F2
Sutton Pl *LEIN* LE4 ... 126 A5
Sutton Rd *ARN* NG5 ... 25 K5
    CDON/KEG DE74 ... 86 A6
    LEIS LE2 ... 131 L8
Swain's Av
    MAPPK/POR/STA NG3 ... 51 L1
Swainson Rd *LEIN* LE4 ... 126 C7
Swain St *LE1* ... 7 H6
Swale Cl *LEIS* LE2 ... 139 H1
Swallow Cl *BLWL* NG6 ... 36 B4
    MCKLVR DE3 ... 56 E4
    RLBORO LE12 ... 113 K5
Swallow Dl *COAL* LE67 ... 100 B8
Swallowdale Dr *LEIN* LE4 ... 124 F1
Swallowdale Rd *DERBYSE* DE24 ... 71 H3
Swallow Dr *RLEINE/SYS* LE7 ... 120 D3
Swallow Gdns *CARL* NG4 ... 37 M6
Swallows Cl *LEIW* LE3 ... 129 J6
Swallow Wk *RLBORO* LE12 ... 94 E6
Swan Cl *RLBORO* LE12 ... 105 J7
    RLBORO LE12 ... 113 K5
Swan Meadow *CARL* NG4 ... 52 D3
Swanmore Rd
    NORM/LIT DE23 ... 56 E7
Swannington Rd *LEIW* LE3 ... 125 G8
Swannymote Rd *COAL* LE67 ... 108 E1
Swanscombe Rd *LEIS* LE2 ... 131 H6
Swansdowne Dr
    CFTN/RUD NG11 ... 64 D5
Swan St *LBORO* LE11 ... 9 H2
    LEIW LE3 ... 6 C4
    RLBORO LE12 ... 106 C7
    RLBORO LE12 ... 114 A4
Swan Wy *COAL* LE67 ... 108 D7
    RLEINE/SYS LE7 ... 120 C3
Swanwick *DERBYE* DE21 ... 44 E6
Swarkestone Br
    MELB/CHEL DE73 ... 82 B2
Swarkestone Dr *NORM/LIT* DE23.. 71 G2
Swarkestone Rd
    MELB/CHEL DE73 ... 72 D6
Swayfield Cl *MCKLVR* DE3 ... 55 M4
Sweetbriar Cl *DERBYSE* DE24 ... 72 E2
Sweetbriar Rd *LEIW* LE3 ... 131 G4
Sweet Leys Dr *RLBORO* LE12 ... 88 C4
Sweet Leys Rd *WBRGFD* NG2 ... 51 G6
Swenson Av *NOTTE* NG7 ... 50 C5
Swift Cl *RLEINE/SYS* LE7 ... 120 D3
Swift Cl *EWD/SEL/PNX* NG16 ... 21 K3
Swift's Cl *RLBORO* LE12 ... 98 A4
Swigert Cl *BLWL* NG6 ... 35 K2
Swinburne St *DERBY* DE1 ... 2 E7
    MAPPK/POR/STA NG3 ... 51 K1
Swinburne Wy *ARN* NG5 ... 37 G1
Swinderby Dr *DERBYE* DE21 ... 44 F6
Swindon Cl *EWD/SEL/PNX* NG16 ... 21 M8
Swinfield Rd *RLBORO* LE12 ... 112 E1
Swinford Av *LEIS* LE2 ... 137 H5
Swingate *EWD/SEL/PNX* NG16 ... 34 A2
Swingbridge Rd *LBORO* LE11 ... 95 K8
Swinney Bank *BPR/DUF* DE56 ... 17 L2
Swinney La *BPR/DUF* DE56 ... 17 L2
Swinstead Rd *LEIE* LE5 ... 133 H3
Swithland Av *LEIN* LE4 ... 125 J6
Swithland Cl *COAL* LE67 ... 116 C7
    LBORO LE11 ... 103 G2
Swithland Dr *WBRGFD* NG2 ... 65 J3
Swithland La *RLEINE/SYS* LE7... 113 C6
Swithland Rd *COAL* LE67 ... 109 G7
    RLEINE/SYS LE7 ... 118 C3
Sword Cl *LEIW* LE3 ... 124 A8
Sybil Rd *LEIS* LE2 ... 130 F6
Sycamore Av *DERBYW* DE22 ... 43 H4
    RDERBYSW DE65 ... 70 B5
    RIPLEY DE5 ... 11 H7
Sycamore Cl
    COT/KEY/RAD NG12 ... 53 K5
    HUCK/RAV NG15 ... 23 J2
    LEIS LE2 ... 132 D6
    RDERBYSW DE65 ... 69 G3
    RLEINE/SYS LE7 ... 120 F5
Sycamore Ct *DERBYE* DE21 ... 59 J2
Sycamore Crs *LGEAT* NG10 ... 47 L8
Sycamore Dr *GBY/RBY* LE6 ... 123 K5
    ILK DE7 ... 33 M8
Sycamore Gv *GBY/RBY* LE6 ... 123 K4
Sycamore Pl
    MAPPK/POR/STA NG3 ... 37 G7
Sycamore Rd *CDON/KEG* DE74 ... 84 C7
    EWD/SEL/PNX NG16 ... 33 M3
    LGEAT NG10 ... 76 A2
    RLEINE/SYS LE7 ... 119 L7
The Sycamores
    EWD/SEL/PNX NG16 ... 21 J8
Sycamore St *RLEIW/BBY* LE8 ... 136 F7
Sycamore Wy *LBORO* LE11 ... 103 L8
    RLEIW/BAR LE9 ... 141 M1
Sydenham Rd *DERBYW* DE22 ... 42 E8
Sydney Cl *MCKLVR* DE3 ... 56 D4
Sydney Gv *COT/KEY/RAD* NG12 ... 53 J4
Sydney Rd *BWSH/BRSTN* DE72 ... 60 E8
    WOL/BIL/BRX NG8 ... 49 M2
Sykefield Av *LEIW* LE3 ... 131 G3
Syke Rd *ARN* NG5 ... 24 D7
Sylvan Av *LEIE* LE5 ... 132 B1
Sylvan St *LEIW* LE3 ... 131 G1
Sylvan Wy *LEIW* LE3 ... 129 M3
Synge Cl *CFTN/RUD* NG11 ... 64 A7
Syon Park *WBRGFD* NG2 ... 65 G2
Syston Av *RLEINE/SYS* LE7 ... 114 A3
Syston St East *LE1* ... 7 K3
Syston St West *LEI* LE1 ... 7 H1
Sywell Av *LBORO* LE11 ... 102 F4
Sywell Dr *WGSTN* LE18 ... 138 C5

T

Tadcaster Av *LEIS* LE2 ... 137 H4
Taddington Rd *DERBYE* DE21.. 44 C7

Taft Av *LGEAT* NG10 ... 61 M1
Taft Leys Rd *RLBORO* LE12 ... 88 D5
Tailby Av *LEIE* LE5 ... 126 C7
Talbot Ct *COT/KEY/RAD* NG12... 53 J4
Talbot Dr *BSTN/STPLFD* NG9 ... 48 B5
Talbot La *COAL* LE67 ... 100 A8
    LEI LE1 ... 6 C6
Talbot St *COAL* LE67 ... 108 B1
    DERBY DE22 ... 2 C4
    LEIN LE4 ... 125 L4
    NOTT NG1 ... 4 E6
Talgarth Cl *DERBYE* DE21 ... 45 G5
Tamar Cl *DERBYW* DE22 ... 43 H3
Tamarix Cl *CARL* NG4 ... 38 E5
Tamar Rd *LEIN* LE4 ... 126 C5
    LEIS LE2 ... 139 H2
Tame Cl *CFTN/RUD* NG11 ... 64 C3
Tamerton Rd *LEIS* LE2 ... 137 J2
Tamworth Rd *RLBORO* LE12 ... 101 K5
Tamworth Gv *CFTN/RUD* NG11 ... 64 D5
Tamworth Rd
    BWSH/BRSTN DE72 ... 75 H7
    LGEAT NG10 ... 76 A2
Tamworth St *BPR/DUF* DE56 ... 29 J4
Tangmere Crs
    WOL/BIL/BRX NG8 ... 35 J6
Tanner's La *RLBORO* LE12 ... 94 E6
Tansey Crs *RLEIW/BAR* LE9 ... 140 A5
Tansley Av *ILK* DE7 ... 31 L6
    WGSTN LE18 ... 137 L6
Tansley Ri *DERBYE* DE21 ... 44 D6
Tants Meadow *BPR/DUF* DE56... 30 C1
Tantum Av *HEANOR* DE75 ... 20 A8
Tanwood Rd
    BSTN/STPLFD NG9 ... 62 F6
Tanyard Cl *CDON/KEG* DE74 ... 84 F3
Taplow Cl *MCKLVR* DE3 ... 56 A5
Tarbat Rd *LEIE* LE5 ... 127 H8
Tarbert Cl *WBRGFD* NG2 ... 50 F5
Target St *NOTTE* NG7 ... 50 C2
Tarina Cl *MELB/CHEL* DE73 ... 72 E6
Tarragon Rd *LEIS* LE2 ... 6 B9
Tasman Cl *MCKLVR* DE3 ... 56 D4
Tatham's La *ILK* DE7 ... 33 J5
Tatlow Rd *LEIW* LE3 ... 130 A1
Tattershall Dr *BSTN/STPLFD* NG9.. 49 M8
    NOTTE NG7 ... 4 C7
Tattle Hl *ILK* DE7 ... 46 D5
Taunton Cl *DERBYSE* DE24 ... 59 G7
    WGSTN LE18 ... 138 A6
Taunton Rd *LEIW* LE3 ... 130 F3
Taupo Dr *HUCK/RAV* NG15 ... 23 G2
Taurus Cl *LEIS* LE2 ... 65 K1
Tavern Av *WOL/BIL/BRX* NG8 ... 36 A5
Taverner Cl *RLEINE/SYS* LE7 ... 123 H8
Taverners Crs *NORM/LIT* DE23 ... 57 H7
Taverners Rd *LEIN* LE4 ... 119 G8
Tavistock Av
    MAPPK/POR/STA NG3 ... 37 G6
    RIPLEY DE5 ... 11 C4
Tavistock Cl *DERBYSE* DE24 ... 71 H4
    HUCK/RAV NG15 ... 23 H2
Tavistock Dr *LEIE* LE5 ... 132 C4
    MAPPK/POR/STA NG3 ... 37 G6
Tavistock Rd *WBRGFD* NG2 ... 65 K1
Tawny Wy *NORM/LIT* DE23 ... 56 E8
Tay Cl *DERBYSE* DE24 ... 71 H5
Taylor Cl *RLEINE/SYS* LE7 ... 120 E4
    WBRGFD NG2 ... 51 L3
Taylor Crs *BSTN/STPLFD* NG9 ... 48 C7
Taylor La *HEANOR* DE75 ... 20 B4
Taylor Rd *LEI* LE1 ... 7 H2
Taylor's Bridge Rd *WGSTN* LE18.. 137 L6
Taylors Cl *RLEIW/BAR* LE9 ... 140 B5
Taylor's Cft *CALV/BJ* NC14 ... 26 F3
Taylor St *ASHB* DE6 ... 54 C1
Taylor St *DERBYSE* DE24 ... 58 B5
    ILK DE7 ... 33 K6
Tayside Cl *DERBYSE* DE24 ... 71 H4
Tay Wk *DERBYW* DE22 ... 43 J4
Teak Cl *MAPPK/POR/STA* NG3 ... 5 K2
Tealby Cl *BLWL* NG6 ... 23 K8
Teal Cl *CARL* NG4 ... 52 F1
    COAL LE67 ... 108 D7
    LEIW LE3 ... 129 J5
Teal Wy *RLEINE/SYS* LE7 ... 120 C3
Teasel Cl *RLEIW/BAR* LE9 ... 135 L7
Tebbs Cl *RLEIW/BBY* LE8 ... 143 G3
Technology Rd
    BSTN/STPLFD NG9 ... 63 L2
Tedworth Av *DERBYSE* DE24 ... 71 H5
Tedworth Gn *LEIN* LE4 ... 125 H2
Teesbrook Dr
    WOL/BIL/BRX NG8 ... 48 F3
Teesdale Cl *LEIS* LE2 ... 6 D9
Teesdale Ct *BSTN/STPLFD* NG9 ... 62 E3
Teesdale Rd *ARN* NG5 ... 36 E5
    LGEAT NG10 ... 75 L1
Teignmouth Cl *LEIE* LE5 ... 132 D4
Telford Cl *MCKLVR* DE3 ... 56 C6
Telford Dr *EWD/SEL/PNX* NG16 ... 21 M4
Telford Wy *LEIE* LE5 ... 133 J2
Tempest Rd *LEIN* LE4 ... 125 K1
Templar Cl *DERBYSE* DE24 ... 71 G5
Templar Rd *BSTN/STPLFD* NG9... 63 M1
Templar Wy *COAL* LE67 ... 108 D2
Templar Wy *RLEINE/SYS* LE7 ... 119 H1
Temple Cl *RLBORO* LE12... 102 A6
Temple Crs *EWD/SEL/PNX* NG16 ... 35 J3
Temple Hl *COAL* LE67 ... 108 D1
Templemen Cl
    CFTN/RUD NG11 ... 64 F8
Templeoak Dr
    WOL/BIL/BRX NG8 ... 49 G4
Temple Rd *LEIS* LE2 ... 132 C2
Templestowe Ct *DERBYSE* DE24 ... 58 B8
Tenbury Crs *WOL/BIL/BRX* NG8 ... 35 M6
Tenby Dr *DERBY* DE21 ... 45 G5
Tendring Dr *WGSTN* LE18 ... 138 D4
Tene Cl *ARN* NG5 ... 25 K5
Tennessee Rd *DERBYE* DE21 ...... 44 F6
Tennis Court Dr *LEIE* LE5 ... 126 E8
Tennis Dr *NOTTE* NG7 ... 4 C7
Tennyson Av *CARL* NG4 ... 38 D6
Tennyson Ct *HUCK/RAV* NG15... 23 H1
Tennyson Dr *BSTN/STPLFD* NG9.. 63 H5

Tennyson Rd *ARN* NG5... 37 J3
    LBORO LE11 ... 8 B2
Tennyson Sq
    EWD/SEL/PNX NG16 ... 34 A3
Tennyson St *DERBYSE* DE24 ... 58 B8
    ILK DE7 ... 33 J4
    LEIS LE2 ... 7 L9
    NOTTE NG7 ... 4 C4
    RLEIW/BAR LE9 ... 135 L6
Tenter Cl *ARN* NG5 ... 24 D7
    LGEAT NG10 ... 76 B2
Tentercroft Av *RLEINE/SYS* LE7 .. 121 G3
Tenter La *BPR/DUF* DE56... 10 B6
Terrace St *NOTTE* NG7 ... 4 B1
Terrian Crs *WBRGFD* NG2 ... 51 K8
Terry Pl *DERBYSE* DE24 ... 58 D8
Terton Rd *ARN* NG5 ... 24 D7
Tetbury Dr *RLBORO* LE12... 101 K5
Tettenbury Rd *ARN* NG5 ... 36 D4
Tetuan Rd *LEIW* LE3 ... 131 G1
Teversal Av *NOTTE* NG7 ... 4 A7
Tevery Cl *BSTN/STPLFD* NG9 ... 48 C7
Teviot Pl *DERBYE* DE21 ... 44 E5
Teviot Rd *ARN* NG5 ... 36 D2
Tewkesbury Cl *WBRGFD* NG2 ... 65 L1
Tewkesbury Crs *DERBYE* DE21... 44 B7
Tewkesbury Dr *BLWL* NG6 ... 36 C3
    EWD/SEL/PNX NG16 ... 22 C8
Tewkesbury Rd *LGEAT* NG10... 76 C3
Tewkesbury St *LEIW* LE3 ... 6 B1
Thackeray's Av *LEIS* LE2 ... 37 J1
Thackeray St *DERBYSE* DE24 ... 71 L2
    LEIS LE2 ... 131 K6
    NOTTE NG7 ... 4 B5
Thames Cl *DERBYW* DE22 ... 56 D2
Thames St *BLWL* NG6 ... 23 M8
    LEI LE1 ... 6 F5
Thane Rd *BSTN/STPLFD* NG9 ... 64 B1
    NOTTE NG7 ... 64 C1
Thanet Dr *DERBYSE* DE24 ... 72 E1
Thatcher Cl *LEIN* LE4 ... 124 F3
Thatchers' Cnr
    RLEINE/SYS LE7 ... 115 H8
Thaxted Cl *WOL/BIL/BRX* NG8 ... 49 H3
Thelda Av *COT/KEY/RAD* NG12 ... 80 C4
Thetford Cl *ARN* NG5 ... 37 L1
Third Av *BLWL* NG6 ... 23 L8
    BSTN/STPLFD NG9 ... 64 A1
    CARL NG4 ... 37 M7
    CARL NG4 ... 38 A7
    CARL NG4 ... 38 D6
Thirlbeck Cl *COT/KEY/RAD* NG12 ... 67 L6
Thirlmere Cl *COAL* LE67 ... 109 G6
    WBRGFD NG2 ... 66 A2
Thirlmere Av *DERBYW* DE22 ... 43 J4
Thirlmere Cl *LGEAT* NG10... 61 M5
    MAPPK/POR/STA NG3 ... 37 K8
Thirlmere Dr *LBORO* LE11 ... 103 H7
    LGEAT NG10... 61 M5
    RLBORO LE12 ... 105 H7
    WGSTN LE18 ... 138 C4
Thirlmere St *LEIS* LE2 ... 131 J4
Thirsk Cl *DERBYSE* DE24 ... 58 B8
Thistle Bank *RLBORO* LE12 ... 88 C4
Thistle Cl *EWD/SEL/PNX* NG16 ... 21 M7
    RLEINE/SYS LE7 ... 118 D5
    RLEIW/BAR LE9 ... 135 L7
Thistledown Cl *DERBYW* DE22 ... 43 L5
Thistledown Rd
    CFTN/RUD NG11 ... 64 C8
Thistle Green Cl *HEANOR* DE75... 20 F6
Thistle Rd *ILK* DE7 ... 47 L3
Thomas Cl *MAPPK/POR/STA* NG3... 5 K3
Thomas Cook Cl
    MELB/CHEL DE73 ... 82 E8
Thomas Parkyn Cl
    CFTN/RUD NG11 ... 79 J8
Thomas Rd *CDON/KEG* DE74...... 86 A6
    COAL LE67 ... 108 C2
Thomasson Rd *LEIE* LE5 ... 132 F1
Thomas St *LBORO* LE11 ... 104 B4
Thompson Av *RLBORO* LE12 ... 100 F1
Thompson Cl *BSTN/STPLFD* NG9.. 63 G4
    RLBORO LE12 ... 112 D1
Thompson Gdns *ARN* NG5 ... 24 E6
Thompson St
    EWD/SEL/PNX NG16 ... 20 F4
Thomson Cl *LEIN* LE4 ... 126 B1
Thomson Dr *RIPLEY* DE5 ... 11 M8
Thore Cl *DERBYE* DE21 ... 44 F6
Thoresby Av *CARL* NG4 ... 38 B5
    WBRGFD NG2 ... 51 K4
Thoresby Cl *COT/KEY/RAD* NG12 .. 53 L3
    RIPLEY DE5 ... 11 J6
Thoresby Ct
    MAPPK/POR/STA NG3 ... 37 H7
Thoresby Crs
    BWSH/BRSTN DE72 ... 60 D8
Thoresby Dl *HUCK/RAV* NG15 ... 15 M8
Thoresby Rd *BSTN/STPLFD* NG9.. 49 G6
    LGEAT NG10 ... 61 M8
Thoresby St *LEIE* LE5 ... 132 C1

Thornhill Rd *DERBYW* DE22 ... 57 G3
    NORM/LIT DE23 ... 57 G6
Thornhills *RLEIW/BAR* LE9 ... 135 L5
Thornhills Gv *RLEIW/BAR* LE9 .. 135 L5
Thornholme Cl *LEIN* LE4 ... 125 G3
Thornley St *NOTTE* NG7 ... 36 C8
Thorn St *NORM/LIT* DE23 ... 57 K5
Thornthwaite Cl
    WBRGFD NG2 ... 66 A1
Thornton Av *ARN* NG5 ... 25 H6
Thornton Cl *COAL* LE67 ... 109 G6
Thornton Dr *RLEIW/BAR* LE9 ... 136 A7
Thornton La *COAL* LE67 ... 122 A4
Thorntons Cl
    COT/KEY/RAD NG12 ... 67 L5
Thorntree Cl *BWSH/BRSTN* DE72.. 61 K6
Thorn Tree Gdns
    EWD/SEL/PNX NG16 ... 21 K3
Thorntree La *DERBY* DE1 ... 2 F4
Thornville Cl *LEIN* LE4 ... 126 C6
Thorny Cl *LBORO* LE11 ... 103 H1
Thorold Cl *CFTN/RUD* NG11 ... 64 C7
Thoroton Rd *WBRGFD* NG2 ... 51 K6
Thoroton St *NOTTE* NG7 ... 4 C5
Thorpe Acre Rd *LBORO* LE11 ... 8 A1
Thorpe Cl *ARN* NG5 ... 24 E7
Thorpe Crs
    MAPPK/POR/STA NG3 ... 37 M5
Thorpe Dr *MCKLVR* DE3 ... 56 C4
    WGSTN LE18 ... 138 B3
Thorpe Field Dr *LEIN* LE4 ... 120 D7
Thorpe Hl *LBORO* LE11 ... 103 G4
Thorpe Hill Dr *HEANOR* DE75 ... 20 C8
Thorpelands Dr
    DERBYW DE22 ... 43 J6
Thorpe La *RLEINE/SYS* LE7 ... 121 H8
Thorpe Leys *LGEAT* NG10... 76 B2
Thorpe Rd *EWD/SEL/PNX* NG16 ... 21 K3
    RLBORO LE12 ... 101 L4
Thorpe's Rd *HEANOR* DE75 ... 20 B6
Thorpe St *ILK* DE7 ... 33 J4
    LEIW LE3 ... 6 B7
Thorpe Wy *BPR/DUF* DE56 ... 17 M2
    RLEIW/BAR LE9 ... 136 B3
Thorpewell *LEIE* LE5 ... 132 C1
Thrapston Av *ARN* NG5 ... 25 K5
Threadgold Cl *LEIN* LE4 ... 124 F1
Three Tunes Rd
    MAPPK/POR/STA NG3 ... 21 L5
Threlkeld Cl *WBRGFD* NG2 ... 66 A1
Thrumpton Av *LGEAT* NG10... 62 D6
Thrumpton Dr *WBRGFD* NG2 ... 50 F6
Thrushton Cl
    RDERBYSW DE65 ... 70 A5
Thrussington Rd
    RLEINE/SYS LE7 ... 115 G5
Thruxton Cl *DERBYSE* DE24 ... 73 G1
Thurcaston La *RLEINE/SYS* LE7 .. 118 F3
Thurcaston Rd *LEIN* LE4 ... 125 J3
Thurcroft Cl *DERBYW* DE22 ... 57 G1
    LEIS LE2 ... 137 H4
Thurgarton Av *WBRGFD* NG2 ... 51 K3
Thurgarton St *WBRGFD* NG2 ... 51 K3
Thurland St *NOTT* NG1 ... 5 H6
Thurlaston La *RLEIW/BAR* LE9 ... 134 E8
    RLEIW/BAR LE9 ... 135 H3
Thurlby Rd *LEIE* LE5 ... 126 B8
Thurlestone Dr
    MAPPK/POR/STA NG3 ... 38 A1
Thurloe Ct *CFTN/RUD* NG11 ... 65 G4
Thurlow Cl *LEIS* LE2 ... 139 H3
Thurlow Ct *DERBYE* DE21 ... 44 E6
Thurlow Rd *LEIS* LE2 ... 131 L6
Thurman Dr *COT/KEY/RAD* NG12 .. 67 K4
Thurman St *ILK* DE7 ... 47 L1
    NOTTE NG7 ... 4 A3
Thurmaston Bvd *LEIN* LE4 ... 126 D3
Thurmaston La *LEIE* LE5 ... 126 E6
    LEIN LE4 ... 126 D4
Thurnby Hl *RLEINE/SYS* LE7 ... 133 J2
Thurnby La *LEIS* LE2 ... 133 J6
Thurncourt Cl *LEIE* LE5 ... 127 C8
Thurncourt Gdns *LEIE* LE5 ... 127 K8
Thurncourt Rd *LEIE* LE5 ... 127 C8
Thurnview Rd *LEIE* LE5 ... 133 C4
Thursby Rd *CFTN/RUD* NG11 ... 64 C2
Thurstone Furlong
    MELB/CHEL DE73 ... 72 C6
Thymus Wk *CFTN/RUD* NG11 ... 64 A6
Thyra Gv *BSTN/STPLFD* NG9 ... 63 L1
    MAPPK/POR/STA NG3 ... 37 H6
Tiber St *DERBYSE* DE24 ... 73 H2
Tichborne St *LEIS* LE2 ... 7 J8
Tickham Av *DERBYSE* DE24 ... 71 C5
Ticknall La *RIPLEY* DE5 ... 18 F6
Tickow La *RLBORO* LE12 ... 101 J5
Tideswell Rd *DERBYE* DE21 ... 44 D6
Tidworth Cl *WOL/BIL/BRX* NG8 ... 49 L1
Tigers Cl *WGSTN* LE18 ... 137 J5
Tigers Rd *WGSTN* LE18 ... 137 J5
Tilberthwaite Cl *WBRGFD* NG2 .. 66 A1
Tilbury Crs *LEIN* LE4 ... 126 E2
Tilbury Pl *DERBYSE* DE24 ... 72 E2
Tilbury Ri *WOL/BIL/BRX* NG8 ... 35 L4
Tilford Crs *LEIS* LE2 ... 137 H5
Tilford Gdns *BSTN/STPLFD* NG9 .. 62 C1
Tilford Rd *HUCK/RAV* NG15 ... 15 H1
Tiller Cl *NORM/LIT* DE23 ... 70 F1
Tilett Rd *LEIS* LE2 ... 130 B5
Tilley Cl *LEIW* LE3 ... 130 A4
Tillingham Rd *LEIE* LE5 ... 126 D7
Tilling Rd *LEIN* LE4 ... 125 C3
Tilstock Ct
    EWD/SEL/PNX NG16 ... 22 E7
Tilton Dr *LEIS* LE2 ... 138 E4
Tilton Gv *ILK* DE7 ... 47 C2
Timbersbrook Cl *DERBYE* DE21 ... 44 E6
Timber St *RLBORO* LE12 ... 137 K6
Timberwood Dr *GBY/RBY* LE6 ... 123 J5
Timsbury Crt *DERBYE* DE21 ... 44 C5
Tinker's Dell *RLEINE/SYS* LE7 ... 115 H7
Tinkersway *WBRGFD* NG2 ... 50 E5
Tinsell Brook *RDERBYSW* DE65 ... 68 B6
Tinsley Rd *EWD/SEL/PNX* NG16 ... 21 L6
Tintagel Cl *NORM/LIT* DE23 ... 57 M5

Tintagel Gn *CFTN/RUD* NG11 ... 64 C5
Tintern Dr *WOL/BIL/BRX* NG8 ... 36 B5
Tipnall Rd *CDON/KEG* DE74 ... 84 E4
Tippett Ct *MAPPK/POR/STA* NG3.. 51 K1
Tip Tree Cl
    EWD/SEL/PNX NG16 ... 22 D8
Tiptree Cl *LEIN* LE4 ... 125 H5
Tiree Cl *BSTN/STPLFD* NG9 ... 48 B5
    DERBYSE DE24 ... 71 K3
Tishbite St *BLWL* NG6 ... 23 M8
Tissington Dr *DERBYE* DE21 ... 44 F4
Tissington Rd *NOTTE* NG7 ... 36 E7
Titchfield St *HUCK/RAV* NG15 ... 15 M8
Tithby Dr *ARN* NG5 ... 25 J4
Tithebarn La *ASHB* DE6 ... 54 A2
Tithe Cl *COAL* LE67 ... 100 A7
Tithe St *LEIE* LE5 ... 126 E8
The Tithings *RLEIW/BBY* LE8 ... 146 E6
    LEIN LE4 ... 126 A5
Tiverton Av *COAL* LE67 ... 108 E5
    LEIS LE2 ... 126 A5
Tiverton Cl *HUCK/RAV* NG15 ... 23 H2
    LEIS LE2 ... 139 G2
    MCKLVR DE3 ... 56 B3
    RLEIW/BAR LE9 ... 135 K7
Tiverton Rd *LBORO* LE11 ... 103 K8
Tivoli Gdns *DERBYW* DE22 ... 43 J8
Toad La *CALV/BJ* NC14 ... 27 L2
Tobermory Wy *DERBYSE* DE24 ... 71 H4
Tobias Cl *ARN* NG5 ... 24 D7
Todd Cl *CFTN/RUD* NG11 ... 64 A7
Toft Cl *COT/KEY/RAD* NG12 ... 67 G3
Toft Rd *BSTN/STPLFD* NG9 ... 62 E4
The Tofts *WGSTN* LE18 ... 138 B6
The Toft *RLBORO* LE12 ... 100 F1
Tolcarne Rd *LEIE* LE5 ... 127 C7
Tolchard Cl *LEIS* LE2 ... 132 E2
Tollemache Av *LEIN* LE4 ... 125 J5
Toller Rd *LEIS* LE2 ... 132 A6
    RLBORO LE12 ... 112 C2
Tollerton Gn *BLWL* NG6 ... 36 B2
Tollerton La *COT/KEY/RAD* NG12 .. 66 B7
Tollerton Rd *COT/KEY/RAD* NG12 .. 66 B1
Tollhouse Hl *NOTT* NG1 ... 4 F6
Tolton Rd *LEIE* LE5 ... 125 H3
Tolwell Rd *LEIN* LE4 ... 125 G1
Tomlin Rd *LEIN* LE4 ... 126 C6
Tomlinson Av *CFTN/RUD* NG11... 77 L6
Tom Paine Cl *LEIW* LE3 ... 130 B5
Tonbridge Dr *DERBYSE* DE24 ... 72 E2
Tonbridge Mt *WOL/BIL/BRX* NG8.. 49 H5
Tonnelier Rd *NOTTE* NG7 ... 50 C6
Toothill Rd *LBORO* LE11 ... 9 J1
Top Cl *LEIW* LE3 ... 130 B6
Top Farm Ct *BPR/DUF* DE56 ... 18 E7
Tophall Dr *RLEIW/BBY* LE8 ... 143 J4
Top Manor Cl
    BWSH/BRSTN DE72 ... 60 A2
Top Rd *CFTN/RUD* NG11 ... 79 C1
Top Valley Dr *ARN* NG5 ... 24 C7
Top Valley Wy *ARN* NG5 ... 24 C8
Tor Av *ALFN* DE55 ... 11 M1
Torbay Crs *ARN* NG5 ... 36 F2
Torcross Cl *LEIW* LE3 ... 124 C7
Torkard Dr *ARN* NG5 ... 24 D7
Toronto Cl *LEI* LE1... 7 H3
Torridon Cl *DERBYSE* DE24... 71 K3
Torrington Av *COAL* LE67 ... 108 E5
Torrington Cl *WGSTN* LE18 ... 138 B7
Torvill Dr *WOL/BIL/BRX* NG8 ... 49 J2
Toston Dr *WOL/BIL/BRX* NG8 ... 50 A3
Totland Dr *BLWL* NG6 ... 36 B6
Totland Rd *BSTN/STPLFD* NG9 ... 49 G5
    LEIE LE5 ... 125 C7
Totley Cl *BLWL* NG6 ... 24 A5
Totnes Cl *HUCK/RAV* NG15 ... 23 J1
Totnes Rd *MAPPK/POR/STA* NG3.. 51 M2
Toton Cl *BLWL* NG6 ... 36 B2
Toton La *BSTN/STPLFD* NG9 ... 62 D2
Tottle Gdns *NOTTE* NG7 ... 50 B1
Tottle Rd *NOTTE* NG7 ... 50 E7
    WBRGFD NG2 ... 51 C4
Tournament Rd *LEIW* LE3 ... 124 B8
Tovey Crs *LEIS* LE2 ... 137 H3
Tower Crs
    EWD/SEL/PNX NG16 ... 34 E3
Towers Cl *RLEIW/BAR* LE9 ... 129 J3
Towers Dr *RLEIW/BAR* LE9 ... 129 J3
Tower St *DERBYSE* DE24 ... 58 B8
    LEI LE1... 6 F9
Towe's Mt *CARL* NG4 ... 38 C8
Towle Cl *BWSH/BRSTN* DE72... 59 M6
Towle St *LGEAT* NG10 ... 75 L3
Towlsons Cft *BLWL* NG6 ... 36 B4
Towles Pastures
    CDON/KEG DE74 ... 84 E4
Town End Rd
    BWSH/BRSTN DE72 ... 60 F8
Town Green St *RLEINE/SYS* LE7 .. 119 J2
Townsend Cl *LEIN* LE4 ... 126 B2
Townsend Gv
    MELB/CHEL DE73 ... 72 E5
Townsend Rd *RLEIW/BAR* LE9 ... 135 L4
    RLEIW/BAR LE9 ... 140 B6
Townside Cl *LGEAT* NG10 ... 75 M3
Town St *BPR/DUF* DE56 ... 29 J4
    BPR/DUF DE56... 30 A1
    BSTN/STPLFD NG9 ... 48 F7
    LGEAT NG10 ... 61 M1
The Town *DERBYE* DE21 ... 30 A8
Town Vw *EWD/SEL/PNX* NG16 ... 22 D8
Towpath Cl *LBORO* LE11 ... 104 A2
Towpath Link *WGSTN* LE18 ... 137 L7
Towson Av *EWD/SEL/PNX* NG16 .. 21 C5
Towson Fld *RLBORO* LE12 ... 88 C4
Trafalgar Cl *NOTTE* NG7 ... 4 A4
Trafalgar Rd *BSTN/STPLFD* NG9 .. 62 E3
    LGEAT NG10 ... 76 B1
Trafalgar Sq *LGEAT* NG10 ... 62 C8
Trafalgar Ter *LGEAT* NG10 ... 62 C8
Traffic St *DERBY* DE1 ... 3 G4
    WBRGFD NG2 ... 51 G4
Trafford Gdns
    WOL/BIL/BRX NG8 ... 36 B8
Trafford Rd *LEIE* LE5 ... 126 D8

Trafford Wy *NORM/LIT* DE23 .... 57 G7
Tranby Gdns *WOL/BIL/BRX* NG8.... 49 K3
Tranter Pl *LEIN* LE4 .... 126 B5 🔟
Travell's Hl *RLBORO* LE12 .... 87 L8
Travers Rd *LGEAT* NG10 .... 61 L1
Treasure Cl *LEIW* LE3 .... 124 A8
Treaty Rd *LEIW* LE3 .... 124 B8
Tredegar Dr *DERBYE* DE21 .... 44 F5
Tredington Rd *LEIW* LE3 .... 124 B6
Treegarth Sq *ARN* NG5 .... 24 F6 🔟
Treetops Cl *LEIE* LE5 .... 126 E8
Tree View Cl *ARN* NG5 .... 25 G6 🔟
Trefan Gdns *ARN* NG5 .... 24 E8
Trefoil Cl *LEIE* LE5 .... 127 G5
Trefoil Ct *NORM/LIT* DE23 .... 56 E8 🔟
Tregaron Cl *DERBYE* DE21 .... 45 G5
Tregony Wy *DERBYSE* DE24 .... 71 H5
Trelawn Cl *ARN* NG5 .... 37 H5 🔟
Trelissick Cl *LEIN* LE11 .... 102 F2 🔟
Tremaine Dr *WGSTN* LE18 .... 138 A6 🔟
Tremayne Rd *WOL/BIL/BRX* NG8 .. 49 J1
Trenant Rd *WGSTN* LE18 .... 137 J3
Trenchham Gdns *CALV/BJ* NG14 ... 39 H4
Trent Av *LEIN* LE4 .... 119 G8
Trent Bvd *WBRGFD* NG2 .... 51 L6
Trent Br *WBRGFD* NG2 .... 51 J6
Trent Bridge Ct
   NORM/LIT DE23 .... 57 G7 🔟
Trent Cl *DERBYSE* DE24 .... 71 H5
   LEIS LE2 .... 139 H2
   BSTN/STPLFD NG9 .... 63 J4
Trent Dr *HUCK/RAV* NG15 .... 23 H4
   NORM/LIT DE23 .... 71 H2
Trent Gdns *CALV/BJ* NG14 .... 39 K3
Trentham Dr *WOL/BIL/BRX* NG8 .. 36 A8
Trentham Gdns
   WOL/BIL/BRX NG8 .... 36 A8
   CALV/BJ NG14 .... 39 M3
   CDON/KEG DE74 .... 84 C2
   LGEAT NG10 .... 76 C4
   MELB/CHEL DE73 .... 83 C5
   WBRGFD NG2 .... 51 K4
Trenton Cl *BSTN/STPLFD* NG9 ..... 48 E6
Trenton Dr *LGEAT* NG10 .... 62 E7
Trenton Green Dr
   DERBYE DE21 .... 58 F1 🔟
Trent Ri *DERBYE* DE21 .... 59 K3
   ILK DE7 .... 47 H3
   WBRGFD NG2 .... 51 K3
Trentside *WBRGFD* NG2 .... 51 J7
Trentside North *WBRGFD* NG2 ..... 51 J6
Trent St *DERBYSE* DE24 .... 58 E8
   LGEAT NG10 .... 62 C7
   NOTT NG1 .... 5 J9
Trent Vale Rd *BSTN/STPLFD* NG9 .. 63 L3
Trent Valley Wy
   BSTN/STPLFD NG9 .... 63 G8
   CFTN/RUD NG11 .... 77 G2
   COT/KEY/RAD NG12 .... 39 L7
   WBRGFD NG2 .... 52 A5
Trent View Gdns
   COT/KEY/RAD NG12 .... 53 L2
Trescoe Ri *LEIW* LE3 .... 130 C2
Tresillian Cl *DERBYW* DE22 .... 43 J5
Tressall Cl *ILK* DE7 .... 33 L7
Tressall Rd *COAL* LE67 .... 108 E4
Tressell Wy *LEIW* LE3 .... 130 B5 🔟
Trevanth Rd *LEIN* LE4 .... 126 D5
Trevelyan Rd *WBRGFD* NG2 .... 51 K7
Treveris Dr *DERBYE* DE21 .... 59 K3 🔟
Trevino Dr *LEIN* LE4 .... 126 B2
Trevone Av *BSTN/STPLFD* NG9 .... 62 C1
Trevor Rd *BSTN/STPLFD* NG9 ..... 63 K2
   WBRGFD NG2 .... 65 L1
Trevose Gdns *ARN* NG5 .... 37 H4
   LEIE LE5 .... 127 H8
Treyford Cl *CFTN/RUD* NG11 .... 64 E3 🔟
The Triangle *ILK* DE7 .... 47 L1
Tricornia Dr *BLWL* NG6............. 35 M3
Trigo Cl *LEIN* LE4 .... 124 E3 🔟
Trillium Cl *LEIE* LE5 .... 127 G4 🔟
Tring V *ARN* NG5 .... 24 F6
Trinity Av *NOTTE* NG7 .... 50 D4 🔟
Trinity Cl *ILK* DE7 .... 33 J4 🔟
   RLEINE/SYS LE7 .... 120 F4
Trinity Crs *CARL* NG4 .... 27 G3
   RLBORO LE12 .... 97 M4
Trinity La *LEI* LE1 .... 6 F9
Trinity Rd *RLEINE/BAR* LE9 .... 136 C5
   RLEIW/BBY LE8 .... 136 D7
Trinity Sq *NOTT* NG1 .... 5 G6
Trinity St *DERBY* DE1 .... 3 H6
   LBORO LE11 .... 9 L4
Trinstead Wy *ARN* NG5 .... 25 G8
Tristram Cl *LEIW* LE3 .... 129 L5
Triumph Rd *LEIW* LE3 .... 124 A8
   NOTTE NG7 .... 50 B3
Trojan Wy *RLEINE/SYS* LE7 .... 120 C5
Troon Cl *EWD/SEL/PNX* NG16 .... 22 C8 🔟
   NORM/LIT DE23 .... 56 E7
Troon Wy *LEIN* LE4 .... 126 B3
Trough La *EWD/SEL/PNX* NG16 ... 22 D7
Trough Rd *EWD/SEL/PNX* NG16 ... 22 E8
Troutbeck *COT/KEY/RAD* NG12 .. 67 L4 🔟
Troutbeck Crs
   BSTN/STPLFD NG9 .... 49 G8
Troutbeck Gv
   NORM/LIT DE23 .... 56 E8 🔟
Trowbridge Cl *DERBYE* DE21 .. 44 C5 🔟
Trowell Av *ILK* DE7 .... 47 L2
   WOL/BIL/BRX NG8................ 48 F2
Trowell Gv *BSTN/STPLFD* NG9 ... 48 B4
   LGEAT NG10 .... 61 M6
Trowell La *RLBORO* LE12 .... 95 J1
Trowell Park Dr
   BSTN/STPLFD NG9 .... 48 B5 🔟
Trowell Rd *BSTN/STPLFD* NG9 .... 48 B5
   WOL/BIL/BRX NG8................ 49 G2
Trowels La *DERBYW* DE22 .... 57 G3
Trueman Gdns *ARN* NG5 .... 37 M1
Trueman St *ILK* DE7 .... 33 K3 🔟
Trueway Dr *RLBORO* LE12 .... 102 A5
Trueway Dr South
   RLBORO LE12 .... 102 A5
Trueway Rd *LEIE* LE5 .... 132 C5

Truman Cl *MAPPK/POR/STA* NG3.... 5 J4
Truman Dr *HUCK/RAV* NG15 .... 23 L1
Truman St *EWD/SEL/PNX* NG16 .... 22 B8
   ILK DE7 .... 33 L6 🔟
Truro Cl *RLBORO* LE12 .... 88 C6
Truro Crs *DERBYE* DE21 .... 45 G4
   NOTTE NG7 .... 36 C8 🔟
Trusley Gdns *NORM/LIT* DE23 ..... 71 H2
Tuckers Cl *LEIN* LE11 .... 9 M6
Tuckers Rd *LBORO* LE11 .... 9 M5
   LBORO LE11 .... 104 B5
Tuckett Rd *RLBORO* LE12 .... 111 K5
Tuckey Cl *RLEIW/BAR* LE9 .... 140 B7
Tudor Cl *CARL* NG4 .... 52 C2
   LEIE LE5 .... 6 B6
   LGEAT NG10 .... 62 C6
Tudor Dr *HUCK/RAV* NG15 .... 23 G2 🔟
Tudor Dr *LEIS* LE2 .... 138 F1
   RLEIW/BAR LE9 .... 142 B6
Tudor Falls *HEANOR* DE75 .... 20 C4
Tudor Field Cl
   MELB/CHEL DE73 .... 72 E6 🔟
Tudor Gv *GBY/RBY* LE6 .... 123 J6
   NOTT NG1 .... 4 F3
Tudor Pl *ILK* DE7 .... 47 G2
Tudor Rd *DERBYE* DE21 .... 58 E1
   LEIW LE3 .... 6 A4
   LEIW LE3 .... 51 K8
Tudor Sq *WBRGFD* NG2 .... 51 K8 🔟
Tudwal Cl *ARN* NG5 .... 24 E8
Tufnell Gdns *DERBYW* DE22 ... 42 F8 🔟
Tulip Av *MAPPK/POR/STA* NG3 ..... 5 K2
Tulip Rd *EWD/SEL/PNX* NG16 ...... 33 M2
Tulla Cl *DERBYSE* DE24 .... 71 J5
Tunnel Rd *NOTTE* NG7 .... 4 D7
Tunstall Crs *LEIN* LE4 .... 126 C7 🔟
   WOL/BIL/BRX NG8................ 35 L6
Tunstall Dr *BLWL* NG6 .... 36 D4
Tunstall Rd *ARN* NG5 .... 37 K3
Turnberry Cl *BSTN/STPLFD* NG9 .. 63 G1
   ILK DE7 .... 33 G5
Turnberry Ct
   COT/KEY/RAD NG12 .... 66 A4
Turnberry Rd *BLWL* NG6 .... 36 B1
Turnbull Dr *LEIW* LE3 .... 130 D7
Turnbury Wy *LEIE* LE5 .... 132 C5 🔟
Turner Av *EWD/SEL/PNX* NG16.... 20 E4
   LBORO LE11 .... 9 H7
Turner Cl *BSTN/STPLFD* NG9 ..... 62 C1
   RLBORO LE12 .... 104 D8
Turner Dr *EWD/SEL/PNX* NG16.... 21 M8
Turner Ri *LEIS* LE2 .... 138 F3
Turner Rd *LEIE* LE5 .... 126 D8 🔟
   LGEAT NG10 .... 76 A3
Turners La *ALFN* DE55 .... 11 L1
Turner St *DERBYSE* DE24 .... 72 B1
   HUCK/RAV NG15 .... 15 L8 🔟
   LEIE LE5 .... 6 F9
Turney St *WBRGFD* NG2 .... 51 H6
Turnpike La *BSTN/STPLFD* NG9 ... 49 L7
Turnpike Wy *COAL* LE67 .... 116 C7
Turn St *RLEINE/SYS* LE7 .... 120 E3
Turolough Rd *COAL* LE67 .... 100 C8
Turpin Av *CARL* NG4 .... 38 B4 🔟
Turton Cl *EWD/SEL/PNX* NG16 .... 20 E4
Turvey La *RLBORO* LE12 .... 94 B5
Turville Cl *WGSTN* LE18 .... 138 C7 🔟
Turville Rd *LEIW* LE3 .... 130 F4
Tuskar Rd *LEIE* LE5 .... 127 H8
Tuxford Cl *DERBYE* DE21 ..... 44 F6 🔟
Tuxford Gdns *LEIN* LE4 .... 126 E4
Tuxford Wk
   MAPPK/POR/STA NG3 .... 51 K1 🔟
Tweeds Muir Cl
   DERBYE DE21 .... 44 D5 🔟
Twentylands Dr *RLBORO* LE12 .... 88 B6
Twickenham Dr
   DERBYW DE22 .... 56 E1 🔟
Twickenham Rd *LEIS* LE2 .... 137 G5
Twin Oaks Cl *NORM/LIT* DE23 ..... 56 D8
The Twitchell
   BSTN/STPLFD NG9 .... 63 J3 🔟
Twycross Rd *ARN* NG5 .... 24 F8 🔟
Twycross St *LEIE* LE2 .... 7 L7
Twyford Cl *COAL* LE67 .... 109 G6
   HEANOR DE75 .... 20 A7
   ILK DE7 .... 32 B7 🔟
Twyford Gdns
   CFTN/RUD NG11 .... 64 C3 🔟
Twyford Rd *LGEAT* NG10 .... 75 K3
Twyford St *NORM/LIT* DE23 .... 2 F8
Tyburn Cl *ARN* NG5 .... 24 E6
Tyers Cl *RLEIW/BAR* LE9 .... 134 E4
Tyes End *LEIN* LE4 .... 124 E4
Tyler Av *LBORO* LE11 .... 103 K2
Tyler Ct *RLBORO* LE12 .... 102 A1
Tyler Rd *GBY/RBY* LE6 .... 123 H7
Tylers Rd *RLBORO* LE12 .... 100 F1
Tymdale Cha *DERBYSE* DE24 ... 71 G5 🔟
Tyndale St *LEIW* LE3 .... 6 A8
Tyndale Cl *LEIS* LE2 .... 139 H2
   LGEAT NG10 .... 75 L1
   WOL/BIL/BRX NG8................ 36 B7
Tyndale Rd *LBORO* LE11 .... 103 G2
Tyne Gdns *HUCK/RAV* NG15 ...... 23 H4
Tyringham Rd *WGSTN* LE18....... 138 C5
Tyrrell St *LEIW* LE3 .... 6 A4
Tysoe Hl *LEIW* LE3 .... 124 B6
Tythorn Dr *WGSTN* LE18 .... 137 L2

U

Uffa Magna *MCKLVR* DE3 .... 56 A6 🔟
Ulldale Ct *BSTN/STPLFD* NG9 ...... 62 F3
Ullscarf Cl *WBRGFD* NG2 .... 66 A2 🔟
Ullswater Av *RLBORO* LE12 .... 105 H6
Ullswater Cl *CARL* NG4 .... 38 D5 🔟
   DERBYE DE21 .... 44 B5 🔟
   WBRGFD NG2 .... 66 B1 🔟
Ullswater Crs *BSTN/STPLFD* NG9 .. 48 A8
Ullswater Dr *DERBYE* DE21 .... 59 J1
   HUCK/RAV NG15.................. 15 K8
   LEIS LE2 .... 139 G2
Ullswater St *LEIS* LE2 .... 6 C9
Ulvers Cft *COAL* LE67 .... 116 C6

Ulverscroft Dr *GBY/RBY* LE6 ...... 123 K5 🔟
Ulverscroft La *COAL* LE67 .... 116 E2
Ulverscroft Rd *LBORO* LE11 .... 103 J7
Una Av *LEIW* LE3 .... 130 F3
Underhill Av *NORM/LIT* DE23 ...... 57 K8
Underhill Cl *NORM/LIT* DE23 ...... 71 J1
Underwood Crs
   RLEIW/BAR LE9 .... 140 C7
Underwood Dr *RLEIW/BAR* LE9 ... 140 B6
Unicorn St *LEIN* LE4 .... 120 B7
Union Cl *HUCK/RAV* NG15 .... 15 L5
Union Rd *ILK* DE7 .... 33 J8
   MAPPK/POR/STA NG3 .... 5 J5
   NOTT NG1 .... 5 J5
Union St *BSTN/STPLFD* NG9 .... 63 K1
   LBORO LE11 .... 9 G3 🔟
   LGEAT NG10 .... 62 C7
   MELB/CHEL DE73 .... 82 E8
Unitt Rd *RLBORO* LE12 .... 112 F3
Unity Crs *MAPPK/POR/STA* NG3 ... 38 A5
Unity Rd *LEIW* LE3 .... 124 A7
University Bvd
   BSTN/STPLFD NG9 .... 49 M7 🔟
   NOTTE 50 A7
University Cl *RLEINE/SYS* LE7 .... 120 F4
University Rd *LBORO* LE11 .... 8 A6
   LEIE LE1 .... 131 L4
Upex Cl *RLEIW/BAR* LE9 .... 142 D3
Upland Dr *COAL* LE67 .... 116 B6
Uplands Av *NORM/LIT* DE23 ...... 71 G1
Uplands Gdns *NORM/LIT* DE23 .... 2 B9
Uplands Rd *LEIS* LE2 .... 137 K2
Upminster Dr *ARN* NG5 .... 25 K6
Upper Bainbridge St
   NORM/LIT DE23 .... 2 D9
Upper Barn Cl *HEANOR* DE75 .... 20 D5 🔟
Upper Boundary Rd
   DERBYW DE22 .... 2 A5
Upper Brown St *LEI* LE1 .... 6 E7
Upper Canaan *CFTN/RUD* NG11 ... 65 H7
Upper Charnwood St *LEIS* LE2 .... 7 K5
Upper Church St
   RLEINE/SYS LE7 .... 120 F3
Upper College St *NOTT* NG1 .... 4 E6
Upper Dale Rd *NORM/LIT* DE23 ... 57 K6
Upper Dunstead Rd
   EWD/SEL/PNX NG16 .... 20 F3
Upper Eldon St *WBRGFD* NG2...... 5 M7
Upper George St *LEI* LE1 .... 7 G3 🔟
Upper Gn *LBORO* LE11 .... 103 H7
Upper Hall Cl *BPR/DUF* DE56 ..... 30 A1
Upper Hollow *NORM/LIT* DE23 .... 57 G6
Upper King St *LEI* LE1 .... 6 F9
Upper Marehay Rd *RIPLEY* DE5 ... 19 G1
Upper Moor Rd *DERBYSE* DE24 ... 72 C1
Upper Nelson St *HEANOR* DE75 ... 20 B5
Upper New Wk *LEI* LE1 .... 7 J9
Upper Orchard St
   BSTN/STPLFD NG9 .... 48 C8 🔟
Upper Parliament St *NOTT* NG1 .... 4 F6
Upper Tichborne St *LEIS* LE2 .... 7 K8
Upperton Ri *LEIW* LE3 .... 131 H4
Upperton Rd *LEIW* LE3 .... 131 H4
Upper Wellington St
   LGEAT NG10 .... 62 A6
Uppingham Cl *LEIE* LE5 .... 133 G2
Uppingham Crs *WBRGFD* NG2 ..... 65 H2
Uppingham Dr *RLEINE/BAR* LE9 .. 141 H7
Uppingham Gdns *WBRGFD* NG2 ... 51 H5
Uppingham La *LEIE* LE5 .... 126 B8
Uppingham Rd *LEIE* LE5 .... 133 K2
Upton Cl *HEANOR* DE75 .... 20 E6 🔟
Upton Dr *ARN* NG5 .... 37 H2 🔟
   WGSTN LE18 .... 138 D5
Utah Cl *LEIN* LE4 .... 124 A8
   RDERBYSW DE65 .... 68 C5 🔟
Utile Gdns *BLWL* NG6 .... 23 L8 🔟
Uttoxeter Cl *LEIN* LE4 .... 126 B2
Uttoxeter New Rd
   DERBYW DE22 .... 57 G4
Uttoxeter Old Rd *DERBY* DE1 ..... 57 H3
Uttoxeter Rd *MCKLVR* DE3 .... 56 C6 🔟
   MCKLVR DE3 .... 56 C5 🔟
Uxbridge Rd *LEIN* LE4 .... 126 A3

V

Vale Cl *EWD/SEL/PNX* NG16 .... 21 M5
   LEIE LE5 .... 127 G8
Vale Crs North
   WOL/BIL/BRX NG8................ 50 B1
Vale Crs South
   WOL/BIL/BRX NG8................ 50 B1
Vale Gdns *CARL* NG4 .... 52 B2
Valence Rd *LEIW* LE3 .... 130 F3
Valentine Dr *LEIS* LE2 .... 138 D1 🔟
Valentine Rd *LEIN* LE4 .... 133 H2
Valerie Rd *BWSH/BRSTN* DE72 ... 73 K8
Vale Rd *CARL* NG4 .... 52 C2
Valeside Gdns *CARL* NG4 .... 52 C2
The Vale *ILK* DE7 .... 33 M8
Valetta Rd *ARN* NG5 .... 25 M8
Valiant Cl *LEIN* LE4 .... 124 A8
Valjean Crs *LEIW* LE3 .... 129 J5
Valley Dr *EWD/SEL/PNX* NG16 .... 21 M6
   LEIW LE3 .... 130 A5
Valley Gdns *WBRGFD* NG2 .... 65 M2
Valley Rd *ARN* NG5 .... 37 G3
   BSTN/STPLFD NG9 .... 62 E2
   CARL NG4 .... 37 M6
   COAL LE67 .... 116 C1
   COT/KEY/RAD NG12 .... 53 L2
   COT/KEY/RAD NG12 .... 65 L3
   DERBYE DE21 .... 58 F1
   EWD/SEL/PNX NG16 .... 22 B8
   ILK DE7 .... 47 J2
   LBORO LE11 .... 103 J7
   LEIN LE4 .... 126 F3
   NORM/LIT DE23 .... 57 H6
Valley Vw *BPR/DUF* DE56 .... 17 L5
   ILK DE7 .... 47 J2
Valley View Dr *ILK* DE7 .... 31 L6
Valley View Rd *ALFN* DE55 .... 12 A3
Valley Wy *COAL* LE67 .... 108 B2
Valmont Rd *ARN* NG5................ 36 E4

   BSTN/STPLFD NG9 .... 48 E7
Vancouver Av
   COT/KEY/RAD NG12 .... 53 J4
   DERBYE DE21 .... 59 H4
Vancouver Rd *LEIS* LE2 .... 7 H2
Vandyke Rd *LEIS* LE2 .... 138 F3
Vanguard Rd *LGEAT* NG10 ..... 76 B3 🔟
Varden Av *BSTN/STPLFD* NG9 .... 49 L6
Varley St *DERBYE* DE24 .... 58 B8
Varney Rd *CFTN/RUD* NG11 .... 64 D4
Vaughan Rd *BSTN/STPLFD* NG9 .. 62 E3
   LEIS LE2 .... 131 J8
Vaughan St *COAL* LE67 .... 108 A7
   LEIW LE3 .... 6 A5
Vaughan Wy *LEI* LE1 .... 6 D5
Vauxhall St *NOTTE* NG7 .... 42 E8
Vedonis Pk *HUCK/RAV* NG15 ...... 23 J2
Ventnor Ri *ARN* NG5 .... 36 D3
Ventnor Rd South *LEIS* LE2 .... 138 B1 🔟
Ventnor St *LEIE* LE5 .... 132 B2
Venus Cl *BLWL* NG6 .... 36 C2 🔟
Verbena Cl *MAPPK/POR/STA* NG3 ... 5 J1
Verbena Dr *NORM/LIT* DE23 ...... 71 H3
Vercor Cl *COAL* LE67 .... 109 H6
Verdale Av *LEIN* LE4 .... 126 D2
Verder Gv *ARN* NG5 .... 24 C7
Verdon Crs *COAL* LE67 .... 108 F6
Vere St *BLWL* NG6 .... 35 M1 🔟
Vermont Dr *DERBYE* DE21 .... 59 G1 🔟
Verne Cl *CARL* NG4 .... 38 A8
Vernon Av *BLWL* NG6 .... 36 C4
   BSTN/STPLFD NG9 .... 63 K1 🔟
   CARL NG4 .... 38 D7
   CFTN/RUD NG11 .... 50 F7
Vernon Ct
   EWD/SEL/PNX NG16 .... 35 K4 🔟
Vernon Dr *DERBYE* DE21 .... 59 K3 🔟
   EWD/SEL/PNX NG16 .... 35 K4
Vernon Park Dr *BLWL* NG6 .... 36 C4
Vernon Rd *BLWL* NG6 .... 36 C4
   LEIS LE2 .... 131 J8
Vernon St *DERBY* DE1 .... 2 B3
   ILK DE7 .... 33 K3
   LEIW LE3 .... 6 A4
   NOTT NG1 .... 4 E6 2
Verona Av *CARL* NG4 .... 52 D1
Veronica Dr *CARL* NG4 .... 38 B6
   EWD/SEL/PNX NG16 .... 22 A7 🔟
Vestry Rd *DERBYE* DE21 .... 44 C5
Vestry St *LEI* LE1 .... 7 H8
Vetch Cl *RLEINE/BAR* LE9 .... 135 K7 🔟
Vetchfield Cl *DERBYSE* DE24 ... 71 K5 🔟
Vicarage Av *ILK* DE7 .... 33 H3
   NORM/LIT DE23 .... 2 B9
Vicarage Cl *ARN* NG5 .... 36 D4
   BPR/DUF DE56 .... 17 L3 🔟
   GBY/RBY LE6 .... 123 J8
   GBY/RBY LE6 .... 129 J1
   ILK DE7 .... 31 K1
   MAPPK/POR/STA NG3 .... 5 C3 🔟
   RLEINE/SYS LE7 .... 120 E3
Vicarage Ct *MCKLVR* DE3 ...... 56 B6 🔟
Vicarage Dr *CALV/BJ* NG14 .... 39 J3
   DERBYE DE21 .... 44 E8
Vicarage Gdns *HEANOR* DE75 .... 20 D6
Vicarage Gn
   COT/KEY/RAD NG12 .... 65 M4 🔟
Vicarage La *BPR/DUF* DE56 .... 29 J3
   CFTN/RUD NG11 .... 64 F7
   COT/KEY/RAD NG12 .... 53 K4
   DERBYE DE21 .... 29 M7
   EWD/SEL/PNX NG16 .... 12 D3
   LEIE LE5 .... 126 F7
   LEIN LE4 .... 125 L4
   RLBORO LE12 .... 100 F1 🔟
   RLEINE/SYS LE7 .... 121 H7
   RLEIW/BBY LE8 .... 136 D7
Vicarage Ms *ALFN* DE55 .... 12 C1
Vicarage Rd *BPR/DUF* DE56 .... 17 K7
   MCKLVR DE3 .... 56 A5
   MELB/CHEL DE73.................. 72 D5
Vicarage St *BSTN/STPLFD* NG9 ... 63 J1
   COAL LE67 .... 108 D2
   ILK DE7 .... 33 H3
Vicarwood Av *BPR/DUF* DE56 ... 18 A8 🔟
   DERBYW DE22 .... 43 K6
Vicary La *RLBORO* LE12 .... 112 A4
Vickers St
   MAPPK/POR/STA NG3 .... 37 H7 🔟
Victor Av *DERBYW* DE22 .... 43 K7
Victor Crs *LGEAT* NG10 .... 62 A3
Victoria Av *BWSH/BRSTN* DE72 ... 59 M5
   BWSH/BRSTN DE72 .... 60 E8 🔟
   LEIS LE2 .... 7 J8 🔟
   WBRGFD NG2 .... 51 K3 🔟
Victoria Cl *ARN* NG5 .... 25 K5
   COAL LE67 .... 108 B2
   MCKLVR DE3 .... 56 C3
Victoria Crs *ARN* NG5 .... 37 H5
   EWD/SEL/PNX NG16 .... 12 D3
Victoria Dr *GBY/RBY* LE6 .... 123 K5
Victoria Emb *WBRGFD* NG2 .... 51 G6
Victoria Gdns *LEIS* LE2 .... 132 A4
Victoria Park Wy *CARL* NG4 .... 52 F1
Victoria Pas *LEI* LE1 .... 36 F4
Victoria Rd *ARN* NG5 .... 36 F4
   BWSH/BRSTN DE72 .... 60 E8
   CARL NG4 .... 38 E8
   CFTN/RUD NG11 .... 79 J6
   COAL LE67 .... 108 B6
   EWD/SEL/PNX NG16 .... 13 K1
   LGEAT NG10 .... 61 M2
   RIPLEY DE5 .... 11 G5
   RLBORO LE12 .... 111 K7
   RLEIW/BBY LE8 .... 136 D7
   WBRGFD NG2 .... 51 J8
Victoria Rd East *LEIE* LE5 .... 126 C7
Victoria Rd North *LEIN* LE4 .... 125 L4
Victoria St *BSTN/STPLFD* NG9 .... 48 B8 🔟
   CARL NG4 .... 38 D6
   CDON/KEG DE74 .... 84 C7
   COT/KEY/RAD NG12 .... 53 K4
   DERBY DE1 .... 2 E4
   EWD/SEL/PNX NG16 .... 13 D3
   EWD/SEL/PNX NG16 .... 21 K4

   EWD/SEL/PNX NG16 .... 21 G4
   EWD/SEL/PNX NG16 .... 34 E1
   HUCK/RAV NG15 .... 15 K7
   ILK DE7 .... 33 K4
   LBORO LE11 .... 9 J5
   LEIN LE4 .... 120 C7
   LGEAT NG10 .... 75 M2
   MELB/CHEL DE73................. 82 E8
   NOTT NG1 .... 5 H7
   RIPLEY DE5 .... 11 K5
   RLBORO LE12 .... 112 F1
   RLEINE/SYS LE7 .... 120 F4
   RLEIW/BAR LE9 .... 136 A8
   RLEIW/BBY LE8 .... 145 K8
   WGSTN LE18 .... 138 B4
Victor Rd *LEIW* LE3 .... 124 B7
Victors Cl *LEIS* LE2 .... 137 G3
Victory Av *RIPLEY* DE5 .... 11 K6
Victory Cl *LGEAT* NG10 .... 76 B2
Victory Rd *BSTN/STPLFD* NG9 .... 63 L3
   DERBYSE 57 M8
Viking Rd *WGSTN* LE18 .... 137 L3
Village Cl *COT/KEY/RAD* NG12 ... 65 M4
Village Farm Cl *RLBORO* LE12 .... 87 K6
Village Rd *CFTN/RUD* NG11 .... 64 B5 🔟
Village St *COT/KEY/RAD* NG12 ... 65 L4
   DERBYSE 57 K7
The Village *ILK* DE7 .... 32 C8
   ILK DE7 .... 46 D5
Villa Rd *COT/KEY/RAD* NG12 ...... 80 D3
   MAPPK/POR/STA NG3 .... 5 G2
Villa St *BSTN/STPLFD* NG9 .... 49 K8
   BWSH/BRSTN DE72 .... 60 F8
Villiers Rd *ARN* NG5 .... 37 H3
   WBRGFD NG2 .... 65 L1
Vincent Av *BSTN/STPLFD* NG9 ... 63 K2 🔟
   DERBYE DE21 .... 59 J4
   ILK DE7 .... 33 K7
Vincent Cl *BPR/DUF* DE56 ...... 18 E7 🔟
   LEIS LE2 .... 130 F1
Vincent St *NORM/LIT* DE23 .... 57 K6
   LEIW LE3 .... 56 F8
Vine Crs *LGEAT* NG10 .... 61 M1
Vine Farm Cl
   COT/KEY/RAD NG12 .... 67 J4
   ILK DE7 .... 47 H1
Vinehouse Cl *RLEINE/SYS* LE7 .. 118 F4
The Vineries *RLEIW/BBY* LE8 .... 143 H4 🔟
Vines Cross *WOL/BIL/BRX* NG8 .. 49 J5 🔟
Vine St *LEI* LE1 .... 6 E7
Vine Ter *HUCK/RAV* NG15 .... 15 M8
Vine Tree Ter *RLBORO* LE12 ...... 97 G5
Viola Cl *DERBYE* DE21 .... 45 G4
Violet Av *EWD/SEL/PNX* NG16 .... 21 M6
Violet Cl *BLWL* NG6 .... 36 B4 🔟
Violet Rd *CARL* NG4 .... 38 B6
   WBRGFD NG2 .... 51 L7
Violet St *NORM/LIT* DE23 .... 57 K6
Viscount Rd *CDON/KEG* DE74 ..... 84 F8
Vivian Av *NOTTE* NG7 .... 36 F7
Vivian St *DERBYE* DE21 .... 43 M7
Vostock Cl *LEIS* LE2 .... 7 K6
Vulcan Cl *BLWL* NG6 .... 36 C3
Vulcan Rd *LEIE* LE5 .... 7 K3
   LEIE 7 L4
Vulcan St *NORM/LIT* DE23 .... 57 M6 🔟
Vulcan Wy *COAL* LE67 .... 108 B5
Vyse Dr *LGEAT* NG10 .... 76 A1

W

Waddington Dr *WBRGFD* NG2 ..... 65 H3
Wade Av *ILK* DE7 .... 33 L8
   NORM/LIT DE23 .... 57 G5
Wadebridge Gv
   DERBYSE DE24 .... 73 G2 🔟
Wade Dr *MCKLVR* DE3 .... 56 C5
Wade St *LEIN* LE4 .... 125 K4 🔟
   NORM/LIT DE23 .... 57 G6
Wadham Rd *ARN* NG5 .... 37 J2
Wadhurst Gdns
   MAPPK/POR/STA NG3 .... 5 K4
Wadhurst Gv
   WOL/BIL/BRX NG8................ 49 H5 🔟
Wadkins Wy *RLEINE/SYS* LE7 ... 133 L2
Wadsworth Rd
   BSTN/STPLFD NG9 .... 48 D7
Wagstaff La
   EWD/SEL/PNX NG16 .... 12 F3
Wagtail Cl *DERBYSE* DE24 .... 71 H3
Wain Br *RLEIW/BBY* LE8 .... 145 H2
Wain Dr *LBORO* LE11 .... 95 G8
Wainfleet Cl *ILK* DE7 .... 33 G4
Waingrove *CFTN/RUD* NG11 .... 64 E4
Waingroves Rd *RIPLEY* DE5 .... 11 L7
   RIPLEY DE5 .... 19 M1
Wakami Crs *MELB/CHEL* DE73 .... 72 E5
Wakefield Av
   COT/KEY/RAD NG12 .... 53 L3
Wakefield Cft *ILK* DE7 .... 33 G4
Wakefield Pl *LEIN* LE4 .... 126 A5 🔟
Wakeley Cl *RLEIW/BAR* LE9 ..... 135 L8 🔟
Wakelin Cl *BWSH/BRSTN* DE72 .. 74 D6
Wakerley Rd *LEIE* LE5 .... 132 D3
Wakes St *WGSTN* LE18 .... 138 B4
Walbrook Cl *WOL/BIL/BRX* NG8 .. 35 L4
Walbrook Rd *NORM/LIT* DE23 ..... 57 K6
Walcote Cl *BPR/DUF* DE56 .... 18 A2
Walcote Dr *WBRGFD* NG2 .... 65 G4
Walcote Rd *LEIN* LE4 .... 126 C5
Waldale Dr *LEIS* LE2 .... 132 A5
Waldeck Rd *ARN* NG5 .... 36 F6
Waldemar Gv
   BSTN/STPLFD NG9 .... 63 L1 🔟
Waldorf Av *DERBYSE* DE24 .... 58 E8
Waldron Dr *LEIS* LE2 .... 139 G2
Wale Rd *RLEIW/BBY* LE8 .... 136 D8
Walesby Crs *WOL/BIL/BRX* NG8 .. 50 A1
Walgrave Wk *ARN* NG5 .... 24 F8 🔟
Walk Cl *BWSH/BRSTN* DE72 .... 60 E8
Walker Av *RIPLEY* DE5 .... 11 J5
Walker Cl *ILK* DE7 .... 47 K3
Walker Gv *BSTN/STPLFD* NG9 .... 62 C1 🔟

Walker La *DERBY* DE1 .... 2 D2
Walker Rd *LEIN* LE4 .... 125 K1
Walkers La *RLEINE/SYS* LE7 .... 119 J2
Walker St *EWD/SEL/PNX* NG16 ...... 21 L5
 WBRGFD NG2 .... 5 L6
Walkers Wy *RLEINE/SYS* LE7 .... 120 F3
Walker's Yd *COT/KEY/RAD* NG12 .. 53 K4
Walk Mill Dr *HUCK/RAV* NG15 ... 15 M6
The Walk *BPR/DUF* DE56 .... 18 F7
Wallace Av *CARL* NG4 .... 38 D8
Wallace Dr *GBY/RBY* LE6 ...... 123 G2
 RLBORO LE12 .... 114 A6
Wallace Gdns
 BSTN/STPLFD NG9 .... 62 D6
Wallace Rd *LBORO* LE11 .... 9 G6
Wallace St *CFTN/RUD* NG11 .... 77 M5
 DERBY DE22 .... 57 C2
Wallan St *NOTTE* NG7 .... 50 C1
Wallet St *CARL* NG4 .... 38 E8
Wallett Av *BSTN/STPLFD* NG9 .. 49 K7
Wallett St *WBRGFD* NG2 .... 51 H5
Wallfields Cl *RDERBYSW* DE65 . 70 B4
Wallingford Rd *LEIN* LE4 ..... 125 K5
Wallis Cl *BWSH/BRSTN* DE72 ... 60 E8
 RLEINE/SYS LE7 .... 118 F4
Wallis St *BLWL* NG6 .... 36 C3
Wall St *RIPLEY* DE5 .... 11 H5
Walnut Av *DERBYSE* DE24 ...... 58 F8
 LEIN LE4 .... 119 K7
Walnut Cl *BWSH/BRSTN* DE72 ... 73 M7
 COAL LE67 .... 116 B7
 ILK DE7 .... 33 L8
 LEIS LE2 .... 138 E2
 MELB/CHEL DE73 .... 72 E7
 RDERBYSW DE65 .... 69 K2
Walnut Dr *BSTN/STPLFD* NG9 ... 48 F7
Walnut Gv *COT/KEY/RAD* NG12 .. 53 K4
 LEIS LE2 .... 136 F3
Walnut Leys *RLEINE/BAR* LE9 .. 142 B5
Walnut Rd *BPR/DUF* DE56 ...... 17 M4
 LBORO LE11 .... 103 L7
Walnut St *DERBYSE* DE24 ...... 58 A8
 LEIS LE2 .... 131 J4
Walnut Tree Gdns *BLWL* NG6 ... 23 K8
Walnut Wy *RLEIW/BBY* LE8 ..... 142 F1
Walpole Ct *LEIW* LE3 .... 130 D2
Walpole St *DERBYE* DE21 ...... 3 M1
Walsgrave Av *LEIE* LE5 .... 133 H2
Walsham Cl *BSTN/STPLFD* NG9 .. 62 F5
Walsham Ct *DERBYE* DE21 ...... 44 A7
Walshe Rd *LEIE* LE5 .... 132 F1
Walsingham Crs *LEIW* LE3 ..... 129 M4
Walsingham Rd *ARN* NG5 .... 37 L2
Walters Av
 EWD/SEL/PNX NG16 .... 21 J1
Walters Crs *EWD/SEL/PNX* NG16 .. 13 H1
Walter St *BWSH/BRSTN* DE72 ... 60 D8
 DERBY DE1 .... 43 J8
 NOTTE NG7 .... 4 D4
Waltham Av *DERBYSE* DE24 ..... 71 K3
 LEIW LE3 .... 130 E1
Waltham Cl *WBRGFD* NG2 .... 65 M1
Walthamstow Dr *DERBYW* DE22 .. 56 F1
Walton Av *MAPPK/POR/STA* NG3 . 51 K2
Walton Cl *RLEIW/BAR* LE9 ..... 129 K3
Walton Cl *ILK* DE7 .... 32 B7
Walton Dr *COT/KEY/RAD* NG12 .. 80 D4
 NORM/LIT DE23 .... 57 J8
 CDON/KEG DE74 .... 84 B8
Walton La *LBORO* LE12 .... 105 H3
Walton Rd *ARN* NG5 .... 25 L6
 DERBYE DE21 .... 58 D2
Walton St *LGEAT* NG10 .... 62 B6
Walton Wy *RLBORO* LE12 .... 113 H7
Wand St *LEIN* LE4 .... 125 L6
Wanlip Av *LEIN* LE4 .... 119 L8
Wanlip La *LEIN* LE4 .... 119 M8
 RLEINE/SYS LE7 .... 119 M5
Wanlip Rd *RLEINE/SYS* LE7 .... 120 B4
Wanlip St *LEI* LE1 .... 7 G2
Wansbeck Cl *NOTTE* NG7 .... 4 C5
Wansbeck Gdns *LEIE* LE5 ...... 127 C3
Wansfell Cl *MCKLVR* DE3 ...... 56 C6
Wanstead Rd *LEIW* LE3 .... 129 L2
Wanstead Wy *ARN* NG5 .... 24 C6
Ward Av *HUCK/RAV* NG15 .... 15 K6
 MAPPK/POR/STA NG3 .... 37 M4
Ward Cl *LEIS* LE2 .... 131 G8
Wardens Wk *LEIW* LE3 .... 129 M4
Wardle Gv *ARN* NG5 .... 25 L7
Wardlow Av *DERBYE* DE21 ...... 44 E7
Wardlow Rd *ILK* DE7 .... 33 H4
Wards Closes *WGSTN* LE18 ..... 138 C7
Ward's Crs *RLBORO* LE12 ...... 114 B4
Ward's End *LBORO* LE11 .... 9 J4
Ward's La *BWSH/BRSTN* DE72 ... 61 H7
 MELB/CHEL DE73 .... 82 D5
Ward St *DERBYW* DE22 .... 2 B5
 NOTTE NG7 .... 36 C7
Wardswood Cl
 BWSH/BRSTN DE72 .... 60 B6
Wardwick *DERBY* DE1 .... 2 C3
Wareham Cl *WBRGFD* NG2 .... 65 G2
 WOL/BIL/BRX NG8 .... 35 L4
Wareham Rd *RLEINE/BBY* LE8 ... 142 F1
Warkton Cl *BSTN/STPLFD* NG9 .. 63 G2
Warmsley Av *WGSTN* LE18 ...... 138 A3
Warner Cl *RLEIW/BBY* LE8 ..... 142 E2
Warner Pl *LBORO* LE11 .... 9 M3
Warners La *LBORO* LE11 .... 9 J2
Warner St *DERBYW* DE22 .... 2 C8
 MCKLVR DE3 .... 56 B6
 RLBORO LE12 .... 105 H8
Warren Av *ARN* NG5 .... 36 E5
 BSTN/STPLFD NG9 .... 48 B8
 LEIN LE4 .... 126 E2
Warren Avenue Extension
 BSTN/STPLFD NG9 .... 48 B8
Warren Cl *COAL* LE67 .... 116 C7
 LEIE LE5 .... 126 E2
Warren Ct *BSTN/STPLFD* NG9 ... 48 B8
Warrender Cl *BSTN/STPLFD* NG9 .. 49 G6
Warren Dr *LEIN* LE4 .... 126 E2
Warrener Gv *ARN* NG5 .... 24 C7

Warren Hl *GBY/RBY* LE6 .... 117 K2
Warren Hills Rd *COAL* LE67 ... 109 H5
Warren La *CDON/KEG* DE74 ..... 75 M7
 COAL LE67 .... 100 D8
 LEIN LE4 .... 129 J5
Warren Park Wy
 RLEIW/BAR LE9 .... 135 L2
Warren Rd *HUCK/RAV* NG15 ..... 23 H2
 RLEIW/BAR LE9 .... 136 B6
Warren St *DERBYSE* DE24 ...... 58 D7
 LEIE LE5 .... 6 A5
The Warren
 COT/KEY/RAD NG12 .... 67 K5
 RLEINE/SYS LE7 .... 115 G8
Warren Vw *LEIN* LE4 .... 126 E2
Warrington Dr *GBY/RBY* LE6 ... 123 J5
Warrington Rd *BLWL* NG6 ...... 24 A8
Warser Ga *NOTT* NG1 .... 5 J7
Warton Av
 MAPPK/POR/STA NG3 .... 37 K7
Warwick Av *ARN* NG5 .... 37 J2
 BSTN/STPLFD NG9 .... 49 K7
 NORM/LIT DE23 .... 57 H6
 RLBORO LE12 .... 112 C1
Warwick Dr *ILK* DE7 .... 33 G4
Warwick Gdns *BPR/DUF* DE56 ... 18 B2
 COT/KEY/RAD NG12 .... 67 K6
Warwick Rd *LGEAT* NG10 .... 62 D8
 MAPPK/POR/STA NG3 .... 37 H5
 RLEIW/BAR LE9 .... 141 H7
 RLEIW/BAR LE9 .... 142 B1
 RLEIW/BBY LE8 .... 146 B7
 WGSTN LE18 .... 137 M4
Warwick St *DERBYSE* DE24 ..... 58 B5
 LEIE LE5 .... 6 A5
 NOTTE NG7 .... 50 C5
Warwick Wy *LBORO* LE11 .... 103 H2
Wasdale Cl *WBRGFD* NG2 .... 66 A2
Wash Br *CALV/BJ* NG14 .... 27 L3
Washdyke La *HUCK/RAV* NG15 ... 15 J7
Washford Rd *RDERBYSW* DE65 ... 68 F5
Washington Av *DERBYE* DE21 ... 58 F1
Washington Cl *MELB/CHEL* DE73 .. 82 E8
Washington Dr
 BSTN/STPLFD NG9 .... 48 D6
Wasnidge Cl
 MAPPK/POR/STA NG3 .... 5 K5
Watchcrete Av
 RLEINE/SYS LE7 .... 121 H2
Watcombe Circ *ARN* NG5 .... 36 F5
Watcombe Rd *ARN* NG5 .... 37 G6
Watendlath Cl *WBRGFD* NG2 .... 66 A2
Waterfield Cl *LEIS* LE2 ...... 132 F2
Waterfield Rd *RLEINE/SYS* LE7 .. 118 D5
Waterford Dr *DERBYE* DE21 .... 58 E3
Waterford St *BLWL* NG6 .... 36 C4
Watergate *RLEINE/SYS* LE7 .... 115 J8
Watergate La *RLEIW/BAR* LE9 .. 130 B8
Watergo La *MCKLVR* DE3 .... 56 A8
Waterhouse La *CARL* NG4 ...... 38 E5
Watering La *BPR/DUF* DE56 .... 30 B1
Water La *COT/KEY/RAD* NG12 ... 53 J5
 RLBORO LE12 .... 106 D7
Waterloo Cl *DERBY* DE1 .... 43 M8
Waterloo Crs *RLEINE/SYS* LE7 . 143 H4
 WGSTN LE18 .... 138 C3
Waterloo La *BSTN/STPLFD* NG9 . 48 C1
Waterloo Prom *NOTTE* NG7 ..... 4 C4
Waterloo Rd *BSTN/STPLFD* NG9 . 63 L2
 HUCK/RAV NG15 .... 15 L5
 NOTTE NG7 .... 4 C3
Waterloo Spinney La
 RLBORO LE12 .... 111 M3
Watermeadow Rd
 DERBYSE DE24 .... 72 E2
The Watermeadows
 LGEAT NG10 .... 61 M7
Watermead Wy *LEIN* LE4 .... 125 M3
Water Orton Cl
 BSTN/STPLFD NG9 .... 62 C4
Waterside *EWD/SEL/PNX* NG16 .. 12 D3
Waterside Cl *DERBYW* DE22 .... 43 L5
 LBORO LE11 .... 103 M2
 LGEAT NG10 .... 61 M4
 RLBORO LE12 .... 66 A1
Waterside Gdns *NOTTE* NG7 .... 50 C6
Waterside Rd *LEIN* LE4 .... 126 E3
Waterway St *WBRGFD* NG2 ...... 51 H5
Waterway St West
 WBRGFD NG2 .... 51 G5
The Waterway *LGEAT* NG10 ..... 62 A3
Waterworks Rd *COAL* LE67 ..... 108 E8
Watery Gate La *RLEIW/BAR* LE9 .. 134 C7
Watery La *ASHB* DE6 .... 38 B8
Watford Rd *WOL/BIL/BRX* NG8 .. 35 M5
Watkinson St *HEANOR* DE75 .... 20 B5
Watkin St *MAPPK/POR/STA* NG3 . 5 H4
Watling St *LEI* LE1 .... 6 E2
 RLBORO LE12 .... 113 J5
Watnall Rd *EWD/SEL/PNX* NG16 . 15 G1
 HUCK/RAV NG15 .... 23 J4
Watson Av *HEANOR* DE75 .... 20 D5
 MAPPK/POR/STA NG3 .... 51 M1
Watson Rd *ILK* DE7 .... 33 G5
 LEIN LE4 .... 126 A5
Watson St *DERBY* DE1 .... 2 B1
 DERBYW DE22 .... 43 J8
Watten Cl *DERBYSE* DE24 ...... 71 K5
Watts Cl *LEIN* LE4 .... 126 A5
Waughs Dr *RLBORO* LE12 .... 113 H7
Waveney Cl *ARN* NG5 .... 37 L1
 DERBYW DE22 .... 43 M2
Waveney Ri *LEIS* LE2 .... 139 H1
Waverley Av *BSTN/STPLFD* NG9 . 63 L1
 CARL NG4 .... 38 E6
Waverley Cl *LBORO* LE11 ...... 102 F2
Waverley Rd *RLEIW/BBY* LE8 ... 143 G1
 WGSTN LE18 .... 137 K5
Waverley St *DERBYSE* DE24 .... 58 A8
 LGEAT NG10 .... 61 M6
 NOTTE NG7 .... 4 D3
Waverley Ter *NOTT* NG1 .... 4 F5
Wavertree Cl *RLEIW/BAR* LE9 .. 142 B3
Wavertree Dr *LEIN* LE4 .... 125 M4
Wayfarer Dr *RLEINE/SYS* LE7 .. 115 J7

Wayfaring Rd *DERBYSE* DE21 ... 44 E6
Wayne Cl *CFTN/RUD* NG11 ...... 64 C6
The Wayne Wy *LEIE* LE5 .... 132 D1
 LEIN LE4 .... 119 L8
Wayside Dr *LEIN* LE4 .... 126 B1
 LEIS LE2 .... 139 G2
Wayzgoose Dr *DERBYSE* DE21 ... 3 K3
Weardale Av *ARN* NG5 .... 36 E5
Weaver Cl *LBORO* LE11 .... 9 K9
Weaver Rd *LEIE* LE5 .... 127 H8
Weavers Cl *BPR/DUF* DE56 ..... 18 A1
 BWSH/BRSTN DE72 .... 60 B6
 RLBORO LE12 .... 88 D4
Weaver's La
 EWD/SEL/PNX NG16 .... 14 D4
 HUCK/RAV NG15 .... 14 D2
Weaverthorpe Rd *ARN* NG5 ..... 37 L2
Webb Cl *LEIS* LE2 .... 129 M5
Webb Rd *WOL/BIL/BRX* NG8 ..... 49 M1
Webb St *HUCK/RAV* NG15 .... 15 J1
Webbs Wy *RLEINE/BAR* LE9 ..... 140 B5
Webster Av
 EWD/SEL/PNX NG16 .... 21 K6
Webster Rd *LEIN* LE4 .... 130 C3
Webster St *DERBY* DE1 .... 2 D6
Weedon Cl
 MAPPK/POR/STA NG3 .... 51 L1
Weekday Cross *NOTT* NG1 ...... 5 J8
Weightman Dr
 EWD/SEL/PNX NG16 .... 21 M8
Weirfield Rd *DERBYW* DE22 .... 43 L5
Weir Rd *RLEINE/BBY* LE8 ...... 146 E8
Welbeck Av *CARL* NG4 .... 38 B5
 ILK DE7 .... 47 H2
 LEIN LE4 .... 125 J5
Welbeck Cl *MAPPK/POR/STA* NG3 .. 5 G3
 RLEIW/BBY LE8 .... 143 G1
Welbeck Gdns
 BSTN/STPLFD NG9 .... 62 D4
Welbeck Gv *DERBYW* DE22 ...... 43 H4
Welbeck Rd *COT/KEY/RAD* NG12 . 53 L3
 LGEAT NG10 .... 61 M4
 WBRGFD NG2 .... 51 J7
Welby Av *NOTTE* NG7 .... 4 A8
Welch Av *BSTN/STPLFD* NG9 .... 48 C7
Welcombe Av *LEIW* LE3 .... 130 D6
Weldbank Cl *BSTN/STPLFD* NG9 . 62 F2
Weldon Av *RLBORO* LE12 .... 114 B3
Weldon Rd *LBORO* LE11 .... 95 J8
 WGSTN LE18 .... 138 B4
Welford Ct *LEIS* LE2 .... 131 M8
Welford Pl *LEI* LE1 .... 6 E7
Welford Rd *LEI* LE1 .... 6 F8
 LEIS LE2 .... 131 K5
 RLEIW/BBY LE8 .... 136 F7
 WGSTN LE18 .... 138 A1
 WGSTN LE18 .... 138 B5
Welham Crs *ARN* NG5 .... 25 L8
Welland Cl *MCKLVR* DE3 .... 56 B4
Welland Rd *RDERBYSW* DE65 .... 68 B6
 RLBORO LE12 .... 113 H1
Welland St *LEIS* LE2 .... 7 K8
Welland Vale Rd *LEIE* LE5 .... 133 H3
Wellbrook Av *RLBORO* LE12 .... 114 B4
Welldon St *RIPLEY* DE5 .... 19 L3
Wellesbourne Dr *LEIW* LE3 .... 124 B6
Wellesley Av *NORM/LIT* DE23 .. 57 H8
Wellesley Crs
 WOL/BIL/BRX NG8 .... 35 H5
Welles St *LEI* LE1 .... 6 D6
Wellgate Av *LEIN* LE4 .... 119 K7
Wellhouse Cl *WGSTN* LE18 ..... 138 A7
Wellin Cl *COT/KEY/RAD* NG12 .. 65 M4
Wellinger Wy *LEIW* LE3 .... 130 C3
Wellington Circ *NOTT* NG1 .... 4 E7
Wellington Cl *BPR/DUF* DE56 .. 17 K3
Wellington Crs *WBRGFD* NG2 ... 51 K8
Wellington Pl
 EWD/SEL/PNX NG16 .... 21 K5
Wellington Sq *NOTTE* NG7 ..... 4 C6
Wellington St *BSTN/STPLFD* NG9 .. 62 A1
 DERBY DE1 .... 3 J6
 EWD/SEL/PNX NG16 .... 21 K4
 HEANOR DE75 .... 20 B5
 LBORO LE11 .... 9 K4
 LEI LE1 .... 6 F7
 LGEAT NG10 .... 62 A5
 MAPPK/POR/STA NG3 .... 5 H4
 RIPLEY DE5 .... 11 J6
 RLEINE/SYS LE7 .... 120 E4
Wellington Vls *NOTTE* NG7 .... 4 C6
Wellin La *COT/KEY/RAD* NG12 .. 65 M4
Well La *BPR/DUF* DE56 .... 17 K8
 WGSTN LE18 .... 144 D4
Wellsic La *RLEINE/SYS* LE7 ... 119 J1
Wellspring Dl *BSTN/STPLFD* NG9 .. 62 C2
Well Spring Hl *WGSTN* LE18 ... 138 C1
Wells Rd *MCKLVR* DE3 .... 56 C5
The Wells Rd
 MAPPK/POR/STA NG3 .... 37 K5
Well St *DERBY* DE1 .... 43 L8
 RIPLEY DE5 .... 11 H6
Well Yard Rd *RLBORO* LE12 .... 102 A4
Welney Cl *MCKLVR* DE3 .... 56 B7
Welshpool Rd *DERBYE* DE21 .... 58 D1
Welstead Av *WOL/BIL/BRX* NG8 . 35 L5
Welton Gdns *BLWL* NG6 .... 23 L7
Welwyn Av *DERBYSE* DE24 ...... 72 C3
 DERBYW DE22 .... 43 H4
Welwyn Rd *WOL/BIL/BRX* NG8 ... 49 J2
Wembley Gdns
 BSTN/STPLFD NG9 .... 48 F5
 DERBYW DE22 .... 56 E1
Wembley Rd *ARN* NG5 .... 37 M2
 LEIW LE3 .... 129 M2
Wemyss Gdns
 WOL/BIL/BRX NG8 .... 50 B5
Wendling Gdns *ARN* NG5 .... 24 F5
Wendover Cl *MCKLVR* DE3 ...... 56 A6
Wendover Dr *WOL/BIL/BRX* NG8 . 35 M5
Wendys Cl *LEIE* LE5 .... 127 H8
Wenlock Cl *EWD/SEL/PNX* NG16 . 22 A7
 MCKLVR DE3 .... 56 C6
Wensleydale Cl
 WOL/BIL/BRX NG8 .... 36 B6
Wensleydale Rd *LGEAT* NG10 ... 75 M1

 WGSTN LE18 .... 138 D6
Wensley Dr *DERBYE* DE21 ...... 59 K4
Wensley Ri *LEIS* LE2 .... 137 G5
Wensley Rd *ARN* NG5 .... 37 K3
Wensor Av *RLEINE/SYS* LE7 .... 49 K7
Wentbridge Rd *LEIN* LE4 ...... 126 B4
Went Rd *LEI* LE1 .... 119 J7
Wentworth Cl *MCKLVR* DE3 ..... 56 D6
Wentworth Ct
 EWD/SEL/PNX NG16 .... 34 C1
Wentworth Cft *HEANOR* DE75 ... 20 E4
Wentworth Gn *RLEIW/BAR* LE9 .. 129 H3
Wentworth Rd *ARN* NG5 .... 36 F5
 BSTN/STPLFD NG9 .... 63 G1
 COAL LE67 .... 108 A7
 LEIW LE3 .... 131 C1
 RLEIW/BBY LE8 .... 145 L8
Wentworth St *ILK* DE7 .... 33 L5
Wentworth Wy
 COT/KEY/RAD NG12 .... 65 M4
Werburgh Cl *DERBYW* DE22 ..... 59 H3
Werburgh St *DERBYW* DE22 ..... 2 C5
Wesleyan Chapel Wk
 BSTN/STPLFD NG9 .... 48 B8
Wesley La *GBY/RBY* LE6 .... 123 G7
 RLBORO LE12 .... 94 E6
 RLBORO LE12 .... 102 F1
 RLEIW/BAR LE9 .... 140 C8
Wesley Pl *BSTN/STPLFD* NG9 ... 48 C7
Wesley Rd *DERBYSE* DE24 ...... 72 F2
Wesley St *ARN* NG5 .... 36 F6
 EWD/SEL/PNX NG16 .... 21 G4
 ILK DE7 .... 33 J3
 LEIN LE4 .... 125 K4
Wesley Wy *CFTN/RUD* NG11 ..... 79 H1
 COAL LE67 .... 116 C7
Wessex Dr *LEIW* LE3 .... 130 C2
Wessington Ms *DERBYW* DE22 ... 43 J6
West Av *BSTN/STPLFD* NG9 ..... 48 C7
 BWSH/BRSTN DE72 .... 60 D7
 DERBY DE1 .... 2 C1
 LEIS LE2 .... 131 M5
 LGEAT NG10 .... 61 L1
 MELB/CHEL DE73 .... 72 C4
 RDERBYSW DE65 .... 68 A5
 RIPLEY DE5 .... 11 G6
 WGSTN LE18 .... 137 M4
West Bank Av *DERBYW* DE22 .... 43 K7
West Bank Rd *DERBYW* DE22 .... 43 J7
West Bank Ms *CDON/KEG* DE74 .. 86 A5
West Bank Rd *DERBYW* DE22 .... 43 J2
Westbourne Pk *DERBYW* DE22 ... 56 D1
Westbourne Rd
 EWD/SEL/PNX NG16 .... 13 L5
Westbourne St *LEIN* LE4 ...... 125 L7
Westbridge Cl *LEI* LE1 .... 6 C7
Westbury Cl *BSTN/STPLFD* NG9 . 62 F2
Westbury Dr *DERBYW* DE22 ..... 57 H4
Westbury Gdns *BPR/DUF* DE56 .. 18 A2
Westbury Rd *ARN* NG5 .... 36 D5
 LEIS LE2 .... 131 L6
Westbury St *DERBYW* DE22 ..... 57 H4
Westby La *EWD/SEL/PNX* NG16 .. 34 C3
Westcliffe Av *CARL* NG4 ...... 38 B4
 COT/KEY/RAD NG12 .... 53 L3
West Cl *COT/KEY/RAD* NG12 .... 80 C5
 DERBYW DE22 .... 43 J5
Westcotes Dr *LEIW* LE3 .... 131 G3
West Crs *BSTN/STPLFD* NG9 .... 63 M2
West Croft Av *NORM/LIT* DE23 . 71 H2
Westcross Av *BSTN/STPLFD* NG9 .. 48 C7
West Cross La *RLEINE/SYS* LE7 .. 113 G8
Westdale Cl *LGEAT* NG10 ...... 75 L2
Westdale Ct *CARL* NG4 .... 38 B5
Westdale Crs *CARL* NG4 .... 38 C6
Westdale La East *CARL* NG4 ... 38 A5
Westdale La West
 MAPPK/POR/STA NG3 .... 38 A4
Westdale Rd
 EWD/SEL/PNX NG16 .... 12 F5
Westdene Av *DERBYSE* DE24 .... 72 B2
Westdown Dr *LEIN* LE4 .... 126 C2
West Dr *LEIE* LE5 .... 126 E7
 MCKLVR DE3 .... 56 B5
West End *BSTN/STPLFD* NG9 .... 63 K2
 RLBORO LE12 .... 93 K3
West End Ar *NOTT* NG1 .... 4 F7
West End Crs *ILK* DE7 .... 33 H7
West End Dr *BWSH/BRSTN* DE72 . 74 C4
 ILK DE7 .... 33 H7
West End St *BSTN/STPLFD* NG9 . 62 A1
Westerby Cl *WGSTN* LE18 ...... 138 B3
Westerdale Rd *WGSTN* LE18 .... 138 D5
Westerfield Wy *CFTN/RUD* NG11 .. 64 E3
Westerham Cl
 WOL/BIL/BRX NG8 .... 35 H8
Westerham Rd *CFTN/RUD* NG11 .. 78 F1
Westerhope Cl
 COT/KEY/RAD NG12 .... 66 A3
Westerlands *BSTN/STPLFD* NG9 . 62 D2
Western Bvd *BLWL* NG6 .... 36 C5
 LEIS LE2 .... 6 C9
 WOL/BIL/BRX NG8 .... 36 C5
Western Dr *HEANOR* DE75 ...... 20 D7
 RLEIW/BBY LE8 .... 136 F6
Western Flds *CFTN/RUD* NG11 .. 78 F1
Western Gdns
 WOL/BIL/BRX NG8 .... 36 B7
Westernhay Rd *LEIS* LE2 ...... 132 A6
Western Park Av *LEIW* LE3 .... 130 C2
Western Rd *LEIS* LE2 .... 131 H4
 MCKLVR DE3 .... 56 C5
 NORM/LIT DE23 .... 2 D8
Western St *NOTT* NG1 .... 5 J6
Western Ter *NOTTE* NG7 .... 4 C7
Westfield Av *HEANOR* DE75 .... 20 D7
 RLEIW/BAR LE9 .... 143 H1
 WGSTN LE18 .... 137 M3
Westfield Cl *ILK* DE7 .... 47 G1
 RLEINE/SYS LE7 .... 115 K7
Westfield Dr *ILK* DE7 .... 33 H5
 LBORO LE11 .... 8 E4
Westfield La *RLEINE/SYS* LE7 . 119 G2

Westfield Rd *LEIW* LE3 .... 130 E2
Westfields La *CALV/BJ* NG14 .. 26 E3
West Furlong
 COT/KEY/RAD NG12 .... 67 L6
West Ga *LGEAT* NG10 .... 62 C8
Westgate Av *LEIN* LE4 .... 119 J7
Westgate Rd *LEIS* LE2 .... 137 M1
Westgate St
 MAPPK/POR/STA NG3 .... 5 L3
Westgreen Av *DERBYSE* DE24 ... 72 B2
West Gv *DERBYSE* DE24 .... 72 B2
Westhall Rd *MCKLVR* DE3 ...... 56 B8
Westhay Ct *WOL/BIL/BRX* NG8 .. 50 A2
West Hi *RIPLEY* DE5 .... 11 M8
Westhill Rd *LEIW* LE3 .... 130 E1
Westholme Gdns
 WOL/BIL/BRX NG8 .... 50 A1
West Holme St *LEI* LE1 .... 6 A7
Westhorpe Dr *LGEAT* NG10 ..... 62 A7
Westland Av *HUCK/RAV* NG15 ... 23 H3
West Langton Rd
 RLEIW/BBY LE8 .... 147 J8
West Lawn *RDERBYSW* DE65 ..... 70 A5
West Leake La *CFTN/RUD* NG11 . 77 G7
 RLBORO LE12 .... 87 J4
West Leake Rd *RLBORO* LE12 ... 87 M6
Westleigh Av *DERBYW* DE22 .... 57 G1
 LEIW LE3 .... 131 G4
Westleigh Rd *LEIW* LE3 .... 131 G4
 WGSTN LE18 .... 137 J6
 WOL/BIL/BRX NG8 .... 35 J5
Westley Crs *DERBYE* DE21 ..... 30 B5
Westmeadow La *RLBORO* LE12 ... 93 K4
Westmeath Av *LEIE* LE5 .... 132 F1
Westminster Av *LGEAT* NG10 ... 62 A7
Westminster Cl
 MAPPK/POR/STA NG3 .... 5 M1
Westminster Dr *WGSTN* LE18 ... 137 H6
Westminster Rd *LEIS* LE2 ..... 132 C6
Westminster St
 DERBYSE DE24 .... 58 D7
West Moor *WBRGFD* NG2 .... 52 B2
Westmorland Av *LBORO* LE11 ... 8 B9
 DERBY DE1 .... 43 K8
 LEIS LE2 .... 126 A5
 WGSTN LE18 .... 137 K5
Westmorland Wy
 EWD/SEL/PNX NG16 .... 12 F4
Westoby Cl *RLBORO* LE12 ...... 102 B4
Weston Av *NOTTE* NG7 .... 4 C3
Weston Cl *ARN* NG5 .... 37 J3
 LEIS LE2 .... 139 J3
 RLEINE/SYS LE7 .... 115 K6
Weston Crs *LGEAT* NG10 .... 75 K3
Weston Park Av *DERBYSE* DE24 . 72 B4
Weston Ri *MELB/CHEL* DE73 .... 72 E7
Weston Rd *BWSH/BRSTN* DE72 ... 83 K1
Weston Spot Cl *RIPLEY* DE5 ... 11 H8
Weston St *HEANOR* DE75 .... 20 E7
West Orch *RLBORO* LE12 .... 114 A6
Westover Rd *LEIW* LE3 .... 130 D5
West Pk *WBRGFD* NG2 .... 51 H8
West Park Rd *DERBYW* DE22 .... 43 J7
Westray Cl *BSTN/STPLFD* NG9 .. 48 F4
West Rd *DERBYE* DE21 .... 59 H2
West Rw *DERBYW* DE22 .... 43 L6
West Service Rd *DERBYE* DE21 . 58 E5
West St *ALFN* DE55 .... 12 A1
 ARN NG5 .... 25 J8
 EWD/SEL/PNX NG16 .... 20 F7
 HEANOR DE75 .... 20 B5
 HUCK/RAV NG15 .... 15 L8
 ILK DE7 .... 33 K6
 LEI LE1 .... 6 F9
 RLEINE/SYS LE7 .... 120 E3
 RLEIW/BAR LE9 .... 135 L5
 RLEIW/BBY LE8 .... 136 F6
 WBRGFD NG2 .... 5 L7
West Ter *HUCK/RAV* NG15 ...... 15 L8
 ILK DE7 .... 33 K6
West Thorpe *RLBORO* LE12 ..... 90 F8
West Vw *WBRGFD* NG2 .... 65 H1
West View Av *LEIS* LE2 .... 136 F4
 NORM/LIT DE23 .... 56 F8
Westview Ct *CARL* NG4 .... 38 D7
West View Rd *CARL* NG4 .... 38 D7
Westville Dr *HUCK/RAV* NG15 .. 23 J4
Westville Gdns
 MAPPK/POR/STA NG3 .... 5 J2
West Wk *LEI* LE1 .... 7 H9
Westway *COT/KEY/RAD* NG12 .... 67 G5
Westwick Rd *WOL/BIL/BRX* NG8 . 49 G1
Westwick St *ILK* DE7 .... 47 L1
Westwood Dr *DERBYSE* DE24 .... 72 B2
Westwood Rd *WBRGFD* NG2 ...... 51 L3
Wetherby Cl
 EWD/SEL/PNX NG16 .... 22 C8
 RLEINE/SYS LE7 .... 121 J1
 WOL/BIL/BRX NG8 .... 35 M7
Wetherby Rd *DERBYSE* DE24 .... 58 B8
 LEIN LE4 .... 126 B4
Wetherlam Cl *WBRGFD* NG2 ..... 51 G8
Wexford Cl *LEIS* LE2 .... 139 H3
Weyacres *BWSH/BRSTN* DE72 .... 59 M6
Weybridge Cl *ILK* DE7 .... 32 B7
Weymouth Cl *WGSTN* LE18 ...... 138 B7
Weymouth St *LEIN* LE4 .... 125 M7
Whaddon Dr *LBORO* LE11 .... 9 L8
Whall Cl *RLBORO* LE12 .... 112 C2
Wharfdale *WOL/BIL/BRX* NG8 ... 48 F4
Wharfedale Cl *DERBYW* DE22 ... 43 M3
Wharfedale Rd *LGEAT* NG10 .... 75 L1
Wharf La *COT/KEY/RAD* NG12 ... 53 C4
Wharf Rd *NOTTE* NG7 .... 4 F9
Wharf St *LEIN* LE4 .... 120 B7
Wharf St North *LEI* LE1 ...... 7 G3
Wharf St South *LEI* LE1 ...... 7 G4
The Wharf *BWSH/BRSTN* DE72 ... 74 C6
Wharf Wy *LEIS* LE2 .... 136 F5
Wharncliffe Rd *ILK* DE7 ...... 33 J7
 LBORO LE11 .... 9 L4
Whatton Oaks *RLBORO* LE12 .... 113 J1
Whatton Ri *ARN* NG5 .... 36 F5
Whatton Rd *CDON/KEG* DE74 .... 86 A8
 RLBORO LE12 .... 94 C5
Wheatacre Rd *CFTN/RUD* NG11 .. 64 D6
Wheat Cl *WOL/BIL/BRX* NG8 .... 49 H2

Wheatcroft Vw
  CFTN/RUD NG11 ...... 65 G4
Wheatcroft Wy *DERBYE* DE21 ..... 44 A5
Wheatfield CI *LEIW* LE3 ..... 124 A8
Wheatfields Rd
  MAPPK/POR/STA NG3 ..... 37 L8
Wheatgrass Rd
  BSTN/STPLFD NG9 ..... 62 F2
Wheathill Gv *NORM/LIT* DE23 ..... 70 E1
Wheatland CI *DERBYE* DE24 ..... 71 G5
  LEIS LE2 ..... 139 H2
Wheatland Rd *LEIN* LE4 ..... 125 H2
Wheatlands Dr *RLEIW/BBY* LE8 ..... 143 H3
Wheatley Dr *CARL* NG4 ..... 38 A8
Wheatley Gv *BSTN/STPLFD* NG9 ..... 63 K3
Wheatley Rd *LEIN* LE4 ..... 125 H3
Wheatley's Rd *LEIN* LE4 ..... 126 B1
Wheatsheaf CI *DERBYE* DE24 ..... 85 G5
Wheatsheaf Ct *CALV/BJ* NG14 ..... 39 K3
Wheat St *LEI* LE1 ..... 7 G4
Wheeldale CI *WGSTN* LE18 ..... 138 D5
Wheeldale CI
  WOL/BIL/BRX NG8 ..... 48 F3
Wheeldon Av *BPR/DUF* DE56 ..... 17 M3
  DERBYW DE22 ..... 43 J8
Wheeler Av *NORM/LIT* DE23 ..... 21 M6
Wheeler Ga *NOTT* NG1 ..... 5 G7
Wheldon Av *CARL* NG4 ..... 38 A5
Whenby CI *MCKLVR* DE3 ..... 56 A5
Whernside CI *DERBYSE* DE24 ..... 73 C1
Whernside Rd *ARN* NG5 ..... 37 J2
Whetstone CI
  WOL/BIL/BRX NG8 ..... 35 H4
Whetstone Dr *COAL* LE67 ..... 108 C6
Whetstone Gorse La
  RLEIW/BBY LE8 ..... 142 E5
Whiles La *LEIN* LE4 ..... 119 M8
Whilton Ct *BPR/DUF* DE56 ..... 18 B3
Whilton Crs *ILK* DE7 ..... 32 B7
Whinbush Av *DERBYE* DE24 ..... 72 C2
Whinchat CI *LEIE* LE5 ..... 7 M4
Whinfell CI *CFTN/RUD* NG11 ..... 64 D5
Whinham Av *RLEIW/BAR* LE9 ..... 141 H8
Whinlatter Dr *WBRGFD* NG2 ..... 66 A1
Whiston CI *ARN* NG5 ..... 37 J5
Whiston Ri *NORM/LIT* DE23 ..... 57 L5
Whitaker Gdns *NORM/LIT* DE23 ..... 2 A9
Whitaker Rd *NORM/LIT* DE23 ..... 57 J5
Whitaker St *NORM/LIT* DE23 ..... 57 L5
Whitbread St *NOTTE* NG7 ..... 5 H5
Whitby Av *DERBYE* DE21 ..... 44 A6
Whitby CI *RLBORO* LE12 ..... 102 F2
  RLEIW/BAR LE9 ..... 141 J7
  WOL/BIL/BRX NG8 ..... 48 F3
Whitby Crs *ARN* NG5 ..... 37 L4
Whitby Rd *EWD/SEL/PNX* NG16 ..... 21 L4
Whitcombe Gdns *ARN* NG5 ..... 24 E6
Whitcroft CI *COAL* LE67 ..... 116 C7
Whitcroft's La *COAL* LE67 ..... 110 B8
Whiteacres *RLEIW/BBY* LE8 ..... 142 C3
White Barn Dr *RLEIW/BAR* LE9 ..... 142 B4
Whitebeam CI
  RLEIW/BAR LE9 ..... 135 L7
Whitebeam Rd *LEIS* LE2 ..... 132 E8
Whitechapel CI
  WOL/BIL/BRX NG8 ..... 36 B5
Whitecross St *DERBY* DE1 ..... 2 D7
Whitefield Rd *LEIN* LE4 ..... 125 K4
White Furrows
  COT/KEY/RAD NG12 ..... 67 J5
Whitegate *LBORO* LE11 ..... 9 L1
White Gates *RIPLEY* DE5 ..... 11 M7
Whitegate V *CFTN/RUD* NG11 ..... 64 B6
Whitehall Rd *LEIE* LE5 ..... 132 F3
Whitehead CI *ILK* DE7 ..... 33 H5
Whitehead CI *WGSTN* LE18 ..... 137 M4
Whitehead Dr
  EWD/SEL/PNX NG16 ..... 13 H7
White Horse La *LEIN* LE4 ..... 125 M1
Whitehouse Av *LBORO* LE11 ..... 9 M6
Whitehouse CI *DERBYE* DE24 ..... 72 B3
White House CI *GBY/RBY* LE6 ..... 123 J4
Whitehouse Ri *BPR/DUF* DE56 ..... 17 J1
Whitehurst St *DERBYSE* DE24 ..... 58 B8
Whitelands *COT/KEY/RAD* NG12 ..... 67 L5
White La *BPR/DUF* DE56 ..... 16 B4
Whiteley Rd *RIPLEY* DE5 ..... 11 K8
White Lodge Gdns
  WOL/BIL/BRX NG8 ..... 35 H8
Whitely CI *BSTN/STPLFD* NG9 ..... 48 C8
Whitemoor Av
  WOL/BIL/BRX NG8 ..... 36 B7
Whitemoor Hall
  BPR/DUF DE56 ..... 18 B2
Whitemoor La *BPR/DUF* DE56 ..... 18 B2
Whitemoor Rd *BLWL* NG6 ..... 36 B5
Whitemoss CI *WOL/BIL/BRX* NG8 ..... 49 J4
Whiteoaks CI *LEIS* LE2 ..... 139 G4
White Rd *ARN* NG5 ..... 36 C4
Whitesand CI *LEIW* LE3 ..... 124 B6
White's Av
  MAPPK/POR/STA NG3 ..... 51 M1
White's Cft *CALV/BJ* NG14 ..... 26 F3
White St *DERBYW* DE22 ..... 43 J8
  RLBORO LE12 ..... 112 D1
  RLEIW/BBY LE8 ..... 146 D7
Whiteway *DERBYW* DE22 ..... 43 J5
Whitewell Gdns
  DERBYE DE24 ..... 73 G2
Whitfield CI *CFTN/RUD* NG11 ..... 64 F1
Whiting Av *BSTN/STPLFD* NG9 ..... 62 D5
Whitley CI *LEIE* LE5 ..... 124 F7
Whitman CI *LEIW* LE3 ..... 130 B1
Whitmore Rd *DERBYE* DE21 ..... 58 D1
Whitstable CI *NORM/LIT* DE23 ..... 57 H8
Whittaker La *DERBYE* DE21 ..... 30 B5
Whittaker Rd *BSTN/STPLFD* NG9 ..... 62 E4
Whitteney Dr *LEIS* LE2 ..... 137 H3
Whittier Rd *LEIS* LE2 ..... 131 K8
  WBRGFD NG2 ..... 51 L4

Whittingham Rd
  MAPPK/POR/STA NG3 ..... 37 L4
Whittington St *GBY/RBY* LE6 ..... 123 C6
Whittington Dr *DERBYSE* DE24 ..... 72 B2
Whittlebury Dr *NORM/LIT* DE23 ..... 56 D8
Whittle CI *RLEIW/BBY* LE8 ..... 142 D1
Whitton CI *ARN* NG5 ..... 24 F6
  BSTN/STPLFD NG9 ..... 63 G5
Whitwell CI *WOL/BIL/BRX* NG8 ..... 35 M4
Whitwell Rd *WOL/BIL/BRX* NG8 ..... 35 M6
Whitwell Rw *LEIW* LE3 ..... 137 J2
Whitwick Moor *COAL* LE67 ..... 100 B8
Whitwick Rd *COAL* LE67 ..... 108 B6
  COAL LE67 ..... 116 A1
Whitwick Wy *LEIW* LE3 ..... 125 G7
Whitworth Dr *CALV/BJ* NG14 ..... 39 C5
  COT/KEY/RAD NG12 ..... 53 J5
Whitworth Ri *ARN* NG5 ..... 24 D7
Whitworth Rd *ILK* DE7 ..... 47 K1
Whyburn La *HUCK/RAV* NG15 ..... 15 G8
Whyburn St *HUCK/RAV* NG15 ..... 24 A1
Whysall St *HEANOR* DE75 ..... 20 C5
Whyston Ct *HUCK/RAV* NG15 ..... 23 G2
Whyteleafe Gv
  DERBYE DE21 ..... 44 F6
Wichnor CI *CFTN/RUD* NG11 ..... 64 C3
Wicken Ri *WGSTN* LE18 ..... 138 C3
Wickersley CI *DERBYE* DE22 ..... 43 J5
Wicket Gv *NOTTE* NG7 ..... 50 C3
Wickham Rd *LEIS* LE2 ..... 138 F3
Wicklow CI *RLBORO* LE12 ..... 102 A5
Wicklow Dr *LEIE* LE5 ..... 132 C1
Wickstead CI
  MAPPK/POR/STA NG3 ..... 37 K4
Wicksteed CI *BPR/DUF* DE56 ..... 18 B2
Widdowson CI *BLWL* NG6 ..... 23 K1
Widdybank CI *DERBYW* DE22 ..... 43 G5
Widecombe La *CFTN/RUD* NG11 ..... 64 B7
Wide La *RLBORO* LE12 ..... 94 E6
  RLBORO LE12 ..... 98 E3
Wide St *RLBORO* LE12 ..... 94 E7
Widford CI *LEIE* LE5 ..... 126 E7
Widmerpool La
  COT/KEY/RAD NG12 ..... 80 F6
The Widon *LBORO* LE11 ..... 103 J7
Wighay Rd *HUCK/RAV* NG15 ..... 15 K5
Wightman CI *RLBORO* LE12 ..... 101 M4
  RLEIW/BAR LE9 ..... 140 B4
Wigley CI *MAPPK/POR/STA* NG3 ..... 5 M3
Wigley Rd *LEIE* LE5 ..... 127 C2
Wigman Rd *WOL/BIL/BRX* NG8 ..... 35 H7
Wigmore La *MCKLVR* DE3 ..... 56 A4
Wigston La *LEIS* LE2 ..... 137 H1
Wigston Rd *LEIS* LE2 ..... 138 E2
  RLEIW/BBY LE8 ..... 136 F7
  WGSTN LE18 ..... 138 D3
Wigston St *LEI* LE1 ..... 7 G6
Wilberforce Rd *LEIS* LE2 ..... 131 H4
Wilcox Dr *EWD/SEL/PNX* NG16 ..... 13 L6
Wilde Crs *EWD/SEL/PNX* NG16 ..... 13 L1
Wilden Crs *CFTN/RUD* NG11 ..... 64 C4
Wilders Lea Ct *BPR/DUF* DE56 ..... 17 L5
Wildman St *NOTTE* NG1 ..... 4 C4
Wildpark La *ASHB* DE6 ..... 41 G1
Wildsmith St *DERBYSE* DE24 ..... 58 E7
Wild St *DERBYW* DE22 ..... 57 H2
Wilford Crs *CFTN/RUD* NG11 ..... 65 G7
Wilford Crs East *WBRGFD* NG2 ..... 51 J6
Wilford Crs West *WBRGFD* NG2 ..... 51 G6
Wilford Gv *WBRGFD* NG2 ..... 51 H6
Wilford La *WBRGFD* NG2 ..... 51 G8
Wilford Rd *CFTN/RUD* NG11 ..... 64 F4
  WBRGFD NG2 ..... 50 F5
Wilfred St *NORM/LIT* DE23 ..... 57 M5
Wilfrid Gv *WBRGFD* NG2 ..... 65 J3
Wilhallow La
  EWD/SEL/PNX NG16 ..... 13 J4
Wilkins CI *DERBYSE* DE24 ..... 58 C8
Wilkins Gdns
  CFTN/RUD NG11 ..... 64 A6
Wilkinson Av
  BSTN/STPLFD NG9 ..... 63 K1
Wilkinson St *WOL/BIL/BRX* NG8 ..... 36 B6
Willaston CI *BLWL* NG6 ..... 36 A3
Willbert Rd *ARN* NG5 ..... 25 L1
Willerby Rd *ARN* NG5 ..... 37 L2
Willersley Dr *WBRGFD* NG2 ..... 51 C5
Willesden Av *DERBYW* DE22 ..... 42 E8
Willesden Gn
  EWD/SEL/PNX NG16 ..... 35 H4
Willetts Rd *DERBYE* DE21 ..... 44 E8
Willey La *EWD/SEL/PNX* NG16 ..... 13 L8
William Av *EWD/SEL/PNX* NG16 ..... 21 K5
William Booth Rd
  WBRGFD NG2 ..... 51 L3
William CI *CARL* NG4 ..... 38 F7
  RLEIW/SYS LE7 ..... 121 J1
William Rd *BSTN/STPLFD* NG9 ..... 48 B8
  WBRGFD NG2 ..... 51 J7
Williams CI *ALFN* DE55 ..... 12 B1
  RLEIW/BAR LE9 ..... 141 M1
Williams Rd *BSTN/STPLFD* NG9 ..... 62 F4
William St *BPR/DUF* DE56 ..... 17 K3
  DERBY DE1 ..... 2 B1
  HUCK/RAV NG15 ..... 15 L8
  LBORO LE11 ..... 9 G4
  LEIE LE5 ..... 7 H5
  LGEAT NG10 ..... 62 A5
  RLEIW/BAR LE9 ..... 135 M8
Willington Rd *RDERBYSW* DE65 ..... 69 C3
  RDERBYSW DE65 ..... 70 A7
Willn CI *COAL* LE67 ..... 108 F7
Willn St *NORM/LIT* DE23 ..... 57 K6
Willoughby Av *LGEAT* NG10 ..... 62 A5
  NOTTE NG7 ..... 4 A8
Willoughby CI
  BWSH/BRSTN DE72 ..... 61 K7
  NOTTE NG7 ..... 49 M7
Willoughby Gdns *LEIW* LE3 ..... 129 L4
Willoughby Rd *RLEIW/BBY* LE8 ..... 143 G4
  WBRGFD NG2 ..... 65 K1
Willoughby St
  BSTN/STPLFD NG9 ..... 63 L1
  ILK DE7 ..... 33 L6
  NOTTE NG7 ..... 4 A9
Willow Av *BSTN/STPLFD* NG9 ..... 62 B1
  CARL NG4 ..... 38 E7
  HUCK/RAV NG15 ..... 23 H2
  LGEAT NG10 ..... 62 B6
  RIPLEY DE5 ..... 11 H8
Willow Brook
  COT/KEY/RAD NG12 ..... 80 E5

Willow Brook CI *LEIW* LE3 ..... 124 A5
Willowbrook CI
  RDERBYSW DE65 ..... 68 A5
  RLEIW/BAR LE9 ..... 141 K8
Willowbrook Gra
  MELB/CHEL DE73 ..... 72 E6
Willow Brook Rd *LEIE* LE5 ..... 7 M2
Willowbrook Vw *LEIE* LE5 ..... 133 J1
  CALV/BJ NG14 ..... 39 K2
  COT/KEY/RAD NG12 ..... 53 K5
  DERBYW DE22 ..... 43 K5
  RLBORO LE12 ..... 88 B7
  RLEIW/BAR LE9 ..... 142 A1
Willow Ct *LEIS* LE2 ..... 7 J7
Willow Crs *CARL* NG4 ..... 27 C8
  CARL NG4 ..... 38 E5
Willow Cft *DERBYSE* DE24 ..... 73 C3
Willowcroft *RLBORO* LE12 ..... 112 C2
Willowcroft Rd *DERBYE* DE21 ..... 59 H4
Willowdene *COT/KEY/RAD* NG12 ..... 67 L4
Willow Dr *GBY/RBY* LE6 ..... 123 J6
  HUCK/RAV NG15 ..... 14 D1
  RLEIW/BBY LE8 ..... 143 J5
Willowfields *RDERBYSW* DE65 ..... 68 B5
Willow Gn *COAL* LE67 ..... 109 C5
Willow Gv *BPR/DUF* DE56 ..... 17 L5
  RLEINE/SYS LE7 ..... 113 C6
Willowherb CI *DERBYSE* DE24 ..... 71 K5
Willow Hill CI *BLWL* NG6 ..... 35 L1
Willow La *CARL* NG4 ..... 38 D5
Willow Park Dr *WGSTN* LE18 ..... 138 B5
Willow Park Wy
  BWSH/BRSTN DE72 ..... 73 L8
Willowpit La *RDERBYSW* DE65 ..... 54 B8
Willow PI *WGSTN* LE18 ..... 138 B5
Willow Pool La *RLBORO* LE12 ..... 95 C2
Willow Rd *CARL* NG4 ..... 38 D7
  CDON/KEG DE74 ..... 84 F2
  LBORO LE11 ..... 103 L7
  NOTTE NG7 ..... 50 C6
  RLBORO LE12 ..... 105 H6
  RLEIW/BBY LE8 ..... 136 F5
  WBRGFD NG2 ..... 65 J4
Willow Rw *DERBY* DE1 ..... 2 D2
Willowsend CI
  RDERBYSW DE65 ..... 70 B6
The Willows *RLBORO* LE12 ..... 105 K1
Willowtree CI *LEIE* LE5 ..... 127 C5
Willow Wk *RLEINE/SYS* LE7 ..... 120 D4
Willow Wong *CALV/BJ* NG14 ..... 39 K2
Wilson Av *NORM/LIT* DE23 ..... 57 C7
Wilson Dr *ALFN* DE55 ..... 11 M1
Wilson Rd *NORM/LIT* DE23 ..... 57 G7
Wilson St *ARN* NG5 ..... 37 M2
  LEIW LE3 ..... 130 D5
  MCKLVR DE3 ..... 56 A7
Wilson Rd *DERBYE* DE21 ..... 44 D7
  EWD/SEL/PNX NG16 ..... 21 K6
  WGSTN LE18 ..... 137 M3
Wilson St *DERBY* DE1 ..... 2 D5
  LEIS LE2 ..... 7 L5
Wilsthorpe Rd
  BWSH/BRSTN DE72 ..... 61 J7
  DERBYE DE21 ..... 44 D8
  LGEAT NG10 ..... 61 M7
  LGEAT NG10 ..... 75 M1
Wilstone CI *LBORO* LE11 ..... 103 G4
Wilton Av *LBORO* LE11 ..... 8 C8
Wilton CI *DERBYSE* DE24 ..... 71 C5
  LEIS LE2 ..... 139 C2
Wilton St *BLWL* NG6 ..... 36 C3
  ILK DE7 ..... 33 K6
Wiltshire Av
  EWD/SEL/PNX NG16 ..... 12 F3
Wiltshire Rd *DERBYE* DE21 ..... 44 B8
  LEIN LE4 ..... 125 H5
  WGSTN LE18 ..... 137 M4
Wimbledon Dr
  EWD/SEL/PNX NG16 ..... 35 J4
Wimbledon Rd *ARN* NG5 ..... 36 E4
  DERBYW DE22 ..... 56 E1
Wimborne CI *WBRGFD* NG2 ..... 65 C2
  WGSTN LE18 ..... 138 A6
Wimborne Rd *LEIS* LE2 ..... 138 B1
Wimbourne CI *MELB/CHEL* DE73 ..... 72 E6
Wimbourne Rd *NOTTE* NG7 ..... 4 A3
Wimpole Gdns *DERBYW* DE22 ..... 56 F1
Wimpole Rd
  BSTN/STPLFD NG9 ..... 49 H6
Wincanton CI *DERBYSE* DE24 ..... 58 B8
Winchcombe Wy *DERBYE* DE21 ..... 44 E5
Winchendon CI *LEIE* LE5 ..... 126 C7
Winchester Av
  BSTN/STPLFD NG9 ..... 49 J7
  LEIW LE3 ..... 130 F4
  RLEIW/BBY LE8 ..... 143 G5
Winchester CI *RLBORO* LE12 ..... 88 C6
Winchester Ct *ARN* NG5 ..... 37 J4
Winchester Crs *DERBYE* DE21 ..... 44 B7

  ILK DE7 ..... 33 L7
Winchester Rd *RLEIW/BBY* LE8 ..... 137 C8
  RLEIW/BBY LE8 ..... 143 C3
Winchester St *ARN* NG5 ..... 37 H4
Windermere Av *ILK* DE7 ..... 47 C2
Windermere CI *CARL* NG4 ..... 38 D5
  WBRGFD NG2 ..... 52 B8
Windermere Crs *DERBYW* DE22 ..... 43 J4
Windermere Dr *DERBYE* DE21 ..... 59 J2
  RLEIW/BAR LE9 ..... 141 H3
Windermere Rd
  BSTN/STPLFD NG9 ..... 49 H6
  HUCK/RAV NG15 ..... 15 K7
  LGEAT NG10 ..... 61 L5
  NOTTE NG7 ..... 36 E7
  RLBORO LE12 ..... 105 H7
  WGSTN LE18 ..... 138 D4
Windermere St *LEIS* LE2 ..... 131 J4
Winder's Wy *LEIS* LE2 ..... 137 H2
Windlea Rd *ALFN* DE55 ..... 12 A1
Windleden Rd *LBORO* LE11 ..... 102 F5
Windley Crs *DERBYW* DE22 ..... 43 H8
Windley Dr *ILK* DE7 ..... 33 H4
Windley La *BPR/DUF* DE56 ..... 28 C1
Windmill CI *LEIE* LE5 ..... 137 K1
  WGSTN LE18 ..... 137 L2
Windmill Bank *WGSTN* LE18 ..... 138 C6
Windmill
  BWSH/BRSTN DE72 ..... 60 A2
  CDON/KEG DE74 ..... 84 F5
  GBY/RBY LE6 ..... 123 H7
  LEIN LE4 ..... 120 D7
  MAPPK/POR/STA NG3 ..... 51 K2
  RLBORO LE12 ..... 113 H4
Windmill Ct *COT/KEY/RAD* NG12 ..... 80 D5
Windmill End *RLEINE/SYS* LE7 ..... 113 J8
Windmill Gdns *RLEIW/BBY* LE8 ..... 146 E5
Windmill Gv *HUCK/RAV* NG15 ..... 23 L1
Windmill Hill La *DERBYW* DE22 ..... 57 G1
Windmill Ri *BPR/DUF* DE56 ..... 17 L2
  GBY/RBY LE6 ..... 123 J4
  RLEINE/SYS LE7 ..... 111 K6
Windmill Vw *BPR/DUF* DE56 ..... 10 C7
  WBRGFD NG2 ..... 51 L3
Windmill Wy *CDON/KEG* DE74 ..... 85 M5
Windrush CI
  BSTN/STPLFD NG9 ..... 49 H6
  DERBYW DE22 ..... 43 M2
Windrush Dr *LEIS* LE2 ..... 139 H2
Windsmoor Rd
  EWD/SEL/PNX NG16 ..... 13 H7
Windsor Av *GBY/RBY* LE6 ..... 123 J5
  LEIN LE4 ..... 125 M5
  MELB/CHEL DE73 ..... 82 E7
  NORM/LIT DE23 ..... 56 F7
Windsor CI *BSTN/STPLFD* NG9 ..... 47 M2
  BWSH/BRSTN DE72 ..... 60 A6
  COAL LE67 ..... 108 F6
  HEANOR DE75 ..... 20 C4
  HUCK/RAV NG15 ..... 15 M7
  LEIS LE2 ..... 139 C4
  RLBORO LE12 ..... 112 F1
  RLBORO LE12 ..... 113 H7
Windsor Crs *ARN* NG5 ..... 37 L2
  BSTN/STPLFD NG9 ..... 48 C8
  ILK DE7 ..... 47 H3
Windsor Dr *DERBYE* DE21 ..... 59 K1
  RLBORO LE12 ..... 101 C5
Windsor Rd *LBORO* LE11 ..... 103 H2
Windsor St *BSTN/STPLFD* NG9 ..... 48 B8
  BSTN/STPLFD NG9 ..... 63 L1
Windy La *DERBYE* DE21 ..... 30 A6
Winforde Crs *LEIW* LE3 ..... 130 B3
Wingbourne Wk *BLWL* NG6 ..... 24 A6
Wingerworth Park Rd
  DERBYE DE21 ..... 59 J2
Wingfield Dr
  BSTN/STPLFD NG9 ..... 49 L6
  DERBYE DE21 ..... 44 D6
  ILK DE7 ..... 33 J8
Wingfield St *LEIN* LE4 ..... 125 M5
Wings Dr *HUCK/RAV* NG15 ..... 23 H3
Winifred Crs *CALV/BJ* NG14 ..... 39 K3
Winifred St *HUCK/RAV* NG15 ..... 23 M1
  LEIS LE2 ..... 6 D9
Winrow Gdns *BLWL* NG6 ..... 36 A4
Winscale Av *ARN* NG5 ..... 24 E7
Winscombe Mt *CFTN/RUD* NG11 ..... 64 B8
Winsford CI *WOL/BIL/BRX* NG8 ..... 35 M5
Winslow Dr *WGSTN* LE18 ..... 138 C3
Winslow Gn *DERBYE* DE21 ..... 58 F1
Winstanley Dr *LEIW* LE3 ..... 130 D3
Winster Av *CARL* NG4 ..... 38 B6
Winster CI *BPR/DUF* DE56 ..... 17 M2
  BSTN/STPLFD NG9 ..... 49 K6
Winster Dr *LEIN* LE4 ..... 120 C7
Winster Rd *DERBYE* DE21 ..... 44 C6
Winster Wy *LGEAT* NG10 ..... 75 K2
Winston Av *RLEIW/BAR* LE9 ..... 141 G3
Winston CI *BSTN/STPLFD* NG9 ..... 48 C7
  MAPPK/POR/STA NG3 ..... 38 A1
Winterbourne Dr
  WGSTN LE18 ..... 138 A6
Winterburn Gdns
  RLEIW/BBY LE8 ..... 136 D8
Winterburn Wy *LBORO* LE11 ..... 102 F4
Winter Closes
  EWD/SEL/PNX NG16 ..... 13 K6
Winterfield CI *LEIW* LE3 ..... 130 F4
Wintergreen Dr *NORM/LIT* DE23 ..... 70 D1
Wintersdale Rd *LEIE* LE5 ..... 133 C1
Winterton CI *ARN* NG5 ..... 37 K1
  LEIN LE4 ..... 120 D7
Winterton Ri *ARN* NG5 ..... 24 F8

Winthorpe Rd *ARN* NG5 ..... 25 L8
Winton Av *LEIW* LE3 ..... 130 F5
Wintringham Crs *ARN* NG5 ..... 37 L2
Wirksworth Rd *BPR/DUF* DE56 ..... 16 C6
  BPR/DUF DE56 ..... 29 H4
  ILK DE7 ..... 47 G3
Wisgreaves Rd *DERBYSE* DE24 ..... 58 D7
Wishford Av *NOTTE* NG7 ..... 50 C4
Wisley CI *CFTN/RUD* NG11 ..... 65 G4
Wistow CI *WGSTN* LE18 ..... 144 E4
  WOL/BIL/BRX NG8 ..... 36 C7
Wistow Rd *RLEIW/BBY* LE8 ..... 145 H1
  WGSTN LE18 ..... 138 B6
  WGSTN LE18 ..... 144 E4
Witham CI *RDERBYSW* DE65 ..... 68 C5
Witham Dr *NORM/LIT* DE23 ..... 71 H1
Withcote La *LEIE* LE5 ..... 133 C2
Withens CI *LEIE* LE5 ..... 124 E8
Witherdell *LEIN* LE4 ..... 124 C4
Withern Rd *WOL/BIL/BRX* NG8 ..... 35 K6
Withers Wy *LEIW* LE3 ..... 130 B6
Withington CI *LEIE* LE5 ..... 130 B5
Witney CI *ARN* NG5 ..... 24 C8
  DERBYE DE21 ..... 58 A7
Wittering CI *LGEAT* NG10 ..... 76 C2
Witton Ct *DERBYSE* DE24 ..... 71 H3
Wiverton Rd *NOTTE* NG7 ..... 51 J2
Woburn CI *COT/KEY/RAD* NG12 ..... 66 A3
  LBORO LE11 ..... 103 C3
  LEIS LE2 ..... 137 C3
  WGSTN LE18 ..... 138 C5
Woburn Cft *LGEAT* NG10 ..... 61 L5
Woburn PI *DERBYW* DE22 ..... 56 F2
Woburn Ri *ARN* NG5 ..... 37 M2
Wodehouse Av *CFTN/RUD* NG11 ..... 77 M5
Wokingham Av *LEIS* LE2 ..... 137 H5
Wolds Dr *COT/KEY/RAD* NG12 ..... 80 D4
Wolds La *COT/KEY/RAD* NG12 ..... 67 H7
  COT/KEY/RAD NG12 ..... 80 D7
Wolds Ri *DERBYE* DE21 ..... 59 H1
The Wolds *RLEINE/SYS* LE7 ..... 115 J7
Wolfa St *DERBY* DE1 ..... 2 C5
Wollacombe CI
  MAPPK/POR/STA NG3 ..... 38 B4
Wollaton Av *CARL* NG4 ..... 38 B4
  LBORO LE11 ..... 103 C3
Wollaton CI *LEIW* LE3 ..... 123 M7
Wollaton Ct *BLWL* NG6 ..... 36 C1
Wollaton Crs
  BSTN/STPLFD NG9 ..... 49 J7
Wollaton Hall Dr
  WOL/BIL/BRX NG8 ..... 50 B4
Wollaton Paddocks
  WOL/BIL/BRX NG8 ..... 49 C3
Wollaton Ri *WOL/BIL/BRX* NG8 ..... 49 J5
Wollaton Rd *BSTN/STPLFD* NG9 ..... 49 J7
  DERBYE DE21 ..... 44 D7
Wollaton St *NOTT* NG1 ..... 4 F6
Wollaton V *WOL/BIL/BRX* NG8 ..... 48 F3
  WOL/BIL/BRX NG8 ..... 49 K6
Wolsey Av *NOTTE* NG7 ..... 4 B5
Wolsey CI *GBY/RBY* LE6 ..... 123 J5
  LEIW LE3 ..... 129 K5
  RLEIW/BBY LE8 ..... 145 K7
Wolsey Dr *GBY/RBY* LE6 ..... 122 F6
Wolsey La *RLEIW/BBY* LE8 ..... 145 K7
Wolsey Rd *COAL* LE67 ..... 108 A5
Wolsey St *LEIW* LE4 ..... 6 A3
Wolsey Wy *LBORO* LE11 ..... 9 M3
  RLEINE/SYS LE7 ..... 120 D4
Wolverley Gra *DERBYSE* DE24 ..... 73 H1
Wolverton Rd *LEIW* LE3 ..... 131 C5
Woodale CI *NORM/LIT* DE23 ..... 70 D1
Wood Av *NOTTE* NG10 ..... 61 L1
Woodbank *LEIS* LE2 ..... 136 F5
Woodbank Dr
  WOL/BIL/BRX NG8 ..... 49 H5
Woodbank Rd *GBY/RBY* LE6 ..... 123 H4
  WGSTN LE18 ..... 138 A1
Woodborough La *ARN* NG5 ..... 25 M4
Woodborough Rd *LEIE* LE5 ..... 132 C3
  MAPPK/POR/STA NG3 ..... 5 J2
Woodboy St *LEI* LE1 ..... 7 C2
Woodbridge Av *CFTN/RUD* NG11 ..... 64 C4
Woodbridge CI
  MELB/CHEL DE73 ..... 72 D6
Woodbridge Rd *LEIN* LE4 ..... 125 M4
Woodbrook Rd *LBORO* LE11 ..... 8 D9
Woodchester Dr *DERBYSE* DE24 ..... 73 H1
Woodchurch Rd *ARN* NG5 ..... 24 F6
Wood CI *RLBORO* LE12 ..... 102 B4
Wood Close Camp
  DERBYE DE21 ..... 30 A8
Woodcote Rd *LEIW* LE3 ..... 130 D8
Woodcote Wy *NORM/LIT* DE23 ..... 56 E8
Wood Cft *NORM/LIT* DE23 ..... 57 H7
Woodcroft Av *LEIS* LE2 ..... 137 L1
The Woodcroft *CDON/KEG* DE74 ..... 93 G2
Wood End *LEIW* LE3 ..... 124 E8
Wood End Rd *HEANOR* DE75 ..... 20 C5
Woodfall La *DERBYW* DE22 ..... 28 D5
Woodfield CI *RLEIW/BAR* LE9 ..... 135 M7
Woodfield Dr *RIPLEY* DE5 ..... 11 L6
Woodfield Rd *LEIS* LE2 ..... 132 F8
  RLEINE/SYS LE7 ..... 119 J1
  WOL/BIL/BRX NG8 ..... 35 J6
Woodford CI *ARN* NG5 ..... 24 C6
  WGSTN LE18 ..... 138 A7
Woodford Rd *ARN* NG5 ..... 37 L2
  DERBYW DE22 ..... 42 E8
  HUCK/RAV NG15 ..... 23 M1
Wood Ga *LBORO* LE11 ..... 9 J4
Woodgate *LEIW* LE3 ..... 6 B2
  RLEINE/SYS LE7 ..... 119 J1
Woodgate CI
  COT/KEY/RAD NG12 ..... 67 J4
Woodgate Dr *LEIN* LE4 ..... 119 K7
  MELB/CHEL DE73 ..... 72 E6
Woodgate La
  COT/KEY/RAD NG12 ..... 67 H4
Woodgate Rd *RLBORO* LE12 ..... 88 A7
Woodgon Rd *RLEINE/SYS* LE7 ..... 124 B1
Woodgreen Rd *LEIN* LE4 ..... 126 B6
Woodhall CI *LEIW* LE3 ..... 130 B2
Woodhall Dr *NORM/LIT* DE23 ..... 56 C7
Woodhall Rd *WOL/BIL/BRX* NG8 ..... 49 M2
Woodhedge Dr
  MAPPK/POR/STA NG3 ..... 37 L7

Wood HI *LEIE* LE5 .... 7 M4
Woodhouse Cl *COAL* LE67 ...... 116 C6 ⑥
Woodhouse La *ASHB* DE6 .... 54 E2
  LBORO LE11 .... 110 F1
Woodhouse Rd *BPR/DUF* DE56 .... 18 E8
  COAL LE67 .... 108 F7
  RLBORO LE12 .... 112 C2
  RLEIW/BAR LE9 .... 135 K8
Woodhouse St
  MAPPK/POR/STA NG3 .... 51 K2
Woodhouse Wy
  EWD/SEL/PNX NG16 .... 35 H4
Woodhurst Cl *DERBYE* DE21 .... 44 B6
Woodkirk Rd *CFTN/RUD* NG11 .... 64 D5
Woodland Av
  BWSH/BRSTN DE72 .... 60 A5
  BWSH/BRSTN DE72 .... 61 K7
  ILK DE7 .... 33 H3 ⑥
  LEIS LE2 .... 132 A6
  RLEIW/BAR LE9 .... 135 M7
Woodland Cl *COAL* LE67 .... 116 C7
  COT/KEY/RAD NG12 .... 53 M4
  COT/KEY/RAD NG12 .... 67 K5 ⑥
Woodland Dr
  EWD/SEL/PNX NG16 .... 35 K3
  LEIW LE3 .... 130 B5
  MAPPK/POR/STA NG3 .... 37 H6
Woodland Gv *ARN* NG5 .... 37 H3
  BSTN/STPLFD NG9 .... 63 H2
Woodland Rd *DERBYW* DE22 .... 43 J7
  LEIE LE5 .... 126 B8
  WBRGFD NG2 .... 51 K6
Woodlands Av *DERBYSE* DE24 .... 72 C3
Woodlands Cl *DERBYE* DE21 .... 29 M7 ⑥
  MELB/CHEL DE73 .... 82 E6
  RLBORO LE12 .... 98 A4 ⑥
Woodlands Dr *GBY/RBY* LE6 .... 123 H3
  LBORO LE11 .... 9 G7
  RLBORO LE12 .... 102 A2 ⑥
Woodlands Farm Cl
  HUCK/RAV NG15 .... 23 H3 ⑥
Woodlands La *DERBYW* DE22 .... 29 H8
  MELB/CHEL DE73 .... 72 E7
  RLEIW/BAR LE9 .... 129 J1 ⑥
Woodlands Rd *DERBYW* DE22 .... 43 H1
The Woodlands *BLWL* NG6 .... 36 A2
  COT/KEY/RAD NG12 .... 53 J4 ⑥
  MELB/CHEL DE73 .... 82 F7
  RLEIW/BAR LE8 .... 143 H3 ⑥
  WGSTN LE18 .... 138 D3 ⑥
Woodlands Wy
  MELB/CHEL DE73 .... 82 E7
Woodland Wy *BPR/DUF* DE56 .... 29 K1
  CARL NG4 .... 38 E6
  CFTN/RUD NG11 .... 77 K7
  HUCK/RAV NG15 .... 15 K8
  ILK DE7 .... 31 H2
  RIPLEY DE5 .... 10 E3
  RLBORO LE12 .... 112 F3
Woodlane Gdns
  MAPPK/POR/STA NG3 .... 37 K8 ⑦
Woodlea Gv *DERBYE* DE21 .... 30 A7
Woodleigh *COT/KEY/RAD* NG12 .... 80 C5
Woodley Rd *GBY/RBY* LE6 .... 123 G7
Woodley Sq *BLWL* NG6 .... 24 A5
Woodley St *CFTN/RUD* NG11 .... 65 G8
Wood Link *BLWL* NG6 .... 23 J8
Woodman's Cha
  RLEINE/SYS LE7 .... 115 H8
Woodmans Wy
  RLBORO LE12 .... 102 A2 ⑦
Woodminton Dr
  MELB/CHEL DE73 .... 72 D4 ⑥

Woodnewton Dr *LEIE* LE5 .... 133 H3
Wood Nook Cl
  EWD/SEL/PNX NG16 .... 13 K1
Woodpecker Cl *LEIW* LE3 .... 129 J5
Woodpecker HI *ILK* DE7 .... 46 E5
Woodrising Cl *DERBYE* DE21 .... 44 F4 ⑩
Wood Rd *DERBYE* DE21 .... 44 E7
  DERBYE DE21 .... 59 L1
Woods Cl *LEIS* LE2 .... 139 G1
Woodsend Cl *CALV/BJ* NG14 .... 39 K3
Woodsford Gv *CFTN/RUD* NG11 .... 64 C5
Woodshawe Ri *LEIW* LE3 .... 130 C4
Woodshop La *MELB/CHEL* DE73 .. 82 B1
Woodside *EWD/SEL/PNX* NG16 .... 21 J5
  ILK DE7 .... 31 H4
  RLBORO LE12 .... 105 G7
Woodside Av
  COT/KEY/RAD NG12 .... 53 M4
  EWD/SEL/PNX NG16 .... 34 E1
  RIPLEY DE5 .... 11 H7
Woodside Cl *LEIW* LE4 .... 126 B6
  RLEIW/BAR LE9 .... 135 K7
Woodside Crs *ILK* DE7 .... 33 H2 ⑥
  LGEAT NG10 .... 61 M7
Woodside Dr *ARN* NG5 .... 25 H7
  DERBYW DE22 .... 43 L3
Woodside Rd *BSTN/STPLFD* NG9 .. 48 K7
  BSTN/STPLFD NG9 .... 62 E3
  CALV/BJ NG14 .... 39 H4
  COT/KEY/RAD NG12 .... 53 M3
  LEIS LE2 .... 139 H4
  LEIS LE2 .... 61 L2
Woods La *DERBYW* DE22 .... 2 C7
Woods Meadow
  DERBYSE DE24 .... 73 H2 ⑥
Woodsorrel Dr *DERBYE* DE21 .... 44 F4
Woodstock Av *NOTTE* NG7 .... 50 C1
Woodstock Cl *DERBYW* DE22 .... 43 H3
  LEIN LE4 .... 125 J3
Woodstock Rd
  BSTN/STPLFD NG9 .... 62 C4
Woodstock St *HUCK/RAV* NG15 .... 23 M1
Wood St *DERBY* DE1 .... 3 G2
  EWD/SEL/PNX NG16 .... 21 K4
  ILK DE7 .... 33 K6
  LEI LE1 .... 6 F3
  RIPLEY DE5 .... 11 H5
  RIPLEY DE5 .... 11 M7
Woodthorne Av *DERBYSE* DE24 .... 72 C3
Woodthorpe Av *ARN* NG5 .... 37 J3
  DERBYE DE21 .... 58 D1
  LBORO LE11 .... 9 K9
Woodthorpe Ct *ARN* NG5 .... 37 J4 ⑧
Woodthorpe Dr *ARN* NG5 .... 37 H3
Woodthorpe Gdns *ARN* NG5 .... 37 J4
Woodthorpe Rd *ARN* NG5 .... 37 K4
  LBORO LE11 .... 9 K8
Wood Vw *COT/KEY/RAD* NG12 .... 65 M4
Woodview *COT/KEY/RAD* NG12 .. 67 L4
Woodville Cl
  BSTN/STPLFD NG9 .... 63 G1 ⑥
Woodville Dr *ARN* NG5 .... 37 C4 ⑥
Woodville Gdns *WGSTN* LE18 .... 138 A2
Woodville Rd *ARN* NG5 .... 37 G5 ⑫
  LEIW LE3 .... 131 G1
Woodward Av *RLBORO* LE12 .... 112 C1
Woodward St *WBRGFD* NG2 .... 51 H6
Woodyard La *WOL/BIL/BRX* NG8 .. 49 L2
Woodsdale Cl *RLEINE/SYS* LE7 .. 118 C8
Wooliscroft Wy *ILK* DE7 .... 33 C5 ⑥
Woollaton St *HUCK/RAV* NG15 ... 15 M8
Woolmer Rd *WBRGFD* NG2 .... 51 C6
Woolpack La *NOTT* NG1 .... 5 J7

Woolrych St *NORM/LIT* DE23 .... 57 K5
Woolsington Cl
  WOL/BIL/BRX NG8 .... 35 H5 ⑭
Woolsthorpe Crs *ILK* DE7 .... 47 H3
Wootton Cl *RLBORO* LE12 .... 88 C5 ⑥
  RLEIW/BBY LE8 .... 142 D1
  WOL/BIL/BRX NG8 .... 35 H8
Wootton Ri *LEIS* LE2 .... 137 H2 ⑥
Worcester Av *LEIN* LE4 .... 120 A7
  RLEINE/SYS LE7 .... 119 M6
Worcester Crs *DERBYE* DE21 .... 44 B7
Worcester Dr *WGSTN* LE18 .... 137 K5
Worcester Gdns *ARN* NG5 .... 37 J2
  LEIS LE2 .... 131 H8
Worcester Rd *ARN* NG5 .... 37 J2
Wordsworth Av *DERBYSE* DE24.... 71 J2
  HUCK/RAV NG15 .... 23 H1
Wordsworth Crs
  RLEIW/BAR LE9 .... 135 L6 ⑥
Wordsworth Dr
  DERBYSE DE24 .... 71 L2 ⑥
Wordsworth Rd *ARN* NG5 .... 25 H8
  EWD/SEL/PNX NG16 .... 34 A2
  LBORO LE11 .... 8 A2
  LEIS LE2 .... 131 L6
  NOTTE NG7 .... 50 C1
  WBRGFD NG2 .... 65 J1
Worksop Rd
  MAPPK/POR/STA NG3 .... 51 K2 ⑥
Worrall Av *ARN* NG5 .... 25 K8
  LGEAT NG10 .... 62 B6
Worrall Cl *LEIW* LE3 .... 130 B3
Worrall Rd *LEIW* LE3 .... 130 B3
Worsley Wy *RLEIW/BBY* LE8 .... 142 E1
Worthington St *LEIS* LE2 .... 7 L7
Worth St *CARL* NG4 .... 38 C7
Wortley Av *BSTN/STPLFD* NG9 .. 48 B4
Wortley Cl *COAL* LE67 .... 108 C6
  ILK DE7 .... 33 L7
  RLBORO LE12 .... 102 A1 ⑥
Worwood Dr *WBRGFD* NG2 .... 65 G2
Wossock La *RLBORO* LE12 .... 87 K2
Woulds Fld *COT/KEY/RAD* NG12.. 67 K6
Wragley Wy *DERBYSE* DE24 .... 71 G5
The Wranglands
  RLEIW/BBY LE8 .... 145 L8
Wray Cl *MAPPK/POR/STA* NG3 ..... 5 M5
Wreake Dr *RLEINE/SYS* LE7 .... 115 L4
Wreake Rd *RLEINE/SYS* LE7 .... 120 C7
Wreford Crs *LEIE* LE5 .... 127 J8
Wren Cl *LEIS* LE2 .... 131 J8
  RLEINE/SYS LE7 .... 120 C3
Wren Park Cl *BPR/DUF* DE56 .... 17 H1
  RDERBYSW DE65 .... 70 B6
Wrenthorpe V *CFTN/RUD* NG11 ... 64 C6
Wretham Cl *MCKLVR* DE3 .... 56 B7 ⑥
Wright Av *RIPLEY* DE5 .... 11 K6
Wright Cl *RLEIW/BBY* LE8 .... 142 D3
Wright La *LEIS* LE2 .... 139 H3
Wrights Acre *RLBORO* LE12 ..... 113 M3 ⑥
Wrights Cl *RLBORO* LE12 .... 112 D2
Wrights Orch
  COT/KEY/RAD NG12 .... 80 C5
Wright St *CARL* NG4 .... 38 E8 ⑪
  RIPLEY DE5 .... 11 M8
Wroughton Ct
  EWD/SEL/PNX NG16 .... 21 L5 ⑥
Wroxall Wy *LEIW* LE3 .... 125 G7
Wroxham Cl *DERBYSE* DE24 .... 72 B3
Wroxham Dr *WOL/BIL/BRX* NG8 .. 49 H4
Wyaston Cl *DERBYW* DE22 .... 43 J6 ⑥
Wyatt Cl *LEIS* LE2 .... 132 C1
Wyatt Rd *COAL* LE67 .... 108 C6
Wych Elm Rd *LEIS* LE2 .... 132 E8

Wychwood Dr
  BSTN/STPLFD NG9 .... 48 B5
Wychwood Rd *RLEIW/BBY* LE8 .. 142 E2
Wycliffe Av *RLBORO* LE12 .... 105 H7
Wycliffe Gv
  MAPPK/POR/STA NG3 .... 37 J5 ⑥
Wycliffe St *LEI* LE1 .... 6 E6 ⑥
  NOTTE NG7 .... 36 D6
Wycombe Cl *CFTN/RUD* NG11 .... 64 B7
Wycombe Rd *LEIE* LE5 .... 126 C7
Wye Dean Dr *WGSTN* LE18 .... 138 B5
Wye Gdns *NOTTE* NG7 .... 50 B1
Wye St *DERBYSE* DE24 .... 58 E7
Wyggeston Rd *COAL* LE67 .... 108 B7
Wykeham Cl *RLEIW/BBY* LE8 .... 142 F1
Wykeham Rd *ARN* NG5 .... 37 L2 ⑥
Wykes Av *CALV* NG4 .... 38 D5
Wylam Cl *LEIW* LE3 .... 124 E7
Wymar Cl *LEIN* LE4 .... 125 G4
Wymeswold La *RLBORO* LE12 .... 97 L7
Wymeswold Rd
  COT/KEY/RAD NG12 .... 90 A7
  RLBORO LE12 .... 97 J5
  RLBORO LE12 .... 98 A3
Wymondham Cl *ARN* NG5 .... 37 L1 ⑥
Wynbreck Dr
  COT/KEY/RAD NG12 .... 80 D4
Wyndale Dr *ILK* DE7 .... 47 C1
  RLEINE/SYS LE7 .... 120 F2 ⑥
Wyndale Rd *LEIS* LE2 .... 131 M8
Wyndham Cl *LEIS* LE2 .... 133 G3
Wyndham Rd *RLEINE/SYS* LE7 .. 102 F1 ⑥
Wyndham St *DERBYSE* DE24 .... 58 E8
The Wyndings *ARN* NG5 .... 37 K3 ⑥
Wynfield Rd *LEIW* LE3 .... 130 F2
Wyngate Dr *LEIW* LE3 .... 130 F2
Wynndale Dr *ARN* NG5 .... 36 E4
Wynthorpe Ri *LEIW* LE3 .... 130 E3
Wynton Av *DERBYSE* DE24 .... 58 D7
Wynton Cl *RLEIW/BBY* LE8 .... 143 G1 ⑥
Wynward Cl *ILK* DE7 .... 33 G4 ⑥
Wynwood Cl
  BSTN/STPLFD NG9 .... 62 F5 ⑥
Wynwood Rd
  BSTN/STPLFD NG9 .... 62 F5 ⑥
Wyrale Dr *WOL/BIL/BRX* NG8 .... 35 J6
Wysall La *COT/KEY/RAD* NG12 .... 80 B8
  COT/KEY/RAD NG12 .... 90 A2
Wysall Rd *COT/KEY/RAD* NG12 .. 79 M7
  COT/KEY/RAD NG12 .... 90 F3
  RLBORO LE12 .... 97 J2
Wyston Brook *RDERBYSW* DE65 .. 68 B6
Wythburn Cl *LBORO* LE11 .... 8 A9
Wyton Cl *ARN* NG5 .... 36 E2
Wyvelle Crs *CDON/KEG* DE74 .... 86 A4 ⑥
Wyvern Av *LEIN* LE4 .... 126 B5
  LGEAT NG10 .... 76 B1 ⑥
Wyvern Cl *EWD/SEL/PNX* NG16 .... 21 K6
Wyvernhoe Dr *RLBORO* LE12 .... 112 C2
Wyvern Wy *DERBYE* DE21 .... 58 E4
Wyville Cl *NOTTE* NG7 .... 50 C2 ⑥
Wyville Rw *LEIW* LE3 .... 130 E6

Yarwell Cl *DERBYE* DE21 .... 44 B6
  MAPPK/POR/STA NG3 .... 38 A8 ⑥
Yarwell Dr *WGSTN* LE18 .... 138 C5
Yatesbury Crs
  WOL/BIL/BRX NG8 .... 35 J6 ⑥
Yates St *NORM/LIT* DE23 .... 57 L6
Yaxley Cl *RLEINE/SYS* LE7 .... 133 K1
Yeates Cl *LEIW* LE3 .... 130 B6
Yelverton Av *LEIE* LE5 .... 133 G4
Yeoman Av *BLWL* NG6 .... 24 D3 ⑥
Yeoman La *LEI* LE1 .... 6 F5
Yeoman's Dl *RLEINE/SYS* LE7 .... 115 H7
Yeoman St *LEI* LE1 .... 6 F5
Yeovil Cl *DERBYE* DE24 .... 59 G8 ⑥
Yew Barrow Cl *WBRGFD* NG2 .... 66 A2
Yew Cl *ARN* NG5 .... 37 H5
  LEIW LE3 .... 129 K6
  RLBORO LE12 .... 88 B7
Yewdale Cl *CFTN/RUD* NG11 ...... 64 B7
  WBRGFD NG2 .... 66 A2 ⑩
Yewdale Gv *DERBYE* DE21 .... 45 G4 ⑰
Yews Cl *MELB/CHEL* DE73 .... 72 E6
The Yews *LEIS* LE2 .... 138 F1
Yew Tree Av *ARN* NG5 .... 37 G6 ⑥
  BWSH/BRSTN DE72 .... 60 B2
Yew Tree Cl *COT/KEY/RAD* NG12 .. 53 H5
  DERBYSE DE24 .... 59 G8 ⑩
Yew Tree Dr *LEIW* LE3 .... 130 A1
Yew Tree La
  BWSH/BRSTN DE72 .... 73 K3 ⑥
  CARL NG4 .... 38 E5
  CFTN/RUD NG11 .... 64 A5
Yew Tree Rd *HUCK/RAV* NG15...... 23 M2
Yonge Cl *COT/KEY/RAD* NG12 .... 53 J5 ⑦
York Av *BSTN/STPLFD* NG9 ...... 63 K3 ⑥
  EWD/SEL/PNX NG16 .... 12 F5
  LGEAT NG10 .... 61 L2
York Cl *CARL* NG4 .... 38 D5 ⑥
  RLBORO LE12 .... 88 B6
  RLBORO LE12 .... 113 H7
  WGSTN LE18 .... 137 J6
York Dr *WOL/BIL/BRX* NG8 .... 35 H5
Yorke St *HUCK/RAV* NG15 .... 23 L1
York Pl *COAL* LE67 .... 109 H6
York Rd *DERBYE* DE21 .... 44 D8
  LBORO LE11 .... 8 F3
  LEI LE1 .... 6 E7
  LGEAT NG10 .... 62 A6
Yorkshire Rd *LEIN* LE4 .... 126 A6
York St *CARL* NG4 .... 38 E8
  DERBY DE1 .... 2 B3
  LEI LE1 .... 6 F7
  NOTT NG1 .... 5 G3
Youlgreave Cl *DERBYE* DE21 .... 44 D6 ⑥
Young Cl *BLWL* NG6 .... 35 K2
Young St *NORM/LIT* DE23 .... 57 K6
Ypres Rd *DERBYW* DE22 .... 43 G5
Yukon Wy *LEI* LE1 .... 7 H3 ⑥
Yvonne Crs *CARL* NG4 .... 38 D8 ⑥

Z

Zetland Cl *COAL* LE67 .... 108 A7
Zetland Crs *DERBYSE* DE24 .... 71 G5
Zouch Rd *RLBORO* LE12 .... 94 E4
Zulla Rd *MAPPK/POR/STA* NG3 .... 37 G7
Zulu Rd *NOTTE* NG7 .... 36 D5 ⑥

Index - featured places

Abbey Business Park
  LEI LE1 .... 6 E2
Abbey Primary School
  LEIN LE4 .... 125 L6
Abbey Road CP School
  WBRGFD NG2 .... 65 L1
A B C Cinemas
  NOTT NG1 .... 4 F7
Abington Gm High School
  WGSTN LE18 .... 138 A6
Adam House Medical Centre
  LGEAT NG10 .... 61 M2
Adco Business Centre
  NOTTE NG7 .... 36 C8
Adult Education College
  LEI LE1 .... 6 F7
Albany Junior Mixed School
  BSTN/STPLFD NG9 .... 48 B7
Albion Leisure Centre
  ILK DE7 .... 33 K7
Aldercar Infant School
  EWD/SEL/PNX NG16 .... 20 E3
Aldercar Secondary School
  EWD/SEL/PNX NG16 .... 20 E3
Alderman Derbyshire School
  BLWL NG6 .... 24 A7
Alderman Newtons School
  LEIW LE3 .... 124 D8
Alderman Richard Hallam
  Primary School
  LEIN LE4 .... 125 G6
Alderman Whitelower School
  BSTN/STPLFD NG9 .... 49 K7
Alderman White School
  BSTN/STPLFD NG9 .... 63 G1
Allenpark Infant School
  DERBYSE DE24 .... 72 C1
All Hallows Primary School
  CARL NG4 .... 38 D6
All Saints C of E Primary School
  RLEIW/BAR LE9 .... 140 B8

All Saints C of E
  Primary School
  WGSTN LE18 .... 138 A5
Alpine House Surgery
  RLBORO LE12 .... 113 J3
Alvaston & Boulton Sports Club
  DERBYSE DE24 .... 58 E6
Alvaston Junior & Infant School
  DERBYSE DE24 .... 59 G8
Alvaston Medical Practice
  DERBYSE DE24 .... 58 F8
Amber Business Centre
  ALFN DE55 .... 12 A2
The Angel Row Art Gallery
  NOTT NG1 .... 4 F7
Annie Holgate Junior
  & Infant School
  HUCK/RAV NG15 .... 23 K1
Anstey Nomads Football Club
  RLEINE/SYS LE7 .... 118 D8
Apex Business Park
  CFTN/RUD NG11 .... 64 F4
Appletree Medical Practice
  BPR/DUF DE56 .... 29 K4
Arboretum Primary School
  NORM/LIT DE23 .... 57 L5
Arkwright Primary School
  WBRGFD NG2 .... 51 H6
Army Training Corps
  COAL LE67 .... 108 B8
Arnold & Carlton College
  ARN NG5 .... 25 K8
Arnold & Carlton College
  CARL NG4 .... 52 D2
Arnold & Carlton College
  MAPPK/POR/STA NG3 .... 38 A4
Arnold Christ the King
  Comprehensive School
  ARN NG5 .... 25 M8
Arnold Health Centre
  ARN NG5 .... 25 K7

Arnold Hill School
  ARN NG5 .... 37 L1
Ar Razi Medical Centre
  LEIE LE5 .... 132 B4
Arthur Mee Secondary
  Girls School
  BSTN/STPLFD NG9 .... 48 B8
Arts Theatre
  NOTT NG1 .... 5 H7
Ascot Park Estate
  LGEAT NG10 .... 62 A1
Ashbrook Junior
  & Infant School
  BWSH/BRSTN DE72 .... 59 M5
Ashcroft Primary School
  DERBYSE DE24 .... 71 J5
Ashfield District Council
  HUCK/RAV NG15 .... 15 L8
Ashfield District Council
  HUCK/RAV NG15 .... 23 M1
Ashfield School
  LEIE LE5 .... 132 D3
Ashforth Business Centre
  MAPPK/POR/STA NG3 .... 5 J3
Ash Lea School
  COT/KEY/RAD NG12 .... 67 K5
Ashmount School
  LBORO LE11 .... 9 G8
Asian Temple
  LEIE LE5 .... 132 C1
Assarts Farm Medical Centre
  EWD/SEL/PNX NG16 .... 35 H3
Assembly Rooms
  DERBY DE1 .... 2 E3
Asterdale Leisure Centre
  DERBYE DE21 .... 59 K4
Asterdale School
  DERBYE DE21 .... 59 K4
Aston Hall Hospital
  BWSH/BRSTN DE72 .... 83 L1

Aston on Trent Primary School
  BWSH/BRSTN DE72 .... 73 L7
Attenborough
  Preparatory School
  BSTN/STPLFD NG9 .... 63 J5
Audley Centre
  DERBY DE1 .... 2 F4
Auster Industrial Estate
  LEIN LE4 .... 126 D1
Avenue Road School
  LEIS LE2 .... 131 M6
Awsworth Junior
  & Infant School
  EWD/SEL/PNX NG16 .... 34 A3
Awsworth Trading Estate
  ILK DE7 .... 33 K5
Aylestone Leisure Centre
  LEIS LE2 .... 131 K7
Babington Community College
  LEIN LE4 .... 124 F4
Babington Hospital
  BPR/DUF DE56 .... 17 J4
Badger Brook County
  Primary School
  RLEIW/BBY LE8 .... 142 D2
Bagthorpe Primary School
  EWD/SEL/PNX NG16 .... 13 L3
Bailey Brook Industrial Estate
  HEANOR DE75 .... 20 F5
Baitul Mukaram Mosque
  LEIS LE2 .... 7 L8
Bakersfield Medical Centre
  MAPPK/POR/STA NG3 .... 52 A1
Balloon Wood Industrial Estate
  BSTN/STPLFD NG9 .... 48 F3
Banks Road Infant School
  BSTN/STPLFD NG9 .... 62 D5
The Banks Surgery
  RLBORO LE12 .... 114 A4
Bar Lane Industrial Estate
  BLWL NG6 .... 36 B5

Barleycroft CP School
  LEIN LE4 .... 125 G4
Barrington Business Park
  LEIN LE4 .... 124 F2
Barrington Park
  Industrial Estate
  LEIN LE4 .... 124 F2
Barrow Health Centre
  RLBORO LE12 .... 105 G8
Barrow Road Business Park
  RLBORO LE12 .... 113 M4
Beacon Hill County Park
  RLBORO LE12 .... 111 G5
Beardall Street
  Secondary School
  HUCK/RAV NG15 .... 15 M8
Beauchamp School
  & Community College
  LEIS LE2 .... 138 F4
Beaufort Junior
  & Infant School
  DERBYE DE21 .... 44 A7
Beaufort Street
  Business Centre
  DERBYE DE21 .... 3 L1
Beaumont Leys
  Health Centre
  LEIN LE4 .... 125 G4
Beaumont Leys
  Secondary School
  LEIN LE4 .... 124 F4
Beaumont Lodge
  Primary School
  LEIN LE4 .... 124 F1
Beaumont Surgery
  LEIN LE4 .... 124 F1
Becket Primary School
  DERBYW DE22 .... 2 C6
Becket RC
  Comprehensive School
  CFTN/RUD NG11 .... 64 E2

The Becket Upper School
   WBRGFD NG2 .... 51 H7
Beechdale Swimming Centre
   WOL/BIL/BRX NG8 .... 50 A1
Beechwood Infant School
   RLEIW/BBY LE8 .... 143 J5
Beeston Clinic
   BSTN/STPLFD NG9 .... 63 K1
Beeston Fields Infant School
   BSTN/STPLFD NG9 .... 49 K7
Belgrave C of E Primary School
   LEIN LE4 .... 125 K4
Belgrave Rugby Football Club
   LEIN LE4 .... 125 K3
Belper Long Row
   Primary School
   BPR/DUF DE56 .... 17 K2
Belper Meadows Sports Club
   BPR/DUF DE56 .... 17 J5
Belper Natural Health Centre
   BPR/DUF DE56 .... 17 J4
Belper Pottery Primary School
   BPR/DUF DE56 .... 18 A3
Belper School
   BPR/DUF DE56 .... 18 A3
Belper Sports Centre
   BPR/DUF DE56 .... 18 B3
Belper Town Council
   BPR/DUF DE56 .... 17 L3
Belton Primary School
   RLBORO LE12 .... 100 F1
Belvoirdale County
   Primary School
   COAL LE67 .... 108 B7
Bembrose Community School
   RDERBYSW DE65 .... 68 A5
Bemrose Community School
   DERBYW DE22 .... 57 H3
Bendbow Rise Infant School
   LEIW LE3 .... 130 B4
Benjamin Outram
   Business Centre
   RIPLEY DE5 .... 11 J8
Bennerley Fields School
   ILK DE7 .... 33 K3
Bennerley School
   ILK DE7 .... 33 K3
Bentinck Primary School
   NOTTE NG7 .... 4 B3
Berridge Infant School
   NOTTE NG7 .... 36 C7
Berridge Junior School
   NOTTE NG7 .... 36 C8
Bestwood Park Health Centre
   ARN NG5 .... 24 F8
Bestwood Swimming Pool
   ARN NG5 .... 36 F1
The Big Wood School
   ARN NG5 .... 24 F5
Bilborough Medical Centre
   WOL/BIL/BRX NG8 .... 35 H8
Bilborough Sixth Form College
   WOL/BIL/BRX NG8 .... 35 G8
Birstall Parish Council
   LEIN LE4 .... 119 M8
Bishop Ellis RC Primary School
   RLEINE/SYS LE7 .... 120 D7
Bishop Lonsdale C of E School
   DERBYW DE22 .... 2 A8
Bispham Drive Junior School
   BSTN/STPLFD NG9 .... 62 C4
Blaby District Council
   RLEINE/BBY LE8 .... 135 M7
Blaby Industrial Park
   RLEINE/BBY LE8 .... 136 F6
Blaby Parish Council
   RLEIN/BBY LE8 .... 142 E1
Blessed Robert Widmerpool RC
   Primary School
   CFTN/RUD NG11 .... 64 C7
Bluebell Gallery
   DERBYW DE22 .... 43 L5
Boars Head Industrial Estate
   DERBYE DE21 .... 3 H2
Boberas Studio Gallery
   NOTT NG1 .... 5 J7
Bonnington Junior School
   BLWL NG6 .... 35 M1
Booth Wood County
   Primary School
   LBORO LE11 .... 103 G4
Borrow Wood Junior
   & Infant School
   DERBYE DE21 .... 59 K2
Bosworth College
   RLEIN/BAR LE9 .... 128 A4
Bosworth Primary School
   WBRGFD NG2 .... 50 F6
Boulton Clinic
   DERBYSE DE24 .... 72 D1
Boulton Junior & Infant School
   DERBYSE DE24 .... 72 E1
Bowling Alley
   LEI LE1 .... 6 D4
Bowling Alley
   NOTT NG1 .... 5 K7
Brackenfield School
   LGEAT NG10 .... 61 M6
Brackensdale Junior
   & Infant School
   DERBYW DE22 .... 56 F1
Bradshaw Retail Park
   DERBY DE1 .... 2 F6
Bramble Business Centre
   DERBY DE1 .... 2 E4
Bramcote C of E School
   BSTN/STPLFD NG9 .... 48 F7
Bramcote Hills
   Comprehensive School
   BSTN/STPLFD NG9 .... 48 F5
Bramcote Hills Primary School
   BSTN/STPLFD NG9 .... 48 F6
Bramcote Leisure Centre
   BSTN/STPLFD NG9 .... 48 E6
Bramcote Park Comprehensive
   School
   BSTN/STPLFD NG9 .... 48 E6

Braunstone Frith Junior School
   LEIW LE3 .... 130 A1
Braunstone Kingsway
   County Primary School
   LEIW LE3 .... 130 C5
Braunstone Town Council
   LEIW LE3 .... 130 C6
Breadsall C of E Primary School
   ILK DE7 .... 44 C3
Breadsall Hilltop Junior
   & Infant School
   DERBYE DE21 .... 44 C6
Brewhouse Yard Museum
   NOTTE NG7 .... 4 F9
Bridge Junior School
   LEIE LE5 .... 7 M3
Brinkhill School
   CFTN/RUD NG11 .... 64 D4
Brinsley Primary School
   EWD/SEL/PNX NG16 .... 13 J7
British Gypsum Business Park
   CFTN/RUD NG11 .... 77 M8
Broad Marsh Shopping Centre
   NOTT NG1 .... 5 H8
Brockington High School &
   Community College
   RLEIW/BAR LE8 .... 136 A5
Brookfield Primary School
   MCKLVR DE3 .... 56 B7
Brookhill Leys Infant School
   EWD/SEL/PNX NG16 .... 21 L6
Brookhill Leys Junior School
   EWD/SEL/PNX NG16 .... 21 L5
Brooklands County
   Infant School
   LGEAT NG10 .... 76 B1
Brooklands Junior School
   LGEAT NG10 .... 62 B8
Brooklyn Surgery
   HEANOR DE75 .... 20 D5
Brooksby Primary School
   CFTN/RUD NG11 .... 64 D4
Brookshill Primary School
   LEIS LE2 .... 138 F4
Brookside Primary School
   RLBORO LE12 .... 88 C6
Brookside School
   ILK DE7 .... 44 C3
Brookside School
   LEIS LE2 .... 139 H1
Broomfield College
   ILK DE7 .... 44 F2
Broomfield County
   Primary School
   RLEINE/SYS LE7 .... 115 J8
Broom Leys County
   Junior School
   COAL LE67 .... 108 E6
Broomleys Surgery
   COAL LE67 .... 108 E6
Broxtowe Borough Council
   BSTN/STPLFD NG9 .... 63 K1
Broxtowe Borough Council
   EWD/SEL/PNX NG16 .... 21 L5
Broxtowe Borough Council
   EWD/SEL/PNX NG16 .... 34 C1
Broxtowe College
   BSTN/STPLFD NG9 .... 63 J2
Broxtowe College
   BSTN/STPLFD NG9 .... 63 K1
Bulwell Business Centre
   BLWL NG6 .... 23 L8
Bulwell Health Centre
   BLWL NG6 .... 35 M1
Bunny C of E Primary School
   CFTN/RUD NG11 .... 79 J7
Burford Primary School
   ARN NG5 .... 37 G1
Burleigh Community College
   LBORO LE11 .... 103 G4
Burton Joyce Primary School
   CALV/BJ NG14 .... 39 K3
Burton on the Wolds
   County Primary School
   RLBORO LE12 .... 105 K1
Bushloe High School
   WGSTN LE18 .... 137 M5
The Business Centre
   LEI LE1 .... 6 E8
B U S M Business Park
   LEIN LE4 .... 125 L6
Buswells Lodge
   Primary School
   LEIN LE4 .... 124 E4
Byron Industrial Estate
   ARN NG5 .... 25 L8
CAB
   DERBY DE1 .... 2 F5
CAB
   NOTT NG1 .... 5 G8
Canal Museum
   NOTT NG1 .... 5 G9
Canalside Industrial Estate
   LGEAT NG10 .... 48 A8
The Carillon
   LBORO LE11 .... 9 H4
Carlton Digby Day School
   MAPPK/POR/STA NG3 .... 38 A4
Carlton Hill Surgery
   CARL NG4 .... 38 A8
Carlton Le Willows School
   CARL NG4 .... 38 F6
Carlton Netherfield
   Junior School
   CARL NG4 .... 38 E8
Carlyle Infant School
   NORM/LIT DE23 .... 56 F7
Carrington Primary School
   ARN NG5 .... 36 F6
Castle
   LEI LE1 .... 6 C7
Castle Clinic
   NOTT NG1 .... 4 D6
Castle Donington
   Community College
   CDON/KEG DE74 .... 84 F4
Castle Gallery
   NOTT NG1 .... 5 H7

Castle Meadow Retail Park
   WBRGFD NG2 .... 50 F4
Castle Museum and art gallery
   NOTT NG7 .... 4 F9
Castle Park Industrial Estate
   WBRGFD NG2 .... 50 F6
Castle Rock High School
   COAL LE67 .... 109 H5
Cathedral Road Clinic
   DERBY DE1 .... 2 D2
Catherine Infant School
   LEIN LE4 .... 125 M7
Catherine Junior School
   LEIN LE4 .... 125 M7
Catherine Street
   Industrial Estate
   LEIN LE4 .... 126 B5
Cavendish Close Infant School
   DERBYE DE21 .... 44 E7
Cavendish Close Junior School
   DERBYE DE21 .... 44 E7
Chaddesden Medical Centre
   DERBYE DE75 .... 58 C1
Charles Keene College
   LEI LE2 .... 6 F1
Charlotte County Infant School
   ILK DE7 .... 33 J5
Charlton House Medical Centre
   LGEAT NG10 .... 62 D7
Charnwood Borough Council
   LBORO LE11 .... 9 K4
Charnwood Community Council
   LBORO LE11 .... 9 H4
Charnwood Health Centre
   LEIE LE5 .... 7 M3
Charnwood Primary School
   LEIS LE2 .... 7 K4
Charnwood Surgery
   DERBY DE1 .... 2 E6
Charnwood Surgery
   RLBORO LE12 .... 113 J6
Chaucer Infant School
   ILK DE7 .... 33 K7
Chaucer Junior School
   ILK DE7 .... 33 K6
Chellaston Infant School
   MELB/CHEL DE73 .... 72 D5
Chellaston School
   MELB/CHEL DE73 .... 72 D6
Cherry Tree Infant School
   DERBYE DE21 .... 58 F2
Cherry Tree Junior School
   DERBYE DE21 .... 58 F2
Chettles Industrial Estate
   NOTTE NG7 .... 50 B2
Chevin Golf Club
   BPR/DUF DE56 .... 29 J2
The Chilwell Alderman
   Pounder Infant School
   BSTN/STPLFD NG9 .... 62 F2
Chilwell College House
   Junior School
   BSTN/STPLFD NG9 .... 63 H2
Chilwell Comprehensive School
   BSTN/STPLFD NG9 .... 63 H1
Chilwell Meadows Surgery
   BSTN/STPLFD NG9 .... 62 F1
Christ the King School
   LEIW LE3 .... 130 F1
Church Hill County
   Infant School
   LEIN LE4 .... 120 C8
Church House Surgery
   CFTN/RUD NG11 .... 79 C1
Church of England
   Primary School
   COAL LE67 .... 108 C1
Church of England
   Primary School
   RLBORO LE12 .... 114 A7
Church Street Medical Centre
   EWD/SEL/PNX NG16 .... 21 J1
Churchwide Business Park
   BLWL NG6 .... 36 C5
Church Wilne Water Sports Club
   BWSH/BRSTN DE72 .... 75 H2
Cinema
   DERBY DE1 .... 2 E5
City Farm
   MAPPK/POR/STA NG3 .... 5 M5
City Gallery
   LEI LE1 .... 7 G6
City of Leicester School
   LEIE LE5 .... 133 G3
City Road Industrial Park
   DERBY DE1 .... 43 L8
Civil Service Sports Ground
   WBRGFD NG2 .... 65 G1
Clarendon City College
   NOTT NG1 .... 5 J7
Clarendon College
   ARN NG5 .... 36 F7
Clarendon Park Medical Centre
   LEIS LE2 .... 131 L6
Clifton Medical Centre
   CFTN/RUD NG11 .... 64 C7
Cloudside Junior School
   LGEAT NG10 .... 61 M1
Club House
   BLWL NG6 .... 24 B8
Club House
   COT/KEY/RAD NG12 .... 80 F5
Club House
   RLBORO LE12 .... 117 L7
Clyde Street Medical Centre
   LEI LE1 .... 7 H4
Coalville Business Park
   COAL LE67 .... 108 A6
Coalville Community Hospital
   COAL LE67 .... 108 B6
Cobden County Primary School
   LBORO LE11 .... 9 L3
Cockshut Lane Business Centre
   MELB/CHEL DE73 .... 82 E7
Codnor Infant & Junior School
   RIPLEY DE5 .... 11 M7
Coleman Primary School
   LEIE LE5 .... 132 C1

Coleman Road Surgery
   LEIE LE5 .... 132 D2
College of Continuing
   Education
   HUCK/RAV NG15 .... 15 M8
College of Further Education
   NOTT NG1 .... 5 K6
College Street Health Centre
   LGEAT NG10 .... 62 A6
Colwick Business Park
   CARL NG4 .... 52 D2
Colwick Parish Council
   CARL NG4 .... 52 D3
Colwick Vale Surgery
   CARL NG4 .... 52 C2
Community Centre
   LEIW LE3 .... 6 A4
Concordia Industrial Estate
   LGEAT NG10 .... 76 A2
Co-operative College
   RLBORO LE12 .... 96 D3
Corfield C of E Infant School
   HEANOR DE75 .... 20 B6
Coroners Service
   LEIS LE2 .... 6 E9
Cosby County Primary School
   RLEIW/BAR LE9 .... 142 A5
Cosby Golf Club
   RLEIW/BAR LE9 .... 142 B6
Cossall Industrial Estate
   ILK DE7 .... 33 M5
Cossington Street
   Sports Centre
   LEIN LE4 .... 125 M6
Costock C of E Primary School
   RLBORO LE12 .... 89 G6
Cotgrave C of E
   Primary School
   COT/KEY/RAD NG12 .... 67 J4
Cotmanhay County
   Infant School
   ILK DE7 .... 33 J2
Cotmanhay County
   Junior School
   ILK DE7 .... 33 J2
Council Offices
   LEIS LE2 .... 7 L5
Countesthorpe
   Community College
   RLEIW/BBY LE8 .... 143 G4
The Countrymans Gallery
   RLEIW/BBY LE8 .... 146 E6
County Hall
   LEIW LE3 .... 124 B5
County Hall
   WBRGFD NG2 .... 51 J6
County Infant School
   COT/KEY/RAD NG12 .... 67 K4
County Primary School
   COAL LE67 .... 108 A3
County Primary School
   COT/KEY/RAD NG12 .... 80 F5
County Primary School
   GBY/RBY LE6 .... 117 H7
County Primary School
   RLBORO LE12 .... 95 H4
County Primary School
   RLEIW/BAR LE9 .... 129 H2
County Primary School
   RLEIW/BAR LE9 .... 142 B3
Covenant College
   NOTT NG1 .... 4 F3
Crescent Junior School
   LEIW LE3 .... 130 C3
Cricket Club
   RLEIW/BBY LE8 .... 146 C7
Croft C of E Primary School
   RLEIW/BAR LE9 .... 141 G4
The Croft Medical Centre
   LEIS LE2 .... 139 G3
Cromford Road
   Industrial Estate
   EWD/SEL/PNX NG16 .... 20 F3
Crossdale Drive Primary School
   COT/KEY/RAD NG12 .... 80 C3
Crown & County Court
   NOTT NG1 .... 5 H9
Crown Court
   DERBY DE1 .... 2 E2
Crown Courts
   LEI LE1 .... 7 G8
Crown Hills School
   LEIE LE5 .... 132 D3
The Curzon C of E
   Primary School
   DERBYW DE22 .... 43 H1
Dale Medical Centre
   NORM/LIT DE23 .... 2 D9
Dale Primary School
   NORM/LIT DE23 .... 57 J5
The Dales Medical Centre
   ILK DE7 .... 32 B8
Dallimore Primary School
   ILK DE7 .... 47 H3
Danemill CP School
   RLEIW/BAR LE9 .... 135 L4
Danemill CP School
   RLEIW/BAR LE9 .... 135 M5
Dar-es-salam Mosque
   LEIS LE2 .... 7 K9
Darul Uloom School
   LEIN LE4 .... 125 L5
Daybrook Business Centre
   ARN NG5 .... 37 H1
Dayncourt School
   COT/KEY/RAD NG12 .... 53 L4
De Lisle RC School
   LBORO LE11 .... 8 A4
The Delves School
   ALFN DE55 .... 11 K1
De Montfort Hall
   LEI LE1 .... 131 M4
De Montfort University
   LEI LE1 .... 6 D7
De Montfort University
   LEI LE1 .... 6 D8
De Montfort University
   LEIS LE2 .... 6 C9

De Montfort University
   LEIS LE2 .... 6 C8
Denby Free C of E Junior
   & Infant School
   RIPLEY DE5 .... 19 H6
The Derby Chest Clinic
   DERBY DE1 .... 2 E5
Derby City Council
   DERBY DE1 .... 2 D3
Derby City Council
   DERBY DE1 .... 2 E3
Derby City Council
   DERBY DE1 .... 2 D2
Derby City Council
   DERBY DE1 .... 3 G5
Derby City Council
   DERBY DE1 .... 3 G3
Derby City Council
   DERBY DE1 .... 3 G3
Derby City Council
   DERBYE DE21 .... 44 B8
Derby City Council
   DERBYSE DE24 .... 58 C6
Derby City Council
   DERBYSE DE24 .... 58 A7
Derby City Council
   DERBYW DE22 .... 43 K8
Derby City Council
   DERBYW DE22 .... 56 E1
Derby City General Hospital
   DERBYW DE22 .... 56 F5
Derby College
   DERBYE DE21 .... 3 L2
Derby College
   of Further Education
   DERBY DE1 .... 2 D6
Derby College Wilmorton
   DERBYSE DE24 .... 58 D5
Derby County Football Club
   DERBYSE DE24 .... 58 C4
Derby County Football Club
   NORM/LIT DE23 .... 57 M6
Derby Crown Court
   DERBY DE1 .... 3 G3
Derby Independent
   Grammar School for Boys
   NORM/LIT DE23 .... 56 D8
Derby Moor Community School
   NORM/LIT DE23 .... 56 F8
Derby Playhouse Theatre
   DERBY DE1 .... 3 G5
Derby Regional
   Swimming Pool
   DERBYSE DE24 .... 72 A1
Derby Rowing Club
   DERBY DE1 .... 43 L8
Derbyshire County Council
   DERBYE DE21 .... 43 M8
Derbyshire County Council
   DERBYE DE21 .... 58 F1
Derbyshire County Council
   DERBYW DE22 .... 57 H4
Derbyshire County Council
   LGEAT NG10 .... 62 B7
Derbyshire County
   Cricket Club
   DERBYE DE21 .... 3 K1
Derbyshire Royal
   Infirmary NHS Trust
   DERBY DE1 .... 3 G6
Derbyshire Royal
   Infirmary NHS Trust
   DERBYSE DE24 .... 58 B7
Derby Small Business Centre
   DERBY DE1 .... 3 H6
Derby Small Business Centre
   NORM/LIT DE23 .... 57 M6
Derby & South Derbyshire
   Magistrates Court
   DERBY DE1 .... 2 F3
Derby Superbowl
   NORM/LIT DE23 .... 57 L8
Derby Trading Estate
   DERBYE DE21 .... 43 M8
Derrymount Mixed School
   ARN NG5 .... 25 K6
Derwent Bus Centre
   DERBY DE1 .... 3 G1
Derwent Business Park
   RIPLEY DE5 .... 11 H6
Derwent Community School
   DERBYE DE21 .... 44 A8
Derwent Medical Centre
   DERBY DE1 .... 2 E1
Derwentside Industrial Estate
   BPR/DUF DE56 .... 17 K6
Derwent Street Surgery
   LEIS LE2 .... 7 M7
Digby Industrial Estate
   EWD/SEL/PNX NG16 .... 22 B8
Diseworth Junior School
   CDON/KEG DE74 .... 93 G1
Djanogly City
   Technology College
   NOTTE NG7 .... 36 E6
The Donington Collection
   Racing Car Museum
   CDON/KEG DE74 .... 84 B7
Douglas Primary School
   NOTTE NG7 .... 4 B6
Dovedale CP School
   LGEAT NG10 .... 75 L1
Dovelands Primary School
   LEIW LE3 .... 130 F2
Draycott Parish Council
   BWSH/BRSTN DE72 .... 60 F8
Draycott Primary School
   BWSH/BRSTN DE72 .... 60 F8
Duffield Art Gallery
   BPR/DUF DE56 .... 29 H5
Duffield Road Industrial Estate
   DERBYE DE21 .... 44 A1
Dunkirk Primary School
   NOTTE NG7 .... 50 C6
Earls Close Industrial Estate
   LEIN LE4 .... 120 C8
Earls Close Industrial Estate
   LEIN LE4 .... 120 D7

East Derbyshire Magistrates
ILK DE7...........................33 J7
Eastfield County
Primary School
LEIN LE4...........................120 E7
East Goscote Parish Council
RLEINE/SYS LE7................115 J8
East Midlands
International Airport
CDON/KEG DE74...............85 G7
East Midlands Nuffield Hospital
NORM/LIT DE23....................70 D1
East Park Road Surgery
LEIE LE5..........................132 B2
Eastwood Comprehensive
Lower School
EWD/SEL/PNX NG16...........21 L4
Eastwood
Comprehensive School
EWD/SEL/PNX NG16...........21 J4
Eastwood Health Centre
EWD/SEL/PNX NG16...........21 L5
Eastwood Junior School
EWD/SEL/PNX NG16...........21 K5
Eastwood & Kimberley
Community College
EWD/SEL/PNX NG16...........21 K4
Eastwood & Kimberley
Community College
EWD/SEL/PNX NG16...........34 D1
Eastwood Town Cricket Club
EWD/SEL/PNX NG16...........21 L4
The Ecclesbourne School
BPR/DUF DE56.....................29 J4
Ecclesbourne Surgery
BPR/DUF DE56.....................29 J4
Eden Surgery
ILK DE7...........................47 K1
Edgewood Drive
Primary School
HUCK/RAV NG15................23 H3
Edna G Olds School
NOTTE NG7...........................4 A9
Edwalton Primary School
COT/KEY/RAD NG12.............66 A3
Elizabeth Woodville
County Primary School
GBY/RBY LE6....................123 J4
Ellerslie Cricket Club
WBRGFD NG2.....................51 K7
Ellesmere College
LEI LE3..........................130 F5
Elliot Durham Swimming Pool
MAPPK/POR/STA NG3............37 J6
Elliott Durham School
MAPPK/POR/STA NG3............37 J5
Ellis Guilford School
BLWL NG6.........................36 A5
The Elms Infant School
MAPPK/POR/STA NG3.............5 H1
Elvaston Castle Working Estate
Museum
BWSH/BRSTN DE72..............73 L1
Elvaston Cricket Club
BWSH/BRSTN DE72..............59 K8
Emily Fortey School
LEIW LE3.........................130 D1
Enderby Leisure Centre
RLEIW/BAR LE9.................135 M4
Endland Industrial Estate
DERBYW DE22.....................57 H3
English Martyrs RC School
LEIW LE3.........................124 F6
English Martyrs RC School
LGEAT NG10.......................61 M6
Erewash Borough Council
ILK DE7...........................33 K8
Erewash Borough Council
ILK DE7...........................33 J8
Erewash Borough Council
ILK DE7...........................33 K7
Erewash Borough Council
LGEAT NG10.......................62 A2
Erewash Borough Council
LGEAT NG10.......................62 B7
Erewash Museum
ILK DE7...........................33 K7
Ernehale County Junior
& Infant School
ARN NG5..........................37 L1
Eskdale CP School
BSTN/STPLFD NG9................62 F2
Etwall Leisure Centre
RDERBYSW DE65..................68 F3
Etwall Primary School
RDERBYSW DE65..................68 F3
Evington Gallery
LEIS LE2.........................132 C8
Evington Valley
Primary School
LEIE LE5.........................132 B4
Exchange Arcade
NOTT NG1...........................5 H7
The Eye Gallery
DERBY DE1..........................2 E3
Eyres Monsell Junior School
LEIS LE2.........................137 H3
Eyres Monsell Primary School
LEIS LE2.........................137 H3
Faircharm Industrial Estate
LEIW LE3.........................131 H5
Fairfield CP School
BSTN/STPLFD NG9................62 B1
Fairfield Preparatory School
LBORO LE11........................9 K5
Fairfield School
WGSTN LE18......................137 L4
Fairham Community College
CFTN/RUD NG11...................64 D8
Family Medical Centre
DERBYSE DE24.....................58 E7
Farnborough
Comprehensive School
CFTN/RUD NG11...................64 E5
Fernvale CP School
RLEINE/SYS LE7.................133 K1

Fernwood
Comprehensive School
WOL/BIL/BRX NG8................49 H3
Fernwood Infant School
WOL/BIL/BRX NG8................49 J3
Fernwood Junior School
WOL/BIL/BRX NG8................49 H3
Field House County
Infant School
ILK DE7...........................47 K1
Findern CP School
RDERBYSW DE65..................70 C7
Firbeck School
WOL/BIL/BRX NG8................48 F3
Fire Station
LEI LE1..........................131 L4
Fire Station
NOTT NG1...........................5 G5
Firfield Primary School
BWSH/BRSTN DE72................61 J8
Firs Estate Primary School
DERBYW DE22.......................2 B8
Fleckney C of E Primary School
RLEIW/BBY LE8..................145 J7
Fleckney Leisure Centre
RLEIW/BBY LE8..................145 K6
Flower Gallery
DERBYW DE22.......................2 A2
Flower Gallery
MAPPK/POR/STA NG3............37 G6
Focus Gallery
NOTT NG1...........................4 E6
Folville Junior School
LEIW LE3.........................130 E5
The Ford College
LBORO LE11........................8 A7
Forest Hill Golf Club
COAL LE67.......................122 A6
Forest House Surgery
RLBORO LE12.....................102 A4
Forest Lodge Primary School
LEIW LE3.........................124 C7
Forest School
NOTTE NG7..........................4 C1
Forest Way Special School
COAL LE67........................108 E7
Fosse Health Trust
LBORO LE11........................9 K3
Fosse Medical Centre
LEIW LE3.........................131 G1
Fosse Park Shopping Centre
RLEIW/BAR LE9..................136 D2
Fosse Primary School
LEIW LE3...........................6 A2
Foxwood School
BSTN/STPLFD NG9................48 F6
Framework Knitters Museum
CFTN/RUD NG11...................79 G1
Frederick Harrison
Infant School
BSTN/STPLFD NG9................48 D7
Friargate Gallery
DERBY DE1..........................2 D3
Friar Gate Surgery
DERBY DE1..........................2 C3
Friargate Surgery
DERBY DE1..........................2 C2
Friar Lane Football Club
LEIS LE2.........................131 K7
Friesland School
BWSH/BRSTN DE72................61 L2
Fullhurst Community College
LEIW LE3.........................130 F4
The Galleries of Shire Hall
NOTT NG1...........................5 J8
The Gallery
DERBY DE1..........................2 F4
The Gallery
ILK DE7...........................33 J8
The Gallery
LEIW LE3...........................6 A7
The Gamston Medical Centre
WBRGFD NG2......................66 A1
Garendon High School
LBORO LE11......................103 G3
Gartree High School
LEIS LE2.........................138 F4
Gas Research Centre
LBORO LE11......................102 F6
Gateway Christian School
ILK DE7...........................46 D5
Gateway Sixth Form College
LEIS LE2...........................6 D7
Gayton Junior School
NORM/LIT DE23....................71 H1
George Spencer
Secondary Mixed School
BSTN/STPLFD NG9................62 C2
Gilbros Business Centre
LEI LE1............................7 G4
Gilthill Primary School
EWD/SEL/PNX NG16..............22 B8
Gladstone Street Surgery
RLBORO LE12......................94 E6
Glaisdale Business Centre
WOL/BIL/BRX NG8................49 H2
Glaisdale School
WOL/BIL/BRX NG8................35 K8
Glapton Primary School
CFTN/RUD NG11...................64 B5
Glebelands Primary School
LEIN LE4.........................119 G7
Glenfield CP School
LEIW LE3.........................123 M7
Glenfield Hall CP School
LEIW LE3.........................124 C6
Glenfield Hospital NHS Trust
LEIW LE3.........................124 C5
Glen Hills Primary School
LEIS LE2.........................136 E4
Glenmere School
WGSTN LE18......................138 D4
Golf Course
RLBORO LE12.....................114 E1
Gorse Hill Hospital
LEIW LE3.........................124 D3
Gotham CP School
CFTN/RUD NG11...................77 L6

Gotham Cricket Club
CFTN/RUD NG11...................77 M5
Government Office
NOTT NG1...........................4 F6
Grace Dieu Manor School
COAL LE67........................100 D7
Granby CP Junior School
ILK DE7...........................33 J4
Granby Halls Leisure Centre
LEIS LE2.........................131 K4
Granby Junior School
LEIS LE2.........................131 H8
Grange Business Park
RLEIW/BBY LE8..................136 D6
Grange Primary School
LGEAT NG10.......................62 D7
Greasley Beauvale D H
Lawrence Infant School
EWD/SEL/PNX NG16..............21 M4
Greasley Beau Vale
Junior School
EWD/SEL/PNX NG16..............22 A5
Greasley Sports Centre
EWD/SEL/PNX NG16..............21 M5
Greencroft Junior
& Primary School
CFTN/RUD NG11...................64 D4
Greengate Medical Centre
LEIN LE4.........................119 L7
Greenholme School
NOTTE NG5........................50 C4
Green Lane Gallery
DERBY DE1..........................2 E6
Green Lane School
LEIE LE5...........................7 M3
Green Lane Surgery
BPR/DUF DE56.....................17 K3
The Green Surgery
COAL LE67........................116 B7
Greenwood Dale Gm School
WBRGFD NG2......................51 L3
Greenwood Infant School
WBRGFD NG2......................51 L2
Greenwood Junior School
WBRGFD NG2......................51 K3
Greenwood & Sneinton Family
Medical Centre
MAPPK/POR/STA NG3............51 K2
Greystoke CP School
RLEIW/BAR LE9..................136 A7
Greythorn Primary School
WBRGFD NG2......................65 G2
Groby Brookvale High School
GBY/RBY LE6....................123 H5
Groby Community College
GBY/RBY LE6....................123 H4
Groby Road Surgery
LEIW LE3...........................6 A1
Groby Trading Estate
GBY/RBY LE6....................123 J3
Group Surgery & Clinic
DERBYW DE22......................43 H5
The Grove Hospital
BWSH/BRSTN DE72................74 B6
Gulzar-e-madina Mosque
LEIS LE2...........................7 L7
Guru Nanak Gurdwara Temple
LEI LE1............................6 C5
Guthlaxton College
WGSTN LE18......................137 M6
G X Superbowl
NOTTE NG7........................50 C6
Haddon Primary School
CARL NG4.........................38 B6
Hallam Fields Junior School
ILK DE7...........................47 K2
Hall Orchard C of E
Primary School
RLBORO LE12.....................105 H8
The Hall
COT/KEY/RAD NG12...............52 F4
Hama Medical Centre
EWD/SEL/PNX NG16..............34 E1
Hamilton Community School
LEIE LE5.........................127 J5
Hardwick Infant School
NORM/LIT DE23....................57 K6
Harrington County
Junior School
LGEAT NG10.......................61 M6
Harry Carlton
Comprehensive School
RLBORO LE12......................88 D5
Harry Mitchell College
BSTN/STPLFD NG9................49 M7
Hartley Business Centre
ARN NG5..........................36 F5
Harvey Haddon Sports Centre
WOL/BIL/BRX NG8................35 K8
Hathern C of E Primary School
RLBORO LE12......................94 E6
Hawthorne Primary School
BLWL NG6.........................24 C3
Haydn Junior School
ARN NG5..........................36 F5
Hayes College
LEIW LE3.........................131 G3
Haymarket Shopping Centre
LEI LE1............................6 F5
Haymarket Theatre
LEI LE1............................6 E4
Haywood Comprehensive
School
ARN NG5..........................37 G2
Hazel Primary School
LEIS LE2.........................131 K4
Heage Primary School
BPR/DUF DE56.....................10 B5
The Health Centre
WBRGFD NG2......................51 J8
Heanor Gate Industrial Estate
HEANOR DE75.....................20 B6
Heanor Gate School
HEANOR DE75.....................20 A6
Heanor Health Centre
HEANOR DE75.....................20 C6

Heanor & Langley Mill District
Memorial Hospital
HEANOR DE75.....................20 D6
Heanor Leisure Centre
HEANOR DE75.....................20 D6
Heanor Town Sports Ground
HEANOR DE75.....................20 C6
Heatherbrook Primary School
& Community Centre
LEIN LE4.........................124 D1
Heatherbrook Surgery
LEIN LE4.........................118 F8
Heathfield Primary School
ARN NG5..........................36 D4
Hemington Primary School
CDON/KEG DE74...................85 H2
Henry Mellish School
BLWL NG6.........................36 B2
Herbert Strutt Primary School
BPR/DUF DE56.....................17 J5
Herrick Primary School
LEIN LE4.........................126 B3
Heymann Primary School
WBRGFD NG2......................65 H3
Highbank Primary School
CFTN/RUD NG11...................64 B8
Highbury Hospital
BLWL NG6.........................36 A3
Highcliffe CP School
LEIN LE4.........................119 K8
Highcroft Surgery
LEIS LE2.........................139 G3
Highfield County Junior
& Infant School
LGEAT NG10.......................62 A5
Highfield Rangers F C
LEIN LE4.........................126 C3
Highfields Medical Centre
LEIS LE2...........................7 L6
Highgate Primary School
RLBORO LE12.....................114 B3
Highgate Surgery
RLBORO LE12.....................114 B4
High Pavement Sixth
Form College
ARN NG5..........................36 E2
High School Sports Ground
ARN NG5..........................36 E3
Hill Lane Industrial Estate
COAL LE67.......................116 B5
Hill Rise School
ARN NG5..........................25 K4
Hillside Medical Centre
BSTN/STPLFD NG9................48 D8
Hilton Industrial Estate
RDERBYSW DE65..................68 A4
Hilton Primary School
RDERBYSW DE65..................68 B5
Hind Leys Community College
RLBORO LE12.....................102 B3
Hindu Temple
LEI LE1............................7 G5
The Hindu Temple
MAPPK/POR/STA NG3............51 K1
HM Prison
LEIS LE2...........................6 F9
HM Young Offenders Institution
& Remand Cen (Glen Parva)
WGSTN LE18......................137 J3
Hogarth Primary School
MAPPK/POR/STA NG3............37 L8
Holbrook C of E Infant School
BPR/DUF DE56.....................18 A4
The Holgate School
HUCK/RAV NG15...................23 J1
Hollybrook Medical Centre
NORM/LIT DE23....................70 D1
Hollygirt School
MAPPK/POR/STA NG3..............5 G2
Holme Pierrepont C of E School
COT/KEY/RAD NG12...............52 E6
Holmfield CP School
LEIW LE3.........................129 M4
Holy Cross RC School
COAL LE67........................108 D2
Holy Cross RC School
HUCK/RAV NG15...................15 M6
Holywell County
Primary School
LBORO LE11......................103 G7
Holywell Primary School
EWD/SEL/PNX NG16..............22 D8
Horsendale Primary School
EWD/SEL/PNX NG16..............35 J4
Horsley C of E Primary School
DERBYE DE21......................30 D1
Horsley Lodge Golf Club
ILK DE7...........................30 F3
Horsley Woodhouse
Primary School
ILK DE7...........................31 H1
Hucknall Leisure Centre
HUCK/RAV NG15...................15 M7
Hucknall National
Secondary School
HUCK/RAV NG15...................15 K6
Hucknall Town Football Club
HUCK/RAV NG15...................23 K2
Humberstone Infant
& Primary School
LEIE LE5.........................126 A4
Humphrey Perkins School
RLBORO LE12.....................105 G7
Huncote CP School
RLEIW/BAR LE9..................135 H7
Huncote Leisure Centre
RLEIW/BAR LE9..................135 G7
Hunters Lodge Medical Centre
LEIW LE3.........................129 K5
Huntingdon Junior School
MAPPK/POR/STA NG3..............5 H4
Husseini Mosque
LEIE LE5.........................125 L5
The Hyson Green St Marys
Catholic Primary School
NOTTE NG7........................36 D7
Ice Stadium
NOTT NG1...........................5 K7

Ilkeston Bowl
ILK DE7...........................33 J8
Ilkeston Community Hospital
ILK DE7...........................33 H3
Ilkeston School
ILK DE7...........................33 H7
Ilkeston Swimming Pool
ILK DE7...........................33 J6
Imperial Avenue Infant School
LEIW LE3.........................130 F4
Industrial Estate
HEANOR DE75.....................20 B6
Industrial Estate
RIPLEY DE5.......................10 F6
Industrial Estate
RLEIW/BBY LE8..................142 C2
Industrial Museum
DERBY DE1..........................2 F2
Inglehurst Junior
& Infant School
LEIW LE3.........................124 F8
Inland Revenue
LEI LE1............................6 D4
Inland Revenue
WBRGFD NG2......................50 F4
Iona School
MAPPK/POR/STA NG3............51 L2
Ironville & Codnor Park
Primary School
EWD/SEL/PNX NG16..............12 D3
Irwin College
LEIS LE2...........................7 K9
Irwin College
LEIS LE2.........................131 M4
Ivy Grove Surgery
RIPLEY DE5.......................11 H6
Ivy House School
NORM/LIT DE23.....................3 J9
James Peacock County School
CFTN/RUD NG11...................64 F8
Jamia Hanfia
Taleem-ul-islam Ahle Sunnat
Wal Jamaat Mosque
NORM/LIT DE23.....................2 D8
Jamia Mosque
LEIE LE5.........................132 B1
Jesse Gray Primary School
WBRGFD NG2......................65 J2
The Jessop Medical Practice
RIPLEY DE5.......................11 H6
Jewry Wall Museum
LEI LE1............................6 C6
John Carrol Leisure Centre
NOTTE NG7..........................4 A5
John Clifford Primary School
BSTN/STPLFD NG9................63 L1
John Doran Gas Museum
LEIS LE2.........................131 J5
John Ellis Community College
LEIN LE4.........................125 L5
John Flamsteed
Community School
RIPLEY DE5.......................18 E5
John Port School
RDERBYSW DE65..................68 F3
John Ryle Health Centre
CFTN/RUD NG11...................64 C6
John Storer Clinic
NOTT NG1...........................4 E7
Judgemeadow
Community College
LEIE LE5.........................133 G2
Junior & Infant School
BPR/DUF DE56.....................18 E7
Kedleston Hall (NT)
DERBYW DE22......................42 C2
Kedleston Park Golf Club
DERBYW DE22......................42 E2
Kegworth County
Primary School
CDON/KEG DE74...................86 A5
Kegworth Museum
CDON/KEG DE74...................86 A5
Kegworth Squash Club
CDON/KEG DE74...................86 A5
Ken Martin Swimming Pool
BLWL NG6.........................24 C4
Kensington Junior School
ILK DE7...........................33 L8
Kestrel Business Park
CARL NG4.........................52 C2
Keyworth County
Infant School
COT/KEY/RAD NG12...............80 C4
Keyworth Health Centre
COT/KEY/RAD NG12...............80 C5
Keyworth Parish Council
COT/KEY/RAD NG12...............80 C5
Kibworth C of E
Primary School
RLEIW/BBY LE8..................146 D6
Kibworth High School
RLEIW/BBY LE8..................146 E7
Kilby C of E School
WGSTN LE18......................144 D3
Killisick Junior School
ARN NG5..........................25 M6
Kilnbrook Avenue
ARN NG5..........................25 M6
Kimberley
Comprehensive School
EWD/SEL/PNX NG16..............34 E1
Kimberley Health Clinic
EWD/SEL/PNX NG16..............34 E1
Kimberley Primary School
EWD/SEL/PNX NG16..............34 D1
Kimberley Recreation Centre
EWD/SEL/PNX NG16..............34 E1
King Edward Park
Primary School
MAPPK/POR/STA NG3..............5 M6
King Edward VII
Community College
COAL LE67........................109 G5
King Richard Infant School
LEIW LE3...........................6 A7
Kings Mead Clinic
DERBY DE1..........................2 C1

Kingsmead Industrial Estate
DERBY DE22 .... 57 H1
Kings Mead Infant School
DERBY DE1 .... 2 C1
The Kings School
WBRGFD NG2 .... 51 H6
Kingsway Hospital
DERBYW DE22 .... 57 G3
Kingsway Industrial Park
DERBYW DE22 .... 56 F2
Kingsway Retail Park
DERBYW DE22 .... 57 G2
Kingsway Surgery
LEIW LE5 .... 130 E8
Kingswell School
ARN NG5 .... 25 K8
Kirk Hallam Community School
ILK DE7 .... 47 H1
Kirk Hallam Ladywood
County School
ILK DE7 .... 47 H2
Kirk Langley C of E
Primary School
ASHB DE6 .... 41 K5
K M Sports Club
RLEIW/BAR LE9 .... 129 J1
Knighton Fields
Primary School
LEIS LE2 .... 131 K7
Lace Centre
NOTT NG1 .... 4 F8
Lace Hall
NOTT NG1 .... 5 H8
Lace Market Theatre
NOTT NG1 .... 5 J8
Lady Bay Junior
& Infant School
WBRGFD NG2 .... 51 L6
Lady Bay Surgery
WBRGFD NG2 .... 51 M6
Ladycross Infant School
LGEAT NG10 .... 61 M1
Lady Jane Grey CP School
GBY/RBY LE6 .... 123 J5
Ladylea Industrial Estate
ILK DE7 .... 18 F8
Lakeside Business Park
LEIN LE4 .... 120 A8
Lakeside Infant School
LGEAT NG10 .... 75 M2
Lambley Primary School &
Community Centre
CARL NG4 .... 26 E8
Lancaster Boys School
LEIS LE2 .... 131 L8
Lancaster Sports Centre
DERBY DE1 .... 2 D2
Landau Forte College
DERBY DE1 .... 2 F1
Langley Infant School
HEANOR DE75 .... 20 E6
Langley Mill Junior
Mixed School
EWD/SEL/PNX NG16 .... 20 F4
Langley Mill Junior School
EWD/SEL/PNX NG16 .... 20 E3
Langley Park Industrial Estate
EWD/SEL/PNX NG16 .... 20 F4
Langmoor Primary School
LEIS LE2 .... 138 D2
Lantern Lane Primary School
RLBORO LE12 .... 88 D5
Larkfields Junior School
EWD/SEL/PNX NG16 .... 34 F1
Larklands County
Infant School
ILK DE7 .... 33 L7
Latimer CP School
RLEINE/SYS LE7 .... 124 C2
Launde Primary School
LEIS LE2 .... 138 F1
The Lawrence Museum
EWD/SEL/PNX NG16 .... 21 K4
Law School
NOTT NG1 .... 4 F5
Leen Mills Junior
& Infant School
HUCK/RAV NG15 .... 15 M7
Lees Brook Community School
DERBYE DE21 .... 44 F7
Leeson Clinic
LEIW LE3 .... 131 G4
Leicester Central Mosque
LEIS LE2 .... 7 J6
Leicester City Council
LEI LE1 .... 6 F7
Leicester City Council
LEI LE1 .... 7 J3
Leicester City Council
LEIE LE5 .... 127 H6
Leicester City Council
LEIN LE4 .... 6 B1
Leicester City Council
LEIN LE4 .... 125 K5
Leicester City Council
LEIN LE4 .... 125 J2
Leicester City Council
LEIN LE4 .... 125 H4
Leicester City Council
LEIN LE4 .... 125 L6
Leicester City Council
LEIS LE2 .... 7 H7
Leicester City Council
LEIS LE2 .... 7 K6
Leicester City Council
LEIS LE2 .... 131 K5
Leicester City Council
LEIS LE2 .... 137 K1
Leicester City Council
LEIW LE3 .... 6 A9
Leicester City Council
LEIW LE3 .... 124 E7
Leicester City Council
LEIW LE3 .... 124 D7
Leicester City Council
LEIW LE3 .... 130 E4
Leicester City Council
LEIW LE3 .... 130 A1

Leicester City Council
LEIW LE3 .... 130 C4
Leicester City Council
LEIW LE3 .... 130 G3
Leicester City Council
LEIW LE3 .... 131 G3
Leicester City Council
RLEIW/BBY LE8 .... 146 E8
Leicester City Council
WGSTN LE18 .... 137 J3
Leicester City Football Club
LEIS LE2 .... 131 J4
Leicester City Museum
LEI LE1 .... 7 G8
Leicester College
LEIS LE2 .... 131 K4
Leicester College
LEIW LE3 .... 6 A9
Leicester County Council
LEIS LE2 .... 132 B6
Leicester Exhibition Centre
LEI LE1 .... 7 G5
Leicester Frith Hospital
LEIW LE3 .... 124 D5
Leicester General Hospital
NHS Trust
LEIE LE5 .... 132 E3
Leicester Grammar
Junior School
LEIE LE5 .... 133 G3
Leicester Grammar School
LEI LE1 .... 6 D6
Leicester High School for Girls
LEIS LE2 .... 132 C7
Leicester Ivanhoe C C
LEIW LE3 .... 129 H5
Leicester Leys Leisure Centre
LEIN LE4 .... 124 E2
Leicester Markazi Mosque
LEIS LE2 .... 7 L5
Leicester Mosque
LEIS LE2 .... 132 B2
Leicester Race Course
LEIS LE2 .... 138 C1
Leicester Royal Infirmary
NHS Trust
LEIS LE2 .... 6 E9
Leicester Royal Infirmary Staff
Residence
LEIS LE2 .... 131 J4
Leicester Rugby Football Club
LEIS LE2 .... 131 K4
Leicestershire County Council
LBORO LE11 .... 9 J2
Leicestershire County Council
LBORO LE11 .... 103 M2
Leicestershire County Council
LEI LE1 .... 6 D6
Leicestershire County Council
LEIE LE5 .... 126 C8
Leicestershire County Council
LEIN LE4 .... 124 F2
Leicestershire County Council
LEIS LE2 .... 7 J7
Leicestershire County Council
LEIS LE2 .... 137 J1
Leicestershire County Council
LEIW LE3 .... 124 C5
Leicestershire County Council
RLBORO LE12 .... 111 M3
Leicestershire County Council
RLEINE/SYS LE7 .... 119 M4
Leicestershire County Council
RLEIW/BAR LE9 .... 135 M7
Leicestershire County Council
WGSTN LE18 .... 137 L4
Leicestershire County Council
WGSTN LE18 .... 137 M6
Leicestershire County
Cricket Club
LEIS LE2 .... 131 J7
Leicestershire
Health Authority
LEI LE1 .... 6 F8
Leicestershire
Health Authority
LEIE LE5 .... 132 E2
Leicestershire Museums
LEI LE1 .... 6 D6
Leicestershire Museums Arts &
Records Service
LEIS LE2 .... 7 H8
Leicestershire & Rutland
Health Care NHS Trust
LEIE LE5 .... 126 D6
Leicester University
LEI LE1 .... 7 H9
Leics Museum of Technology
LEIN LE4 .... 125 K5
Leisure Centre
ARN NG5 .... 25 K7
Leisure Centre
LBORO LE11 .... 9 H5
Lenton Business Centre
NOTTE NG7 .... 50 C3
Lenton Health Centre
NOTTE NG7 .... 4 A7
Lenton Infant School
NOTTE NG7 .... 50 D4
Lenton Leisure Centre
NOTTE NG7 .... 4 A9
Leysland Clinic
RLEIW/BBY LE8 .... 143 G3
Leysland High School
RLEIW/BBY LE8 .... 143 G3
Limehurst High School
LBORO LE11 .... 9 H1
Lime Leigh Medical Centre
LEIW LE3 .... 131 G4
Linby Papplewick
C of E School
HUCK/RAV NG15 .... 15 M4
Linden Junior School
RLEIW/BBY LE8 .... 143 J3
Linden Primary School
LEIE LE5 .... 132 E4
Lings Bar Hospital
WBRGFD NG2 .... 66 A1

Little Eaton Primary School
DERBYE DE21 .... 30 A7
Little Hill CP School
WGSTN LE18 .... 138 A6
Littleover Community School
NORM/LIT DE23 .... 56 D7
Littleover Medical Centre
NORM/LIT DE23 .... 56 F6
The Little Theatre
LEI LE1 .... 7 G7
Littlewick Medical Centre
ILK DE7 .... 33 K8
London Road
Private Hospital
LEIS LE2 .... 132 B6
Long Eaton Community School
LGEAT NG10 .... 62 B8
The Long Eaton & District
Arts Council
LGEAT NG10 .... 62 C8
Longlane C of E Primary School
ASHB DE6 .... 40 B7
Longmoor Primary School
LGEAT NG10 .... 62 A4
Longslade Community College
RLEINE/SYS LE7 .... 119 M6
Long Street Surgery
WGSTN LE18 .... 138 A5
Long Whatton C of E School
RLBORO LE12 .... 94 A4
Lons County Infant School
RIPLEY DE5 .... 11 H5
Loscoe C of E Primary School
HEANOR DE75 .... 19 M3
Loughborough C of E School
LBORO LE11 .... 8 F4
Loughborough College
of Art & Design
LBORO LE11 .... 8 F4
Loughborough College
of Further Education
LBORO LE11 .... 8 E5
Loughborough Health Centre
LBORO LE11 .... 9 K3
Loughborough High School
LBORO LE11 .... 9 K5
Loughborough Hospital
LBORO LE11 .... 8 D2
Loughborough Mosque
& Islamic Cultural Association
LBORO LE11 .... 9 L4
Loughborough
Motorway Trading Estate
RLBORO LE12 .... 101 L5
Loughborough Town Hall
LBORO LE11 .... 9 J3
Loughborough University
LBORO LE11 .... 8 D3
Loughborough University
LBORO LE11 .... 8 C5
Loughborough University
LBORO LE11 .... 8 F7
Loughborough University
LBORO LE11 .... 8 A5
Loughborough University
LBORO LE11 .... 8 C6
Loughborough University
LBORO LE11 .... 103 C5
Lower School
RLBORO LE12 .... 76 B1
Lum Farm Leisure Centre
RIPLEY DE5 .... 19 J2
Lutterworth Road Surgery
LEIS LE2 .... 137 G2
Lutterworth Road Surgery
RLEIW/BBY LE8 .... 136 F8
Lynncroft Primary School
EWD/SEL/PNX NG16 .... 21 L4
Mackworth College Derby
DERBYW DE22 .... 56 D2
Madford Business Park
ARN NG5 .... 37 H1
Magazine Gatehouse
LEIS LE2 .... 6 D7
Main Shopping Centre
DERBY DE1 .... 3 G4
Main Street Surgery
RLEIW/BBY LE8 .... 139 L6
Manhattan Gallery
NOTT NG1 .... 5 H7
Manorbrooke School
LEIS LE2 .... 132 A7
Manorfield C of E
Primary School
RLEIW/BAR LE9 .... 140 B5
Manor High School
LEIE LE5 .... 133 H8
The Manor Surgery
BSTN/STPLFD NG9 .... 63 K1
Manvers Junior School
COT/KEY/RAD NG12 .... 67 K4
Maplewell Hall School
RLBORO LE12 .... 111 J8
Mapperley C of E
Primary School
ILK DE7 .... 32 D4
Mapperley Park
Medical Centre
MAPPK/POR/STA NG3............ 5 H1
Mapperley Plains
Primary School
MAPPK/POR/STA NG3............ 37 M4
Margaret Glen-bott School
WOL/BIL/BRX NG8 .... 49 M3
Markaz-e-badri-dawoodi
Bohra Mosque
LEI LE1 .... 6 F7
Markeaton Primary School
DERBYW DE22 .... 43 J8
Market
DERBY DE1 .... 2 F4
Market
NOTT NG1 .... 5 H6
Markets and Corn Exchange
LEI LE1 .... 6 E6
Marlow Road Industrial Estate
LEIW LE3 .... 131 H5

Marlpool Junior School
HEANOR DE75 .... 20 E6
Marriott Primary School
LEIS LE2 .... 137 J1
Martin High School
RLEINE/SYS LE7 .... 118 B8
Martinshaw CP School
GBY/RBY LE6 .... 123 H3
Mary Howitt
Infant Community School
HEANOR DE75 .... 20 B5
Mary Linwood School
WGSTN LE18 .... 137 K3
Mayflower Junior School
LEIE LE5 .... 132 D3
Meadowbank Day Hospital
WBRGFD NG2 .... 50 F6
Meadow County
Primary School
WGSTN LE18 .... 138 C4
Meadow Farm Community
Primary School
DERBYE DE21 .... 58 D3
Meadow Lane County
Infant School
BSTN/STPLFD NG9 .... 63 J3
Meadow Lane Industrial Estate
LBORO LE11 .... 104 A1
Meadows Primary School
WBRGFD NG2 .... 51 H5
The Meadows Primary School
BPR/DUF DE56 .... 29 H4
Meadow Trading Estate
WBRGFD NG2 .... 51 J5
Media Centre
NOTT NG1 .... 5 J7
Medway Primary School
LEIS LE2 .... 7 L8
Melbourne Junior
& Infant School
MELB/CHEL DE73 .... 82 F7
Melbourne Park Medical Centre
WOL/BIL/BRX NG8 .... 36 A6
Melbourne Street Surgery
LEIS LE2 .... 7 L5
Melbury Primary School
WOL/BIL/BRX NG8 .... 35 H7
Mellers Primary School
NOTTE NG7 .... 4 A4
Mellor Infant School
LEIN LE4 .... 125 M4
Menphys Special School
for the Handicapped
WGSTN LE18 .... 138 A3
Mental Health Clinic
BSTN/STPLFD NG9 .... 63 K2
Mercenfield CP School
COAL LE67 .... 116 B7
Merridale Medical Centre
LEIW LE3 .... 130 F6
The Merrill Community
School & Sixth Form College
DERBYSE DE24 .... 72 C1
Merrydale Junior
& Infant School
LEIE LE5 .... 126 C7
Merton County
Primary School
RLEINE/SYS LE7 .... 120 F5
Michael House School
HEANOR DE75 .... 32 E1
Mickleover Primary School
MCKLVR DE3 .... 56 B5
Mickleover Surgery
MCKLVR DE3 .... 56 C5
Middleton School
WOL/BIL/BRX NG8 .... 50 A3
Milford County School
BPR/DUF DE56 .... 17 L8
Milford Primary School
CFTN/RUD NG11 .... 64 C7
Millennium Business Centre
DERBYE DE21 .... 58 C3
Millfield County
Primary School
LEIW LE3 .... 130 C7
Millgate School
LEIS LE2 .... 131 L7
Mill Hill Industrial Estate
RLEIW/BAR LE9 .... 135 L3
Mill Lane Industrial Estate
GBY/RBY LE6 .... 123 L6
The Moat Community College
LEIS LE2 .... 7 J6
Moderns Rugby Football Club
CFTN/RUD NG11 .... 50 F7
Montage Gallery
DERBY DE1 .... 2 E2
Montrose Primary School
LEIS LE2 .... 137 H1
The Moore Clinic
BPR/DUF DE56 .... 17 K3
Moorgreen Industrial Park
EWD/SEL/PNX NG16 .... 21 M2
Moorhead Primary School
DERBYSE DE24 .... 72 D1
Morley Primary School
ILK DE7 .... 31 H8
Mornington Primary School
EWD/SEL/PNX NG16 .... 35 H3
Mosque
LEIS LE2 .... 7 K6
Mosque
NORM/LIT DE23 .... 2 F9
Mosque
NOTT NG1 .... 5 J5
Mount St Bernard Abbey
COAL LE67 .... 109 H2
Mountsorrel Health Centre
RLBORO LE12 .... 113 J8
Mountsorrel Primary School
RLBORO LE12 .... 113 H5
Mowacre Community
& Sports Centre
LEIN LE4 .... 125 J1

Mowacre Hill Primary School
LEIN LE4 .... 125 H2
Mundella Community College
LEI LE1 .... 126 D7
Mundy C E Junior School
HEANOR DE75 .... 20 C6
Murray Park
Community School
MCKLVR DE3 .... 56 D3
Museum & Art Gallery
DERBY DE1 .... 2 E3
Museum of Costume
LEI LE1 .... 6 D6
Museum of Law
NOTT NG1 .... 5 H8
Museum of Nottingham
Lace & Shop
NOTT NG1 .... 5 H8
Narborough Hall Gallery
RLEIW/BAR LE9 .... 135 M8
Narborough Health Centre
RLEIW/BAR LE9 .... 136 A7
Narborough Parish Council
RLEIW/BAR LE9 .... 135 M7
Narborough Road
Doctors Surgery
LEIW LE3 .... 131 G4
N A Temple
NOTT NG1 .... 5 G7
National Junior & Infant School
HUCK/RAV NG15 .... 15 L7
National Water Sports Centre
COT/KEY/RAD NG12 .... 52 C5
Natural History Museum
WOL/BIL/BRX NG8 .... 49 L4
Nature Care Clinic
LEI LE1 .... 6 E7
Netherfield Infant School
CARL NG4 .... 38 D8
Netherfield Medical Centre
CARL NG4 .... 38 E8
Nethergate School
CFTN/RUD NG11 .... 64 D6
Netherhall Road Surgery
LEIE LE5 .... 127 H6
Nether Hall School
LEIE LE5 .... 127 H6
Newarke House Museum
LEI LE1 .... 6 D7
Newbridge High School
COAL LE67 .... 108 B7
Newchase Business Park
DERBYSE DE24 .... 58 A6
New College Nottingham
ARN NG5 .... 36 F7
New College Nottingham
BLWL NG6 .... 36 A3
Newcroft County
Primary School
RLBORO LE12 .... 102 A4
New Parks Clinic
LEIW LE3 .... 124 D7
New Parks
Community College
LEIW LE3 .... 124 D8
New Parks House
Primary School
LEIW LE3 .... 124 E7
New Parks Leisure Centre
LEIW LE3 .... 124 D8
Newry Junior School
WGSTN LE18 .... 137 K2
Newstead Primary School
HUCK/RAV NG15 .... 15 H1
New Walk Centre
LEI LE1 .... 6 F7
Nightingale Business Park
DERBYSE DE24 .... 58 B7
Nightingale Infant School
DERBYSE DE24 .... 58 A8
Nightingale Junior School
DERBYSE DE24 .... 58 A7
Noel Baker Community School
DERBYSE DE24 .... 72 D3
Normanton Junior School
NORM/LIT DE23 .... 57 J8
Northfield House
Junior School
LEIN LE4 .... 126 B6
Northgate Primary School
NOTTE NG7 .... 36 D6
North West Leicestershire
Training College
COAL LE67 .... 108 A6
Nottingham Bluecoat School
WOL/BIL/BRX NG8 .... 36 A7
Nottingham Business Centre
NOTTE NG7 .... 50 C3
Nottingham City Council
ARN NG5 .... 37 J4
Nottingham City Council
BLWL NG6 .... 36 C4
Nottingham City Council
EWD/SEL/PNX NG16 .... 21 L5
Nottingham City Council
MAPPK/POR/STA NG3............ 5 L3
Nottingham City Council
MAPPK/POR/STA NG3............ 5 G1
Nottingham City Council
MAPPK/POR/STA NG3............ 5 K1
Nottingham City Council
MAPPK/POR/STA NG3............ 5 H3
Nottingham City Council
MAPPK/POR/STA NG3............ 51 L2
Nottingham City Council
NOTT NG1 .... 4 F8
Nottingham City Council
NOTT NG1 .... 4 E5
Nottingham City Council
NOTT NG1 .... 4 F6
Nottingham City Council
NOTT NG1 .... 5 G8
Nottingham City Council
NOTT NG1 .... 5 G7
Nottingham City Council
WBRGFD NG2 .... 51 K6
Nottingham City Council
WBRGFD NG2 .... 51 K3

Nottingham City Council
  WOL/BIL/BRX NG8 ...... 35 K7
Nottingham City Council
  WOL/BIL/BRX NG8 ...... 49 K4
Nottingham City Hospital
  Mobility Centre
  ARN NG5 ...... 36 F3
Nottingham City Hospital
  NHS Trust
  ARN NG5 ...... 36 E2
Nottingham
  Community College
  MAPPK/POR/STA NG3 ...... 5 L6
Nottingham Community
  Health NHS Trust
  NOTTE NG7 ...... 4 B6
Nottingham County Council
  WBRGFD NG2 ...... 51 J6
Nottingham Forest
  Football Club
  WBRGFD NG2 ...... 51 J6
Nottingham General Hospital
  NOTTE NG7 ...... 4 E8
Nottingham Health Authority
  NOTT NG1 ...... 4 F8
Nottingham High School
  NOTT NG1 ...... 4 E3
Nottingham High School
  for Girls
  NOTT NG1 ...... 4 F3
Nottingham Law School
  NOTT NG1 ...... 4 E5
Nottingham Magistrates Court
  WBRGFD NG2 ...... 51 G4
Nottingham Nuffield Hospital
  ARN NG5 ...... 37 H2
Nottingham Playhouse Theatre
  NOTT NG1 ...... 4 F6
Nottingham R F C
  BSTN/STPLFD NG9 ...... 63 K2
Nottinghamshire
  County Council
  ARN NG5 ...... 25 L8
Nottinghamshire
  County Council
  ARN NG5 ...... 37 G1
Nottinghamshire
  County Council
  CFTN/RUD NG11 ...... 64 C6
Nottinghamshire
  County Council
  COT/KEY/RAD NG12 ...... 52 B7
Nottinghamshire
  County Council
  COT/KEY/RAD NG12 ...... 81 G6
Nottinghamshire
  County Council
  WBRGFD NG2 ...... 5 G9
Nottinghamshire
  County Council
  WBRGFD NG2 ...... 51 J7
Nottinghamshire
  County Council
  WBRGFD NG2 ...... 51 J7
Nottinghamshire
  County Council
  WBRGFD NG2 ...... 51 J7
Nottinghamshire
  County Council
  WBRGFD NG2 ...... 51 K7
Nottinghamshire
  County Council
  WBRGFD NG2 ...... 65 K2
Nottinghamshire
  County Council
  WOL/BIL/BRX NG8 ...... 49 L3
Nottinghamshire County
  Cricket Club
  WBRGFD NG2 ...... 51 J6
Nottingham South
  Industrial Estate
  CFTN/RUD NG11 ...... 64 F3
Nottingham Theatre Club
  NOTT NG1 ...... 5 H8
Nottingham Trent University
  CFTN/RUD NG11 ...... 63 M5
Nottingham Trent University
  CFTN/RUD NG11 ...... 64 B4
Nottingham Trent University
  NOTT NG1 ...... 4 F5
Nottingham Trent University
  NOTT NG1 ...... 4 E4
Nottingham Trent University
  NOTT NG1 ...... 4 E5
Nottingham University Hospital
  NOTTE NG7 ...... 50 B5
Notts County Football Club
  WBRGFD NG2 ...... 51 J5
Nuffield Hospital
  LEIE LE5 ...... 126 F7
Nursery
  DERBY DE1 ...... 2 E1
Nutbrook Cricket Club
  ILK DE7 ...... 32 F7
Oadby Health Centre
  LEIS LE2 ...... 138 D2
Oadby Town Football Club
  WCSTN LE18 ...... 138 D3
Oadby & Wigston
  Borough Council
  WCSTN LE18 ...... 137 M5
Oakmeadow Surgery
  LEIW LE3 ...... 124 A8
Oaks Industrial Estate
  LBORO LE11 ...... 103 K1
Oaks Industrial Estate
  RLEIW/BAR LE9 ...... 135 L8
The Oaks Medical Centre
  BSTN/STPLFD NG9 ...... 49 K8
Oakwood Infant School
  DERBYSE DE24 ...... 72 E1
Oakwood Junior School
  DERBYSE DE24 ...... 72 E1
Oakwood Leisure Centre
  DERBYE DE21 ...... 44 E5
Oakwood Medical Centre
  DERBYE DE21 ...... 44 D6

Oakwood Surgery
  DERBYE DE21 ...... 44 E6
Ockbrook School
  BWSH/BRSTN DE72 ...... 60 A2
Odeon Cinema
  NOTT NG1 ...... 5 G7
Odeon Multiplex
  LEIS LE18 ...... 131 K5
Old Ashby Road Surgery
  LBORO LE11 ...... 102 F5
Old Basford Health Centre
  BLWL NG6 ...... 36 C5
Old Hall Mill Business Park
  DERBYE DE21 ...... 30 A8
Old Rectory Museum
  LBORO LE11 ...... 9 J1
The Old School Surgery
  RLEIW/BAR LE9 ...... 140 B5
The Old School Surgery
  RLEIW/BBY LE8 ...... 146 E7
Old Vicarage School
  DERBYW DE22 ...... 43 K4
Old Wyggestonians
  Sports Club
  WCSTN LE18 ...... 138 D3
The Open University
  NOTT NG7 ...... 4 B8
The Open University
  NOTT NG7 ...... 36 F7
Orchard Business Park
  ILK DE7 ...... 33 H6
Orchard Close Surgery
  RLBORO LE12 ...... 95 G1
Orchard CP School
  CDON/KEG DE74 ...... 84 E3
Orchard Surgery
  CDON/KEG DE74 ...... 86 B5
Ormonde Fields Golf Club
  RIPLEY DE5 ...... 12 B3
Orton Industrial Estate
  COAL LE67 ...... 108 B6
Osmaston Road Surgery
  DERBY DE1 ...... 2 F6
Our Lady of Perpetual Succour
  RC Primary School
  BLWL NG6 ...... 36 B1
Our Ladys Convent School
  LBORO LE11 ...... 9 J6
Outwoods Edge
  Primary School
  RLBORO LE12 ...... 103 L8
Overdale Junior
  & Infant School
  LEIS LE2 ...... 138 A1
Oxley School
  RLBORO LE12 ...... 101 L4
Parish Council
  LEIN LE4 ...... 125 M1
Parkdale Primary School
  CARL NG4 ...... 52 B1
Parker Drive Business Centre
  LEIN LE4 ...... 125 J5
Parker Industrial Estate
  DERBYE DE21 ...... 43 M7
Park Farm Medical Centre
  DERBYW DE22 ...... 43 H5
Parkfields Surgery
  DERBYSE DE24 ...... 58 E7
Parkham Gallery
  EWD/SEL/PNX NG16 ...... 21 J1
Park House Medical Centre
  CARL NG4 ...... 38 D7
Parkland County
  Primary School
  WCSTN LE18 ...... 137 K6
Parklands County
  Infant School
  LGEAT NG10 ...... 61 M6
Park Lane Surgery
  DERBYW DE22 ...... 43 K3
The Park Medical Practice
  BWSH/BRSTN DE72 ...... 59 L5
The Park Medical Practice
  DERBYE DE21 ...... 58 E1
Park Surgery
  HEANOR DE75 ...... 20 D1
Parkview Surgery
  EWD/SEL/PNX NG16 ...... 21 L3
Parsons Gallery
  GBY/RBY LE6 ...... 129 J1
Pasley Road Health Centre
  LEIS LE2 ...... 137 H3
Pastures CP School
  RLEIW/BAR LE9 ...... 135 K5
Peak Practice
  RIPLEY DE5 ...... 11 L6
Peartree Clinic
  NORM/LIT DE23 ...... 57 L6
Pear Tree Junior
  & Infant School
  NORM/LIT DE23 ...... 57 L6
Pear Tree Medical Centre
  NORM/LIT DE23 ...... 57 L6
Peckleton Lane Business Park
  RLEIW/BAR LE9 ...... 128 A8
Peoples College
  NOTT NG1 ...... 5 G8
Peoples College for Further
  Education
  NOTT NG1 ...... 4 E7
Percy Street School
  BLWL NG6 ...... 36 B4
Perkins Industrial Estate
  DERBYE DE21 ...... 44 A7
Perry Road Surgery
  ARN NG5 ...... 37 G4
Peter Baines Industrial Estate
  DERBY DE1 ...... 2 D6
Phoenix Arts Centre
  LEI LE1 ...... 6 E7
Phoenix School
  CARL NG4 ...... 38 D5
Pickfords House Museum
  DERBY DE1 ...... 2 C3
Picture House
  LEI LE1 ...... 6 E5
Pilkington Librarye
  LBORO LE11 ...... 103 G5

Pinfold Medical Practice
  LBORO LE11 ...... 9 K3
Pinfold Trading Estate
  BSTN/STPLFD NG9 ...... 48 C7
Piper Way School
  LEIW LE3 ...... 130 D1
Plumtree School
  COT/KEY/RAD NG12 ...... 80 C1
Police Museum
  LEI LE1 ...... 2 E2
Portland Leisure Centre
  NOTTE NG7 ...... 51 H5
Portland Primary School
  WOL/BIL/BRX NG8 ...... 49 G1
Portway Infant School
  DERBYW DE22 ...... 43 J3
Portway Junior School
  DERBYW DE22 ...... 43 J3
Po Sorting Office
  DERBY DE1 ...... 3 H7
Power Station
  CFTN/RUD NG11 ...... 76 E6
Primary School
  LBORO LE11 ...... 9 H2
Primary School
  NOTTE NG7 ...... 50 C2
Prime Business Centre
  DERBYE DE21 ...... 58 F3
Prime Industrial Estate
  NORM/LIT DE23 ...... 58 A5
Priory Junior School
  CARL NG4 ...... 38 D6
Priory RC Primary School
  EWD/SEL/PNX NG16 ...... 21 L6
Puppets Theatre
  MAPPK/POR/STA NG3 ...... 5 J3
Queen St Baths
  DERBY DE1 ...... 2 E2
Queens Drive Industrial Estate
  WBRGFD NG2 ...... 50 E6
Queens Leisure Centre
  DERBY DE1 ...... 2 E2
Queensmead Infant School
  LEIW LE3 ...... 130 D3
Queens Medical Centre
  NOTTE NG7 ...... 50 B5
Queens Road Surgery
  LEIS LE2 ...... 131 M5
Quorn Parish Council
  RLBORO LE12 ...... 112 E2
Racecourse Industrial Park
  DERBYE DE21 ...... 44 A7
Radcliffe Junior School
  COT/KEY/RAD NG12 ...... 53 K5
Radcliffe on Trent Golf Club
  COT/KEY/RAD NG12 ...... 53 M5
Raf Building
  COAL LE67 ...... 108 E7
Rail Museum
  ALFN DE55 ...... 11 L3
Ramcharia Sikh Temple
  NORM/LIT DE23 ...... 57 L5
Ratby CP School
  GBY/RBY LE6 ...... 123 G6
Ratby Sports Club
  GBY/RBY LE6 ...... 123 G7
Ratby Surgery
  GBY/RBY LE6 ...... 123 H8
Ratcliffe College
  RLEINE/SYS LE7 ...... 114 E5
Ravensdale Junior
  & Infant School
  MCKLVR DE3 ...... 56 C4
Rawlins School
  RLBORO LE12 ...... 112 D1
Rawlins School
  & Community College
  RLBORO LE12 ...... 112 E1
Redhill Comprehensive School
  ARN NG5 ...... 25 J6
Red Hill Field CP School
  RLEIW/BAR LE9 ...... 135 L7
Redhill Leisure Centre
  ARN NG5 ...... 25 J6
Redhill Primary School
  BWSH/BRSTN DE72 ...... 60 B3
Redlands County
  Junior School
  RLBORO LE12 ...... 114 A4
Redwood Junior
  & Infant School
  DERBYSE DE24 ...... 71 J4
The Regent Clinic
  of Cosmetic Surgery
  NOTTE NG7 ...... 4 D7
Regent College 6th
  Form College
  LEI LE1 ...... 131 L4
Register Office
  NOTT NG1 ...... 4 F4
Registry Office
  LEI LE1 ...... 6 E7
Reigate Junior & Infant School
  DERBYW DE22 ...... 42 D8
Richard Herrod Leisure Centre
  CARL NG4 ...... 38 A7
Richard Hill C of E School
  RLEINE/SYS LE7 ...... 118 F5
Richardson Endowed
  Primary School
  ILK DE7 ...... 31 K1
Riddings Infant School
  ALFN DE55 ...... 12 A1
Riddings Junior School
  ALFN DE55 ...... 12 B1
Ridgeway Infant School
  NORM/LIT DE23 ...... 71 H1
The Ridgeway Surgery
  RLEINE/SYS LE7 ...... 119 G1
Ripley Hospital
  RIPLEY DE5 ...... 11 G6
Ripley Junior and Infant School
  RIPLEY DE5 ...... 11 G7
Ripley Leisure Centre
  RIPLEY DE5 ...... 11 H6
Ripley Mill Hill School
  RIPLEY DE5 ...... 11 L7

Rise Park Junior
  & Infant School
  ARN NG5 ...... 24 C6
Risley Lower Grammar
  C of E Primary School
  BWSH/BRSTN DE72 ...... 61 J3
Riverlyn Medical Centre
  BLWL NG6 ...... 35 M1
Riversdale Surgery
  BPR/DF56 ...... 17 J3
Riverside County
  Junior School
  LEIN LE4 ...... 119 M8
Robert Bakewell
  Primary School
  LBORO LE11 ...... 103 H1
Robert Mellors Primary School
  ARN NG5 ...... 25 L7
Robert Shaw Primary School
  WOL/BIL/BRX NG8 ...... 50 A1
Robert Shaw School
  WOL/BIL/BRX NG8 ...... 50 B1
Robin Hood Industrial Estate
  MAPPK/POR/STA NG3 ...... 5 L5
Robin Hood School
  ARN NG5 ...... 36 E1
Robinsons Industrial Estate
  NORM/LIT DE23 ...... 58 A5
Rolleston Junior School
  LEIS LE2 ...... 137 H5
Rookery Lane Surgery
  GBY/RBY LE6 ...... 123 J4
Rosebery County
  Junior School
  LBORO LE11 ...... 8 E2
Rosehill Clinic
  MAPPK/POR/STA NG3 ...... 5 M4
Rosehill Infant School
  NORM/LIT DE23 ...... 3 G8
Rothley C of E School
  RLEINE/SYS LE7 ...... 119 J1
Rothley Parish Council
  RLEINE/SYS LE7 ...... 119 J1
Rothley Park Club House
  RLEINE/SYS LE7 ...... 119 H3
Roundhill College
  RLEINE/SYS LE7 ...... 120 D6
Round Hill Primary School
  BSTN/STPLFD NG9 ...... 49 J8
Rowlatts Hill Primary School
  LEIE LE5 ...... 132 E1
Rowley Fields
  Community College
  LEIW LE3 ...... 130 F7
Royal Crown Derby
  NORM/LIT DE23 ...... 3 G8
Ruddington Medical Centre
  CFTN/RUD NG11 ...... 65 G8
Ruddington Parish Council
  CFTN/RUD NG11 ...... 65 G8
Rushcliffe Golf Club
  RLBORO LE12 ...... 88 B3
Rushcliffe School
  WBRGFD NG2 ...... 65 K3
Rushey Mead Health Centre
  LEIN LE4 ...... 126 B3
Rushey Mead Primary School
  LEIN LE4 ...... 126 A5
Rusheymead
  Recreation Centre
  LEIN LE4 ...... 126 A3
Rushey Mead
  Secondary School
  LEIN LE4 ...... 126 A4
Rylands Junior School
  BSTN/STPLFD NG9 ...... 63 L3
Sacred Heart RC
  Primary School
  CARL NG4 ...... 38 B8
Sacred Heart R C
  Primary School
  LBORO LE11 ...... 9 G8
Sacred Heart RC School
  LEIE LE5 ...... 7 M4
S A I Medical Centre
  NORM/LIT DE23 ...... 57 L5
St Albans Primary School
  DERBYE DE21 ...... 58 D1
St Andrews C of E
  Primary School
  ILK DE7 ...... 45 M2
St Andrews Special School
  DERBYE DE21 ...... 44 C6
St Anns Well Infant School
  MAPPK/POR/STA NG3 ...... 5 M2
St Augustine School
  MAPPK/POR/STA NG3 ...... 5 H1
St Augustine School
  MAPPK/POR/STA NG3 ...... 37 G7
St Barnabas Catholic Cathedral
  NOTT NG1 ...... 4 E6
St Barnabas C of E
  Primary School
  LEIE LE5 ...... 126 C8
St Bartholomews
  Primary School
  LBORO LE12 ...... 112 C2
St Benedict School
  & Sixth Form Centre
  DERBYW DE22 ...... 43 K6
St Botolphs C of E
  Primary School
  RLBORO LE12 ...... 102 A3
St Chads C of E Infant School
  NORM/LIT DE23 ...... 2 D9
St Clares RC Primary School
  COAL LE67 ...... 108 B7
St Clares School
  MCKLVR DE3 ...... 56 D5
St Crispins School
  LEIS LE2 ...... 131 M5
St Edward RC School
  MAPPK/POR/STA NG3 ...... 51 K1
St Edwards Junior School
  CDON/KEG DE74 ...... 84 F4
St Elizabeths School
  BPR/DF56 ...... 17 K2

St Georges RC School
  NORM/LIT DE23 ...... 57 G8
St Georges Retail Park
  LEIE LE5 ...... 7 J5
St Giles School
  DERBYE DE23 ...... 44 A6
St Helens Business Centre
  DERBY DE1 ...... 2 D1
St James C of E Infant School
  NORM/LIT DE23 ...... 3 G7
St John Fisher RC
  Primary School
  DERBYSE DE24 ...... 59 G7
St John Fisher RC
  Primary School
  WCSTN LE18 ...... 138 C3
St John Houghton RC School
  ILK DE7 ...... 47 G1
St Johns C of E Primary School
  BPR/DUF DE56 ...... 17 M2
St Johns C of E Primary School
  RIPLEY DE5 ...... 11 K5
St Johns C of E School
  BSTN/STPLFD NG9 ...... 48 C8
St Johns College
  BSTN/STPLFD NG9 ...... 48 F8
St Johns School
  LEIS LE2 ...... 132 A5
St John the Baptist
  Junior & Infant School
  LEIS LE2 ...... 132 A5
St John the Baptist
  Primary School
  CARL NG4 ...... 52 C2
St Josephs RC Primary School
  LEIE LE5 ...... 127 H7
St Josephs School
  NORM/LIT DE23 ...... 2 D7
St Lawrence C of E
  Primary School
  LGEAT NG10 ...... 76 B1
St Leonards C of E School
  RLBORO LE12 ...... 112 C8
St Lukes Church
  DERBYW DE22 ...... 2 B6
St Lukes C of E School
  RLEINE/SYS LE7 ...... 133 K2
St Margarets Baths
  LEI LE1 ...... 6 D4
St Margarets Business Centre
  LEI LE1 ...... 6 E3
St Margarets Sports Centre
  LEI LE1 ...... 6 D2
St Martins School
  DERBYSE DE24 ...... 58 D7
St Martins Shopping Centre
  LEI LE1 ...... 6 E6
St Mary De Castro Church
  LEI LE1 ...... 6 C7
St Marys C of E School
  BLWL NG6 ...... 23 M7
St Marys Fields Infant School
  LEIW LE3 ...... 131 G5
St Marys RC Primary School
  DERBY DE1 ...... 2 D1
St Mathews Sports Hall
  LEI LE1 ...... 7 H3
St Matthews Business Centre
  LEI LE1 ...... 6 F5
St Michael & All Angels
  C of E School
  RLEINE/SYS LE7 ...... 115 L5
St Patricks RC Primary School
  LEIN LE4 ...... 125 M5
St Patricks RC School
  CFTN/RUD NG11 ...... 50 F7
St Pauls C of E Primary School
  RLBORO LE12 ...... 111 L6
St Pauls RC
  Comprehensive School
  LEIE LE5 ...... 133 G3
St Peter & St Paul
  C of E Primary School
  RLEINE/SYS LE7 ...... 120 E2
St Peters C of E Primary School
  RLEIW/BBY LE8 ...... 136 D8
St Peters C of E Junior School
  NORM/LIT DE23 ...... 57 G6
St Peters Health Centre
  LEIS LE2 ...... 7 J7
St Peters Junior School
  CFTN/RUD NG11 ...... 65 H7
St Peters Junior School
  LEIS LE2 ...... 7 K7
St Teresas RC Primary School
  WOL/BIL/BRX NG8 ...... 35 L7
St Thomas Moore RC School
  LEIS LE2 ...... 132 A7
St Thomas RC Primary School
  ILK DE7 ...... 47 J1
St Werburgh's Arcade
  DERBY DE1 ...... 2 D3
St Werburghs C of E School
  DERBYE DE21 ...... 59 H2
St Winifrides RC
  Primary School
  RLBORO LE12 ...... 101 M3
Salvation Army
  DERBY DE1 ...... 2 F5
Salvation Army
  NOTT NG1 ...... 5 J5
Sandfield Close Primary School
  LEIN LE4 ...... 126 C2
Sandiacre Friesland
  Sports Centre
  BWSH/BRSTN DE72 ...... 61 K2
Sawley County Junior
  & Infant School
  LGEAT NG10 ...... 75 L3
Sawmills Industrial Park
  HEANOR DE75 ...... 20 B4
Scargill C of E Primary School
  ILK DE7 ...... 32 B8
Scotholme Primary School
  NOTT NG7 ...... 36 D7
Scraptoft Golf Club
  RLEINE/SYS LE7 ...... 127 L5

Scraptoft Lane
  Doctors Surgery
    LEIE LE5 .... 127 H8
Scraptoft Lane Surgery
    LEIE LE5 .... 127 G8
Scraptoft Valley Infant School
    LEIE LE5 .... 127 H7
Seagrave CP School
    RLBORO LE12 .... 106 D7
Seagrave Primary School
    WOL/BIL/BRX NG8 .... 35 H5
Sgcs Business Park
    BSTN/STPLFD NG9 .... 63 L3
Shardlow Business Park
    BWSH/BRSTN DE72 .... 74 B6
Shardlow County
  Primary School
    BWSH/BRSTN DE72 .... 74 C6
Shelthorpe Primary School
    LBORO LE11 .... 9 L8
Shenton Primary School
    LEIE LE5 .... 7 L3
Shepshed Dynamo F C
    RLBORO LE12 .... 102 A3
Sherwin Sports Centre
    NORM/LIT DE23 .... 57 M7
Sherwood Bear Clinic
    NOTT NG1 .... 5 H7
Sherwood Rise Medical Centre
    NOTTE NG7 .... 36 E6
Shipstones Business Centre
    NOTTE NG7 .... 36 C6
Shires Shopping Centre
    LEI LE1 .... 6 E5
Shonki Business Centre
    LEI LE1 .... 6 E2
Showcase Cinemas
    NORM/LIT DE23 .... 57 L8
Showcase Cinemas
    NOTTE NG7 .... 50 C7
Shree Sanatan Mandir Temple
    LEIN LE4 .... 125 M7
Sikh Temple
    LEIN LE4 .... 126 A5
Sileby Parish Council
    RLBORO LE12 .... 114 A4
Silverhill Primary School
    MCKLVR DE3 .... 56 A4
Sinfin Community School
    DERBYSE DE24 .... 71 J4
Sinfin Primary School
    DERBYSE DE24 .... 71 K2
Slater Primary School
    LEIW LE3 .... 6 C3
Snape Wood Medical Centre
    BLWL NG6 .... 23 K7
Snapewood Primary School
    BLWL NG6 .... 23 L8
S N College
    NOTT NG1 .... 5 G7
Sneinton C of E Primary School
    MAPPK/POR/STA NG3 .... 51 K3
Sneinton Health Centre
    WBRGFD NG2 .... 5 L7
Sofa Gallery
    DERBYSE DE24 .... 58 B6
South Derbyshire
  Health Authority
    DERBY DE1 .... 3 H7
South Derbyshire
  Mental Health NHS Trust
    DERBYW DE22 .... 56 F3
South East Derbyshire College
    HEANOR DE75 .... 20 C6
South East Derbyshire College
    ILK DE7 .... 33 K8
Southern Derbyshire
  Health Authority
    DERBY DE1 .... 2 F5
Southern Derbyshire
  Health Authority
    DERBY DE1 .... 2 F3
Southern Derbyshire
  Mental Health NHS Trust
    MCKLVR DE3 .... 56 F3
Southern Derbyshire NHS Trust
    ILK DE7 .... 33 J8
Southfields College
    LEI LE1 .... 6 E3
Southgate Infant School
    DERBYSE DE24 .... 58 D7
South Leicester Rugby Club
    WGSTN LE18 .... 138 B7
South Nottingham College
    WBRGFD NG2 .... 65 H2
South Notts College
    CFTN/RUD NG11 .... 64 E6
Southwark Infant School
    BLWL NG6 .... 36 B3
Southwark Junior School
    BLWL NG6 .... 36 B3
South Wigston Health Centre
    WGSTN LE18 .... 137 L5
South Wigston High School
    WGSTN LE18 .... 137 J6
South Wilford Endowed
  C of E Aided Primary School
    CFTN/RUD NG11 .... 50 F8
Southwold Primary School
    WOL/BIL/BRX NG8 .... 50 B2
South Wolds
  Comprehensive School
    COT/KEY/RAD NG12 .... 80 D4
Sparkenhoe Community
  Primary School
    LEIS LE2 .... 7 K8

Spence Street Sports Centre
    LEIE LE5 .... 126 B8
Spinney Hill Primary School
    LEIE LE5 .... 132 B2
Springfield Junior
  & Infant School
    BLWL NG6 .... 24 A6
Springfield Primary School
    DERBYE DE21 .... 59 H2
Springfield Road
  Health Centre
    LEIS LE2 .... 132 A5
Springfield Surgery
    BLWL NG6 .... 24 A8
Spring Street Primary School
    HUCK/RAV NG15 .... 15 K8
Stafford Leys CP School
    LEIW LE3 .... 129 K5
Standhill Infant School
    MAPPK/POR/STA NG3 .... 37 M8
Stanhope Primary School
    CARL NG4 .... 38 B4
Stanley Common C of E
  Primary School
    ILK DE7 .... 31 L6
Stanstead Primary School
    ARN NG5 .... 24 C7
Stanton Vale School
    ILK DE7 .... 47 K1
Stapleford Health Centre
    BSTN/STPLFD NG9 .... 62 B1
Stapleford Town Council
    BSTN/STPLFD NG9 .... 48 B8
Station Road Surgery
    LEIW LE3 .... 124 B5
Station Road Surgery
    RLBORO LE12 .... 112 E1
Stenhouse Medical Centre
    ARN NG5 .... 25 J7
Stenson Fields Community
  Primary School
    DERBYSE DE24 .... 71 H5
Stephenson College
    COAL LE67 .... 108 B7
Stevenson Junior School
    BSTN/STPLFD NG9 .... 48 D7
Stewart Avenue Surgery
    RLEIW/BAR LE9 .... 135 L5
Stokes C of E Primary School
    RLEIW/BBY LE8 .... 136 E7
Stokes Drive Surgery
    LEIW LE3 .... 124 F7
Stokes Wood Primary School
    LEIW LE3 .... 124 F7
Stonebow Primary School
    RLBORO LE12 .... 102 E1
Stonebridge Mental
  Health Centre
    MAPPK/POR/STA NG3 .... 51 K2
The Stonehill High School
    RLEINE/SYS LE7 .... 119 M6
Stoneygate College
    LEIS LE2 .... 132 A5
Stoneygate Football Club
    RLEINE/SYS LE7 .... 127 L7
Stoneygate School
    LEIS LE2 .... 132 A5
Stoneygate School
    RLEIW/BBY LE8 .... 146 A1
Street Lane Primary School
    RIPLEY DE5 .... 18 F2
Strelley Health Centre
    WOL/BIL/BRX NG8 .... 35 H6
Stretton Hall
    NORM/LIT DE23 .... 57 J8
Sunnyhill Infant School
    NORM/LIT DE23 .... 57 J8
Sunnyside Primary
  & Infant School
    BSTN/STPLFD NG9 .... 62 F1
Sutton Bonington
  Primary School
    RLBORO LE12 .... 94 F1
Swanwick Primary School
    ALFN DE55 .... 11 H1
Swarkestone Boat Club
    MELB/CHEL DE73 .... 82 B3
Swimming Baths
    CFTN/RUD NG11 .... 64 D5
Sycamore Junior
  & Infant School
    MAPPK/POR/STA NG3 .... 5 K3
Syston Health Centre
    RLEINE/SYS LE7 .... 120 F3
Tales of Robin Hood
    NOTT NG1 .... 4 F7
Taylor Primary School
    LEI LE1 .... 7 J2
Temple House Clinic
    NORM/LIT DE23 .... 2 E7
The Temple
    LEIS LE2 .... 7 L5
The Temple
    NORM/LIT DE23 .... 2 E9
Tennis Club
    NOTTE NG7 .... 4 D7
The Textile Museum
    NOTT NG1 .... 4 F8
Theatre Royal
  and Concert Hall
    NOTT NG1 .... 4 F6

Thistly Meadow
  Primary School
    RLEIW/BBY LE8 .... 137 C8
Thornfield Industrial Estate
    MAPPK/POR/STA NG3 .... 51 K2
Thringstone CP School
    COAL LE67 .... 100 B7
Thrussington C of E Primary
  School
    RLEINE/SYS LE7 .... 115 K3
Thurcaston & Cropston Parish
  Council Memorial Hall
    RLEINE/SYS LE7 .... 118 E5
Thurlaston C of E
  Primary School
    RLEIW/BAR LE9 .... 134 E4
Thurnby Lodge CP School
    LEIE LE5 .... 133 H1
Thurnby Lodge Surgery
    LEIE LE5 .... 133 J1
Thythorn Field CP School
    WGSTN LE18 .... 138 B8
Tollerton Primary School
    COT/KEY/RAD NG12 .... 66 C5
Tomlinson Industrial Estate
    DERBYE DE21 .... 43 M5
Top Valley
  Comprehensive School
    ARN NG5 .... 24 C6
Top Valley Health Centre
    ARN NG5 .... 24 D7
Torkard Hill Medical Centre
    HUCK/RAV NG15 .... 23 L1
Toton Chetwynd Road
  Primary School
    BSTN/STPLFD NG9 .... 62 E5
Tracey Quaife Theatre School
    NOTT NG1 .... 5 K8
Trading Estate
    LBORO LE11 .... 8 D2
Trading Estate
    LEIS LE2 .... 7 J6
Trent Bridge Primary School
    WBRGFD NG2 .... 51 H7
Trent College
    LGEAT NG10 .... 62 A6
Trent Lane Industrial Estate
    CDON/KEG DE74 .... 84 F1
Trent Pool Sports Centre
    WBRGFD NG2 .... 51 K5
Trent Vale Infant School
    BSTN/STPLFD NG9 .... 63 M3
Trinity Hospital
    LEI LE1 .... 6 C7
Trinity School
    WOL/BIL/BRX NG8 .... 35 L4
Troon Way Business Centre
    LEIN LE4 .... 126 D3
Trowell C of E School
    BSTN/STPLFD NG9 .... 48 B3
U C I Cinemas
    DERBYE DE21 .... 44 A6
Underwood C of E
  Primary School
    EWD/SEL/PNX NG16 .... 13 K6
Unit G Belgrave
  Industrial Centre
    LEIN LE4 .... 125 L5
University Chaplaincy
    BSTN/STPLFD NG9 .... 49 L8
University Exhibition Centre
    LEI LE1 .... 6 C6
University of Derby
    DERBY DE1 .... 2 C2
University of Derby
    DERBYW DE22 .... 2 B2
University of Derby
    DERBYW DE22 .... 2 A2
University of Derby
    DERBYW DE22 .... 2 A1
University of Derby
    DERBYW DE22 .... 57 H3
University of Derby
    MCKLVR DE3 .... 56 D4
University of Derby
    NORM/LIT DE23 .... 2 A9
University of Derby
    NORM/LIT DE23 .... 57 H5
University of Leicester
    LEI LE1 .... 6 F8
University of Leicester
    LEI LE1 .... 7 G9
University of Leicester
    LEI LE1 .... 131 L4
University of Leicester
    LEIS LE2 .... 131 K6
University of Leicester
    LEIS LE2 .... 132 B7
University of Leicester
    LEIS LE2 .... 132 A7
University of Nottingham
    BSTN/STPLFD NG9 .... 49 L6
University of Nottingham
    BSTN/STPLFD NG9 .... 49 L7
University of Nottingham
    NOTTE NG7 .... 49 M7
University of Nottingham
    NOTTE NG7 .... 49 M6
University of Nottingham
    NOTTE NG7 .... 49 M6

University of Nottingham
    NOTTE NG7 .... 50 A5
University of Nottingham
    RLBORO LE12 .... 86 F6
Uplands Primary School
    LEIE LE5 .... 7 L7
Uppingham Road
  Health Centre
    LEIE LE5 .... 126 C8
Valley Surgery
    BSTN/STPLFD NG9 .... 63 G2
Vaughan College
    LEIW LE3 .... 6 C5
Vernon Park Trading Estate
    BLWL NG6 .... 36 C4
Vernon Street Medical Centre
    DERBY DE1 .... 2 B3
Victoria Clinic
    LEIS LE2 .... 131 M5
The Victoria Gallery
    NOTT NG1 .... 5 J5
Victoria Health Centre
    NOTT NG1 .... 5 H5
Victoria Leisure Centre
    NOTT NG1 .... 5 K6
Victoria Shopping Centre
    NOTT NG1 .... 5 H5
Vidya Medical Centre
    DERBY DE1 .... 2 F7
The Village Community School
    NORM/LIT DE23 .... 57 K7
Vulcan Business Centre
    LEIE LE5 .... 7 K3
Waingroves Primary School
    RIPLEY DE5 .... 11 L7
Walnut Street Medical Centre
    LEIS LE2 .... 131 J4
Walter Evans C of E School
    DERBYW DE22 .... 43 K5
Walter Halls Primary School
    MAPPK/POR/STA NG3 .... 37 J5
Warren Primary School
    ARN NG5 .... 24 E5
Water Leys Primary School
    WGSTN LE18 .... 137 M3
Waterside Retail Park
    ILK DE7 .... 33 L6
Waverley Street Clinic
    DERBYSE DE24 .... 58 A8
Welbeck School
    WBRGFD NG2 .... 51 G5
Welford Road Surgery
    LEIS LE2 .... 137 M1
Wellbeck Surgery
    ARN NG5 .... 37 G5
Wellside Medical Centre
    DERBY DE1 .... 2 E6
West Bridgford School
    WBRGFD NG2 .... 65 H3
Westbrook School
    LGEAT NG10 .... 62 A8
Westcotes Health Centre
    LEIW LE3 .... 131 G3
Westcotes School
    LEIS LE2 .... 131 H4
Westdale Infant School
    MAPPK/POR/STA NG3 .... 38 A4
Westgate Junior
  & Infant School
    ARN NG5 .... 24 D7
West Hallam Cricket Club
    ILK DE7 .... 32 B8
West Hallam Medical Centre
    ILK DE7 .... 32 C8
Westleigh Business Park
    RLEIW/BBY LE8 .... 136 F6
Westleigh Rugby Club
    RLEIW/BBY LE8 .... 136 E8
Westleigh Rugby Football Club
    RLEIW/BBY LE8 .... 142 E2
Weston on Trent Parochial
  Primary School
    BWSH/BRSTN DE72 .... 83 J3
West Park Community School
    DERBYE DE21 .... 59 H2
West Park Leisure Centre
    LGEAT NG10 .... 61 M8
The Wheldon School
    CARL NG4 .... 38 A6
Whetstone Parish Council
    RLEIW/BBY LE8 .... 136 D7
Whitegate Junior
  & Infant School
    CFTN/RUD NG11 .... 64 B7
Whitehall Primary School
    LEIE LE5 .... 132 F3
Whitemoor Court
  Industrial Estate
    NOTTE NG7 .... 36 C7
Whitemoor Primary School
    WOL/BIL/BRX NG8 .... 36 B6
Whitwick Business Park
    COAL LE67 .... 108 B5
Whitwick Health Centre
    COAL LE67 .... 108 C2
Wholesale Fruit
  and Flower Market
    WBRGFD NG2 .... 51 J4
Whyburn Primary School
    HUCK/RAV NG15 .... 15 K8

Wigston Central Surgery
    WGSTN LE18 .... 138 B4
Wigston College
  of Further Education
    WGSTN LE18 .... 137 M5
Wigston Swimming Pool
    WGSTN LE18 .... 137 M5
Wilberforce Road Surgery
    LEIS LE2 .... 6 B9
Wilford Business Park
    CFTN/RUD NG11 .... 64 F4
Wilford Meadows School
    CFTN/RUD NG11 .... 51 G7
William Booth
  Birthplace Museum
    WBRGFD NG2 .... 5 M7
William Booth
  Birthplace Museum
    WBRGFD NG2 .... 51 K3
William Booth Infant School
    WBRGFD NG2 .... 5 M8
William Crane School
    WOL/BIL/BRX NG8 .... 35 M6
William Gilbert End C of E
  Primary School
    BPR/DUF DE56 .... 29 J3
William Lilley Infant School
    BSTN/STPLFD NG9 .... 62 B1
William Sharp School
    WOL/BIL/BRX NG8 .... 35 G8
Willowbrook Primary School
    LEIE LE5 .... 133 J1
Willow Farm CP School
    CARL NG4 .... 38 E5
Willow Sports Centre
    DERBY DE1 .... 2 D2
The Will Practice
    BSTN/STPLFD NG9 .... 63 G4
Wilmorton Primary School
    DERBYSE DE24 .... 58 B6
Wilson Street Surgery
    DERBY DE1 .... 2 E5
Wilson Street Surgery
    DERBYSE DE21 .... 44 D6
Wilsthorpe
  Comprehensive School
    LGEAT NG10 .... 61 M6
Windley Junior School
    NOTTE NG7 .... 4 C4
Windmill Road Industrial Estate
    LBORO LE11 .... 104 B4
Winstanley High School
    LEIW LE3 .... 130 C3
Wollaton Cricket Club
    WOL/BIL/BRX NG8 .... 49 J3
Wollaton Vale Health Centre
    WOL/BIL/BRX NG8 .... 49 H4
Wolsey House Primary School
    LEIW LE3 .... 125 J4
Women & Medkill Practice
    CFTN/RUD NG11 .... 64 E4
Woodborough Road Clinic
    ARN NG5 .... 37 H5
Woodborough Woods School
    CALV/BJ NG14 .... 26 F3
Woodbrook Vale High School
    RLBORO LE12 .... 103 K8
Woodhouse Parish Council
    RLBORO LE12 .... 111 L2
Woodland Grange CP School
    LEIS LE2 .... 139 H3
Woodlands
  Community School
    DERBYW DE22 .... 43 H3
Woodlands Day Hospital
    RLEIW/BAR LE9 .... 135 L7
Woodstock CP School
    LEIN LE4 .... 125 J3
Woodview Business Centre
    ARN NG5 .... 24 E6
Woolden Hill CP School
    RLEINE/SYS LE7 .... 118 C7
Wreake Valley College
    RLEINE/SYS LE7 .... 121 G2
Wren Park Primary School
    MCKLVR DE3 .... 56 E5
Wycliffe Community College
    LEIW LE3 .... 130 D2
Wyggeston Hospital
    LEIW LE3 .... 131 G2
Wyggeston Queen
  Elizabeth I College
    LEI LE1 .... 131 L5
Wymeswold C of E School
    RLBORO LE12 .... 98 A4
Wymeswold Industrial Park
    RLBORO LE12 .... 97 L6
Wyvern Business Park
    DERBYE DE21 .... 58 E4
Wyvern Primary School
    LEIN LE4 .... 126 B5
YMCA
    LEI LE1 .... 7 G7
YMCA
    NOTT NG1 .... 4 F3
YMCA
    NOTT NG1 .... 5 G5
Zen Gallery
    LGEAT NG10 .... 62 B7

Page 14

F6
1 Barton St
2 Beauford Sq
3 Bridewell La
4 Harington Pl
5 Kingsmead Sq
6 Kingsmead St
7 Old Bond St
8 Parsonage La
9 Princes St
10 Queen St
11 Quiet St
12 St John's Pl
13 Saw Cl
14 Trim Br
15 Trim St
16 Westgate Buildings
17 Westgate St

Page 15

G6
1 Abbey St
2 Boat Stall La
3 Cheap St
4 Grand Pde
5 Green St
6 High St
7 New Bond St
8 Northgate St
9 Northumberland Pl
10 Orange Gv
11 Spring Gardens Rd
12 Union St
13 Upper Borough Walls

G7
1 Abbeygate St
2 Abbey Gn
3 Amery La
4 Church St
5 Henry St
6 Kingston Rd
7 Manvers St
8 New Orchard St
9 Pierrepont Pl
10 Pierrepont St
11 Southgate
12 Stall St
13 Swallow St
14 Terrace Wk
15 York St

Page 30

C5
1 Boursland Cl
2 Campion Dr
3 Foxborough Gdns
4 Perrys Lea
5 Primrose Cl
6 Teal Cl

Page 34

D6
1 Cherry Rd
2 Chestnut Dr
3 Meadow Rd
4 The Parade
5 River Rd
6 Streamside Rd
7 Wistaria Av

Page 42

A7
1 Chantry La
2 Chepstow Pk
3 Goodwood Gdns
4 Haylock Cl
5 Plumpton Ct
6 Redcar Ct
7 Sedgefield Gdns
8 Wetherby Cl
9 Wincanton Ct

Page 51

F4
1 Ellbridge Cl
2 Halwyn Cl
3 Yeomans Cl

J7
1 Anglesea Pl
2 Belgrave Hl
3 Highland Crs
4 Highland Sq
5 Hughenden Rd
6 Mornington Rd
7 Normanton Rd
8 Quarry Steps
9 Redland Ter
10 Richmond Dl
11 St Vincent's Hl
12 Westbury Rd
13 York St

K3
1 Blandford Cl
2 Grange Cl North
3 Waterford Rd

K7
1 East Shrubbery
2 Evans Rd
3 Hartington Pk
4 Luccombe Hl
5 Shrubbery Cottages
6 West Shrubbery
7 Woodland Ter

Page 52

A3
1 Croft Vw

D1
1 St Aldwyn's Cl

D2
1 Caine Rd

D3
1 Crofton Av

D4
1 Draycott Rd
2 Uphill Rd

D6
1 Hopetoun Rd
2 Osborne Av
3 St Bartholomew's Rd

D7
1 Ashley Court Rd
2 Ashley Grove Rd
3 Ashley Pde
4 Cumberland Gv
5 Fairlawn Rd
6 Falkland Rd
7 Milverton Gdns
8 Old Ashley Hl
9 Richmond Av
10 Richmond Rd
11 St Andrew's Rd
12 St Werburgh's Rd
13 Sommerville Rd South
14 York St

E1
1 Austen Gv
2 Cropthorne Rd South
3 Thackeray Wk

E2
1 Masefield Wy
2 Rose Mead
3 Shearmore Cl
4 Taunton Wk

Page 53

C7
1 Apsley St
2 Argyle St
3 Bay Gdns
4 Berkeley Gn
5 Boswell St
6 Caraway Gdns
7 Coriander Wk
8 East Park Dr
9 Fountaine Ct
10 Freeland Buildings
11 Juniper Ct
12 St Leonard's Rd

H3
1 Bryansons Cl
2 Countess Wk
3 Princess Gdns

J4
1 Blackberry La
2 Cromwells Hide
3 Frome Pl
4 Glenside Pk
5 Kite Hay Cl
6 Lark's Fld
7 Pennyroyal Gv
8 Spires Vw

K2
1 Broadways Dr

K3
1 Curlew Cl
2 Lapwing Gdns
3 Ronald Rd
4 Whinchat Gdns
5 Witherlies Rd

K5
1 Adelaide Pl
2 Albert Ter
3 Featherstone Rd
4 Langdale Rd
5 Wharf Rd

K7
1 Irena Rd
2 Madeline Rd

Page 54

A2
1 Blenman Cl
2 Probyn Cl
3 Scott Lawrence Cl
4 Stourden Cl

A4
1 Claverham Rd
2 College Av
3 Guinea La

A5
1 Hinton Cl
2 Hockey's La

A6
1 Acton Rd
2 Ivy La
3 Justice Rd
4 Poplar Pl

A7
1 Dean's Dr

B2
1 Churchside

B3
1 Lanaway Rd
2 Little Hayes
3 Oldbury Court Dr

B4
1 Cunningham Gdns

B5
1 Bridges Ct
2 Chasefield La
3 Daws Ct
4 Parkhurst Av
5 Vicars Cl

B6
1 Filwood Ct
2 William St

B7
1 Forest Wk
2 Lyncombe Wk

C1
1 Beckspool Rd

C2
1 Quarry Rd
2 Tuckett La

C3
1 Bracey Dr
2 Bridges Dr
3 Grangewood Cl
4 Shimsey Cl
5 Urfords Dr

C4
1 Pemberton Ct

C5
1 Edgeware Rd

C6
1 Acacia Cl
2 The Chase
3 Glendale
4 The Greenway
5 Market Sq
6 Quadrant East
7 The Rosery

C7
1 Coulson Wk
2 Henshaw Cl
3 Welton Wk
4 Wentforth Dr
5 Willow Gv
6 Woodland Cl

D1
1 Bromley Heath Rd
2 Pilgrims Wy
3 Quaker's Cl
4 Scantleberry Cl

D2
1 Cleeve Wood Rd
2 Heath Ct

D3
1 Chestnut Rd
2 Conifer Cl
3 Edmund Cl

Page 55

F3
1 Stanbridge Cl
2 Woodhall Cl

Page 65

H4
1 Albemarle Rw
2 Cornwallis Av
3 Cumberland Pl
4 Dowry Sq
5 Freeland Pl
6 Glendale
7 Hopechapel Hl
8 Hope Sq
9 Hotwell Rd
10 Joy Hl
11 North Green St
12 Oxford Pl
13 The Paragon
14 Royal York Crs
15 South Green St
16 Victoria Ter
17 Windsor Ter

J4
1 Ambra V
2 Ambra V South
3 Ambra V West
4 Camden Ter
5 Clifton Hl
6 Clifton Vale Cl
7 Cliftonwood Ter
8 Dowry Rd
9 Polygon Rd
10 Royal York Vls
11 St Vincent's Rd
12 Saville Pl

J6
1 Ashton Gate Ter
2 Baynton Rd
3 Leigh St
4 North Rd
5 St Francis Rd
6 Wells St

K2
1 Alma Road Av
2 Melrose Av
3 Oakfield Pl
4 Westbourne Pl

K4
1 Bellevue Cottages
2 Cliftonwood Crs
3 Gasferry Rd
4 Glentworth Rd
5 Gorse La
6 John Carr's Ter
7 St Edward's Rd
8 Southernhay
9 Southernhay Av

K7
1 Crowther St
2 Dartmoor St
3 Dorset St
4 Jasper St
5 Lindrea St
6 Martin St
7 The Nursery
8 Parker St
9 Pembery Rd
10 Stanley St North
11 Thistle St
12 Upper Sydney St

Page 66

A3
1 Berkeley Av
2 Berkeley Sq
3 Lodge Pl
4 Lodge St
5 Old Park Hl
6 Park La
7 Park Street Av
8 Royal Fort Rd
9 There-and-back-again La

A4
1 Bigwood La
2 Brandon Steep
3 Charlotte St South
4 College Sq
5 Culver St
6 Denmark Av
7 Frogmore St
8 Gaunt's La
9 Hobb's La
10 Lower College St
11 Lower Lamb St
12 Orchard Av
13 Orchard La
14 Orchard St
15 Partition St
16 Unity St
17 Upper Wells St
18 York Pl

Page 42

A7
1 Chantry La

Page 30

A6
1 Argyle St
2 Dean St
3 Fairfield St
4 Kingston Rd
5 Merrywood Cl
6 Morley Rd
7 Mount Pleasant Ter
8 Murray St
9 Summer St

B1
1 Arley Cottages
2 Arley Pk
3 Elmgrove Rd
4 Fremantle La
5 Fremantle Rd
6 St Matthew's Av
7 Southfield Rd
8 Victoria Gdns
9 Winsley Rd

B2
1 Barton St
2 Cherry La
3 Clevedon Ter
4 Cottage Pl
5 Earl St
6 Henrietta St
7 Hillgrove St North
8 King Sq
9 King Square Av
10 Lower Gay St
11 Marlborough Hill Pl
12 Montague Hl
13 Montague Hl South
14 Montague St
15 Princess Rw
16 Spring Hl
17 Terrell St
18 Whitson St

B3
1 All Saints' St
2 Bell La
3 Blackfriars
4 Bridewell St
5 Cannon St
6 Christmas St
7 Fiennes Ct
8 High St
9 Host St
10 Lewins Mead
11 Nelson St
12 Newmarket Av
13 Pithay
14 Pithay Ct
15 Quay St
16 St Stephen's St
17 Silver St
18 Union St

B4
1 Bathwell Rd
2 Clyde Ter
3 Fairfoot Rd
4 Fordell Pl
5 Goolden St
6 Knowle Rd
7 Vale St

C1
1 Armidale Av
2 Barnabas St
3 Bath Buildings
4 Dalrymple Rd
5 Drummond Rd
6 Norrisville Rd
7 Woodmancote Rd

C2
1 Callowhill Ct
2 George Whitefield Ct
3 Hanover Ct
4 Marybush La
5 Merchant St
6 Old King Street Ct
7 Philadelphia St
8 Quakers' Friars
9 Wellington Rd
10 Whippington Ct

C4
1 Church St
2 Ferry St
3 Long Rw
4 Narrow Pln
5 St Thomas St East
6 Three Queens' La
7 Tower St

D1
1 Albany Rd
2 Albert Rw
3 Ashfield Pl
4 Brook La
5 Cairns' Crs
6 Corey Cl
7 Franklyn La
8 London Rd
9 Tudor Rd
10 Winkworth Pl

D2
1 Beggarswell Cl
2 Charlotte St
3 Cheapside
4 East St
5 Elton St
6 Eugene St
7 Frome St
8 Wilson Pl

D3
1 Asher La
2 David St
3 Eyer's La
4 Gloucester La
5 Hawkins St
6 Redcross St
7 St Matthias Pk
8 Tucker St
9 Waterloo St
10 Willway St

D4
1 Broad Pln
2 Louisa St
3 Midland St
4 New Kingsley Rd
5 New Thomas St
6 Poets' Cl
7 Providence Pl
8 Straight St

D5
1 Chatterton Sq
2 Chatterton St
3 Lower Station Approach Rd

D6
1 Bellevue Ter
2 Bushy Pk
3 Cheapside St
4 Dunmore St
5 Higham St
6 Vernon St

Page 67

F1
1 Chapel Rd
2 Church Av
3 Earl St
4 Greenbank Av West
5 Henrietta St
6 Lawrence Av
7 Moorhill St
8 Normandy Rd
9 Northcote St
10 St Mark's Ter
11 St Nicholas Pk
12 Warwick Av
13 Warwick Rd
14 Woodborough St

F2
1 Abraham Cl
2 Adelaide Pl
3 All Hallows Rd
4 Brighton Pk
5 Cattybrook St
6 Clayton St
7 Combfactory La
8 Eastbourne Rd
9 Elmgrove Av
10 Luxton St
11 Owen St
12 Pountney Dr
13 Thomson Rd
14 Tyndall Rd
15 Vining Wk
16 Westbourne Rd
17 Windsor Gv

F3
1 Arthur Skemp Cl
2 Atchley St
3 Bright St
4 Charlton St
5 Church St
6 Earl Russell Wy
7 Ernest Barker Cl
8 Morton St
9 Payne Dr
10 Robert St
11 Roman Rd
12 Strawbridge Rd
13 William Mason Cl

F4
1 Beaconsfield St
2 Bradhurst St
3 Canterbury St
4 Cockworthy St
5 Fripp Cl
6 Goulter St
7 Holmes St
8 Maze St
9 Napier St
10 Parkers Barton
11 Victor St

G3
1 Beam St
2 Brook St
3 Brunswick St
4 Byron St
5 Cambridge St
6 Cowper St
7 Hanover St
8 Howett Rd
9 Lancaster St
10 Matthew's Rd
11 Milton Pk
12 Morse Rd
13 Osprey Rd
14 Oxford St
15 Verrier Rd
16 Weight Rd
17 Witchell Rd
18 York St

H2
1 Altringham Rd
2 Bourneville Rd
3 Charterhouse Rd
4 Congleton Rd
5 Earlstone Crs
6 Hammersmith Rd
7 Mary St
8 Neath Rd
9 Oakleigh Av
10 Stretford Av
11 Tintern Av
12 Trelawney Av
13 Westminster Rd
14 Whitehall Gdns
15 Woodbine Rd

H5
1 Buckingham Rd
2 Westwood Crs

J2
1 Hudd's Vale Rd
2 Oakland Rd
3 Snowberry Wk

J3
1 Bennett Rd
2 Burgess Green Cl
3 Pilgrims Whf

Page 68

B7
1 Rowan Wy
2 Sycamore Cl

D1
1 Victoria Rd

E6
1 Avonlea
2 Briarfield Av
3 Creswicke Av
4 Hunters Cl
5 Laburnum Rd
6 Lower Chapel Rd
7 Martins Cl

D1
1 Brighton Rd
2 Chesham Wy
3 Gladstone Rd
4 Hampton St
5 Kennington Av
6 Kimberley Av
7 Morley Ter
8 Wesley Hl
9 Worcester Rd

D2
1 Bank Rd
2 Ellesmere Rd
3 Halls Rd
4 Parklands
5 West St

D5
1 Alexandra Rd
2 Grange Ct
3 Whitefield Rd
4 Whitucks Rd

D6
1 Hale Cl
2 Headington Cl

E1
1 Collingwood Av
2 Frys Hl
3 Holly Crs
4 Runnymede

E2
1 Macrae Ct
2 Staynes Crs

E3
1 Bellevue Cl
2 Berkeley Rd

Page 69

F3
1 Brake Cl
2 Bredon Cl
3 Gee Moors
4 Kingsleigh Ct
5 Kingsleigh Gdns
6 Ladd Cl
7 Norton Cl
8 Penard Wy
9 Shilton Cl
10 Woodstock Rd

F6
1 Alwins St
2 Bramley Ct
3 Britten Cr
4 Drummond Ct
5 Dudley Ct
6 Frampton Ct
7 Godfrey Ct
8 Greve Ct
9 Harris Ct
10 Hicks Ct
11 Laphams Ct
12 Logus Ct
13 Lynch Ct
14 Miles Ct
15 Park Farm Ct
16 Pippin Ct
17 Press Moor Dr
18 Stibbs Ct
19 Tindell Ct
20 Turners Ct
21 Woodington Ct

G5
1 Betjeman Ct
2 Churchill Ct
3 Coronation Ct
4 Dylan Thomas Ct
5 Earlstone Crs
6 Henry Williamson Ct
7 Laurie Lee Ct

G7
1 Bakersfield
2 Beaumont Cl
3 Fairoaks
4 Pennngrove
5 Redwood Cl
6 Rutherford Cl
7 Springville Cl

J5
1 The Dell
2 Makin Cl
3 Neads Dr

J6
1 Brendon Cl
2 Hawkins Cl

J7
1 Brookfield Wk
2 The Clamp
3 Chequers Cl
4 The Croft

Page 70

E2
1 Bradford St
2 Braikenridge Rd
3 Britannia Wy
4 Bryant Gdns
5 Stickland
6 Wickfield
7 Woodington St

Page 71

F1
1 Churchill Cl
2 Coleridge Vale Rd East
3 Elm Tree Rd
4 Hillview Av
5 Kingsley Rd
6 Melbourne Ter
7 New Rd

F2
1 Closemead
2 Corner Cft
3 Cooksons
4 Leach Cl
5 Newlands Gn
6 Orchard Rd
7 The Paddock
8 Pedder Rd
9 Stonebridge
10 Tone Rd

Page 73

G2
1 Chantry Cl
2 Chapel Barton
3 Elm Cl
4 Goss Cl
5 Goss Vw
6 May Tree Cl
7 Yew Tree Cl
8 Yew Tree Ms

Page 74

A1
1 Birch Dene
2 The Birches
3 Cerney Gdns
4 Chesterton Dr
5 Chestnut Cha
6 Coates Gv
7 The Oaks
8 Redwood Cl
9 Rowan Cl
10 Sawyers Cl

A2
1 Cairn Cl
2 Cleeve Pl
3 Cricklade Ct
4 Falmouth Cl
5 Gleneagles Cl
6 Kemble Cl
7 St Agnes Cl
8 St Andrews Cl
9 St Ives Cl
10 Sherston Cl
11 Sunningdale Cl
12 Truro Rd
13 Vynes Cl
14 Woodford Cl

Page 77

H5
1 Costland Dr
2 Marlepit Gv
3 Sandburrows Wk
4 Spartley Wk

K1
1 Bedminster Down Rd
2 Brighton Ter
3 Churclands Rd
4 Derry Rd
5 Hardy Rd
6 Harptree Gv
7 Hengaston St
8 Highridge Rd
9 Osborne Ter
10 South Liberty La
11 Temple St
12 Trafalgar Ter
13 Winterstoke Rd

K6
1 Farmwell Cl
2 Flowerwell Rd
3 Fulford Rd
4 Fulford Wk
5 Gander Cl
6 Gatehouse Ct
7 Lyveden Gdns
8 Vigor Rd
9 Whitland Av

Page 78

B5
1 Elgar Cl
2 Inns Court Dr
3 Stainer Cl
4 Travers Cl
5 Wilbye Gv

D3
1 Barnstaple Wk
2 Corsley Wk
3 Dunster Rd
4 Hartcliffe Wk
5 Neston Wk

E1
1 Stoneleigh Wk

E2
1 Green Wk
2 Greenwood Rd
3 Preston Wk
4 The Square
5 Teignmouth St

E4
1 Parsons Paddock
2 Portmeirion Cl

Page 79

F3
1 Allanmead Rd
2 Drayton Cl
3 Edgewood Cl

F7
1 Foxcombe Rd

H4
1 Fontmell Cl
2 Hanford Ct
3 Morden Wk
4 Roundmoor Gdns

K1
1 Clothier Rd

K2
1 Emery Rd

Page 99

H7
1 Cheltenham St
2 Hayden Cl
3 Junction Av
4 Westmoreland Rd
5 Westmoreland Station Rd
6 Westmoreland St

J4
1 All Saints Rd
2 Ballance St
3 Bella Vista Rd
4 Burlington St
5 Great Bedford St
6 Harley St
7 Lansdown Pl East
8 Lansdown Pl West
9 Morford St
10 Northampton Buildings
11 Northampton St
12 Park Street Ms
13 St Stephen's Cl

J5
1 Alfred St
2 Bartlett St
3 Bennett St
4 Brock St
5 Catharine St
6 Circus Ms
7 Circus Pl
8 Gloucester St
9 Guinea La
10 Hay Hl
11 John St
12 Milsom St
13 Old King St
14 Queen's Pde
15 Queen's Parade Pl
16 Rivers Street Ms
17 Russell St
18 Saville Rw
19 Upper Church St

J6
1 Amery La
2 Barton St
3 Bath St
4 Beauford Sq
5 Beau St
6 Bilbury La
7 Bridewell La
8 Burton St
9 Chapel Rw
10 Cumberland Rw
11 Harington Pl
12 Helting Ct
13 Hot Bath St
14 Kingsmead Sq
15 Kingsmead West
16 Kingsmead West
17 Monmouth St
18 Old Bond St
19 Palace Yard Ms
20 Parsonage La
21 St John's Pl
22 St Michael's Pl
23 Saw Cl
24 Trim Br
25 Trim St
26 Trinity Cl
27 Trinity St
28 Union St
29 Upper Borough Walls
30 Westgate Buildings
31 Wood St

K4
1 Alpine Gdns
2 Bedford St
3 Clarence St
4 Gay's Hl
5 Lower Hedgemead Rd
6 Margaret's Hl
7 Nelson Pl
8 Nelson Ter
9 Pera Pl

Page 104

C5
1 Cambridge Pl
2 Connaught Pl
3 Grove Rd
4 High St
5 Knightstone Rd
6 Market La
7 Old Post Office La
8 St Margaret's Ter
9 Victoria Rd
10 Wadham St
11 West St

D5
1 Albert Quadrant
2 Burlington St
3 Edinburgh Pl
4 Gerard Rd
5 Glebe Rd
6 Hans Price Cl
7 Hopkins St
8 King's La
9 Longton Grove Rd
10 Orchard Pl
11 Poplar Pl
12 Prospect Pl
13 Tivoli La
14 Victoria Quadrant
15 Worthy La

Page 105

F5
1 Maple Cl
2 Summerlands Rd
3 Sycamore Cl

H5
1 Saxon Rd

Page 99

E7
1 Boucher Pl
2 Boyce Dr
3 Cleave St
4 Dorset Gv
5 Durham Rd
6 Hereford Rd
7 John St
8 Lancaster Rd
9 Lynmouth Rd
10 Merstham Rd
11 Norman Rd
12 Ryland Pl
13 Seddon Rd
14 Stafford Rd
15 Tewkesbury Rd
16 Treefield Pl
17 Trentham Cl
18 Warminster Rd
19 Weedon Cl
20 York St

D4
1 Christchurch Av
2 Christchurch La
3 Downend Park Rd
4 Nelson Rd
5 Tyler's La

D5
1 Alexandra Cl
2 Kensington Rd
3 Nelson Rd
4 North Vw
5 Pendennis Av

D6
1 Beazer Cl
2 Colston Cl
3 Leicester Sq
4 Portland Pl
5 Wesley Cl

D7
1 Norman Gv
2 Wellington Rd
3 Whitfield Cl
4 The Wickets
5 Woodland Av

E1
1 Sandholme Cl
2 Sandringham Pk

E2
1 Oakdale Ct

E3
1 Buckingham Pl
2 Westerleigh Rd
3 Woodlands

E4
1 Clarence Gdns
2 Heathcote Rd

E5
1 Byron Pl
2 Eastleigh Cl
3 Fiennes Cl
4 Irving Cl
5 James Cl
6 Saunders Rd
7 Shipnran Ct
8 Teewall Cl

E6
1 Gladstone Dr
2 Gloucester Rd
3 St Stephens Cl
4 Wiltshire Pl
5 Woodchester

E7
1 Blackthorn Wk
2 Deerhurst
3 Frys Hl
4 Pembroke Rd
5 Tyndale Rd

F3
1 Stanbridge Cl
2 Woodhall Cl

Page 106

A2
1 Atholl Cl
2 Constable Dr
3 Gainsborough Dr
4 Gleneagles Cl
5 Kielder Dr
6 Landseer Cl
7 Lynch Cl
8 Meadowbank
9 Reubens Ct
10 St Andrews Cl
11 Turnbury Cl
12 Turner Ct

A4
1 Bittern Cl
2 Blueberry Wy
3 Cormorant Cl
4 Curlew Gdns
5 Downs Cl
6 Lark Rd
7 Swift Cl
8 Teal Cl

B2
1 Becket Dr
2 Bishop Av
3 Blythe Gdns
4 Dormer Cl
5 Hogarth Ms
6 The Larches
7 Lester Dr
8 Parsons Gn
9 St Michael's Av
10 Torrington Crs
11 Vicarage Cl
12 Wentworth Cl

C1
1 Austen Dr
2 Denning Ct
3 Fenners
4 The Fielders
5 Gill Ms
6 Goddard Dr
7 Kent Wy
8 Longdown Dr
9 Marindrin Dr
10 Portishead Rd
11 Sadbury Cl
12 The Saffrons
13 Saxby Cl
14 Spinners End
15 Taylor Ct
16 Tremlett Ms
17 Wainwright Cl
18 Wellard Cl

C3
1 Griffin Cl
2 Thorn Cl

C4
1 Collett Cl
2 Ellis Pk
3 Hawksworth Dr
4 Jesmond Rd

K1
1 Blake End
2 Collingwood Cl
3 The Dell
4 Frobisher Cl
5 Harwood Gdns
6 Jellicoe Ct
7 The Lindens
8 Mountbatten Cl
9 Nelson Cl
10 Ramsay Cl
11 Tovey Cl
12 Willowdown

K3
1 Deacons Cl
2 Hawthorn Hl
3 Hill Rd East
4 Lawrence Close Ms
5 Martins Gv
6 Nutwell Sq

K4
1 Bunting Ct
2 Linnet Cl
3 Mayfield Av
4 Nightingale Cl
5 Nutwell Sq

K5
1 Artemesia Av
2 Bailey Cl
3 Falcon Crs
4 Finch Cl
5 Greengage Cl
6 Lombardy Cl
7 Magpie Cl
8 Merlin Cl
9 Sutton Cl
10 Swan Cl
11 Thrush Cl
12 Wagtail Gdns

K6
1 Damson Rd
2 Magnolia Cl

Notes